W9-BEV-414

Hardy's Skiing & Snowboarding Guide 2009

796.93
H273
2009

Cadogan Guides is an imprint of
New Holland Publishers (UK) Ltd
London • Cape Town • Sydney • Auckland

New Holland Publishers (UK) Ltd
Garfield House
86–88 Edgware Road
London W2 2EA

80 McKenzie Street
Cape Town 8001
South Africa

Unit 1, 66 Gibbes Street
Chatswood, NSW 2067
Australia

218 Lake Road
Northcote
Auckland
New Zealand

cadogan@nhpub.co.uk
www.cadoganguides.com
t 44 (0)20 7724 7773

Distributed in the United States by Globe Pequot, Connecticut

Copyright © 2008 in text: Peter and Felice Hardy
Copyright © 2008 in photographs: individual photographers as credited below
Copyright © 2008 New Holland Publishers (UK) Ltd

Cover photograph: Warren Smith by Melody Sky
Other photographs: p.1 © swimnews; p.15 © Konstantin Shishkin; p.18 ©: Matthew Veldhuis, Konstantin Shishkin, Hermann Danzmayr; p.25 © rob bossi; p.26 © C Dingwall, Jiri Pavlik; p.31© Matthew Veldhuis, steve estvanik; p.32 © Geir Olav Lyngfjell; p.33 © Hermann Danzmayr; p.44 © Robert Taylor; p.45 © SVolker; p.61 © Wolfgang Amri, Danila; p.80 © Peter Brett Charlton; p.83 © Razvan Stroie; p.107 © Steve Rosset; p.121 © robcocquyt; p.130 © Gail Johnson, Elena Elisseeva; p.141 © Elena Elisseeva; p.145 © Peter Salaj; p.154 © Kheng Guan Toh; p.155 © Stephen Meese; p.193 © Boussac; p.209 © Jeffrey Van Daele; p.228 © Baudot; p.237 © Stephen Meese; p.253 © Jerome Scholler; p.256 © Matthew Veldhuis; p.269 © Marco_Sc, Jakub Cejpek; p.279 © Marco_Sc; p.295 © Konstantin Shishkin; Roca; p.309 © Ilya D. Gridnev; p.320 © Robert Zywucki; p.329 © Salvador Garcia Gil; p.334 © Atlaspix; p.383 © jackweichen_gatech; p.398 © Robert Fullerton; Nick Lamb; p.455 © Franck Chazot; p.516 © Blaz Kure

Art director: Sarah Gardner
Editor: Nicola Jessop
Editorial Assistant/Advertising: Claire S. Bicknell
Proofreading: Susannah Wight

Printed in Italy by Legoprint
A catalogue record for this book is available from the British Library

ISBN: 978-1-86011-408-3

The author and publishers have made every effort to ensure the accuracy of the information in this book at the time of going to press. However, they cannot accept any responsibility for any loss, injury or inconvenience resulting from the use of information contained in this guide.

Please help us to keep this guide up to date. We have done our best to ensure that the information in this guide is correct at the time of going to press. But laws and regulations are constantly changing, and standards and prices fluctuate. We would be delighted to receive any comments. Authors of the best letters will receive a copy of the Cadogan Guide of their choice.

All rights reserved. No part of this publication may be reproduced, stored in a retrieval system, or transmitted, in any form or by any means, electronic or mechanical, including photocopying and recording, or by any information storage and retrieval system except as may be expressly permitted by the UK 1988 Copyright Design & Patents Act and the USA 1976 Copyright Act or in writing from the publisher. Requests for permission should be addressed to Cadogan Guides/New Holland Publishers, Garfield House, 86–88 Edgware Road, London, W2 2EA United Kingdom.

Scott Dunn

Inspirational holidays since 1986...

Imagine the ultimate winter holiday... experience impeccable Scott Dunn service... enjoy exquisite food in outstanding chalets... be pampered in handpicked hotels... and have your little ones looked after.

We have superb chalets and hotels in the finest resorts in the Alps – Courchevel 1850, St Anton, Val d'Isere, Meribel, Zermatt, Lech, Zurs, St Moritz, the Dolomites, Portes du Soleil, and some fantastic new editions in the US and Canada – Whistler, Jackson Hole and Aspen.

To ensure you don't miss out this season, call us now on 020 8682 5050 or visit www.scottdunn.com/ski

EXCLUSIVE OFFER TO JOIN THE SKI CLUB OF GREAT BRITAIN

The Ski Club of Great Britain is for skiers and snowboarders of all ages and abilities. Over 34,000 snowsports lovers a year benefit from the Club's unrivalled knowledge of the skiing and snowboarding world.

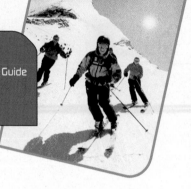

EXCLUSIVE OFFER

For readers of the Great Skiing and Snowboarding Guide
Half-price membership for one year*

Individual: £27.50 Family: £42.50

WHY JOIN THE SKI CLUB?

SKI CLUB REPS

Ski Club Reps in 37 resorts take you skiing, finding you the best snow and runs of the day

SAVE UP TO 10% ON YOUR HOLIDAY

Save on holidays booked with 60 tour operators

RESORT ADVICE

Get advice on where to ski at www.skiclub.co.uk or by talking to our knowledgeable information department

SKI FRESHTRACKS HOLIDAYS

Take advantage of our off-piste expertise and ski with others of the same ability. Improve your skiing on an instructional holiday or try something different on a ski tour or ski safari

AND THERE'S MORE...

COMPREHENSIVE INSURANCE

OVER 1000 DISCOUNTS INCLUDING SKI HIRE, AIRPORT PARKING, CAR HIRE AND UK SLOPES

SKI+BOARD MAGAZINE

DETAILED ONLINE SNOW REPORTS

RESORT EVENTS, PARTIES, BARBECUES AND SPECIAL EVENTS IN THE UK

FREE SUBSCRIPTION TO WWW.SKITV.CO.UK

SKI CLUB OF GREAT BRITAIN
HALF-PRICE
MEMBERSHIP OFFER

* This offer is subject to the production of the corner flash on this page and to signing a direct debit for second and subsequent subscriptions. The offer expires on 30 April 2009 and may not be used in conjunction with any other offers and is for new members to the Ski Club only. For further information, call the Ski Club Membership Department on 0845 45 807 82 or visit www.skiclub.co.uk.

Photo credits: Victor Cortez www.alpinephotoshop.com

Sail to France for less

book online or call
0870 870 10 20

Norfolkline Terms and Conditions apply. £5 administration fee applys to telephone bookings.

norfolkline.com

DOVER - DUNKERQUE FERRIES

ALPINE Tracks

At Alpine Tracks we pride ourselves on our high level of service with our customary personal touch.

The Mountain Lodge - Ski in Ski Out 4 star Luxury in the heart of the Portes du Soleil. Spa, swimming pool, cinema, underground parking, in chalet ski hire set at 1650m and 1 lift from Avoriaz The Mountain Lodge is set in a stunning location in Les Crosets

For a personal approach for your next ski holiday contact Alpine Tracks on **0800 0282546**

or visit **www.alpinetracks.com**

THE PERFORMANCE SKI COACHING SPECIALISTS

WARREN SMITH SKI ACADEMY

ABOUT THE ACADEMY

The Warren Smith Ski Academy brings together some of the sports top coaching professionals, athletes and UIAGM mountain guides to create the ultimate performance coaching team. The Academy coaches and develops many different levels from early intermediate recreational skiers to ski instructors and professional World Cup athletes.

The performance coaching, combined with continuous biomechanical analysis and video feedback, helps develop your technique and unblock aspects of your skiing. This optimises your skiing performance, gains you consistency + confidence and reduces the risk of injury.

WHAT THE ACADEMY OFFERS

The Academy offers many courses throughout the year which include ski technique solutions for the following aspects of skiing:

CONFIDENCE BUILDING / GETTING OFF THE PLATEAU
CARVING / ON PISTE PERFORMANCE / DYNAMICS
INTRODUCTION TO OFF-PISTE / MOGULS / STEEPS
FREERIDE PERFORMANCE / HELI SKIING
ISIA + ISTD INSTRUCTOR TRAINING
SKI BIOMECHANICS ANALYSIS / VIDEO ANALYSIS
FREESTYLE SNOWPARK / BACK COUNTRY FREESTYLE
GAP YEAR INSTRUCTOR TRAINING PROGRAMS

WHY CHOOSE THE ACADEMY

1. The Warren Smith Ski Academy coaching reputation, see the reviews online: **www.warrensmith-skiacademy.com/read-the-course-reviews.htm**
2. The courses offer guaranteed skier improvement because they combine: **Ski Technique / Ski Biomechanics / Ski Physiology / Video Analysis**
3. What the students themselves have to say about the course: **www.warrensmith-skiacademy.com/gap/gap-program_08.htm**

ACADEMY LOCATIONS

WINTER
Verbier, Switzerland
Zinal, Switzerland
Niseko, Japan

SPRING
Chill Factore, Manchester
SNO!zone, Castleford
SNO!zone, Milton Keynes
SNO!zone, Braehead

SUMMER
Saas-Fee, Switzerland
Wanaka, New Zealand

AUTUMN
Chill Factore, Manchester
SNO!zone, Castleford
SNO!zone, Milton Keynes
SNO!zone, Braehead

Photo: www.melodysky.com Skier: Warren Smith Location: Niseko, Japan

RECOMMENDED BY

THE INDEPENDENT
Men's Health
Time Out
THE TIMES

Esquire

The Mail ON SUNDAY

WWW.WARRENSMITH-SKIACADEMY.COM

IS POWERED BY THE FOLLOWING LEADING BRANDS

U.K. LAND ESTATES
uk-land-estates.co.uk

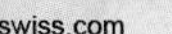
swiss.com

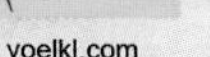
voelkl.com

oakley.com

mammut.ch

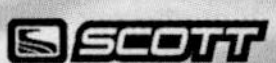
scottusa.com

zipfit.com

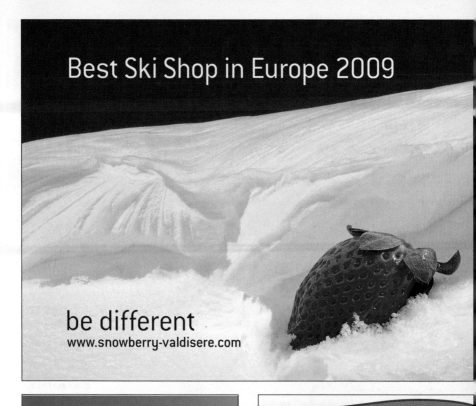

Best Ski Shop in Europe 2009

be different

www.snowberry-valdisere.com

THE SEASON WORKERS' WEBSITE:

- jobs
- cv advice
- snow reports equipment
- cookery courses
- seasonal accommodation
- webcams
- chat
- shopping

To apply **NOW** visit **natives.co.uk**
or email jobs@natives.co.uk or call 08700 463377

natives.co.uk
the season workers' website

Major Resorts - Great Prices

SkiCollection

Only 4 Star Ski Apartments

Resorts throughout the French Alps include Meribel, Val d'Isere, Tignes, Les Arcs, La Plagne, Courchevel, Val Thorens, Les Menuires, Chamonix, Alpe d'Huez, Flaine...

Accommodation only or self-drive package deals

www.skicollection.co.uk

0844 576 0175

ABTA W5537

For *cheap flights* to Chambery

Book online at

www.

.co.uk

Gatwick to Chambery	Stansted to Chambery	Bristol to Chambery	Manchester to Chambery
from £29 one way	from £29 one way	from £34 one way	from £39 one way

And more Service!

Ski & boot carriage *on all* snowjet flights

20Kgs baggage allowance

Book *online now* at

www.snowjet.co.uk

Quoted prices valid at 6th May 2008. Snowjet is a trading name of Satellite Travel, one of the largest suppliers of flights to ski tour operators for over 20 years.

Book with confidence, Snowjet is ATOL protected.

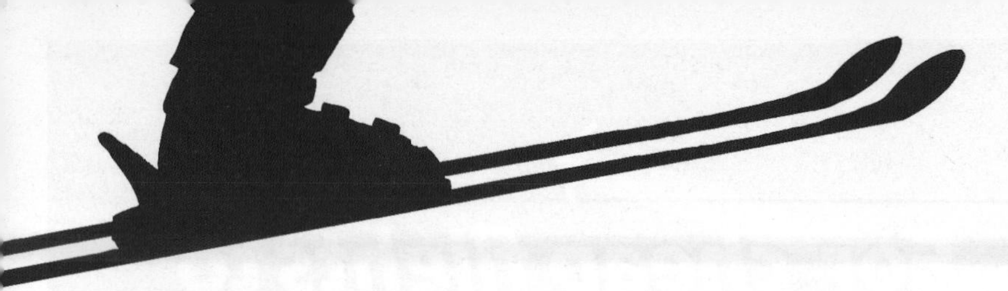

This winter, take the fast run to France.

Folkestone – Calais in only 35 minutes!

- Direct motorway access
- No luggage, roof box or ski supplement
- Up to three shuttles per hour
- Fare covers 1 car, up to 9 skiers and 18 skis
- Book your ski travel early to get our best prices
  call 08705 34 35 36
  or visit eurotunnel.com/ski

Travel from

£49 per car, single

EURO TUNNEL

call 08705 34 35 36 or book on-line at eurotunnel.com

THE MOTORISTS' NO.1 CHOICE FOR CROSSING THE CHANNEL

Contents

Introduction

The Top Resorts

Andorra

Austria

Canada

Eastern Europe

France

Italy

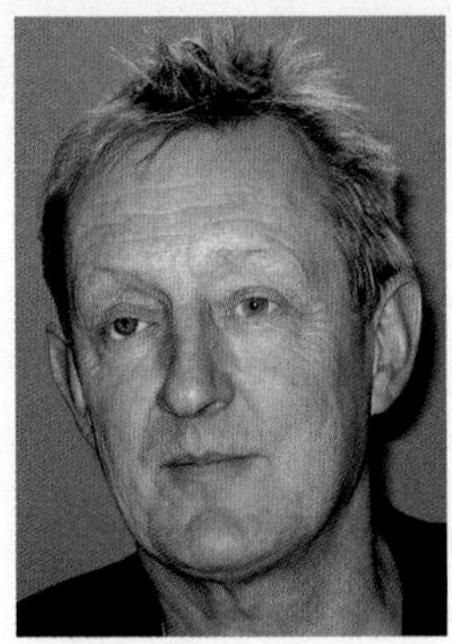

About the authors

Peter and Felice Hardy are both full-time travel writers and are acknowledged worldwide as the two most authoritative experts on ski resorts and the ski industry. They have spent many years skiing in some 500 resorts around the globe. In an average 18-week winter, Peter alone commutes from Britain to some 45 resorts on both sides of the Atlantic. When they are not up to their knees in fresh powder somewhere in the Alps, the Rockies or the Andes, they can be found at their rural home in Hampshire with their three children and three dogs, all of whom are expert skiers and accomplished snowboarders (not the dogs).

Peter and Felice are the joint authors of some 20 travel books and co-editors of the ski information website *www.welove2ski.com*. Peter is the ski correspondent of the *Daily Telegraph* and the *Daily Mail*. Felice writes regularly in the London *Evening Standard* and for an enormous number of lifestyle and travel magazines, including *Harper's Bazaar, Vanity Fair, BA High Life, Condé Nast Traveller, Country Life* and *Tatler*.

Introduction

It doesn't get much better than this. Just when the pundits were telling us that skiing as we know it was finished in Europe because of global warming, Nature struck back with a vengeance. By early November 2007 much of Austria was positively buried in the white stuff. Kitzbühel, a resort often criticized by this guide because of its low altitude and consequent questionable snow record, was digging out its lifts a full month before its normal starting date. By the time we got to the Tyrol in the middle of November, the whole of Austria was being buffeted by a blizzard that got the season off to the kind of start of which you can only dream. And then it got better.

The only downside – if you can call it that – was a long period of mid-winter sunshine. In Europe the sun refused to hide during the whole month of February, with one blue-sky day following another. But finally the snow returned and kept on returning until long after the final lifts shut down for the summer. The only true exception was Andorra, which suffered by far its worst winter in recent years – it had the sunshine, but without the snow. Indeed, there were times when a Flymo would have produced more off-piste entertainment than a pair of Völkls. But it is a tribute to Andorra's snowmaking that almost all runs remained open – even if there were at times little more than stubborn ribbons of white stamped on an otherwise green mountainside. Even here, it came right in the end. The picture on the far side of the Atlantic was equally – if not more – rosy, with regular top-ups throughout a hugely productive winter. Jackson Hole and Fernie broke all records. Whistler had a ball, positioning itself nicely for the upcoming Olympics in 2010.

So, where do we go from here? The answer, weather-wise, is forwards with extreme caution. Let's not kid ourselves. Global warming hasn't gone away, it's just played truant (or hookey, if you come from North America) for a single season.

At the time of writing, we cannot say that conditions in the coming season will even begin to match those of last winter; hopefully it will also be good. But the spectre of climate change has not gone away.

If you are planning to buy property you would be wise to look at 1750m or above – not that many people are rushing to buy ski chalets and apartments in Europe at present. The strength of the euro also means that the cost of a chalet, along with the average ski holiday this winter, rises by at least 15 per cent on last year. But skiers and snowboarders are a resilient lot. We're not going to let price get in the way, although rising fuel costs may have considerable influence on where we choose to go.

North America seems the obvious choice this winter. Check out Revelstoke Mountain Resort, which we consider to be the most exciting development on either side of the Atlantic in the past 20 years. Avoid Europe over half-term: for the first time in at least five years, the Government has squeezed almost every school in the country into one February week. Prices are ridiculously high and overcrowding on the slopes in big name French resorts will be nothing short of dangerous.

Ski safely, have fun, and for up-to-the-minute snow reports and further news on resorts and holidays, check out our ski information website at *www.welove2ski.com*

Hardy's Skiing & Snowboarding Awards 2009

Hardy's Skiing & Snowboarding Awards are judged by a panel of experts, including the authors of the guide, and take into account nominations supplied by readers. These prestigious awards go to the resorts, hotels and restaurants that demonstrate particular merit. One winner has been selected for each category, one in Europe and one in North America.

Readers are invited to submit their nominations for Hardy's Skiing & Snowboarding 2010 Awards. Please send them by email to *pictures@skishoot.co.uk*

BEST SKI RESORT

Europe: Verbier, Switzerland
North America: Banff-Lake Louise, Alberta

BEST SMALL RESORT

Europe: Samoëns, France
North America: Jasper, Alberta

BEST FAMILY RESORT

Europe: Courchevel 1650
North America: Snowmass, Colorado

MOST PROMISING RESORT

Europe: Grimentz, Switzerland
North America: Revelstoke, BC

BEST SKI HOTEL

Europe: Hotel Bella Tola, St Luc, Switzerland, and Hotel Manali, Courchevel 1650, France
North America: Fox Hotel & Suites, Banff, Alberta

BEST SKI SPA

Europe: Hotel Tschuggen, Arosa
North America: Red Earth Spa, Banff, Alberta

BEST MOUNTAIN RESTAURANT

Europe: L'Olympic, Verbier, Switzerland
Japan: Northern Resort, Niseko

BEST RESORT RESTAURANT

Europe: Hotel Neige et Roc, Samoëns, France
North America: Maple Leaf Grille, Banff, Alberta

BEST APRÈS-SKI VENUE

Europe: Le Farinet, Verbier, Switzerland
North America: Garibaldi Lift Company, Whistler, BC

BEST SKI SCHOOL

Europe: Oxygène, Val d'Isère and La Plagne, France
North America: Jackson Hole Mountain Sports School, Wyoming

BEST SKI SHOP

Europe: Francis Sport, Courchevel 1650 and Snowberry, Val d'Isère, France
North America: Ski Hub, Banff

The Best

These are the resorts or ski areas we consider to be the best in a variety of categories. The 10 entries in each are listed alphabetically rather than in order of merit.

First-timers

Bansko
Beaver Creek
Big White
Flaine
Livigno
Mayrhofen
Pal-Arinsal/Vallnord
Poiana Brasov
Saas-Fee
Westendorf

Intermediates

Banff–Lake Louise
Courchevel
La Plagne
Park City Resort
Sauze d'Oulx
Serre Chevalier
Soldeu/Grandvalira
Söll/SkiWelt
Vail
Wengen

Challenge-hunters

Aspen
Chamonix
Jackson Hole
St Anton
Snowbird and Alta
Taos
Telluride
Val d'Isère
Verbier
Zermatt

Mixed groups

Les Arcs/Paradiski
Aspen
Banff-Lake Louise
Courchevel
Flaine
Lech and Zürs
Morzine
Park City
Vail
Whistler

Snowboarders

Avoriaz
Axamer Lizum
Breckenridge
Chamonix
Davos
Mammoth
St Anton
Serre Chevalier
Verbier
Whistler

Steep and deep

Alagna
Chamonix
Jackson Hole
Kicking Horse
La Grave
Revelstoke
Snowbird and Alta
Val d'Isère
Verbier
Whistler

Mogul-hoppers

Avoriaz
Breckenridge
Killington
Klosters
Mürren
Red Resort
St Anton
Taos
Telluride
Verbier

Ski to lunch

Cortina d'Ampezzo
Courchevel
Courmayeur
Kicking Horse
Klosters
Megève
St Anton
St Moritz
The Canyons
Zermatt

Luxury

Aspen
Beaver Creek
Courchevel 1850
Deer Valley
Gstaad
Jackson Hole
Lech and Zürs
Méribel
St Moritz
Zermatt

Après-ski gourmets

Aspen
Banff
Courchevel
Courmayeur
Kitzbühel
Megève
Park City
St Anton
Telluride
Zermatt

Party-goers

Banff
Baqueira-Beret

Chamonix
Ischgl
Kitzbühel
Pas de la Casa/
  Grandvalira
St Anton
Sauze d'Oulx
Verbier
Zermatt

Ski and shop

Arinsal/Andorra La Vella
Aspen
Breckenridge
Cortina d'Ampezzo
Jackson Hole
Livigno
Madonna di Campiglio
Megève
Park City
Whistler

Ski and spa

Arosa
Aspen
Bad Gastein
Banff
Grindelwald
Megève
St Moritz
Snowbird
Telluride
Whistler

Cosmopolitan sophistication

Aspen
Courchevel 1850
Davos
Grindelwald
Kitzbühel
St Moritz
Sun Valley
Telluride
Whistler
Zermatt

Families with young children

Åre
Beaver Creek
Geilo
La Tania
Lake Louise
Obergurgl
Sun Peaks
Tignes
Valmorel
Villars

Families with older children

Courchevel 1650
Flims
Les Gets
Saalbach
Schladming
Soldeu/Vallnord
Tignes
Vail
Vaujany
Whistler

Non-skiers

Åre
Aspen
Banff
Cortina d'Ampezzo
Kitzbühel
Megève
St Moritz
Seefeld
Telluride
Zermatt

Value

Arinsal/Vallnord
Bansko
Barèges
Fernie
Levi
Livigno
Niederau
Poiana Brasov
Red Resort
Serre Chevalier

Snow-sure

Cervinia
Kaprun
Neustift/Stubai
Obergurgl-Hochgurgl
Obertauern
Passo Tonale
Niseko
Saas-Fee
Tignes/Val d'Isère
Val Thorens

Romantic

Alpbach
Courmayeur
Jackson Hole
Kitzbühel
Megève
Saas-Fee
St Luc/Grimentz
Telluride
Zell am See
Zermatt

Off the beaten track

Alagna
Crested Butte
Kicking Horse
La Grave
Red Resort
Rusutsu
Sainte-Foy
St-Gervais
St-Martin-de-Belleville
Taos

Resorts in exotic locations

Banff-Lake Louise
Chamonix
Cortina d'Ampezzo
Grindelwald
Heavenly
Las Leñas
Niseko
Portillo
Ruapehu
Thredbo

Purpose-built convenience

Big White
Courchevel
Flaine
Kicking Horse
La Plagne
Les Arcs
Obertauern
Snowbird
Tignes
Valmorel

State-of-the art lifts

Bansko
Copper Mountain
Keystone
Kicking Horse
Kronplatz
The Canyons
Tremblant
Trois Vallées
Saalbach-Hinterglemm
Yellowstone Club

Village back doors to large ski areas

Champagny/Montchavin (Paradiski)
Champéry (Portes du Soleil)
Corvara (Sella Ronda)
Dorfgastein (Gasteinertal)
Ellmau (SkiWelt)
Flachau/Wagrain (Salzburger Sportwelt)
St-Martin-de-Belleville (Trois Vallées)
Samoëns (Flaine)
Stuben (St Anton)
Vaujany (Alpe d'Huez)

Close to an interesting city/ airport convenience

Baqueira-Beret (Granada)
Chamonix (Geneva)
Cortina d'Ampezzo (Venice)
Mont-Ste-Anne (Québec City)
Park City Resorts (Salt Lake City)
Sauze d'Oulx (Turin)
Seefeld (Innsbruck)
Valle Nevado (Santiago)
Whistler (Vancouver)
Winter Park (Denver)

Heli- or cat-skiing

Fernie
Grand Targhee
Humber Valley
Kicking Horse
La Thuile
Panorama
Revelstoke
Sun Peaks
Whistler
Zermatt

Buying into the Ski Property Boom

By Sean Newsom

For many skiers, it has become a potent dream: the idea of not just skiing a mountain, but owning a little piece of it too. Buying property, be it a flat or fully fledged chalet, in a resort has become so popular of late that both the Alps and the Rockies have been swept by a construction boom – and each summer the hills are alive not with music but the clank and hammer of new builds. The rising value of the euro has currently put on hold the plans of many British skiers who had dreamt of an Alpine hideaway. Others have simply turned their attention to Canada and the US where prices are currently more attractive.

But before you rush to join the ranks of skiers with second homes, just pause for breath a moment and answer one simple question. Do you really need to do this? Sure, if you're looking at the mountain market purely as an investment, then fine: provided you buy in the right place (more of which in a moment), it's a sound idea. But if you're driven simply by a love of snow, chair lifts and gravity-driven excitement, then you should think very carefully about nailing your skiing adventures down to a single location. After all, half the fun of skiing lies in the exploration of new slopes, new mountains, new countries even. It's this experience that drives a book like *Hardy's Skiing & Snowboarding Guide*, and it has certainly helped make skiing and boarding a life-changing experience for me over the years. Do you really want to lay all of that aside in favour of one resort?

My own feeling is that younger skiers should keep their cash in their wallets and concentrate on spreading their wings. It's only later, when they've got children, that a ski property makes sense. Actually, at that point it makes very good sense indeed. Being in one place will allow you to develop relationships with kindergartens, ski schools and restaurants, and to gain a knowledge of snow conditions that you will benefit from for years. You can then let the kids off the leash, kick back on a sunny terrace somewhere, and relax.

So if you are in the market for a second home for your family, what are the most important considerations? First is travel. Will you always be happy to fly to your home? It's an important issue, with fears of global warming pricking the conscience of even the most hardened consumers and the price of air travel set to rise over the next few years. There are practical issues to consider too – such as how to get a family's clobber from the UK to your second home. Most people would be well advised to keep their transport options open, and restrict their search to an area west of Verbier. Frankly, driving any further than this is a drag, and taking the train will involve spending at least one night in a couchette carriage.

The second consideration is whether or not you want a second home for the summer as well as for skiing. If the only thing you care about is snow, then the advice is simple: aim high, and keep to the famous names. Unless you're a hedge fund manager, this will mean compromising on the size of your property, but who cares how big the sitting room is if you're going to be outside all day? Far better to have a shoebox in Tignes or Val d'Isère, in the heart of one of the world's great lift systems, than be rattling around in some overblown chalet in a low-altitude resort, wondering when it's going to stop raining.

There's an added advantage to this policy, too – everyone else also wants to ski the big names, which means it'll be much easier to let your property in the weeks when you're not there.

But of course there's more to the mountains than winter and if you have your eye on long, green summers, mountain-biking, hiking, swimming or even playing golf, then you need to be a little more subtle in your search. A lot of the most snowsure resorts in the western Alps are bleak, tree-less spots and can be hard on both head and heart when the snows melt. So you need to try to find a spot which is a little lower, sheltered by trees, and yet offers good skiing, or which, failing that, is only a short commute from somewhere that does.

Several resorts fit the bill nicely. Les Arcs, for example, has a buzzing summer scene, and less hard-core scenery than the likes of Tignes. The choice of properties has dramatically improved here of late, too. Sainte-Foy, on the road up to Val d'Isère, is a lovely spot in both summer and winter, though property prices have jumped here in recent years. Vaujany, linked by cable car to Alpe d'Huez, is another mountain village with huge potential. A couple of hours with a map and this guide will help you to locate a clutch of others.

Whatever you do, avoid two common pitfalls. The first is to fall for property developers' hype about brand-new resorts, unless they're in western Canada or the American Rockies – or linked to an established ski area. Second, think carefully before committing to North America in general. At the moment, the expanding resorts of western Canada, such as Revelstoke, are a sound investment. But do you really want to sit on a plane for nine hours every time you want a break in your lovely ski pad?

And one more thing. If you do find somewhere gorgeous, close to the lifts, in a stunning resort, can I come and stay?

For ski property specialists in the UK see Directory, page 533*. Bear in mind that most specialize in new developments. To properly explore the resale market, you'll need to contact local estate agents. It's best to Google for contacts, or call the local tourist office.*

For the widest choice of ski holidays, and ski properties for sale, in the finest resorts

Register now for early releases and pre-season discounts

Property sales:
020 7590 1624
www.ernalowproperty.co.uk

Ski holidays:
0845 863 0525
www.ernalow.co.uk

Family Skiing

By Felice Hardy

The number of families taking a childcare-inclusive ski holiday in recent years has increased to the point where demand during the peak weeks is beginning to outstrip supply. If you are hoping to go to the Alps over New Year or at February half-term, a call to any of the specialist family tour operators couldn't be soon enough. This winter, for the first time in the past six years, schools throughout the country will be taking the same half-term week beginning 14/15 February. Competition for the pick of chalet and hotel beds is high and prices have spiralled.

It helps if the parents are themselves experienced skiers. Getting children dressed, breakfasted, booted and off to ski school each morning complete with lift pass, skis, mittens and a pair of goggles is hard work. Getting all of you there on time and into separate ski classes is virtually impossible. You need expert help.

Crèches and classes

We recommend going with a tour operator who offers dedicated childcare. More than 30 operators have a crèche or nanny service. Most provide baby care, as well as indoor and outdoor play for children up to six years old. This takes place from around 9am to 4.30pm, which gives parents enough time to go skiing.

Non-skiing children under the age of four require full-day care with lunch provided. Skiing children under eight may be happy to go to lessons in the morning, but few will have the energy for a whole day on the slopes. Ideally, you should find an operator with staff who pick up your child at lunchtime and then either return him or her to ski school in the afternoon or provide entertainment or activities such as skating or tobogganing until you return.

The tour operator's crèche – and indeed the resort kindergarten – provides cots for little ones to have a rest during the day. Potties, high chairs and bottle-warmers are usually also provided, as well as toys, books, games, colouring equipment and videos. Bring your own nappies and milk formula. Trying to buy your usual size or brand in a ski resort can be difficult.

When to start

Doting parents have been known to start their children skiing when they are still in nappies – more for their own benefit than for their child's. If you really have to, **Bobo's Miniclub**, **t** +43 (0)4285 8241, *www.skiarena.at*, in Nassfeld, Austria, offers lessons for two-year-olds. However, you run the risk of putting your child off the sport for years to come. The ideal age to start is between five and eight years old.

Where to stay

The overall success of your holiday is dependent on choosing the right resort. Proximity to the nursery slopes, the lifts and ski school rendezvous point is a great energy-saver for families with children of all ages.

No.1 FOR FAMILY SKIING

ESPRIT

Ski

17 Top resorts in Switzerland, France, Austria and Italy

Market-leading, dedicated child care in every resort!

- ★ *We focus 100% on families, guaranteeing complete dedication to family needs*
- ★ *Exclusive Esprit Nurseries with qualified English-speaking nannies*
- ★ *Exclusive Esprit ski classes, with maximum 6 or 8 children per qualified instructor*
- ★ *Children's afternoon Activity Clubs & evening 'Cocoa Clubs' in every resort*
- ★ *Free evening Baby-Listening / Child Patrol Service available*
- ★ *Strict child care ratios & procedures based on 26 years' child care experience*

Fly direct from all over the country – Gatwick, Stansted, Bristol, Birmingham, Manchester, Edinburgh, and *NEW* - Southampton.

Call: 01252 618 300 Visit: espritski.com

The best hotels have a relaxed atmosphere and plenty of like-minded families around you. If you are taking a baby or toddler they can pre-book extras such as cots and high-chairs. Check whether evening babysitting is available so that you can escape when you need to. An in-house crèche, larger-than-normal 'family rooms' or two linked rooms are big bonuses.

Apartments provide flexible accommodation best suited to families with older children, allowing the option of eating in or out each evening. Cooking for your family saves money, and it is fun – as well as educational – to shop in foreign supermarkets.

Chalets are the home-from-home option and you won't have to worry about your noisy children running around and disturbing other guests. The living areas usually have satellite television, DVD and CD players; some even have games rooms and other useful extras. An early children's supper is provided, and the chalet staff will sometimes babysit for an extra fee.

Which area?

Andorra

No longer has a price advantage, but several resorts have linked to form impressive intermediate ski areas. Last season the snow cover was poor.

Highlighted resort: Soldeu in the Grandvalira region.

Austria

The traditional place to learn. It is pretty and jolly, with comfortable and friendly family-run hotels and some great hotel spas for parents to relax in after skiing.

Highlighted resorts: Mayrhofen, Obergurgl, Saalbach and Schladming.

Eastern Europe

Much lower prices, with Bansko in Bulgaria now competing in terms of ski infrastructure with comparably sized alpine resorts. However, it can be very crowded.

France

The most popular country for British families, with some of the best-equipped crèches in Europe, but the 'you are here to learn' attitude of some ski schools can be off-putting. No longer cheap; go for a catered chalet to save on other costs in euros.

Highlighted resorts: Les Gets, Courchevel, La Tania, Mèribel, Morzine, Tignes, Valmorel and Vaujany.

Italy

Not great for small children, as many resorts (Ortisei is an exception) do not have childcare owing to the Italian penchant for bringing granny along on the family holiday as babyminder.

Scandinavia

Most Norwegians and Swedes are fluent English-speakers (this matters enormously to you if you are four years old and have been left for the week in a strange environment). Safety is paramount, with free helmets offered wherever you go. Alternative activities include husky sleigh rides and dog-sledding, which are lots of fun.

Highlighted resorts: Åre, Hemsedal and Geilo.

Call us on 0845 64 437 64

Well located chalets, inclusive childcare, great service, fabulous food and superb skiing.

Visit us online www.skifamille.co.uk

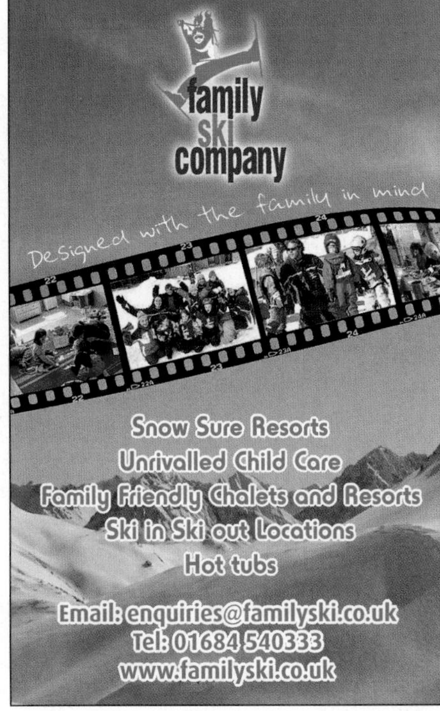

Switzerland

Used to be seen as the expensive option, but the most fashionable French resorts have caught up, price-wise. The country offers efficiency, excellent skiing, and traditional villages full of atmosphere.

Highlighted resorts: Arosa, Flims, Villars and Zermatt.

North America

This is where to find value for money this season, and North America also provides a less frenetic alternative in high season. Nowhere in Europe can beat the enthusiastic welcome your child will receive, and the advantage of tuition in your native language outweighs almost everything else.

Highlighted resorts: (younger kids) Beaver Creek, Deer Valley, Banff–Lake Louise; (older kids) Fernie, Snowmass, Vail and Whistler.

How to dodge the crowds

There are several ways to minimize the inconvenience of the half-term and New Year crowds. The first is to choose a resort with a really modern lift system (*see* 'The Best: State-of-the-art lifts') that can cope with large numbers swiftly and efficiently. The second is to opt for a lesser-known resort (*see* 'The Best: Village back doors'), which is part of a bigger ski area. The third is to go for a resort off the beaten track (*see* 'The Best: Off the beaten track'). The fourth is to go to North America.

Potential problems

The younger the child, the more likely you are to encounter a hitch, including dehydration from the high altitude. Avoid taking little ones under 18 months to very high resorts (2000m or above) as it can be stressful for them and if they have a cold they can get ear infections, which will ruin everyone's holiday.

Teen scene

It is important for them to be seen in all the right places – so check 'The Best: Party-goers'. If you don't want to waste their expensive lift passes, parents should insist that adolescents vacate their beds and hit the slopes by 10am. Do not stay in a hotel (the extras of drinks and telephone calls may necessitate a second mortgage); opt for an apartment or chalet instead.

Other activities

Choose a location with alternatives activities on offer. Snow-tubing is the tobogganing of the 21st century, and can be enjoyed by children from four years. You sit comfortably cocooned inside a rubber ring with handles and rocket down a man-made course. Dog-sledding is fun for all ages, with older children able to drive their own dog team in some Canadian resorts.

Corporate Skiing

By Peter Hardy

Standing at the top of a vertiginous *couloir* above Zermatt, the multi-choice business option is a familiar one for a high-flying investment banker used to taking momentous decisions under pressure. The Swiss ski instructor looks as relaxed as a mountain goat on this near vertical slope as she explains to the sweating, white-faced figure perched on the ledge above her what his immediate future holds.

'OK, you've got two options here. One: you can go for it. In order not to fall – and you really don't want to think of falling here – you've got to commit yourself totally to that first turn. Don't just think about the initial one, visualize the second and third turns as well. Use the edges of both skis. You're a good skier; you can do it. The only problem you have is in your mind. Two: you can climb back up, take the easy way down and meet the rest of us later at the bottom. No one is going to think the less of you for it'.

Understandably, The Banker's not so sure about that. His MD has already gone down.

Corporate team-building and brainstorming, for five partners or 1,500 employees, is one of the biggest growth areas in skiing, with a collection of specialist tour operators cashing in on the demand for executive outward-bound courses in a hedonistic high-altitude environment.

The bonding takes place in only the most upmarket resorts and, as most companies are time-poor, they usually opt for a long weekend rather than a full week. There is almost no limit to what can be planned, from champagne on the transfers to private jets and helicopters, guiding and instruction, picnics on the piste, evening menus complete with company logo, and ski races.

Six-star luxury is second nature to **Descent International**, the most hedonistic of all chalet operators. In its time the company has arranged husky safaris, organized firework displays, booked magicians, and shipped in five tons of sand to transform a mountain restaurant into Rick's Bar from *Casablanca*. They organize everything from private jets and helicopter transfers to digging a fire-pit in the snow and barbecuing a whole sheep, as they were once asked to do. On arrival, Descent brings the ski shop to the chalet so clients can choose equipment in comfort.

Equally deluxe is **Scott Dunn** with a gilt-edged client list headed by Deutsche Bank. A favourite activity is privately booking the lift from Zermatt up to Furi, then walking down to the charming restaurant of Zum See for dinner, carrying flares.

Tailor-made whiz **Momentum** has looked after the Google ski trip, an annual gathering on snow of 1,500 Google executives. Momentum first made its mark on the corporate scene by starting the annual City Ski Championships in Courmayeur, where ski-minded Square Mile companies get a chance to compete against each other in a testosterone- and Veuve Clicquot-fuelled environment.

THE CORPORATE
SKI COMPANY

If you want to organise a winter event then you must call the specialist.

- With over 13 years of experience in planning and operating over 200 winter sports events, we have the knowledge and contacts required
- We work in Europe, Canada and the USA
- All programmes can combine skiing and non-skiing, meetings and presentations with social and fun activities

For more details contact:
Charlie Paddock
The Corporate Ski Company
TEL: 020 8542 8555 Fax: 020 8542 8102
e-mail: ski@vantagepoint.co.uk
www.thecorporateskicompany.co.uk

4481 ATOL PROTECTED

eventia

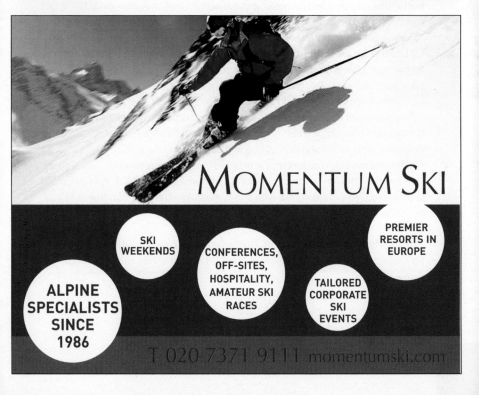

MOMENTUM SKI

SKI WEEKENDS

CONFERENCES, OFF-SITES, HOSPITALITY, AMATEUR SKI RACES

PREMIER RESORTS IN EUROPE

TAILORED CORPORATE SKI EVENTS

ALPINE SPECIALISTS SINCE 1986

T 020 7371 9111 momentumski.com

For the past 13 years, **The Corporate Ski Company** has organized some 35 winter events each season for high-profile clients including major financial institutions. They pride themselves on being led by brief rather than by destination. This means that they will propose the place that best suits their client's needs. Last season they organised events from 20 up to 180 people. These included a CEO forum in Kitzbuhel, and an Olympic taxi-bob experience in Italy. They organized an ice hockey game for an incentive weekend in Chamonix, which was followed by a casino night in a restaurant that they had taken over exclusively for the evening.

Last winter, The Corporate Ski Company launched its Winter Alternatives corporate programme to Iceland, Finnish Lapland and Lillehammer in Norway. Activities include snowmobiling, super jeep safaris, biathlon, reindeer sleigh rides and bobsleigh.

Altitude Inspires is a platinum-level newcomer with an impeccable pedigree. **Exosphere**, its sister company, is a bespoke travel company that is so exclusive that it is by invitation only. Clients of Altitude include a number of top City institutions, as well as other FTSE 250 companies. Managing director John Saunders was brought up in Switzerland, and the company's strength lies in its network of high-level contacts in the Alps. Activities include ski guiding with former Olympic downhill champions Pirmin Zurbriggen in Switzerland and Patrick Ortlieb in Austria. The company also arranges VIP ski events at the World Economic Forum in Davos.

Powder Byrne's most unusual demands included a company flag flown on top of a hotel, and a sunrise breakfast on a glacier complete with chefs and waiters.

Ski 2's flexible approach means they are always completely understanding about fluctuating numbers and names of group members that may change up to the last minute. They have years of experience in organizing groups up to 200 people.

Flexible operator **Ski Weekend** has taken groups from six to 60, mainly to Davos, Cortina d'Ampezzo, St Moritz and Chamonix. On one occasion they had to create an ice bar with a Swiss bank's logo on it; on another they held a Burns Night dinner up the mountain – complete with haggis.

Chamonix operator **Mountain Leap Events** has in the past held a mountaintop banquet reached by snowmobile. Once – for a product launch – they buried a car on the hillside for an alpine treasure hunt. Their clients include Barclays Capital, Goldman Sachs, Mako, Vodafone, CIT, 3i and Boeing.

Jeffersons has organized corporate trips to St Moritz, the resort that sets a world standard for indulgence. Travel is by private jet from Farnborough, Biggin Hill, Luton or Stansted, direct to the resort, with a 10-minute limo transfer from tiny St Moritz airport to the hotel. Champagne, wine and a Jeffersons hamper are all on board the flight.

Back in the *couloir* above Zermatt, The Banker takes a deep breath, thinks of his colleagues waiting down below, pictures his annual bonus, and skis it with surprising ease.

Corporate operators

Altitude Inspires, **t** +44 (0)20 7591 4970, *www.altitudeinspires.com*
The Corporate Ski Company, **t** +44 (0)20 8542 8100, *www.thecorporateskicompany.co.uk*
Descent International, **t** +44 (0)20 7384 3854, *www.descent.co.uk*
Flexiski, **t** +44 (0)1273 244 668, *www.flexiski.com*
Jeffersons, **t** +44 (0)870 850 8181, *www.jeffersons.com*
Kaluma Travel, **t** +44 (0)870 442 8044, *www.kalumatravel.co.uk*
Made to Measure, **t** +44 (0)1243 533 333, *www.mtmholidays.co.uk*
Momentum Ski, **t** +44 (0)20 7371 9111, *www.momentumski.com*
Mountain Leap Events, **t** +44 (0)20 7931 0621, *www.mountainleap.com*
The Oxford Ski Company, **t** +44 (0)870 787 1785, *www.oxfordski.com*
Pollen-Brooks Leisure, **t** +44 (0)1344 849 135, *www.pollenbrooks.com*
Powder Byrne, **t** +44 (0)20 8246 5300, *www.powderbyrne.com*
Scott Dunn Corporate, **t** +44 (0)20 8682 5080, *www.scottdunn.com*
Ski 2, **t** +44 (0)1962 713 330, *www.ski-2.com*
Ski Verbier, **t** +44 (0)20 7385 8050, *www.skiverbier.com*
Ski Weekend, **t** +44 (0)870 060 0615, *www.skiweekend.com*
White Roc Weekends, **t** +44 (0)20 7792 1188, *www.whiteroc.co.uk*

The Ski Club of Great Britain icon, which appears in the Top Resorts chapters of this guide, highlights resorts where you will find a representative of the Ski Club of Great Britain. *See* p. 4 for details of the Ski Club of Great Britain 2009 offer.

01

The Top Resorts: Andorra

Pal-Arinsal and Ordino-Arcalis

* BEST FOR

First-timers, families, nightlife (Pal-Arinsal) and competent skiers and riders (Ordino-Arcalis)

ESSENTIALS

Altitude: Pal-Arinsal 1940m (6,363ft) –2624m (8,609ft); Ordino-Arcalis 1950m (5,084ft)–2573m (8,442ft)
Further information: t +376 878 000, *www.vallnord.com*
Lifts in area: 38 (3 cableways, 17 chairs, 18 drags) serving 89km of piste
Lift pass: Vallnord €138–162, child 6–11yrs €102–123, both for six days
Access: Toulouse airport 3½hrs, Barcelona airport 3hrs

Profile

Friendly area with good nightlife, an excellent nursery and easy intermediate slopes

Resorts

The village of Arinsal and the linked ski area of Pal joined forces with the valley town of La Massana and the quite separate ski area of Ordino-Arcalis to form the single lift pass region of Vallnord.

It's all part of the dramatic £112 million regeneration of Andorra in recent years as a serious ski destination. It has unceremoniously binned its bargain basement image, and the once humble resort of Arinsal, still renowned for its low-cost nightlife, has even managed to twin itself with glitzy Gstaad in Switzerland.

The problem last season was the snow – or rather the lack of it. Winter didn't truly arrive until Easter, then, just as everyone was packing up and heading home at the end of the season the skies opened. However, it is a tribute to the extraordinarily efficient artificial snow system here and elsewhere in Andorra that nearly all runs remained open throughout the season. But at times, if you ventured off the carefully farmed pistes, you would have had more luck with a seven iron or a sit-on mower than a pair of Salomons.

Most skiers and riders choose to stay in Arinsal, an attractive little resort with easy gondola access to some easy beginner and low intermediate pistes. 'I could not recommend this place highly enough,' said a reader.

A sleek 12-person gondola connects La Massana into the Pal-Arinsal circuit, making it an alternative and convenient place in which to stay. It is also a convenient base for the more demanding and much underrated ski area of Ordino-Arcalis, situated a 20-minute drive away up a remote valley. Arcalis has recently received an investment of €3 million for more snow cannons and restaurant improvements.

When the snow is good and the sun is shining, the easy, undulating pistes can match those of any resort. But no amount of investment can give the mountains here the thrilling high-altitude terrain of the Alps.

One of the major reasons to choose the Vallnord region is its proximity to the capital, Andorra La Vella. Here you can shop your heart out on the Avenida Carlemany. Boutiques sell designer names like Versace, Armani, Ralph Lauren and Dolce & Gabbana at discount prices.

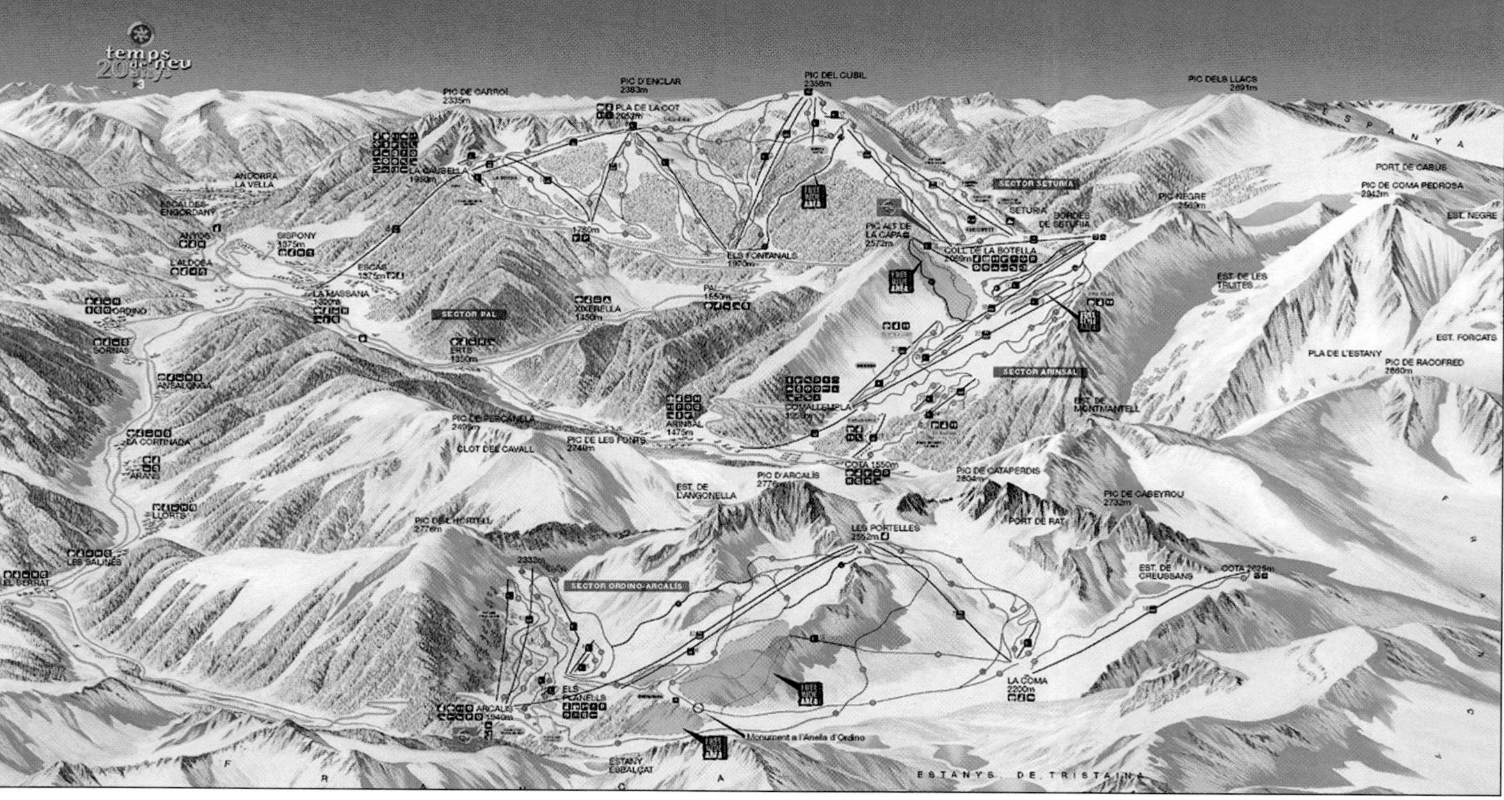
VALLNORD Mountain Park
temps de neu
PIC DE CARROI
2335m
PIC D'ENCLAR
2383m
PLA DE LA COT
PIC DEL CUBIL
2358m
PIC DELS LLACS
2691m
ESPANYA
PORT DE CABÚS
PIC DE COMA PEDROSA
2942m
EST. NEGRE
SECTOR SETURIA
PIC NEGRE
SETURIA
BORDES DE SETURIA
ANDORRA LA VELLA
ESCALDES-ENGORDANY
LA CAUBELLA
ANYÓS
BISPONY
1375m
L'ALDOSA
ESCÀS
1375m
LA MASSANA
ELS FONTANALS
1970m
PIC ALT DE LA CAPA
2572m
COLL DE LA BOTELLA
2069m
EST. DE LES TRUITES
ORDINO
SECTOR PAL
XIXERELLA
1450m
PAL
1550m
SORNÀS
ERTS
1350m
ANSALONGA
SECTOR ARINSAL
PLA DE L'ESTANY
PIC DE RACOFRED
2860m
EST. FORCATS
COMALLEMPLA
ARINSAL
1475m
PIC DE PERCANELA
PIC DE LES FONTS
2749m
EST. DE MONTMANTELL
LA CORTINADA
CLOT DEL CAVALL
ARANS
COTA 1550m
PIC D'ARCALÍS
2776m
PIC DE CATAPERDIS
2804m
EST. DE L'ANGONELLA
PIC DE CABEYROU
2732m
LLORTS
PIC DEL HORTELL
2776m
LES PORTELLES
2552m
PORT DE RAT
LES SALINES
EL SERRAT
2332m
SECTOR ORDINO-ARCALÍS
EST. DE CREUSSANS
COTA 2625m
ELS PLANELLS
LA COMA
2200m
ARCALÍS
1940m
Monument a l'Anella d'Ordino
ESTANY ESBALÇAT
ESTANYS DE TRISTAINA
FRANÇA

Mountain

Although the resort is busy, the lift system is efficient and so there is not too much queuing. Arinsal's skiing begins with a gondola ride from the middle of the village up to the mid-mountain station at 1950m. A new six-person chair will be in place for the 2008–9 season.

Lifts from here bring you up towards the 2569m Pic Negre and allow for some smooth novice and easy runs back down to 1950m. In good snow conditions the descent through the trees to the valley is hugely enjoyable.

From the top of Arinsal, a cable car spans the valley to the Col de La Botella and the start of the Pal ski area. Although the El Cubil six-pack replaced an old quad last season and the runs here are slightly more demanding, the whole area is best suited to beginners and low intermediates.

Ordino-Arcalis is of considerably more interest for advanced skiers. Its remote position and limited base facilities deter most foreign tourists except the Spanish from across the border. This is where you will find Andorrans skiing at weekends.

A couple of black runs on the front face of the 2552m mountain provide a serious challenge, as well as several long reds served by modern quad-chairs. A new gondola is on the drawing board, but has yet to materialize.

Vallnord has a high percentage of riders among its clientele. The 40,000m^2 FreeStyle Area at Arinsal contains a half-pipe, jumps and other obstacles.

'The runs are always well groomed and the area has great artificial snowmaking capabilities,' said a reporter, and 'the lifts are quick and every year become a bit more modernized'. This is set to improve further, with €6 million currently being invested in new lifts, snow-cannon and restaurants, so watch this space.

Learn

'Pal–Arinsal has more than enough ski runs for beginners,' said a reader. **Arinsal, t** +376 737 029, and **Pal, t** +376 737 008, ski schools have lots of experience in teaching foreign skiers. **Arcalis, t** +376 739 600, is the third school.

Children

Babyclub cares for children from 12 months at Comallempla above Arinsal and Els Planells at Pal. **Snowpark ski kindergarten** is from four years at Pal, all **t** +376 737 014. Ordino-Arcalis has a **Jardin d'Enfants, t** +376 739 600.

Lunch

At Arinsal, the midday meal is multicultural. Eat Chinese at **Xina Igloo** and Tex-Mex at **MexicObelix**, British burgers at **Panoramix**, pork n' beans in the **Far West**, or pasta at **Bella Italia**, **t** +376 737 020, for all. **La Borda, t** +376 737 020, at Pal serves chicken tikka, Thai red curry, and authentic Catalan cuisine of sausages and peppery salads. At Ordino-Arcalis, **La Coma, t** +376 850 201, specializes in barbecued meat.

Dine

Xalet restaurant in Arinsal is reportedly not the cheapest place to eat, but the food is said to be superb, 'a great place for a special occasion or a wee treat'. The incomparable **El Rusc, t** +376 838 200, in La Massana, is one of the finest restaurants in Andorra. Starters include oyster soup with saffron, a main course of steamed cod with rosemary, tomato, olives and port wine jus. **La Borda, t** +376 737 020, in Pal, is also open in the evenings.

Party

'Après in Arinsal is excellent, with friendly bar staff, loads of promotions and freebies, and superb prices,' said a reporter; 'friendly and affordable' said another. The nightlife involves sustained drinking and was rated in bars such as **El Cau** and **Quo Vadis**. **Surf** and the **Derby** are also popular. In La Massana the action is at **El Cocktail de l'Avi** and **El Xtu en el Complejo Tabola**.

Escaldes-Engordany, on the outskirts of Andorra La Vella, is home to **Caldea**, **t** +376 800 999, a futuristic spa inspired by Gaudì and made with glass and metal. Inside are Turkish, Roman, Aztec and Icelandic baths, and a thermal lagoon.

Sleep

- ★★★★ **Hotel Princesa Parc** and **Princesa Diana**, **t** +376 736 400, *www.hotelprincesaparc.com*, in Arinsal, attracts 93 per cent of its visitors from the UK. The establishment is a mélange of eccentric styles, with a bar called The Bog. Rooms are pleasant, staff are helpful and it's very close to the gondola.
- ★★★★ **Hotel Rutllan**, **t** +376 835 000, *www.hotelrutllan.ad*, is the best hotel in La Massana and ideally situated close to the gondola.
- ★★★ **Husa Xalet Verdù Hotel**, **t** +376 737 140, *www.hotelhusaxalet.es*, in Arinsal is ideal, with really friendly staff, nice rooms, and although not exactly Michelin-star quality, the food isn't bad.
- ★★★ **Poblado apartments**, **t** +376 835 122, in Arinsal, are recommended.
- ★★ **Residència Janet**, **t** +376 835 088, is a small, family-run apartment building at Erts between Arinsal and La Massana.
- ★★ **Hotel Coma Pedrosa**, **t** +376 835 123, was praised by readers surprised at the quality of the hotel. 'The rooms were newly furnished, it was clean, and the staff were really friendly.'

Pas de la Casa

Profile

Frontier town with cheap and unsophisticated nightlife at the foot of Andorra's largest ski area. Suitable for anyone looking for raw partying with piste-bashing, also for bargain-hunting shoppers

Resort

Andorra has dramatically reinvented itself as a world class destination. Pas de la Casa-Grau Roig on the French frontier shares the Grandvalira lift pass with neighbouring Soldeu-El Tarter. The skiing also extends to Canillo, Porte des Neiges and to outlying Encamp in the middle of the country. The ski area has expanded into France with the construction of a six-pack lift on Mt Pedrus on the far side of the River Arèges, which marks the frontier. It is the first of three lifts that will give access to 12 slopes in the Porte des Neiges sector.

✻ BEST FOR

20-somethings, beginners and intermediates, spirited nightlife, value

ESSENTIALS

Altitude: 2095m (6,872ft)–2580m (8,465ft)
Further information: Grandvalira, **t** +376 808 900, *www.grandvalira.com*
Lifts in area: 58 (4 cableways, 30 chairs, 24 drags) serving 193km of piste
Lift pass: Grandvalira adult €175–180, child 6–11yrs €131–138, both for six days. All Andorra passes €152 for 5 consecutive days
Access: Toulouse airport 3hrs, Barcelona airport 3hrs

GRANDVALIRA

SOLDEU
GRAU ROIG
CANILLO
MONTMALUS 2781
PIC NEGRE D'ENVALIRA 2822
PIC DE LES ABELLETES 2596
PIC BLANC
PIC DE LA MENERA 2774
PIC BAIX DEL CUBIL
CIRC DEL COLELLS
PESSONS 2307
EMPORTONA
COLLADA D'ENRADORT 2447
ESTANY DE LES ABELLETES
COMA III 2300
COLL BLANC 2528
RIOLET 2150
PESSONS
CUBIL 2100
GRAU ROIG 2120
LLAC DEL CUBIL
C. DE LES SOLANELLES 2458
TOSSAL DE LA LLOSADA 2560
CIRC DELS CORTALS
PIC D'ENCAMPADANA 2491
SOLANA DE LA GARGOTA
ELS CORTALS
PORTELLA 2465
ROCS NEGRES
CAP DE REP
TOSA DELS ESPIOLETS 2457
ESPIOLETS 2250
RIBA ESCORXADA 2100
EL FORN 2000
ENCAMP 1300
FONT NEGRE 2140
PORT D'ENVALIRA 2408
PLA DE LES PEDRES 2150
COSTA RODONA 2218
TÚNEL D'ENVALIRA
BORDES D'ENVALIRA
PAS DE LA CASA
SOLDEU 1800
EL TARTER
CANILLO 1500
SANT PERE
ST JOAN DE CASELLES
L'ALDOSA
ELS PLANS
INCLES
RANSOL
MERITXELL
PRATS
Frédérique et Pierre Novat 04.05 ©

ANDORRA

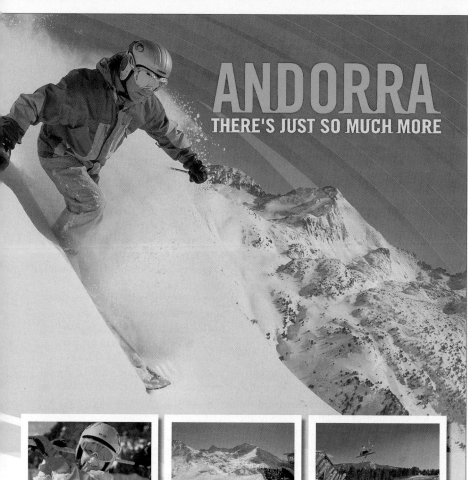

THERE'S JUST SO MUCH MORE

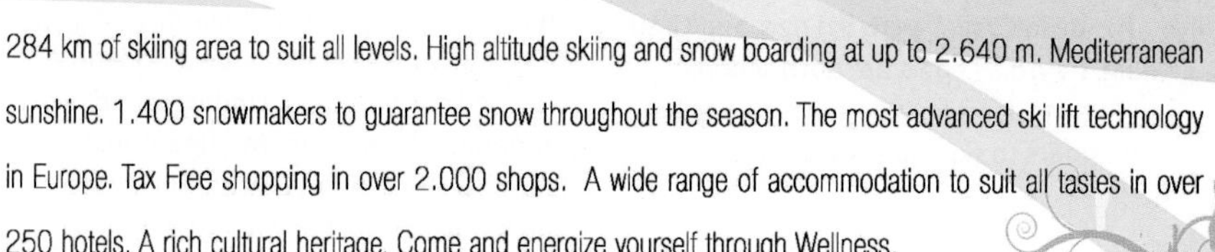

284 km of skiing area to suit all levels. High altitude skiing and snow boarding at up to 2.640 m. Mediterranean sunshine. 1.400 snowmakers to guarantee snow throughout the season. The most advanced ski lift technology in Europe. Tax Free shopping in over 2.000 shops. A wide range of accommodation to suit all tastes in over 250 hotels. A rich cultural heritage. Come and energize yourself through Wellness.

Andorra is featured in all the main UK tour operator brochures.

For more information on skiing in Andorra and on how to put together your own package visit:
www.skiandorra.ad

For more general information on Andorra visit: www.andorra.ad

Live Vallnord

VALLNORD

Ski Andorra

New lifts and hotels abound, but Pas remains a concrete dormitory with duty-free booze and some of best skiing in the principality. It is ideal for 20-somethings; other areas in Grand Valira are better suited to families and older skiers and riders.

Mountain

Mountain access from the town is by a choice of chair lifts that take you up to the ridge overlooking the hamlet of Grandvalira-Grau Roig. From here you can either explore the lift-served terrain on either side of the ridge or take the Cubil quad-chair and work your way across to the wooded slopes above Soldeu. The terrain park is on the Tubs piste at Pas. The developing ski area on the French side of the frontier is a great improvement.

Last year a serious shortage of natural snow throughout most of the season was a major problem – one blue-sky day followed another until the heavens finally opened in the dying days of the season. But, thanks to some highly efficient snow-making, *pisteurs* managed to keep almost all runs open.

Learn

Pas de la Casa, **t** +376 871 920, and **Grau Roig**, **t** +376 872 920, are both schools with considerable experience in teaching foreigners to ski and snowboard.

Children

Pas de la Casa, **t** +376 871 920, and **Grau Roig**, **t** +376 872 920, crèches care for children from 12 months to thee years. The new **Mickey Snow Club** in Grandvalira-Grau Roig and the **Jardin de Neige** ski kindergarten (**t** +376 872 920 for both) offer an introduction to skiing from three years of age.

Lunch

Llac de Pessons, **t** +376 759 015, near Grandvalira-Grau Roig, is the best mountain restaurant in Andorra. It serves fine grilled meats and enjoys dramatic views across the lake.

Dine

'The food was average and overpriced,' said a reporter. 'If you want to prepare for the day ahead, go to Paddy's for a hearty English/Irish breakfast, reasonably priced with a good atmosphere.' **Chez Paulo**, **t** +376 855 596, offers pizzas and French cuisine. **El Carlit**, **t** +376 855 211, is renowned for its mussels and trout with almonds. **Refugo Calones**, **t** +376 856 040, has fondues and raclette. **La Tagliatelle**, **t** +376 750 656, serves pizza and pasta dishes. **L'Husky**, **t** +376 855 248, was recommended for good people and good prices and rated 'fantastic' in the evening.

Party

'The après-ski in Pas is great, with free shots galore. The clubs are open until dawn and every night is busy,' commented a happy reporter. 'I have never been anywhere where they serve so many free drinks,' said another; 'après-ski, quite simply brilliant,' said a third. **Milwaukee** is the largest and most crowded bar, while the **Underground** is pronounced 'good fun'. **Mulligans Irish Pub**, **KYU Disco-pub**, **Havana**, **The Pirate** and **Kamikaze Surf** all provide serious competition. For live entertainment visit **La Marseilles**. **KSB** bar overlooks the slopes and serves brilliant steaks cooked on an open fire. **Pas 83**, on the slopes, has very welcoming staff and a cosy open fire. The **Outdoor Centre** offers paintballing in the snow. **The Grandvalira Circuit** offers ice-driving and is located at Port d'Envalira, a five-minute drive from Pas de la Casa.

Sleep

★★★★ **Hotel Himalaia Pas, t** +376 735 515, *www.hotansa.com*, has a pool, sauna and a gym.

★★★★**Aparthotel Alaska, t** +376 756 056, is situated in the upper part of town and houses La Tagliatelle restaurant.

★★★★**Hotel Font d'Argent, t** +376 739 739, *www.fontdargent.com*, is an attractive boutique hotel.

★★★**Hotel Cristina, t** +376 736 800, is a friendly hotel at the top of town.

★★★**Hotel Parma, t** +376 855 323, is just 200m from the pistes, with clean, tidy rooms, excellent staff and very good food.

★★**Hotel Camelot, t** +376 755 435, offers smallish rooms that are, nonetheless, very clean and warm with immaculate bathrooms and plentiful hot water.

Soldeu-El Tarter

Profile

This is the skiing capital of the new Andorra, a village with considerable charm that provides the most agreeable base in the principality. It suits those in search of creature comforts and good, easy skiing. Nightlife is less brash than in neighbouring Pas de la Casa-Grau Roig

Resort

Soldeu is a smart little resort just over the pass from Pas de la Casa, but a world away in style. The ribbon of stone-and-wood buildings stretching along the main road to adjoining El Tarter has undergone a physical and social transformation. 'A great resort to visit,' said one reporter, 'I will definitely be going back.'

New lifts and hotels abound, and the resort now has a five-star hotel with a four-storey spa centre of the kind of imperial proportions you might only encounter in Ancient Rome.

Like other Andorran resorts, Soldeu is still popular with budget skiers, but you have to ask yourself for how much longer. The new Andorra, recipient of lavish £112 million funding in recent years, is in danger of losing sight of why it was ever popular in the first place – for low prices.

Soldeu is part of the Grandvalira, a single ski pass area that includes Pas de la Casa, Grau Roig, El Tarter, the ancient community of Canillo further along the valley, and Porte de Neige in France. The skiing can also be accessed by gondola from Encamp in the middle of the country.

Andorra normally has reliable cover but for the last two seasons it has suffered from a shortage of natural snow. It was a tribute to its sophisticated snow-making machinery that most runs stayed open.

✻ BEST FOR

Beginners and low intermediates, families, night-owls, value

ESSENTIALS

Altitude: 1710m (5,610ft)–2580m (8,465ft)
Further information: Grandvalira, **t** +376 808 900, *www.grandvalira.com*
Lifts in area: 60 (4 cableways, 30 chairs, 26 drags) serving 193km of piste
Lift pass: Grandvalira adult €191–196, child 6–11yrs €135–141, both for six days. All Andorra passes €152 for five consecutive weekdays
Access: Toulouse airport 3hrs, Barcelona airport 3hrs

Mountain

The skiing is reached by a gondola or chair from Soldeu and by the same choice from El Tarter. From the mid-mountain station of Espiolets, lifts fan out in both directions towards Pas and further down the valley to Canillo, where a gondola leads back into the area.

The undulating terrain above and below the tree-line is best suited to beginners and intermediates. However, the substantial size of the Grandvalira should keep more advanced skiers fully occupied. Off-piste opportunities through the trees are particularly good, and new snow does not get tracked out within hours.

Recent lift improvements include the £3.8 million 10-person gondola, which takes skiers up the mountain from El Tarter.

Learn

Soldeu Ski School, **t** +376 890 591, deservedly has the reputation of being the best in Andorra and one of the top half-dozen learning academies in Europe. The set-up is highly praised by readers for its professionalism.

Much of this is due to the enthusiasm of its veteran teaching director, Yorkshireman Gordon Standeven. Some 100 of the 240 instructors are native English-speakers. **Canillo**, **t** +376 890 691, and **El Tarter**, **t** +376 890 641, also have good reputations. All of them become very crowded over February half-term.

Children

Mickey Snow Club in Soldeu, **t** +376 890 59, Canillo, **t** +376 890 691, and El Tarter, **t** +376 890 641, cares for non-skiing children aged two to three years, and the **Jardin de Neige** ski kindergarten from three years. **El Tarter**'s snowboard tuition is recommended by readers for its great board school for kids and consistently friendly, helpful staff.

Lunch

Roc de les Bruixes, **t** +376 890 696, above Canillo, is warmly recommended, along with refurbished **Solanelles**, **t** +376 759 008, in the Encamp sector. **Hotel Bruxelles**, **t** +376 851 010, is recommended at lunchtime for its great pizzas and fast service. **Gall de Bosc**, **t** +376 890 607, above Soldeu, has Catalan mountain cuisine and spectacular views. Try *faves* (warm bean, pea and ham salad) or *trixat* (bubble-and-squeak topped with slivers of black pudding). 'Avoid the mountain fast food,' warned a reader, darkly.

Dine

Soldeu's **Cort de Popaire**, **t** +376 851 211, is renowed for its grilled lamb and steaks. **La Fontanella**, **t** +376 871 787, in the Hotel Piolets, serves pasta and pizza. **Fat Albert's**, **t** +376 851 765, is rated for its great pizzas and heavenly rosemary bread, as is **Sol i Neu**, **t** +376 851 325, ('the more formal restaurant upstairs was outstanding, with great service and really interesting food'). **La Llar del Artesa**, **t** +376 851 078, just out of town at Bordes d'Envalira, has good-value Catalan mountain dishes. **Borda de l'Horto**, **t** +376 851 622, outside El Tarter, serves grilled meat and fish and is popular with the locals.

Party

Soldeu's main street is lined with shops, bars and restaurants. Nightlife is frenetic all season but, unlike brasher Pas, revellers here are not confined to the 16–25 age bracket. Venues include **The Avalanche**, **Roc Bar**, **Aspen** ('fun on Friday after the ski school races'), **Ice Berg**, **Pussy Cat** and the popular **Villager** bar. Most atmospheric is **Fat Albert's**, a cavernous barn with videos and live music and a reliable choice for après-ski drinking.

Caldea spa, **t** +376 800 999, in Escaldes-Engordany on the outskirts of the capital of Andorra La Viella, has a 600 sq metre, 68°C thermal pool and is one of the largest spas in Europe.

Sleep

All accommodation can be booked through a central reservations office, **t** +376 890 501.

Soldeu:

★★★★★**Sport Hotel Hermitage**, **t** +376 870 670, *www.sporthotels.ad*, under the same ownership as the Sport Hotel, is the resort's first five-star, with 120 suites. It is linked internally to a colossal four-storey spa with 18 treatment rooms and a giant basement pool.

★★★★**Sport Hotel Village**, **t** +376 870 500, *www.sporthotels.ad*, has a vast lobby with hacienda-style atrium. The wood-panelled bedrooms are large and comfortable. The main mountain access gondola is 50m away.

★★★★**Hotel Piolets Park**, **t** +376 872 787, *www.ahotels.ad*, has comfortable rooms and contains a steak house, swimming pool and gym.

★★★★**Hotel Himalaia Soldeu**, **t** +376 878 515, *www.himalaiahotels.ad*, has been refurbished and has a buffet-style restaurant.

★★★**Hotel Bruxelles**, **t** +376 851 010, *www.hotelbruxelles.ad*, was highly rated: 'A small personal place with the best food in Soldeu – not just my opinion but that of most instructors I've talked to,' said one reader.

★★★**Hotel Soldeu Maistre**, **t** +376 801 963, is very clean and comfortable, with an excellent choice of food.

Canillo:

★★★★**Hotel Font d'Argent**, **t** +376 753 753, *www.fontdargent.com*, in the old town centre, was new last season.

★★★**Hotel Bonavida**, **t** +376 851 300, is a cosy place with a pool.

El Tarter:

★★★★**Hotel Llop Gris**, **t** +376 751 515, *www.llopgris.com*, is convenient for the slopes, with squash courts and a pool.

★★★★**Hotel Nordic**, **t** +376 739 500, *www.grupnordic.ad*, has wood-and-stone décor and an entrance hall dominated by a Rolls-Royce.

★★★★**Hotel Euro Ski**, **t** +376 736 666, *www.hotansa.com*, is highly recommended by one reporter.

★★★**Hotel del Tarter**, **t** +376 802 080, *www.hotel-eltarter.com*, has a well-regarded restaurant.

★★★**Hotel del Clos**, **t** +376 851 500, is ski-in, ski-out and modern.

Encamp:

★★★★**Hotel Guillem**, **t** +376 832 133, 500m from the Funicamp lift, has a heated pool, sauna and hot tub.

02 The Top Resorts: Austria

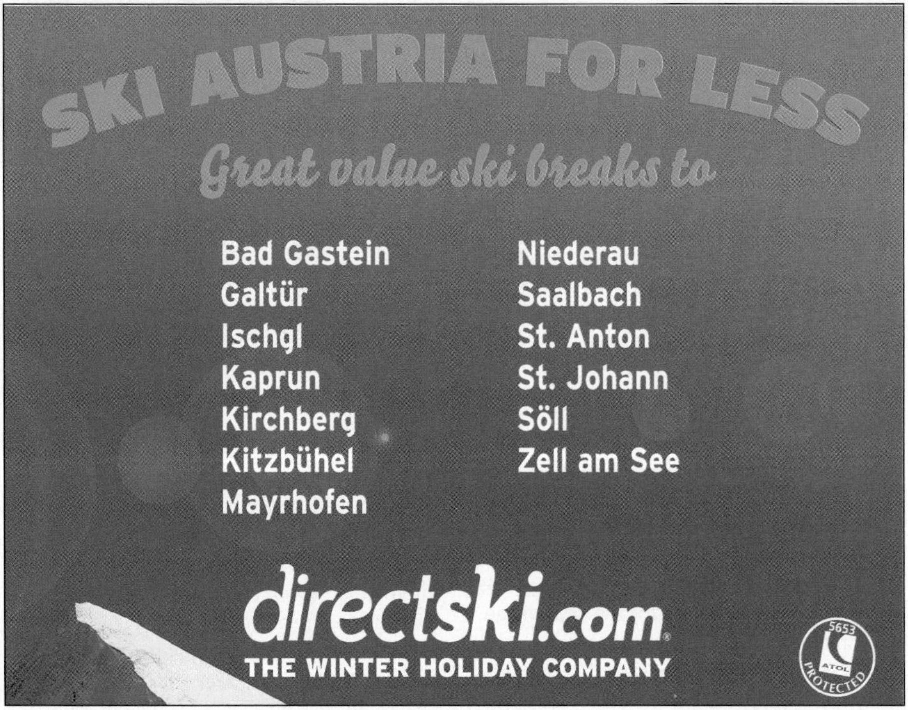

SKI AUSTRIA FOR LESS

Great value ski breaks to

Bad Gastein
Galtür
Ischgl
Kaprun
Kirchberg
Kitzbühel
Mayrhofen
Niederau
Saalbach
St. Anton
St. Johann
Söll
Zell am See

directski.com®
THE WINTER HOLIDAY COMPANY

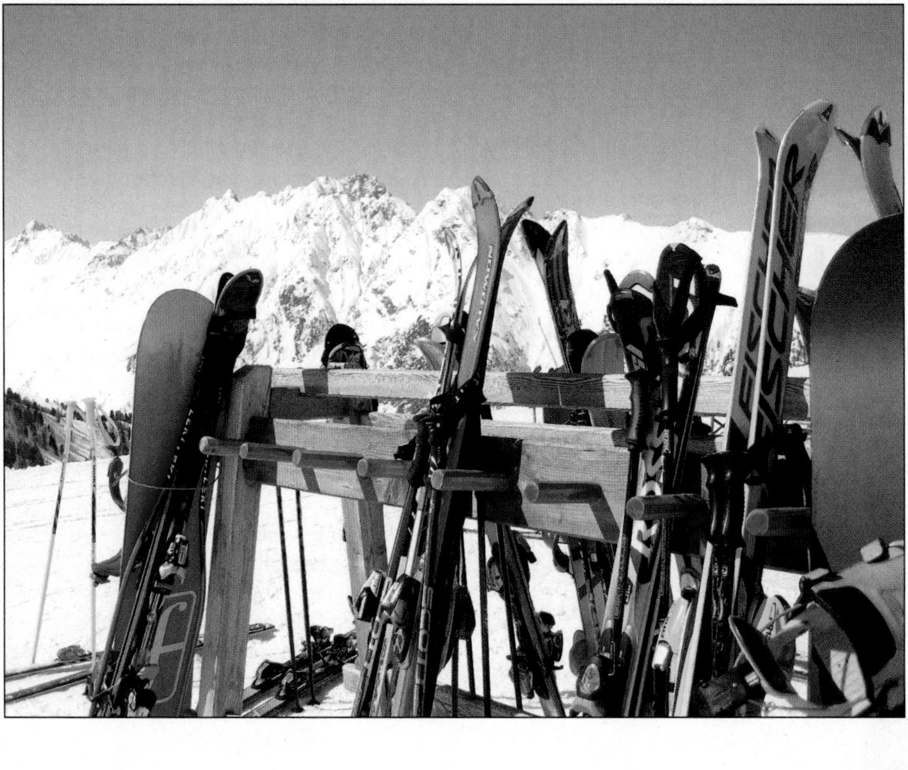

Alpbach

***BEST FOR**

Authentic Tyrolean ambience, intermediates, families, romantics

ESSENTIALS

Altitude: 1000m (3,281ft)–2100m (6,890ft)
Further information: **t** +43 (0)5336 20094, *www.alpbachtal.at/alpbach*

Lifts in area: 18 (3 cableways, 5 chairs, 10 drags) serving 45km of piste
Lift pass: adult €135–151.50, child 6–15yrs €68–76, both six days
Access: Innsbruck airport 40mins

Profile

Typically Tyrolean village with loads of alpine charm. Family-friendly with good intermediate skiing, and surprisingly varied off-piste possibilities

Resort

Alpbach is officially the prettiest village in Austria, a small, friendly resort with enduring charm that has maintained close ties with British skiers for more than 50 years. The overriding key to its success is that in the early 1970s the wise village fathers took an ice axe to future development plans in their determination to avoid the commercial path taken by some of its Tyrolean rivals. As a result it remains a largely unspoilt, traditional village where farming continues outside the ski season.

Daily life still revolves around the church, which is backed by two buttressed village inns where, between services, drink has been taken and gossip exchanged for 1,100 years.

Mountain

If you need a lot of variety in your skiing, then Alpbach is not to be recommended. However, if you need a relaxing holiday with skiing available, then it is an ideal choice.

With the exception of a single nursery slope in the middle of the village, the skiing takes place a five-minute free bus ride away on the Wiedersbergerhorn.

Mountain access is by a two-stage gondola that brings you up to Hornsboden at 1850m. A small network of lifts rise a further 150m on the Wiedersbergerhorn, and runs overall are more challenging than in the better-known nearby resorts of similar size.

Alpbach still has plenty of novice terrain, but the skiing is best suited to intermediates. 'Not enough ski variety available,' complained one reader. Experts will find off-piste opportunities adjacent to the marked runs, however.

The eight-person Pöglbahn gondola takes you from the hamlet of Inneralpbach (now a separate resort in its own right) to a mid and a top station on the Wiedersbergerhorn.

The local piste map understates the potential of the region, which includes lifts in neighbouring Reith. Our favourite piste is the former FIS downhill course, which tracks the fall line of the main mountain access gondola to the Wiedersbergerhorn. The Galtenerg drag was replaced by a quad-chair last season. Plans remain on the drawing board to link the Alpbach Valley by gondola with the adjoining Wildschönau.

Learn

Alpbach-Inneralpbach Ski School, **t** +43 (0)5336 5515, has a fine reputation, with visitors impressed by the quality of teaching and **Alpbach Aktiv Ski School**, **t** +43 (0)5336 5351, is the alternative.

Children

Juppi Kid's Club, **t** +43 (0)5337 62674, and **Kids Center Alpbach**, **t** +43 (0)5336 5351, care for children from two years. Both ski schools give lessons from four years, with free helmets provided.

Lunch

The choices include **Berggasthaus Hornboden**, **t** +43 (0)5336 5366, near the top of the access gondola, **Gasthof Almhof** by the Wiedersbergerhorn mid station, **t** +43 (0)5336 5379, and **Schihütte Böglalm**, **t** +43 (0)664 9161743, at Inneralpbach.

Dine

Try **Gasthof Wiedersbergerhorn**, **t** +43 (0)5336 5612, at Inneralpbach, or **Jo Margreiter's Hotel Post**, **t** +43 (0)5336 5203. **Gasthaus Rossmoos**, **t** +43 (0)5336 5305, and **Gasthof Jakober**, **t** +43 (0)5336 5171, both have fine food.

Party

The liveliest bars are the **Messnerwirt**, the **Postalm**, and the **Waschkuchl**. However, outside high season, nightlife can be quiet mid-week.

Sleep

★★★★**Hotel Galtenberg**, **t** +43 (0)5336 5610, *www.galtenberg.com*, in Inneralpbach, is rated 'outstanding' with 'excellent childcare'. The gondola is about 250m away.

★★★★**Hotel Alphof**, **t** +43 (0)5336 5371, *www.hotel-alphof.at*, is in a peaceful location.

★★★**Romantikhotel Böglerhof**, **t** +43 (0)5336 52270, *www.boeglerhof.at*, is ski in, ski out, with a pool and spa.

★★★**Hotel Post**, **t** +43 (0)5336 5203, is in the heart of the village, with a popular bar and restaurant.

★★★**Gästehaus Larch**, **t** +43 (0)5336 5875, *www.gaestehaus-larch.at*, offers B&B or self-catering.

★★**Haus Schönblick**, **t** +43 (0)5336 5324, was rated 'wonderful, with spacious, modern, self-catered rooms – and only three minutes from the bus stop'.

The Gasteinertal

Profile

Skiing suited mainly to intermediates, especially for those wanting to clock up a high daily mileage. Ideal resort for non-skiers who like walking, spas and eating

Resort

The ancient watering-hole of Bad Gastein is the original and still the most important of the four resorts dotted

*** BEST FOR**

Long-distance cruisers, waterbabes, ski gourmets, non-skiers

ESSENTIALS

Altitude: 840m (2,756ft)–2686m (8,810ft)

Further information: **t** +43 (0)6432 339 3560, *www.gastein.com*

Lifts in area: 44 (1 funicular, 10 cableways, 18 chairs, 15 drags) serving 201km of piste. Skiverbund Amadé region 276 (30 cableways, 74 chairs, 172 drags) serving 860km

Lift pass: Skiverbund Amadé adult €169.50–182, child 6–15yrs €88–94.50, both for six days

Access: Salzburg airport 1½hrs, railway station in Bad Gastein

Ski, Berge & Thermen.

GASTEIN

www.skigastein.com

Kreuzkogel 2.686 m
Schareck 3.122 m
Sportgastein
1.590 m
Graukogel 2.492 m
Silberpfennig 2.600 m
Stubnerkogel 2.246 m
Autoschleuse Richtung Mallnitz
Heilstollen
Sportgastein
Mautstelle
FunCenter
Böckstein
Breitfeldkogel 2.412 m
Kötschachtal
Felsentherme
Skischaukel Stubnerkogel-Angertal-Schlossalm
Hohe Scharte 2.300 m
Bad Gastein
1.002 m
Bad Bruck
Kötschachdorf
Skizentrum Angertal
1.175 m
Schlossalm 2.050 m
Kleine Scharte
Skischaukel Dorfgastein-Großarltal
Kreuzkogel 2.027 m
Fulseck 2.033 m
Bad Hofgastein
860 m
Kitzstein 1.320 m
Alpen Therme
Großarl
Salzburg
Dorfgastein
830 m
Salzburg - München
Alpen Solarbad

LEGENDE

Standseilbahn
Seilbahn
Kabinenbahn
Schlepplift
Doppel-Sessellift
Dreier-Sessellift
Vierer-Sessellift
Sechser-Sessellift
Rodelbahn
Flutlichtanlage
Parkplatz
Skibus
Skischule
Schwimmbad
Bahnhof
Skiverleih
Langlaufloipe
Piste leicht
Piste mittel
Piste schwierig
Schneesport Schule
Top-Rent Skiverleih
Carvingstrecke
FunCenter Stubnerkogel Bergstation
KIDS Park
beschneite Abfahrten
familienfreundliche Skihütten
Skiroute – markiert, nicht angelegt, nicht präpariert, nicht kontrolliert, Schutz vor Lawinengefahr

· Skizentrum Angertal · Felsentherme · Alpen Solarbad

THE GASTEINERTAL

along this scenic valley, which sits on a giant reservoir of bath-temperature thermal water, a 90-minute drive from Salzburg. The Romans, the Habsburgs and later the Nazis viewed it as the ideal holiday hideaway. An impressive 23 million litres of this curative water bubbles up each day from 17 springs. This is piped to the leading hotels and to public indoor and outdoor baths. You can enjoy the surreal experience of soaking at the foot of the pistes while snow falls around you.

Johann Strauss and Franz Schubert were both inspired to compose here. Hotel Mozart is named not after the supreme maestro, but after his mother, who was a regular guest. Visitors should be aware that the hotels, an interesting mix of revamped imperial and gleaming modern, are set on extraordinarily steep gradients. If you don't like walking in ski boots, choose your base with care ('the steep hills make walking difficult unless you are very fit'). However, it is possible to leave equipment ovenight close to the lifts. 'The town lacks a central focal point and the intimate feel of the smaller Austrian ski resorts,' commented a reporter. The streets are flanked by smart boutiques and expensive jewellery shops.

Bad Hofgastein, further along the valley, is a modern and spacious resort built at a less challenging angle. It shares the main alpine ski area but is more suited to families and those who enjoy cross-country skiing, snowshoeing and walking. It also has good ice rinks, a sophisticated sports centre and its own assortment of thermal pools and accompanying health treatments.

Dorfgastein is contrastingly different – a sleepy farming settlement by the entrance to the valley. It has considerable rural charm as well as some of the best skiing in the area, which stretches across the shoulder of the 2027m Kreuzkogel to link with the village of Grossarl.

Sportgastein, at the head of the valley, is a high-altitude ski area rather than a resort, a lift station built on the site of a medieval gold mine that was briefly reopened by Hermann Goering in the Second World War in the hope of finding fresh natural resources to fund the war machine of the Third Reich. Health-conscious visitors should pay a visit to the nearby Healing Galleries, a naturally heated underground chamber reached by a 2km train journey into the mountain. The Gastein resorts are included in the regional Amadé lift pass.

Mountain

The valley is best suited to high-mileage intermediates looking for a large ski area with plenty of challenges. It is not such a good resort, however, for beginners; the nursery slopes are either too steep (Bad Gastein), too flat (Angertal) or too short (Dorfgastein), and there are no good progression runs to move on to. Advanced skiers and riders should head to Sportgastein and Graukogel, which both have fine off-piste runs in the right conditions. A general lack of ski convenience makes the resort unsuitable for first-time beginners.

Learn

Bad Gastein, **t** +43 (0)6434 2260, **Bad Hofgastein**, **t** +43 (0)6432 6339, and **Dorfgastein**, **t** +43 (0)6433 7538, are the three main ski and board schools. Small and friendly **Schlossalm**, **t** +43 (0)6432 3298, operates from Bad Hofgastein and **Dorf Aktiv**, **t** +43 (0)6433 20048, has a strong following in Dorfgastein.

Guiding is available through the ski schools or from **L. Kravanja**, **t** +43 (0)6434 2941, **F. Sendlhofer**, **t** +43 (0)6434 2879, and **Hans Zlöbl**, **t** +43 (0)6434 5355.

Children

The geography of the valley with its separate ski areas does not make the Gasteinertal a good choice for a family holiday with small children. However, the three main ski schools operate ski- and non-ski kindergartens for children from three years, with lessons from four years. **Hotel Grüner Baum, t** +43 (0)6434 2516, has a crèche for guests. **The Fun Centre** at the Stubnerkogel lift has a kids' cinema, table tennis, a climbing wall and a ball pond. **Restaurant Angertal, t** +43 (0)6432 7475, in the futuristic Angertal Ski Centre, offers supervised meals for children aged three to 12 years.

Lunch

The Gasteinertal is dotted with welcoming huts serving typical mountain fare. **Aeroplanstadl, t** +43 (0)6432 8603, on the home run to Bad Hofgastein, has to be visited not just for its *Apfelstrudl* but for its extraordinarily original *Damen* and *Herren*. We also recommend the **Jungerstube, t** +43 (0)6433 7370, and the **Wengeralm, t** +43 (0)6433 7257, as well as the cosy **Waldgasthof Angertal, t** +43 (0)6432 8418, for its homemade *Gulaschsuppe*.

Dine

Lutter & Wegner, t +43 (0)6434 5101, at the Villa Solitude, is a favourite of ours, along with the **Fischerstüberl, t** +43 (0)6434 4505, the **Orania Stüberl, t** +43 (0)6434 2717, and the **Medeterran, t** +39 (0)6434 30004, by the waterfall. **Gisela & Co, t** +43 (0)6434 225 350, and the **Bahnhofrestaurant, t** +43 (0)6434 2166, are also recommended. **Bellevue Alm, t** +43 (0)6434 3881, and the **Hofkeller, t** +43 (0)6434 203 7245, both specialize in fondue. The restaurant in **Hotel Grüner Baum, t** +43 (0)6434 2516, has won awards as one of the outstanding dining rooms in the region.

Party

The bars at and near the **Felsentherme outdoor baths** are the focal point as skiers return from the slopes. The action moves on to a huge assortment of bars and clubs in town. **Haeggbloms, Oslags, Silver Bullet** ('recommended for kicking live music'), **Eden's Pub** ('for a quiet drink') and the **Gatz Music Club** are among the most popular. **Ritz**, in the Hotel Salzburgerhof, has regular live music and the bar here is worth a try for a bit of self-indulgence and good cocktails. The British-owned **Tannburg Hotel** near the top of the town claims to have the cheapest beer. Bad Hofgastein has five discos and a dozen bars.

Sleep

Bad Gastein has an unusually wide range of hotels, pensions and student hostels as befits a resort that caters for wealthy middle-aged bankers, euro-skint British snowboarders, and everybody in between. Some arduous uphill walking is unavoidable, although the ski bus operates between 8am and 6pm daily.

Bad Gastein:

********Arcotel-Elizabethpark, t**** +43 (0)6434 2551, *www.arcotel.at*, is modern and central; facilities include an indoor pool and wellness centre.

********Hotel Wildbad, t**** +43 (0)6434 3761, *www.hotel-wildbad.com*, is much nearer the lifts and recommended for its half-board cuisine that includes tea as well as dinner.

********Hotel Grüner Baum, t**** +43 (0)6434 2516, *www.grunerbaum.com*, is a 19th-century imperial hunting lodge in its own rural hamlet just outside the resort. The stylish hotel has a spa and a children's club, and attracts a chic celebrity crowd.

****Villa Solitude, t +43 (0)6434 5101, *www.villasolitude.com*, is a magnificently restored 19th-century town house near the casino and the waterfall.

***Hotel Mozart, t +43 (0)6434 2686, *www.hotelmozart.at*, is conveniently located and reasonably priced.

***Pension Kurhaus Orania, t +43 (0)6434 2224, *www.gastein.com*, is convenient, friendly, well run and good value.

Bad Hofgastein:

*****Grand Park Hotel, t +43 (0)6432 6356, *www.grandparkhotel.at*, is the smartest address as well as being on the edge of the piste.

****Österreichischer Hof, t +43 (0)6432 62160, *www.oehof.co.at*, is warmly recommended.

****Hotel Alte Post, t +43 (0)6432, *www.bergwelthotels.at*, is a traditional hotel in the town centre.

Dorfgastein:

****Hotel Römerhof, t +43 (0)6433 7777, *www.roemerhof.com*, has an indoor pool and spa.

****Dorfhotel Kirchenwirt, t +43 (0)6433 7251, *www.kirchenwirt-gastein.at*, is friendly and family-run.

***Gasthof Steindlwirt, t +43 (0)6433 7219, *www.steindlwirt.com*, has a cheerful children's playroom and provides everything from baby baths to bottle-warmers.

***Landgasthof Gasteiner Einkehr, t +43 6433 7248, *www.einkehr.com*, is situated close to the main lift.

***Gasthof Mühlbachstüeberl, t +43 (0)6433 7367, *www.muehlbachstueberl.com*, has a reputation for fine food.

Ischgl

Profile

A resort surrounded by beautiful scenery and a large intermediate ski area. It boasts the biggest terrain park in Europe as well as some of the wildest après-ski. Not a place for those on a budget

Resort

Ischgl is considered internationally to be Austria's second most important resort after St Anton. The two ski centres, which are only 45km apart, developed along parallel lines during the early 20th century. But St Anton found international fame while Ischgl remained largely the private haunt of ski-tourers.

Today it has a sophisticated lift system, and the old farming village houses a collection of smart hotels and cavernous bars. An airport-style pedestrian walkway, cut through the rock around which the town was built, provides easy access to pistes, shops and restaurants – regardless of where you choose to stay. If St Anton is

*BEST FOR

Table-dancers, intermediates, off-piste, ski gourmets

ESSENTIALS

Altitude: 1400m (4,592ft)–2864m (9,394ft)
Further information: t +43 (0)50 990 100, *www.ischgl.com*
Lifts in area: 40 (5 cableways, 23 chairs, 12 drags) serving 235km in Ischgl-Samnaun
Lift pass: Silvretta Regional (covers Galtür, Ischgl, Kappl, Samnaun, See) adult €189–219.50, child 8–17yrs €125, both for six days
Access: Innsbruck airport 90mins, Zurich Zurich airport 2½hrs, Landeck station 30km, frequent buses from station

Silvretta Arena
ISCHGL
SAMNAUN

MUTTLER
3294 m
STAMMERSPITZE 3254 m
PIZ TASNA
FLUCHTHORN
3398 m
PIZ VAL GRONDA
2811 m
ZAHNJOCH
PALINKOPF 2864 m
ZEBLASJOCH
2539 m
HEIDELBERGER HÜTTE
2264 m
VAL MAISAS
VAL CHAMINS
ZEBLASWIESEN
INNERES
VIDERJOCH
2704 m
HÖLLENSPITZE
FIMBAALP
2123 m
SAMNAUN DORF 1840 m
PIZ OT
2758 m
VESIL
GREITSPITZ
2872 m
SALAAS
FIMBATAL
STRASSE NACH
SPISS/PFUNDS
& VINADI
SAMNAUN RAVAISCH
SAMNAUN PLAN
SAMNAUN COMPATSCH
SAMNAUN LARET
PIZ MUNSCHUNS
2656 m
ALP TRIDA SATTEL
2488 m
HÖLLENKAR
GAMPENALP
1975 m
GRIVALEA 2700 m
Projekt
Laret Muller
ALP TRIDA ECK
OBSTACLE
PARK
DREIKÖPFL
2970 m
PAZNAUNER
THAYA 2000 m
BODENALP
1840 m
Rennstrecke
IDJOCH 2760 m
OBERALP 2380 m
ALP BELLA
ALP TRIDA
2263 m
Funpark
VISNITZKOPF 2744 m
MULLER
VIDERJOCH 2732 m
Skischule
FLIMSPITZ
2928 m
IDALP
2320 m
TSCHAMATSCHKOPF
2640 m
BÜRKELKOPF
3033 m
NEU
VELILLSCHARTE
2556 m
PARDATSCHGRAT
2624 m
NEU
GALTÜR 1584 m
MITTELSTATION
PARDATSCHALP
MATHON 1454 m
WESTL. VISNITZJOCH
BÜRKELSPITZEN
2933 m
VESULSPITZE
3089 m
PAZNAUNTAL
VELILLSPITZE
2704 m
VELILLTAL
UNTERE
VELILLALP
NEU
KAPPL 8 km
SEE 15 km
LANDECK/ARLBERG
FERNPASS
ISCHGL.com
1400 m

the skiing capital of Europe, then Ischgl – against strong opposition from its rival – wears the après-ski crown and waves the sceptre of a never-empty *Stein* of beer: the resort is linked on piste across the Swiss frontier to the duty-free village of Samnaun. It is also connected to the small resort of Galtür by a free shuttle bus during the day.

Mountain

The ski area has been hugely improved in recent years, with lifts being upgraded and pistes widened on an annual basis. Main mountain access is by three swift gondolas from different parts of town that take you up to Idalp, the mid-mountain station at 2320m that forms the hub of the lift system. One of these, the Fimbabahn, was completely renewed last season.

Lifts extend up to and over the ridge that forms the territorial frontier with Switzerland. Some of the best skiing is at Palinkopf, which at 2864m is the highest point, reached by two chairlifts from Idalp. Long red and black runs sweep down into the beautiful Fimbatal on the edge of the ski area. Some of the most rewarding off-piste runs here can be found off the Gampenbahn chair.

However, whenever the day dawns bright and sunny, it seems that almost everyone in the resort heads over to Samnaun to indulge in a cheese-rich Swiss mountain lunch and to fill their rucksacks with duty-free cigarettes, drink, perfume and electrical goods at supposedly bargain prices.

The return journey begins with a ride on what was the world's first double-decker cable car. Multiple chairlifts – Ischgl had the first eight-seater – help to ferry skiers homewards. 'The snow is always reliable although the reds down to town at the end of the day can be difficult and worn,' said a reporter. These are indeed narrow and steep – too difficult for many of Ischgl's habitual clients, but that does not stop them trying and falling in the path of others.

This is a serious snowboarding resort. Boarders Paradise at Idjoch has a half-pipe and over 30 obstacles and is one of the largest in the Alps.

Learn

Ischgl Ski School, **t** +43 (0)5444 5257, has plenty of good English speakers, but don't expect to pick up any cutting-edge techniques from most of the locally born instructors.

Children

The **Ski Kindergarten**, **t** +43 (0)5444 5257, at Idalp is run by the ski school and provides all-day care with lunch for children aged from three years. Ski lessons start at four years.

Lunch

The restaurant in the giant glass-and-steel Pardatschgrat complex at the top of the gondola is called **Panorama-Restaurant Alp Trida Sattel**, **t** +41 (0)81 868 5117, and it has the rustic **Gourmet-Stüberl'n** on the first floor. **La Marmotte** in the Bergrestaurant Alp Trida, **t** +41 (0)81 868 5221, and **Bodenalp**, **t** +43 (0)5444 5285, in the Fimbertal are also suitable escapes from the ubiquitous self-services.

Across the frontier, **Hotel Samnaunerhof**, **t** +41 (0)81 861 8181, is good for *Rösti* and **Hotel Chasa Montana**, **t** +41 (0)81 861 9000, has great pizzas.

Dine

Paznauner Stube, **t** +43 (0)5444 600, in the Trofana Royal, has one Michelin star.

Feuer & Eis, t +43 (0)5444 591 956, and **Salz & Pfeffer**, t +43 (0)5444 591 956, both have good pizzas. **Gasthaus Alt-Paznaun**, t +43 (0)5444 5380, has a comprehensive menu of regional and international dishes. **Hotel Madlein**, t +43 (0)5444 5226, serves light Austrian food inspired by the Far East. The **Goldener Adler**, t +43 (0)5444 5217, is known for its baked fresh trout. The rustic **Heidelberger Hütte**, t +43 (0)5444 5418, **Bodenalp**, t +43 (0)5444 5285, and **Vider Alp**, t +43 (0)5444 5385, are mountain huts offering fondue evenings. Reporters recommend **Baurakucha Loba**, t +43 (0)5444 5289, for local Austrian food, and **La Nona**, t +43 (0)5444 5247, for pizzas.

Party

'Where to start? So many to choose from and all great,' was how one reporter put it. By 4pm Germans and Austrians are in full swing, dancing on table-tops to jaded euro anthems and New Wave Oompah while downing litres of beer and shots of schnapps. Go-go girls clad in minimalist parodies of Austrian national dress are an intrinsic part of Ischgl's tea-time scene.

The **Schatzi Bar** in the Hotel Elisabeth ('the dancing girls were great fun'), **Kitzloch**, **Kuhstall** at the Sporthotel Suvretta ('lively après-ski and late-night party atmosphere'), **Trofana Alm** ('worth a trip if you want to dance and get close to someone new'), the **Eisbar** and **Niki's Stadl** form the hardcore of this sozzled spectacle. Those still sober enough (and others, too) then tackle the famous toboggan run on Mondays and Thursdays. The track from the top of the Silvrettabahn is a gruelling 7km, with a vertical drop of nearly 1000m.

Remaining energy is expended on the late-night dance floors of **Pacha** in the Hotel Madlein, **Feuer & Eis**, **Hölle** and **Trofana Arena** in the Trofana Royal. **Guxa** is a cocktail and cigar bar. Every winter the resort holds open-air pop concerts featuring big name stars. Previous performers include Sting, Elton John, Sugababes, Scissor Sisters and Melanie C.

Sleep

★★★★**Trofana Royal**, t +43 (0)5444 600, *www.trofana.at*, has an extensive wellness centre – anti-ageing is the speciality.

★★★★**Hotel Madlein**, t +43 (0)5444 5226, *www.madlein.com*, is a minimalist hotel with Oriental overtones.

★★★★**Hotel Elisabeth**, t +43 (0)5444 5411, *www.ischglelisabeth.com*, is a popular resort meeting-place.

★★★★**The Goldener Adler**, t +43 (0)5444 5217, *www.goldener-adler.at*, is in a 350-year-old building with an ultra-modern interior and a wellness centre.

★★★★**Hotel Jägerhof**, t +43 (0)5444 513 650, *www.hoteljaegerhof-ischgl.at*, is conveniently placed for the underground walkway and has a friendly atmosphere.

★★★★**Hotel Seiblishof**, t +43 (0)5444 5425, *www.seiblishof.com*, has a separate children's restaurant.

Kitzbühel

Profile

Architecturally the most beautiful ski resort in Austria, with lots of alpine charm, scenic skiing and lively après-ski

Resort

Watching the Hahnenkamm on TV, the toughest of all the downhills on the

World Cup circuit, it's easy to see why Kitzbühel holds a special place in the hearts of racers. Austrian Olympic hero Franz Klammer, who in the 1970s made the course his own, once famously said that every one of them who got to the bottom was a winner. The Blue Riband event on the racing calendar signals a bacchanalian frenzy among supporters, who party a whole January weekend away in the picturesque medieval town with its heavily buttressed walls and delicate frescoes.

This annual television portrayal gives the erroneous impression that Kitz is a resort reserved strictly for experts who can jump 75 metres over the jaws of the Mausefalle and then tackle the reverse camber of the Steilhang at 80mph. In fact, nothing could be further from the truth. When not prepared for competition, the notorious Streif race course reverts to its more sedate role as a *Familienabfahrt* – a family run. Without the wickedly iced surface and with the jumps cordoned off, almost anyone who can ski parallel will enjoy themselves here on the Hahnenkamm as well as on the Kitzbüheler Horn, the town's second classic ski area. Kitzbühel also has excellent beginner slopes as well as a few serious piste challenges for experts.

This attractive medieval silver-mining town, set against the dramatic backdrop of the Wilderkaiser mountains, has been a ski centre ever since local hero Franz Reisch managed to acquire a pair of long wooden skis from Norway in 1893. His antics on the Horn incited a combination of curiosity and amusement that quickly spread across the Tyrol. These days, wealthy couples in designer ski suits and fur coats browse expensive boutiques in the pedestrianized centre and dine in Kitzbühel's sumptuous restaurants.

*BEST FOR

Authentic Tyrolean ambience, all levels of skier and rider, party-goers, non-skiers

ESSENTIALS

Altitude: 760m (2,493ft)–2,000m (6,562ft)
Further information: t +43 (0)5356 777, *www.kitzbuehel-alpen.com*
Lifts in area: 54 (9 cableways, 30 chairs, 15 drags) serving 168km of piste in linked area
Lift pass: area pass covers Jochberg, Kitzbühel, Kirchberg, Pass Thurn. Adult €187, child 6–15yrs €93.50, both for six days
Access: Salzburg airport 1½hrs, Innsbruck airport 2hrs, Munich airport 2½hrs, railway station in Kitzbühel

Mountain

Kitzbühel's critics used to argue that the town rested on its laurels for much of the second half of the 20th century. For those who come here to actually ski rather than revel in its scenic surroundings, Kitzbühel had until recently been seriously lacking in modern lifts. However, major changes abound. 'The lifts have been massively upgraded since my previous visit in the 80s,' said a reporter, 'and new fast chairlifts relieve old bottlenecks. Few queues seen – and none over five minutes despite half-term.' Kitzbühel-based skiers can now complete the ski safari to Jochberg and Pass Thurn in both directions. The Jufenalm triple-chair was replaced last season by a six-pack, and a new eight-person chair also opened up.

A gondola connects the ski manufacturing town of Mittersill with Pass Thurn and Kitzbühel. The Ki-West gondola also links Kirchberg with Westendorf and the other resorts of the Wilder Kaiser Brixental SkiWelt. The addition of SkiWelt's 150 lifts make this a sizeable intermediate region in an increasingly competitive market at a time when Big is considered essential to being Beautiful.

KITZBÜHEL

Gr. Rettenstein 2366 m
Kl. Rettenstein 2216 m
Großvenediger 3674 m
RESTERHÖHE 1894 m
Zweitausender 2004 m
Felbertauern
MITTERSILL
PASS THURN
Bärenbadkogel 1883 m
Schwarzkogel 2030 m
NEU 3S
NEU
Wurzhöhe 1739 m
PENGELSTEIN 1938 m
ASCHAU
Steinbergkogel 1972 m
Ehrenbachhöhe 1802 m
Alte Wacht
JOCHBERG 923 m
GAISBERG
Skirast
HAHNENKAMM 1668 m
Hechenmoos
Stuckkogel 1888 m
BICHLALM 1595 m
AURACH 800 m
Hochetzkogel
KITZBÜHEL 800 m
AQUARENA
KIRCHBERG 837 m
Innsbruck-München
Trattalm
1773 m
Raintal
2000
KITZBÜHELER HORN SNOWBOARD AREA
Salzburg Wien
Schwarzsee
REITH
N

For the present, the area is not yet fully linked. You still have to rely on a bus between Kirchberg and the base of the Ki-West lift, however Westendorf is connected to the rest of SkiWelt by a new gondola this season across the Brixen Valley.

The 2000m Hahnenkamm is the main ski area, and it is best reached by a six-person gondola from the centre of town. However, at busy times it can make sense to employ one of a number of alternative routes. The Fleckalmbahn gondola near the neighbouring town of Kirchberg takes you directly to the top of the mountain. The Wagstäst chair at Jochberg provides a back door into the system, as does the Pengelstein gondola that rises from a car park beyond Kirchberg on the main road to Aschau.

The Kitzbüheler Horn, the town's second mountain, is on the far side of the valley and reached from the centre by regular ski bus. A gondola followed by a cable car brings you up to the summit. But the views from the top are better than the skiing. Apart from a token black run, the area consists of banal blue and red trails that meander through summer pastures.

However, the presence of a half-pipe, a boardercross course and a terrain park makes the Horn of major interest to riders and twin-tippers.

Learn

Kitzbühel's assorted ski schools have all amalgamated under the banner of **Rote Teufel/The Red Devils, t** +43 (0)5356 62500, with 350 instructors. Under centralized management there has been some improvement in standards.

Children

The ski school has a kindergarten and runs group lessons. One reporter said, 'My three kids – all first time on snow – were very well looked after by the Red Devils ski school, having lots of fun and making great progress.' **Anita Halder, t** +43 (0)5356 75063, provides private childcare.

Lunch

'The large numbers of super mountain restaurants make it way more attractive than most resorts,' said a reporter.

Sohnbühel, t +43 (0)5356 62776, on the Hahnenkamm, has a good sun terrace and great food. **Hochkitzbühel, t** +43 (0)5356 695 7230, at the top of the Hahnenkamm gondola, serves typical Austrian dishes and also has a popular sun terrace.

Staudachstub'n, t +43 (0)5357 2084, on the main run down to the Fleckalm gondola, is recommended; **Streifalm, t** +43 (0)5356 64690, is famous for its home-made ravioli. **Seidlalm, t** +43 (0)5356 63135, on the Hahnenkamm, is renowned for its cheese dishes and has great views of the resort.

Dine

Rosengarten, t +43 (0)5357 2527, in the Hotel Taxacherhof at Kirchberg, is one of the finest restaurants in the Tyrol. Acclaimed chef Simon Taxacher has created his own outstanding style of Austrian nouvelle cuisine. **Golf-Hotel Rasmushof, t** +43 (0)5356 652 5249, at the bottom of the Streif, has great food and a traditional atmosphere. **Hotel zur Tenne, t** +43 (0)5356 64444, in Kitzbühel's Vorderstadt, is known for its fresh trout and is a favourite. **Huberbräu-Stüberl, t** +43 (0)5356 65677, serves simple dishes at reasonable prices. **La Fonda, t** +43 (0)5356 73673, in the Hinterstadt, serves

Mexican food. **Lois Stern, t** +43 (0)5356 74882, serves Asian fusion cuisine. **Barrique, t** +43 (0)5356 62658, has real Italian pizzas.

Party

Reporters commented on 'the beauty and buzz of the town'. **The Londoner**, Kitzbühel's long-established British pub, is overshadowed these days by **The Pavillon**, beside the Hahnenkamm lift, and **Brass Monkeys**, which are both serious contenders for best après-ski bar. The Pavillion is 'great for après-ski as soon as you get off the mountain'. Others include **Flannigans**, the tiny **Waschkuchl**, **Stamperl**, **S'Lichtl**, **Jimmy's**, **Funferl**, **Bergsinn** and **Barrique**. The coolest nightclub is **Club Take Five**. **Olympia**, **Royal** and **Club Python** are the alternatives. **The Casino** has been entirely revamped and now offers a sophisticated evening out in contemporary surroundings. **Aquarena Leisure Complex, t** +43 (0)5356 64385 has a 25m pool and offers a full range of spa treatments.

Sleep

*******Grand SPA Resort A-ROSA, t** +43 (0)5356 656 600, *www.a-rosa.de*, is a fine modern building on the golf course just outside the town.

*******Romantikhotel Tennerhof, t** +43 (0)5356 63181, *www.tennerhof.com*, was originally an elegant Tyrolean country house.

*******Hotel Weisses Rössl, t** +43 (0)5356 625 410, *ww.weisses-roessl.com*, is the other sophisticated hotel. Its facilities include the two-storey Cheval Blanc spa with an indoor pool and pool bar.

******Golf-Hotel Rasmushof, t** +43 (0)5356 652 5249, *www.austria-tourist.net*, is off the beaten tourist track – a smart, welcoming establishment that is a favourite with the Hahnenkamm racers.

******Sport-und-Beautyhotel Schweizerhof, t** +43 (0)5356 62735, *www.hotel-schweizerhof.at*, is comfortable, handy for the town centre and offers excellent food.

******Hotel Goldener Greif, t** +43 (0)5356 64311, *www.hotel-goldener-greif.at*, is warmly traditional.

******Hotel Jägerwirt, t** +43 (0)5356 64067, *www.hotel-jaegerwirt.at*, has its own Irish pub, Sigi's Sport Bar.

******Schloss Lebenberg, t** +43 (0)5356 6901, *www.tiscover.com/schloss-lebenberg*, is a converted hunting lodge with a medieval-style interior complete with four-poster beds, and a health centre.

******Hotel Zur Tenne, t** +43 (0)5356 64444, *www.hotelzurtenne.com*, in the town centre, is a comfortable designer hotel. Many bedrooms have open fireplaces, and some suites have whirlpools and steam baths.

******Villa Mellon, t** +43 (0)5356 66821, *www.villa-mellon.at*, is a private house formerly owned by the banking family. Decorated like a hunting lodge, it offers *haute cuisine* and beautiful views.

******Golfhotel Bruggerhof, t** +43 (0)5356 62806, outside town, is recommended for the quality of its food.

******Hotel Kaiserhof, t** + 43 (0)5356 75503, is in a fantastic position next to the Hahenkammbahn. It has good-sized rooms and a lovely pool.

Alpeniglu Village, t +49 (0)711 3416 9090, *www.alpeniglu.com*, consists, conditions permitting, of glittering ice buildings and snow sculptures. The village has an ice church, shop, restaurant and bar as well as accommodation. Rooms are covered in icy works of art, complete with carved snow furniture. When night falls, candles create the romantic lighting.

Lech and Zürs

＊BEST FOR

Older intermediates, comfort-seekers, free-spenders, families

ESSENTIALS

Altitude: Lech 1450m (4,756ft), Zürs 1720m (5,642ft)–2450m (8,036ft)
Further information: t +43 (0)5583 2161-0, *www.lech-zuers.at*
Lifts in area: 85 lifts serving 276km and 85 lifts in Arlberg Ski Pass area
Lift pass: Arlberg Ski Pass (covers Lech and Zürs, Klösterle, Pettneu, St Anton, St Christoph, Stuben) adult €92–204, child 7–14yrs €115–122, both for six days; 6yrs and under €10 for whole season
Access: Innsbruck airport 2hrs, Zurich airport 2½hrs, Langen station 17km by Postbus

Profile

Two adjoining resorts for comfort-seekers who prefer a flattering piste to a tricky challenge. Not for those on a tight budget

Resort

Lech is an attractive traditional village tucked away in a narrow valley on the banks of a river, with a large collection of sumptuous four- and five-star hotels.

Zürs is perched 5km away at a snow-sure high altitude on the Flexen Pass, in a region that looks more towards Switzerland than to the rest of Austria and is best reached by car or train from Zurich. It shares its ski area with larger Lech and is included with St Anton in the regional Arlberg Ski Pass.

This is one of the birthplaces of modern skiing. Victor Sohm, a founding father of the original technique, gave the first lessons in Zürs on the open slopes of the Trittkopf and Hexenboden over 100 years ago. His international clients were mainly wealthy British, Swiss and Germans wanting to learn the new sport and relax in beautiful surroundings. In this respect, not much has changed.

Today, the two villages are the most exclusive resorts in Austria, with six five-star hotels between them. Both attract a higher age group than nearby St Anton and consequently the slopes are very civilized. 'It may be more expensive to stay here than other places, but I thought it was great value taking into account the lack of queues and the quality of service and attention to detail,' said a reporter.

For many years, Princess Caroline of Monaco has been the unofficial patron of Zürs, while Princess Diana was her counterpart in Lech. The Dutch and Jordanian royal families, as well as former tennis champion Boris Becker and Russian prime minister Vladimir Putin, are numbered among the fans of the region.

The terrain here is markedly easier than in St Anton. 'The piste skiing is not really challenging but is certainly enjoyable. It's easy to find you are the only people on a piste,' said a reporter. As a result, large numbers of skiers and riders based in St Anton come here for the day, but overcrowding is not an issue.

Zürs is no more than a huddle of smart hotels and precious little else. In Lech, hotels, restaurants and the slopes are set on either side of the little river that meanders through the centre, past a magnificent onion-domed church.

Oberlech, on the higher summer pastures, provides a traffic-free environment. 'The resort was good, but not quite top of the pile,' says a reporter, 'the plus points included convenience –

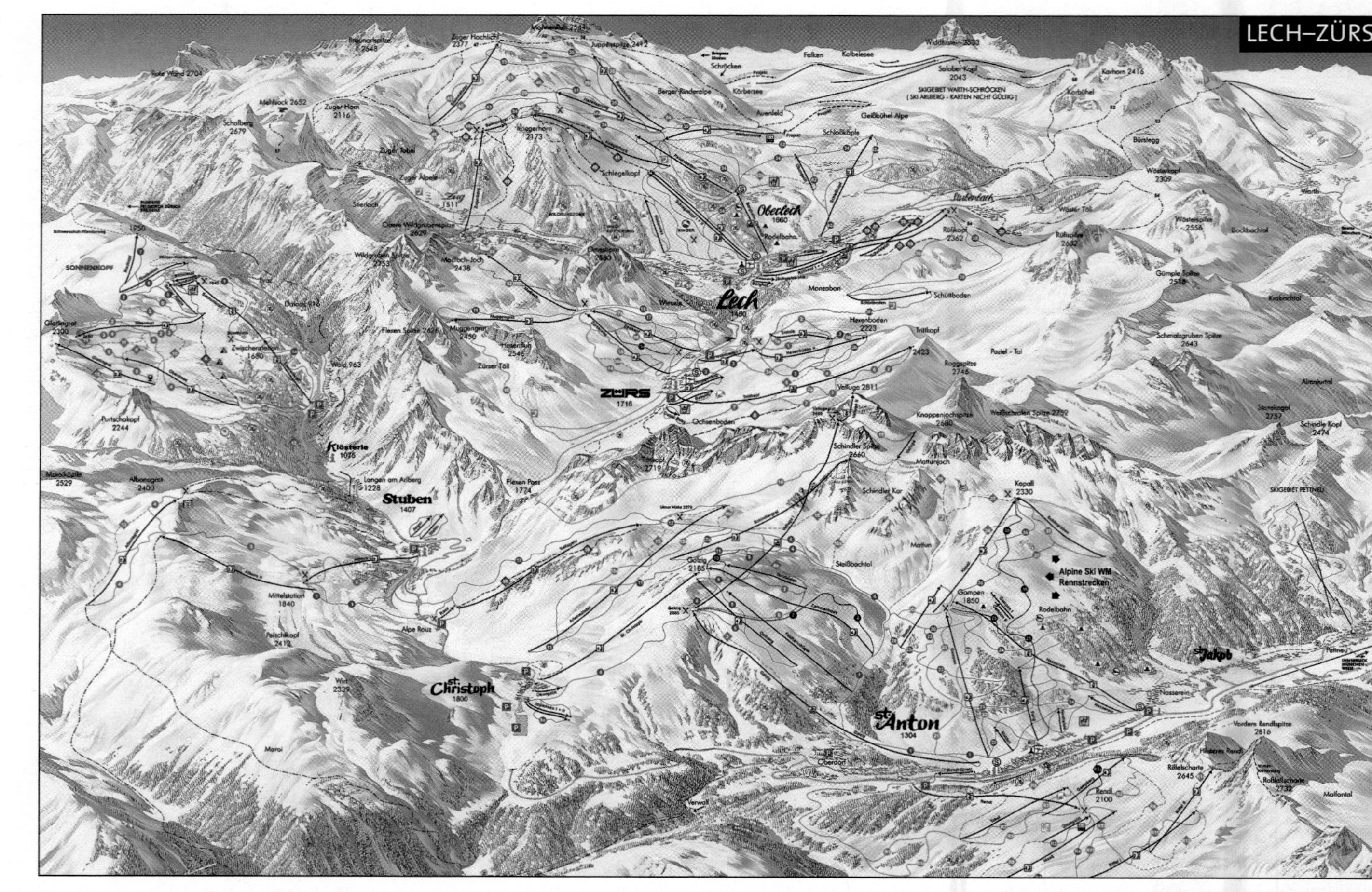

LECH–ZÜRS
Lech
1450
Oberlech
1660
ZÜRS
1716
Stuben
1407
St. Christoph
1800
St. Anton
1304
St. Jakob
Klösterle
1076
Langen am Arlberg
1228
Zug
1511
SKIGEBIET WARTH-SCHRÖCKEN
(SKI ARLBERG - KARTEN NICHT GÜLTIG)
SKIGEBIET PETTNEU
Alpine Ski WM
Rennstrecken
Valluga 2811
Flexen Pass
1724
Alpe Rauz
Kapall
2330
Galzig
2185
Gampen
1850
Rendl
2100
Albonagrat
2400
Mittelstation
1840
Hexenboden
2223
Zuger Hochlicht
2377
Rüfikopf
2362
Schindler Spitze
2660
Roggspitze
2746
Vordere Rendlspitze
2816

SKI SOLUTIONS .com
Use the Ultimate
Human Ski-Holiday
Search Engine
020 7471 7700
skihols@skisolutions.com
ABTA C6711 ATOL Protected 4055

not much walking/bussing around required.' Winter access is only by cable car, and luggage is cunningly transported to your hotel through a network of tunnels beneath the piste.

Zug, a tiny hamlet reached along a narrow lane through the woods from Lech, offers an alternative tranquil base that is linked into the lift system. There is also a pleasant scenic cross-country trail to Zug.

The galleried road across the Flexen Pass is prone to the occasional closure due to avalanche danger. Skiers wanting to explore further afield can join the St Anton ski area by taking a 20-minute bus ride to Alpe Rauz. It is possible for experts to ski home off-piste – with a guide – from the top station of the 2811m Valluga.

Mountain

Zürs and Lech provide a pleasant playground of three mountains that can be skied in a clockwise direction only. The more challenging slopes are at the Zürs end of the circuit and on the Kriegerhorn and Zuger Hochlicht. The easiest runs are to be found on the sunny meadows surrounding Oberlech.

Many of the chairlifts are heated: 'The first time we'd experienced it, and I'm a fan!' said a reporter.

From Lech, the circuit begins with a ride up the twin Rüfikopf cable cars. A combination of easy pistes takes you over the Schüttboden and Hexenboden and down into Zürs.

From Zürs, you take either the Seekopf or Zürsersee chairs followed by the Madloch chair for the long itinerary run down to Zug and on towards Lech.

It's worth noting that unpatrolled ski itineraries are marked by orange triangles and either orange or black broken lines. Most of these runs are so well skied that they are effectively pisted, but you should check the small print of your insurance policy to ensure that you are covered.

In good snow conditions, the area has sufficient challenge for accomplished skiers. Zürs has the steep black Sonnenberg, but otherwise the most challenging routes are all marked as itineraries.

Off-piste skiing through the woods is forbidden for environmental reasons and anyone caught doing so is liable to forfeit their lift pass, but there is plenty of enjoyable open terrain away from the marked runs.

Beginners have good nursery slopes at Oberlech as well as a dedicated area behind the church in Lech. The Boarderland terrain park on the Schlegelkopf in Lech has a quarter-pipe and a wide range of obstacles. 'The off-piste is excellent. Acres of accessible powder left untouched for days,' enthused a reader.

Learn

The traditional ski schools are **Lech**, **t** +43 (0)5583 2355, **Oberlech**, **t** +43 (0)5583 200, and **Zürs**, **t** +43 (0)5583 2611. Newer is **AlpinCenter Lech**, **t** +43 (0)5583 39880.

It is a reflection of their financial status that some 80 per cent of visitors to Zürs and 50 per cent to Lech choose to take private rather than group lessons. What they get for their money is year-to-year continuity, but this is by no means the kind of cutting-edge technique that wins medals for Austria. However, we have received some favourable comments: 'We were very impressed with the standard of tuition from the Lech ski school, as well as the patience and friendliness of the instructors,' said one satisfied student.

Children

'The skiing is outstanding, especially for a family or group of mixed abilities,' said a reporter.

Children six years and under ski for €10 for the whole season. **Kinderland Oberlech, t** +43 (0)5583 2007, accepts children aged from four-and-a-half years. **Miniclub Lech, t** +43 (0)5583 3530, provides a programme of play and skiing for children from three years. **Little Zürs Kindergarten, t** +43 (0)5583 224 515, also takes children from three years.

Lunch

Reporters complain that there is a real lack of restaurants on mountain. The pick of the lunch spots are attached to hotels. **Alter Goldener Berg, t** +43 (0)5583 2205, at Oberlech is recommended, along with the nearby **Bergkristall, t** +43 (0)5583 2678, **Montana, t** +43 (0)5583 2460, and the **Sonnenburg, t** +43 (0)5583 2147. In Zürs, **Gasthof Seekopf, t** +43 (0)5583 2143, and **Trittalm, t** +43 (0)5583 2831, are rated.

Dine

'Plenty of decent restaurants and understated bars,' said one reader, and 'We were braced for sky-high prices having read other people's reviews but didn't actually find them that bad,' said another. Most of the best restaurants are in the hotels. These include the **Post, t** +43 (0)5583 2206, **Arlberg, t** +43 (0)5583 2134, and **Brunnenhof, t** +43 (0)5583 2349, in Lech, as well as the **Rote Wand, t** +43 (0)5583 3435, in Zug, the **Albona Nova, t** +43 (0)5583 2341, and **Chesa** in Hotel Edelweiss, **t** +43 (0)5583 2662, in Zürs.

Other restaurants in Lech include tiny **Hüs Nr. 8, t** +43 (0)5583 33220, opposite the Post, serving grilled meat and light regional cooking with a superb wine list ('wonderful for lunch or après-ski drinks'). **Fux, t** +43 (0)5583 2992, offers Asian fusion dishes. **Don Enzo Due, t** +43 (0)5583 2225, has great pizzas. **Rudi's Stamperl, t** +43 (0)5583 3666, is warmly recommended for its duck and venison dishes. In Oberlech, **Ilga, t** +43 (0)5583 31210, has great fondues and raclette.

Party

'Nightlife is virtually non-existent,' said one reporter. However, the evening gets under way with drinking at the ice bar outside the Tannbergerhof and 5pm tea-dancing inside the hotel. For hot chocolate and Glühwein, the outdoor bar at the Hotel Krone was recommended. The Ice Bar at the top of the Schlegelkopf lift is 'unique, and worth a visit'. The **Schneggarei** bar by the Schlegelkopf lift catches the crowd as they come off the slopes. Later on, the action switches to **Klausur** in the Schneider-Almhof, **Fux** and **Pfefferköndl. Archiv** stays open until 2am. You can dance at the **Tannbergerhof, Hotel Krone** and Egon Zimmerman's **Scotch Club**.

In Zürs, **Vernissage** in Skiclub Alpenrose, the bar in the Hotel Hirlanda and **Kaminstüble** in the Schweizerhaus are all popular.

Disco Zürsserl in Sporthotel Edelweiss is the late-night venue. A collective taxi service called 'James' runs until 4am and takes you back to your hotel for a flat fee.

Sleep

★★★★★**Schneider-Almhof, t** +43 (0)5583 3500, *www.almhof.at*, has rooms decorated with natural materials, wooden furniture and stone-made accessories.

★★★★★**Hotel Gasthof Post, t** +43 (0)5583 22060, *www.postlech.com*, is small but sumptuous and attracts an older clientele.

★★★★★**Hotel Arlberg, t** +43 (0)5583 2134, *www.arlberghotel.at*, is on the edge of the piste and has comfortable suites and a gourmet restaurant. Reporters testify to being extremely well looked after here.

★★★★**Sporthotel Kristiania, t** +43 (0)5583 2561, *www.kristiania.at*, is a boutique hotel founded by 1952 Olympic champion Othmar Schneider.

★★★★**Hotel Pension Haldenhof, t** +43 (0)5583 24440, *www.haldenhof.at*, is friendly and family-run.

★★★★**Romantik-Hotel Krone, t** +43 (0)5583 2551, *www.romantikhotelkronelech.at*, is on the river bank opposite the church and has a Moroccan-influenced spa.

★★★★**Hotel Tannbergerhof, t** +43 (0)5583 3313, *www.tannbergerhof.com*, is a principal resort rendezvous.

★★★**Hotel-Café Stülzis, t** +43 (0)5583 2471, *www.stuelzis.com*, has large, clean, comfortable rooms, a wellness suite, and excellent half-board food and wine.

★★★**Pension Fortuna, t** +43 (0)5583 2424, was rated 'clean, family-run, and in short, just perfect'.

Oberlech:

★★★★**Hotel Sonnenburg, t** +43 (0)5583 2147, *www.sonnenburg.at*, is the best hotel in the hamlet. Facilities include an indoor pool and two saunas with 'fog grottos'.

Zug:

★★★★**Hotel Rote Wand, t** +43 (0)5583 3435, *www.rotewand.com*, has a swimming pool, indoor golf, wellness centre and a minimalist apartment wing.

Zürs:

★★★★★**Thurnhers Alpenhof, t** +43 (0)5583 21910,*www.thurnhersalpenhof.com*, is a favourite and a member of *Leading Hotels of the World*.

★★★★★**Hotel Lorünser, t** +43 (0)5583 22540, *www.loruenser.at*, is worthy of its rating.

★★★★★**Hotel Zürserhof, t** +43 (0)5583 25130, *www.zuerserhof.at*, continues to have a popular following.

★★★★**Arlberghaus, t** +43 (0)5583 2258, *www.arlberghaus.com*, has a rooftop curling rink.

★★★★**Sporthotel Edelweiss, t** +43 (0)5583 2662, is convenient for the nightlife.

Mayrhofen

Profile

Large intermediate ski area with a well-regarded ski school make this a good place to learn and to take children, but the nightlife is noisy. This is not a resort for advanced skiers and riders or for people looking for skiing convenience

Resort

The once quaint village of Mayrhofen was one of the original migration points for British skiers back in the 1970s and early 1980s. In those days, Austria in general and the Tyrol in particular attracted more British skiers than anywhere else in the world.

The mass market has long since deserted rival resorts in the region in favour of the more demanding slopes of France, but curiously the allure of Mayrhofen has never faded; it is described as 'a very pretty village, with lots of nice hotels and a good variety of shops'. An unfettered nightlife and reasonable accommodation, as well as good tuition and childcare, gloss over the fact that Mayrhofen itself is one of the worst resorts for skiing convenience in the Alps,

*BEST FOR

Beginners and intermediates, nightlife, families

ESSENTIALS

Altitude: 630m (2,066ft)–2500m (8,202ft)
Further information: **t** +43 (0)5285 6760, *www.mayrhofen.at*
Lifts in area: 48 in Mayrhofen (8 cableways, 18 chairs, 22 drags) serving 157km of piste. 639km in the whole Zillertal area
Lift pass: Zillertal Superskipass adult €176, youth 15–17yrs €140.50, child 6–14yrs €88, all for six days
Access: Innsbruck airport 1hr, Munich and Salzburg airports 2½hrs, railway station in resort

with heavy high-season queues to go up and down the main access lift.

Its big plus point is that outlying hamlets have been incorporated into the ski area branded as Zillertal 3000, making it the largest complex in the valley. The glacier at Hintertux is also within easy reach and, regardless of the vagaries of nature, you can ski there throughout the year. The key is to think of the entire Ziller Valley as the ski area and Mayrhofen as the hub. 'In four weeks we never queued once to go up or down a lift, largely because we generally skied in the other less crowded areas that are easily accessed by the efficient bus and train service,' said one reporter.

The Zillertal Superskipass covers all 11 different villages in the valley. Buses are frequent and a free train goes down the valley to Zell am Ziller and to the mainline station at Jenbach.

Mountain

Mayrhofen's own ski area is split between two mountains. Beginners must make their way to the edge of town to the Ahorn, a 2000m peak now served by a modern cableway ('the new lift system has made a huge difference to this great resort' – the biggest in Austria). The top is given over to snow-sure nursery runs. The 5.5km red Ebenwald piste from the top to the valley gives more accomplished skiers and riders a reason to explore Ahorn.

'The skiing is diverse and the infrastructure efficient – though Penken queues can be a pain,' said a reader. The main skiing takes place on slopes on the other side of the valley, reached by the modern Penkenbahn gondola from the centre of town. Unfortunately the topography dictates that there is no home run and skiers must return by lift at the end of the day – and cope with further high-season queues. Alternative access is provided by gondolas from Finkenberg and Vorderlanersbach up the valley, and from Schwendau further down the Zillertal. You can, snow conditions permitting, ski back down to these bases, but must then take a usually overcrowded peak-hour bus back to Mayrhofen.

The Vans Penken terrain park, with a 130m half-pipe and served by a dedicated four-person chair, has been voted the best in the German-speaking Alps. If you can't leave your work behind on holiday or need to commune with iTunes, it is worth noting that one of the first wireless hotspots in a ski area is situated on Penken.

Learn

Four schools with over 100 instructors between them cope with the annual influx of predominantly beginner and lower intermediate clients as well as a few experts who are drawn to the recommended **Mount Everest** ski school, **t** +43 (0)5285 62829. Its charismatic owner, Peter Habeler, climbed Everest without oxygen in 1978. His school teaches all standards and he personally guides off-piste tours with overnight stops in a mountain hut. The other

MAYRHOFEN
Mayrhofner Bergbahnen
Rastkogel 2762 m
RASTKOGEL 1300 - 2500 m
Pangert 2250 m
Grüblspitze 2395 m
EGGALM 1300 - 2300 m
Beilspitzlift 2.300 m
Egger Skialm
Bergrestaurant Eggalm
DSB Lattenalm
2000 m
Eggalmbahn
Hintertuxer Gletscher
nach Hintertux
Tux-Lanersbach 1300 m
Tux-Vorderlanersbach 1300 m
Christlerhof
2er Lämmerbichl
SL Lämmerbichl
8er Horbergjoch 2500 m
8er Wanglspitz
150er-Tux
Horbergjoch 2590 m
HORBERG 620 - 2278 m
Horbergtal
6 SB Unterbergalm
2100 m
Babylift
Bergrestaurant Lämmerbichl
Penkenjoch 2095 m
Gspielkopf
Nordhangbahn
4 SB Sun-Jet
Mittertrettlift
6 SB Gerent
NEU
6 SB Schneekar
Gerentberg 1934 m
8 SB Tappenalm
Knorren 2081 m
6 SB Knorren
DSB Katzenmooslift
8 EUB Finkenberg
Hasenmuldenlifte
3 SB Penken
4 SB Lärchwald
Rastkogelbahn
Mittelstation 1750 m
PENKEN 630 - 2095 m
6 SB Penken express
Penkenhof
1.800 m
Babylift
1620 m
Schwendberg
Finkenberger Almbahn
PENKEN
Penkenbahn
Horbergbahn
AHORN 670 - 1965 m
Filzenstadl
Übungsland Ahorn
Ahornhütte
1965 m
Ahornlifte
DSB Ebenwald
Projekt
AHORN
Projekt Ahornbahn neu
Ahornbahn
Wiesenhof
Brunnhaus
Persal
Finkenberg 840 m
Dorf
Dorflift
Hochsteg
Gstan
nach Ginzling
Kreuzlau
Bahnhof
Ziller
Zillertalbahn
MAYRHOFEN 630 m
Schwendau 630 m
Schwendberg
Mühlbach
Burgstall
630 m
Ramsau 630 m
Eckartau
Hollenzen
Zillergrund
Laubichl
nach Brandberg

schools are **Roten Profis**, **t** +43 (0)5285 63900, Max Rahm's **Mayrhofen Total**, **t** +43 (0)5285 63939, and **Mayrhofen 3000**, **t** +43 (0)5285 64015.

Children

Back in the 1970s, Mayrhofen pioneered the first ski kindergarten in the Alps. The resort maintains its long tradition of childcare, which remain as good as any in the Alps. **Wuppy's Kinderland**, **t** +43 (0)5285 63612, takes children from three months to seven years. **Roten Profis**, **t** +43 (0)5285 63800, looks after children from 12 months, and **Mayrhofen Total**, **t** +43 (0)5285 63939, accepts children from two years.

Lunch

Some 28 huts are dotted around the mountainside. **Ahornhütte**, **t** +43 (0)5285 62333, on the Ahorn is owned by ex-World Cup racer Uli Spiess. **Josef's Biohütte**, **t** +43 (0)5285 62309, has organic fare. **Schneekarhütte**, **t** +43 (0)5285 64940, is renowned for its fresh prawns and salmon steaks. On Penken, the **Penkentenne**, **t** +43 (0)5285 62115, and Hilde's **Skitenne**, **t** +43 (0)664 385 7574, are both recommended. **Grillholfalm**, **t** +43 (0)664 3126426, by the terrain park, has good pizzas. **Christa's Skialm**, **t** +43 (0)5285 63033, and **Schiestl's Sunnalm**, **t** +43 (0)5282 4182, are popular. The **White Lounge** igloo bar has inside and outside seating, plays music, and holds art exhibitions.

Dine

Most visitors to Mayrhofen eat at their hotels. **Ciao**, **t** +43 (0)5285 63299, is a friendly Italian. **Café Dengg**, **t** +43 (0)5285 64866, has fine pizzas. **Coup & More** in Alpenhotel Kramerwirt, **T** +43 5285 6700, is simple with good food and excellent staff. The modern **Sport Bar Grill**, **t** +43 (0)5285 6705, in Fun & Spa Hotel Strass, serves international food until 2am. **Bruggerstube**, **t** +43 (0)5285 63793, and **Eckartauerhof**, **t** +43 (0)5285 62435, are atmospheric.

Party

The town is disciplined in its control of après-ski, thus allowing satisfaction for families and couples. 'Everyone piles into the bars at 4pm, drinks till 8pm, then eats and goes to sleep,' said a reporter, but 'Apres ski is lively and would go on all night if you so wished,' remarked another. The action starts up the mountain at **Penken** before spreading to the **Ice Bar** at the foot of Penken gondola. The latest addition is the White Lounge, an igloo 2000m up the mountain. Reporters praise the **Apres Ski** bar in Hotel Brucke at the bottom of Ahorn cable car. Also try the **Speak Easy** in the Sporthotel Strass, **Happy End**, **Niki's Schirmbar**, **Mo's** and the **Piccadilly Pub**. **Schlüsselalm** and **Sports Arena** are the discos.

The **Erlebnis Mayrhofen** pool complex is the best waterpark in this part of Austria.

Sleep

*******Elisabethhotel**, **t** +43 (0)5285 6767, *www.elisabethhotel.com*, is a charming Tyrolean hotel with a fine pool and spa.

******Alpendomizil Neuhaus**, **t** +43 (0)5285 6703, *www.hotel-neuhaus.at*, enjoys fantastic food, friendly staff and great facilities, including a highly popular crèche. It is a 10-minute stroll to get to the lift, but this means the noisier pubs are not on the doorstep.

******Fun & Spa Hotel Strass**, **t** +43 (0)5285 6705, *www.hotelstrass.com*, is next to the Penken lift.

★★★★**Hotel Berghof**, **t** +43 (0)5285 62254, *www.berghof.cc*, is family-run, with comfortable rooms and three indoor tennis courts.

★★★★**Alpenhotel Kramerwirt**, **t** +43 (0)5285 6700, *www.kramerwirt.at*, was established by the Kröll family in 1624 and is stylishly traditional.

★★★★**Hotel Manni**, **t** +43 (0)5285 63301, *www.mannis.at*, has great food, first-class service and a central location.

★★★★**Hotel Pramstraller**, **t** +43 (0)5285 62119, *www.pramstraller.at*, is a two-minute walk from the centre and offers good accommodation, a central location and a well-stocked breakfast.

★★★★**Hotel Pension Waldheim**, **t** +43 (0)5285 62211, *www.waldheim.at*, is close to the adventure pool.

★★★**Hotel-Gasthof Perauer**, **t** +43 (0)5285 62566, *www.perauer.at*, is a converted Tyrolean hotel. It offers regional, international and vegetarian cuisine.

★★★**Gasthof Brücke**, **t** +43 (0)5285 62232, *www.gasthof-bruecke.com*, has 'a brilliant atmosphere and friendly, helpful staff'.

Neustift and the Stubaital

Profile

Large attractive village close to Innsbruck, with its own simple ski area and the snow-sure Stubai Glacier. Neustift is the first Disney-franchised resort in Europe

* BEST FOR

Families, beginners and intermediates, guaranteed snow-cover (Stubai Glacier)

ESSENTIALS

Altitude: Fulpmes 937m (3,074ft)–2200m (7,218ft), Neustift 1000m (3,281ft)–3333m (10,499ft), Schönberg 1113m (3,651ft)
Further information: Stubaital, **t** +43 (0)501 8810, *www.stubai.at*
Lifts in area: 44 (9 cableways, 9 chairs, 26 drags) serving 147km
Lift pass: Superskipass Stubai adult €156.60–174, child 10–14yrs €78.30–87, both for six days
Access: Innsbruck airport 20mins, Munich airport 1½hrs

Resort

Neustift is the most important community in the Stubaital, the broad valley between Innsbruck and the Brenner Pass to Italy. The large, attractive village is gateway to the Stubai Glacier, a training centre for national ski teams. Schönberg, Fulpmes, Mieders and Telfes villages are dotted along the valley and act as further bed-bases.

Mountain

Apart from the glacier, situated a 20-minute drive away, Neustift has its own little ski area on the Elfer that stretches over undulating pastures ('runs not exceptionally challenging, but great for the less experienced'). Schlick 2000 at Fulpmes is in a sheltered bowl on the 2230m Sennjoch. The Serlesbahnen in Mieders offers some good pistes, cross-country tracks and toboggan runs. All the lower ski areas are ideal for families with young children.

The Stubai Glacier is served by twin gondolas that form part of a network of 21 lifts serving 110km of piste. It is a good out-of-season training area for racers and offers a snow guarantee from October until June.

Learn

If you are a complete beginner, there are probably better places to learn. 'The lack of English visitors means you could be in a class where you are the only English-speaking person,' says a reporter.
The Stubai has five ski schools: **Neustift Stubaier Gletscher**, **t** +43 (0)5226 8108, **Neustift Olympia**, **t** +43 (0)676 330 5112, **Alpin Schischule Neustift**, **t** +43 (0)5226 3461, the **Stubai**, **t** +43 (0)664 333 2222, and **Fulpmes** ski school, **t** +43 (0)5225 62317.

Children

The **Mickey Mouse Ski Club**, **t** +43 (0)5226 8108, based up on the glacier, teaches kids from four years to learn to ski while having fun. The children's magic carpet lift is inside a tunnel and the nursery slope has ski-through Disney characters. Non-skiers from three years are cared for in the slope-side **Ski Club Micky Maus Clubhaus**.

Lunch

Fulpmes has 10 self-service restaurants on the mountain at Schlick 2000. There are five eateries on the **Stubai Glacier**, including the **Jochdohlenhütte t** +43 (0)5226 8141. 'On-mountain restaurants were efficient with very short queues,' said a reader.

Dine

In Neustift, **Grillstube**, **t** +43 (0)5226 3147, has great steaks and **Café Anni Platzl**, **t** +43 (0)5226 3613, has good pizzas, but the restaurant in the **Hotel Jagdhof**, **t** +43 (0)5226 2666, serves the best food in town. Restaurants in Mieders include the **Gletscherblick**, **t** +43 (0)699 1133 1101.

Party

'The village is very quiet, not buzzing with much nightlife at all,' complained one reader. **Aumi's Pub**, **Rossini** and **Dorf Pub** are the main meeting places in Neustift. **The Umbrella** bar and disco in Mutterberg, the **Nachtkastl** and **Rumpl** discos are the late-night spots. In Fulpmes, **Café Corso**, **Kuhstall**, **Leo'Stadl** and the **Tatort** provide the action.

Sleep

★★★★★**Hotel Jagdhof & Spa**, **t** +43 (0)5226 2666, *www.hotel-jagdhof.at*, in Neustift village centre, has excellent food and a fabulous spa.

★★★★**Alpenhotel Tirolerhof**, **t** +43 (0)5226 3278, *www.alpenhotel-tirolerhof.com*, is said to be good value with excellent service and Tyrolean-style accommodation.

★★★★**Sporthotel Neustift**, **t** +43 (0)5226 2510, *www.sporthotelneustift.at*, has a wellness suite and an entire floor for non-smokers.

★★★★**Alpenhotel Mutterberg**, **t** +43 (0)5226 8116, *www.stubaital.at/mutterberg*, is a comfortable hotel for keen skiers who prefer to stay at the base of the Stubai lifts.

★★★★**Alpenhotel Tirolerhof**, **t** +43 (0)5225 62422, *www.tirolerhoffulpmes.at*, in Fulpmes, has been refurbished.

★★★★**Sporthotel Cristall**, **t** +43 (0)5225 634 240, *www.sporthotelcristall.at*, is also recommended.

Niederau

Profile

Traditional village that attracts a large influx of young British skiers and riders. Neighbouring Auffach and Oberau provide further skiing

Resort

Niederau is a modest traditional village in the Wildschönau region, which includes the surrounding Tyrolean communities of Thierbach, Oberau and Auffach. Together they have acted as a winter playground for overseas visitors for 70 years. Much of the appeal has been based on lower-than-average prices and benign but beautiful slopes. Plans have been approved in principle to connect the Wildschönau to the neighbouring and perceivedly smarter Alpbach valley, a move that should be beneficial to both. Lift-builder Doppelmayr has produced the blueprints, but both resorts seem reluctant to commit.

Mountain

All the villages are linked by free ski-bus. Main mountain access from Niederau is by a modern eight-person gondola. From the summit of the Markbachjoch you have a choice of three pisted and one unpisted run back to the valley. The old single-chair is due to be replaced this winter.

Auffach has the pick of the skiing ('lovely big slopes'). A gondola takes you through the woods to a network of five draglifts and two chairs. Oberau has five short drags, while skiing in Thierbach is confined to just one draglift. Riders congregate in Auffach, which has a terrain park with a half-pipe.

*** BEST FOR**

Traditional Tyrolean ambience, beginners and low intermediates, families

ESSENTIALS

Altitude: 830m (2,722ft)–1903m (6,243ft)
Further information: t +43 (0)5339 82550, *www.wildschoenau.com*
Lifts in area: 26 (2 cableways, 3 chairs, 21 drags) serving 70km of piste
Lift pass: area adult €135.40–150.40, youth €108.40–120.40, child from 6yrs €79–87.80, all for six days
Access: Innsbruck airport 45mins, Wörgl station 10mins

Learn

'I was looking for a confidence-building week and I was not disappointed,' said a reporter, 'The ski schools are second to none and turn a great week into a perfect one.' Niederau has two ski and board schools: **Aktiv**, **t** +43 (0)5339 2701, and **1st Skischool Wildschönau**, **t** +43 (0)5339 2200, with its equally excellent instructors.

Children

Niederau's **crèche** takes children from two years. The Wildschönau ski school runs **Bobo's Kinderclub** for two- to six-year-olds.

Lunch

In Niederau, **Anton-Graf-Hütte**, **t** +43 (0)5339 2547, and **Markbachjochalm**, **t** +43 (0)5339 8202, offer wholesome fare.

Dine

Hotel Wastlhof, **t** +43 (0)5339 8247, has the best cuisine. **Hotel Austria**, **t** +43 (0)5339 8188, houses the most popular restaurant in Niederau. There are two

Italian eateries, **Ferrari**, **t** +43 (0)5339 2733, in **Niederau**, and **Italia 90**, **t** +43 (0)5339 8109, in Oberau.

Party

Bobo's Heustadl at the gondola base in Niederau and the **Gruttn-Bar** in Auffach draw skiers off the slopes long before the lifts stop for the day. **Sno Blau** in Hotel Tirolerhof, the **Starchent Weinstüberl** and the **Keller Bar** are the hotspots in Oberau. **O'Mailleys Irish Pub** ('small, intimate and very friendly, with live music every night'), **Dorfstub'n**, the **Stadl Bar** ('caters for the Drum n' Bass group') and the **Cave Bar** ('absorbs all the alcohol-seeking night owls wishing to party through the early hours') provide the late-night entertainment in Niederau.

Sleep

Auffach:

*****Auffacherhof**, **t** +43 (0)5339 8837, *www.auffacherhof.at*, is in the centre of the village.

Niederau:

******Hotel Sonnschein**, **t** +43 (0)5339 8353, *www.harmony-hotels.com*, has an indoor pool, playroom, and good-sized bedrooms, but staying here involves an uphill walk to the lifts.

******Hotel Wastlhof**, **t** +43 (0)5339 8247, *www.hotelwastlhof.at*, is more conveniently located beside a lift linking to the main gondola. It has a pool and a large all-weather horse-riding arena.

*****Hotel Alpenland**, **t** +43 (0)5339 8258, *www.alp1.at*, is well situated but food can be a bit plain and unimaginative.

*****Hotel Hafenwirt**, **t** +43 (0)5339 8315, was rated clean but basic, with good food. 'Ticks all the boxes on my wish-list. The food was simple and hearty and the ambience was warm,' said a reporter.

Hotel Hannes, **t** +43 (0)5339 8232, *www.hotel-hannes.at*, is praised for the warmth of its welcome: 'the owner made us feel like a family member'.

Oberau:

******Hotel Silberberger**, **t** +43 (0)5339 8407 *www.silberberger.at*, is charming and traditional.

*****Hotel Tirolerhof**, **t** +43 (0)5339 81180, *www.hoteltirolerhof.at*, is ski-in ski-out and the main resort meeting place.

*****Gasthof Kellerwirt**, **t** +43 (0)5339 8116, *www.kellerwirt.com*, is a former monastery.

Obergurgl-Hochgurgl

Profile

Charming high-altitude family resort with magnificent glacial scenery, a long ski season that stretches to late April, cheerful après-ski and good ski-touring

Resort

'Best for families, beginners to lower intermediates,' said a reporter, and 'good value for what is quite a classy resort. The best bit is there are hardly any boarders,' said another.

Obergurgl is set around a fine church at 1930m in the high 67km Ötz Valley close to the frontier with Italy, an easy drive from Innsbruck. Back in 1931, Swiss aviation pioneer Auguste Piccard first put Obergurgl on the ski map when he landed his hot-air balloon on the Gurgler-Ferner glacier after achieving a world altitude record of 16000m. In a triumphant rescue

OBERGURGL-HOCHGURGL

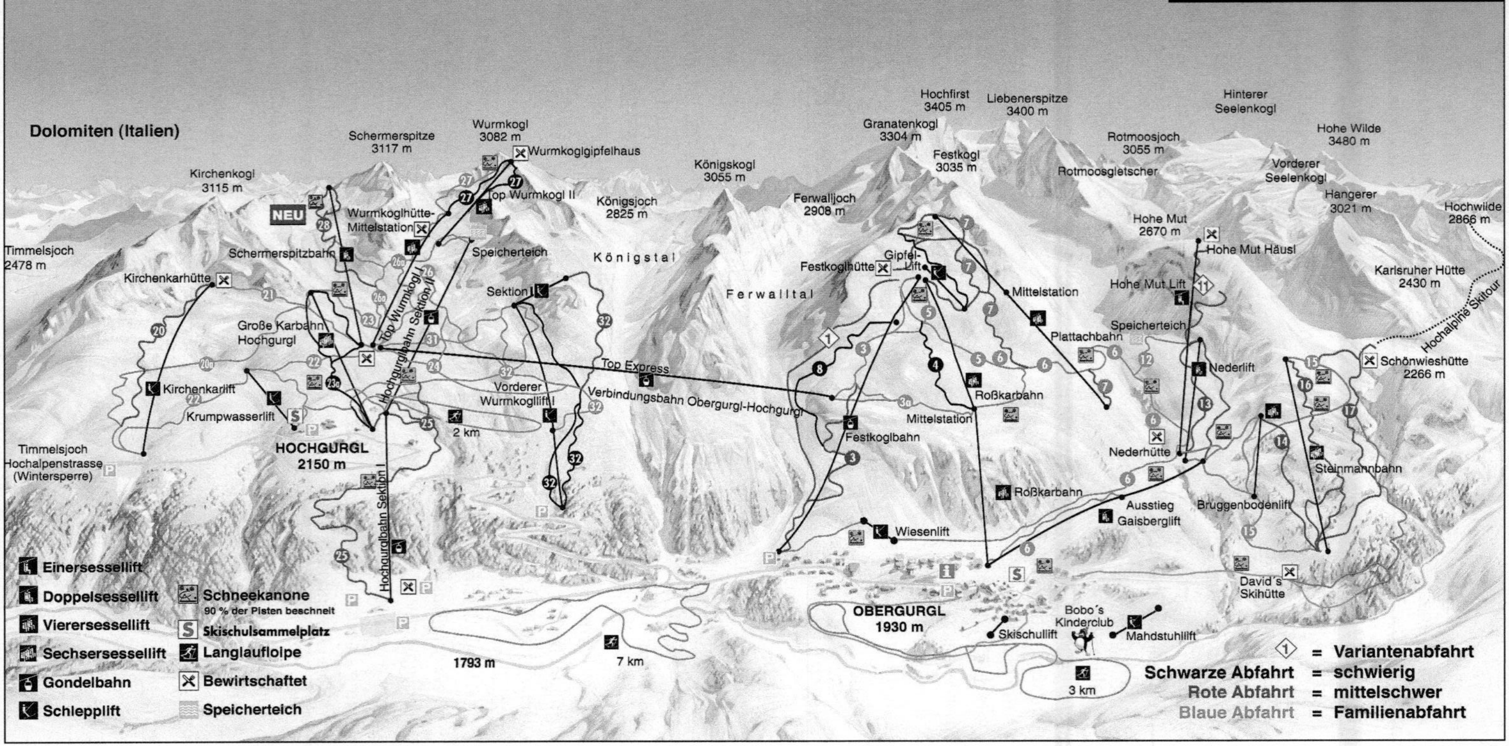

Dolomiten (Italien)

Timmelsjoch
2478 m

Kirchenkogl
3115 m

Schermerspitze
3117 m

Wurmkogl
3082 m

Wurmkoglgipfelhaus

Königskogl
3055 m

Königsjoch
2825 m

Königstal

Ferwalljoch
2908 m

Ferwalltal

Granatenkogl
3304 m

Hochfirst
3405 m

Festkogl
3035 m

Liebenerspitze
3400 m

Rotmoosjoch
3055 m

Rotmoosgletscher

Hinterer
Seelenkogl

Vorderer
Seelenkogl

Hohe Wilde
3480 m

Hangerer
3021 m

Hochwilde
2866 m

Hohe Mut
2670 m

Hohe Mut Häusl

Hohe Mut Lift

Karlsruher Hütte
2430 m

Hochalpine Skitour

Schönwieshütte
2266 m

NEU

Wurmkoglhütte-
Mittelstation

Schermerspitzbahn

Top Wurmkogl II

Top Wurmkogl I

Hochgurglbahn Sektion II

Speicherteich

Kirchenkarhütte

Große Karbahn
Hochgurgl

Kirchenkarlift

Krumpwasserlift

Timmelsjoch
Hochalpenstrasse
(Wintersperre)

HOCHGURGL
2150 m

Hochgurglbahn Sektion I

Sektion I

Vorderer
Wurmkogllift I

Top Express

Verbindungsbahn Obergurgl-Hochgurgl

2 km

Festkoglhütte

Gipfel-
Lift

Mittelstation

Plattachbahn

Roßkarbahn

Festkoglbahn

Speicherteich

Nederlift

Nederhütte

Ausstieg
Gaisberglift

Bruggenbodenlift

Steinmannbahn

David´s
Skihütte

Wiesenlift

OBERGURGL
1930 m

Bobo´s
Kinderclub

Skischullift

Mahdstuhllift

1793 m

7 km

3 km

Einersessellift

Doppelsessellift

Vierersessellift

Sechsersessellift

Gondelbahn

Schlepplift

Schneekanone
90 % der Pisten beschneit

Skischulsammelplatz

Langlaufloipe

Bewirtschaftet

Speicherteich

1 = Variantenabfahrt

Schwarze Abfahrt = schwierig

Rote Abfahrt = mittelschwer

Blaue Abfahrt = Familienabfahrt

✻ BEST FOR

Reliable snow-cover, families with young children, ski-tourers

ESSENTIALS

Altitude: 1930m (6,330ft)–3080m (10,104ft)
Further information: t +43 (0)57200 100, *www.obergurgl.com*
Lifts in area: 22 (7 cableways, 8 chairs, 7 drags) serving 110km of piste
Lift pass: adult €190.50–212, child 9–16yrs €115, both for six days
Access: Innsbruck airport 1½hrs, Ötztal station 54km, with the new Öztal Shuttle

operation, local guide Hans Falkner led the explorers across to crevasses to safety and glory. More recently, Oetzi, the 5,300-year-old hunter whose perfectly preserved body was found on one of the 23 glaciers above the resort, has brought renewed fame to the valley.

Higher Hochgurgl is a collection of ski-in, ski-out hotels perched on the mountainside and linked by gondola to Obergurgl. Much of the appeal of the joint resort lies in secure snow conditions that last from November to the beginning of April. Obergurgl has a few shops, an open-air ice rink, indoor golf and a horse-riding arena.

Mountain

'Queues almost non-existent even in half-term week,' enthused a reporter. This is an easy family ski area with few challenges on piste but plenty of opportunities for guided excursions into magnificent terrain leading up to the Italian frontier. The skiing takes place in three topographically separate but lift-linked areas spread across the northwestern side of the Ötztal. Obergurgl's main sector is reached either by a gondola at the beginning of the village or by a two-stage chair from the centre. From the top you can reach two further lifts and together these give access to a pleasant choice of blue and red cruising runs, as well as a couple of steeper blacks.

From mid-mountain, the 3.6km Top Express gondola spans two valleys to reach Hochgurgl. The glacial terrain here is much more extensive with plenty of long, mainly blue, descents. The two-stage Hochgurglbahn gondola allows swift access from the valley to the modest collection of draglifts, chairs and gondolas – including a new gondola – and a continuous vertical drop of 1500m. 'The red run through the trees from Hochgurgl down to Untergurgl is really good,' said a reader.

The third smaller area of Gaisberg lies to the south of Obergurgl and is reached by gondola from the village centre. Gaisberg offers delightful blue runs as well as three more challenging reds between the trees, served by the swift six-person Steinmannbahn chair. There's a red run, but also a glorious off-piste route from the Hohe Mut down to near the Schönwieshütte.

Learn

Obergurgl Ski School, t +43 (0)5256 6305 ('superb tuition'), and **Hochgurgl Ski School**, t +43 (0)5256 6265, have been successfully teaching the basics to international visitors for generations, but don't expect to learn cutting-edge technique here. 'The ski school was brilliant for all of us, and our instructor exceptional; he was 77,' commented a reporter.

Children

Bobo's Kinderclub, t +43 (0)5256 6305, provides care for non-skiing children from four years. The ski school accepts children as young as three years. The resort allows children aged nine and under to ski for free – a higher age limit than in many other resorts. A number of hotels operate their own crèches. These are usually free of charge for older children, but you need to check ages carefully before booking. They include **Alpina**, **Austria**, **Bellevue**, **Bergwelt**, **Crystal** and **Hochfirst** as well as **Hotel Edelweiss & Gurgl** and **Top Hotel Hochgurgl**.

Lunch

Gletscherhäusl Hohe Mut, **t** +43 (0)5256 6274, is a popular lunch venue with magnificent views at the top of the Gaisberg sector. It is reached by a chairlift but the only route from here is an unclassified itinerary run. Less accomplished skiers are advised to take the lift back down. **The Schönwieshütte**, **t** +43 (0)664 442 8113, is a touring refuge renowned for its *Gulaschsuppe* and *Kaiserschmarren* (plum pancakes).

David's Skihütte, **t** +43 (0)5256 6332, offering excellent food, is at the bottom of the Steinmannlift. The popular lunch venue also has lively après-ski. **Festkoglalm**, **t** +43 (0)5256 6370, and **Nederhütte**, **t** +43 (0)5256 6425, are also recommended.

In Hochgurgl, the **Wurmkoglhütte**, **t** +43 (0)5675 6100, offers traditional mountain fare. From the new **Top Mountain Star**, **t** +43 (0)5256 6265, restaurant in Top Hotel Hochgurgl you can see the Dolomites.

Dine

With only a handful of exceptions, the restaurants in both Obergurgl and Hochgurgl are located within the hotels. **Dorf-Alm**, **t** +43 (0)5256 6570, offers regional dishes and cheese fondue. **Pizzeria Romantika** in the Hotel Madeleine, **t** +43 (0)5256 63550, and **Pizzeria Belmonte**, **t** +43 (0)5256 6533, both have good pizzas.

Party

Nightlife is generally muted and one reader described it as 'not a resort for party animals'. The **Nederhütte** and other mountain restaurants start the ball rolling with music and dedicated drinking in the late afternoon. Later on, the **Josl-Keller** has the best atmosphere. **Krump'n'Stadl** is crowded and noisy. **Austria-Keller** in Obergurgl and **African Bar** in Hochgurgl have dancing and stay open into the early hours.

Sleep

Hochgurgl:

★★★★★**Top Hotel Hochgurgl**, **t** +43 (0)5256 6265, *www.tophotelhochgurgl.com*, is the only five-star in the area and leads the field. It has a crèche and health club, and was rated 'fantastic, with an amazing fondue'.

★★★★**Hotel Riml**, **t** +43 (0)5256 6261, *www.hotel-riml.com*, is in a great location on the piste at Hochgurgl. The hotel claims to be a well-balanced 'energy zone' with a colour scheme designed for relaxation, and strategically placed 'energy pyramids'. There is also indoor golf.

★★★**Alpenhotel Laurin**, **t** +43 (0)5256 6227, *www.laurin.at*, in Hochgurgl, serves first-rate food.

Obergurgl:

★★★★**Art & Relax Hotel Bergwelt**, **t** +43 (0)5256 6274, *www.hotelbergwelt.com*, is a traditional hotel with great ambience and a good pool.

★★★★**Hotel Deutschmann**, **t** +43 (0)5256 22943, *www.hotel-deutschmann.com*, is warmly recommended ('virtually ski in-ski out – decor chintzy, rooms pretty basic for a four-star but food very good and plentiful').

★★★★**Hotel Alpenland**, **t** +43 (0)5256 6337, *www.hotelalpenland.at*, was praised for its superb location, outstanding food and service, spotless rooms and basement bowling alley.

★★★★**Hotel Alpina**, **t** +43 (0)5256 6000, *www.hotelalpina.com*, runs its own children's programme. It is a first class hotel, run by a charming family, with good food and superb service.

★★★★**Austria-Bellevue Hotel**, **t** +43 (0)5256 6282, *www.austria-bellevue.com*, dates back to 1561 and is first class – excellent food, efficient service, clean rooms and a great spa. Better for families than for couples seeking romance.

★★★★**Hotel Crystal**, **t** +43 (0)5256 6454, *www.hotel-crystal.com*, is a monster of a building, but extremely comfortable ('the hotel was fantastic').

★★★★**Hotel Edelweiss & Gurgl**, **t** +43 (0)5256 6223, *www.edelweiss-gurgl.com*, in the centre, is one of the resort's original hotels. 'Just brilliant,' enthused a reporter, 'great staff, great food, great room, wonderful pool complex and exceptional spa.'

★★★★**Hotel Hochfirst**, **t** +43 (0)5256 63250, *www.hochfirst.com*, has the best pool in the resort and an amazing spa.

★★★★**Hotel Jenewein**, **t** +43 (0)5256 6203, *www.hotel-jenewein.com*, offers exceptional half-board cuisine.

★★★★**Hotel Madeleine**, **t** +43 (0)5256 63550, *www.hotel-madeleine.com*, has pristine accommodation, excellent food and very pleasant staff.

★★★**Burghotel Alpenglühn**, **t** +43 (0)5256 6301, *www.burghotel-tirol.at*, offers fantastic hospitality, spotless rooms and a wonderfully warm welcome.

Obertauern

Profile

Purpose-built resort with convenient, if unadventous, snow-sure skiing and an impressive lift system. Not suitable for non-skiers

Resort

When snow-cover is light elsewhere in Austria, this high-altitude ski area has virtually guaranteed conditions. Its position on a mountain pass in the Niedere Tauern mountain range, 90km south of Salzburg, attracts a favourable micro-climate.

Until local ski enthusiasts 'colonized' the pass in the early 1930s the only building was Hotel Tauernpasshöhe. During the intervening decades a straggle of hotels and bars has sprung up along the roadside to give Obertauern more of an American ski resort atmosphere. The resort is recommended for families, intermediates and beginners looking for an all-round fun holiday, but probably not for experts.

*BEST FOR

Reliable snow-cover, convenience, beginners and intermediates, late skiing

ESSENTIALS

Altitude: 1740m (5,708ft)–2313m (7,587ft)
Further information: **t** +43 (0)6456 7252, *www.obertauern.com*
Lifts in area: 26 (1 cableway, 19 chairs, 6 drags)
Lift pass: adult €156.50–172.50, children up to 15yrs €86.50, both for six days
Access: Salzburg airport 90km, Radstadt station 20km

Mountain

The peaks on both sides of the road rise to over 2200m and the lifts complete a circuit that can be skied in either direction. There is a very good hands-free lift system with barely a draglift to be found. Plenty of novice terrain can be found close to the village centre as well as a couple of testing blacks. The area provides lots of variety as well as some sensational off-piste. Poor piste signage and bad grooming were reporters' main gripes.

Learn

All the ski schools have different meeting points, so if you want to avoid a trek with skis in the morning choose one which meets near your hotel. Competition among teaching academies is healthily high, but of the five main schools **Krallinger, t** +43 (0)6456 7258, receives the most praise: 'Very good – Cody was the best instructor I'd ever had', along with **CSA Willi Grillitsch, t** +43 (0)6456 7462 ('would particularly recommend instructor Ziggy who has been at the resort for 25 years. He books in advance for lunch so you can eat immediately'). **Frau Holle, t** +43 (0)6456 766 384, **Koch, t** +43(0)6456 72285, and **Top, t** +43 (0)6456 7678, are worthy contenders. **Blue Tomato, t** +43 (0)6456 20036, is for boarders, and **Snowkite School Tony Ully, t** +43 (0)676 340 8779, is the first school of its type in Austria.

Children

Kinderland Crèche, t +43 (0)6456 725 224, cares for children from three. **CSA Willi Grillitsch, t** +43 (0)6456 7462, has a non-ski kindergarten. All the ski schools run ski kindergartens.

Lunch

The resort has over 20 enticing restaurants ('a great atmosphere in the mountain restaurants'). **Lürzer Alm, t** +43 (0)6456 7289, and **Hochalm, t** +43 (0)6456 731 8522, have good food. **Almrausch, t** +43 (0)6456 7407, is also open in the evening. Also try **Flubachalm, t** +43 (0)6456 7217, and **Edelweisalm, t** +43 (0)6456 20026.

Dine

Bacchuskeller, t +43 (0)6456 7561, and **Restaurant Sailer, t** +43 (0)6456 7328, are both recommended. **Edelweiss-Stüberl, t** +43 (0)6456 7245, and **Wagner Stub'n, t** +43 (0)6456 7256, each have reasonable prices.

Party

'The apres-ski is unbeatable,' said a reporter. The **Edelweissalm** and the **Achenrainhütte** are lively in the late afternoon. 'Make sure you're at the Edelweissalm by 3pm for a table, then you need to be prepared to climb on top of the table by 4pm when the Euro-pop starts – and dance,' said one reporter. **Der Turm** and **Römerbar** are popular. The **Lürzer Alm** is 'one of the resort's highlights' and Gruber Stadl is said to have 'a great atmosphere'. The evening then progresses to **Monkey's Heaven** in Hotel Rigele Royal. The night-skiing on Thursday and Tuesday is rated 'awesome'.

Sleep

******Alpenhotel Römerhof, t** +43 (0)6456 72380, *www.roemerhof.at*, has a traditional interior and a piste-side terrace.

******Andi's Skihotel Krallinger, t** +43 (0)6456 7303, *www.krallinger.com*, is excellently located, small and friendly, with traditional Tyrolean decor. The Krallinger ski school meets outside the door.

★★★★**Hotel Kohlmayr, t** +43 (0)6456 7272, *hotel-kohlmayr.at*, is a great hotel with exceptional food and convenient slope access.

★★★★**Hotel Latschenhof, t** +43 (0)6456 7334, *www.latschenhof.com*, was said to be very comfortable, with good, plentiful food and an excellent bar.

★★★★**Hotel Rigele Royal, t** +43 (0)6456 73540, *www.rigele-royal.com*, is good value, with spacious rooms and a spa with indoor-outdoor pool.

★★★★**Sporthotel Edelweiss, t** +43 (0)6456 7245, *www.luerzer.at*, is situated beside the village nursery slope.

★★★★**Sporthotel Cinderella Spa & Resort, t** +43 (0)6456 20000, *www.cinderella.at*, is decorated true to its fairytale name. The dining room has low turreted walls painted with pastel frescoes.

★★★★**Sportinghotel Marietta, t** +43 (0)6456 7262, *www.marietta.at*, is a lavish place at the foot of the slopes.

Saalbach-Hinterglemm

Profile

Adjoining villages sharing an extensive ski circuit with confidence-building slopes, reliable snow-cover and a modern lift system. Great for ski-to-lunchers and night-owls, but not for anyone who is early-to-bed

*BEST FOR

All levels of skier and rider, dedicated lunchers, night-owls

ESSENTIALS

Altitude: 1,003m (3,280ft)–2100m (6,890ft)

Further information: t +43 (0)6541 68068, *www.saalbach.com*

Lifts in area: 55 (15 cableways, 16 chairs, 24 drags) serving 200km of piste

Lift pass: area (Skicircus Saalbach Hinterglemm Leogang) adult €156.40–195.50, youth 16–18yrs €121.20–151.50 child 6–15yrs €78.20–97.80, all for six days

Access: Salzburg airport 1½hrs, Zell am See station 19km

Mountain

The skiing here is ideal for adventurous intermediates who want to feel that they are travelling somewhere each day rather than skiing the same stretch of mountainside over and over again. The main circuit is made up of easy blue and undemanding red runs that can be tackled by anyone who can ski parallel. Unlike a lot of other circuits, such as the Sella Ronda in Italy, you don't have to complete it – just descend to the valley floor and hop home on a free ski-bus.

Whether you start from Saalbach or Hinterglemm, you move seamlessly into the 200km circuit – few areas in Austria can match the modern lift system, which is being continuously upgraded ('great variety of piste and off-piste, very good lift system'). Recent innovations include a gondola on Hochalm, a couple of chairlifts upgraded to six-packs, and extended snowmaking. The Westgipfelbahn gondola has replaced two old chairs. A six-pack has also taken over from the old Kar and Weissbach lifts on the 1910m Wildenkarkogel.

The clockwise circuit from Saalbach starts with a two-stage gondola ride to Schattberg Ost. From Hinterglemm the Westgipfelbahn gondola provides greatly improved access. On the other side of the

SAALBACH-HINTERGLEMM

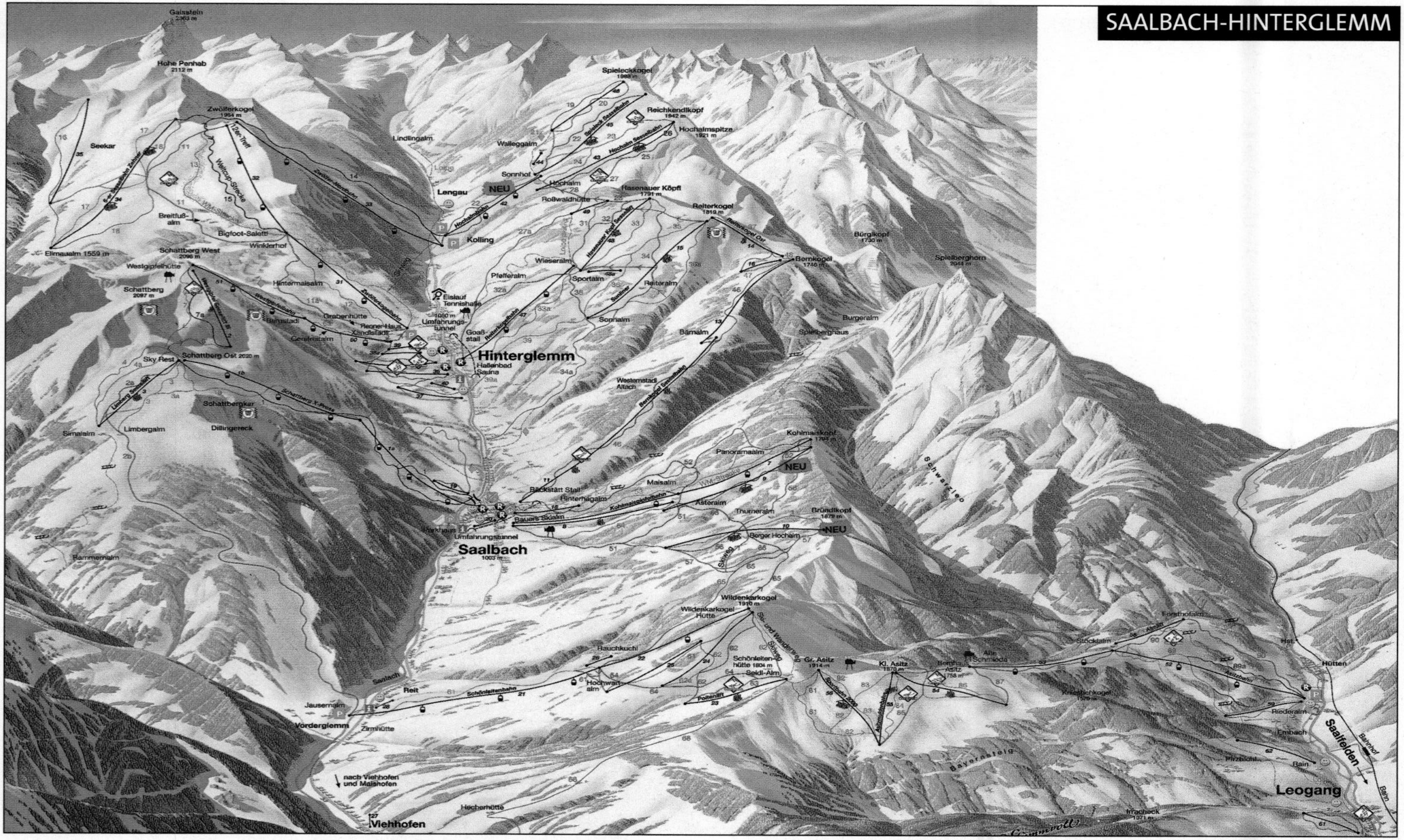

Gaisstein 2363 m
Hohe Penhab 2112 m
Zwölferkogel 1984 m
12er-Treff
Weltcup-Strecke
Seekar
Elmaualm 1559 m
Breitfuß-alm
Bigfoot-Saletti
Winklerhof
Schattberg West 2096 m
Westgipfelhütte
Schattberg 2097 m
Hintermaisalm
Grabenhütte
Reiner Haus
Kindlstadl
Gerstreitalm
Sky Rest
Schattberg Ost 2020 m
Schattberg X-Press
Schattbergkar
Simalalm
Limbergalm
Dillingereck
Rammernalm
Lindlingalm
Lengau
Kolling
NEU
Walleggalm
Sonnhof
Hochalm
Spieleckkogel 1998 m
Reichkendlkopf 1942 m
Hochalmspitze 1921 m
Hasenauer Köpfl 1791 m
Roßwaldhütte
Reiterkogel 1819 m
Bürglkopf 1730 m
Spielberghorn 2044 m
Bernkogel 1740 m
Wieseralm
Sportalm
Reiteralm
Pfefferalm
Sonnalm
Eislauf Tennishalle
1060 m
Umfahrungs-tunnel
Goaß-stall
Hinterglemm
Hallenbad Sauna
Bärnalm
Burgeralm
Spielberghaus
Westernstadl Altach
Kohlmaiskopf 1794 m
Panoramaalm
Maisalm
Bäckstätt Stall
Hinterhagalm
Bauers Skialm
Asteralm
Thurneralm
Bründlkopf 1879 m
Berger Hochalm
Parkhaus
Umfahrungstunnel
Saalbach
1003 m
Schwarzleo
Wildenkarkogel 1910 m
Wildenkarkogel Hütte
Rauchkuchl
Hochwart-alm
Schönleiten-hütte 1804 m
Seidl-Alm
Gr. Asitz 1914 m
Kl. Asitz 1870 m
Alte Schmiede
Stöcklalm
Forsthofalm
Saalach
Reit
Schönleitenbahn
Jausernalm
Vorderglemm
Zirmhütte
Polten-lift
Bayernsteig
Riederalm
Embach
Pirzbichl
Rain
Hütten
Saalfelden
Bahnhof
Bahn
Leogang
Irracheck 1071 m
nach Viehhofen und Maishofen
Hecherhütte
Viehhofen

valley the Bernkogel triple-chair, followed by one of the few remaining draglifts, brings you up to the 1740m summit of Bernkogel and the start of the anti-clockwise circuit.

This is a good resort for snowboarding, with a terrain park situated just above Hinterglemm and another served by the six-person Asitzmuldenbahn between Vorderglemm and Leogang. The nearby quad Polten lift gives access to a boardercross course, while the half-pipe is beneath the Bernkogel chair. The valley offers considerable opportunities for cross-country and the resort has three dedicated toboggan runs. The north side of the valley offers some outstanding powder runs.

Learn

Saalbach has no fewer than seven competing ski schools, while Hinterglemm has two and the hamlet of Vorderglemm has one. The continued survival of all of them gives an indication of the popularity of the Glemmtal during the main holiday period. In Saalbach a beginner recommends **Aamadall Snow Academy**, **t** +43 (0)6541 668 256 ('I was very impressed with the set up'). Others include **Green Discount**, **t** +43 (0)664 499 8465, **Zink**, **t** +43 (0)664 162 3655, and **Fürstauer**, **t** +43 (0)6541 8444 ('highly recommended for instruction and guides'). In Hinterglemm, **Snow & Fun**, **t** +43 (0)6541 634 640, has an enduring reputation. Off-piste guiding is available through **Sepp Mitterer**, **t** +43 (0)664 242 0236.

Children

In Hinterglemm, **Hotel Lengauerhof**, **t** +43 (0)6541 7255, and **Hotel Glemmtalerhof**, **t** +43 (0)6541 71350, both have crèches. **Annaliese Kröll**, **t** +43 (0)6541 7183, provides babysitting.

Lunch

'Great, affordable mountain eating everywhere,' was how one reporter summed it up. The ski circuit is dotted with 41 huts that vary from proper restaurants to the simplest of snack bars. **Pfefferalm**, **t** +43 (0)664 452 9649, an ancient farmhouse above Hinterglemm, is a favourite. **Rosswaldhütte**, **t** +43 (0)6541 6959, situated beside the Rosswald lift, has good food and staff in traditional dress. **Sportalm**, **t** +43 (0)6541 7972, **Thurner Alm**, **t** +43 (0)6541 8418, **Gerstreit Alm**, **t** +43 (0)6541 6565, and **Maisalm**, **t** +43 (0)6541 7409, are all recommended.

Dine

In Saalbach, **La Trattoria Italiana** and **Vitrine Asia Wok** are both in the Alpenhotel, **t** +43 (0)6541 6666, and make a change from traditional Austrian mountain fare. **Bäckstättstall**, **t** +43 (0)6541 7652, is the smart eatery option.

In Hinterglemm we recommend the **Fuhrmannstube** in Hotel Dorfschmiede, **t** +43 (0)6541 740 862. **Restaurant Kendler**, **t** +43 (0)6541 6225, has a rustic atmosphere; signature dishes include roast venison and sole.

Party

'Saalbach definitely parties hard, people were still staggering around in ski boots late into the evening.' Late afternoon comes to alcoholic life in **Hinterhagalm** above Saalbach, at **Bauer's Schialm** by the church, and at **Veltins** ('basically a small tumbledown shack'). It's equally noisy at the rustic **GoassStall** and **Hexenhäusl** in Hinterglemm. The snow bar outside **Hotel zur Dorfschmiede** is always busy as the

lift closes. Later on, attention in Saalbach focuses on The **Alibi Bar** and the Kuhstall. **Bobby's Pub** and **Zum Turm** (a converted jail) are lively. In Hinterglemm the **Glemmerkeller**, **Road King** and **Tanzhimmel** attract the late-night crowd.

The Nightliner bus service operates along the valley road between the two villages until late evening and until 2.30am on Saturday nights.

Sleep

Saalbach:

********Kunst-Hotel Kristiana**, t +43 (0)6541 6253, *www.kunsthotel.at*, has a typically Tyrolean interior transformed by a modern art collection.

******Gartenhotel Theresia**, t +43 (0)6541 74140, *www.hotel-theresia.co.at*, is a stylish hotel filled with contemporary art. It has won awards for the use of organic produce in its kitchen and offers especially good family facilities.

******Saalbacherhof**, t +43 (0)6541 7111, *www.saalbacherhof.at*, has a pool surrounded by rocks and is very comfortable, with superb cuisine.

******Alpenhotel**, t +43 (0)6541 6666, *www.alpenhotel.at*, is a multiple nightlife centre.

Hinterglemm:

******Sport & Vitalhotel Ellmau**, t +43 (0)6541 7226, *www.sporthotel-ellmau.at*, has an impressive spa, and a kitchen specializing in healthy cuisine including Ayurvedic food. There's a children's funpark with tubing and snowmobiling, a children's gym and sauna.

******Hotel Glemmtalerhof**, t +43 (0)6541 7135, *www.alpinparadies.at*, is long established and conveniently situated in the village centre.

******Hotel Panther**, t +43 (0)6541 6227, *www.hotel-panther.at*, is well located for the lifts and pubs, although 'the rear-facing rooms are a little exposed to late-night street revellers'.

******Blumenhotel Tirolerhof**, t +43 (0)6541 64970, *www.blumenhotels.at*, has a wellness spa and a heated outdoor pool.

******Hotel Zur Dorfschmiede**, t +43 (0)6541 74080, *www.wolf-hotels.at*, also in Hinterglemm village centre, has outstanding half-board cuisine and comfortable rooms.

St Anton

Profile

A lively town with some of the most challenging skiing and nightlife in Europe. Not recommended for beginners or anyone of a nervous disposition

Resort

The Arlberg is the major European home of skiing. While the Swiss caught on to the idea of what were originally called

*** BEST FOR**

Sophisto-cats, strong intermediates and experts, off-piste, party-goers

ESSENTIALS

Altitude: 1304m (4,278ft)–2811m (9,222ft)

Further information: +43 (0)5446 22690, *www.stantonamarlberg.com*

Lifts in area: 85 on Arlberg Ski Pass (10 cableways, 39 chairs, 36 drags) serving 280km of piste

Lift pass: Arlberg Ski Pass (covers Lech and Zürs, Pettneu, St Anton, St Christoph, Stuben, Sonnenkopf-Klösterle) adult €192–204, child 7–14yrs €115–122, both for six days; 6yrs and under €10 for whole season

Access: Innsbruck airport 1hr, Friedrichshafen airport 1½hrs, Zurich airport 2–3hrs, Munich airport 3–4hrs, railway station in resort

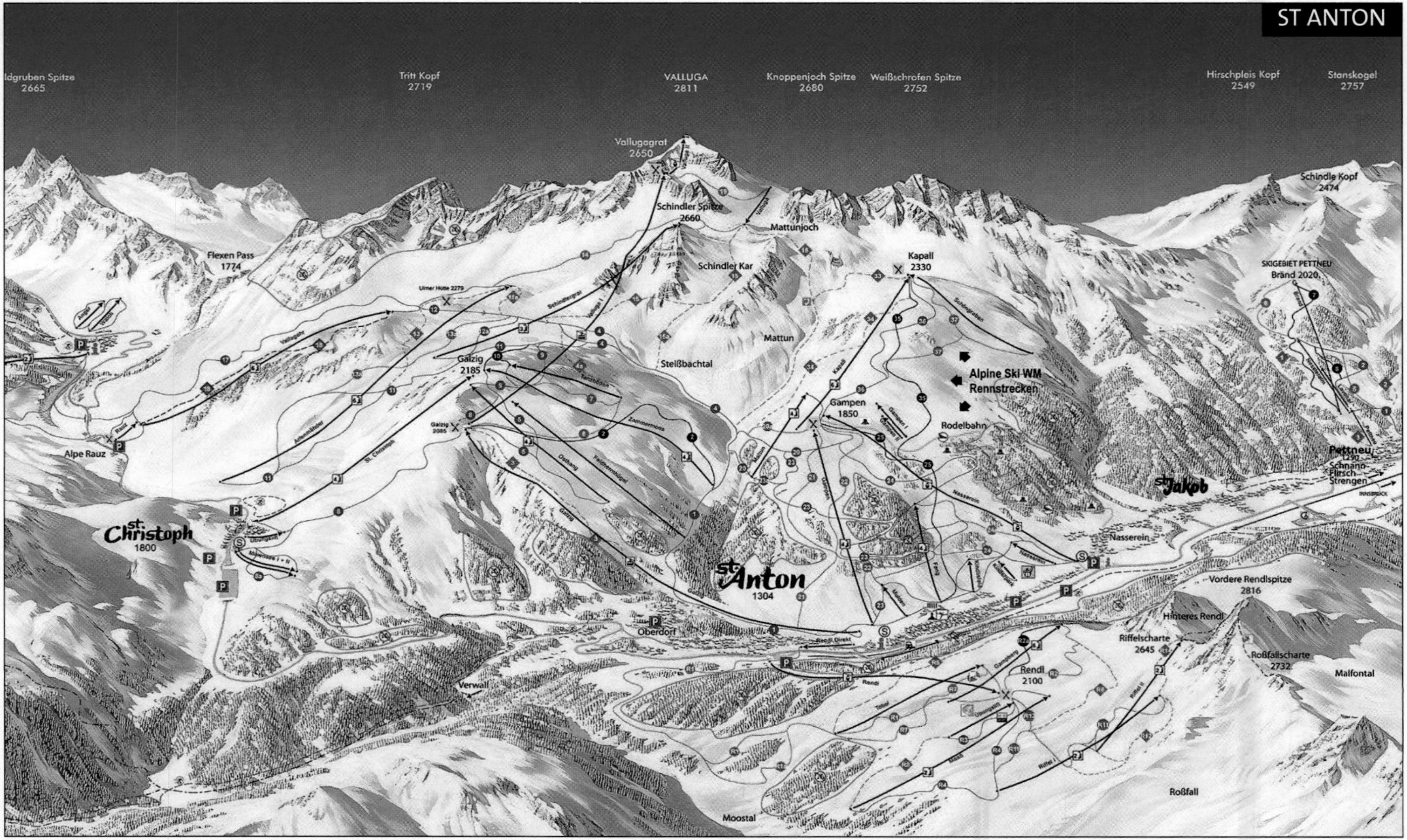

ST ANTON

ldgruben Spitze 2665
Tritt Kopf 2719
VALLUGA 2811
Knoppenjoch Spitze 2680
Weißschrofen Spitze 2752
Hirschpleis Kopf 2549
Stanskogel 2757
Vallugagrat 2650
Schindler Spitze 2660
Mattunjoch
Schindle Kopf 2474
Flexen Pass 1774
Schindler Kar
Kapall 2330
SKIGEBIET PETTNEU Brand 2020
Ulmer Hütte 2279
Mattun
Steißbachtal
Galzig 2185
Alpine Ski WM Rennstrecken
Gampen 1850
Rodelbahn
Galzig 2085
Alpe Rauz
Pettneu
Schnann
Flirsch
Strengen
St. Jakob
St. Christoph 1800
St. Anton 1304
Nasserein
Vordere Rendlspitze 2816
Hinteres Rendl
Oberdorf
Riffelscharte 2645
Roßfallscharte 2732
Rendl 2100
Malfontal
Verwall
Roßfall
Moostal

The St Anton chalet specialist providing a superior standard of comfort, care & cuisine

01449 711 952
www.albustravel.com

ATOL Protected 5510

'Norwegian snow shoes' at the start of the 1890s, they had little idea what to do with them. It was ski instructors in St Anton who perfected the original technique that allowed you not only to go downhill, but also to turn (almost) at will.

The first races were held in the neighbouring hamlet of St Christoph in 1903. But it wasn't until 1921 that the great Hannes Schneider opened his Arlberg Ski School on the slopes below Galzig, and St Anton began to shape the history of modern skiing.

Back in the 1950s, St Anton earned itself a place among the top five ski resorts in the world. It is remarkable, given the enormous development of the sport in both hemispheres over the past half century, that it easily holds on to its position. In the hall of fame, St Anton rubs shoulders with Chamonix, Val d'Isère/Tignes, Verbier, Zermatt, Jackson Hole and Whistler as one of the world's Truly Greats.

Anyone going for the first time should be aware that the terrain here varies from quite steep to the near sheer. It is not a place for novices and certainly not a place for wobbly second-weekers looking for a little confidence-building. St Anton is popular with experienced snowboarders, but if you can't manage steep moguls then stay away.

The village itself is a blend of old and new, much improved by the relocation of the railway line that used to bisect it. The attractive centre is pedestrianized during the day, with a modest selection of sports shops and boutiques, as well as some fine old hostelries and modern bars.

St Anton stretches in both directions, to the outlying and popular alternative bed-base of Nasserein as well as in the west towards Mooserkreuz. A ski-bus runs throughout the day and a night bus until 2am, but some walking is inevitable. However, it's possible to leave skis and boots in storage overnight near the bottom of the Galzig gondola.

Mountain

Much has been done to update St Anton's lift system. Most of this effort was concentrated into the build-up to the 2001 Alpine World Championships. The venerable Galzigbahn cable car built in 1937 was replaced in late 2006 by a 24-person jumbo gondola with a revolutionary ferris wheel design. This dispenses with the tedium of having to climb a staircase from the piste in order to reach the cabins. It has transformed mountain access and disposed of high-season lift queues.

The ski area is in two sections, one on either side of the St Anton Valley. Rendl, the smaller and easier of these, is a pleasant suntrap with a choice of red and blue runs reached by a gondola which rises inconveniently a short bus ride or awkward walk in boots from outside the village. Rendl has a terrain park and is popular with riders.

However, most skiers head each morning for the opposite side of the valley. A quad-chair followed by a six-pack take you up Gampen and Kapall for the easiest intermediate skiing in the main area. That said, the long black descent from the top follows the course used for the downhill races in the World Championships.

This sector connects – by piste and chair from Gampen, or by gondola from St Anton – with 2185m Galzig, the true hub of the ski area. From here you can ski down to the charming hamlet of St Christoph. Alternatively you can take the cable car up to the 2811m Valluga, the highest point in the ski area. From the top station it is possible to ski off the back down to Zürs, but you have to be accompanied by a guide.

It is fair to describe almost all St Anton's skiing as difficult, and the standard of skier and rider is high. The main runs become bumped up within hours of a major snowfall. The powder skiing is phenomenal, with unlimited possibilities, ('the best and most extensive skiing ever'). This is high alpine terrain, so avalanche danger is ever present, and a guide is essential when straying beyond the ropes.

'Really surprised a resort with such a big name does not have a half-pipe or a decent park,' was the only criticism, 'If you like freestyle this may not be the resort for you'.

Learn

St Anton is renowned for being a higher-level skier's resort and the teaching is generally good. The two ski schools retain their separate identities, but are under the same ownership. The original **Arlberg Ski School**, **t** +43 (0)5446 3411 ('fab off-piste classes'), founded by Hannes Schneider, has 250 instructors. **Franz Klimmer's St Anton**, **t** +43 (0)5446 3563, has 60 teachers. Both offer a high level of tuition, although standards can fall during peak weeks. The British-run **Piste to Powder Mountain Guided Adventures**, **t** +43 (0)6641 7462 820, or **t** +44 (0)1661 824 318, teaches off-piste and offers guiding to small groups. Reporters rate it highly.

Children

'I cannot praise the Arlberg kids ski school enough – it's heaps better than France or Switzerland,' said a reporter. **Kinderwelt**, **t** +43 (0)5446 2526, run by the Arlberg school, has a kindergarten at the ski school meeting place, on the Gampen, in Nasserein, and at St Christoph. Small skiers are accepted once they are out of nappies. **Kiki Club**, **t** +43 (0)5446 3563, operated by the St Anton school, runs ski classes for older children.

Lunch

The best mountain meal in the Arlberg is at **Galzig** in the Verwall Stube, **t** +43 (0)5446 235 2501 – modern Austrian cuisine with an emphasis on fresh fish and seafood. Also recommended are **Kaminstube**, **t** +43 (0)5446 2681, and **Rodelhütte**, **t** +43 (0)699 1085 8855, for good value, exceptional food and traditional Austrian atmosphere, as well as **Albona-Grat**, **t** +43 (0)5582 761, and **Ulmerhütte**, **t** +43 (0)5446 30200, on the descent from the Schindler Spitze. **Sennhütte**, **t** +43 (0)5446 2048, has live music. Our favourite lunch spot is the sunny terrace of the **Arlberg-Hospiz-Alm**, **t** +43 (0)5446 2611, in St Christoph, where waiters wear Austrian national dress and the descent to the loo is by a helter-skelter slide. The **Maiensee Stube**, **t** +43 (0)5446 2804, also in St Christoph, and the **Hotel Post**, **t** +43 (0)5582 761, in Stuben, both have a warm atmosphere and good food.

Dine

By night the Werner family's **Arlberg-Hospiz-Alm**, **t** +43 (0)5446 2611, in St Christoph, puts on the tablecloths and becomes a serious gourmet restaurant with an astonishing wine cellar. In St Anton, the warehouse-style **Benvenuto**, **t** +43 (0)5446 30203, serves mainly Oriental dishes. Family-run **Floriani**, **t** +43 (0)5446 2330, is recommended, as is **Hazienda**, **t** +43 (0)5446 2968, which serves excellent steaks and seafood. **The Museum**, **t** +43 (0)5446 2475, is like eating in someone's large private home. **Sportcafé Schneider**, **t** +43 (0)5446 2548, is in the pedestrian zone. **Café Aquila**, **t** +43 (0)5446 2217, is decorated 1960s style. The **Funky Chicken**, **t** +43 (0)664 404 3360, is popular with snowboarders and has some of the best-value food in town. Nasserein's **San Antonio**, **t** +43 (0)5446 3474, is a popular pizzeria.

Party

The afternoon warms up with a Glühwein at the **Sennhütte** before the descent into degenerate behaviour at the infamous **Krazy Kanguruh** and/or the **Mooserwirt** on the meadow above the resort. The party gets truly under way with raucous music and much drinking and dancing as the light fades. Most make it back down the nursery slope in one piece, ready for a full evening of entertainment ahead. Hotspots include the **Piccadilly**, **Funky Chicken**, **Bar Cuba**, **Hazienda**, **Train** and **Vino**. **Scotty's Bar** in the Hotel Rosanna is also a popular meeting place. The **Kandahar** comes to life in the early hours as other establishments close.

Sleep

*******Hotel Arlberg-Hospiz**, **t** +43 (0)5446 2611, *www.hospiz.com*, in St Christoph, counts Russian prime minister Vladimir Putin among its patrons.

*******Hotel St Antoner Hof**, **t** +43 (0)5446 2910, *www.st.antonerhof.at*, is comfortable and modern.

*******Arlberg Lodges**, **t** +44 (0)20 8682 5050, *www.scottdunn.com*, is a complex of four superlative catered chalets on the outskirts of town.

******Hotel Post**, **t** +43 (0)5446 2213, *www.hotel-post.co.at*, is close to the lifts.

******Hotel Alte Post**, **t** +43 (0)5446 2553, *www.hotel-alte-post.at*, is the original coaching inn. It's well located and has a good spa.

******Hotel Karl Schranz**, **t** +43 (0)5446 25550, *www.arlberg.com/hotel.karl.schranz*, owned by the former world champion, has pleasant rooms and good food but is slightly out of town.

******Hotel Arlberg**, **t** +43 (0)5446 22100, *www.arlberg.com*, has a relaxed atmosphere and is furnished in traditional Tyrolean style. 'Very good food and service,' said a reader.

******Hotel Tyrol**, **t** +43 (0)5446 2340, *www.tyrolhotel.com*, near the church, is a pleasant place to stay – very friendly, with helpful staff.

******Hotel Bergschlössl**, **t** +43 (0)5446 2220, *www.bergschloessl.at*, is well located next to the Galzig cable car and is owned by Johanna Moosbrugger, whose brother owns Gasthof Post in Lech. Bedrooms are spacious and individually decorated.

******Hotel Schwarzer Adler**, **t** +43 (0)5446 22440, *www.schwarzeradler.com*, is central, friendly and comfortable, with a great pool. A large number of visitors to the resort choose to stay in catered chalets.

St Johann in Tirol

Profile

Unpretentious Tyrolean village of frescoed houses surrounded by less attractive suburbs. There is a modern lift system, benign slopes, and three surrounding resorts of Oberndorf, Kirchdorf and Erpfendorf

Resort

St Johann in Tirol found popularity with foreign visitors in the 1970s and 1980s before fading from the frame. But now, thanks to new lifts and a reaffirmed sense of identity, it is enjoying a fresh lease of winter life.

The pretty Tyrolean village with its ornately frescoed watering holes and old coaching inns is marred by traffic and industrial estates on the outskirts, but the centre retains considerable charm.

Mountain

This is a particularly good area for beginners to low intermediates, with a series of dedicated nursery slopes on the gentle meadows behind the station and in the hamlet of Eichenhof.

Mountain access is by a two-stage gondola, which brings you up to the 1700m summit of Harschbichl. Reporters complain of queues at around 10am each morning during high season. It is advisable to take the alternative, and usually near-deserted, eight-seater gondola that rises from Penzing on the edge of Oberndorf.

The resort has a terrain park beneath the Penzing chair and a half-pipe at Eichenhof. Cross-country skiing is extensive, with 275km of prepared trails just outside the village.

Learn

St Johann has five ski schools: **St Johann**, **t** +43 (0)5352 64777, **Eichenhof**, **t** +43 (0)5352 65930, **Wilder Kaiser**, **t** +43 (0)5352 64888, **Ski-Akademie St Johann in Tirol**, **t** +43 (0)5352 624 888, and **White Eagle**, **t** +43 (0)664 762 0481.

Children

St Johann ski school, **t** +43 (0)5352 64777, runs **Bobo's Ski Kindergarten**, which takes children from four years. Eichenhof's **Kinderland**, **t** +43 (0)5352 65930, also cares for children from four years.

*BEST FOR

Beginners and low intermediates, families

ESSENTIALS

Altitude: 670m (2,198ft)–1,700m (5,576ft)
Further information: **t** +43 (0)5352 633 350, *www.ferienregion.at*
Lifts in area: 17 lifts (3 cableways, 4 chairs, 10 drags) serving 60km of piste. 60 lifts and 170km of piste in linked Schneewinkel area
Lift pass: Schneewinkel adult €142–166, child €71–83, both for six days
Access: Innsbruck airport 1hr, Salzburg airport 1hr, Munich airport 1½hrs, railway station in resort

Lunch

The **Harschbichlhütte**, **t** +43 (0)5352 64671, has great *Gulaschsuppe*. **Koasaburg**, **t** +43 (0)5352 63940, has home-cooked food and a sunny terrace. **Grander Schupf**, **t** +43 (0)5352 63925, and **Bassgeigeralm**, **t** +43 (0)5352 62117, are recommended.

Dine

Lange Mauer, **t** +43 (0)5352 62174, serves Chinese cuisine. **La Rustica-Antonio**, **t** +43 (0)5352 62843, and **Rialto**, **t** +43 (0)5352 64168, are pizzerias. **Edelweiss**, **t** +43 (0)5352 63580, serves mountain dishes.

Party

Popular bars include **Bunny's**, **Humungus**, **Max Pub** and **Rogi's Stadl**. The **Scala-Bar Club** provides the late-night entertainment.

Sleep

******Sporthotel Austria**, **t** +43 (0)5352 62507, *www.sporthotelaustria.at*, is traditional and in a central yet quiet location. Facilities include an indoor pool and family apartments with two adjoining bedrooms.

★★★★**Hotel Gasthof Park**, t +43 (0)5352 62226, *www.park.at*, is near the gondola.

★★★**Hotel Post**, t +43 (0)5352 62230, *www.hotel-post.tv*, dates from 1225 and is beautifully frescoed on the outside, with each room individually decorated.

★★★**Hotel Fischer**, t +43 (0)5352 62332, *www.hotel-fischer.com*, is located in the pedestrian area and has comfortable rooms.

Schladming

* BEST FOR

Intermediates, mountain huts, families, cross-country skiers

ESSENTIALS

Altitude: 745m (2,224ft)–2,015m (6,609ft)

Further information: t +43 (0)3687 23310, *www.schladming-rohrmoos.com*

Lifts in area: 109 (9 cableways, 25 chairs, 57 drags, 18 children's lifts) serving 223km of piste

Skiverbund Amadé region: 270 (37 cableways, 90 chairs, 143 drags) serving 860km of piste

Lift pass: Skiverbund Amadé adult €176–189, child €81.50–98, both for six days

Access: Salzburg airport 1hr, Munich airport 2½hrs, railway station in resort

Profile

Large intermediate playground included in the 276-lift Skiverbund Amadé lift pass. Glacier skiing and extensive cross-country trails nearby, but the terrain is not suited to advanced skiers

Resort

Schladming is a fine medieval town with an industrial and cultural life of its own rather than a village that has expanded into a ski resort. It has two beautiful Romanesque and Gothic churches and a magnificent 18th-century town square.

'Schladming is an exciting, entertaining resort in the bottom of the valley, with shops, a leisure centre, and plenty of mountain restaurants,' was how one reporter summed it up. The town makes a charming base from which to explore not just the rather banal skiing immediately around it, but also other areas such as Flachau/Wagrain and the Gasteinertal. All are included in the regional lift pass and are situated just a short drive away.

Be warned: this is a resort much loved by the Austrians, and the slopes can be very crowded during the national school holidays in February. However, 'the locals are very friendly and there aren't too many English in the resort,' said a reader.

Mountain

The central Planai ski area is reached by a gondola that rises from the edge of town. Alternatively, you can drive up an all-weather road to a car park just below the mid-station. A network of modern, mainly high-capacity chairs serve easy blue and red runs that wind down between the trees.

Pistes and a chairlift provide links to the peaks of Hauser Kaibling on one side and Hochwurzen and Reiteralm on the other. Fageralm, a few kilometres further along the valley towards Radstadt and Salzburg, is another small but enjoyable ski area.

In the other direction, towards Linz and Graz, lies the pretty village of Haus-im-Ennstal, flanked by two gondolas that rise to the top of Hauser Kaibling. Beyond Haus, the 1986m Galsterbergalm above Pruggern provides slightly more

Schladming-Dachstein Tauern
mit der 4-Berge-Skischaukel
GALSTERBERGALM 1986 m
HAUSER KAIBLING 2015 m
PLANAI 1894 m
HOCHWURZEN 1850 m
REITERALM 1860 m
FAGERALM 1885 m
NATURPARK SÖLKTÄLER
ROHRMOOS 1050 m
FORSTAU 930 m
AICH 750 m
GRÖBMING
STODERZINKEN 2045 m
HAUS/ENNSTAL 752 m
SCHLADMING 745 m
PICHL 800 m
GLEIMING 810 m
Rittisberg 1600 m
RAMSAU AM DACHSTEIN 1100 m - 1300 m
DACHSTEINGLETSCHER 2700 m

demanding terrain. Schladming is 'a great resort for people who can happily ski red runs' rather than a resort for off-piste skiers. In the main ski area above the resort, leaving the marked piste is positively discouraged. Planai and the Dachstein Glacier both have good half-pipes. Schladming has opened the world's first Music Slope, with 'spirited rhythms and cheerful music' to ski to.

The Ramsau plateau, situated just a few minutes' drive from Schladming, is one of Austria's most scenic cross-country areas, and is a former venue for the World Championships. It has 145km of snow-sure marked trails between 1100m and 1300m. High-altitude skiing is possible on the adjoining Dachstein Glacier, reached by cable car from Turlwand.

Learn

Hopl, **t** +43 (0)3687 23582, and **Tritscher**, **t** +43 (0)3687 22137, provide a full range of ski and snowboard lessons. **Blue Tomato**, **t** +43 (0)3687 24223, is the specialist board school. Off-piste guiding is available from **Helli Team Bedarfsflug**, **t** +43 (0)3687 81323.

Children

Meine Kleine Schule, **t** +43 (0)3687 24407, and **Frau Ladreiter**, **t** +43 (0)3687 61313, are the resort's two non-ski kindergartens. **Trischer** ski school operates a highly acclaimed ski kindergarten.

Lunch

Schladming has an abundance of friendly huts scattered across the mountainside and should win a prize for being one of the only resorts in the world to list mountain restaurants with telephone numbers on the piste map. 'Great variety and atmosphere and the prices are extremely reasonable,' said a reader. **Seiterhütte**, **t** +43 (0)3687 61615, below the summit of Hochwurzen, has a welcoming sun terrace. **Märchenwiese Hütte**, **t** +43 (0)3687 61251, near the lift of the same name, has reliable home cooking. **Onkel Willy's Hütte**, **t** +43 (0)3687 23105, has live music and a sunny terrace. **Eiskarhütte**, **t** +43 (0)6454 7234, at Reiteralm, is recommended.

Dine

L'Osteria da Giorgio, **t** +43 (0)3687 23173, and **Va Bene**, **t** +43 (0)3687 23226, provide an Italian alternative to Austrian mountain fare, along with **Giovanni's Pizza & Pasta**, **t** +43 (0)3687 24638. **Planaistub'n Charly Kahr**, **t** +43 (0)3687 23544, is a favourite of Californian Governor Arnold Schwarzenegger when he returns to these parts. **Arnoldstub'n Charly Kahr**, **t** +43 (0)3687 23544, is under the same ownership. The **Rôtisserie Royer Grill**, **t** +43 (0)3687 2000, in Sporthotel Royer, is recommended. **Kirchenwirt**, **t** +43 (0)3687 22435, has good-quality food, a warm atmosphere and excellent service. **China Restaurant Peking**, **t** +43 (0)3687 22688, rings the changes.

Party

Hohenhaus Tenne is the big new après venue, set on five floors with eight bars, a dance bar and a restaurant called **Mak Planai**. Otherwise, there is **Onkel Willy's Hütte** on Planai and the **Schirmbar, which** draw a large crowd long before the lifts close. Later on the action moves to **Charly's Treff** which is a resort meeting point, along with **La Porta**, **Das Beisl**, **Mariah's Mexican**, the **Hanglbar**, **Ferry's**, **Twister Bar**, **Siglu** and the **Sonderbar Disco**. The 8km toboggan run from the top of Hochwurzen is open in the evenings. Schladming has a good swimming pool made of stainless steel.

Sleep

★★★★**Sporthotel Royer**, **t** +43 (0)3687 2000, *www.royer.at*, has a pool, indoor tennis and squash, bowling alley and a wellness centre. It is crowded with Russians in January.

★★★★**Hotel-Restaurant Alte Post**, **t** +43 (0)3687 22571, *www.alte-post.at*, is an old coaching inn in the main square, with a fine restaurant and wellness centre.

★★★★**Hotel zum Stadttor**, **t** +43 (0)3687 24525, *www.hotelzumstadttor.at*, is a family-run hotel next to the church.

★★★**Appartement-Hotel Ferienalm**, **t** +43 (0)3687 23517, *www.ferienalm.com*, has a panoramic view of Schladming and the Planai ski area and is five minutes by ski bus from the Planai gondola.

★★★**Gasthof zum Kaiserweg**, **t** +43 (0)3687 22038, *www.kaiserweg.at*, is in a quiet position five minutes from the centre. It has simple rooms, and a good restaurant with all fresh ingredients and everything homemade.

Seefeld

Profile

Attractive old town with elegant hotels and a sophisticated nightlife. This is the cross-country ski capital of the Austrian Alps, with downhill skiing best suited to the less experienced

* BEST FOR

Beginners, low intermediates, families, value, night-owls, non-skiers, langlaufers

ESSENTIALS

Altitude: 1200m (3,937ft)–2100m (6,890ft)
Further information: **t** +43 (0)508 800, *www.seefeld.com*
Lifts in area: 32 (1 mountain railway, 2 cableways, 6 chairs, 23 drags) serving 48km of piste
Lift pass: adult €169.50, child 7–15yrs €101.50, both for six days
Access: Innsbruck airport 20mins, railway station in resort

Resort

Seefeld is a mini-Kitzbühel, with a modest amount of downhill skiing and 280km of cross-country tracks set around a large village with frescoed medieval architecture above the Inn valley.

Visitors come here not just for the skiing, but for an all-round winter holiday complete with sleigh rides, winter walks, skating, tobogganing, exotic spa treatments, a casino, and a clutch of superlative hotels and restaurants. Even non-skiers will have a ball, with candlelight walks, and restaurants with typical Austrian theme nights.

Mountain

The serious skiers here are *langlaufers* who want to explore the 266km of marked tracks in the area. The 3km floodlit *loipe* opens six evenings a week.

Downhill skiers have three small areas. Novices congregate at Geigenbühel. Gschwandtkopf is a hill next to the cross-country track used mainly by the ski school. Rosshütte is the more extensive area, with some more challenging runs, a long off-piste trail, night-skiing and a snowboard park. The Rosshütten-Express six-person chair has replaced a fixed double and a draglift and is a great improvement.

Learn

Seefeld, t +43 (0)5212 2412, is the largest school and has a good reputation. **Sport Aktiv, t** +43 (0)6991 461 000, is based in the Gschwandtkopf area. **Mösern, t** +43 (0)5212 4736, has a beginner slope in the hamlet of the same name and also teaches on the Gschwandtkopf.

Children

Ski School Seefeld, t +43 (0)5212 2412, offers childcare with or without lessons, as well as a games zone and designated pistes.

Lunch

Sonnenalm, t +43 (0)5212 2490, is an enticing mountain restaurant on the Gschwandtkopf. **Rosshütte, t** +43 (0)5212 24160, has been completely refurbished.

Dine

Krachele Moos, t +43 (0)5212 4680, **Triendlsäge, t** +43 (0)5212 2580, and **Südtiroler Stubn, t** +43 (0)5212 50446, serve typical Tyrolean dishes. Gourmets can try the **Alte Stube** in the Casinohotel Karwendelhof, **t** +43 (0)5212 2655. **Café Nanni, t** +43 (0)5212 2229, and **Café Moccamühle** in Hotel Elite, **t** +43 (0)5212 2901, are popular for their cakes and *Apfelstrudl*. The gourmet restaurant **Ritter Oswald Stube** in the Klosterbräu, **t** +43 (0)5212 26210, has a 500-year-old wine cellar housing 9,000 bottles.

Party

Batzenhäusl, and hotels **Kaltschmid** and **Klosterbräu**, all have live music. The **Tenne** has tea-dancing, **Siglu** is always crowded, and late-night entertainment is focused on the **Jeep**, **Buffalo** and **Full Moon** discos. The sports centre has a renovated Olympic-sized pool, as well as saunas, skating and curling.

Sleep

★★★★★**Dorint Vital Royal & Spa, t** +43 (0)5212 44310, *www.sofitel.com*, has a large pool and a spa specializing in Chinese treatments.

★★★★★**Hotel Klosterbräeu, t** +43 (0)5212 26210, *www.klosterbraeu.com*, is a former 16th-century monastery with sumptuous bedrooms.

★★★★**Hotel Bergland, t** +43 (0)5212 2293, *www.h-bergland.at*, has received praise for its exceptional food, and keenness to cater for guests' individual needs.

★★★★**Hotel A-Vita Viktoria, t** +43 (0)5212 4441, *www.viktoria.at*, has suites with apt names such as Laura Ashley, La Dolce Vita and St-Paul-de-Vence.

★★★★**Casinohotel Karwendelhof, t** +43 (0)5212 2655, *www.karwendelhof.com*, is in the pedestrian precinct.

★★★★**Hotel Inntalerhof, t** +43 (0)5212 4747, *www.inntalerhof.com*, is a family-run hotel in the village of Mösern just outside Seefeld – a really good place for a relaxing stay; great food and wellness centre, extremely friendly staff, super views and very well priced.

★★★★**Hotel Kaltschmid, t** +43 (0)5212 2191, *www.kaltschmid.info*, has a free kindergarten.

★★★★**Gartenhotel Tümmlerhof, t** +43 (0)5212 2571, *www.tuemmlerhof.at*, offers daycare.

★★★★**Wellnesshotel Schönruh, t** +43 (0)5212 2447, *www.kaltschmid.info*, is slightly starchy and formal, but the staff are excellent.

Sölden

*BEST FOR

Snow-sure slopes, long season, vibrant après-ski

ESSENTIALS

Altitude: 1377m (4,517ft)–3250m (10,663ft)
Further information: t 43 (0)57200 200, *www.soelden.com*
Lifts in area: 34 (7 cableways, 19 chairs, 8 drags) serving 146km of piste
Lift pass: adult €184.50–205.50, child 7–17yrs €111–143, both for six days
Access: Innsbruck airport 1hr, Ötztal station 45mins

Profile

High-altitude destination for all standards and for those who want jolly après-ski. Two glaciers offering snow-sure skiing and boarding throughout a long season

Resort

High-altitude Sölden is renowned for reliable snow-cover and unfettered nightlife, two products that endear it to substantial numbers of fun-loving visitors who ski hard and party even harder. 'Solden gets the thumbs up from us, it's a great skiing destination. Not the prettiest of Austrian resorts but if it's skiing you're after, look no further,' enthused a reader.

However, the lack of charm is far outweighed by the quality of the skiing and the accommodation.

Hochsölden is a car-free satellite set on summer pastures above the village with a handful of ski-in, ski-out hotels and panoramic views of the Ötztal.

Mountain

'In terms of skiing, this resort has it all, said a reporter. 'The three mountains are well connected, without any annoying little paths between lifts. The lifts are virtually all modern and fast.' Sölden's reputation for snow-sure skiing hinges on the presence of the adjoining Tiefenback and Rettenbach glaciers. These were incorporated some years ago into the resort's mainstream terrain by the addition of a gondola that spans the Rettenbach valley.

However, the resort's own skiing goes up to 3058m, allowing for an impressive vertical drop of 1680m. Sölden's skiing is suited to all standards, with plenty of intermediate terrain and a few testing blacks. The total kilometres feels longer than stated because it is not padded with the tedious, linking blue tracks that you find in many resorts.

Mountain access is by two gondolas, one at either end of the village. The excellent Giggijoch gondola gets you up the mountain in under 10 minutes. Giggijoch terrain park, reached by the Hainbachkar chair, has a half-pipe and a boardercross course. Another terrain park is built each autumn on the Rettenbach glacier.

Learn

Sölden has five schools: **Sölden-Hochsölden**, **t** +43 (0)5254 2364, **Yellow Power**, **t** +43 (0)664 442 4866, **Skiaktiv**, **t** +43 (0)5253 6313, **Vacancia Total**, **t** +43 (0)5254 3100, and **Freeride Center Tirol**, **t** +43 (0)650 266 5292. All have established reputations.

Children

Sölden-Hochsölden ski school, has a non-ski kindergarten for children from six months. It also runs **Bobo's Ski Kindergarten** for children from three years. Yellow Power operates **Fiddel Bambini Club** ski kindergarten on Giggijoch for little ones from three years.

Lunch

Mountain huts are in abundance. **Gampe Thaya, t** +43 (0)5254 5010, has plenty of atmosphere. **Heide Alm, t** +43 (0)5254 508875, offers beautiful views.

Dine

Mangia Bene, t +43 (0)5254 5010, serves pasta and fish. **La Tavola, t** +43 (0)5254 2674, has pizzas and Austrian specialities. **Pizzeria Gusto, t** +43 (0)5254 2272, and **Gasthof Waldcafé, t** +43 (0)5254 2319, are recommended, along with the **Schnalser Stube** in the Hotel Liebe Sonne, **t** +43 (0)5254 2203.

Party

Après-ski begins at **Giggi Tenne**, **Felsenstüberl**, **Grüner's Almstube**, **Kuhstall**, **Philipp** at Innerwald, and at the **Cuckoo Bar** at the bottom of the Gigijoch gondola ('the best place'). Later on, some 12 nightclubs, including the popular **Bierhimml**, keep visitors on their feet until the early hours. There are some cosy bars such as **The Grizzly**, with its fireplace and candles, and the unpromising-sounding **Harley Davison Bar**, which actually offers brilliant service. In Hochsölden the action centres around **Eugens Obstlerhütte**. The **Snowrock Café** has a good mixture of music, live or mixed. For the later venues the main club is **Partyhaus**, for a younger crowd.

Sleep

*****__Central Sölden, t__ +43 (0)5254 22600, *www.central-soelden.at*, has a vast spa.

****__Hotel Regina, t__ +43 (0)5254 2301, *www.hotel-regina.com*, has a pool and is convenient for the Gaislachkoglbahn.

****__Hotel Stefan, t__ +43 (0)5254 2237, *www.hotel-stefan.at*, is close to the Giggijoch lift station and has good food.

**__Gasthof Sonnenheim, t__ +43 (0)5254 2276, *www.kraxner.com/sonnenheim*, is a recommended budget option. 'I honestly don't think we could have eaten better anywhere else in Solden,' said a reader, and 'wonderfully comfortable,' added another.

Söll and the SkiWelt

Profile

Large linked ski area that is good value for money. Not the place if you're looking for alternative activities to skiing and partying

Resort

By virtue of being the largest bed-base in the region, Söll is the uncrowned capital of what is still Austria's largest interconnected ski area. The network of lifts spans the mainly gentle mountain-sides surrounding seven resorts near Kitzbühel.

Two further resorts, Westendorf (now, in turn, linked to Kirchberg and Kitzbühel) and Kelchsau, are linked into the system only by bus but consider themselves part of the network and are included in the lift

✱ BEST FOR

Beginners, low intermediates, families, value, night-owls

ESSENTIALS

Altitude: 703m (2,306ft)–1829m (6,001ft)
Further information: t +43 (0)5358 505, *www.wilderkaiser.info*
Lifts in area: 90 (1 funicular, 11 cableways, 38 chairs, 39 drags) serving 250km of piste in the SkiWelt Wilder Kaiser–Brixental.
Lift pass: SkiWelt adult €154.50–181.50, child 6–16yrs, €77–145.50, both for six days
Access: Innsbruck airport 1hr, Salzburg airport 1hr, Munich airport 1½hrs, Wörgl railway station 20mins

pass. There have been complaints that the regional lift map is of little assistance: 'We kept getting lost, but it didn't matter as we kept finding new runs,' said a reporter. In a bid to attract more families, the region has dramatically reduced the cost of a six-day child's lift pass.

This is prime cruising country over undulating summer pastureland, best suited to skiers who have progressed from the nursery slopes and are in need of daily confidence-building mileage.

Söll is a large, friendly village set around an onion-domed church in the middle of a wide valley. The ski area is 1km away and best reached by ski-bus ('this can be a very crowded and unpleasant experience in the rush hour – think Tube journey with skis and poles').

Back in the 1980s the resort was an annual mustering point for British and Dutch youth who did more drinking than skiing. For a while it shrugged off its overtly laddish image, but we continue to receive reports that Söll is reverting to type. 'The profile of visitors appears to be getting more and more beery with each year that passes,' was one typical comment.

Mountain

'The three mountains are well connected and give you some great skiing,' said a reader. Mountain access is by a two-stage gondola, which brings you swiftly up to Hohe Salve, the high point of the linked area. The other linked villages of Going, Ellmau, Scheffau, Itter, Hopfgarten and Brixen-im-Thale all line the valley around the dome-shaped massif. Each of these resorts provides alternative access into the system, either by gondola or by funicular from Ellmau, or by quad-chair from Going.

The resorts are linked on the main road by postbus, but not by free ski-bus, so in the afternoon it is advisable to keep an eye on your watch.

All of them, except south-facing Hopfgarten and Brixen, have dedicated nursery slopes at the bottom of the mountain. Scheffau, our favourite here, is set back on the other side of the valley and has its novice area on a sloping meadow beneath the church. The home run back to Söll is marked red on the piste map. It is covered by snow-cannon, but lack of natural cover can lead to difficult icy conditions. Regular blue-run skiers are advised to return to the valley by gondola.

This is not a place for advanced skiers, who, despite the beauty of the scenery, will soon tire of the lack of challenge. Lärchenhang, on the north side of Hohe Salve, is a short and testing pitch. Other steep terrain as well as some rewarding off-piste can be found with the help of a guide. The terrain park and half-pipe at Söll are situated above Salvenmoos.

If you don't want to ski alone, the SkiWelt has introduced a 'find-a-ski-mate' scheme. The area has seven fixed meeting points and you are given an appropriate sticker for your jacket. Further information at *www.skiwelt.at*.

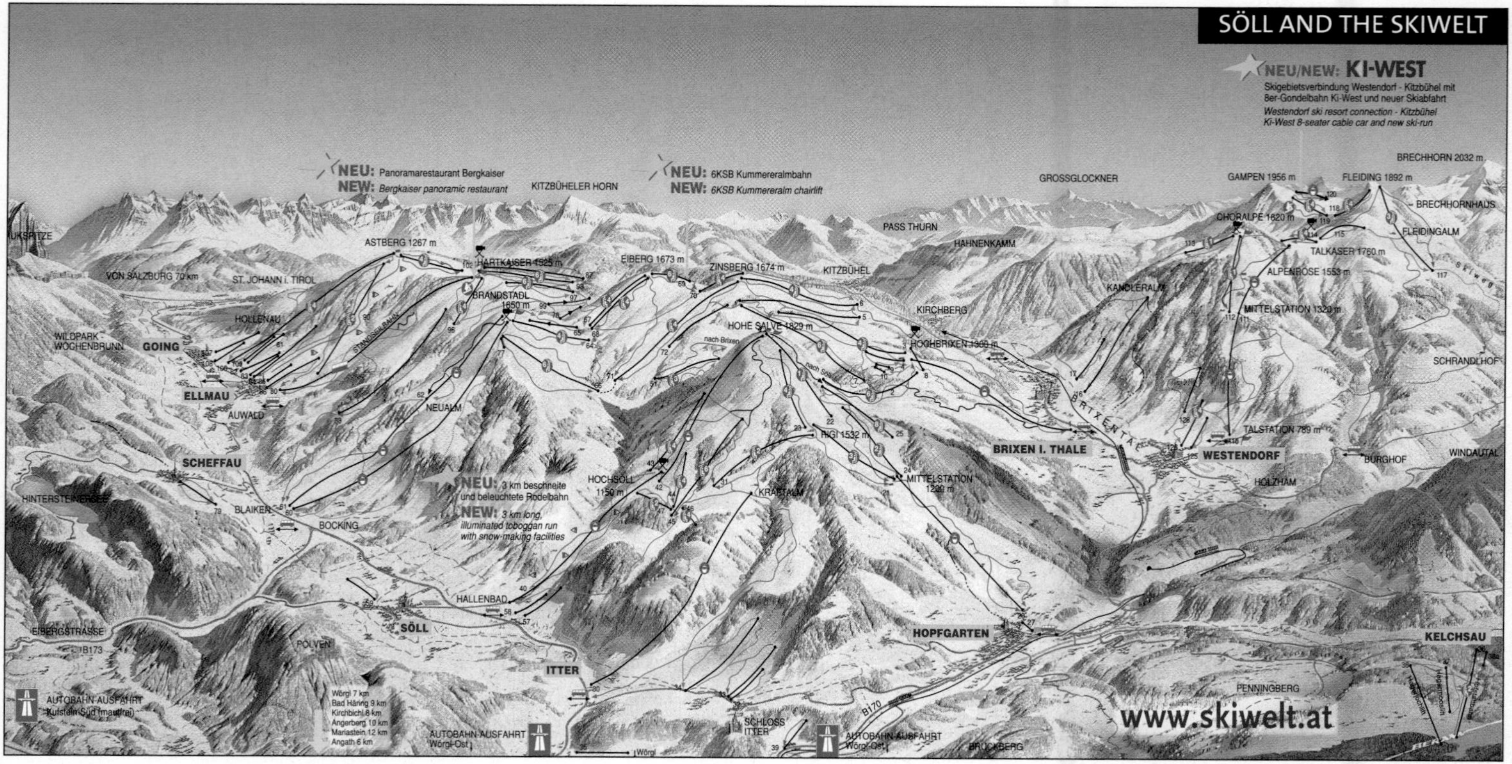

SÖLL AND THE SKIWELT

NEU/NEW: KI-WEST
Skigebietsverbindung Westendorf - Kitzbühel mit 8er-Gondelbahn Ki-West und neuer Skiabfahrt
Westendorf ski resort connection - Kitzbühel Ki-West 8-seater cable car and new ski-run

NEU: Panoramarestaurant Bergkaiser
NEW: *Bergkaiser panoramic restaurant*

NEU: 6KSB Kummereralmbahn
NEW: *6KSB Kummereralm chairlift*

NEU: 3 km beschneite und beleuchtete Rodelbahn
NEW: *3 km long, illuminated toboggan run with snow-making facilities*

KITZBÜHELER HORN
GROSSGLOCKNER
BRECHHORN 2032 m
GAMPEN 1956 m
FLEIDING 1892 m
BRECHHORNHAUS
CHORALPE 1620 m
FLEIDINGALM
TALKASER 1760 m
ALPENROSE 1553 m
MITTELSTATION 1320 m
PASS THURN
HAHNENKAMM
KANDLERALM
SCHRANDLHOF
KIRCHBERG
KITZBÜHEL
ASTBERG 1267 m
HARTKAISER 1525 m
EIBERG 1673 m
ZINSBERG 1674 m
VON SALZBURG 70 km
ST. JOHANN i. TIROL
BRANDSTADL 1650 m
HOLLENAU
WILDPARK WOCHENBRUNN
GOING
HOHE SALVE 1829 m
HOCHBRIXEN 1300 m
ELLMAU
AUWALD
NEUALM
RIGI 1532 m
TALSTATION 789 m
BRIXEN I. THALE
WESTENDORF
BURGHOF
WINDAUTAL
HOLZHAM
SCHEFFAU
HINTERSTEINERSEE
HOCHSÖLL 1150 m
KRAFTALM
MITTELSTATION 1200 m
BLAIKEN
BOCKING
HALLENBAD
SÖLL
EIBERGSTRASSE
B173
POLVEN
HOPFGARTEN
KELCHSAU
ITTER
PENNINGBERG
AUTOBAHN-AUSFAHRT Kufstein Süd (mautfrei)
Wörgl 7 km
Bad Häring 9 km
Kirchbichl 8 km
Angerberg 10 km
Mariastein 12 km
Angath 6 km
AUTOBAHN-AUSFAHRT Wörgl-Ost
SCHLOSS ITTER
B170
AUTOBAHN-AUSFAHRT Wörgl-Ost
BRUCKBERG
Wörgl

www.skiwelt.at

Learn

The various ski schools here have amalgamated into the **Söll-Hochsöll**, **t** +43 (0)5333 5454, which over the past 40 years has acquired considerable experience in teaching foreigners to ski. As a place to get to grips with the basics, we warmly recommend it. However, like a lot of Austrian ski schools in major beginner and intermediate resorts, there seems to be little emphasis on adapting teaching methods to encompass the latest generation of skis.

Children

'A great place to take the family skiing, super kids' club and loads of fun to be had on the slopes,' one reporter commented. **Bobo Miniclub**, **t** +43 (0)6457 2090, is run by the ski school and cares for children from five years. Small guests at the Alphotel can join the **Smiley Tiny Tots Ski School**, **t** +43 (0)5517 5449, from two years.

Lunch

The mountainside is dotted with welcoming huts and larger self-service restaurants. **Gründalm**, **t** +43 (0)5333 5060, and **Gipfelrestaurant Hohe Salve**, **t** +43 (0)5333 5949, are both recommended. **Schernthannstuberl**, **t** +43 (0)5333 5273, is a welcome spot on a cold day. **Stöcklalm**, **t** +43 (0)5333 5127, and **Kraftalm**, **t** +43 (0)5332 75152, are both extremely busy from 11.30am onwards.

Dine

Most restaurants are in the hotels. **Giovanni**, **t** +43 (0)5333 57050, **Venezia**, **t** +43 (0)5333 6191, and **Hexenalm**, **t** +43 (0)5333 5544, are all good pizzerias. **Schindlhaus**, **t** +43 (0)5333 516 136, offers more gourmet fare. **Panoramabad Café**, **t** +43 (0)5333 544 212, is out of the way but worth the walk for coffee and cakes. The village, thankfully, also has some more adult places now in the shape of **Bella Vita**, **t** +43 (0)5333 20360, with excellent food, and **Rossini's**, **t** +43 (0)5333 5139, across the road.

Party

Nightlife is good, if you're up to it. **Whisky Mühle** is the original venue, with live music most nights including UK bands. However, not all comments were favourable: 'I used to enjoy the Whisky Mühle, but this year's display involved pie-eyed drunkenness and lots of hooded teenagers.' Après-ski begins much earlier at **Hexenalm** by the gondola station, and at **Hexenkessel** and **Salvenstadl**, enjoyable, if you can bear the smoke and the din. **The Moonlight Bar** is a noisy pub and the **Sports Bar** shows Premier League football and has Guinness on tap. **Buffalo's** is run by one of the ski teachers.

Sleep

******Hotel Postwirt**, **t** +43 (0)5333 5081, *www.hotel-postwirt-soell.at*, in the village centre, is brilliant – lovely food, and plenty of it, as well as a friendly bar. There is also an outdoor pool heated to 33°C.

******Hotel AlpenSchlössl**, **t** +43 (0)5333 6400, *www.hotel-alpenschloessl.com*, is more luxurious, with an indoor pool complex and frescoed Sleeping Beauty Tower Rooms.

******Alphotel**, **t** +43 (0)5517 5449, *www.alphotel.at*, is a member of Kinderhotels, which offer indoor 'splash pools', children's menus and organized activities, a children's ski school and soft drinks round the clock.

★★★**Hotel Feldwebel**, **t** +43 (0)5333 5224, is a newly converted traditional building in the village centre, recommended for its rooms and half-board food.

★★**Hotel Gänsleit**, **t** +43 (0)5333 5471, is a five-minute walk from the village centre and welcomes children.

Wagrain and the Salzburger Sportwelt

*BEST FOR

Austrian village ambience, high-mileage cruisers

ESSENTIALS

Altitude: 650m (2,132ft)–2188m (7,177ft)
Further information: **t** +43 (0)6457 2929, *www.salzburgersportwelt.at*
Lifts in area: 90 (14 cableways, 34 chairs, 43 drags) serving 350km of piste. Skiverbund Amadé region 276 (30 cableways, 74 chairs, 172 drags) serving 865km
Lift pass: Skiverbund Amadé adult €176–189, child €91–98, both for six days
Access: Salzburg airport 45mins

Profile

Large intermediate ski area covering a dozen villages within easy reach of Salzburg. The main resorts are linked by lift, while regular buses serve the outlying corners of the ski area. Towns and villages vary in character

Resort

This easily accessible ski area is extremely popular with Austrians from Salzburg and elsewhere, but much underrated by overseas visitors. St Johann im Pongau is the regional capital of this corner of the country and is a ski resort in its own right. However, the cathedral city was burnt to the ground in 1852 and lacks the medieval charm of Salzburg or Innsbruck. It has its own small ski area, and from the pistes above the town you get a panoramic view of the cathedral.

Of far more interest to the skier are the outlying villages of Alpendorf, Wagrain, Kleinarl, Flachau and Zauchensee, which are linked from valley to valley by a complex network of modern lifts. Other resorts, including Radstadt/Altenmarkt and Filzmoos, add extra variety and are alternative places in which to stay. All are included in the regional Skiverbund Amadé lift pass.

Wagrain and Flachau are the most centrally placed and convenient resorts. Altenmarkt and Radstadt, linked by piste and lift across the 1677m Kemahdhöhe, are pleasant little market towns. Their main ski area of Zauchensee is a few minutes' bus ride away. Filzmoos, hot-air balloon capital of the Austrian Alps and a winter bolthole for Viennese aristocracy in the first years of the 20th century, shares its ski area with neighbouring Neuberg, just off the edge of the circuit.

Mountain

The whole Wagrain region comprises a dozen resorts served by 90 lifts covering undulating pastures and woodland as well as a handful of rounded 2000m summits. Runs here are of limited challenge to true experts, although that did nothing to arrest the development of

Austrian downhill hero Hermann Maier, who was raised, and still lives, in Flachau.

However, the area should prove enormously enjoyable for the vast majority of skiers. Lifts are mainly fast and modern, allowing you to travel a considerable distance from scenic valley to valley in a single day. The postbus service is efficient, but it makes sense to keep track of time when venturing far from home.

Learn

Each of the resorts has at least one ski school. Wagrain has **Skischule Wagrain**, **t** +43 (0)6413 7100. Flachau has six including **Hermann Maier**, **t** +43 (0)6457 2812. St Johann has four including **Alpendorf**, **t** +43 (0)6412 8455, and its board school, **Vitamin B**. Schools In Altenmarkt include **Der Erste S**, **t** +43 (0)6452 60700. In Zauchensee the choice is between **Happy Maier**, **t** +43 (0)6452 4315, and **Radstadt Pichler**, **t** +43 (0)6452 7382.

Children

Wagrain Ski Kindergarten, **t** +43 (0)6413 7100, cares for children from three years. In Flachau the ski schools accept children from four years. **Bobo Miniclub** , **t** +43 (0)6457 2090, is the non-ski kindergarten. Altenmarkt's **Balla Kindergarten**, **t** +43 (0)6452 4737, cares for children from three years. In Alpendorf, **Wellness & Sporthotel Alpina**, **t** +43 (0)6412 8282, runs a supervised activity programme for its small guests.

Lunch

The mountainside is dotted with welcoming huts. In the Flachau area try **Hoflalm**, **t** +43 (0)6457 2332, **Hubertusalm**, **t** +43 (0)6457 2756, and the **Griessenkar Hütte, t** +43 (0)6457 2575. In the Wagrain area, **Almstadl**, **t** +43 (0)6413 7444, is recommended. In Zauchensee, both **Arlhofhütte**, **t** +43 (0)6452 54856, and **Hochnösslerälm**, **t** +43 (0)6452 6242, have plenty of atmosphere.

Dine

In Wagrain, **Gasthof Kalkhofen**, **t** +43 (0)6413 8206, dates back to the 16th century and serves traditional dishes. **Haar-Trog Alm**, **t** +43 (0)6413 7286, has pasta and Asian fusion cuisine. **Mennerhäusl**, **t** +43 (0)6413 8965, is recommended. **H.C. Andersen**, **t** +43 (0)6413 8170, specializes in fresh fish. In Flachau, **Alter Jagdhof, t** +43 (0)6457 2228, serves mainly Italian cuisine. Rustic **Hoagascht–Das Restaurant**, **t** +43 (0)6457 32490, has Asian, Italian and Austrian fare. **Hotel Schartner**, **t** +43 (0)6452 5469, in Altenmarkt, is famed for its modern Austrian cuisine.

Party

Wagrain's returning skiers head for the outdoor **Schirmbar** at the end of the day. The **Haar-Trog Alm** and the **Kuhstall** are both extremely lively, while the **Point** has live music and karaoke. You can dance on the floor or on the tables at the **Tenne**. In Flachau, **Franzl's Schirmbar**, **Dampfkessel**, **Bergwerk**, **Ema's Pub** and **Double Dutch** are the hotspots. Late-nighters dance at **Burg** and **Yeti's Partyhaus**. Altenmarkt's après spots include **Napa Valley**, **S'Kessei** and **Webers Bar**. St Johann has plenty of places to eat out, and shops for the girls.

Sleep

Alpendorf:

******Wellness & Sporthotel Alpina**, **t** +43 (0)6412 8282, *www.sporthotel-alpina.com*, contains apartments, a playroom and an impressive indoor pool.

Altenmarkt:

★★★★**Hotel Alpenrose**, t +43 (0)6452 4027, *www.hotel-alpenrose.at*, has a wellness and fitness centre and serves 'creative cuisine'.

Flachau:

★★★★**Vierjahreszeiten**, t +43 (0)6457 2981, *www.vierjahreszeiten.co.at*, has a central but quiet location.

★★★★**Hotel Tauernhof**, t +43 (0)6457 2311, *www.tauernhof.at*, calls itself 'a four-star base camp for sporty guests'.

★★★★**Flachauerhof**, t +43 (0)6457 2225, *www.flachauerhof.at*, is a traditional establishment in the village centre.

★★★**Hotel Wieseneck**, t +43 (0)6457 2276, is in a peaceful, ski-in ski-out position.

Wagrain:

★★★★**Wagrainerhof**, t +43 (0)6413 8204, *www.wagrainerhof.com*, has good half-board food and welcomes children.

★★★★**Hotel Alpenhof Edelweiss**, t +43 (0)6413 8447, *www.alpenhof.edelweiss*, has a relaxed atmosphere and the restaurant uses local organic produce.

★★★★**Hotel Alpina**, t +43 (0)6413 8337, *www.hotelalpina.at*, has a large pool and spa.

★★★★**Sporthotel Wagrain**, t +43 (0)6413 7333, *www.sporthotel.at*, has a 1000 sq m wellness centre and miniclub.

★★★**Hotel Sonne**, t +43 (0)6413 8242, *www.wagrain.at/hotel/sonne*, is a pleasant establishment with a sauna, gym and sun terrace.

Westendorf

Profile

Appealing village with lots of Tyrolean atmosphere. Has its own modest skiing, and is linked by bus into the giant SkiWelt circuit and to Kirchberg and Kitzbühel

Resort

'Westendorf has a magical charm which a lot of the Austrian villages have, but this one has the magnetism to keep you wanting more,' was how one reporter put it. Westendorf has the best and highest skiing in the SkiWelt, a network of lifts covering nine villages. It is linked to Kirchberg by piste and the Ki-West gondola that in turn connects by a 1km bus ride to the Kitzbühel/Pass Thurn ski area. However its allegiance is still to the SkiWelt, and a new gondola linking to Brixen and the rest of SkiWelt opens for the 2008–9 season.

The attractive village has plenty of atmosphere and has been popular with foreign skiers since the 1960s. Many families congregate here during school holidays, but be warned that noisy high

* BEST FOR

Beginners, intermediates, families, high-season party-goers

ESSENTIALS

Altitude: 789m (2,589ft)–1892m (6,207ft)

Further information: t +43 (0)5334 6230, *www.kitzbuehel-alpen.com*, *www.westendorf.com*

Lifts in area: 90 (1 funicular, 12 cableways, 38 chairs, 39 drags) serving 250km of piste in the SkiWelt Wilder Kaiser-Brixental

Lift pass: SkiWelt adult €154.50–181.50, child 6–16yrs, €77–145.50, both for six days

Access: Innsbruck airport 45mins. Wörgl station 15mins

season après-ski can last well into the night. However, reporters were unanimous in their praise, calling it 'a lovely little bit of paradise'.

Mountain

'Westendorf has something for everyone, from beginners to advanced. A charming little village with some of the best skiing I have done,' said a reporter.

Lazy skiers avoid the 1km walk or bus ride to the gondola, the only means of mountain access, by riding the Schneebergbahn quad up the nursery slope and traversing to the main lift station. The two-stage gondola takes you up to a small network of high-capacity chairs that bring you to the peak of Fleiding, the highest point in the SkiWelt.

The Ki-West gondola tranformed Westendorf from a small Tyrolean village into a link between two giant ski areas. Whether this, in the long term, will change the intimate character of the resort remains to be seen. The new gondola this season connecting it to the rest of the SkiWelt removes the last vestiges of isolation.

Learn

Westendorf has three ski schools: **Ideal**, **t** +43 (0)5334 2919, **Top**, **t** +43 (0)5334 6737, and **Westendorf**, **t** +43 (0)5334 6181, also know as the Reds, which is excellent.

Children

All the ski schools accept children. **Kindergruppe Simba**, **t** +43 (0)5334 20603, cares for non-skiing children from 18 months to four years.

Lunch

Alpenrosenhütte, **t** +43 (0)5334 6488, and **Bergrestaurant Choralpe**, **t** +43 (0)5334 61290, have plenty of atmosphere. **Jausenstation Alte Mittel**, **t** +43 (0)5334 2324, beneath the gondola, is also recommended.

Dine

Most of the restaurants are in hotels, with the **Vital-Landhotel Schermer**, **t** +43 (0)5334 6268, providing gourmet cuisine. **FEINSINN**, **T** +43 (0)5334 30111, is recommended, along with **Gasthof Maierhof**, **t** +43 (0)5334 6412, and **Gery's Inn**, **t** +43 (0)5334 6334.

Party

The après-ski atmosphere is extremely lively, with plenty of bars for a pint or a Schnapps on your last run down. The food and drinks are reasonably priced. The hotel bars and the **Village Pub** are the main meeting points, along with **Bruchstall** après-ski bar next to the nursery slope. The other places are **Kibo** and **FeinSinn**.

Early evening après ski is best at **Gerry's Inn** ('a must after a hard day on the piste') adjacent to the nursery slope in the village centre.

The noisy **Wunderbar** disco stays open until 6am. **Café Friends** and **Kibo Bar** are quieter and more elegant. The Tyrolean evening at the **Gassnerwirt** is highly recommended: 'The food was delicious and all the ladies in our group have fond memories of the handsome dancers in their *Lederhosen*.'

Sleep

★★★★**Hotel Glockenstuhl**, **t** +43 (0)5334 6175, *www.glockenstuhl.at*, comes highly praised for its warm family environment and friendly staff. 'What a hotel! Remarkable meals, the rooms have recently been refurbished and there's a huge heated pool.'

★★★★**Hotel Jakobwirt**, **t** +43 (0)5334 6245, *www.jakobwirt.at*, is on the edge of the piste and is warmly recommended for its food and facilities ('well run hotel with an excellent evening meal and service second to none').

★★★★**Vital-Landhotel Schermer**, **t** +43 (0)5334 6268, *www.vitalhotel schermer.at*, is on the edge of the village with a major wellness centre offering thalasso therapy treatments.

★★★**Vital Hotel Sportalm**, **t** +43 (0)5334 6495, *www.sportalm-schwaigeralm.at*, next to the Alpenrose piste, has a spa.

★★★**Hotel Post**, **t** +43 (0)5334 6202, *www.hotelpost.co.at*, built in 1593, has 40 rooms, including some that sleep six. It is friendly and good for beginners as it is so close to the nursery slopes.

Zell am See and Kaprun

Profile

A pretty resort (Zell) on the shore of Austria's most scenic lake. It offers substantial, mainly easy, skiing backed up by snow-sure glacial and summer skiing on the Kitzsteinhorn at Kaprun. Good nightlife and alpine atmosphere

Resort

Zell am See–Kaprun is one of those rare places where in summer you can ski in the morning and sunbathe, swim and sail in the afternoon. The lakeside town acts as the tourist gateway to the Grossglockner, Austria's highest mountain, and attracts a year-round clientele that is as sedate in summer as it is lively in winter. Above it rises the dome of the 2000m Schmittenhöhe, a charming and mainly wooded ski area best suited to intermediates but with dedicated learning areas at base and mid-mountain.

Zell am See was first established by a monastic order in the 8th century and had considerable commercial importance in medieval times. The legacy of fine old buildings has been transformed over the years into a See-side Kitzbühel. It has smart hotels and boutiques as well as villas dotted along the shore that are the holiday homes of wealthy Salzburgers.

Less cosmopolitan Kaprun, 8km up the road, is more of a traditional ski village, with its own little mountain. However, focus here is up the valley on the 3000m Kitzsteinhorn Glacier, where skiing continues throughout most of the year. Non-skiers can take day trips to Salzburg or Kitzbühel.

*BEST FOR

Beginners and intermediates, beautiful scenery, certain snow-cover (Kaprun Glacier)

ESSENTIALS

Altitude: 758m (2,487ft)–3029m (9,938ft)
Further information: **t** +43 (0)43 6542 770, *www.zellamsee-kaprun.info*
Lifts in area: 54 in Zell am See/Kaprun (13 cableways, 18 chairs, 24 drags) serving 77km of piste in Zell am See, 59km in Kaprun
Lift pass: Europa Sport Region (covers Kaprun, Zell am See) adult €172–192, child 6–15yrs €86–96, both for six days; free for under 6yrs if accompanied by adult
Salzburg Superski Card (covers 2200km of piste) adult €204, child €102, all six days
Access: Salzburg airport 1hr, railway station in Zell am See

ZELL AM SEE AND KAPRUN

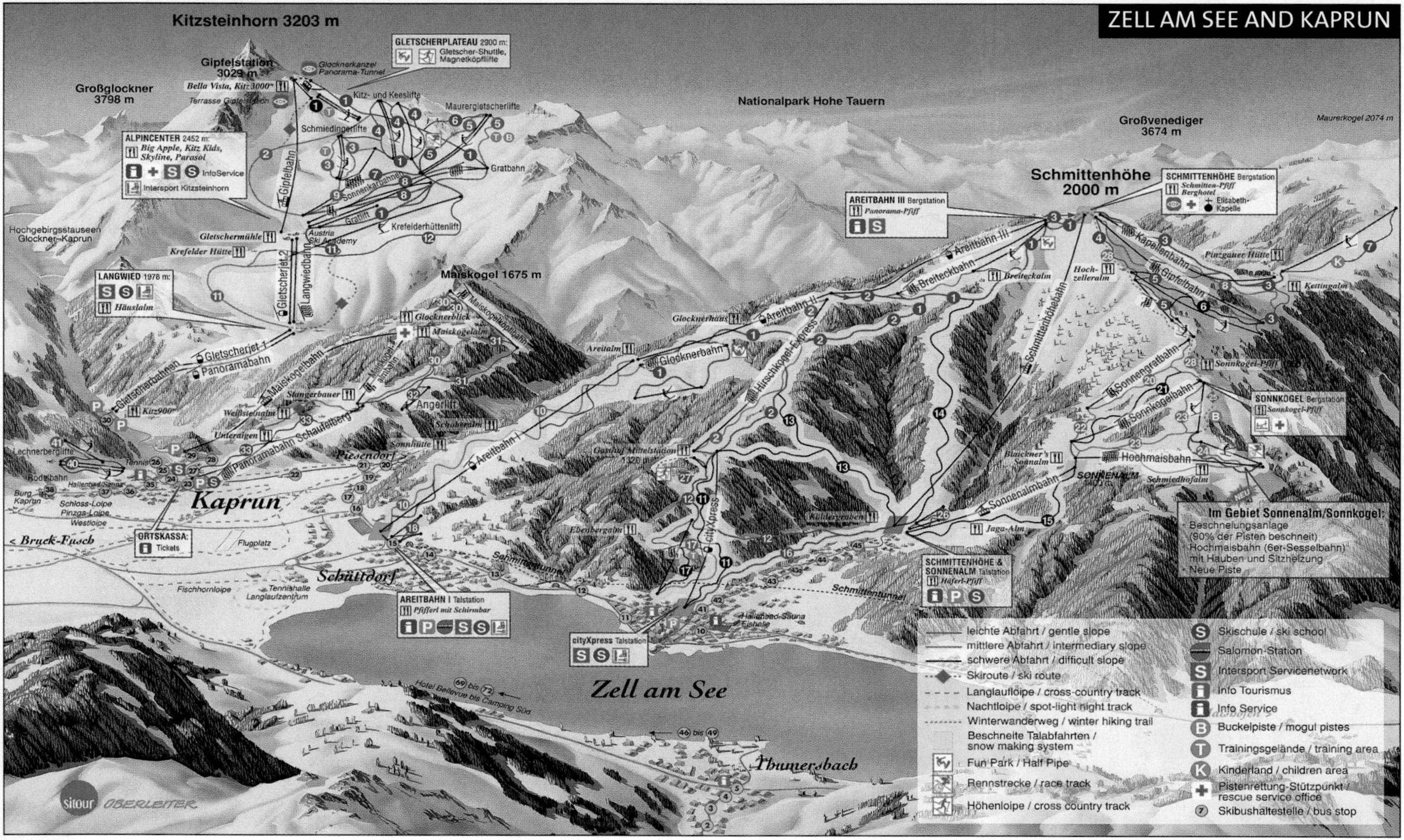

Kitzsteinhorn 3203 m

Gipfelstation 3029 m

Großglockner 3798 m

Nationalpark Hohe Tauern

Großvenediger 3674 m

Maurerkogel 2074 m

Schmittenhöhe 2000 m

Maiskogel 1675 m

GLETSCHERPLATEAU 2900 m: Gletscher-Shuttle, Magnetköpflifte

ALPINCENTER 2452 m: Big Apple, Kitz Kids, Skyline, Parasol
InfoService
Intersport Kitzsteinhorn

LANGWIED 1978 m:
Häuslalm

AREITBAHN III Bergstation
Panorama-Pfiff

SCHMITTENHÖHE Bergstation
Schmitten-Pfiff
Berghotel
Elisabeth-Kapelle

SONNKOGEL Bergstation
Sonnkogel-Pfiff

SCHMITTENHÖHE & SONNENALM Talstation
Häferl-Pfiff

AREITBAHN I Talstation
Pfifferl mit Schirmbar

cityXpress Talstation

ORTSKASSA:
Tickets

Im Gebiet Sonnenalm/Sonnkogel:
- Beschneiungsanlage (90% der Pisten beschneit)
- Hochmaisbahn (6er-Sesselbahn) mit Hauben und Sitzheizung
- Neue Piste

Kaprun

Zell am See

Schüttdorf

Thumersbach

< Bruck-Fusch

leichte Abfahrt / gentle slope	Skischule / ski school
mittlere Abfahrt / intermediary slope	Salomon-Station
schwere Abfahrt / difficult slope	Intersport Servicenetwork
Skiroute / ski route	Info Tourismus
Langlaufloipe / cross-country track	Info Service
Nachtloipe / spot-light night track	Buckelpiste / mogul pistes
Winterwanderweg / winter hiking trail	Trainingsgelände / training area
Beschneite Talabfahrten / snow making system	Kinderland / children area
Fun Park / Half Pipe	Pistenrettung-Stützpunkt / rescue service office
Rennstrecke / race track	Skibushaltestelle / bus stop
Höhenloipe / cross country track	

sitour OBERLEITER

Mountain

A modern gondola rises from Zell, but the quickest way to the top of the mountain is by ski-bus to Schüttdorf and a three-stage gondola. Alternatively, you can catch a bus and join one of the two cable cars from Schmittental, the base of the main ski area, but this is prone to overcrowding at peak times.

A glance at the piste map gives the erroneous impression that the skiing here is testing. While the western shoulder of the mountain is given over to easy blue and red runs, the front face features seven blacks. In fact, in many other resorts most of these would be graded as moderate reds. The severe classification is only barely justified in icy conditions when cover is thin. The whole area is ideally suited to intermediates.

Kaprun has its own winter area on Maiskogel, reached by a six-pack with pull-down Perspex covers. The glacier is served by twin cableways that take you up to the Alpincenter mid-mountain hub at 2452m. A network of lifts fan out between here and the 3029m top statlon. The Kristallbahn six-person covered chair with heated seats has replaced the long and chilly Krefelderhütten drag. In winter conditions you can ski all the way down to the cable car station at Langwied. Terrain parks are located on the Kitzsteinhorn and at Jumping City on the Schmittenhöhe, where there is also a half-pipe.

Learn

Of the 10 schools in both resorts, **Sport-Alpin Zell am See**, t +43 (0)664 453 1419, receives the most praise ('excellent'), along with **Kitzsteinhorn**, t +43 (0)6547 862 1363, in Kaprun. **Ski Safari, t** +43 (0)664 336 1487, teaches off-piste and has a strong reputation. **Oberschneider**, t +43 (0)6547 82320, is strongly recommended. **Snowboard Academy**, t +43 (0)664 253 0381, is the dedicated school.

Children

The **Sport-Alpin**, t +43 (0)664 453 1419 ('superb for the kids') and **Zell-am-See**, t +43 (0)6542 56020, in Zell, plus five schools in Kaprun, offer lessons to children from three years. **Play & Fun**, t +43 (0)6542 56020, is the non-ski kindergarten. **Joys**, t +43 (0)664 332 5665, was a new kindergarten last season. **Babyboom**, t +43 (0)664 376 2553, provides baby-sitting.

Lunch

Readers rated the mountain restaurants as both warm and welcoming. On Schmittenhöhe, try **Ebenbergalm, t** +43 664 351 2307, **Jagaalm**, t +43 (0)6542 72969, for local game dishes, **Schmiedhofalm**, t +43 (0)6542 72868, for Pinzgauer specialities and panoramic views, and **Hochzeller Alm, t** +43 (0)6542 72113, for home cooking. **The Breiteckalm**, t +43 (0)6542 73419, is recommended. **Pinzgauer Hütte**, t +43 (0)6549 7861, is 'a must for a stop, followed by the ski-pull-on ropes behind a skidoo back to the slopes'. On Maiskogel, **Weisssteinalm Eisbär**, t +43 (0)6547 7439, has plenty of atmosphere. On Kitzsteinhorn, **Gletschermühle, t** +43 (0)6547 862 1371, is popular.

Dine

Nearly all the restaurants are in hotels. In Zell, the **Steinerwirt**, t +43 (0)6542 72502, is recommended, along with the **Kupferkessel**, t +43 (0)6542 72768. **Hotel St Georg, t** +43 (0)6542 7680, **Zur Einkehr**, t +43 (0)6542 72363, **Landhotel Erlhof**, t +43 (0)6542 566370, and the

Salzburgerhof, **t** +43 (0)6542 765, are all worth a visit. Reporters praised **Antonio's**, **t** +43 (0)6542 53650, for its curry.

In Kaprun, **Hotel Orgler**, **t** +43 (0)6547 8205, has some of the best food in the village. **Zucchini**, **t** +43 (0)6547 20010, makes a change from the ubiquitous *Wienerschnitzel*. **Restaurant Dorfkrug**, **t** +43 (0)6547 20081, and **Hillberger's Beisl**, **t** +43 (0)6547 72, are also recommended.

Party

Après-ski is 'not in your face compared to neighbouring resorts like Saalbach'. **Villa CrazyDaisy, Octopussy** and **Diele** are the hotspots. **Gunthers** is 'a must', recommends a reader. **Sunrise** disco and the **Rock-Bar** are also important hang-outs. Kaprun's nightlife is more muted. **Kitsch & Bitter** has regular live bands. The **Baum Bar** caters for night owls. The **Optimum Sports Centre** contains an indoor pool, sauna and fitness centre, as well as a giant outdoor water-slide.

Sleep

Zell am See:

******Grand Hotel**, **t** +43 (0)6542 7880, *www.grandhotel-zellamsee.at*, by the lake, is a short walk to the lift. 'Stunning and in a great location, the food was lovely and the staff helpful.'

*******Hotel Salzburgerhof**, **t** +43 (0)6542 765, *www.salzburgerhof.at*, is by far the most comfortable base and has a sensational spa.

******Romantikhotel Zum Metzgerwirt**, **t** +43 (0)6542 72520, *www.romantik-hotel.at*, has pastel bedrooms, with a fireplace and waterbed in one of the suites.

******Alpin Sporthotel**, **t**+43 (0)6542 769, *www.alpinhotel.at*, has modern bedrooms.

******Hotel Alpenblick**, **t** +43 (0)6542 5433, *www.alpenblick.at*, has wood-panelled rooms and studios.

******Hotel Heitzmann**, **t** +43 (0)6542 72152, *www.zellamsee-hotel.at*, is a small family-run hotel with a friendly atmosphere and first-class food.

******Landgasthof Stadt Wein Hotel**, **t** +43 (0)6542 7620, *www.hotel-stadtwien.at*, is a family-run gem set in the woods above the centre. 'The food and hospitality were wonderful, but get a room away from the first floor as the children's play area gets noisy,' warns a reporter.

******Zum Hirschen**, **t** +43 (0)6542 7740, *www.hotel-zum-hirschen.at*, has 'huge clean rooms and great food'.

*****Hotel Schwebebahn**, **t** +43 (0)6542 72461, *www.schwebebahn.at*, is convenient for the skiing.

******Hotel St Georg**, **t** +43 (0)6542 768, *www.grossglockner.co.at/stgeorg*, has traditional rooms and views of the lake.

******Hotel Berner**, **t** +43 (0)6542 779, *www.bernerhotel.com*, is in a quiet position and has a heated outdoor pool.

******Kinderhotel Hagleitner**, **t** +43 (0)6542 571870, *www.kinderhotel-hagleitner.at*, at Schüttdorf, is good for young families.

******Hotel Fischerwirt**, **t** +43 (0)6542 781, *www.fischerwirt.com*, was highly rated for its lovely rooms, full English breakfast, and a four-course dinner.

******Hotel zum Hirschen**, **t** +43 (0)6542 72152, *www.zum-hirschen.at*, was commended for its good food, with plenty of choices, and helpful staff.

*****Hotel Bellevue**, **t** +43 (0)6542 73104, *www.zellamsee.at/bellevue*, is on the lakeside.

*****Gasthof Der Wildbachhof**, **t** +43 (0)6547 72244, is a 20-minute walk from town, but has friendly staff and is convenient for the slopes.

*****Hotel Schönblick**, **t** +43 (0)6547 57400, in Schüttdorf, received particular praise:

'Nothing was too much trouble. The food was excellent and the hotel had a warm, friendly feel.'

Pension Hubertus, t +43 (0)6547 72427, was rated superb for its great location and good breakfast 'always served with a smile and a personal touch'.

Kaprun:

****Active by Leitner's**, t +43 (0)6547 8782, *www.active-kaprun.at*, is a 1960s-style hotel run like an action-packed club. As well as skiing and snowboarding, the owners can arrange tobogganing and snowball-throwing parties.

****Alpen-Wellness Hotel Barbarahof**, t +43 (0)6547 7248, *www.hotel-barbarahof.at*, offering excellent service and food, has a good spa and is next to the ski school meeting place.

****Hotel Orgler**, t +43 (0)6547 8205, *www.hotel-orgler.at*, is the original village inn with comfortable rooms.

****Hotel Rudolfshof**, t +43 (0)6547 7183, *www.rudolfshof.com*, has good-sized rooms, amazing food, a lovely spa, and is excellent value.

****Hotel Sonnblick**, t +43 (0)6547 8301, *www.hotel-sonnblick.at*, is decorated in modern Tyrolean style.

****Hotel Tauernhof**, t +43 (0)6547 8235, *www.tauernhof-kaprun.at*, is in the centre of the village at the bottom of the nursery slopes, making it ideal for first-time skiers.

***Haus Annelies**, t +43 (0)6547 8689, *www.sbg.at/haus-annelies*, is a very nice B&B, but perhaps more budget than three-star.

03

The Top Resorts: Canada

Banff-Lake Louise, Alberta

🏆 BEST SKI RESORT 2009
🏆 BEST SKI HOTEL 2009
(FOX HOTEL & SUITES, BANFF)
🏆 BEST RESORT RESTAURANT 2009
(MAPLE LEAF GRILLE, BANFF)
🏆 BEST SKI SHOP 2009
(SKI HUB, BANFF)
🏆 BEST SKI SPA 2009
(RED EARTH SPA, BANFF)

***BEST FOR**

Beautiful scenery, all levels of skier and rider, value, nightlife (Banff)

ESSENTIALS

Altitude: 5,350ft (1631m)–8,650ft (2637m)
Further information: t +1 403 762 4421, *www.skibig3.com*
Lifts in area: 30 (2 cableways, 21 chairs, 7 drags) serving 7,748 acres of terrain in area
Lift pass: adult CDN$462–485.10, youth 13–17yrs CDN$411.18–431.76, child 6–12yrs CDN$217.14–228, all for six out of eight days
Access: Calgary airport 1½hrs

Profile

Lake Louise is a peaceful village surrounded by stunningly beautiful scenery. The snow-sure slopes offer great skiing variety and few queues. This is not a place for those who dislike low temperatures

Resort

It is a triumph of successful Canadian marketing that two such totally different resorts in Alberta so far apart from each other should be bracketed together, not to mention similarly separate Sunshine Village, which sits on a mountaintop between them.

'Banff is an ordinary little tourist resort,' wrote the First World War poet Rupert Brooke in the year before his death, 'but Lake Louise – Lake Louise is of another world.' More than 90 winters later, his description is still apt. Banff is a busy little town just inside the gates of the Banff National Park. This is a traditional summer destination for thousands of North Americans, but not until relatively recently one that excited much interest in wintertime. It has its own nearby little ski area of Mount Norquay, which it has unsuccessfully tried to brand as SkiBanff@Norquay.

Since hoteliers discovered that overseas skiers would pay to fill their empty beds during the closed season, Banff has become an important destination for temporary migrants from the slopes of Andorra and Austria in search of fresh low-cost ski fields and an equally frenetic nightlife. Never more so than this season when numbers are fuelled by the high standing of the euro.

Lake Louise lies 56km away across the park down the Trans-Canadian highway, which is dotted with little bridges so that elk and other animals can cross in safety. It is so small that 'village' is an exaggeration: a handful of hotels and a couple of shops that originally owed their *raison d'être* to the Canadian Pacific railway line. It built

Lake Louise Mountain Resort

FRONT SIDE/SOUTH FACE

1100 Skiable Acres

To Powder Bowls, Larch Area and Temple Lodge

Upper Front Side

Saddleback Ridge 8,300ft. 2,530m

Grizzly Gondola Area

West Bowl

Mount Whitehorn 8,765ft 2,672m

Ski Area Boundary

Summit Platter

Top of the World 6-Pack Express

Permanently Closed Avalanche Area

BE AWARE SKI & RIDE WITH CARE

LAKE LOUISE WINTERSTART WORLD CUP

Downhill Course

Grizzly Express Gondola

Lower Front Side

Glacier Express Quad

RCR Rail Park

RCR Race Centre

Wilderness Adventure Park

Base Area

Sunny T-Bar

Base Area 5,400ft / 1,646m

Lodge of the Ten Peaks

Whiskyjack Lodge

Kokanee Kabin

Glacier (Express)

Grizzly Express Gondola

Sunny T-Bar

LAKE LOUISE

South Face

8,650ft 2,637m

7,500ft 2,286m

7,308m 2,227m

6,850ft 2,088m

Whiskyjack Lodge 5,400ft 1,646m

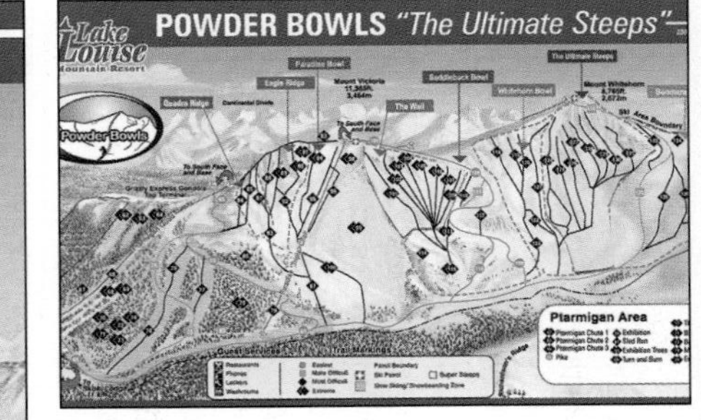

the splendid Victorian hotel, the Château Lake Louise, here so that passengers could rest in comfort while drinking in one of most dramatic glacial vistas of the Rockies. Lake Louise has its own substantial ski area situated an inconvenient five-minute bus ride away from the 'village' and hotels.

Sunshine Village is, again, not a 'village' but the name of the third ski area sandwiched between the two, 16km from Banff and 24km from Lake Louise. Its skiing rivals that of Lake Louise, but the only place to stay is at the ski in, ski out hotel at the mid-mountain base, reached by gondola and far from any serious evening entertainment.

We recommend that visitors stay in Banff and commute to the ski areas. All three share a regional lift pass and are connected by a regular bus service. However, renting a car adds considerable convenience and avoids any hanging around in what can be mind-numbingly low temperatures in mid-winter. We have mixed reports of poor ski and board hire in Banff, with iniquitous 'excess' damage charges on top of local insurance. 'I definitely recommend taking your own skis/boards as rental was very difficult – they seemed to run out of most intermediate/advanced ranges even though it wasn't high season,' said a reporter. However, on a recent visit, we found good equipment hire and very helpful service at The Ski Hub on Banff Avenue. If in doubt, take your own equipment – or rent in the base lodges of the resorts themselves.

Mountain

Mount Norquay is much more than a local hill, but you didn't cross the Atlantic to ride three quad-chairs. Nevertheless we spent an enjoyable morning here repeatedly cruising beautifully groomed but short trails cut through the trees. The pitch dictates whether each is classified as easy or intermediate. Four of the runs get a double-black-diamond rating.

Lake Louise is far more exciting: a multi-mountain area with every type of terrain from gentle tree-lined trails to steep chutes and awesome open bowls. It is all challenging stuff, but less confident skiers should not be scared away. An easy run descends from every lift. The Larch Express Quad gives access to a couple of easy motorways as well as four hugely enjoyable blue trails. 'Lake Louise is vast with long winding runs where you can pick up some great speed, especially on the men's downhill,' said a reader.

For strong intermediates as well as advanced skiers and riders, the pick of the action is off the backside. A host of demanding or downright impossible chutes are reached along the heavily corniced ridge from the top of the Summit Platter lift, the Top of the World Express, and from Paradise Chair. On a big powder day the locals just ski lap after lap here. The Grizzly Express gondola accesses some steep double-diamond-graded tree skiing that is served on the backside by the Ptarmigan quad.

The whole area is popular with snowboarders, but unfortunately, for health and safety reasons, the terrain park at Lake Louise is no more. It seems that its giant kickers collected an unacceptable level of injury. Riders and skiers must now be content with a much blander rail park where you have to register before entry.

Sunshine Village has three separate mountains and, to no one's surprise, a newly extended terrain park. Mount Standish is a rounded, exposed peak with a mixture of terrain for all standards. Look Out Mountain suits strong intermediates and more advanced skiers, although the Angel Chair does have some green runs.

Goat's Eye Mountain is the domain of the hardcore and Delirium Dive is its classic steep. While not in the same league as Corbet's in Jackson Hole, it is spoken of in reverentially hushed tones by the cognoscenti. The ski patrol adds to the hype by insisting that you wear a transceiver and have a shovel and probe in your backpack. In fact, the idea is to confine this pitch to dedicated off-piste enthusiasts who are already sufficiently experienced to have bought their own gear – you can't rent a transceiver anywhere nearby. After a usually tricky entrance it opens into steep bowl with a choice of exits: the more direct involves a walk-out, while a lengthy traverse to the skier's right offers more powder and a speedier return to a lift.

Sunshine Village is 'like one big playground with natural half-pipes and loads of powder where you can go mental,' enthused a reporter.

Another summed up the region: 'No queues, and the slopes were not packed with other skiers. Fabulous and reliable snow, great service and value for money – try getting a cup of coffee on the slopes in France for 75p.'

Learn

Ski and snowboard schools **Lake Louise**, **t** +1 403 522 1333, **Ski Norquay**, **t** +1 403 760 7717, and **Sunshine Village**, **t** +1 403 762 6560, all offer group and private lessons. They were praised by reporters. 'Ski school was incredible. Well organized, very friendly and terrific value for money.' **Club Ski/Snowboard**, **t** +1 403 760 7731, runs three-day courses for groups of similar ability, with guided tours of all three resorts.

Children

At Lake Louise, the **Day Care Center**, **t** +1 403 522 3555, accepts babies from 17 days old. The **Club Ski Junior** programme, **t** +1 403 760 7731, offers a mix of guiding and instruction. **Tiny Tigers Daycare**, **t** +1 403 762 6560, at Sunshine Village, and **Ski Norquay Day Care**, **t** +403 762 4421, supervise children from 19 months.

Lunch

At Mount Norquay, Cascade Lodge houses the **Lone Pine**, **t** +1 403 762 4421, which serves hearty mountain fare.

At Lake Louise, **Sawyers Nook** upstairs at the Temple Lodge, **t** +1 403 522 3555, has wait-service food and an intimate atmosphere. **Kokanee Kabin**, **t** +1 403 522 3555, at the base, has barbecues and beer. **Lodge of the Ten Peaks**, **t** +1 403 522 3555, and the **Whisky Jack Lodge**, **t** +1 403 522 3555, house a cafeteria. The **Great Bear Room**, **t** +1 403 522 3555, has self-service dining with soups, pasta and roast beef.

At Sunshine, all the restaurants are at the mid-mountain base area, **t** +1 403 762 4421 for all. **Lookout Bistro** on the top floor of the Day Lodge has a full menu and a warm fireplace. We recommend the **Eagle's Nest** in Sunshine Inn for a long lunch. **Mad Trapper's Saloon** in Old Sunshine Lodge is a Western-style saloon on two floors with the ubiquitous burger.

Dine

Banff has a wonderfully wide choice of restaurants that reflect its multicultural clientele. **Maple Leaf Grille & Lounge**, **t** +1 403 760 7680, is essentially Canadian, with excellent food and an emphasis on elk, bison, duck and lobster. 'Some of the best food I have eaten,' said a reporter, 'lovely surroundings and fantastic cuisine.' **The Sleeping Buffalo** at the

Buffalo Mountain Lodge, **t** +1 403 410 7417, serves all manner of game in an attractive beamed setting. **Melissa's**, **t** +1 403 762 5511, is a rustic log cabin with great steaks and BBQ ribs. **Le Beaujolais**, **t** +1 403 762 2712, is French, romantic and regularly wins Canadian culinary awards. Try the *osso buco* with polenta at **Giorgio's Trattoria**, **t** +1 403 762 5114. **El Toro**, **t** +1 403 762 2520, is Greek, the **Silver Dragon**, **t** +1 403 762 3939, serves Cantonese Peking cuisine. **Miki**, **t** +1 403 286 2860, is Japanese.

In Lake Louise Village, **The Post Hotel**, **t** +1 403 522 3989, and **Deer Lodge**, **t** +1 403 522 3747, are the pick of a limited choice. **Timber Wolf Pizza**, **t** +1 403 522 3791, at the Lake Louise Inn, is recommended. The **Fairmont Château Lake Louise**, **t** +1 403 522 3511, has four restaurants including the **Walliser Stube Wine Bar**, **t** +1 403 522 1817. **Mountain Restaurant**, **t** +1 403 522 3573, serves Asian fusion cuisine and pasta.

Party

Après-ski in Banff largely revolves around the enormous number of bars along Banff Avenue. These include **Tommy's Neighbourhood Pub** ('best for having a few beers'), the **Magpie & Stump**, the **Rose & Crown** and **St James's Gate** – an Irish pub originally built in Dublin and shipped in pieces over to Canada. **Wild Bill's** has Country and Western bands, and the **Elk & Oarsman** hosts quiz nights and live rock bands. **Hoodoo Lounge** and **Aurora** are both popular clubs. The shopping on Banff Avenue is highly recommended, with some good bargains to be found. The nightlife at Lake Louise is quiet ('not for those looking for a busy nightlife') and restricted to a few hotel bars. A great half day trip is dog-sledding with **Snowy Owl**, **t** +1 403 678 4369, at nearby Canmore.

Sleep

Luxury:

Banff:

Fairmont Banff Springs, **t** +1 403 762 2211, *www.fairmont.com/banffsprings*, Château Lake Louise's majestic 'sister' hotel in Banff, is designed to look like a Scottish castle with one of the best spas in Canada – magical.

Buffalo Mountain Lodge, **t** +1 403 410 7417, *www.crmr.com/lodgebuffalo.php*, is a boutique style ruggedly luxurious place, with open fires and beams.

The Fox Hotel & Suites, **t** +1 403 762 5887, *www.bestofbanff.com*, is a new building on Banff Avenue with enormous rooms and suites, each of them different. The hotel's hot pool centrepiece is inspired by the original springs.

Rimrock Resort Hotel, **t** +1 403 762 3356, *www.rimrockresort.com*, is elegant and modern, located on Sulphur Mountain a short walk from Banff's hot springs.

Lake Louise:

Fairmont Château Lake Louise, **t** +1 403 522 3511, *www.fairmont.com/lakelouise*, is in a quiet wilderness setting with spectacular views over the frozen lake.

The Post Hotel & Spa, **t** +1 403 522 3989, *www.posthotel.com*, also in Lake Louise, is a luxuriously elegant recreation of 1900s style with large rooms.

Moderate/Budget:

Banff:

The Mount Royal, **t** +1 403 762 3331, *www.mountroyalhotel.com*, is ideally placed for Banff's nightlife.

Banff Caribou Lodge, **t** +1 403 762 5887, *www.bestofbanff.com*, is a 15-minute walk from downtown and is rustic Western style. It houses the fabulous Red Earth Spa.

Juniper Inn, **t** +1 403 762 2281, *www.decorehotels.com/juniper*, has newly renovated chalets and suites.

BIG WHITE

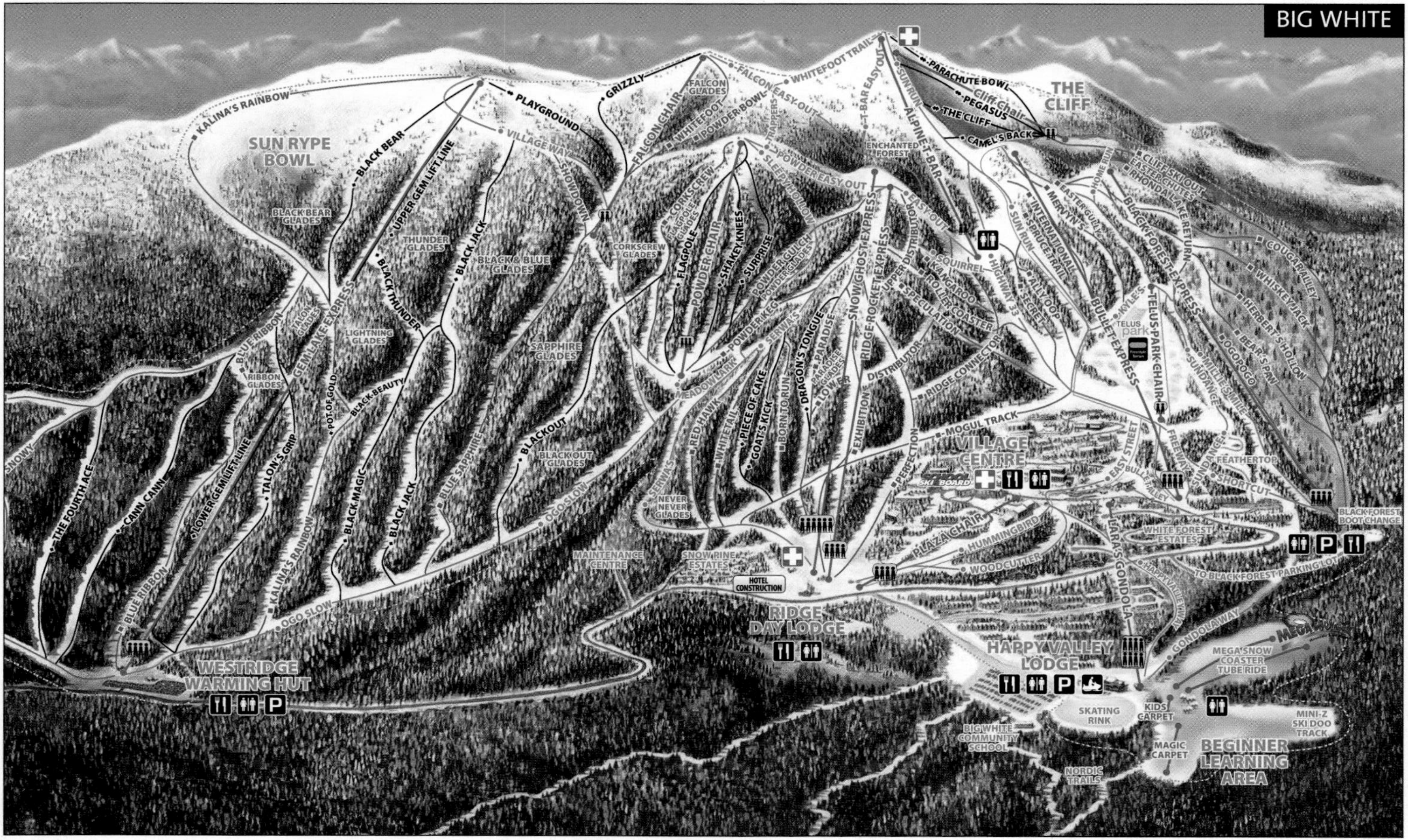

SUN RYPE BOWL
THE CLIFF
KALINA'S RAINBOW
BLACK BEAR
UPPER GEM LIFT LINE
PLAYGROUND
VILLAGE WAY
GRIZZLY
FALCON CHAIR
FALCON GLADES
WHITEFOOT
POWDER BOWL
FALCON EASY-OUT
WHITEFOOT TRAIL
T-BAR EASY OUT
TRAPPERS
SUN RUN
ALPINE T-BAR
PARACHUTE BOWL
Cliff Chair
PEGASUS
THE CLIFF
CAMEL'S BACK
ENCHANTED FOREST
SLEEPY HOLLOW
POWDER EASY OUT
SHOWDOWN
BLACK BEAR GLADES
THUNDER GLADES
BLACK JACK
BLACK & BLUE GLADES
BLACK THUNDER
CORKSCREW GLADES
CORKSCREW
FLAGPOLE GLADES
FLAGPOLE
POWDER CHAIR
SHAKEY KNEES
SURPRISE
POWDER GULCH
POWDER GLADES
POWDER KEG
SNOW GHOST EXPRESS
RIDGE ROCKET EXPRESS
UPPER DISTRIBUTOR
EASY OUT
SQUIRREL
KANGAROO
ROLLER COASTER
SPECULATION
HIGHWAY 33
SECRET
ALLY OOP
SPRUCE TRAIL
INTERNATIONAL
SUN RUN
MERVYN'S
EASTER GULLY
HOME RUN
CLIFF SKI OUT
EASTER CHUTES
RHONDA LAKE RETURN
BLACK FOREST EXPRESS
COUGAR ALLEY
WHISKEY JACK
HERBERT'S HOLLOW
BEAR'S PAW
OGOPOGO
MILLIE'S MILE
SUNDANCE
KYLE'S
TELUS park
BULLET EXPRESS
TELUS PARK CHAIR
BLUE RIBBON
TALON GLADES
GEM LAKE EXPRESS
LIGHTNING GLADES
SAPPHIRE GLADES
RIBBON GLADES
POT OF GOLD
BLACK BEAUTY
MEADOWLARK
DRAGON'S TONGUE
PARADISE
PARADISE GLADES
LOWER
DISTRIBUTOR
RIDGE CONNECTOR
SERWA'S
RED HAWK
WHITETAIL
PIECE OF CAKE
GOAT'S KICK
BORN TO RUN
EXHIBITION
MOGUL TRACK
PERFECTION
VILLAGE CENTRE
SKI BOARD
EASY STREET
BULLET ALLEY
FREEWAY
SUNDANCE
FEATHERTOP
SHORTCUT
BLACK FOREST BOOT CHANGE
SNOWY
THE FOURTH ACE
CANN CANN
LOWER GEM LIFT LINE
TALON'S GRIP
BLACK MAGIC
BLUE SAPPHIRE
BLACKOUT
BLACK OUT GLADES
OGO SLOW
KALINA'S RAINBOW
BLUE RIBBON
SERWAS
NEVER NEVER GLADES
MAINTENANCE CENTRE
SNOW PINE ESTATES
HOTEL CONSTRUCTION
PLAZA CHAIR
HUMMINGBIRD
WOODCUTTER
LARA'S GONDOLA
WHITE FOREST ESTATES
HAPPY VALLEY WAY
TO BLACK FOREST PARKING LOT
GONDOLA WAY
WESTRIDGE WARMING HUT
RIDGE DAY LODGE
HAPPY VALLEY LODGE
MEGA SNOW COASTER TUBE RIDE
SKATING RINK
KIDS CARPET
MINI-Z SKI DOO TRACK
MAGIC CARPET
BEGINNER LEARNING AREA
BIG WHITE COMMUNITY SCHOOL
NORDIC TRAILS

The Rundle Manor Hotel, t +1 403 762 5544, is apartment-style and represents good-value.

Siding 29 Lodge, t +1 403 762 5575, *www.bestwesternsiding29.com*, is a no-frills hotel with an indoor pool.

Lake Louise:

Deer Lodge, t +1 403 522 3747, *www.crmr.com/lodgedeer.php*, is two minutes' walk from the lake shore, and ideal for those wanting a quiet retreat. It has a rooftop hot tub.

Sunshine Village:

Sunshine Village Inn, t +1 403 762 6564, *www.banff_ski_packages/sunshine–inn.php*, is reached by a 15-minute gondola ride from Sunshine base and is the area's only ski in, ski out accommodation. Some rooms have recently been upgraded.

Big White, BC

Profile

Attractive village with doorstep skiing. This is BC's second largest resort. More suited to families than party-goers, with a lack of mountain restaurants and après-ski venues

Resort

Big White is a big hitter among the more recently developed clutch of Canadian resorts that have successfully sought international acclaim. It is hidden away in British Columbia in the beautiful Okanagan Valley, the country's famous wine-growing region.

Big White takes its name from the sometimes all-enveloping moisture-filled cloud, which creates a phantom forest of snow-ghosts – trees frozen into eerie shapes. It is under the same Australian ownership as nearby Silver Star. 'Superb snow, negligible lift lines, good grooming, and excellent accommodation, make this a first-rate destination,' said a reporter.

*** BEST FOR**

Beginners and intermediates, off-piste, families, value for money

ESSENTIALS

Altitude: 4,950ft (1508m)–7,606ft (2319m)
Further information: t +1 250 765 3101, *www.bigwhite.com*
Lifts in area: 13 (1 cableway, 11 chairs, 1 draglift) serving 2,765 acres of terrain
Lift pass: adult CDN$380, youth 13–18yrs CDN$313, child 6–12yrs CDN$169, all for six days
Access: Kelowna airport 35 miles (56km), Vancouver airport 4½hrs

Mountain

This is a small but testing intermediate area with magical charm. Beginners congregate around the Humming Bird quad below the village and in the Happy Valley Beginner area, while others head directly for the Ridge Rocket Express and Snow Ghost Express six-pack, which give smooth access to the main runs. Superb off-piste can be found between the snow-ghosts on Gem Lake, Falcon, Powder or Alpine T-bars, or in the expanses served by the Cliff Chair. Big White has a long history of snowboarding, with the first riders congregating here back in 1983. The terrain park has an Olympic-sized superpipe, a snowcross course and a series of jumps and rails.

Learn

Big White Ski and Snowboard School, **t** +1 250 491 6113, has a sound reputation. It incorporates **Telus Heavy Metal Flight School**, which teaches terrain park technique. **Snow Skool**, *www.snowskool.co.uk*, offers instuctional programmes for gap year students.

Children

Tot Town Day Care, **t** +1 250 491 2711, takes non-skiing children from 18 months. **The Kids' Centre**, **t** +1 250 418 6118, cares for kids from four years all day. Both are warmly recommended.

Lunch

Though there are places on the mountain to grab a snack, such as **West Ridge Warming Hut** and **Black Forest**, most skiers return to the resort. Try **Happy Valley Day Lodge** or **Beano's** in the Village Center Mall, **t** +1 250 765 3101, for all.

Dine

Kettle Valley Steakhouse, **t** +1 250 491 0130, in Happy Valley, has the best gourmet fare. **The Swiss Bear**, **t** +1 250 491 7750, has authentic fondues. **Carvers**, **t** +1 250 491 2009, serves Indo-Canadian cuisine, and **Copper Kettle**, **t** + 1 250 491 8122, offers an intimate slopeside location.

Party

Snowshoe Sam's is the main resort rendezvous, with pool tables and dancing. **Raakels** has DJs or live music most nights.

Sleep

'The accommodation is the best we have come across in North America,' said a reader. We wouldn't go that far, but all of it adjoins the piste and includes a range of pleasant condos. Further details on **t** +1 250 765 8888, *www.bigwhite.com*.

Luxury:

Chateau Big White is the resort's best address at the top of the village. It has a small spa.

Big White Condos throughout the resort include 14 new rental mountain homes.

Sundance Lodge is a family-favourite with waterpark and pool, fitness and games rooms and an in-house cinema.

Moderate/Budget:

Eagles Resort is ski in, ski-out.

Inn at Big White is the only hotel here with a pool.

Whitefoot Lodge is centrally located, with budget prices.

White Crystal Inn has large family rooms.

Fernie, BC

Profile

Good-value but remote resort with uncrowded slopes, extensive piste grooming, a friendly atmosphere and a good snow record. Nightlife has improved in recent years

*BEST FOR

All levels of skier and rider, families, ski convenience (Ski Village)

ESSENTIALS

Altitude: 3,500ft (1068m)–6,316ft (1925m)
Further information: **t** +1 250 423 4655, *www.skifernie.com*
Lifts in area: 10 (6 chairs, 4 drags) serving 2,504 acres of terrain
Lift pass: adult CDN$414–444, youth 13–17yrs CDN$288–318, child 6–12yrs CDN$132, all for six days
Access: Calgary airport 3½hrs

Fernie Alpine Resort Lift System

All lifts operate 9-4 daily

Total Lift Capacity: 13,716 skiers per hour!

Name	Length		Vertical		Ride Time
Mini Moose Conveyor	60'	18m	14'	4m	1 min
Mighty Moose Platter	1000'	300m	150'	50m	4 min
Haul Back T-Bar	1560'	480m	460'	140m	2.5 min
Deer Triple Chair	2978'	908m	672'	205m	7 min
Elk Quad Chair	4630'	1410m	1020'	310m	9 min
Great Bear Express Quad	5085'	1550m	1541'	470m	5 min
Boomerang Triple Chair	4040'	1230m	1640'	500m	8 min
Face Lift Handle Tow	1000'	300m	330'	100m	4 min
Timber Bowl Express Quad	8763'	2671m	2152'	656m	8 min
White Pass Quad	3773'	1150m	1234'	376m	8 min

Resort

'Fernie is my favourite place to ski in North America – and I have skied them all', said a reporter, 'this is a skiers' mountain, with low traffic, high variety, and uniquely good snow. Nightlife and shopping are modest, and the base village is spartan, but the mining town is authentic, and the views are worth the trip'. Fernie is a wonderfully challenging ski area in a remote corner of BC. Few destinations can offer such premium pistes and powder within the infrastructure of a modern ski village that is backed by all the charm and historical association of an attractive Victorian railway town.

Over the past dozen years this small and once unfashionable resort has achieved pipe-dream fame as luxurious apartment blocks and mountain homes have sprouted around the ski village.

Real estate developers are working on a CDN$1.5 billion development between the ski area and the old town that is the setting for a new Greg Norman championship golf course. Nearby Canadian Rockies International Airport has increased its runway to take large airliners, and the region looks set for its biggest boom since the 19th-century Gold Rush.

But where are the new lifts? Fernie's ski area has somehow managed its metamorphosis from ugly duckling to swan with six chairs – none of them covered and only two of them quads. 'Some of the lifts are ancient and slow,' complained a reporter, 'the Elk Lift drips grease so don't sit beneath the cable.' Fernie belongs to Resorts of the Canadian Rockies, which also owns Lake Louise Mountain Resort, Kimberley, Stoneham and Mont-Sainte-Anne. An initial CDN$6 million investment resulted in new base facilities, but so far no fresh uphill transport. Despite all the comfortable living accommodation, it is foolish to suppose that international skiers will continue to support Fernie unless it dramatically overhauls its antiquated lift system. Fernie was tipped by us as the resort waiting to grab Whistler's crown, but it has clearly now been overtaken by exciting new Revelstoke Mountain Resort.

Visitors have the choice of staying in ski-convenient hotel rooms and condos at the base area or in the old town of Fernie, three miles below the resort. By slumbering with minimal change throughout the 20th century, the town has managed to retain its considerable Victorian charm. A regular bus service operates between the mountain village and old Fernie. As one reporter summed it up, 'If you want a quiet resort with awesome skiing then try Fernie.'

Mountain

This is one of these rare resorts that truly suits all levels, and its compact size lends itself particularly well to families. It has a good beginner area at the base, and plenty of tree-skiing for all standards. However, the real action is found in the series of five deep powder bowls that stand side by side beneath the 2000m peaks of Elephant Head, Polar Peak and Grizzly Peak. These provide an astonishing variety of challenging terrain that will keep a strong intermediate or advanced skier happy for a whole season. 'This is wilderness skiing, where you can easily go without seeing another skier on some of the outlying runs. You will wake many mornings to true heli-skiing calibre snow,' said a reader.

Main mountain access is by two successive quads from the base area that take you up into Lizard Bowl, setting for the notorious Face Lift. Originally this was a meat-hook tow, but it now has platters for easier use. The slow and cold Timber Bowl Express quad from the base area brings you to the steep terrain of Siberia Bowl at the other end of the ski area. Fernie is popular with riders and has a rail park reached by the Elk or Bear chairlift.

Learn

Fernie Alpine Resort Winter Sports School, **t** +1 250 423 4655, is warmly recommended for lessons in alpine skiing, snowboarding and telemark. Back-country excursions can be arranged through **Fernie Wilderness Adventures Snowcat Skiing**, **t** +1 250 423 6704, **Island Lake Lodge** and **Powder Cowboy Cat Skiing**, **t** +1 250 423 3700, and through **RK Heli-ski**, **t** +1 250 342 3889, in the nearby resort of Panorama.

Children

Telus Resort Kids Daycare, **t** +1 250 423 4655, looks after small babies and toddlers. The children's ski programme is extensive. The Freeriders Programme is aimed at experienced teenagers.

Lunch

Kelsey's, **t** +1 250 423 2444, at the Cornerstone Lodge in the mountain village, has English-style fish and chips and Mexican dishes as well as chilli and burgers. **Lizard Creek Lodge**, **t** +1 250 423 205, offers 'a nice lunch by a cosy log fire'. The **Lost Boys Café**, **t** +1 250 423 4655, at the top of Timber Express quad, is 'worth a visit for a good chilli and the views'.

Dine

Lizard Creek Lodge, **t** +1 250 423 205, has the finest food in the ski village. **River Rock Bistro**, **t** +1 250 423 6871, in Park Place Lodge, is recommended for steaks and local trout. **Gabriella's**, **t** +1 250 423 7388, is Italian and serves good-value pasta dishes. The **Alpine Lodge**, **t** +1 250 423 4237, above the base area is Asian fusion. Old Fernie has a host of pretty good eateries. In particular, **Yamagoya**, **t** +1 250 430 0090, which serves sushi, is highly recommended. **The Old Elevator**, **t** +1 250 423 7115, features *ahi* tuna carpaccio and pan-seared venison rack. **Curry Bowl**, **t** +1 250 423 2695, is highly rated, as are **Corner Pocket**, **t** +1 250 423 500, which has everything from bison burgers to mussels, and **Mojo Rising**, **t** +1 250 423 7743, which is Creole. **Rip 'n' Richard's Eatery**, **t** +1 250 423 3002, has more basic Canadian fare. The historic **Royal Hotel**, **t** +1 250 423 7743, features modern Australian cuisine.

Party

The **Griz Bar** is where the après-ski starts (and finishes at 6pm), but most of the nightlife is in the town. In the Alpine Village, dog-sledding and ski-jöring take precedence over Alpine Oompah. Try your hand at ice-skating or curling in the old town. In old Fernie, **The Pub**, **Grand Central Hotel & Bar**, **Phat City** and the **Royal Hotel** are popular meeting places – some have live music.

Sleep

Luxury:

Lizard Creek Lodge, **t** +1 250 423 2057, *www.lizardcreek.com*, is the best address on the mountain, with spacious condos, a gym, pool and hot tub. The bar serves snacks while you sit in squashy sofas around the open fire.

Island Lake Lodge, **t** + 1 250 423 3700, *www.islandlakeresorts.com*, is outside Fernie, but close enough for a day's add-on. Perched above a lake, it offers one of the ultimate cat-skiing experiences and is worth a visit. Its three luxurious lodges sleep up to 48 people, and have exquisite dining and a spa.

Moderate/Budget:

Fernie Alpine Lodge, t +1 250 423 4237, *www.alpinelodge.com*, is a ski in, ski out B&B with a warm atmosphere.

Cornerstone Lodge, t +1 250 423 6855, *www.cornerstonelodge.ca*, is at the foot of Deer chair and houses Kelsey's Restaurant.

Juniper Lodge, *www.juniperlodgefernie.com*, at Timberline Lodges is the resort's newest accommodation.

The Old Nurses Residence, t +1 250 423 3091, is a B&B built in 1908, with large, attractively restored rooms.

Park Place Lodge, t +1 250 423 6871, *www.parkplacelodge.com*, is in the old town and has modern rooms.

Red Tree Lodge, t +44 (0)870 241 8070, is a 42-bedroom lodge run by UK tour operator, Nonstopski. It has a laid-back ambience, spacious bedrooms, and a swimming-pool.

Wolf's Den Lodge, t + 1 877 333 239, *www.skifernie.com*, has been upgraded and now offers some of the best-value slopeside accommodation in the resort.

Kicking Horse, BC

Profile

Rugged terrain best suited to good skiers wanting serious challenge, without having to ignore creature comforts. KH has the best mountain restaurant in North America and modern, comfortable accommodation at its base

*BEST FOR

Strong intermediates and experts, ski gourmets

ESSENTIALS

Altitude: 3,902ft (1190m)–8,037ft (2450m)
Further information: **t** +1 250 754 5425, *www.kickinghorseresort.com*
Lifts in area: 4 (1 cableway, 3 chairs) serving 3,800 acres
Lift pass: adult CDN$375, youth 13–17yrs CDN$303, child 7–12yrs CDN$155, all for six days
Access: Calgary airport 3hrs

Resort

When it opened eight years ago, Kicking Horse was billed as the first new resort in the world to be built in a generation. This was not strictly true, but after a tricky start in a bad-snow winter the ski area in a remote corner of BC has far exceeded all expectations and become one of our favourite resorts on both continents. It now has world-class ranking, with tough terrain comparable to Whistler and Jackson Hole.

The secret of its international appeal lies in an agreable blend of Canadian know-how and European sophistication, coupled with substantial Dutch finance. The backbone of KH is a high-speed gondola, which gives a respectable 1260m vertical drop on a ski mountain of perfect shape. The bottom third of the mountain used to be the old community ski hill of Whitetooth above the valley town of Golden. Certainly it needed vision to choose this remote spot.

This is no quaint Victorian mining town awaiting gentrification, but a busy blue-collar railway junction sprawled across both sides of the tracks and lacking even an ounce of charm. But having completed the gondola, the stroke of European-inspired genius was to build, at the top of it, the best mountain restaurant in North America, the Eagle's Eye.

However, no one would willingly choose to spend a week or a fortnight in Golden, although one reporter would disagree: 'Real people and that hometown feel. We loved the place so much that we moved lock, stock and barrel to live in Golden.' Comfortable and luxury accommodation has been constructed at Kicking Horse base. So far this has taken the form of delightful mountain homes and new guest lodges that ring the base area. However, the major luxury hotel promised originally by its developers has failed to materialize. With rival Revelstoke now tipped for stardom, it is now unlikely to do so.

Mountain

A quad-chair serves the beginner area and an old fixed-grip double gives access to some easy and advanced runs on the lower half of the mountain. But Eagle's Eye on the summit is why you make the effort to travel all this way. The gondola does offer an easier route down for the less proficient skier, for those who have either eaten and drunk too much in the restaurant – or those who lose their nerve when they start to discover the nature of the terrain.

The choice of entrées starts right outside the door of the Eagle's Eye restaurant. Wicked black-diamonds fall away from both sides of the ridge to produce some sensational tree- and bowl-skiing. Some of this is steep by any standards, and for anyone lacking in confidence it pays to study the topography before immediately committing yourself to runs that may test your ability to its limits.

Stairway to Heaven, a quad on the far side of the ski area, takes you up to Blue Heaven, the highest point on the mountain. More steep runs follow down through the trees on one side of Redemption Ridge. Another leads down into Feuz Bowl, a glorious powder cache after a fresh fall. Kicking Horse's 2,750-acre ski area is now larger than Breckenridge and, according to one reader, 'a truly great place for anyone who wants challenging skiing'.

There is a wide choice of runs, not least those served by the old Pioneer Chair, which most people seem to ignore in favour of using the gondola. The runs from the Pioneer are excellent and – in the week at least – almost devoid of other skiers.

Learn

Kicking Horse Snow School, t +1 866 754 5425, has established a reputation as a worthy powder academy. Heli-skiing can be arranged through **Purcell Heli Skiing, t** +1 250 344 5410.

Children

The resort has opened a new **Kids' Zone** and the ski school teaches children from three years of age.

Lunch

Horse Thief Café, t +1 250 344 8679, in Glacier Lodge, is open daily for lunch. A mid-mountain yurt called **Heaven's Door** serves sushi. The base lodge has a self-service restaurant. The **Eagle's Eye, t** +1 250 439 5410, at the gondola summit, has a roaring log fire, floor-to-ceiling windows and wooden rafters that all add to the atmosphere. Local game is the culinary speciality.

Dine

The **Eagle's Eye, t** +1 250 439 5410, is also open on weekend evenings. **Corks, t** +1 250 344 7644, and the **Local Hero, t** +1 250 344

KICKING HORSE

Eagle's Eye Restaurant 7,700'

Blue Heaven 8,033'

CPR RIDGE

REDEMPTION RIDGE

Feuz Bowl

Crystal Bowl

Bowl Over

Terminator Ridge

Super Bowl

Golden Eagle Express

Stairway to Heaven

Pioneer

Catamount

Midstation

Whispering Pines

Slow Slope

Magic Carpet "Pony Express"

Day Lodge

Mountaineer

Glacier Lodge

Kicking Horse Trail

Selkirk

Purcell Woods

The Cache

Dogtooth Properties

Vagabond Lodge

Copper Horse Lodge

Highland Lodge

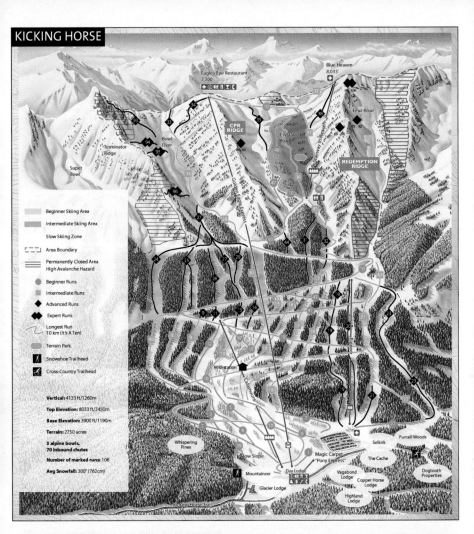

Beginner Skiing Area

Intermediate Skiing Area

Slow Skiing Zone

Area Boundary

Permanently Closed Area High Avalanche Hazard

Beginner Runs

Intermediate Runs

Advanced Runs

Expert Runs

Longest Run 10 km (It's A Ten)

Terrain Park

Snowshoe Trailhead

Cross-Country Trailhead

Vertical: 4133 ft/1260m

Top Elevation: 8033 ft/2450m

Base Elevation: 3900 ft/1190m

Terrain: 2750 acres

3 alpine bowls, 70 inbound chutes

Number of marked runs: 106

Avg Snowfall: 300" (762cm)

7272, are both open for dinner. **Sushi Kuma**, **t** +1 250 344 8678, in Glacier Lodge, is open daily for dinner. Golden boasts a number of coffee shops, bars and cafés, such as **The Taps**, **t** +1 250 344 7155, and **Jita's Café**, **t** +1 250 344 3660. **Eleven22**, **t** +1 250 344 2443, on the edge of town, is strongly recommended. The **Kicking Horse Grill**, **t** +1 250 344 2330, which has a Dutch chef/owner, is highly recommended for its atmospheric log cabin setting and adventurous cuisine.

Party

The **Mad Trapper Pub** in Golden has been the only establishment to rise to the evening needs of skiers and snowboarders. The après-ski options have improved at the base area, with **Extreme Peaks** and the **Copper Horse Lodge** offering well-stocked bars and dining. The **Highland Pub** serves basic meals including fish and chips – and stocks a huge range of single malts.

The **Vagabond Lodge**, near the ski area base, has a bar and games room.

Sleep

Luxury:

Eagle's Eye restaurant, **t** +1 250 439 5400, *www.kickinghorseresort.com/activities/eagleseye*, has two suites where you can stay after dinner and make first tracks down in the morning.

The **ski in, ski out chalets**, **t** +1 250 439 5424, at the area base, are beautifully equipped with large rooms and modern kitchens, outdoor hot-tubs and garages.

Copper Horse Lodge, **t** +1 250 344 7644, *www.copperhorselodge.com*, ('excellent hospitality and food') is a 10-room boutique hotel housing Corks restaurant.

Glacier Lodge, **t** +1 250 439 1160, is in a great location, just 100ft from the Eagle Express Gondola, and comprises a health club, sushi bar and ski shop.

Vagabond Lodge, **t** +1 250 344 2622, *www.vagabondlodge.ca*, has 10 suites and a lounge with fireplace.

Emerald Lake Lodge, **t** +1 403 410 7417, *www.crmr.com/lodgeemerald.php*, about 45km away on the other side of Kicking Horse Pass, is a lakeside mountain retreat built of hand-hewn timber and featuring massive stone fireplaces. Accommodation is in 24 cabin-style buildings.

Budget:

Golden, a 10-minute drive away, has half a dozen B&Bs, and a handful of motels and lodges.

Ramada Golden, **t** +1 250 439 1888, *www.ramadagolden.com*, has an indoor pool.

Prestige Inn, **t** +1 250 344 7990, *www.prestigeinn.com*, has simple rooms.

Panorama, BC

Profile

Purpose-built village close to some of Canada's best heli-skiing. The piste skiing best suits intermediates and families

Resort

Panorama is an attractive village built by developer Intrawest, with comfortable accommodation and some good skiing. It lies a two-hour drive to the southwest of Banff and is on the edge of the Bugaboos.

LAKE LOUISE
CALGARY
MT GOLDIE
BANFF
VIEW 1000 PEAKS
7800 ft/2400m
Summit Hut
Outback Ridge
RADIUM HOT SPRINGS
INVERMERE
TAYNTON BOWL
Never Never Land
Whitetail
Kinnesset
C Spine
Kunuks
Devils Drop
B 2nd
B 1st
Hell High
View of 1000 Peaks
Hell-Face
Halfpipe
Brush Line
Funnel
Star Fire
Cauldron
Landing Strip
Elmo
Orca
Getmedown
Outer Limits
Roy's Run
Tight Spots
Top of the World
Tree Time
SUMMIT QUAD
Picture Perfect
Canadian
Founders Ridge
Cappuccino Hut
Millenium
CHAMPAGNE EXPRESS
Upper Bowl
Sun Bowl Trail
Stump Farm
Schober's Dream
Lower Bowl
Rollercoaster
Mcintosh Way
Strobl Strasse
Ostrander
Delestie
Downhill
Tacky
Skyline
Triple
Sunbird
Whiskey Jack
Fritz's
Little Dipper
SUNBIRD
Stinger
Powder Trail
Horseshoe
Showoff
Old Timer
Hay Fever
Cliff Glade
MILE 1 QUAD EXPRESS
Beginner
RED RIDER
SILVER PLATTER
Magic Carpet
TAYNTON LODGE
HEARTH-STONE
PANORAMA SPRINGS
EARL GREY LODGE
1000 PEAKS LODGE & SUMMIT
SKI TIP TAMARACK LODGE
SKI TIP DAY LODGE
SNOWMOBILE CENTRE
Hoggvilla
Half Pipe
New Timer
Eagle Glade
TOBY
SHOWZONE terrain parks
PINE INN
VILLAGE GONDOLA
AURORA
HORSETHIEF CORE LOUNGE
TOBY CREEK LODGE VILLAGE STORE
CENTRAL CHECK-IN
RIVERBEND
DAY PARKING & GONDOLA ACCESS
HELIPLEX
TO INVERMERE
3800ft/1160m
WOLF EDUCATION CENTRE
GREYWOLF NORDIC CENTRE
WOLF LAKE
GREYWOLF GOLF COURSE

***BEST FOR**

Families, intermediates, base for heli-skiing

ESSENTIALS

Altitude: 3,800ft (1158m)–7,800ft (2360m)
Further information: t +1 250 342 6941, *www.panoramaresort.com*
Lifts in area: 8 (1 cableway, 5 chairs, 2 drags) serving 2,847 acres of terrain
Lift pass: adult CDN$314, youth 13–18yrs CDN$239, child 7–12yrs CDN$139, all for six days
Access: Calgary airport 4hrs

Mountain

The enjoyable, mainly easy and intermediate, trails through the trees offer few challenges but are ideal for anyone wanting the Canadian ski experience in a thoroughly agreeable environment. Taynton Bowl, off the backside with 1,000 acres of chutes, gullies and difficult tree-skiing, is a worthy off-piste playground for more advanced skiers.

The resort is included in the Canadian Rockies Super Pass covering eight other resorts, including Banff-Lake Louise, Fernie, Nakiska, Kimberley and Fortress Mountain.

Learn

The **School of Skiing and Snowboarding**, **t** +1 250 342 6941, organizes group and private lessons.

Children

This is great, safe skiing for families. **Wee Wascals, t** +1 250 341 3041, provides daycare for children from 18 months. **Snowbirds Ski Kindergarten, t** +1 250 342 6941, accepts children from three years.

Lunch

The **Summit Hut, t** +1 250 342 0217, has a limited menu but great views. **Beckie Scott Nordic Centre, t** +1 250 342 6941 ext. 3840, at the base of Sunbird Chair, has a lunchtime BBQ with very good service.

Dine

Wildfire Grill, t +1 250 342 6941, is relaxed and reasonably priced, serving burgers, salads and ribs. **Ferrari's on Toby Creek, t** +1 250 341 3056, is affordable family dining. **Earl Grey Lodge t** +1 250 341 3641, specializes in French and Italian dishes. You can also eat at the **Heli-Plex Restaurant, t** +1 250 342 6941, where the local heli-skiing is based. Also try visiting the town of Invermere for dinner.

Party

This is not a great party resort. The **Crazy Horse Saloon** and **Jackpine Pub** are the main rendezvous points. The **Glacier Nightclub** is a popular venue. You can relax at the **Panorama Springs** outdoor waterpark, or go to the valley town of Invermere to bath in the hot springs.

Sleep

For all accommodation, contact Resort Reservations, **t** +1 250 342 6941.

Luxury:

Riverbend Townhomes on Toby Creek have easy access to the Village Gondola.

Wolf Lake Townhomes are in a ski in, ski out position by the Sunbird chairlift.

Gold Premium Lodging is in condos in the Upper Village.

Earl Grey Lodge t +1 250 341 3641, *www.earlgreylodge.com*, is a privately owned boutique hotel 200m from the main mountain access lift.

Moderate/Budget:

Silver Lodging is at Creekside.

Bronze Lodging is at the Pine Inn at the base of the Mile 1 chair.

Red Resort, BC

*BEST FOR

Advanced skiers and riders, retro-chic, value

ESSENTIALS

Altitude: 3,888ft (11296m)–6,800ft (2266m)
Further information: **t** +1 800 663 0105, *www.redresort.com*
Lifts in area: 5 (4 chairs, 1 drag) serving 1,685 acres of terrain
Lift pass: adult CDN$354, youth 13–18yrs CDN$282, child 7–12yrs CDN$180, all for six or seven days
Access: Castlegar airport 30mins, Spokane airport in Washington State 2½hrs

Profile

Rough, tough skiing for accomplished intermediates to advanced skiers and boarders. Accommodation choice lies between the small ski base area and the historic valley town

Resort

For a while back in 2005 it looked as if this cult resort in BC, with a rugged reputation for some of the steepest terrain in Canada, was going to go out of business. But, to the delight of the people of the nearby town of Rossland, Red was saved in the nick of time by a Californian businessman. He began with a major property development around the base area. Retro-chic is what Red had traded on for a generation – a last frontier of Canadian machismo where slow lifts and mighty moguls were the name of the game. But the commercial reality is that retro-chic makes money for no one.

Mountain

Red and adjoining Granite Mountains can be skied 360 degrees on all faces that are served by only six lifts. During the winter of 2008 the old triple Silverlode chair was upgraded to a quad. Together, the two mountains offer 87 trails, of which a high 45 per cent is graded at least black diamond. The vertical drop is only 887m, but the longest run – Long Squaw – is a respectable 7km. The off-piste opportunities down through the trees are endless and the overall quality of the skiing is nothing short of phenomenal. Red's terrain park on the T-bar slope has 15 rails, funboxes, and table-tops.

'Some of the best skiing and boarding we have ever done. The snow was great, the local skiers polite, with exceptional ability. If you are looking for a change to Whistler and want to ski or board a run through trees and on to an equally empty piste, then come here. A truly fantastic place to slide,' enthused one reporter.

Learn

Red Snowsports School, t +1 800 663 0105, offers lessons and guiding. **Valhalla Powdercats, t** +877 969 7669, and **Big Red Cats, t** + 1 877 969 7669, both offer cat-skiing excursions.

Children

Red Kinder Kids, t +1 800 663 0105, accepts children from 18 months, and combines skiing with childcare for three- to five-year-olds. The **Red Ski Academy, t** +1 250 362 7388, runs race-training courses for young skiers aged 11 to 18 years, local or foreign, in conjunction with academic work.

Lunch

Paradise Lodge has been revamped and provides simple but good food. **Rafters Pizza** at the base-lodge is recommended. For information contact **t** +1 800 663 0105. **Deane Cabin, t** +1 250 362 7384 ext 233, is for those who want to rent their own warm, private cabin for the day. There's room for up to 25 people, and hot and cold drinks and snacks can be ordered on arrival from **Sourdough Alley** and **Rafters Pizza**, with costs added to your final bill.

Dine

The Gypsy at Red, t +1 250 362 3347, is located on the mountain and has good fusion cuisine.

Party

The laid-back town of Rossland has bars like **The Flying Steamshovel** and **The Rock Cut Pub** for pool, and **Nowhere Special Social Club** for dancing.

Sleep

Luxury:

Red Property Management, t +1 250 362 5553, has ski in, ski out options with 'all the room and comfort of home'.

Moderate/Budget:

Prestige Mountain Resort-Rossland, t +1 250 362 7375, has simple rooms.

Black Bear B&B, t +1 250 362 3398, *www.blackbearinn.ca*, is five minutes' drive from Red, was built in 1898 and has an outdoor hot-tub.

Ram's Head Inn, t +1 250 362 9577, *www.ramshead.bc.ca*, a pleasant B&B, is almost ski in, ski out, with communal breakfast dining and a hot tub.

Revelstoke, BC

🏆 MOST PROMISING RESORT 2009

Profile

New and exciting resort based around an old Victorian town and heli-ski centre in a remote corner of BC. Ideal for serious skiers and snowboarders, but not for children or party-goers

Resort

In what we consider to be the most exciting development in snow business on either side of the Atlantic over the past 20 years, brand new billion-dollar Revelstoke Mountain Resort (RMR) is poised to become one of the world's most exciting destinations. What's more, it suits everyone from complete beginner to heli-skiing powder pig.

Within less than a decade we predict that RMR will earn its place as one of the Top Ten Truly Greats alongside Aspen, Jackson Hole, Whistler, St Anton, Chamonix, Courchevel, Val d'Isère, Verbier and Zermatt.

* BEST FOR

Wannabee heli-skiers and riders, reliable snow cover, backwoods beauty

ESSENTIALS

Altitude: 2,562ft (782m)–7,300ft (2225m)
Further information: **t** +1 866 373 4754, *www.revelstokemountainresort.com*
Lifts in area: 5 (1 cable-way, 4 chairs) serving 1,500 acres of terrain
Lift pass: adult CDN$311, youth 13–18yrs CDN$227, child 6–12yrs CDN$167, all for six days
Access: Calgary airport 4½hrs, Kelowna airport 2hrs; Revelstoke airport has bi-weekly flights from Calgary

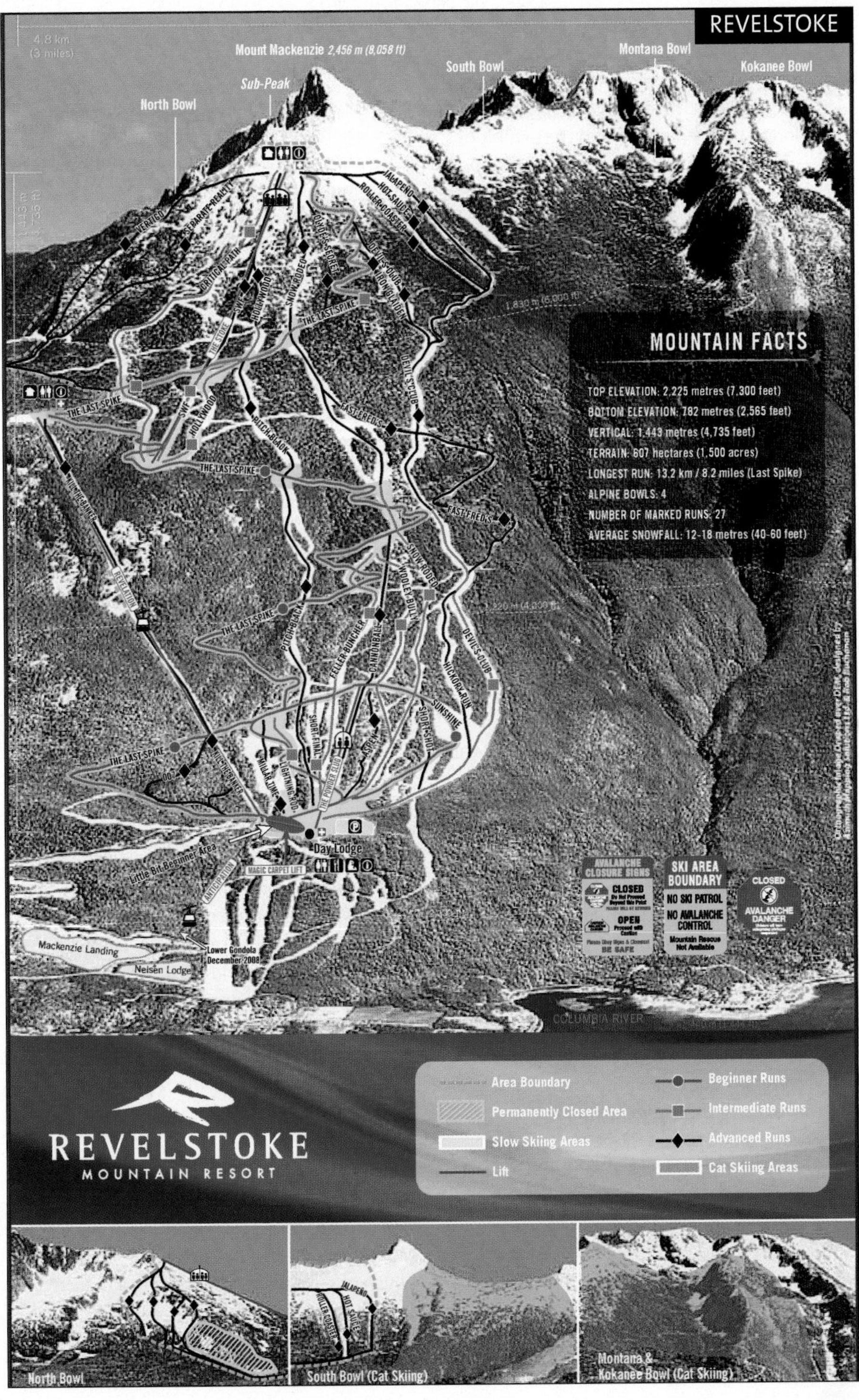
4.8 km (3 miles)
Mount Mackenzie 2,456 m (8,058 ft)
Sub-Peak
North Bowl
South Bowl
Montana Bowl
Kokanee Bowl
1,443 m (4,735 ft)
1,830 m (6,000 ft)
1,220 m (4,000 ft)
MOUNTAIN FACTS
TOP ELEVATION: 2,225 metres (7,300 feet)
BOTTOM ELEVATION: 782 metres (2,565 feet)
VERTICAL: 1,443 metres (4,735 feet)
TERRAIN: 607 hectares (1,500 acres)
LONGEST RUN: 13.2 km / 8.2 miles (Last Spike)
ALPINE BOWLS: 4
NUMBER OF MARKED RUNS: 27
AVERAGE SNOWFALL: 12-18 metres (40-60 feet)
VERTIGO
SEPARATE REALITY
CRITICAL PATH
HOLLYWOOD
SNOW RODEO
DOLCES SECRET
DEVIL'S CLUB
IRON GLADES
ROLLER COASTER
HOT SAUCE
JALAPEÑO
THE LAST SPIKE
THE STORE
SWF
PITCH BLACK
EAST FREDS
FAST FREDS
KILL THE BANKER
REVELATION
WOOLEY BULLY
FELLER BUNCHER
CANNONBALL
HICKORY RUN
SUNSHINE
SHORT SHOT
ASPEN
SHORT FINAL
THE POWDER SLUG
LIGHTNING ROD
MILLAR LINE
007
Day Lodge
MAGIC CARPET LIFT
Little Bit Beginner Area
ANTICIPATION
Lower Gondola December 2008
Mackenzie Landing
Nelsen Lodge
COLUMBIA RIVER
AVALANCHE CLOSURE SIGNS
CLOSED
OPEN
BE SAFE
SKI AREA BOUNDARY
NO SKI PATROL
NO AVALANCHE CONTROL
Mountain Rescue Not Available
CLOSED
AVALANCHE DANGER
REVELSTOKE
MOUNTAIN RESORT
Area Boundary
Permanently Closed Area
Slow Skiing Areas
Lift
Beginner Runs
Intermediate Runs
Advanced Runs
Cat Skiing Areas
North Bowl
South Bowl (Cat Skiing)
Montana & Kokanee Bowl (Cat Skiing)

Until now, not much of note has happened in sleepy, remote Revelstoke in the wilds of British Columbia. Winter is long, summer is brief, and the exhibit of pride in the local museum is a left-handed chain-saw. The 8,500 people who live here on the banks of the great Columbia River have been quietly going about their business of mining and lumber since the last spike in the line of the trans-continental Canadian Pacific Railway was hammered home back in 1885.

Over the past 30 years its situation in a valley sandwiched between the Monashee and Selkirk mountain ranges has made it the world capital of helicopter skiing. Around 12m of snow falls out of the sky during an average winter. But heli-ski numbers are limited and the occasional chatter of a chopper overhead has hardly helped the economy. Trains and timber are not what they were and the town has been in slow decline for decades.

However all that has changed dramatically with the construction of the eight-person Revelation gondola, which rises for two whole miles up tree-lined Mount Mackenzie.

The first of 5,000 homes at the base area are under construction. Hotels will follow. To make RMR truly unique, the developers have bought Selkirk Tangiers and its 500,000-acre tenure of high alpine terrain and forest in both the Selkirks and the Monashees. At the same time it has acquired the local cat-skiing company. The pride of the new homes even have their own heli-pads.

The small town of Revelstoke has an attractive few blocks of faded Victorian buildings. House prices have already doubled and we'll no doubt see lots of gentrification as the bed base expands from the present 800 into thousands.

Mountain

What you find when you ride the Revelation gondola from its temporary base area is a giant of a mountain with unlimited potential on a scale that challenges almost every other major ski destination worldwide.

Two more lifts come on stream for this season, bringing the total to five. These access marked runs and enough off-piste to keep even the hungriest skier or snowboarder happy for a fortnight. So long and challenging is the descent that last season the average visitor managed only 1.5 gondola rides per day. Its vertical drop of 1829m is the longest in North America – and, indeed, one of the longest in the world. To put that in perspective, the drop in Tignes from the Grande Motte to Val Claret is 1400m, Whistler Peak to Whistler Creek is 1609m. Only the thigh-burning descent from the Klein Matterhorn to Cervinia in Italy exceeds Revelstoke.

The new lifts this winter open up what we are assured are plenty of novice and intermediate runs that were lacking last season. On completion in 15 years' time, the resort should boast 21 lifts and 115 runs set in 10,000 skiable acres.

Mark Warner has been the first to spot the potential here for mixing the best of resort skiing with world-class heli-skiing, while Erna Low is taking advantage of the favourable dollar rate to sell ski property here at a time when the high euro has seriously affected the European market for British buyers.

Learn

There's only one ski school, **Revelstoke Mountain Snow School, t** +1 250 837 9400, which offers low-cost tuition and a high standard of teaching.

Children

Revelstoke Mountain Snow School, **t** +1 250 837 9400, teaches skiing from six years and snowboarding from eight years. So far there's no kindergarten, but hotels in town may be able to arrange babysitting.

Lunch

For the moment it's burger, wraps and a daily choice of specials in the **Day Lodge**. Plans are afoot for a wait-service restaurant at the top of the gondola.

Dine

The **One-Twelve in the Regent Inn**, **t** +1 250 837 2107, and the **Dining Room in the Hillcrest Hotel**, **t** +1 250 837 3322, are the best bets for international cuisine because both cater largely for heli-ski guests. **Claudio's Pizza & Pasta Parlour**, **t** +1 250 837 6743, has sound Italian fare. **Three Bears Bistro**, **t** +1 250 837 9575, has an open fire place and welcoming atmosphere. **Bad Paul's Roadhouse Grill**, **t** +1 250 837 9575, is renowned for its steaks. **Hong Kong Restaurant**, **t** +1 250 837 2360, makes a Chinese change from traditional Canadian fare. **Magpie & Stump**, **t** +1 250 837 4067, serves Tex-Mex.

Party

Heli-skiers are usually early-to-bed and holiday nightlife is, to put it mildly, in its infancy in Revelstoke. The **River City Pub** in the Regent Inn is a pleasant bar. **Grizzly's Sports Bar** has two pool tables and is where the locals drink. **Stokers Bar** is a long-established small town strip club, an institution that is popular with the local youth and itinerant truck drivers.

Sleep

The **Nelsen Lodge complex**, **t** +1 866 373 4754, opens the first of three condo-hotels this season.

Hillcrest Hotel and Coast Resort, **t** +1 250 837 3322, *www.hillcresthotel.com*, is the comfortable base for Selkirk-Tangiers Heli-skiing, 'great restaurant and amazing après ski massage. Rooms are simple but lack for nothing', said a reader.

Regent Inn, **t** +1 250 837 2107, *www.regentinn.com*, is a Victorian inn at the centre of the downtown area and one of the resort's main hubs, 'plenty of atmosphere and fine dining'.

Comfort Inn & Suites, **t** +1 250 837 2191, *www.revelstokecomfortinn.com*, recently underwent a CDN$3 million renovation.

Sandman Inn, **t** +1 250 837 5271, *www.sandmanhotels.com*, offers rooms with kitchenettes near the centre of town.

Silver Star, BC

Profile

Attractive neo-Victorian village with convenient skiing and recommended ski school

Resort

Silver Star is one of a trio of resorts in the heart of the the scenic wine-growing country of BC that has come to prominence over the past five years. It's not big, but combined with Big White, its Australian-owned stablemate, this area makes for a great holiday.

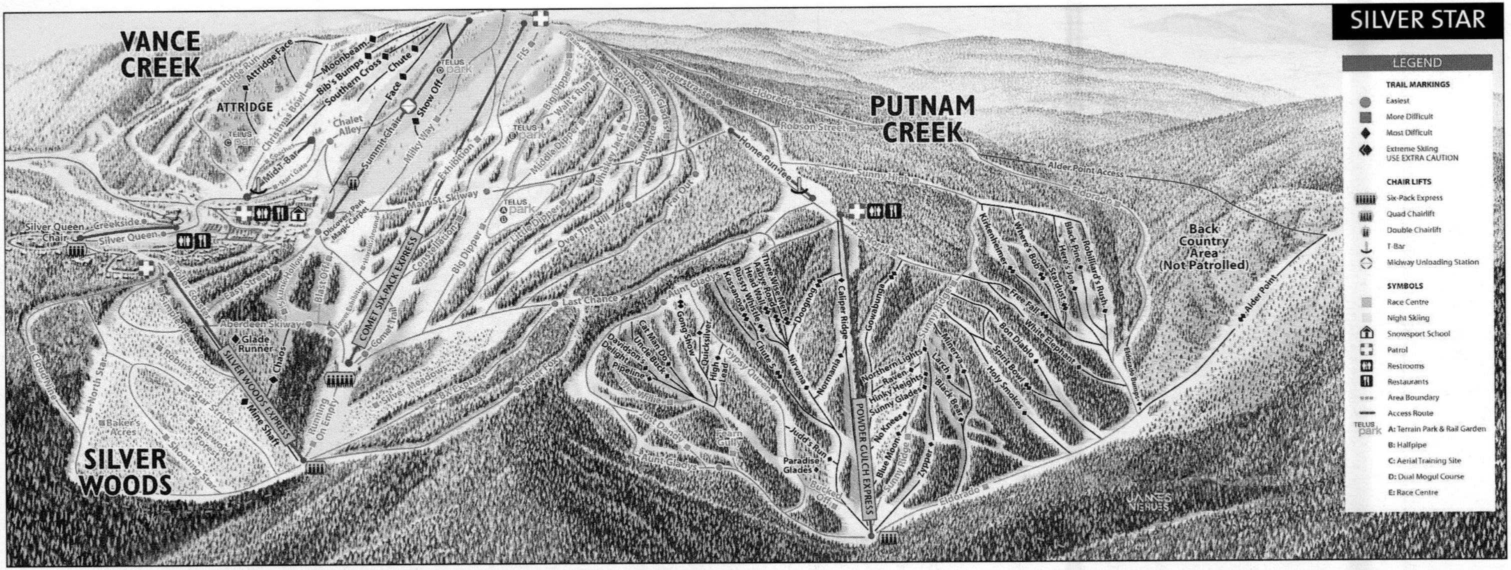

SILVER STAR

VANCE CREEK

PUTNAM CREEK

SILVER WOODS

ATTRIDGE

Back Country Area (Not Patrolled)

COMET SIX-PACK EXPRESS

SILVER WOODS EXPRESS

POWDER GULCH EXPRESS

Silver Queen Chair

LEGEND

TRAIL MARKINGS

- Easiest
- More Difficult
- Most Difficult
- Extreme Skiing USE EXTRA CAUTION

CHAIR LIFTS

- Six-Pack Express
- Quad Chairlift
- Double Chairlift
- T-Bar
- Midway Unloading Station

SYMBOLS

- Race Centre
- Night Skiing
- Snowsport School
- Patrol
- Restrooms
- Restaurants
- Area Boundary
- Access Route

TELUS park

- A: Terrain Park & Rail Garden
- B: Halfpipe
- C: Aerial Training Site
- D: Dual Mogul Course
- E: Race Centre

*** BEST FOR**

Village ambience, all standards of skier and rider, terrain park

ESSENTIALS

Altitude: 3,780ft (1155m)–6,280ft (1915m)
Further information: t +1 250 542 0224, *www.skisilverstar.com*
Lifts in area: 7 (6 chairs, 1 drag) serving 2,725 acres of terrain
Lift pass: adult CDN$380, youth 13–18yrs CDN$313, child 6–12yrs CDN$169, all for six out of seven days
Access: Kelowna airport 55mins

At first sight, the 10-lift resort near Vernon suggests that it is a restored *fin de siècle* mining town. In fact the 'old' vividly painted town houses and streets lit with soft sodium lamps are a complete sham. For a purpose-built resort it has considerable panache, but it is not a place for non-skiers.

Mountain

The ski area, our favourite in the Okanagen Valley, is underrated. The front face comprises the usual North American menu of gladed easy and intermediate runs. However, the backside is much more demanding. Double-diamond runs such as vertiginous Freefall and the infamous Cowabunga are of sufficiently steep pitch to make even the most jaded powderhound think edge control.

The Silver Woods area, served by a high-speed detachable-quad, opened up 360 acres of mainly intermediate terrain with 10 runs and five areas of tree-skiing. The Alpine Meadows quad-chair has greatly improved service to the steep terrain to the skier's right of the recently upgraded Summit Chair. The old Silver Queen chair has also been renovated.

The terrain park is one of the most highly rated in BC and features a rail garden, half-pipe, aerial training site, race centre and a dual mogul race course.

Learn

Silver Star Snowsport School, **t** +1 250 558 6065, has a good reputation for teaching cutting-edge ski and snowboard technique. 'The instructors were excellent,' said a reporter.

Children

'Brilliant for all the family,' said a reader. **Star Kids Center**, **t** +1 250 558 6065, accepts little ones from newborn to six years old, and skiers and riders from four years and is very good for young children.

Lunch

Paradise Camp, **t** +1 250 558 6087, near the top of the Powder Gulch Express, offers the only on-mountain lunch. **Longjohn's Pub**, **t** +1 250 549 2992, is back in the village. **Bugaboos Bakery**, **t** +1 250 545 3208, is the place to go for a snack.

Dine

The Italian Garden Restaurant, **t** +1 250 558 1448, serves pizzas and pasta. **Clementine's**, **t** +1 250 549 5191, has live piano at weekends, and the **Silver Lode Restaurant**, **t** +1 250 549 5105, specializes in international cuisine. The **Silver Grill Steak and Chop House**, **t** +1 250 558 6070, has more formal dining and an impressive wine list. Snowcats takes you up to **Paradise Camp**, **t** +1 250 558 6087, for a multi-course gourmet meal.

Party

The après-ski is what you make it. **Beyond Wrapture Mind and Body Care Day Spa** is one place in which to relax, while the tubing park is another. The action then shifts to a pre-dinner drink in the **Wine Cellar** below the Bulldog Hotel, followed by a few games of pool in the newly-decorated **Saloon**.

Sleep

Bookings for all, t +1 250 558 6083.

Luxury:

Snowbird Lodge is the resort's top hotel, with on-deck hot tubs in some units.

Moderate:

The Silver Star Club Resort , T +1 250 549 5191, is a complex of three buildings in a convenient ski in, ski out position.

Creekside Condos are beside the tubing park and suitable for families.

Victorian Vacation Homes range from simple studios to five-bedroom town houses complete with private hot tubs.

Sun Peaks, BC

* BEST FOR

Comfort-seekers, all levels of skier and rider, cat-skiing

ESSENTIALS

Altitude: 3,933ft (1199m)–7,060ft (2152m)

Further information: t +1 250 578 5474, *www.sunpeaksresort.com*

Lifts in area: 10 (6 chairs, 4 drags) serving 3,678 acres of terrain

Lift pass: adult CDN$408, youth 13–18yrs CDN$324, child 6–12yrs CDN$198, all for six days

Access Kamloops airport 45mins

Profile

An upmarket resort for all standards with luxury accommodation, good restaurants and nightlife, and doorstep skiing. Not the place for non-skiers

Resort

Lying nearly four hours by road from Vancouver, Sun Peaks seems an unlikely location for an international resort. But Nancy Greene, the *grande dame* of Canadian skiing who won Olympic gold in Grenoble, was summoned to promote the resort, while owners the Nippon Cable Company stumped up CDN$ 225 million. The result was a delightful three-mountain ski area set around a well-designed village with world-class accommodation. Recently a further CDN$4 million has been spent on a new lift and new terrain.

To sum it up: 'It is a long way to go but we felt it was worth it,' said reporters, and 'Lovely small village with a European feel. Slopes are not crowded and at times it feels like you are the only people on the whole mountain.'

Mountain

'Absolutely awesome,' was how one reporter put it,' I never ever got bored with so much skiing of every level.' The skiing is suited to strong intermediates who will enjoy the mainly short but searching runs on Sundance and on Mount Tod. Advanced skiers will find plenty of challenging pistes to keep them busy. But the real excitement is the cat-skiing on the upper reaches of Mount Tod.

Novices and wobbly second-weekers will find their ski legs on Mount Morrisey, where the gentlest of scenic trails have been cut through the trees. Sun Peaks has a recently expanded terrain park and a 100m half-pipe.

Learn

Sun Peaks Sports School, t +1 250 578 5505, is for group and private lessons.

'Having never having skied before I found the ski school brilliant. Our instructors were very patient,' said a reporter.

Children

Sundance Playschool, **t** +1 250 578 5433, cares for babies from 18 months. **Sun Tots** gives private ski lessons from three years, and **Sun Kids** (both **t** +1 250 578 5505) accepts children from six years for skiing and eight years for snowboarding ('instructor was fantastic with the children'). **The Kids Ranch** is an animated theme park which opened last season at the top of the Village Platter.

Lunch

Mountain eating is limited to the self-service **Sunburst Restaurant**, **t** +1 250 578 7222, at the top of the Sunburst Express, much improved from past years.

Dine

Sun Peaks Village has an Asian restaurant called **Toro Restaurant**, **t** +1 250 578 7870. **Macker's Bistro**, **t** +1 250 578 7894, in Nancy Green's Cahilty Lodge, has an eclectic menu. **Powder Hounds**, **t** +1 250 578 0014, in the Fireside Lodge, offers a European–Canadian menu.

Party

Mackdaddy's Nightclub in the Delta Sun Peak Resort is the liveliest nightspot.

Sleep

Luxury:

Delta Sun Peaks Resort, **t** +1 250 578 6000, *www.deltasunpeaks.bcresorts.com*, is one of the country's finest ski hotels. The hotel manages a new apartment-style hotel, **The Delta Residences**.

Moderate:

Nancy Greene's Cahilty Lodge, **t** +1 250 578 7454, *www.cahiltylodge.com*, is ski in, ski out.

Fireside Lodge, **t** +1 270 578 7842, *www.woodlandsatsunpeaks.com/lodgesfireside.html*, condos have fully equipped kitchens.

Hearthstone Lodge, **t** +1 250 578 8588, *www.hearthstonelodgeatsunpeaks.com*, is a charming boutique hotel.

Kookaburra Lodge, **t** +1 (0)250 572 7208, *www.kookaburralodge.ca*, offers 15 affordable apartments, ranging from one to four bedrooms.

Tremblant, Québec

Profile

State-of-the-art lift system, beautifully groomed slopes, extensive snowmaking, attractive purpose-built village, and *cuisine québéçoise*. Bitterly cold mid-winter temperatures might deter some people

Resort

Tremblant has achieved phenomenal success. More than a decade has slipped by since developer Intrawest began pumping in tens of millions of dollars in one of its first lucrative explorations of the relationships between real estate, ski areas and golf courses. A whole new village on the Versant Soleil side of the mountain is under construction.

What's surprising is that the company behind Whistler in BC and Arc 1950 in France chose such a modest mountain in

*** BEST FOR**

Ski convenience, groomed slopes, comfort-seekers

ESSENTIALS

Altitude: 870ft (265m)–3,001ft (915m)
Further information: t +1 819 681 2000, *www.tremblant.ca*
Lifts in area: 10 (2 cableways, 8 chairs) serving 628 acres of terrain
Lift pass: adult CDN$367.81, youth 13–17yrs CDN$269.73, children 6–12yrs CDN$220.29, all for six days
Access: Mont Tremblant airport 35 mins, Montreal airport 90 mins

chilly Québec rather than the Rockies. What's even more surprising is that Trembant now ranks close to Whistler as the most popular destination in Canada for European skiers.

Tremblant lies in the Laurentian Mountains, 130km northwest of Montréal. Intrawest retained the original village of Vieux-Tremblant while creating a new one of steeply terraced streets with painted wooden buildings modelled on the old quarter of Québec City. A visit here is a chance to appreciate québéçois culture and cuisine in contrived but charming surroundings. 'Clearly Intrawest have studied up on how Disney would present a theme park in the mountains,' complained a reporter. The ambience is warm, but the same cannot be said about the air temperature in mid-winter. ('On day four of our holiday it was minus 42°C with wind chill. It was almost unbearable to stay still and you had to cover every inch of exposed flesh.') European February half-term is the most popular time to visit, but it can be crowded at weekends ('the busiest weekend by far we have experienced in North America') .

We have received warnings about equipment hire costs. 'The rental price for 13 days for boots alone was nearly $300, so I bought my own brand new ones from the Atomic shop for $299.'

Mountain

The 10-lift ski area (13 if you include children's lifts) stretches in four sectors across both faces of the mountain. The main Équilibre beginner area lies just above the village, and most of the easy intermediate terrain is also on the South Side. The gondola ride up from the village to the Grand Manitou temporarily shelters you from the reality of skiing in a cold climate. But low temperatures do not necessarily equate with high snowfall. To compensate for nature's not infrequent failure, Tremblant has Canada's largest artificial snowmaking system.

The North Side receives little sunshine in winter and, because of this, retains good cover throughout the winter. It offers considerably more scope for strong intermediates and advanced skiers and riders. A couple of trails have short sharp pitches of 42 degrees and call for a high level of technique in the often-icy conditions.

The Edge, served by its own quad-chair, is an area set aside for accomplished skiers and riders. Haute-Tension, an expert run that follows the fall line beneath the lift, is guaranteed to raise blood pressure.

The main terrain park, Adrenaline Park, on the South Side, has the biggest jumps and the highest and longest features. The intermediate park, on the North Side, has a super-pipe and a variety of obstacles. The nearby intermediate runs of Réaction and Sensation on the Edge side wind down through the frozen spruces and provide a dramatic introduction to tree-skiing.

One reporter enthused about the skiing in the nearby Gray Rocks area. 'Midweek, it is as quiet as a private hill and the snow is well kept. Their equipment rental rates are about half Tremblant's and the sheer charm of the place made it preferable to any rip-off resort – it's the antithesis of factory skiing.' Another added: 'Gray Rocks

VERSANT NORD
NORTH SIDE

GRAND MANITOU

VERSANT EDGE / *THE EDGE*

VERS LE VERSANT SUD
TO SOUTH SIDE

BOOMERANG 56

VERS P7O
Sentier pédestre
Nord-Sud

SUPER DEMI-LUNE
SUPER HALFPIPE

75 ANDY HOE

PARC À NEIGE
SNOWPARK

MINI PARC

76 AXEL

68 ROPE TOW

BON VIVANT

EDGE

LA TRAVERSE

SHORTCUT

LOWELL THOMAS

GAGNON

LETENDRE

BUZZ

DUNCAN EXPRESS

EXPO EXPRESS

VERS LE VERSANT SUD
TO THE SOUTH SIDE

FOURCHETTE
DU DIABLE

TREMBLANT

JAMES NIEHUES

TREMBLANT

VERSANT SUD
SOUTH SIDE

VERSANT EDGE / *THE EDGE*

GRAND MANITOU

50 LA GARETTE

DUNZEE 17

13 VERTIGE

VERS LE PIC JOHANNSEN – 4 KM
TO JOHANNSEN PEAK – 4 KM

BON VIVANT

VERSANT SOLEIL / *SOLEIL SIDE*

40 FRANC SUD

41 TOBOGGAN

PORC-À-PIC 44

CASCADES

YO ! 48

LA FLUME

LE SOLEIL

LA CRIQUE

STANDARD

11 BELVÉDÈRE

PARC À NEIGE
SNOWPARK

EXPRESS
FLYING MILE

TÉLÉCABINE EXPRESS
8 minutes pour atteindre le sommet
8 minutes to get to the summit

23 DERNIER CRI

CURÉ DESLAURIERS 33

PROMENADE 25

BOY SCOTT 27

SENTIER DES PRUCHES

PLACE
ST-BERNARD

ONÉSIME

CHALET DES VOYAGEURS

PETIT CHALET
SMALL LODGE

PORTE DU SOLEIL

ACCÈS DIRECT AUX PENTES
DIRECT ACCESS TO THE SLOPES

ACCÈS DIRECT AU VERSANT SOLEIL
DIRECT ACCESS TO SOLEIL SIDE

VERS LE VERSANT NORD
TO THE NORTH SIDE

Aire de débutant
ÉQUILIBRE
Beginner area

Village piétonnier *Pedestrian Village*

JAMES NIEHUES

was superb – we skied there on our first year when we all learned as a family, but it is limited once you progress.'

Learn

Tremblant Snow School, **t** +1 819 681 5666, has a first-rate reputation, but new visitors to this part of Canada may be surprised to discover that some of the instructors are not fluent English-speakers.

Children

Kidz Club, **t** +1 819 681 5666, at the base of the slopes, provides daycare for non-skiing children from 12 months, and runs ski programmes from three years of age. 'The daycare was excellent and conveniently located right next to the ski school meeting point at the top of the village Cabriolet gondola,' said a reader.

Lunch

Mountain eating includes a wide range of cafeteria-style places, including **Le Grand Manitou**, **t** +1 819 681 3000 ext 36393, at the summit. **Le Refuge du Trappeur**, **t** +1 819 861 2000, on the Versant Soleil, is a log cabin that serves soups and drinks by the fireplace.

Dine

The cost of eating out in Tremblant is high, with an eclectic choice of restaurants from pizzas and *cuisine québéçoise* to sushi. **Aux Truffes**, **t** +1 819 681 4544, is for truffles, *foie gras* and game, and **La Forge**, **t** +1 819 681 4900, has steaks and grills. **Plus Minus Café**, **t** +1 819 681 4994, is the resort's oldest chalet, and serves gastronomic organic fare ('very expensive'). **Coco Pazzo**, **t** +1 819 681 4774, offers Italian and vegetarian food, **Sprag & Co**, **t** +1 819 681 4444, specializes in pasta ('a fantastic Carbonara') and **Crêperie Catherine**, **t** +1 819 681 4888, is for Breton crêpes ('the kids adored it'). **Restaurant Yamada**, **t** +1 819 681 4141, is for progressive cuisine – sushi combined with international classics.

Party

Bar Café d'Époque is a main resort meeting place, open from mid-afternoon until 3am with a DJ and dancing. **Le P'tit Caribou** in Vieux-Tremblant offers a more intimate atmosphere. **Microbrasserie La Diable** brews its own beer and is a popular bar before dinner. The pool at **La Source Aquaclub** provides good family entertainment. **Spa Le Scandinave** is a relaxing wellness centre a few kilometres out of town. **Westin Amérispa** and **Fairmont Amérispa** are more convenient. Other activities nearby include dog-sledding, sleigh rides, ice-climbing, tubing, snow-mobiling and moonlit snowshoe hikes. **Acrobranche** is a sensational adventure with zip-wires strung 25–75ft high in the trees.

Sleep

All accommodation, unless otherwise stated, can be booked through Central Reservations, **t** +1 819 681 2000, *www.tremblant.ca/reservations*.

Luxury:

★★★★★**Château Beauvallon**, **t** +1 819 681 6611, *www.chateaubeauvallon.com*, is a member of Small Luxury Hotels of the World and has 70 well-designed suites in a private lakeside setting.

★★★★★**Fairmont Tremblant**, **t** +1 819 681 7000, *www.fairmont.com/tremblant*, on the edge of the piste, with a large spa and outdoor pool, is still the premier hotel address.

★★★★★**Le Westin Resort & Spa**, **t** +1 819 681 8000, *www.westin.com/tremblant*, is a comfortable hotel with a choice of restaurants.

Moderate:

★★★★**Ermitage du Lac**, **t** +1 819 681 2000, set between Lac Tremblant and Lac Miroir, is a sophisticated boutique hotel.

★★★★**Homewood Suites by Hilton**, **t** +1 819 681 0808, *www.homewoodsuites tremblant.com*, are a short walk from the lifts. 'Great rooms, nicely furnished, very clean and really friendly staff. Breakfast was great apart from the people coming down to eat in their pyjamas,' said a reader.

★★★★**Le Lodge de la Montagne** is a ski in, ski out condo hotel next to La Source Aquaclub in the pedestrian area.

★★★★**Marriott Residence Inn** is at the heart of the pedestrian village.

★★★★**La Tour des Voyageurs**, at the entrance to the village, has hotel rooms and condos. A people-mover lift links it to the ski area. 'Perfect for families with kids,' was how one reporter described it.

★★★★**Club Intrawest Tremblant** is 10 minutes' drive away on the shore of Lake Tremblant, with fine views over the lake and to the ski slopes.

Whistler, BC

🏆 BEST APRÈS SKI VENUE 2009 (GARIBALDI LIFT COMPANY)

Profile

Still the top resort in North America. Twin mountains with an enormous vertical act as showcases for every conceivable type of terrain. Its Pacific Rim position makes it a melting pot of different nationalities. Whistler has a vibrant atmosphere, excellent accommodation and restaurants, and a buzzing nightlife – but high prices

Resort

The weather in Whistler is always a subject of conversation. Normally the village, which lies at only 675m – but on the same latitude as Labrador – attracts abundant winter precipitation. Much of this falls as rain in the resort and as powder on top. For the past two winters it consistently had the best snow conditions of any resort in the world. The number of blue-sky days is significantly lower than in Colorado. Mid-winter temperatures can

* BEST FOR

All levels of skier and rider, shoppers, off-piste, foodies

ESSENTIALS

Altitude: 2,228ft (675m)–7,494ft (2284m)

Further information: **t** +1 604 664 5625, *www.whistler blackcomb.com*, *www.whistler.com*

Lifts in area: 38 (3 cableways, 19 chairs, 16 drags) serving 8,171 acres of terrain

Lift pass: adult CDN$474, youth 13–18yrs CDN$396, child 7–12yrs CDN$234, all for six days

Access: Vancouver airport 2hrs

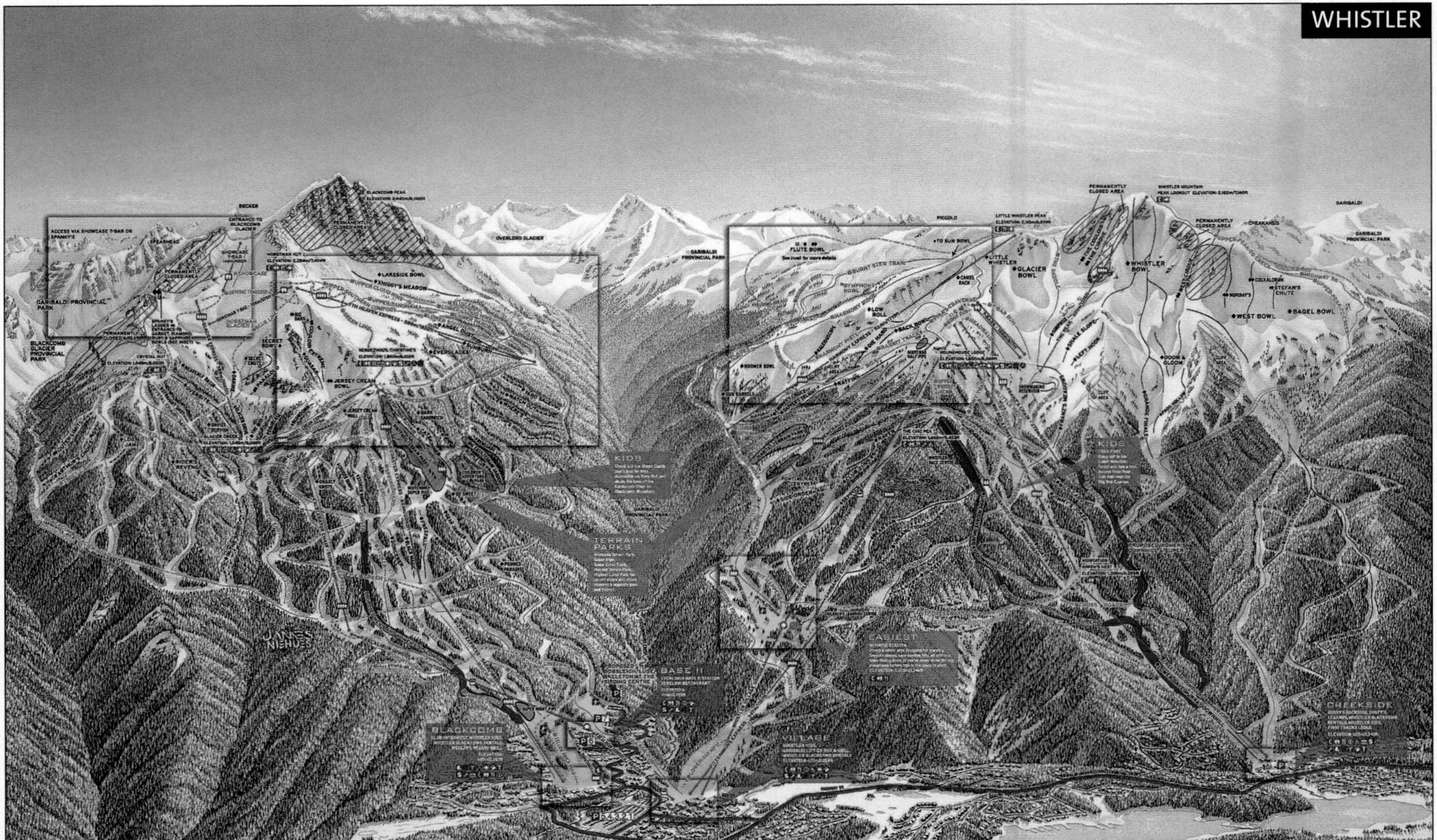
BLACKCOMB PEAK
ELEVATION: 2,440m/8,000ft
DECKER
ENTRANCE TO BLACKCOMB GLACIER
ACCESS VIA SHOWCASE T-BAR OR SPANKY'S
SPEARHEAD
PERMANENTLY CLOSED AREA
GARIBALDI PROVINCIAL PARK
BLACKCOMB GLACIER PROVINCIAL PARK
SECRET BOWL
OVERLORD GLACIER
HORSTMAN HUT
ELEVATION: 2,284m/7,494ft
LAKESIDE BOWL
XHIGGY'S MEADOW
JERSEY CREAM BOWL
GARIBALDI PROVINCIAL PARK
PICCOLO
FLUTE BOWL
TO SUN BOWL
BURNT STEW TRAIL
SYMPHONY BOWL
LOW ROLL
CAMEL BACK
BACK BOWL
BOOMER BOWL
LITTLE WHISTLER PEAK
LITTLE WHISTLER
GLACIER BOWL
PERMANENTLY CLOSED AREA
WHISTLER MOUNTAIN
PEAK LOOKOUT ELEVATION: 2,182m/7,160ft
WHISTLER BOWL
GARIBALDI
GARIBALDI PROVINCIAL PARK
CHEAKAMUS
COCKALORUM
STEFAN'S CHUTE
NORDAY'S
WEST BOWL
BAGEL BOWL
DOOM & GLOOM
GRANDE FINALE
KIDS
TERRAIN PARKS
EASIEST
BASE II
BLACKCOMB
VILLAGE
CREEKSIDE
JAMES NIEHUES

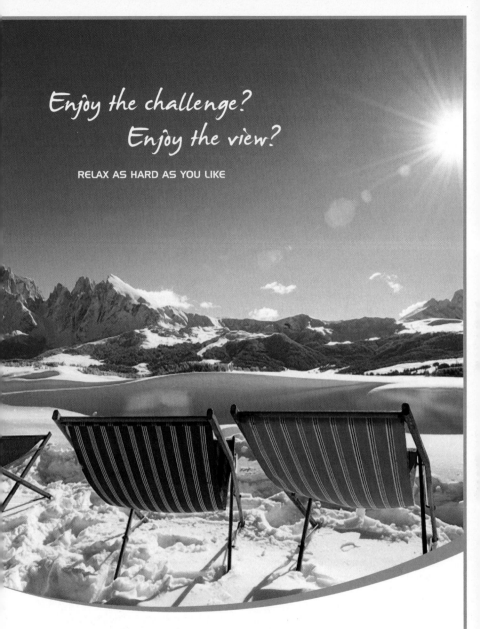

Enjoy the challenge?
Enjoy the view?

RELAX AS HARD AS YOU LIKE

On a Neilson holiday you could spend your time tearing down black runs or pottering down the nursery slopes. Getting cosy in a family-friendly hotel or living it up in a comfy private chalet. Choose from more than 80 different resorts across 13 countries – and whether it's your first time with us or your 20th, get first-class tuition at every level. So whatever you want from a winter break, Neilson have created the perfect holiday for you. It's just a call or a click away.

Call **0845 070 3460** or visit **www.neilson.co.uk**

SAILING ■ WINDSURFING ■ SKI & BOARDING ■ TENNIS ■ BIKING ■ DIVING ■ KIDS' CLUBS ■ WATERSKIING

be chilly, although not as low as in Banff and the central Rockies. Glacier skiing continues on Blackcomb throughout most of the summer.

Whistler is the official Alpine venue for the 2010 Winter Olympics and it is right that the Number One Resort in North America should be hosting the Games. Whistler and Blackcomb mountains have the longest vertical drop on the continent and awesome terrain, making for some of the most unique skiing in the world, together with a cosmopolitan atmosphere. You can stay and eat here better than in almost any other resort on the continent. 'It really is as good as everyone says,' was how one reader summed it up. However: 'It lacks real charm and there's just a hint of Disneyland about it,' said a reporter. The resort is also in danger of pricing itself out of the reach of most people.

Mountain

Whistler and Blackcomb provide enjoyable intermediate and advanced skiing on their gladed lower slopes, but the top halves of both offer contrastingly different experiences. While Whistler is given over to a succession of glorious powder bowls, Blackcomb has steep *couloirs* and long glacial descents. Both offer thrilling top-to-bottom skiing on long cruising trails, and part of the enjoyment of a stay here is deciding which to choose each morning. Both are reached from adjoining lifts in Whistler Village. This winter sees the opening of the 4.4km Peak to Peak gondola, the on-mountain link between Whistler's twin mountains. It has cost CDN$52 million to complete and has been the resort's major expenditure in the run up to the Olympics.

Whistler Village gondola provides the main access to mid-mountain Roundhouse Lodge on Whistler Mountain. At peak times, wise skiers take the underused Fitzsimmons Express quad-chair beside it. This provides a trouble-free back door into the system. Creekside, down Highway 99 from Whistler, is an alternative accommodation base, with car parks designed to attract day visitors from Vancouver and deter them from clogging up Whistler itself. Access from here to the Roundhouse and top lifts is by the Creekside gondola, followed by the Big Red Express quad. Peak to Creek is a 5km intermediate run with a vertical drop of 1650m on the west side of Whistler Mountain.

Blackcomb Mountain is accessed by the Excalibur gondola from Whistler Village or by the Wizard Express chair from Upper Village (formerly Blackcomb Village).

Blackcomb has nursery slopes served by a chair just above the village. Whistler has higher beginner terrain reached by the first stage of the Village gondola. However: ' As beginners/low intermediates Whistler is not the place to go, in my opinion; there are few true beginners' slopes,' said a reader.

Whistler is considered to be one of the top snowboarding resorts in North America, with terrain parks on both mountains, as well as a super-pipe and snowcross course on Blackcomb. The Highest Level Park on Blackcomb is dedicated to expert riders and skiers.

Numerous heli-ski companies operate in and around Whistler, including **Blackcomb Helicopters**, **t** +1 604 938 1700, **Coast Range Heliskiing**, **t** +1 604 894 1144, **Helico Presto**, **t** +1 604 938 2927, **Spearhead Mountain Guides** **t** +1 604 932 8802, **TLH Heliskiing**, **t** +1 250 558 5379, **Whistler Alpine Guides Bureau**, **t** +1 604 932 4040, and **Whistler Heli-skiing**, **t** +1 604 932 4105.

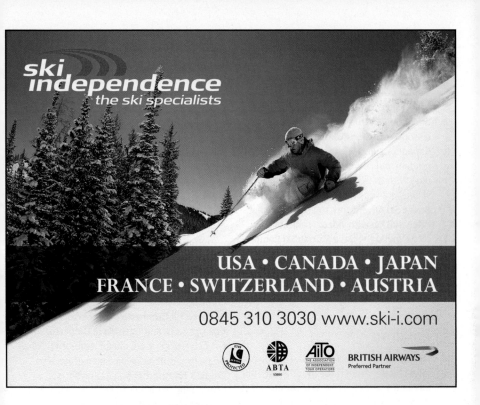

ski independence
the ski specialists

USA • CANADA • JAPAN
FRANCE • SWITZERLAND • AUSTRIA

0845 310 3030 www.ski-i.com

0749 ATOL PROTECTED
ABTA V3690
AITO THE ASSOCIATION OF INDEPENDENT TOUR OPERATORS
BRITISH AIRWAYS Preferred Partner

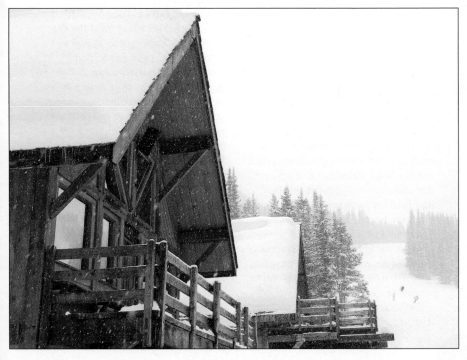

Learn

Whistler Blackcomb Ski and Snowboard School, **t** +1 800 766 0449, has an established academy for cutting-edge ski and riding instruction, although private lessons are expensive. **Extremely Canadian**, **t** +1 604 932 4105, provides guiding and powder instruction ('Two days with these guys will transform your skiing,' praised one reader), while **Lauralee Bowie Ski Adventures**, **t** +1 604 689 7444, offers tuition with video. 'I cannot recommend the **Dave Murray Ski Camp**, **t** +1 604 932 5765, highly enough,' enthused a reporter, 'it turned my wife from a cautious blue hacker to a bumps and powder nut.'

Childcare

Whistler Kids, **t** +1 800 766 0449, looks after children from three months with all-day care and lessons for appropriate ages . It also runs special classes for teenagers. Evening babysitting in your hotel or condo can be arranged through **The Nanny Network**, **t** +1 604 938 2823.

Lunch

A lack of good mountain restaurants is Whistler's only true failing. On Whistler Mountain, the **Roundhouse Lodge**, **t** +1 800 766 0449 offers hamburgers, fresh sushi and pasta in cavernous self-service surroundings. **Steeps**, **t** +1 604 905 2379, in the same building, has wait-service. **Garibaldi Lift Company**, **t** +1 604 905 2220, has good burgers and a warm atmosphere. **Ravens Nest**, **t** +1 800 766 0449, at the top of **Creekside Gondola**, serves soups and stews. **Dusty's**, **t** +1 604 905 2171, at Creekside base, has plenty of ambience.

On Blackcomb, **Christine's Restaurant**, **t** +1 604 938 7437, in Rendezvous Lodge, is the resort's best shot at a wait-service restaurant – but standards of cuisine and service seem to yo-yo. **The River Rock Grill**, **t** +1 800 766 0449, at the Glacier Creek Lodge, is a good self-service ('check out the Asian broth and stir fry'). **Monks Grill**, **t** +1 604 932 9677, in the Upper Village, is recommended.

Dine

Some truly excellent restaurants – from fab sashimi to classic French, and everything in between. If you self-cater, the local supermarket will deliver. In Whistler Village, **Bearfoot Bistro**, **t** +1 604 932 3433, specializes in French and other European cuisine ('up to CDN$200–300 per head'). **Il Caminetto di Umberto**, **t** +1 604 932 4442, and **Trattoria di Umberto**, **t** +1 604 932 5858, are Italian. **Après**, **t** +1 604 935 0200, has Pacific Rim cuisine. **Zueski's Taverna**, **t** +1 604 932 6009, is Greek. **Teppan Village**, **t** +1 604 932 2223, is a Japanese steakhouse. Reporters recommend **Earl's**, **t** +1 604 935 3222 ('plentiful but not cheap'), and **The Keg**, **t** +1 604 932 5151, for steaks, as well as **21 Steps**, **t** +1 604 966 2121, for home-cooked food. If you have a large budget, try **Quatro**, **t** +1 604 905 4844, **Araxi**, **t** +1 604 932 4540, and **Hy's Steakhouse**, **t** +1 604 905 5555. The food in Hy's is superb, but expensive. In Upper Village, try **La Rua**, **t** +1 604 932 5011, for West Coast cuisine, or **Thai One On**, **t** +1 604 932 4822, for Thai. In Whistler Village North, **Sushi-Ya**, **t** +1 604 905 0155, has great food. **Ciao-Thyme Bistro**, **t** +1 604 932 9795, looks like a bikers' café, but is anything but. **Elements**, t +1 808 913 1133, is an acclaimed eatery in the Summit Lodge.

In Whistler Creek, the **Rim Rock Café**, **t** +1 604 932 5565, has seafood and fine European dishes. **Zen Whistler, t** +1 604 932 3667, is Japanese.

COLD COMFORTS
WHISTLER CANADA
SKI HOLIDAYS
Whistler Ski Holiday Specialists
Early Booking Offers Include:
Free Nights
Free Days Skiing
Free Day Ski Guiding
Tailor-make your Whistler Holiday!
Call: 0800 881 8429
www.cold-comforts.com

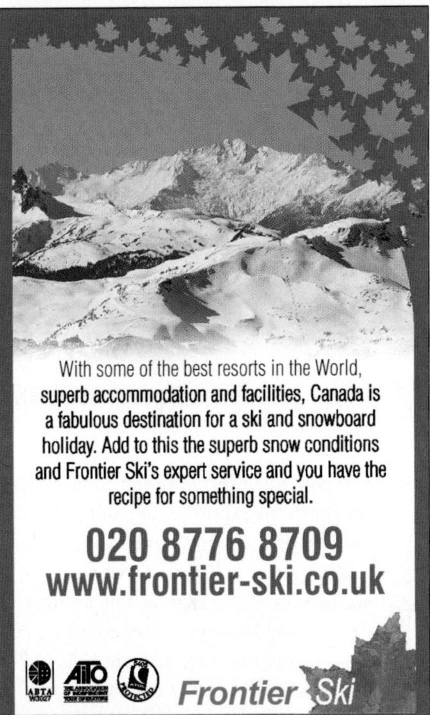
With some of the best resorts in the World, superb accommodation and facilities, Canada is a fabulous destination for a ski and snowboard holiday. Add to this the superb snow conditions and Frontier Ski's expert service and you have the recipe for something special.
020 8776 8709
www.frontier-ski.co.uk
Frontier Ski

Chalet-hotel Salana
Ski Miquel offers an eclectic range of Resorts all around Europe from the exclusive Baqueira to the well known Alpe dHuez. Specialising in en-suite chalet-hotels offering excellent accommodation with wonderful food including wine & coffee, six day ski guiding programme, well timed flights.
Featured Resort- Baqueira Spain from only £460 including flight, transfer, half board.
Fly to Toulouse, enjoy the direct 2hr transfer to resort, stay in our luxurious accommodation, with hot tub, and ski perfectly groomed slopes in one of Europes best kept secrets.
Tel. 01457 821200
Ski MIQUEL
73, High Street, Uppermill, Saddleworth, OL3 6AP
email: ski@miquelhols.co.uk www.miquelhols.co.uk

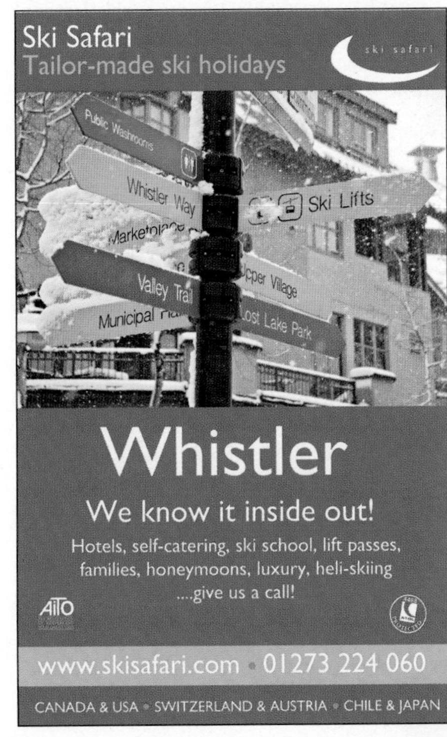
Ski Safari
Tailor-made ski holidays
ski safari
Public Washrooms
Whistler Way
Ski Lifts
Valley Trail
Upper Village
Lost Lake Park
Whistler
We know it inside out!
Hotels, self-catering, ski school, lift passes, families, honeymoons, luxury, heli-skiing
....give us a call!
www.skisafari.com 01273 224 060
CANADA & USA • SWITZERLAND & AUSTRIA • CHILE & JAPAN

Party

'The après ski will not have you dancing on the tables in your ski clobber until 4am,' said a reader. That said, a wide range of clubs, pubs and bars cater for all but the wackiest tastes. Après-ski begins noisily
at the **Dubh Linn Gate** Irish pub, and **Longhorn**, at the base of the Excalibur and Whistler Village gondolas. **Garibaldi Lift Co** in Whistler and **Merlin's** at Blackcomb base have live bands. **The Amsterdam** is worth a look as well. Shopping – which continues until 10pm – is a core part of the evening entertainment. Zip-wiring is an alternative sport in Whistler and an exhilarating way to spend an afternoon.

Later on the action switches to **Garfinkel's**, the **Savage Beagle**, **Tommy Africa's** and **Maxx Fish**. **Moe Joes's** is smaller and more intimate. **Buffalo Bill's** attracts the over-30s. **Citta's Bar** in the Village Square is a friendly hangout for a quiet drink. The **Mallard Bar** in the Château Whistler is more sophisticated and expensive.

Sleep

Luxury:

Fairmont Château Whistler, t +1 604 938 8000, *www.fairmont.com/whistler*, is one of the world's great ski hotels, right on the piste at Blackcomb base, with a good restaurant, heated outdoor pools and an outstanding Vida spa.

The Four Seasons Resort, t +1 604 935 3400, *www.fourseasons.com/whistler*, is slightly less well positioned but a true contender for Whistler's most luxurious hotel. 'What a fantastic experience it was. Pampered? Definitely, but it was lovely,' said a reader.

The Westin Resort & Spa, t +1 604 905 5000, *www.westinwhistler.com*, at Whistler Mountain base, has a shopping mall and is conveniently located.

Adara Hotel, t +1 604 905 4009, *www.adarahotel.com*, is a boutique hotel with contemporary design.

Whistler Chalets, t +1 604 905 5287, *www.whistlerchalets.com*, has a portfolio of luxury self-catering homes.

Moderate:

Delta Whistler Village Suites, t +1 604 905 3987, *www.deltahotels.com*, has a rustic mountain atmosphere. Hy's Steakhouse and Garfunkel's nightclub are both located here. 'Accommodation in Delta Whistler Village Suites was really good – far superior to anything in France for similar money,' said a reporter.

Pan Pacific Mountainside t +1 604 905 2999, *www.panpacificwhistler.com*, and **Pan Pacific Village Centre, t** +1 604 966 5500, are both comfortable, with fireplaces and floor-to-ceiling windows.

Crystal Lodge, t +1 604 932 2221, *www.crystal-lodge.com*, is a boutique hotel that is conveniently located.

Listel Whistler Hotel, t +1 604 932 1133, *www.listelhotel.com*, has a heated outdoor pool and is a short walk from the shops. The Bearfoot Bistro is within the hotel.

Summit Lodge, t +1 888 913 8811, *www.summitlodge.com*, in the heart of Whistler Village North, has a spa and free in-room yoga.

Budget:

Alpine Springs B&B, t +1 604 905 2747, *www.bc-bed-and-breakfast.com*, is in a peaceful setting.

Blue Spruce Lodge B&B, t +1 604 932 3508, *www.bluesprucelodgewhistler.com*, sleeps 8–10 people and is good value.

04

The Top Resorts: Eastern Europe

Bansko, Bulgaria

***BEST FOR**
Beginners and intermediates, value

ESSENTIALS
Altitude: 936m (3,079ft)–2560m (8,399ft)
Further information: t +359 (0)7443 8060, *www.banskoski.com*
Lifts in area: 14 (1 cableway, 7 chairs, 6 drags) serving 70km of piste
Lift pass: adult €144, child up to 12yrs €79.25, both for six days
Access: Sofia airport 160km

Profile

Best-developed ski resort in Eastern Europe, an attractive old town with a modern lift system and hotels of international standard

Resort

Bansko, previously better known for its school of Orthodox icon painting than for its pistes, is now Boomtown Bulgaria, much the most successful and challenging resort in Eastern Europe – and, thanks to an investment of €130 million by a Sofia-based consortium, the only one to have a modern lift system.

What began in the 1980s as a one-lift ski resort in the Pirin Mountains has been transformed in recent years into the ski capital of the Wild East. Foreign investors, spearheaded by the British, have rushed here to buy bargain-priced apartments for holidays and rental income.

A modest €130,000 secures a luxurious two-bedroom apartment by the base of the lifts, provided that you can locate your plot among the cranes and burgeoning concrete shells that blot the landscape.

However, just how profitable – or even secure – these investments are remains to be seen. A report by the Worldwide Fund for Nature claims that two-thirds of the construction is 'essentially illegal' as the building work has been carried out on land that is part of the sacrosanct Pirin National Park. Certainly it would appear that far too much has been built too soon. Until this is resolved, we would suggest a cautious approach to buying.

Reporters complained at the sheer scale of the development. 'Bankso really is a building site – the place is a mess, full of potholed streets, no pavements, and wasteground with rubbish lying around. The old town is not quaint, it's simply older but still as grim a location.'

At peak times you can expect to wait an hour for the gondola that provides the main means of mountain access ('queues, queues, queues, and I mean London rush hour queues! Lifts were packed and slopes were the same – totally full up'). However, you can now drive up to the mid-station where a large car park has been built.

Unlike Borovets, the mountains here are perfectly shaped for snowsports, with the kind of awe-inspiring terrain that befits a future Les Arcs. The resort has a long season that usually runs from mid-December until mid-April.

Investment has been sufficient to encourage the building of a British-designed golf course and the five-star Grand Arena Hotel, which is managed by the German Kempinski group. Plenty of other less exalted, but clean and cheerful, accommodation can be found in the old town with its cobbled streets. Walking along those streets is like entering a scene from *The Third Man*. Ancient houses – most of them ripe for renovation – give the place a time-warped character. It's icy underfoot and you have to watch out for potholes and the odd gaping drain.

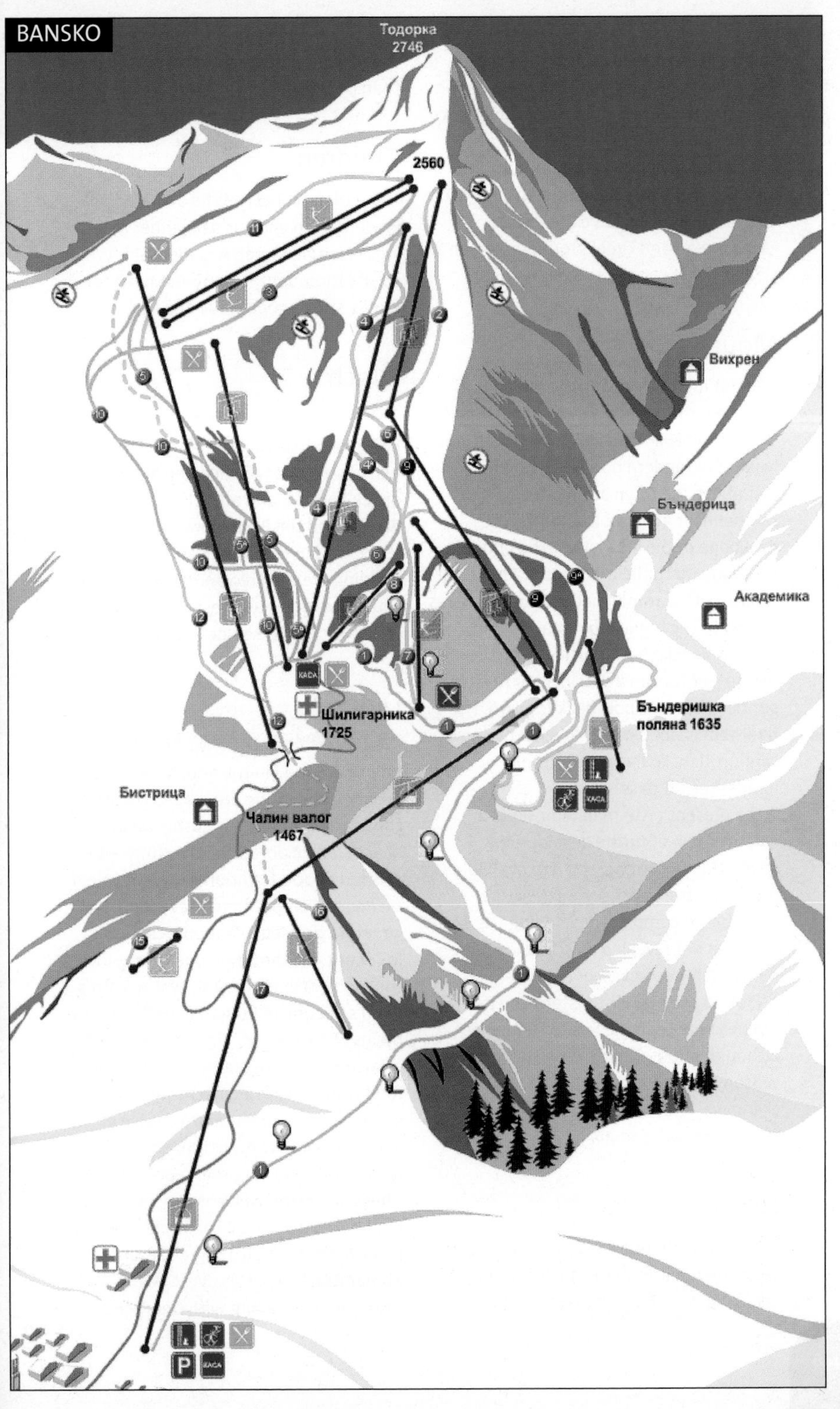
BANSKO
Тодорка
2746
2560
Вихрен
Бъндерица
Академика
Шилигарника
1725
Бъндеришка
поляна 1635
Бистрица
Чалин валог
1467

In the days of the Ottoman Empire, Bansko was an important staging post on the caravan route from Constantinople to Thessaloniki. The downside to any visit here is the tedious two-and-a-half-hour journey southwards on bone-jarring roads from Sofia. Bansko lies close to the Macedonian and Greek frontiers, and on a clear day you can see the Aegean Sea.

Mountain

To put it into a Western perspective, the ski area is of a similar size to Alpbach and larger than Niederau in Austria. A new 'village' of modern hotels is being built just above the town around the Doppelmayr gondola that forms the backbone of the lift system. The gondola takes you up to the mid-mountain area at 1725m, where a small network of lifts takes you on to the highest point at 2560m. At present Bansko has a vertical drop of 1100m – or 1600m if you include the long, gentle coast-and-pole back to town. The final 7km is floodlit and covered by snow-cannon. Bansko has an electronic hands-free lift pass.

The present piste map represents a creative view of future development rather than a current record of available mountain transport. So far, Ulen, the Sofia-based company developing the ski area, has not revealed any detailed plan for a much-needed second gondola.

'I found the main lift system and its queues unacceptable,' stated a reporter, although another said: 'We visited in low season and had a fabulous time. The skiing was great for intermediates and it was not crowded at all.'

Learn

The **Ulen school**, **t** +359 (0)7443 8060, is recommended, with most instructors speaking good English ('ski school was excellent, although groups were bigger than previously').

Children

The **Ulen school** runs its own ski kindergarten and has a beginner area with a magic carpet. A reader said, 'We would thoroughly recommended it for family skiing, good value and fun.'

Lunch

Mountain restaurants, **t** +359 (0)7443 8049 for all, serving simple local dishes at reasonable prices are located at the foot of the gondola and at mid-mountain. **Bla-Bla** and the **Bachvite** waiter-service restaurant in the Banderishka Polyana building are both recommended. A two-course lunch for two costs around £12 including a bottle of local wine.

Dine

Reporters repeatedly warned that half-board food in the hotels was to be avoided, but eating out was so cheap that this was no financial hardship ('great food at very reasonable prices'). Eating out is centred on 100 traditional taverns called *mehanas*. Competition is keen, and 'greeters' dressed in national costume loiter outside the larger ones. Once inside, the ambience is invariably warm, with a good selection of Bulgarian wines. Hearty meals of barbecued lamb and assorted offal are not for the faint-hearted. 'The food was mixed,' said a reporter. 'We had some fantastic meals and a couple of awful ones in the more touristy restaurants,' said another reporter, and 'the food, on the whole is very poor quality, mostly served cold,' said another. **Beli Noshti**, **t** +359 (0)7443 5088, and **Kamenitsa**, **t** +359 (0)7443 4635, are recommended, along with **Georgeo's**

Pizzeria, **t** + 359 (0)7443 2948, **Steak House**, **t** +359 (0)7443 2416, and **Come Prima** in the Kempinski, **t** +359 (0)7443 8933, which has gourmet Italian cuisine.

Party

Happy End and **The Lions Pub**, at the gondola end of town, are Bansko's best shots at international après-ski. More traditional Bulgarian entertainment is to be found in the *mehanas*, which offer live folk music. The best include **Dedo Pene**, **Motikata**, **Kassapinova Kashta**, **Kadiyata**, **Molerite**, **Bai Koce** and **Baryakova Mehana**. The **Torino** cabaret bar attracts smart Sofian weekenders. **Amnesia** and **No Name** are the most popular clubs.

Sleep

*****Kempinski Grand Arena**, **t** +359 (0)7443 8933, *www.kempinski.com*, is a smart place opposite the gondola station. It has an indoor pool, spa and two restaurants. 'First class and does a wicked club sandwich,' said a reader.

****Hotel Avalon**, **t** +359 (0)7498 8399, *http://avalon.bansko.bg*, is British-run and a great place to stay, with friendly staff, reasonable prices and a short walk to the gondola.

****Hotel Bansko**, **t** +359 (0)7443 8054, *www.hotelbansko.bansko.bg*, is popular with the locals and has huge rooms with intricate wood-carved ceilings.

****Hotel Bulgaria**, **t** +359 (0)7498 8010, *www.hotelbulgariabansko.com*, has very good rooms, reasonable food and a pool.

****Hotel Glazne**, **t** +359 (0)7443 8021, *www.glazne.bansko.bg*, has a sports centre, and separate villas for families.

****Lion Hotel**, **t** +359 7443 6800, *www.hotelslion.com*, combines local craftsmanship with modern furnishings and was rated excellent, with very good bed and breakfast.

****Hotel Perun**, **t** +359 (0)7498 8477, *www.hotelperunbansko.com*, is in the town centre, 10 minutes from the gondola. 'Good accommodation but the evening food was dull' said a reporter.

****Hotel Strazhite**, **t** +359 (0)7443 8117, *www.banskoski.com*, has a pool and a bowling alley.

****Hotel Tanne**, **t** +359 (0)7443 8100, *www.hotel-tanne.com*, is decorated in authentic Bulgarian style. Its Tavern restaurant has live music.

Hotel Zornitza, **t** +359 7443 8200, is in the old town and offers clean, cheerful and friendly accommodation.

Bohinj, Slovenia

Profile

Beginner and limited intermediate skiing in a retro-Austrian atmosphere with beautiful scenery, low prices, excellent tuition and a high standard of food and hotels

Resort

Bohinj is pronounced 'Bocking' and lies just 27km beyond the beautiful lakeside town of Bled, dominated by a fairytale castle and an island church. This is the most entertaining of Slovenia's 26 ski areas. Slovenia is reminiscent of Austria 20 years ago. Imagine a ski holiday in quaint traditional alpine surroundings where a lift pass costs €25 a day, a three-course meal with wine €18, and a beer €2.

✻BEST FOR
Beginners, low intermediates, value for money

ESSENTIALS
Altitude: 512m (1,680ft)–1800m (5,905ft)
Further information: **Vogel, t** +386 (0)4572 4236, **Kobla, t** +386 (0)4574 7100, *www.bohinj.si*
Lifts in area: 18 (1 cableway, 7 chairs, 10 drags) serving 65km of piste
Lift pass: adult €147.30, child €103, both for six days
Access: Ljubljana airport 1hr

Mountain

Bohinj's three ski areas are a 10-minute drive apart in the mountains above Lake Bohinj. Vogel, at the eastern end of the lake, is reached by a cable car, which rises from the far end of Lake Bohinj. The 18km area is larger than statistics suggest; you can ski around the shoulder of the mountain down to the cable car station.

Kobla, the country's original ski resort, is our favourite. Its three antiquated double chairlifts add to its charm as you rise from the village to the mountaintop.

The long, steep run down the front face has the pedigree of the FIS downhill course it once was. The third little area of Soriska Planina has three draglifts and 3km of nursery slopes.

Learn

Schools **Vogel, t** +386 (0)4572 1451, **Kobla, t** +386 (0)4574 7100, and **Soriska Planina, t** +386 (0)4511 7835, all offer friendly tuition at a low price.

Children

No special facilities.

Lunch

Mountain huts in Vogel and Kobla provide a good range of hot dishes. **Vogel Bar, t** +386 (0)5063 7921, is recommended.

Dine

Rupa, t +386 (0)4572 3401, at Srednja Vas, has good home-cooked food. **Erlah, t** +386 (0)4572 3309, at the Vogel end of the lake, is renowned for its fresh trout and *strukljі* (filled buckwheat dumplings).

Party

Bohinj has a few bars that liven up at weekends. Bled has a disco and a casino.

Sleep

Bohinj:

- ★★★★**Hotel Bohinj, t** +386 (0)4572 6000, *www.alpinum.net*, is recommended.
- ★★★★**Hotel Jezero, t** +386 (0)4572 9100, *www.bohinj.si*, overlooks the lake and is convenient for both main ski areas.
- ★★★**Hotel Zlatorog, t** +386 (0)4572 3381, is in a beautiful setting near the lake.

Bled:

- ★★★★★**Grand Hotel Toplice, t** +386 (0)4579 1000, *www.hotel-toplice.com*, is a traditional hotel.
- ★★★★**Vila Bled, t** +386 (0)4579 1500, has an intimate atmosphere.

Borovets, Bulgaria

Profile

Unimaginative food and an antiquated lift system are offset by an appealing forest setting, low prices, a lively nightlife and good beginner instruction

✻ BEST FOR
Beginners, value

ESSENTIALS
Altitude: 1323m (4,339ft)–2540m (8,333ft)
Further information: t +359 (0)2 91133, *www.bulgariaski.com*
Lifts in area: 13 (1 cableway, 3 chairs, 9 drags) serving 52km of piste
Lift pass: adults €146, child €88
Access: Sofia airport 1hr

Resort

Borovets is the oldest resort in Bulgaria. Skiing started here as long ago as 1896, and cynics would argue that the lift system has scarcely improved since. The village was originally the site of a hunting lodge of the Bulgarian royal family. It is situated in a pine forest at the foot of Mount Moussala, 73km from Sofia.

It developed into a ski resort in the 1970s and, after the fall of Communism in Eastern Europe, Borovets looked set to attract overseas investment. But it never happened, and now Bansko has stolen its title of top ski destination in Bulgaria. However, development there has finally acted as a spur here. Two new chairlifts and an access gondola have been built, and plans to develop the satellite of Super Borovets are slowly taking shape.

Despite its mountain shortcomings, Borovets has a lively atmosphere and continues to attract a large number of overseas skiers from Britain in particular. Many of these are people who proclaim that they would not ski anywhere else. 'An affordable and unpretentious resort,' said a reporter, 'I was pleasantly surprised and find it difficult to relate to some of the negative reviews that appear.'

Mountain

The antiquated lift system is headed by an ageing gondola and an assortment of chairlifts and venerable draglifts. Inevitably, high season lift queues are irritatingly long, though overall it is a very good destination for beginners to intermediates. The skiing is divided into two separate sectors, linked by a long walk on an ice-rutted road. The Markoudjik sector, reached by a 1970s gondola, offers the best of the resort's skiing, which is mainly above the tree-line with a highest ski point of 2540m. All the nursery slopes are located at the base of the separate Martinovi Baraki area. In good conditions there is plenty of off-piste, including low-cost heli-skiing.

Learn

Borosport Ski School, t +359 (0)7128 2441, has a strong reputation for teaching the basics in a friendly and efficient manner. 'Bobi from Boro Sport was the most patient instructor, he always listened to our fears and was really fun,' said a reporter.

Children

The ski school's **Borosport Ski School & Day Care, t** +359 (0)7128 2441, in the Rila Hotel, accepts non-skiers from 12 months to four years old and skiers from four to eight years.

Lunch

There are a couple of snack bars on the mountain – but it is best to return to the resort.

Dine

'Food and drink is very reasonably priced, but don't expect top quality nosh,' commented a reader. 'Eating out was an interesting experience. What with all the touts trying to get you into their restaurants, the whole experience becomes very trying. But you have the consolation of wide-screen TV showing Sky Sports Premier League football every night in almost every restaurant,' said another. Small restaurants abound serving burgers, pasta and pizzas as well as Bulgarian fare, Turkish and Chinese cuisine. Chips are big here in Bulgaria's biggest potato-growing region. Try the **Hungry Horse**, **Mamacita's**, **Franco's**, **Blue Café** and **White Magic**.

Party

The **Buzz Bar** is the main rendezvous, and the **Happy Duck** is recommended: 'The band was absolutely fantastic and the whole place bursting at the seams.' **Chilli Peppers Bar & Food** has parties from 4pm and karaoke. The **Samakov** and **Rila** hotels have clubs. Happy Hour cocktails are 'an absolute must'.

Sleep

Contact, T +359 (0)2 91133, *www.bulgariaski.com*, for all.

★★★★**Ice Angels Hotel** is one of the smartest hotel in Borovets, situated in the centre.

★★★★**Samokov Hotel** has a pool, bowling alley and nightclub. Food is plentiful, but rooms could do with refurbishment.

★★★★**St George Hotel** is a new hotel in a peaceful setting in the pine forest yet close enough to the lifts.

★★★★**Hotel Rila** is convenient for the skiing. ('Perfectly adequate with good-sized rooms, clean towels every day and an excellent maid service. The food was a little basic but there was plenty of it.')

★★★**Hotel Flora** is 'nice and comfortable, apart from the nightly dog-barking sessions outside,' according to one unhappy reader.

★★★**The Lodge Hotel** is the resort's first boutique hotel.

Poiana Brasov, Romania

Profile

Budget beginner skiing with competent, friendly tuition, blighted by a primitive lift system. High standard of hotels and unlimited nightlife in nearby Brasov

Resort

Poiana Brasov opened as a ski resort in 1906 and has slowly grown into a small town at the foot of 1799m Mount Postavaru in the Carpathian mountains. It lies a 13km drive up a mountain road from the attractive medieval town of Brasov with its famous Black Church, Romania's most important cathedral.

Beautiful surroundings, a high standard of accommodation and cuisine and the friendliness of the people make this one of our favourite destinations in Eastern Europe. However, snowfall is variable.

'If you're looking for a different location, fantastic scenery, fascinating local history, extremely good ski schools, and don't mind roughing it a bit – then perhaps Poiana is worth a go,' said a reporter.

A new international airport is under construction nearby and is scheduled to open in 2009. A new road is also being built from Bucharest.

Mountain

This a pleasant beginner and lower intermediate area for anyone who wants

***BEST FOR**

Beginners, value, hectic nightlife

ESSENTIALS

Altitude: 1021m (3,350ft)–1775m (5,823ft)
Further information: **t** +40 (0)286 417 866, *www.poiana-brasov.com*
Lifts in area: 8 (3 cableways, 5 drags) serving 14km of piste
Lift pass: adult €95, child 6–12yrs €57, both for six days
Access: Bucharest airport 186km

to get to grips with the basics without breaking the bank.

Mount Postavaru is accessed by a gondola and two ancient cable cars. Nursery slopes are located by the Sport and Bradul hotels.

Learn

'For the beginner, there is a nice selection of suitable slopes,' said a reader. The six ski schools teach modern technique and are all of a similar high standard. They are: **Ana Hotels**, **t** +40 (0)268 407 330, **Club Montana Schi**, **t** +40 (0)722 269 411, **Euro Inter Ski**,a **t** +40 (0)268 151 735, **Impera International**, **t** +40 (0)744 321 065, **Poiana SA**, **t** +40 (0)268 262 310, and **Valona Tour**, **t** +40 (0)722 269 411.

Children

All schools take children from four years. Non-skiing activities include tobogganing, paintballing in the woods, and excursions to Dracula's Castle and to Peles Castle at Sinaia.

Lunch

Two mountain restaurants, **Cristianu Mare** and **Postavaru**, serve pizzas, burgers, soup and sandwiches at low prices.

Dine

In Poiana Brasov, **Sura Dacilor**, **t** +40 (0)268 262 327, has Romanian cuisine and folk music. **Coliba Haiducilor**, **t** +40 (0)268 262 1370, also known as the **Outlaws' Hut**, has barbecued bear and traditional dancing. **Vanatorul**, **t** +40 (0)268 262 3540, serves venison, pheasant and wild boar.

In Brasov, **Le Stradivari**, **t** +40 (0)268 476 945, is Italian and specializes in seafood. **Pepper Jack**, **t** +40 (0)268 417 349, has Mexican and Transylvanian cuisine.

Party

'Don't expect lots of lively après-ski; those cosy bars elsewhere seem a world away here,' warned a reporter. In Poiana the **Ciucas**, **Alpin**, **Bradul** and **Poiana** hotel bars are the liveliest. In Brasov, try **Festival 39**, **Cabana** and **Blue Night**. **Blitz** is the hippest late-night spot. Other discos are **Pro-Club**, **Hacienda** and **No Problem**.

Sleep

★★★**Alpin Hotel**, **t** +40 (0)268 262 111, has a pool and a gym, and offers excellent service and good food.

★★★**Hotel Miruna**, **t** +40 (0)268 262 120, *www.mirunahotel.ro*, built four years ago, is recommended.

★★★**Piatra Mare**, **t** +40 (0)268 262 029, *www.piatramare.ro*, has split-level suites with Jacuzzis.

★★★**Sport Hotel**, **t** +40 (0)268 407 330, *www.anahotels.ro*, is convenient for the nursery slopes.

★★★**Tirol Hotel**, **t** +40 (0)268 262 460, has a good restaurant.

★★**Hotel Bradul**, **t** +40 (0)268 407 330, *www.anahotels.ro*, adjoins the Sport Hotel and is well located.

05

The Top Resorts: France

SKI FRANCE FOR LESS

Great value ski breaks to

Alpe d'Huez
Avoriaz
Chamonix
La Tania
Les Arcs 1800
Les Arcs 1950
Les Ménuires
Morzine
Méribel Valley
Tignes
Val Thorens
Val d'Isère

directski.com
THE WINTER HOLIDAY COMPANY

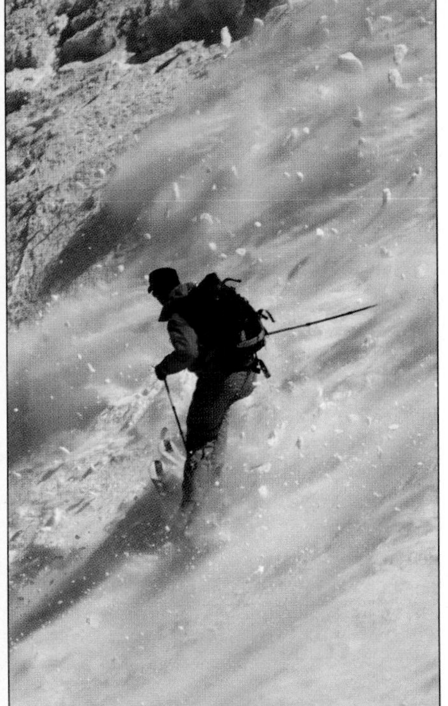

Val d'Isere, Courchevel & Paradiski

• 24 chalets for 6 - 20 people
• Flights from Gatwick, Manchester & Edinburgh to Chambery
• Tailor made weekends & short breaks
• Our 27th season

FINLAYS

AITO 1056

01573 226611

4828 ATOL PROTECTED

www.finlayski.com

Alpe d'Huez

*** BEST FOR**
All standards of skier and rider, eating out

Profile

A large architectural hotpotch with plenty of high-altitude, snow-sure skiing. The lift system extends to some smaller and more pleasing resorts in neighbouring valleys

ESSENTIALS

Altitude: 1120m (3,674ft)–3330m (10,922ft)
Further information: t +33 (0)4 76 11 44 44, *www.alpedhuez.com*
Lifts in area: 81 (16 cableways, 25 chairs, 40 drags) serving 237km of piste
Lift pass: area (covers linked resorts, 2 days in Les Deux Alpes, 1 day in La Grave, the Milky Way, Puy-St-Vincent and Serre Chevalier) adult €203, child 5–15yrs €145, both for six days
Access: Grenoble airport 1½hrs, Lyon airport 2hrs

Resort

Alpe d'Huez is one of France's oldest resorts and is the hub of the fifth-largest ski circuit in the country. Back in 1936, a young engineer called Pomagalski invented the draglift here just days ahead of a rival in Davos. It was also a venue for the 1968 Winter Olympics. However, Alpe d'Huez is better known to millions of cycling fans each July when the 21-bend approach road becomes one of the most energy-sapping climbs of the Tour de France.

Over the years the resort has grown without design along a sunny balcony above the beautiful Oisans Valley. Lifts link the various sectors of the village, which provides a utilitarian base for some excellent skiing for all standards.

Alpe d'Huez stirs up mixed emotions. 'Such a nice friendly resort,' commented a reporter, but another said it was 'not as unsightly as many guidebooks claim, though it does lack alpine charm. The endless ski lifts in every direction through the village seem somewhat unthought out.'

Mountain

Alpe d'Huez is one of the wise resorts that a few years ago started responding to the threat of global warming – and this has paid huge dividends. The lift company took the decision to develop the summer ski area on the glacier above the resort. The plan was to ensure that, even in the worst winters, skiers and riders would have plenty of snow-sure terrain at high altitude. Not, of course, that this mattered last season.

Two quad-chairs serve long runs on the glacier, which can be reached by an extension of the Marmottes gondola at one end of the resort and by the Pic Blanc cable car at the other. Skiers and riders must return to mid-mountain by lift unless they are capable of descending the notoriously difficult and often icy Tunnel run down the front face or the 16km Sarenne that leads into the Sarenne Gorge below the resort.

'A good all-round resort with something for everyone,' was how one reporter summed it up. Alpe d'Huez-based skiers tend to congregate on the easy and intermediate runs directly above the resort, which are served by gondolas from either end. In fact the best skiing is to be found off both sides leading down to the neighbouring villages of Oz, Vaujany and Auris-en-Oisans, as well as the lower satellites of Villard-Reculas and Huez.

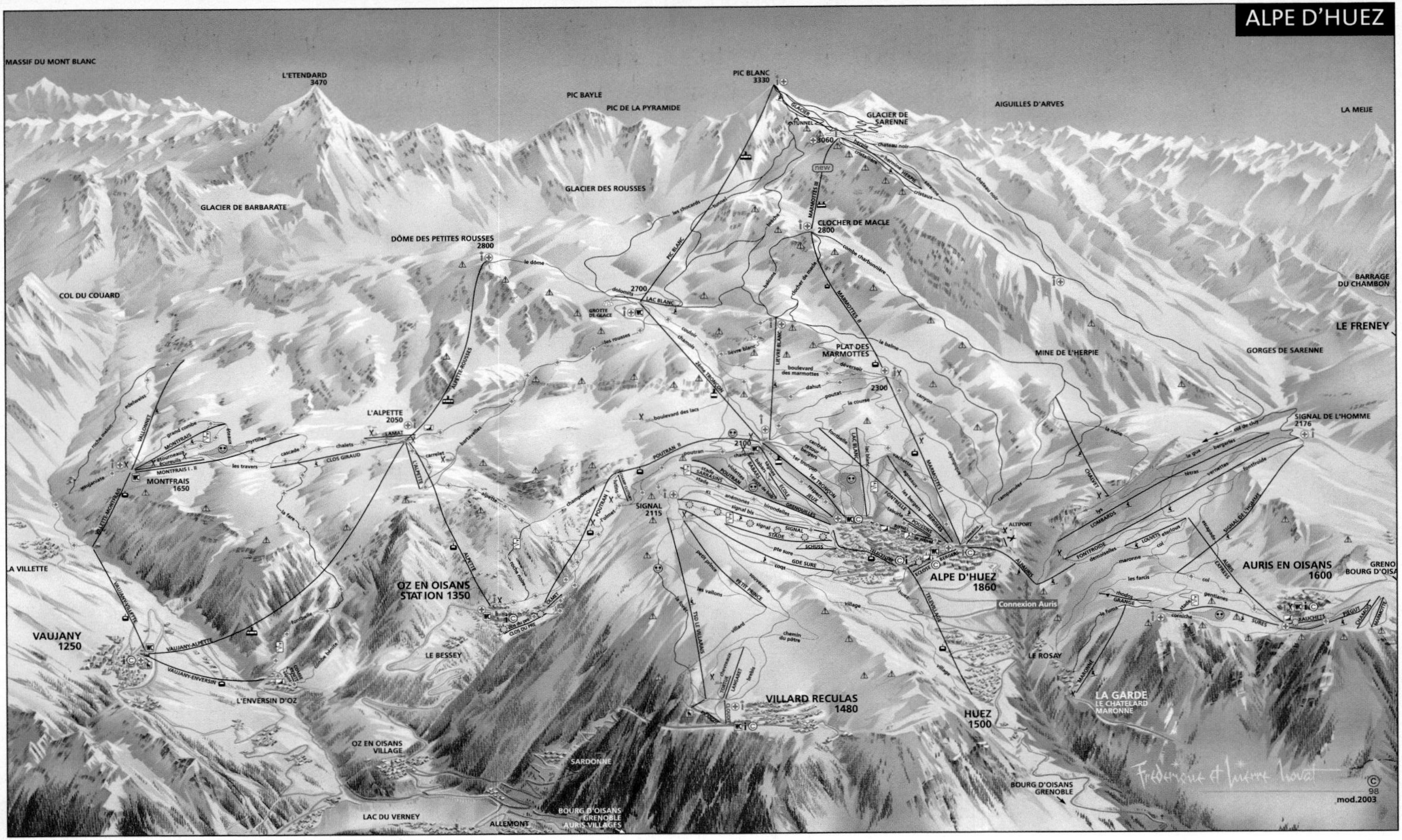

ALPE D'HUEZ

MASSIF DU MONT BLANC
L'ETENDARD 3470
PIC BAYLE
PIC DE LA PYRAMIDE
PIC BLANC 3330
AIGUILLES D'ARVES
LA MEIJE
GLACIER DE SARENNE
GLACIER DES ROUSSES
GLACIER DE BARBARATE
CLOCHER DE MACLE 2800
DÔME DES PETITES ROUSSES 2800
COL DU COUARD
BARRAGE DU CHAMBON
LE FRENEY
GORGES DE SARENNE
MINE DE L'HERPIE
PLAT DES MARMOTTES
2300
2700
L'ALPETTE 2050
2100
SIGNAL DE L'HOMME 2176
MONTFRAIS 1650
SIGNAL 2115
LA VILLETTE
OZ EN OISANS STATION 1350
ALPE D'HUEZ 1860
AURIS EN OISANS 1600
GRENO
BOURG D'OISA
Connexion Auris
VAUJANY 1250
LE BESSEY
LE ROSAY
L'ENVERSIN D'OZ
VILLARD RECULAS 1480
LA GARDE
LE CHATELARD
MARONNE
HUEZ 1500
OZ EN OISANS VILLAGE
SARDONNE
BOURG D'OISANS GRENOBLE
LAC DU VERNEY
ALLEMONT
BOURG D'OISANS GRENOBLE AURIS VILLAGES
© 98 mod.2003

The 3330m Pic Blanc is the starting point for a number of off-piste itineraries. These include the Grand Sablat, the Combe du Loup and a long, tricky descent via the Couloir de Fare. A 20-minute climb from the cable car station takes you to the top of La Pyramide. From here you can ski more than 2000m of vertical down to Vaujany. Alpe d'Huez has a half-pipe on the Signal piste as well as a terrain park at Plat des Marmottes. Slopes immediately above the resort tend to become seriously overcrowded during peak periods. A reporter recommended: 'get away from the main bowl down into Vaujany and Villard Reculas – much less crowded,' and 'The piste grooming was economic to say the least,' said another.

Learn

The **ESF, t** +33 (0)4 76 80 94 23, has a number of English-speaking instructors and receives glowing comments: 'The head of the ski school in the Les Bergers sector was simply the best I have ever encountered anywhere in 30 years of skiing,' and 'instruction was first class,' said another. The **ESI, t** +33 (0)4 76 80 42 77, offers smaller classes and tuition in English, while **British Masterclass, t** +33 (0)4 76 80 93 83, is highly recommended. 'I had six hours of tuition for the same price as 16 hours with other schools, but loved every minute of it.' Guiding is available through the **Bureau des Guides, t** +33 (0)4 76 80 42 55, while **SAF Isère Heliskiing, t** +33 (0)4 76 80 65 49, will pick you up at the end of day ski tours into neighbouring valleys.

Children

The **ESF, t** +33 (0)4 76 80 94 23, accepts children from four years and guarantees 10 or fewer pupils per class. 'Our eldest children were in all-day ski school and made lots of progress,' said a reader. The **ESI, t** +33 (0)4 76 80 42 77, teaches children from three and a half, and **Les Eterlous, t** +33 (0)4 76 80 67 85, alternates skiing and games for little ones from two and a half years. **Les Crapouilloux, t** +33 (0)4 76 11 39 23, is a crèche for children from two and a half years. **Les Intrépides, t** +33 (0)4 76 11 21 61, is the alternative for non-skiers aged six months to three years.

Lunch

'Eating on the mountain is varied depending on how much you want to pay,' said a reader. **La Cabane du Poutat, t** +33 (0)4 76 80 42 88, beneath the Marmottes gondola, has a serious gourmet menu. **La Bergerie, t** +33 (0)4 76 80 36 83, on the way down to Villard-Reculas, is an alpine museum with simple dishes. **Auberge de l'Alpette, t** +33 (0)4 76 80 70 00, above Oz, has the best omelettes and salads on the mountain. The **Chalet du Lac Besson, t** +33 (0)4 76 80 65 37, on the cross-country trail, has an open fireplace and a large sun terrace, though is perhaps not as good as it used to be. **L'Altibar, t** +33 (0)4 76 80 41 15, beside the altiport runway, is a local favourite. **La Fôret de Maronne, t** +33 (0)4 76 80 00 06, is worth a visit. **Le Signal, t** +33 (0)476 80 39 54, offers panoramic views. **Bonsoir Clara, t** +33 (0)4 76 80 37 20, at Villard-Reculas, is recommended.

Dine

Alpe d'Huez has a fine choice of eateries, although 'eating-out can be pricey,' complained a reporter. **Au P'tit Creux, t** +33 (0)4 76 80 62 83, is traditional and cosy, with friendly staff and gourmet food, while **Passe Montagne, t** +33 (0)4 76 11 31 53, is good value. **Les Caves, t** +33 (0)4 76 80 92 44, has fine food and wine.

Le Génépi, **t** +33 (0)4 76 80 36 22, was praised by reporters. **Lily Muldoon's**, **t** +33 (0)4 76 80 35 39, is an Irish restaurant with a popular following.

Party

Alpe d'Huez has a vibrant atmosphere, and après ski ('wicked nightlife') lasts well into the early hours at **The Underground** and **Le Sporting**. Others recommended include **Crowded House**, **Sphere Bar**, **Les Caves**, **Zoo Music Bar**, **Freeride Café** and **L'Etalon**. **Magoos**, the **O Bar**, **The Last Bar** and **O'Sharkeys** are also popular. Reporters recommend **Freeride**, **Etalon**, **Smithys** and **Sadoo**.

Sleep

- ★★★★**Chalets de l'Altiport t** +33 (0)4 79 65 07 65, *www.eurogroup-vacances.com*, is the newest and most luxurious chalet style property in the resort.
- ★★★★**Au Chamois d'Or t** +33 (0)4 76 80 31 32, *www.chamoisdor-alpedhuez.com*, is at the top of the village, with some delightful wood-panelled suites and a good spa.
- ★★★★**Pierre et Vacances Les Bergers**, **t** +33 (0)4 76 80 85 00, *www.pierreetvacances.com*, are the best apartments in the resort.
- ★★★**Le Christina**, **t** +33 (0)4 76 80 33 32, *www.lechristina-alpedhuez.com*, is a chalet-style building with a restaurant serving local cuisine.
- ★★★**Hôtel Le Pic Blanc**, **t** +33 (0)4 76 11 42 42, *www.hmc-hotels.com*, is a very welcoming place.
- ★★★**Le Printemps de Juliette**, **t** +33 (0)4 76 11 44 38, *www.leprintempsdejuliette.com*, is a delightful boutique hotel with just four rooms and four suites.
- ★★★**Les Alpages**, **t** +33 (0)4 76 11 07 99, *www.alpages-hotel.com*, is a charming chalet in the resort centre.

Les Arcs

Profile

Part of the giant Paradiski area that includes La Plagne, offering high-altitude skiing in purpose-built villages. Good terrain for all standards and abundant off-piste opportunities

Resort

Les Arcs was one of France's great new areas developed during the boom years at the end of the 1960s. This was a time when every Parisian and quite a few others flocked to the Alps for at least one week each winter in search of snow, sunshine and a shoebox-sized apartment they could call their own.

Local skier Robert Blanc conceived the idea of building a series of villages at different altitudes on the mountain above his home town of Bourg-St-Maurice. Ex-Olympic champion Emile Allais lent his name to the project and the first village of

✱ BEST FOR

All standards, ski convenience, big ski area, reliable snow-cover

ESSENTIALS

Altitude: 1200m (2,788ft)–3226m (10,581ft)
Further information: **t** +33 (0)4 79 07 12 57, *www.lesarcs.com*
Lifts in area: 141 in Paradiski (1 mountain railway, 16 cableways, 66 chairs, 58 drags) serving 425km of piste
Lift pass: Paradiski unlimited (covers linked Les Arcs/La Plagne area and one day in each of Val d'Isère/Tignes, Pralognan-La Vanoise, Les Saisies), adult €243, child 6–14yrs €182.50, both for 6 days
Access: Chambéry airport 2hrs, Lyon airport 2½hrs, Geneva airport 2½hrs, Bourg-St-Maurice station (for Eurostar) 15km, with buses and funicular to Arc 1600

paradiski
Savoie – France
Versant SUD / Champagny-en-Vanoise
MONT POURRI
GRANDE MOTTE
GRANDE CASSE
BELLECÔTE
3417 m
AIGUILLE ROUGE
3226 m
AIG. DU ST ESPRIT
GLACIER DU VARET
GLACIER DE LA CHIAUPE
GLACIER DE BELLECÔTE
LE TOUGNE
L'ALIET
AIGUILLE GRIVE
2732 m
ROCHE DE MIO
2700 m
POINTE DE FRIOLIN
AIG. ROUSSE
PORTE DU PARC
NATIONAL DE LA VANOISE
ROSUEL
GDE ROCHETTE
2505 m
LES VERDONS
2500 m
BECOIN
2594 m
COL DE FORCLE
2270 m
ARC 2000
ARC 1950
L'ARPETTE
2413 m
LES DEUX TÊTES
2260 m
VILLAROGER
1200 m
LE PLANAY
LE PRÉ
LES LANCHES
site de ski de fond
NANCROIX
LES RAUCHES
PLAN PEISEY
1600 m
VALLANDRY
1600 m
LE MOULIN
VANOISE EXPRESS
PEISEY NANCROIX
LE VILLARET
ARC 1800
ARC 1600
COURBATON
LES CHARMETTES
L'ARPETTE
2385 m
BELLE PLAGNE
2050 m
PLAGNE VILLAGES
2050 m
AIME LA PLAGNE
2100 m
PLAGNE CENTRE
1970 m
PLAGNE SOLEIL
2050 m
PLAGNE BELLECÔTE
1930 m
PLAN BOIS
PLAGNE 1800
LES COCHES
1450 m
MONTCHAVIN
1250 m
MONTORLIN
LES GRANGES
MONTRIGON
MONTVENIX
LE BÉRARD
LE MARTOREY
SEEZ
HAUTEVILLE GONDON
GONDON
LE VILLARD
LANDRY
LES GRANGES
L'ISÈRE
LA ROCHE
LES GRANGES
LES VILLARDS DE MACÔT
VILLARD DE SANGOT
MACÔT LA PLAGNE
SANGOT
PLAGNE MONTALBERT
1350 m
PLANCHAMP
MONTVILLIERS
MONTGILBERT
BELLENTRE
AIME
VERS MOÛTIERS
ALBERTVILLE
BOURG ST MAURICE
Frédérique et Pierre Novat
03
mod.04
LES ARCS
Les Arcs
Peisey Vallandry
la Plagne

Arc 1600 opened in 1968. Les Arcs has come a long way since then.

Villages at 1800 and 2000 were followed much more recently by the development of another at 1950. Intrawest, the giant North American resort developer, chose Les Arcs for the first of what are planned as a number of property-led commercial forays in the Alps.

Arc 1950 is the focal point of the whole resort, with a true village ambience. The last apartment building completed in 2008. It provides sympathetic architecture and reasonably priced apartments finished to a level not previously found in the French Alps. The next Intrawest project here is Edenarc, a new four-star complex of Savoyard-style apartments to be constructed just above Arc 1800 around an 'aqua-relaxation' area.

The timing of the initial construction coincided with the creation of Paradiski, the name given to the combined ski area of Les Arcs and adjoining La Plagne. Both resort lift companies are under the same ownership of the Compagnie des Alpes, who decided to link two of France's largest ski areas together to provide a rival to the Trois Vallées.

A reporter pointed out that being an Intrawest resort, there was a noticeable lack of competition among traders in Arc 1950. Two ski concessions had captured the entire market with accordingly high prices.

The other complaint was that the serviced apartments didn't have any provision for those attempting to provide the service. 'On most mornings, the slow lifts were often shared with waste carts or linen trolleys and as a result were too full to enter. On changeover day, the narrow corridors were so heavily congested with cleaning trolleys that moving suitcases became a real challenge.'

Mountain

Last season the Vanoise Express cable car that links Les Arcs and La Plagne was out of action. Hopefully it will reopen in December 2008.

The 425km of skiing in Paradiski covers every conceivable type of run, but most of it is given over to enjoyable red and blue motorway pistes that are ideal intermediate terrain. Long runs start above the tree-line and descend through the woods to outlying hamlets, and in good mid-winter conditions you can ski all the way down to Bourg-St-Maurice at 850m.

The easy pistes above Arc 1800, served by the Transarc gondola and a whole series of chairs spread across the mountainside, attract the crowds – but more enterprising skiers and riders will explore further afield.

A gondola and a cable car from Arc 2000 take you up to the 3226m Aiguille Rouge, the highest point in the ski area and starting point for some classic steep runs, including a 7km descent down to Le Planay or Le Pré.

The area is so large that even accomplished skiers must work at travelling by lift and piste in a single day from Le Pré at one end of Paradiski to Champagny-en-Vanoise at the other – and back again. Each of the Arc villages has its own dedicated nursery slopes, but the best are found at 1800.

Les Arcs is famous for its speed-skiing track above Arc 2000, the setting over the years for a number of world records. For a modest fee anyone is allowed to have a go from a lower starting point that keeps your speed down to a sensible level. Les Arcs was also a pioneer of snowboarding in Europe. The terrain park is situated between Arc 1800 and Arc 1600.

As one reporter summed it up, 'A vast ski area, superb variety of long runs for all levels, great snow. Enjoy.'

Learn

The **ESF**, t +33 (0)4 79 07 40 31, has a branch in each village. We recommend **ESI Arc Aventures, t** +33 (0)4 79 07 41 28, in Arc 1800, and **Spirit 1950, t** +33 (0)4 79 04 25 72, in Arc 1950. **Initial Snow, t** +33 (0)6 12 45 72 91, is a small school based in Bourg-St-Maurice, with meeting points in Les Arcs. **Privilege, t** +33 (0)4 79 07 23 38, is another small school in Arc 1800. **Darentasia, t** +33 (0)4 79 04 16 81, specializes in off-piste. Guiding can also be arranged through the **Bureau des Guides, t** +33 (0)4 79 07 71 19.

Children

In Arc 1600, **Hôtel La Cachette, t** +33 (0)4 79 07 70 50, cares for children from four months to two years and has a mini-club for under-12s. In Arc 1800, **Les Pommes des Pins, t** +33 (0)4 79 04 24 31, looks after children from 12 months to six years. In Arc 2000, **Les Marmottons, t** +33 (0)4 79 07 64 25, provides a mix of daycare and lessons, but not lunch. In the same satellite, **Garderie 2000, t** +33 (0)4 79 07 64 25, provides a mix of daycare and lessons, but not lunch. **The Cariboos Club, t** +33 (0)4 79 07 05 57, in Arc 1950, welcomes children from nine months to 13 years. **Spirit 1950, t** +33 (0)4 79 04 25 72, in Arc 1950, was said to be 'excellent, although no other English children were in the lessons'.

Lunch

Bélliou La Fumée, t +33 (0)4 79 07 29 130, is a 500-year-old hunting lodge in Pré-St-Esprit just below Arc 2000 where staff somehow manage to negotiate the ladder and higgledy-piggledy scattered tables to serve exquisite dishes. The **Aiguille Grive, t** +33 (0)4 79 07 43 97, has good food in a panoramic setting. **Chalet de Luigi, t** +33 (0)6 08 57 23 36, in Arc 1950, is renowned for its ham-based gourmet cuisine. **Les Chalets de l'Arc**, in Arc 2000, **t** +33 (0)4 79 04 15 40, has a warm atmosphere and serves traditional Savoyard cuisine.

Dine

In Arc 1600, **La Rive** in Hotel La Cachette, **t** +33 (0)4 79 07 70 50, is recommended. In Arc 1800, try **Casa Mia, t** +33 (0)4 79 07 05 75, and **La Marmite, t** +33 (0)4 79 07 44 28.

In Arc 1950, **Chalet de Luigi, t** +33 (0)6 08 57 23 36, is the focal point for fine dining, although Il **Valentino, t** +33 (0)4 79 07 56 48, is much much the best restaurant in the resort. **East, t** +33 (0)4 79 11 19 57, is an oriental fusion restaurant. One reader complained that culinary options for kids are in short supply ('expect them to live on burgers, nuggets and fries all week; Arc 1950 needs Jamie Oliver to open a place'). A worrying criticism came from another reader: 'The restaurants in 1950 were ludicrously expensive, even compared to quality restaurant prices in central London. In fact, the prices in 1950 exceeded all others around the resort by a significant margin – even those in the mountain restaurants where one expects to pay a premium.'

In Arc 2000, **El Latino Loco, t** +33 (0)4 79 07 79 49, has some of the best food in the village.

In Bourg-St-Maurice, **L'Hostellerie du Petit Saint Bernard, t** +33 (0)4 79 07 04 32, is the kind of old-fashioned bourgeois French restaurant that serves snails, frogs' legs and wonderful steaks.

Party

This is definitely not a place for lively après ski. At the end of the day the French seem to disappear into their self-catering apartments and do not reappear until morning. Apart from a few busy bars, the main action – what there is of it – is found in **Apokalypse** and **L'Igloo** at Arc 1800. One reporter recommended the **Red Hot Saloon** as the best bar. **KL** is in Arc 2000. **Chalet de Luigi** at 1950 has a nightclub that is building a reputation as the best in the resort. **O Chaud** in 1950 was said to be 'always very lively'.

Sleep

Most accommodation is in self-catering apartments. Arc 1950 has the newest and the best.

Arc 2000:

★★★★Les Chalets des Neiges, t +44 (0)20 7244 8764, is a complex containing chalet-apartments sharing an indoor pool and bar. They include Chalet Turia and Chalet Charvet, which sleep 10 people each.

Arc 1950:

★★★★Radisson SAS, t +44 (0)20 7584 7820, *www.ernalow.co.uk*, is the most comfortable *résidence* with a pool and underground parking. 'Pretty cool, staff very friendly and the apartments are as good as they get' was one of the favourable comments.

Auberge Jerome, t +44 (0)20 7584 7820, *www.ernalow.co.uk*, offers 'wonderful staff and comfortable apartments, and the outdoor pool is a bonus'.

Arc 1800:

★★★★MGM Les Alpages du Chantel apartments, t +44 (0)20 7584 2841, *www.residences-mgm.com*, are piste-side and have an indoor pool, sauna and massage area ('I would not recommend Chantel 1 and 2 to a beginner or nervous skier. To call these apartments ski in, ski out for these grades is not realistic,' said one reporter).

★★★Hotel du Golf Maeva, t +33 (0)4 79 41 43 43, *www.maeva.com*, is the village's original hotel with sloping walkways rather than staircases. The hotel is in a great location by the lifts, with pleasant rooms and an attractive lounge bar with open fire, but we have received mixed comments about the food.

★★★Grand Hotel Paradiso, t +33 (0)4 79 07 65 00, *www.grand-hotel-lesarcs.com*, is the new incarnation of the Mercure Coralia hotel.

Arc 1600:

★★★★Résidence Lagrange Prestige, t +44 (0)20 7099 2080, is new for this winter.

★★★Hôtel La Cachette, t +33 (0)4 79 07 70 50, *www.lacachette.com*, has a deserved reputation as one of the best hotels in the Alps for families with small children.

★★Hôtel Béguin, t +33 (0)4 79 07 72 61, *www.hotelbeguin.com*, is small and simple.

★★Hôtel Explorers, t +33 (0)4 79 04 16 00, *www.lesarcs.com*, provides cheerful accommodation.

Bourg-St-Maurice:

★★Hostellerie du Petit-St-Bernard, t +33 (0)4 79 07 04 32, *www.hostelleriedu petitstbernard.com*, has a celebrated restaurant.

Hôtel La Petite Auberge, t +33 (0)4 79 07 05 86, on the edge of town, has clean rooms and a good restaurant.

Avoriaz

Profile

Part of the giant Portes du Soleil ski area, this car-free resort is in a dramatic clifftop setting above Morzine

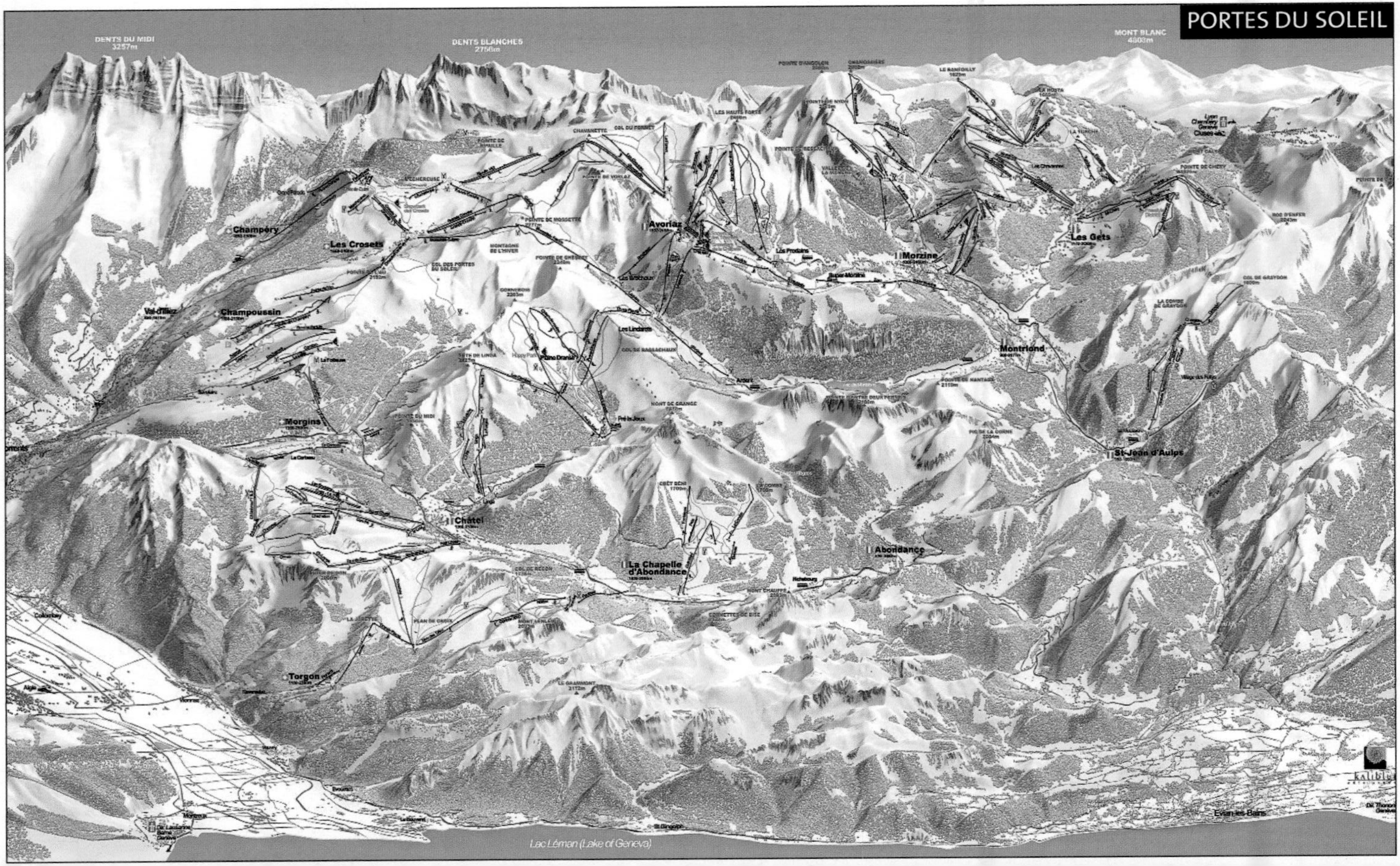

PORTES DU SOLEIL

DENTS DU MIDI 3257m

DENTS BLANCHES 2756m

MONT BLANC 4803m

Champéry

Les Crosets

Val-d'Illiez

Champoussin

Avoriaz

Morzine

Les Gets

Montriond

Morgins

Châtel

St-Jean d'Aulps

La Chapelle d'Abondance

Abondance

Torgon

Evian-les-Bains

Lac Léman (Lake of Geneva)

*** BEST FOR**

Ski convenience, intermediates and advanced, snowboarders

ESSENTIALS

Altitude: 1000m (3,280ft)–2466m (8,090ft)
Further information: t +33 (0)4 50 74 02 11, *www.avoriaz.com*
Lifts in area: 195 in Portes du Soleil area (13 cableways, 80 chairs, 102 drags) serving 650km of piste
Lift pass: Portes du Soleil (covers 14 resorts) adult €189, child 5–15yrs €127, both for six days
Access: Geneva airport 2hrs

Resort

The Portes du Soleil, a trans-frontier alliance of a dozen ski villages in France and Switzerland, largely came into being as a consequence of the 1960 Olympics, which were held 8000km away in Squaw Valley in California.

Jean Vuarnet won gold in the downhill for France and on his return was asked to oversee the creation of a high-altitude *station de ski* above his native Morzine. At the same time it was suggested he might try linking his new ski area to Champéry in Switzerland. He called the new resort Avoriaz, and the Portes du Soleil now includes 195 lifts, which serve a mighty 650km of piste covering a large area of mountainside above Lake Geneva.

Ironically, Vuarnet is better-known today for his sunglasses than for his speed on snow, but it is a tribute to him that his vision all those years ago remains as futuristic-looking today as it did then. Avoriaz clings to the cliff face at the top of the cable car that brings you up from Les Prodains in the Morzine Valley. The French government has already correctly listed it as a Landmark of the 20th Century.

Most of the original 'shoebox' *résidence* buildings have been completely gutted to provide a smaller number of decent-sized apartments. Other new ones in the Falaise and Festival *quartiers* fulfil the much more luxurious expectations of present-day skiers. But the concept remains unchanged: a series of apartment buildings on different levels that are linked by exterior boulevard pistes and interior stairs, lifts and walkways.

You can also drive up to Avoriaz, but the covered parking is expensive and in a pedestrianized resort you have no need of your own transport. Baggage is conveyed to your apartment or hotel by horse-drawn sleigh or snow tractor.

Avoriaz is the best place to base yourself in the Portes du Soleil, which falls short of being one of the world's outstanding ski circuits only because of its altitude. Although the resort is at 1800m, the top of the ski area only goes up to 2466m. Last season, of course, the snow was exceptionally good.

The resort has been a champion of snowboarding since the first boards arrived here in the 1970s, and in 1993 it was the first resort in France to build a dedicated terrain park and half-pipe. The resort now has three terrain parks, including La Chapelle park, which is designed for beginners and intermediates. The Arare, which is 800m long and 80m high, hosts a number of international competitions. New for 2007–8 was a terrain park called Stash. A constantly updated lift system allows you to explore the main villages of the Portes du Soleil and return to base by evening. A few, such as St-Jean-d'Aulps, remain entirely independent and require a separate excursion.

As with Sella Ronda in Italy, completing the tour of the principal French and Swiss resorts in a single day is perfectly possible although much of the day is taken up with riding lifts. It makes more sense to explore one sector of the area at a time. Decide on where you want to go and the quickest way to get there. Comprehensible lift maps covering such a large and diverse area have always been a problem. Every few years the Portes du Soleil radically changes them, but with no discernible improvement. The current generation of maps provide only a rough indication of where you are and where you want to go. Fortunately the piste signage is good.

Border controls are unusual, but not unheard of. We strongly advise you to carry your passport. If you or one of your party has an accident along the way, you could be stranded in another country. Border guards on skis are a rarity and few goods are so much cheaper in one country than the other that it pays to lug them home in a rucksack. However, Switzerland is not part of the EU, and restrictions apply as to what you may take from one country to the other without paying duty.

Both currencies are widely accepted, but you will find the exchange rate more favourable if you tender the appropriate one for lunch or goods purchased.

Mountain

'We have now been to Avoriaz for the past four years and we are finding it hard to book a ski holiday anywhere else,' said a reporter. Avoriaz is suited to all levels of skier and rider, but in particular to intermediates who will enjoy the feeling of 'going somewhere' each day rather than being forced to ski the same slopes over and over again for the whole week. Part of the charm of the resort is that the village streets are pistes – making this the definitive destination for doorstep skiing. The main nursery slopes are above the village, and a number of different lifts serve a series of pleasant green runs that connect to lifts coming up from the valley town of Morzine. Lifts are being steadily updated.

Most of Avoriaz's own intermediate terrain lies on the lift-served slopes leading up to the ridge that marks the Swiss border as well as in the adjoining Les Hauts Forts sector, accessed by a chairlift near the lower 'gate' of Avoriaz. Skiers here can explore some outstanding blue and red runs above and below the tree-line with lots of off-piste variations that are superb after a fresh snowfall. A long and testing black run descends from Le Plan Brazy following the basic steep line of the FIS downhill course and brings you down eventually – by blue run to Les Prodains, where you can take the cable car directly back to Avoriaz.

Adventurous skiers or riders will soon want to explore further afield either by taking the Chaux Fleurie chair to the Col de Bassachaux and Châtel beyond, or by tackling the notorious Wall and heading into Switzerland for a cheesy lunch.

The Wall – its correct name is La Chavanette – has achieved considerable notoriety over the years as one of the most difficult descents marked as a black run on any piste map. In reality its bark is usually much worse than its bite, although the toxicity of the latter is dependent on the quality of the snow.

A piste sign at the top warns that the run should be attempted only by experts. At the start, the angle of descent does not allow you to see what lies ahead. But once you have completed the first half dozen turns it eases into a relatively straightforward but heavily mogulled run.

Alternative routes, including a moderately steep and narrow gully on skier's left, may well be preferable in high season traffic conditions when the moguls on The Wall tend to be poorly cut. If conditions are hard-packed and you don't like what you see – or rather don't see – at the top of The Wall, then you should ride the chair down. More lifts take you up to a point above Les Crosets, Champéry and the rest of the Portes du Soleil.

The hamlet of Les Crosets is little more than a few holiday homes and a hotel that doubles as a lift station. It is surrounded by wide north-facing pistes served by lifts leading back up in the direction of Avoriaz. It's worth spending some time exploring this sector. A chairlift to the Pointe de l'Au takes you deeper into the Portes du Soleil in the direction of little Champoussin and Morgins beyond.

Morgins has an enjoyable north-facing run that takes you down through the woods to the village. On the far side, a lift takes you up to Super-Châtel over the Pas de Morgins and back into France. Alternatively, you can ski down into Switzerland again to the remote purpose-built village of Torgon.

At Châtel you have to cross the village by bus to take the gondola up to Linga and the lifts and piste beyond that complete the circuit to Avoriaz. Plan your day carefully and allow plenty of time.

If you don't manage to finish your tour before the lifts close, you must decide between an expensive taxi ride, an even more expensive phone call to **Mont Blanc Helicopters, t** +33 (0)4 50 74 22 44, or an unscheduled overnight stay. The best powder runs are found on both sides of the Swiss border. The area is prone to considerable avalanche danger, and the services of a qualified guide are essential.

Learn

Avoriaz has the **ESI Ecole de Glisse, t** +33 (0)4 50 74 02 18, which received favourable comments from reporters, and the **ESF, t** +33 (0)4 50 74 05 65. The **Avoriaz Alpine Ski and Snowboarding School** and **Burton Snowboard Center, t** +33 (0)4 50 38 34 91, are warmly recommended.

Children

'I just can't imagine a better family resort,' said a reporter. **Le Village des Enfants/Le Village Snowboard, t** +33 (0)4 50 74 04 46, cares for children from three to 16 years in a dedicated area in the centre of the resort, using methods developed by the French ski champion Annie Famose. 'You couldn't find a better ski school,' said a reader. **Les P'tits Loups, t** +33 (0)4 50 74 00 38, crèche cares for non-skiing children from three months to five years. Last season saw the opening of a dedicated snowpark for kids aged five to 12 years.

Lunch

The main self-service restaurants are prone to overcrowding during high season or when snow-cover is poor elsewhere. It pays to seek out one of the authentic mountain huts. **Coquoz, t** +41 (0)24 479 1255, at Planachaux has a circular open fireplace and good food. The goat-farming hamlet of Les Lindarets has a number of enticing eateries including **La Crémaillère, t** +33 (0)4 50 74 11 68. **L'Abricotine, t** +33 (0)4 50 74 17 43, at Les Brochaux, and **Les Crêtes de Zorre, t** +33 (0)4 50 79 24 73, are also recommended.

Dine

Avoriaz has a wide choice of restaurants. **La Table du Marché, t** +33 (0)4 50 74 08 11, is in Les Dromonts hotel. **Le Bistro, t** +33 (0)4 50 74 14 08, opposite **Le Village des Enfants**, is good but expensive. **La Réserve, t** +33 (0)4 50 74 02 01, has wonderful lamb dishes. **Chez Flo, t** +33 (0)4 50 74 19 24, is also recommended. **Les Intrêts, t** +33 (0)4 50 74 15 45, and **Crêperie La Duchesse Anne, t** +33 (0)4 50 74 12 50, are friendly with marvellous food.

Party

The Place, **Le Shooter's** and **Le Globe Trotters Café** are all popular international pubs with live music. **Le Tavaillon-Pub** attracts predominantly young British customers. **Le Yak** is the late-night venue.

Sleep

Most visitors to Avoriaz stay in apartments. Bookings can be made through **Pierre et Vacances, t** +33 (0)4 50 74 35 35, **Agence Immobilière des Dromonts, t** +33 (0)4 50 74 00 03, **Agence Immobilière des Hauts Forts, t** +33 (0)4 50 74 16 08, and **Selectis, t** +33 (0)4 50 74 26 95. As all the skiing is from your door, location is unimportant.

Hôtel Dromonts, t +33 (0)4 94 97 91 91, *www.christophe-leroy.com/hotel avoriaz*, has a spa, and playroom for kids.

Hôtel Neige & Roc, t +33 (0)4 50 79 03 21, *www.neige-roc.com*, is at the bottom of the cable car at Les Prodains.

Chamonix and Argentière

Profile

Strikingly beautiful glacial scenery and rugged off-piste beneath the soaring peaks of the Mont Blanc massif. This is a high alpine area best suited to strong intermediate and expert skiers and riders looking for new challenges. Beginners and nervous skiers should steer clear

* BEST FOR

Steep 'n' deep, glacial scenery, nightlife, airport access

ESSENTIALS

Altitude: 1035m (3,396ft)–3842m (12,605ft)
Further information: t +33 (0)4 50 53 00 24, *www.chamonix.com*
Lifts in area: 47 (1 funicular, 13 cableways, 17 chairs, 16 drags) serving 155km of piste; 729km in Mont Blanc ski area
Lift pass: Mont-Blanc Unlimited (covers Chamonix, Les Houches, Courmayeur) adult €225, child 4–15yrs €180, family €562
Access: Geneva airport 1hr, railway station in resort

Resort

Chamonix first ventured into tourism in 1741 when two heavily armed English explorers, William Windham and Richard Pococke, took three days rather than the current one hour to reach the valley from Geneva. Pococke, for reasons best known to himself, was dressed as an Arab.

They gazed up at the ice-fields of Mont Blanc, but it was another 45 years before the highest peak in Western Europe was successfully conquered by local crystal collector Jacques Balmat. Since then it has become the climbing – and more recently skiing – capital of the world.

The little town with its *fin de siècle* villas and grand hotels acts as a magnet for powderhounds. They are attracted by the extraordinarily steep and awe-inspiring terrain that takes no prisoners. After a fresh overnight snowfall you must rise long before the sun to cut first tracks. By mid-morning not a bowl or a single gully will be left unsullied by the passage of ski and board.

There are plenty of groomed pistes, but they are much steeper than in most other resorts. This is not the place for those who demand doorstep skiing and enjoy miles of conveniently linked motorways, nor is it a good resort for families or groups of mixed ability.

CHAMONIX

Mont-Blanc 4810m
Dôme du Goûter 4304 m
Grandes Jorasses 4208 m
Dent du Géant 4013 m
Helbronner 3466 m
Blanc du Tacul 4248 m
Aiguille du Goûter 3817 m
Aiguille du Midi 3842 m
St-Gervais
Le Brévent 2525 m
Tramway du Mont-Blanc
Glacier des Bossons
Col Cornu 2414 m
Glacier du Géant Vallée Blanche
Les Houches
Planpraz 2000 m
Chamonix 1035 m
L'Index 2385 m
Plan de l'Aiguille 2317 m
La Salle à Manger
Le Savoy
Aiguille Verte 4121 m
Aiguille du Dru 3754 m
Les Planards
Montenvers 1913 m
Mer de Glace
Les Praz 1060 m
La Flégère 1877 m
Les Grands Montets 3275 m
La Trappe
Bochard 2765 m
Glacier d'Argentière
La Herse 2595 m
Chosalets
Lognan 1972 m
Argentière 1252 m
Le Tour 1462 m
Aiguillette des Posettes 2201 m
La Vormaine
Chalets de Balme
Glacier du Tour
Vallorcine 1264 m
Charamillon 1856 m
Tête de Balme 2270 m
Domaine de Balme 2270 m
Col de Balme 2186 m

Mountain

Chamonix is dominated by the 3842m Aiguille du Midi, reached by cable car from the southern side of town. This is the starting point for the famous Vallée Blanche, a glorious 22km descent past yawning crevasses and house-sized *séracs* (ice boulders) all the way back to Chamonix. Anyone who can ski parallel and who is not afraid of heights can tackle the easiest of the four main routes, but you must take a guide.

At the start you have to negotiate the ice steps cut into the spine of the ridge leading down from the cable car station. They are not difficult, but the 2000m sheer drop to your left can have an unsettling psychological effect. The return to Chamonix is by rack-and-pinion railway from Montenvers or via a short climb and a long descent down a narrow path and piste to a cowbell factory on the outskirts of Chamonix.

But the town's main skiing is on the other side of the valley, reached either from the outskirts of the resort or from a lift station at Les Praz higher up the valley. The Planpraz gondola should have new eight-person cabins for this season, doubling uphill capacity. Linked Le Brévent and La Flégère provide plenty of scope for intermediate and strong skiers. 'My biggest gripe was the lift queues at La Flégère cable car – over one hour at weekends,' grumbled a reader.

However, for powderhounds the main course starts at the little village of Argentière, where an 80-person cable car and a quad-chair give access to Lognan. From this mid-mountain station a cable car (not included in the lift pass) rises to the 3275m Grands Montets, one of the world's greatest ski mountains. The descents from here through the glacier are as staggeringly beautiful as they are demanding. Pas de Chèvre, a run from the top of Bochard via one of several difficult couloirs down to the Mer de Glace, is a Chamonix classic. 'Anyone who can ski a black run competently should persuade a guide to take them to the Pas de Chèvre. Long, hard, but stunningly beautiful,' commented a reporter.

At the head of the valley, Le Tour offers some good novice terrain as well as rewarding runs on the Col de Balme and a long descent to Vallorcine. The Grands Montets and Le Tour both have terrain parks, but the majority of snowboarders here are usually busy elsewhere, climbing up or riding down a vertiginous *couloir*.

Learn

The **ESF**, **t** +33 (0)4 50 53 22 57, offers traditional tuition. **Sensation Ski Ecole Internationale**, **t** +33 (0)4 50 53 56 46, takes a more offbeat approach. **Evolution 2**, **t** +33 (0)4 50 55 90 22, is strongly praised by reporters. The **ESF** also has a branch in **Argentière**, **t** +33 (0)4 50 54 00 12, and **Summit Ski Montagne**, **t** +33 (0)4 50 53 50 14, is the specialist board school. Other schools include **Kailish Adventure**, **t** +33 (0)4 50 53 18 99, and **Stages Bernard Muller**, **t** +33 (0)4 50 53 18 99.

Guiding is available through **Association Internationale des Guides du Mont-Blanc**, **t** +33 (0)4 50 53 27 05, **Compagnie des Guides de Chamonix**, **t** +33 (0)4 50 53 00 88, **Mont Blanc Ski Tours**, **t** +33 (0)4 50 53 82 16, **Roland Stieger**, **t** +33 (0)4 50 55 84 77, **Sensation Ski Ecole Internationale**, **t** +33 (0)4 50 55 94 26, **Stages Vallençant**, **t** +33 (0)4 50 54 05 11, and **Yak & Yeti**, **t** +33 (0)4 50 53 53 67.

Children

'The resort is OK for late-night revellers but not for families,' said a reporter. However, up the mountain, two ski areas, Les Planards and Le Savoy, are reserved for children. The **ESF Piou-Piou Club**, **t** +33 (0)4 50 55 53 57, cares for children from three years old. The ESF runs its **Panda Club** ski kindergarten in Chamonix, **t** +33 (0)4 50 55 86 12, and in Argentière, **t** +33 (0)4 50 54 04 76. Both provide daycare and tuition from three years. **Evolution 2** gives lessons from three years at Chamonix, **t** +33 (0)4 50 55 93 03, and at Argentière, **t** +33 (0)4 50 54 21 36.

Lunch

'Eating on the mountain was extortionate and should be avoided if possible,' complained a reader. However, there are exceptions: at Lognan, **La Crèmerie du Glacier**, **t** +33 (0)4 50 54 07 52, in the woods above the base station of the Lognan cable car, is one of the only restaurants not owned by the lift company. **Plan Joran**, **t** +33 (0)4 50 54 05 77, has good food and a sunny terrace. At Brévent, **La Bergerie de Planpraz**, **t** +33 (0)4 50 53 05 42, is recommended, along with **La Chavanne** at Flégère, **t** +33 (0)4 50 53 06 13. In Chamonix, **Le Robinson**, **t** +33 (0)4 50 53 45 87, on the cross-country track, has a great atmosphere.

Dine

'Dining out in the town was good value with many decent restaurants available,' said a reporter. **La Maison Carrier**, **t** +33 (0)4 50 53 00 03, has outstanding Savoyard cuisine. **L'Auberge du Bois Prin**, **t** +33 (0)4 50 53 33 51, is also warmly recommended, along with **Hotel Eden in Les Praz**, **t** +33 (0)4 50 53 06 40. **Atmosphere**, **t** +33 (0)4 50 55 97 97, serves gourmet food. **La Calèche**, **t** +33 (0)4 50 55 94 68, specializes in traditional Savoyard dishes. **Le Satsuki**, **t** +33 (0)4 50 53 21 99, has sushi. **L'Impossible**, **t** + 33 (0)4 50 53 20 36, is an ancient wooden barn with fine rural fare in Chamonix Sud. **Le Panier des Quatre Saisons**, **t** +33 (0)4 50 53 98 77, has gourmet cuisine at a sensible price. **Le National**, **t** +33(0)4 50 53 02 23, has 'the best steaks in town'. **Casa Valerio**, **t** +33 (0)4 50 55 93 40, has the finest pizzas. The **Rusticana**, **t** +33 (0)4 50 55 88 28, in Argentière, offers fish and chips and Irish stew.

Party

Chamonix has a more lively après ski than almost any other French resort, although not all reporters were in agreement. 'Nightlife was ok but very blokeish.' Start the evening with cocktails at **Chambre Neuf**, **Le Choucas**, **Le Privilege**, **Jekyll** or **Expedition**; Rue du Docteur Paccard is paved with welcoming bars. **La Terrasse** on the main square has good live music, a chill-out area upstairs, and a great cocktail bar. **La Cante** was said to be 'populated like a broiler house but fun'. Other bars include **Elevation** and **Bard'Up**. The **MBC** bar and restaurant on the road towards Les Praz is a favourite with the locals. Real late-nighters end up at the **BPM** or the **Garage** in Chamonix Sud.

In Argentière, **The Office** – under new management this season – is a resort institution where you can drink, eat, listen to live music – or even stay.

Sleep

Chamonix:

Chamonix offers everything, from youth hostels to four-star hotels, plus a wide choice of chalets and apartments. All bookings can be made through **Chamonix Reservations Centre**, **t** +33 (0)4 50 53 23 33.

★★★★**Le Hameau Albert 1er**, **t** +33 (0)4 50 53 05 09, *www.hameaualbert.fr*, is a stylish and atmospheric hotel.

★★★★**L'Auberge du Bois Prin**, **t** +33 (0)4 50 53 33 51, *www.boisprin.com*, has much charm as well as a fine restaurant.

★★★★**Les Balcons du Savoy, t** +33 (0)4 50 55 32 32, *www.lesbalconsdusavoy.com*, are the resort's prime apartments.

★★★★**Grand Hotel des Alpes, t** +33 (0)4 50 55 37 80, *www.grandhoteldesalpes.com*, is new and extremely comfortable.

★★★**Hotel Gustavia, t** +33 (0)4 50 53 00 31, *www.hotel-gustavia.com*, is lively and central; the food is fantastic and the lively après ski bar is separated from the hotel by a soundproof door.

★★★**Park Hotel Suisse, t** +33 (0)4 50 53 07 58, *www.chamonix-park-hotel.com*, is described as 'superb' by reporters.

★★**Hotel Richemond, t** +33 (0)4 50 53 08 85, *www.richemond.fr*, is in the town centre; although slightly dated, the hotel is spotless, the staff are friendly and breakfasts very good.

The Clubhouse, t +33 (0)4 50 90 96 56, *www.theclubhouse.fr*, is a contemporary boutique hotel inside an Art Deco mansion built in 1927. Accommodation is in custom-built bunkhouses. Each has a plasma screen, XBox and 'rainforest' shower.

Argentière:

★★**Hotel Le Dahu, t** +33 (0)4 50 54 01 55, *www.hotel-le-dahu.com*, is warmly recommended.

Le Lavancher:

★★★★**Hotel Jeu de Paume, t** +33 (0)4 50 54 03 76, *www.jeudepaumechamonix.com*, is a romantic boutique hotel with an outstanding gourmet restaurant.

★★★★**Les Chalets de Philippe, t** +33 (0)6 07 23 17 26, *www.chaletsphilippe.com*, are stylishly converted wood-and-stone *mazots* (ancient barns).

La Clusaz

Profile

One of the closest resorts to Geneva airport, with lots of low-level intermediate skiing, good mountain restaurants and modest hotels

Resort

La Clusaz has been a resort since 1908 when local lad Pierre-Noël Vittoz experimented with skis and an invention called *Le Paret*, the first-ever snowbike. The attractive village is built around an early 19th-century church and a mountain stream.

Mountain

The skiing is divided into five sectors. Access to Beauregard and L'Aiguille is by lifts from the resort centre. The other areas (Balme, L'Etale and Croix-Fry/Merdassier) are reached by ski-bus. Most of the skiing is ideal for intermediates. 'What the ski area lacks in challenge, it certainly makes up for in

✱BEST FOR

Easy intermediate skiing, families, airport access

ESSENTIALS

Altitude: 1100m (3,608ft)–2600m (8,528ft)
Further information: **t** +33 (0)4 50 32 65 00, *www.laclusaz.com*
Lifts in area: 84 in La Clusaz (5 cableways, 13 chairs, 27 drags) serving 128km of piste
Lift pass: Aravis (covers La Clusaz, Le Grand-Bornand, Manigod and St-Jean-de-Sixt) adult €146–158, child 5–15yrs €116; La Clusaz adult €137.50–149.50, child 5–15yrs €107
Access: Geneva airport 1hr, railway station at Annecy 30mins

beauty,' said a reporter. The terrain park on Aiguille receives much praise. This season the old cableway and double-chair on L'Etale is being replaced by a chondola and a quad-chair.

Learn

ESF, **t** +33 (0)4 50 02 40 83, is rated excellent, while the **ESI Sno-Académie**, **t** +33 (0)4 50 32 66 05, and **Aravis Challenge**, **t** +33 (0)4 50 02 81 29, are recommended. The others are **Evolution 2**, **t** +33 (0)4 50 23 52 77, **Alter Ego**, **t** +33 (0)6 07 39 72 53, and **Dimension Freeride**, **t** +33 (0)4 50 03 54 39.

Children

The ESF and ESI provide lessons. **Club des Mouflets**, **t** +33 (0)4 50 02 48 91, is the non-ski kindergarten, the **ESF Piou-Piou Club** offers daycare with optional ski lessons, and – unusually – there is a cross-country ski kindergarten for children from four years, **t** +33 (0)4 50 02 40 83 for all.

Lunch

Try **Altitude 1647**, **t** +33 (0)4 50 02 44 00, in the Beauregard area, and **Chalet des Praz**, **t** +33 (0)4 50 02 59 84, an atmospheric Savoyard chalet built in 1792 on the Crêt du Merle piste. **Le Bercail**, **t** +33 (0)4 50 02 43 75, on the Massif de L'Aiguille, is a fine lunching experience.

Dine

Au Cochon des Neiges, **t** +33 (0)4 50 02 62 62, serves Savoyard cuisine. **La Calèche**, **t** +33 (0)4 50 02 42 60, is renowned for its fresh fish and home-made foie gras. **L'Arbé**, **t** +33 (0)4 50 02 60 54, has a chalet ambience. **Le Symphonie** in Hotel Beauregard, **t** +33 (0)4 50 32 68 00, is a gastronomic delight.

Party

Après-bars include **La Grolle**, **Les Caves du Paccaly** and **La Braise**. **Le Pressoir** is a snowboarders' haunt and **Le Grenier** attracts the locals. **L'Ecluse** nightclub has a glass dance floor over the river, and at **Club 18** you can dance away until the early hours.

Sleep

- ★★★**Hôtel Beauregard**, **t** +33 (0)4 50 322 68 00, *www.hotel-beauregard.fr*, has an attractive interior and a pool.
- ★★★**Hôtel L'Alpage de Tante Pauline**, **t** +33 (0)4 50 02 63 28, *www.chaletalpage.com*, has 10 rooms.
- ★★★**Hôtel Vieux Chalet**, **t** +33 (0)4 50 02 41 53, *www.levieuxchalet.fr*, is even smaller, with eight rooms.
- ★★★**Hôtel Alpen Roc**, **t** +33 (0)4 50 02 58 96, *www.hotel-alpenroc.fr*, a stable mate of the Beauregard, is very friendly and punches above its star rating.
- ★★**Hôtel Les Sapins**, **t** +33 (0)4 50 63 33 33, *www.clusaz.com*, is in a good position.

Courchevel

🏆 BEST FAMILY RESORT 2009 (COURCHEVEL 1650)
🏆 BEST SKI HOTEL 2009 (HOTEL MANALI, COURCHEVAL 1650)
🏆 BEST SKI SHOP 2009 (FRANCIS SPORT)

Profile

At its highest level, Courchevel is the most chic and the most expensive resort in France, and it also happens to have

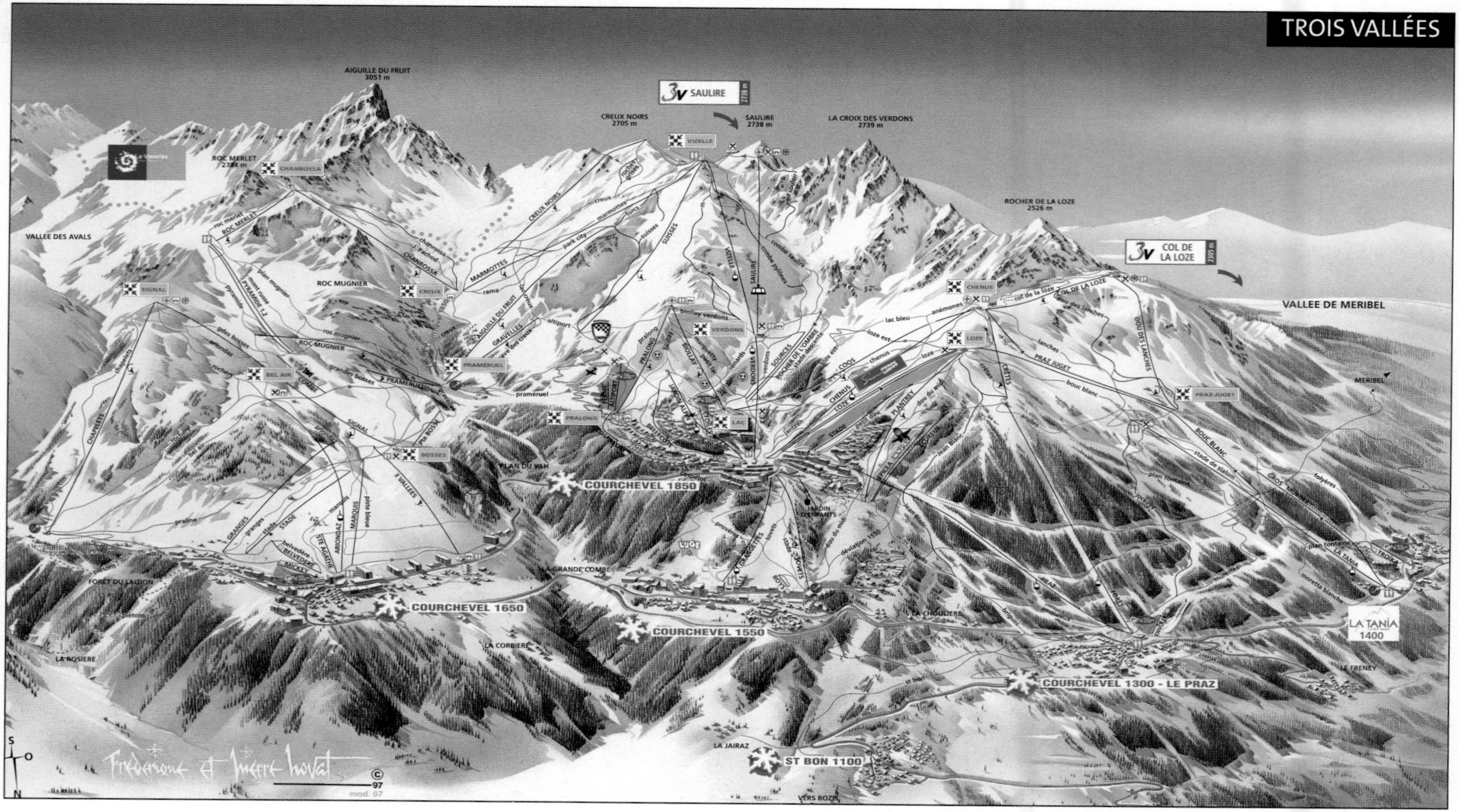

TROIS VALLÉES

AIGUILLE DU FRUIT
3051 m

SAULIRE 2738 m

CREUX NOIRS
2705 m

SAULIRE
2738 m

LA CROIX DES VERDONS
2739 m

ROCHER DE LA LOZE
2526 m

COL DE LA LOZE 2305 m

ROC MERLET
2734 m

VALLEE DES AVALS

ROC MUGNIER

VALLEE DE MERIBEL

MERIBEL

PLAN DU VAH

COURCHEVEL 1850

COURCHEVEL 1650

COURCHEVEL 1550

COURCHEVEL 1300 - LE PRAZ

LA TANIA
1400

ST BON 1100

LA GRANDE COMBE

FORÊT DU LAITION

LA ROSIERE

LA CORBIERE

LA CHOULIERE

LE FRENEY

LA JAIRAZ

VERS BOZEL

JARDIN D'ENFANTS

LUGE

ALTIPORT

S
O
N

© 97
mod. 07

Courchevel

VAL D'ISÈRE AND LA TANIA

- 29 superbly placed chalets
- Genuine, friendly service
- Delicious food and wine
- Sunday flights to Chambéry

WWW.LESKI.COM
Brand new website with videos and online booking

For more information call
01484 548996

INDEPENDENT CHALET SPECIALISTS FOR 25 YEARS

www.leski.com

*** BEST FOR**

Cosmopolitan sophistication (1850), all levels of skiing and riding, families, luxury accommodation

ESSENTIALS

Altitude: 1100m (3,608ft)–2738m (8,983ft)
Further information: t +33 (0)4 79 08 00 29, *www.courchevel.com*
Lifts in area: 165 in Trois Vallées (43 cableways, 68 chairs, 54 drags) serving 600km of piste
Lift pass: Trois Vallées adult €157–295, child 5–13yrs €112–225, both for six days
Access: Chambéry airport 1½hrs, Lyon airport 2hrs, Geneva airport 2½hrs, Eurostar at Moûtiers, 25km

outstanding skiing. But that is just the top bit. Courchevel is made up of four quite separate villages at different altitudes and has something to suit everybody

Resort

Courchevel has been reigning supreme since 1946 as the resort closest to the heart of Parisians. Ever since the Mugnier family first cashed in their cow pastures and agreed to the construction of the first lift, Courchevel has caught the eye of the capital's café society. In present-day terms what we are talking about is Courchevel 1850, the highest of these villages, with direct links to Méribel and the other resorts of the Trois Vallées.

Courchevel 1850 is the only centre here with *Le Jet Set* appeal, a purpose-built portfolio of extraordinarily hedonistic hotels and private chalets perched on the mountainside above the still unspoilt valley town of Bozel. It has few alpine rivals for comfort, cuisine and cost. 'Half way down one of the green runs you stumble across a Vuitton shop. The shopping area is like one big Harvey Nicks...fab!' said a reader. The resort caters for an international clientele that includes Russians, Chinese and Bollywood stars, who don't care what it costs to stay, ski and eat here as long as they enjoy themselves. That's 1850.

Some 200 vertical metres down the mountain in both altitude and social standing comes Courchevel 1650, a more authentic French mountain village with reasonable restaurant prices and affordable chalet accommodation. It also has the best skiing.

Courchevel 1550, which is geographically directly below 1850 and served by a six-person chair, is becoming a serious satellite of its sophisticated sister, while 1650 has opened its first luxury hotel but still retains a more earthy character.

At the bottom of the mountain lies the original farming village of Le Praz or Courchevel 1300. This is a delightful place to stay, with good accommodation and easy access by gondola to Courchevel 1850.

Mountain

The number of lifts and the sheer scale of the skiing in the Trois Vallées is simply staggering. Mere statistics mean nothing; you have to see it for yourself. It is worth noting that the resort lift map takes considerable licence with the compass. Courchevel appears to be the most westerly resort in the region, when in reality it is the most easterly, a fact to be borne in mind when searching for sunshine or north-facing slopes.

From the hub of La Croisette at 1850 a network of gondolas and a cable car take you up to 2738m Saulire. You can either ski down the far side to Méribel and further into the Trois Vallées, or return towards Courchevel. The main arterial run back down to 1850 can become horrendously overcrowded and it pays to spend time around the adjoining 2659m peak, where most slopes are slightly more challenging and therefore less popular.

For accomplished skiers and riders, the black Les Suisses is particularly enjoyable. In the right snow conditions it is possible to ski from Saulire all the way down to St Bon below Courchevel – a vertical drop of over 1600m.

Courchevel is famed for its *couloirs*, three ribbons of snow between the rocks that unfurl from the ridge on the right-hand side of the top station of the cable car. Grand Couloir, Sous le Téléphérique and Emile Allais can be extremely demanding when icy. However, in good mid-winter snow conditions they should present no great problem to an experienced skier or rider. Catch them as soon as they are declared open after a major dump. They quickly become bumped up with some awkward VW-sized moguls in the high reaches. If you fall here, it is a long way down, but there are no obstacles and the likelihood of serious injury is small. However, you should treat the often icy approach route from the cable car with considerable caution.

The Altiport sector of Courchevel just to the east of 1850 is good beginner terrain, with green and easy blue runs that are ideal for building confidence before heading further afield. Topographically, the Trois Vallées is the perfect ski area. The links between different sectors are natural rather than contrived. This allows for more real ski time rather than hours wasted on paths. From almost everywhere there is an easy way down, and anyone who can vaguely ski parallel can explore far afield.

During peak season the cognoscenti head for Courchevel 1650. Its own extensive ski area beneath a trio of peaks is off the Trois Vallées beaten track. The runs on Col de Chanrossa, Signal and Bel Air above the village are suited to all standards and are some of the most enjoyable in the whole region. From Roc Merlet you can ski off-piste on the higher slopes of the Vallée des Avals on a glorious itinerary that brings you back down to 1650.

Snowboarders will find a good supply of natural hits throughout Courchevel. The terrain park at Plantrey now has the only rail-park in the Trois Vallées. Riders also congregate on the snowcross course at Les Verdons and Biolley.

Learn

Ski lesson are big business in Courchevel and there is intense rivalry between the various schools. Large numbers of 'blacks' – unqualified ski bums – also tout for business and should be avoided. The **ESF**, **t** +33 (0)4 79 08 07 72, has branches in all the villages and, with over 700 teachers working during the peak month of February, the quality of instruction can be a matter of chance. We recommend **New Generation**, **t** +33 (0)4 79 01 03 18 ('simply great', according to one reader), owned and operated by British BASI instructors. **Supreme**, **t** +33 (0)4 79 08 27 87, rated 'excellent' is another long-established British school. **Ski Academy**, **t** +33 (0)4 79 08 11 99, has a strong reputation. **Absolute Ski**, **t** +33 (0)6 68 51 74 94, is a small school with local instructors. **Magic in Motion**, **t** +33 (0)4 79 01 01 81, is a favourite with tour operators. Guiding can be arranged through the ski schools or the **Bureau des Guides**, **t** +33 (0)4 79 01 03 66.

Children

Courchevel has the French government's *P'tits Montagnards* award for childcare. It is also home to a revolutionary new type of chairlift with electro-magnets. These lock onto the ski school bibs of small children to keep them safely seated during the upward ride. The ESF runs both non-ski and ski kindergartens. In 1850 **Village des Enfants**, **t** +33 (0)4 79 08 08 47, provides all-day care and an introduction to skiing from three years. **Magic in Motion**, t +33 (0)4 79 01 01 81, runs English-only classes for four- to six-year-olds. **Ski Academy**, t +33 (0)4 79 08 11 99, has morning classes for children from four years as well as dedicated classes for children aged 10 to 13 years and 14 to 16 years. **Supreme**, t +33 (0)4 79 08 27 87, has classes for children aged six to 12 years during school holidays.

In 1650 **Les Pitchounets**, t + 33 (0)4 79 08 33 69, is a dedicated play area for small children. **Le Club des Oursons**, t +33 (0)4 79 08 26 08, teaches children from three years. The **Garderie**, t +33 (0)620 66 37 23, cares for children under 18 months.

In 1550 **Le Club des Piou-Piou**, t +33 (0)4 79 08 21 07, takes children from three to five years for a mix of lessons and snow fun.

Lunch

Courchevel has lots of overpriced self-services and a portfolio of elegant piste-side eateries that cater for a clientèle that sees a gourmet lunch and a €60 bottle of wine as a basic component of the skiing day. Booking is essential. 'Food in 1850 is on the steep side, but very good, wheras 1650 and La Tania offer great value for money,' said a reporter. Best value is **Bel-Air**, t +33 (0)4 79 08 00 93, at the top of the Courchevel 1650 gondola. It serves traditional Savoyard cuisine in a beautiful setting, with friendly staff. **Le Cap Horn**, t +33 (0)4 79 08 33 10, by the Altiport, offers seafood and Asian dishes served by liveried waiters. **Chalet de Pierres**, t +33 (0)4 79 08 18 61, on the descent from Saulire, is a comfortable but costly resort institution with a sunny terrace, more liveried waiters, and an enticing display of desserts. In 1650 **Le Petit Savoyard**, t +33 (0)4 79 08 27 44, and **L'Eterlou**, t +33 (0)4 79 08 25 45, are both reasonably priced with friendly service.

Dine

In 1850 double Michelin-starred **Le Bateau Ivre**, t +33 (0)4 79 00 11 71, in Hôtel Pomme de Pin, has inspirational cooking that stands head and shoulders above its many rivals. **Hôtel Le Chabichou**, t +33 (0)4 79 08 00 55, has a similar double-Michelin-starred accolade. **La Saulire** (known as **Jacques' Bar**), t +33 (0)4 79 08 07 52, is our favourite in 1850; it has an impressive menu and wine list, intimate surroundings and impeccable, friendly service.

In 1650 **Le Manali**, t +33 (0)4 79 08 07 07 is an outstanding newcomer and a rival to the best restaurants in 1850. Elsewhere in 1650 prices are considerably lower. We recommend **L'Eterlou**, t +33 (0)4 79 08 25 45. In 1550 **L'Œil de Bœuf**, t +33 (0)4 79 08 22 10, is in an old mountain barn. In Le Praz, **La Table de Mon Grand-Père** in Hôtel Les Peupliers, t +33 (0)4 79 08 41 42, has a strong following 'but it definitely lost its edge last season after a change of chef'. **La Cave d'à Côté**, t +33 (0)4 79 08 42 90, serves local specialities.

Party

'Après is quiet and fairly expensive in 1850 – choose pubs carefully,' warned a reader, '**Bar Le Jump** in 1850 was reasonable in comparison to the rest of the resort.' At **Prends Ta Luge et Tire-toi** you can check your emails, have a drink or buy a snowboard. The iniquitously expensive **Le Piggys Pub** is popular, and **The Purple** is a 'fashion bar' with a DJ. **Les Caves** is the shockingly expensive, late-night venue.

In 1650 the British relax and check their emails in **Le Bubble**. New on the scene is the stylish bar in the **Manali Hotel**, complete with pool table and a giant video screen. In 1550 après ski centres around the friendly **Taverne**, **Le Barouf** and **Chanrossa**. Family-orientated Le Praz (Courchevel 1300) falls asleep early, but you can enjoy a drink in **L'Escorch'vel**.

Sleep

Courchevel 1850:

★★★★*deluxe* **Hotel Les Airelles**, **t** +33 (0)4 79 09 38 38, *www.airelles.fr*, is tastefully discreet and has undergone a revamp.

★★★★*deluxe* **Le Cheval Blanc**, **t** +33 (0)4 79 00 50 50, *www.chevalblanc.com*, is owned by Bernard Arnault, the man behind LVMH (Louis Vuitton-Moët-Hennessy). The charmingly OTT hotel is made up almost entirely of suites, with a Givenchy spa, and Louis Vuitton and Christian Dior boutiques.

★★★★*deluxe* **Hotel Kilimandjaro**, **t** +33 (0)4 79 01 46 46, *www.hotelkilimandjaro.com*, is a collection of chalets with a restaurant and La Prairie spa.

★★★★*deluxe* **Hotel Le Lana**, **t** +33 (0)4 79 08 01 10, *www.lelana.com*, has a spa with swimming pool.

★★★★*deluxe* **Le Mélézin**, **t** +33 (0)4 79 08 01 33, *www.amanresorts.com*, is the stylish alpine headquarters of Aman Resorts, with a gym and swimming pool.

★★★★*deluxe* **Hotel Le Saint-Joseph**, **t** +33 (0)4 79 08 16 16, in the heart of the village, offers understated luxury combined with a retro style in its 11 rooms and three apartments.

★★★★**Chalet Aurea**, **t** +44 (0)20 8682 5050, *www.scottdunn.com*, is a short walk from the village centre and the main lift. It has a pool, hot tub and steam room.

★★★★**Hotel Chabichou**, **t** +33 (0)4 79 08 00 55, *www.chabichou-courchevel.com*, is in a large chalet-style building, and offers weekly cookery courses.

★★★★**Hotel des Neiges**, **t** +33 (0)4 79 03 03 77, *www.hoteldesneiges.com*, has a gastronomic restaurant and Banyan Spa.

★★★★**Hotel La Sivolière**, **t** +33 (0)4 79 08 08 33, *www.hotel-la-sivoliere.com*, is quiet and luxurious.

★★★★**Hotel des Trois Vallées**, **t** +33 (0)4 79 08 00 12, *www.hoteldestroisvallees.com*, has panoramic views.

★★★**Hotel Les Ducs de Savoie**, **t** +33 (0)4 79 08 03 00, *www.hotel-restaurant-courchevel.net*, has a pool and is in the Jardin Alpin residential area.

★★★**Hotel La Loze**, **t** +33 (0)4 79 08 28 25, *www.la-loze.com*, has a library that doubles as a bar.

Courchevel 1650:

★★★★*deluxe* **Le Manali**, **t** +33 (0)4 79 08 07 07, *www.hotelmanali.com*, is a fabulous and unexpected find in quaint 1650. Its rooms are a choice of Indian, Swiss chalet and Canadian log cabin style and the restaurant is one of the best in the Courchevel area.

★★★**Hotel du Golf**, **t** +33 (0)4 79 00 92 92, *www.hoteldugolf-courchevel.fr*, is ski in, ski out.

★★★**Hotel Le Seizena**, **t** +33 (0)4 79 01 26 36, *ww.hotelseizena.com*, is a friendly B&B with 20 attractive rooms.

★★★**Chalet Rikiki** is right on the edge of the piste, and **Chalet Les Sorbiers** has great views, both **t** +44 (0)870 754 4444, *www.leski.com*.

Le Praz:

★★★**Hôtel Les Peupliers**, **t** +33 (0)4 79 08 41 47, *www.lespeupliers.com*, is delightful.

LES DEUX ALPES

La Meije
3982
Les Ecrins
4102
Le Rateau
3809
Aiguille du Plat
de la Selle
3596
Tête de Lauranours
3323
La Muze
Pic de la Grave
3669
Massif du Soreiller
Glacier
la Meije
Glacier
du Râteau
Dôme de la Lauze
3568
Dôme de Puy Salié
3421
Grotte
de Glace
Table
d'orientation
Le Jandri
3288
Col des Ruillans
3211
Glacier
de la Girose
Glacier
de Mantel
GLACIER
3200m
La Toura
2914
Lac Noir
Snowpark
Tête du Diable
2869
Tête Moute
2813
TOURA
2600m
2800
Refuge
Chancel
Vers La Grave
Clot
de Chalance
DIABLE
2400m
Lac du Plan
LA FÉE
2100m
CRÊTES
2100m
LES 2 ALPES
1650m
PIED
MOUTET
2100m
Mont-de-Lans
1300m
Bons
Cuculet
Lac du Chambon
1040

…néraire La Grave - La Meije
…nditions particulières d'accès
…x remontées mécaniques
…nseignements :
…isse centrale - Le Meijotel

www.2alpe…

Les Deux Alpes

*** BEST FOR**

Novices, intermediate skiers and riders, off-piste, families, guaranteed snow cover, party-goers

ESSENTIALS

Altitude: 1650m (5,412ft)–3600m (11,808ft)
Further information: t +33 (0)4 76 79 22 00, *www.les2alpes.com*
Lifts in area: 50 (7 cableways, 23 chairs, 20 drags) serving 240km of piste in Les Deux Alpes/La Grave
Lift pass: Grande Galaxie (covers linked resorts, Alpe d'Huez, La Grave, 1 day in Puy-St-Vincent and Serre Chevalier) adult €163.80–182, child 5–13yrs €131–145.60, both for six days
Access: Grenoble airport 1½hrs, Lyon airport 2hrs

Profile

Large ski area with snow-sure glacial slopes served by a modern lift system. The nightlife is some of the most frenetic in France

Resort

Les Deux Alpes (L2A) lies between Grenoble and Briançon in a remote corner of the Dauphiné. Its biggest asset is its high altitude, which allows skiing to continue throughout much of the year and makes it a popular venue for out-of-season ski and snowboard camps. It has been a ski resort since 1939 when a primitive rope-tow was installed. Unfortunately this fell down 15 minutes after the opening ceremony. Hostilities with Germany then got in the way of any further development plans until 1946, when a gondola paved the way for Les Deux Alpes to become an important French resort.

The purpose-built village was conceived as a *station de ski* on the sunny balcony above the ancient community of Venosc, to which it is connected by gondola, but not by piste. Venosc, with its cobbled lanes, craft shops and enticing restaurants, provides a welcome contrast and a tranquil alternative bed-base to the functional ski factory above it.

L2A sprawls along a narrow ledge below what were once the high summer pastures of sheep and goat farmers. The village is currently receiving a facelift; exteriors are being smartened up with wood cladding and interiors are more spacious and modern than previously.

The resort is suited to all levels of skier and rider. However, lower intermediates should note that on the main mountain the gradient is 'reversed'. Some of the easiest skiing is higher up – both on and around the glacier. The benefit of this is that complete beginners can learn against the panoramic backdrop of the High Alps rather than on a shaded slope tucked away on the outskirts of a village. The downside is that inexperienced skiers will find the steep final descent to the resort beyond their capabilities. 'The winding green run back to the resort was a tough task – full of snow-ploughers and fallen bodies who were hard to overtake. We came down on the black run instead and found that much easier, even for our novice.' Another alternative is to download by gondola.

Advanced skiers will want to explore the glacial terrain of La Meije, reached by snowcat from the top of the ski area to the 3568m Dôme de la Lauze. From here you can ski all the way down to the ancient climbing village of La Grave.

Here and elsewhere in the L2A area, it is important always to be aware that you are in high mountains where the weather can change within minutes. It is the kind of territory where anyone who goes off-piste without a qualified local mountain guide is risking their life. Even then, it is up to the individual to take overall responsibility for his or her own safety. Mountain guides, like everyone else, are fallible.

Mountain

Gondolas and cable cars provide the main mountain access ('the lift system was fast and efficient with minimal queues'). The most important of these, the Jandri Express jumbo gondola, takes you to an underground funicular station at 3200m for the final ride to the top of the glacier. The whole journey from the village takes around 45 minutes, a practical indication of the enormous vertical drop here. The bulk of the skiing revolves around the hubs of Les Crêtes at 2100m and Toura at 2600m. The terrain flattens out on the lower reaches of the glacier to provide easy pistes where the snow quality is always excellent.

La Fée sector, off the shoulder below Toura, is usually uncrowded and offers some of the best blue and black runs on the mountain. On the other side of the resort, the Pied Moutet sector provides gentle sunny blue runs served by three lifts. From here, snow conditions permitting, you can also ski down to the village of Bons at 1300m.

L2A is an important resort for riders and each October hosts the World Snowboard Meeting. The terrain park has a 120m half-pipe and is one of the most sophisticated in Europe.

Learn

The **ESF, t** +33 (0)4 76 79 21 21, and **ESI St Christophe, t** +33 (0)4 76 79 04 21, are the main teaching establishments. The British-run **European Ski School, t** +33 (0)4 76 79 74 55, offers tuition in English for classes of up to four pupils. **Ski Privilège, t** +33 (0)4 76 79 23 44, and British-run **Easiski, t** +33 (0)6 82 79 57 34, are alternatives. **2 Alpes Snowboard, t** +33 (0)6 15 07 94 42, are the dedicated snowboard academies. Race-training is with **Stages Pierre Alain Carrel, t** +33 (0)4 76 80 51 99, and **Stages Damien Albert, t** +33 (0)4 76 79 50 38. Guiding is through **Bureau des Guides ESF, t** +33 (0)4 76 11 36 29.

Children

L2A has the coveted *Les P'tits Montagnards* award from the French government for excellence in childcare. **Crèche Les 2 Alpes 1800, t** +33 (0)4 76 79 02 62, cares for children aged six months to two years. **Garderie Le Bonhomme de Neige, t** +33 (0)4 76 79 06 77, looks after children from two to six years. **Espace Luge** is a children's play area at the base of the mountain with a trampoline, slalom course, snow-biking, tobogganing, tubing and an inflatable bob-run.

The **ESF, t** +33 (0)4 76 79 21 21, runs ski kindergartens in the village, at Champamé and at Les Crêtes, with lessons for little ones from three years combined with fun in the snow and indoor play and videos. **ESI St Christophe, t** +33 (0)4 76 79 04 21, is for children up to eight years. **The European, t** +33 (0)4 76 79 74 55, also runs classes for children.

Lunch

La Molière, t +33 (0)4 76 80 18 99, is at the foot of the pistes, and **Le Diable au Cœur, t** +33 (0)4 76 79 99 50, at 2400m, has an open fireplace and well-prepared regional cuisine. Both are recommended. **Le Panoramic, t** +33 (0)4 76 79 06 75, at 2600m, is a mountain hut with a great atmosphere and some of the best fare in the resort.

Dine

'Good choice of restaurants, some did have reasonable prices for a change,' said a reader. The gourmet choice is **Le P'tit Polyte**, **t** +33 (0)4 76 80 56 90, which has an excellent wine list. **L'Abri**, **t** +33 (0)4 76 79 21 41, has an alpine ambience. **La Spaghetteria**, **t** +33 (0)4 76 79 05 77, is recommended for pasta, and **Tribeca Caffé**, **t** +33 (0)4 76 80 58 53, for pizzas. **Blu Salmon**, **t** +33 (0)4 76 79 29 56, is typically French, and **Il Caminetto**, **t** +33 (0)4 76 79 51 54, is a typical Italian restaurant. **Smokey Joe's**, **t** +33 (0)4 76 79 21 70, offers good-value Tex-Mex. **La Patate**, **t** +33 (0)4 76 79 23 55 ('a great place to eat'), and **Le Paellou**, **t** +33 (0)4 76 80 51 54, both serve raclette and fondue in an alpine atmosphere. The restaurant in **Hôtel-Chalet Mounier**, **t** +33 (0)4 76 80 56 90, has reasonable prices and a romantic ambience.

Party

We received mixed reportes about the après ski: 'The nightlife is amazing,' said one reporter. 'The nightlife did not live up to the hype', said another, and 'There were few places to entertain those of us over the age of 30.' Popular watering holes include **Pub Le Windsor**, **Smokey Joe's**, **The Secret**, **Smithy's**, **Polar Bear** and **Le Pressoir**. **L'Opéra** is the recommended disco. **L'Avalanche** ('crammed and noisy') has a strong following.

Sleep

Most of the accommodation is in apartments.

★★★**Alpina Lodge**, **t** +33 (0)4 76 79 75 17, *www.les2alpes.com*, contains some very comfortable apartments for two to 10 people.

★★★★**Les Balconnes de Sarenne**, **t** +33 (0)4 76 79 57 97, *www.lesbalconnesdesarenne.com*, are luxury apartments.

★★★★**Hôtel La Farandole**, **t** +33 (0)4 76 80 50 45, *www.utaf.com/lafarandole*, is a traditional chalet with an excellent restaurant and a piano bar.

★★★**Hotel La Brunerie**, **t** +33 (0)4 76 79 22 23, was rated 'an outstanding place to stay, the rooms were perfectly adequate and the amazing food more than made up for what the rooms lacked'.

★★★**Hôtel Le Souleil'Or**, **t** +33 (0)4 76 79 24 69, *www.le-souleil-or.fr*, is a modern hotel with friendly owners and lots of alpine character.

★★★**Hôtel-Chalet Mounier**, **t** +33 (0)4 76 80 56 90, *www.chalet-mounier.com*, was a mountain refuge and alpine farm back in 1879. Today it is attractively decorated, and has a pool and spa.

★★★**Hôtel Muzelle Sylvana**, **t** +33 (0)4 76 80 50 93, *www.skisystem.net*, is 50m from the Diable cable car and has a good wine cellar.

Flaine

Profile

Large ski area with an excellent snow record near the Mont Blanc massif. Suitable for all standards of skier and rider looking for a no-frills holiday in delightful alpine surroundings

Resort

Flying down the red Lucifer run or blue Belzebuth above Flaine, it is easy to imagine you have somehow become entangled in a devilish time warp. While other famous resorts in the French Alps

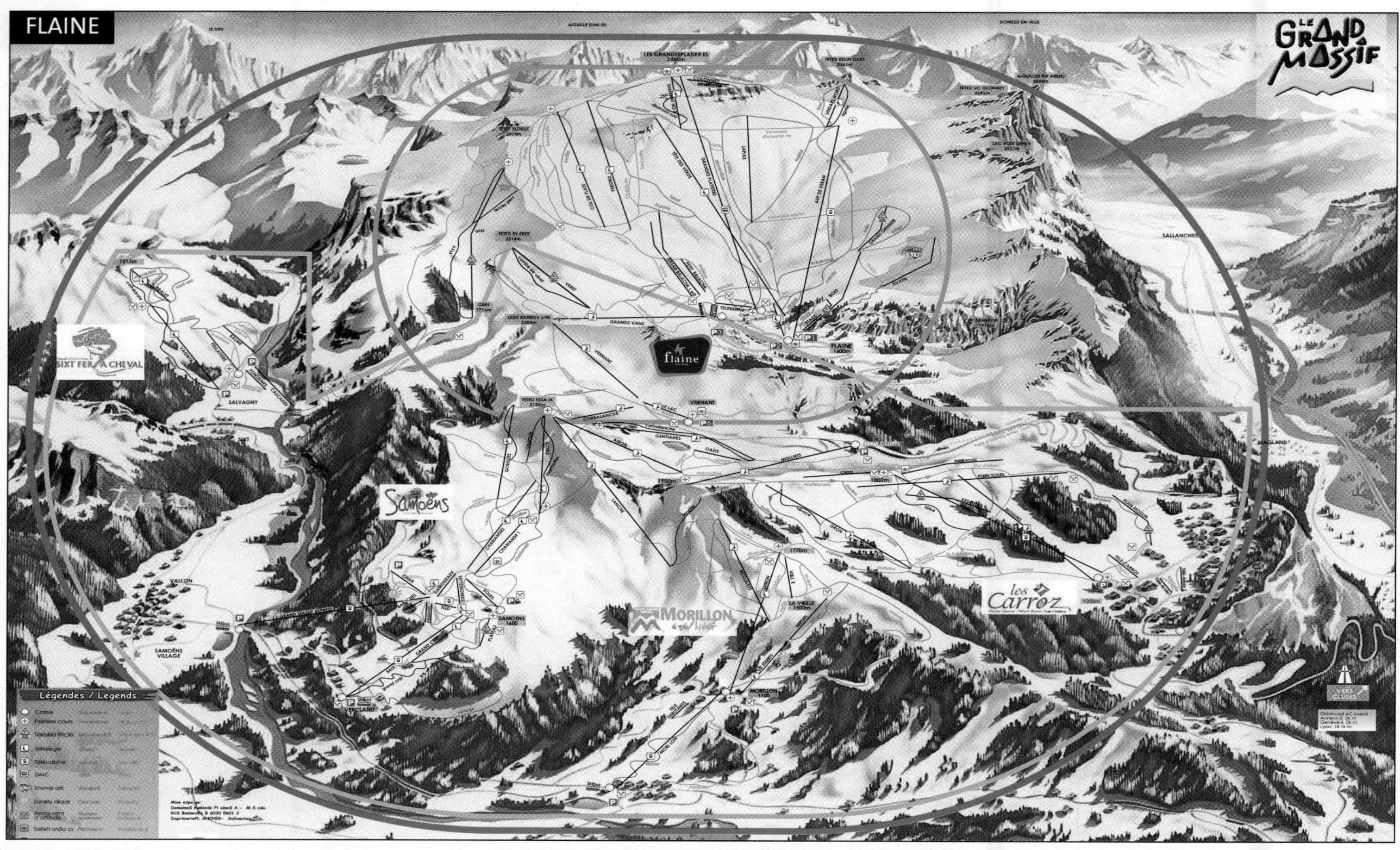

LE GRAND MASSIF
LES GRANDESPLATIER ES 2480m
flaine
FLAINE 1600m
GRANDS VANS
VERNANT
LE LAC
GENTIANES
OASIS
SIXT FER A CHEVAL
SALVAGNY
SIXT
Samoëns
SAMOENS 1600
SAMOËNS VILLAGE
VALLON
VERCLAND
MORILLON été/hiver
MORILLON 1100
LA VIEILLE 1500m
1770m
1900m
1800m
les Carroz
1200m
SALLANCHES
MAGLAND
Légendes / Legends
Caisse
Télésiège
Télécabine
DMC
Snowpark

free style

Le Boqueteau - **Jean Dubuffet**

Big BANG FX - MCI Group Photos : Pascal Lebeau

FLAINE

LE GRAND MASSIF

CULTURE GRAND SKI

*BEST FOR

All levels of skier and rider, big ski area, ski convenience, reliable snow-cover, off-piste, short airport transfer

ESSENTIALS

Altitude: 1600m (5,248ft)–2480m (8,134ft)
Further information: **t** +33 (0)4 50 90 80 01, *www.flaine.com*
Lifts in area: 73 in Le Grand Massif (7 cableways, 28 chairs, 38 drags) serving 265km of piste
Lift pass: Grand Massif (covers Les Carroz, Flaine, Morillon, Samoëns, Sixt) adult €187.20, youth 12–15yrs €147, child 5–11yrs €135, all for six days
Access: Geneva airport 1½hrs, railway station at Cluses 25km, frequent bus service to resort

over the past 40 years have expanded out of all recognition, this temple of Modernism, once worshipped by the British in general and by the Scots in particular, has so far remained largely undeveloped since the 1960s – but not for much longer.

The harsh diamond-shaped apartments conceived by architect Marcel Breuer still sit in a natural bowl on the edge of the Mont Blanc massif, little more than a one-hour drive from Geneva. Depending on your cultural viewpoint they are either an eyesore or a shining example of the Bauhaus School. 'Flaine is an ugly resort, but if you're a keen skier this is more than made up for by the convenience of access to the slopes,' said a reporter, and 'Somehow the austere buildings do fit in with the natural shape of the bowl,' was how another described it.

True, the raw concrete edifices have mellowed in colour, but to us they still look as alien now to their majestic mountain setting as they did when the Beatles ruled the charts.

Until now, the newest addition was the so-called Scandinavian Village, and that was built 20 years ago. This contrastingly pretty but isolated collection of pastel-painted cabins on the outskirts has considerable charm but is in serious need of a makeover. However, all this is about to change and Flaine is suddenly about to become the hottest property in the Alps.

Canadian resort developer Intrawest, the force behind the creation of the successful Arc 1950 village at Les Arcs, picked Flaine for its next major investment in the Alps. The area around the main gondola base station is being redeveloped for 2008–9 and a new 'village', Flaine Montsoleil, is under construction below the Scandinavian Village.

The first apartments – increasing the number of beds in Flaine by 30 per cent – come onstream this winter with the remainder scheduled for completion by 2012. Each building has a different cultural theme – contemporary is the watchword – in keeping with the resort's original avant-garde image. Canny skiers who did not buy in Les Arcs are reaching for their cheque books. Correctly, they surmise that Flaine and the Grand Massif have just as much to offer.

Despite its modest altitude, Flaine has a more reliable snow record than any resort of comparable altitude in France, thanks to the microclimate created by nearby Mont Blanc. Snow-cover is virtually guaranteed from early December until late April. Equally important is the high quality of the ski terrain, which extends to the traditional villages of Samoëns, Morillon, Les Carroz and Sixt.

Mountain

Main mountain access is by gondola, which takes you up to the Grandes Platières at 2480m. This is the starting point for a whole series of runs graded blue, red and black leading down into the main bowl of Flaine. The natural amphitheatre is rimmed by a series of lifts all going up to around 2500m. Good nursery slopes are located in and outside the village, making it an ideal spot for families with young children.

For more adventurous skiers and riders, Flaine is a base for exploring further afield into the Grand Massif. The Intrawest development plan has spurred the Compagnie des Alpes – owners of the lift system – to promise a series of upgrades including a link to the main part of the new village, situated just below the Scandinavian complex.

The main lift out of the bowl is a fast eight-person chair. From the 2204m summit of the Tête des Saix, north-facing runs drop down steep mogul slopes towards Samoëns. Alternatively you can choose easier cruising pistes that bring you all the way down to Morillon or to Les Carroz. The ancient village of Sixt has its own small ski area and is directly linked into the Grand Massif via a piste, but ski-buses provide the only means of return.

Anyone who can ski parallel can enjoy day-long excursions to the far corners of the Grand Massif. However, the lift system is prone to high-season bottlenecks in the afternoon when everyone is heading for home.

Flaine was one of the first resorts in France to embrace snowboarding. The 1500m Jam-Park has a half-pipe and snowcross course. Fantasurf has a half-pipe for children.

Learn

'Plus points are the excellent ski schools,' commented a reader. The **ESF**, **t** +33 (0)4 50 90 81 00, has a large presence. Anglo-Saxon visitors tend to favour the **ESI**, **t** +33 (0)4 50 90 84 41, said to be both good value and well organized, which has small classes of six to seven pupils. We have good reports of **Moniteurs Independants**, **t** +33 (0)6 07 19 56 09, a co-operative of individual teachers run by veteran instructor Guy Pezet. They offer group and private instruction for adults and children. **Stages Francois Simond**, **t** +33 (0)4 50 90 80 97, and **Stages Flaine Super Ski**, **t** +33 (0)6 81 06 19 06, both offer race training. Guiding is available through the ski schools.

Children

'Especially good for families,' said a reader. All the ski schools offer lessons, with the **ESI La Souris Verte**, **t** +33 (0)4 50 90 84 41, offering small groups. The **ESF Rabbit Club**, **t** +33 (0)4 50 90 81 00, is more Gallic. Both offer a collection and drop-off service. **MMV** in Hôtel Aujon and **Le Flaine**, **t** +33 (0)4 92 12 62 12, have mini-clubs for four to 11 years and a youth club for 12 to 14 years. **Club Med**, **t** +33 (0)4 50 90 81 66, has childcare for its small residents. Crystal's Hôtel Totem **Whizz Kids**, **t** +44 (0)870 160 6040, was rated 'first class' by reporters. **Les P'tits Loups**, **t** +33 (0)4 50 90 87 82, accepts children from six months to three years.

Lunch

'Expensive – try the mountain restaurants on the Samoëns side of the mountain, which are about 20 to 30 per cent cheaper,' advised a reporter. **Blanchot**, **t** +33 (0)4 50 90 82 44, is renowned for its onion soup. **Epicéa**, **t** +33 (0)4 50 90 83 79, between Flaine Forêt and Forum, has good pasta. **L'Eloge**, **t** +33 (0)4 50 90 85 91, by the Flaine gondola, provides simple food and service with a smile. **L'Igloo**, **t** +33 (0)4 50 90 14 31, at the top of the Morillon chair, has reasonable food at good prices. **The Oréade**, **t** +33 (0)4 50 90 03 61, at the top of the Kédeuse gondola, serves local mountain dishes. **Le Bissac**, **t** +33 (0)4 50 90 81 32, is a busy self-service with a good range of dishes.

Dine

'Flaine is an expensive resort for eating and drinking and the quality of the food is very variable,' said a reader. In Flaine Forum, try friendly **Chez La Jeanne, t** +33 (0)4 50 90 81 87, for excellent pizzas. **L'Auroch, t** +33 (0)4 50 90 12 83, and **Le Grain de Sel, t** +33 (0)4 50 90 80 49, serve traditional French cuisine. **Chez Daniel, t** +33 (0)4 50 90 81 87, has a warm alpine ambience. **La Pizzeria Chez Pierrot, t** +33 (0)4 50 90 84 56, has the best pizzas in town. **Les Chalets du Michet, t** +33 (0)4 50 90 80 08, has plenty of atmosphere. In Flaine Forêt, **La Perdrix Noire, t** +33 (0)4 50 90 81 81, specializes in Savoyard cuisine and has a fine reputation.

Party

'Not so hot in terms of ambience and nightlife,' said a reporter. Certainly other destinations have livelier après ski. The **White Pub** is recommended. The **Flying Dutchman** has karaoke and **Le Diamant Noir** is busy at weekends and in high season. You can also try your hand at driving a saloon car on ice. The **Ice Driving School, t** +33 (0)4 50 90 44 07, is one of the most famous in France.

Sleep

All the original hotels are now run by tour operators; accommodation can also be booked through **Flaine Reservations, t** +33 (0)4 50 90 89 09, *www.flaine reservations.com*.

★★★**Le Hameau de Flaine, t** +33 (0)4 50 90 40 40, on the mountain at 1800m, has Scandinavian-inspired chalets.

★★**Cap'Vacances Les Lindars, t** +33 (0)4 71 50 80 88, *www.capvacances.com*, is in the centre, with a sun terrace and a theatre.

★★**Le Totem, t** +44 (0)870 160 6040, is run by Crystal Holidays and has good-sized rooms. The food is rated 10 out of 10.

★★**Hôtel-Club Le Flaine MMV, t** +33 (0)4 50 90 47 36, *www.mmv.fr*, has spacious rooms and good food.

★★**Hôtel-Club Aujon MMV, t** +33 (0)4 50 90 80 10, *www.mmv.fr*, has comfortable, clean rooms.

★★**Résidence de la Forêt, t** +33 (0)4 50 90 86 99, situated at the top of the resort, has recently been renovated ('apartments very spacious and modern by normal French standards').

La Grave

Profile

For experts only. Rugged off-piste skiing on the glacial slopes of the mighty 4000m La Meije. The ski area is linked to Les Deux Alpes

Resort

La Meije, which rises above the rugged little village of La Grave between Grenoble and Briançon, was the last great peak of the Alpes to be conquered. Local guide Pierre Gaspard finally reached the 3982m summit in 1877. This corner of L'Oisans is

*BEST FOR

Steep 'n' deep, ski touring, ski mountaineering

ESSENTIALS

Altitude: 1450m (4,757ft)–3550m (11,647ft)

Further information: t +33 (0)4 76 79 90 05, *www.lagrave-lameije.com*

Lifts in resort: 4 (2 cableways, 2 drags) serving 5km of piste

Lift pass: adult or child €162 for six days

Access: Grenoble airport 2hrs

one of the poorest, least populated and most wildly beautiful areas of France, a place of jagged peaks and rushing waterfalls.

La Grave has some of the most demanding high-altitude skiing and snowboarding in Europe, with an extraordinary vertical drop of 2200m through dramatic glacial scenery. The top of the ski area can be reached by a long gondola and draglift from La Grave or by a snowcat from the top of the ski area at Les Deux Alpes. 'The village has real soul,' said a reporter; 'it reminds me of Zinal or Alagna.'

Mountain

The old but efficient gondola takes half an hour to climb from the village of La Grave to the top station. You must then find your own way down between the giant *séracs* and yawning crevasses. The main routes are clearly indicated but stray from the well-beaten path and you may encounter some spectacular *couloirs*. Runs at le Pan de Rideau start with a traverse along the edge of cliffs that requires a certain degree of concentration even for the most experienced powderhound.

From the top of the ski area you can either descend to the valley or ski off the backside with a guide to the remote village of St-Christophe-en-Oisans. You can take a taxi back to Venosc below Les Deux Alpes, climb through the lift system to the glacier, and return to La Grave down the front face of La Meije.

Learn

This is not teaching terrain. You can hire a guide from the **Bureau des Guides**, **t** +33 (0)4 76 79 90 21, but the only tuition is with the **ESF**, **t** +33 (0)4 76 79 92 86, 5km away at Le Chazelet.

Children

The **ESF** in Le Chazelet accepts children from four years. Babysitting can be arranged through the tourist office.

Lunch

The area has three mountain refuges, but most people have lunch in the village.

Dine

La Meije, **t** +33 (0)4 76 79 21 27, is a pizzeria close to the tourist office. The other restaurants are in the hotels.

Party

La Grave itself has little to offer anyone who does not climb or ski off-piste.

Sleep

*****Hôtel Les Chalets de la Meije**, **t** +33 (0)4 76 79 97 97, has double, triple and quadruple rooms, and a restaurant.

****Hôtel Edelweiss**, **t** +33 (0)4 76 79 90 93, *www.hotel-edelweiss.com*, has a bar and restaurant.

La Roche Méane, **t** +33 (0)4 76 79 91 43, *www.rochemeane.com*, is a charming and good-value B&B that was once an old stone barn. It has five bedrooms.

Skiers' Lodge, *www.skierslodge.com*, is said to have excellent four-course meals. Accommodation is basic but satisfactory.

Les Houches

***BEST FOR**

All levels of skier and rider, families, boy/girl racers

ESSENTIALS

Altitude: 1000m (3,281ft)–1860m (6,102ft)
Further information: **t** +33 (0)4 50 55 50 62, *www.leshouches.com*
Lifts in area: 18 (1 mountain railway, 2 cableways, 4 chairs, 11 drags) in Les Houches serving 55km of piste. 729km in Mont Blanc ski area
Lift pass: Mont-Blanc Unlimited (covers Les Houches, Chamonix, Courmayeur) adult €225, child 4–15yrs €180, family €562. Les Houches adult €147.80, child 4–15yrs €103.50
Access: Geneva airport 1hr, railway station in resort

Profile

Family-friendly resort in the Chamonix Valley with good tree-skiing and a revered World Cup downhill course. Ski area linked by lift but not by piste to St-Gervais

Resort

Les Houches is a pleasant family resort with the best tree-skiing in the Mont Blanc region. It has an FIS World Cup downhill course considered by racers to be second only in techical difficulty to the Streif on the Hahnenkamm in Kitzbühel. 'World Cup run, the Kandahar, is brilliant,' said a reader.

Mountain

Main mountain access is by a new cable car or eight-person gondola. Don't be surprised to see a railway carriage slowly crossing the pistes on the mountaintop near the cable car top station. The rack-and-pinion Mont Blanc Tramway, which comes up from St-Gervais, opened in 1904 and is still going strong.

The pistes offer a wide variety of skiing for all levels with some excellent trails winding through the woods. 'There is enough skiing on a local Les Houches pass for a week for intermediate skiers with young families,' said a reporter. The slopes are used by the **British Ski Academy**, **t** +44 (0)20 8399 1181, a skiing school (with academic as well as ski lessons) for young British hopefuls, based in Les Houches.

Learn

ESF, t +33 (0)4 50 54 48 79, and **Evolution 2**, **t** +33 (0)4 50 54 31 44, are the two schools. The **Compagnie des Guides de Chamonix**, **t** +33 (0)4 50 47 21 68, has a branch in Les Houches.

Children

The **ESF Jardin des Neiges**, **t** +33 (0)4 50 54 48 79, is for skiers from three years. **La Garderie des Chavants**, **t** +33 (0)4 50 54 48 19, looks after little ones from three months.

Lunch

Try **Les Vieilles Luges**, **t** +33 (0)6 84 42 37 00, at Maisonneuve, **Le Prarion**, **t** +33 (0)4 50 54 40 07, at Prarion, and **Le Courant d'Air**, **t** +33 (0)4 50 55 99 65, on the Col de Voza. **Le Hors Piste**, **t** +33 (0)4 50 55 55 50 62, is a new eatery at the top of the Maisonneuve chair.

Dine

La Sabaudia, **t** +33 (0)4 50 54 47 72, **Le Delice**, **t** +33 (0)4 50 54 91 52 06, and **La Ferme des Agapes**, **t** +33 (0)4 50 54 50 69, offer regional specialities. **La Ferme de**

Stephane, **t** +33 (0)4 50 54 26 34, is a new restaurant serving high quality cuisine.

Party

Nightlife is limited to just a couple of quiet bars. If you require after-dinner entertainment, head to Chamonix.

Sleep

- ★★★★**Les Granges en Haut**, **t** +33 (0)4 50 54 65 36, *www.grangesdenhaut.com*, is Les Houches' first luxury property – a mountain hamlet of 14 elegant wooden chalets tucked away in the forest.
- ★★★**Hôtel Beau-Site**, **t** +33 (0)4 50 55 51 16, *www.hotel-beausite.com*, is in the heart of the village, with a restaurant and pool.
- ★★★**Hôtel Chris-Tal**, **t** +33 (0)4 50 54 50 55, *www.chris-tal.fr*, has a games room and pool.
- ★★★**Hôtel du Bois**, **t** +33 (0)4 50 54 50 35, *www.hotel-du-bois.com*, is decorated in traditional chalet style, and houses Le Caprice restaurant.
- ★★★**Hôtel Slalom** **t** +33 (0)4 50 54 40 60, *www.hotelslalom.net*, is opposite the main lift and is very comfortable and modern.
- **La Ferme d'en Haut**, **t** +33 (0)4 50 54 74 87, *www.lafermedenhaut.fr*, is an early 19th-century farmhouse with four bedrooms.

Megève

Profile

Family-friendly resort in the Chamonix Valley with good tree-skiing for all levels and a revered World Cup downhill course. Ski area linked by lift to St-Gervais

*BEST FOR

Sophisto-cats, ski gourmets, intermediate cruisers, window-shoppers

ESSENTIALS

Altitude: 1113m (3,651ft)–2350m (7,708ft)
Further information: **t** +33 (0)4 50 21 27 29, *www.megeve.com*
Lifts in area: 111 in Evasion Mont Blanc (13 cableways, 38 chairs, 60 drags) serving 445km of piste; 729km in Mont Blanc ski area
Lift pass: Mont-Blanc Unlimited (covers Les Houches, Chamonix, Courmayeur) adult €225, child 4–15yrs €180, family €562
Access: Geneva airport 1hr, TGV railway station at Sallanches 10km, regular bus service to resort

Resort

Megève vies with Courchevel 1850 for the title of France's smartest resort. It was founded in 1914 by Baroness de Rothschild who, during the years following the First World War, turned it into her own winter salon for European aristocracy. The rich and famous built houses here and, at one point, the resort liked to boast that it was the winter home to more kings and queens – both crowned and uncrowned – than any other resort in Europe.

Its heyday was in the 1950s and 1960s when artist and author Jean Cocteau, along with celebrities such as Charles Aznavour, Sacha Distel, Johnny Hallyday and Brigitte Bardot made it the focus of Parisian café society.

Patronage has continued from other influential families such as Citroën, Tattinger and Benetton. However, the only royals left these days are the House of Saudi, who have a lavish chalet just above the town.

Megève's position, just an hour's drive from Geneva airport, makes it popular with weekenders and families wanting to avoid long transfers. Its only downside is that low altitude can restrict snow-cover in the village. However, it has had reliably good snow cover for the past three

AIG. DE ROSELETTE 2384
MONT JOLY 2525
AIG. CROCHE 2487
CRÊT DU MIDI 1890
2353
CÔTE 2000
L'EPAULE 2112
LES CONTAMINES
MT JOUX 1958
LE PLANAY
ALTIPORT
ROCHEBRUNE 1754
LE TORRAZ 1930
FLUMET
PRAZ S/ ARLY
LE CHRISTOMET 1853
CASSIOZ
FREDDY 1833
MT D'ARBOIS 1840
LE PLANELLET
ST NICOLAS DE VEROCE
LES CHATTRIX
LES COMMUNAILLES
LE VILLARD
LE JAILLET 1580
LA MOTTAZ
LES PLANS
LES PETTOREAUX
LES PRAZ
MEGÈVE
LE BETTEX
MONT D'ARBOIS
LE VERNAY
MONTS ROSSET
PONT D'ARBON
VAUVRAY
CUPELIN
LE CHATELET
LA PRINCESSE
DEMI-QUARTIER
LE FREYNET
ORMARET
ST GERVAIS MONT-BLANC
COMBLOUX
COVAGNET
GARE TGV
LE FAYET

Fréderique et Pierre Novat © 04

Stanford Skiing
The Megève Specialists
- Family-run company
- Catered Chalets
- Professional Chefs
- Hotels, Luxury Apartments
- Flexible Travel
- Weekends & Short Breaks
- Accompanied Skiing
- English Ski Lessons
HOTEL SYLVANA
Chalet les Clochettes & Chalet-Hotel Sylvana
t +44(0)1603 477 471
www.stanfordskiing.co.uk
3978
ATOL
PROTECTED

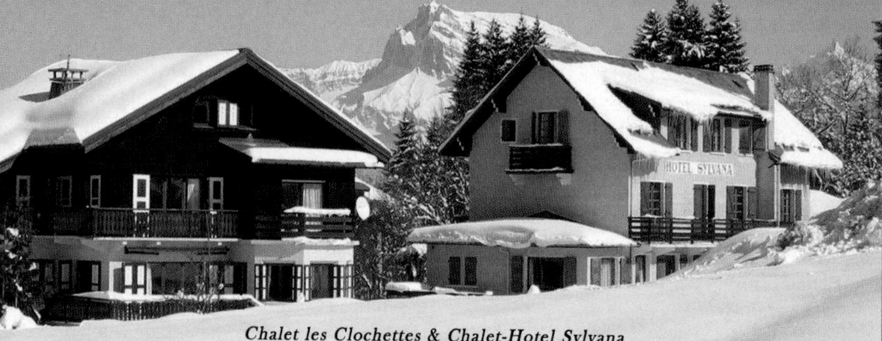

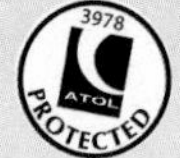

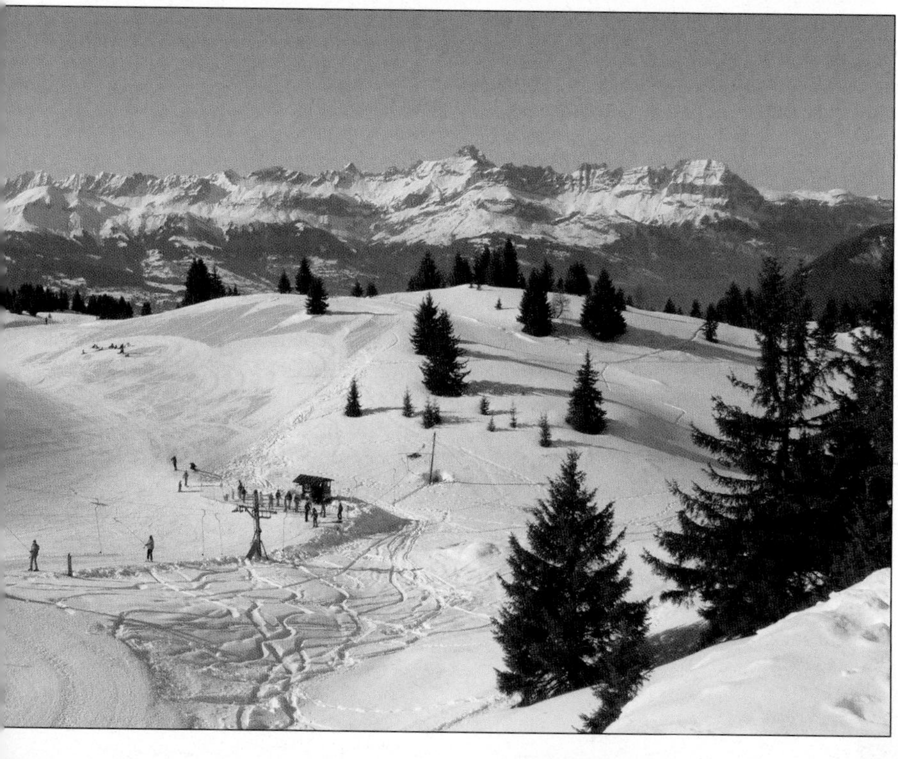

seasons. The focal point of Megève is a central square surrounded by mellow 18th-century buildings, a fine medieval church and the Allard department store where the world's first ski trousers were tailored.

Brightly painted sleighs driven by local farmers ply for hire to reach the lift stations and hotels. They are more fun but more expensive than the free ski buses and regular services to Chamonix and other resorts in the region covered by the extensive regional lift passes.

'High spots were the people, the food and the jazz club – actually it's not just a jazz club but a good live music venue,' said reporters, 'but beware that it is very expensive.'

Mountain

This enormous ski area extends from the spa town of St-Gervais and the village of St-Nicolas-de-Veroce through Mègeve and on to the little resort of La Giettaz where wooded slopes lead down to Praz-sur-Arly in the Val d'Arly. The next step will be for Mègeve to join the 73-lift Espace Diamant circuit that includes Flumet, Notre-Dame-de-Bellecombe, Les Saisies and Crest-Voland.

For the moment, Megève's skiing is divided into three sectors, with two of them, Mont d'Arbois and Rochebrune, joined by cableways.

A gondola from the town centre or a cable car from the outskirts take you up to Rochebrune. The area offers the most attractive runs in the resort and is usually less crowded than Mont d'Arbois. From the top of the gondola, a sequence of further lifts and pistes lead up to Côte 2000, which has some of the most challenging runs in the region.

The main beginner and intermediate area of Mont d'Arbois is reached by cable car and gondola from Rochebune or by a choice of two gondolas from the other side of town. A network of green and blue pistes provide easy skiing back towards Megève, or you can venture almost endlessly further afield. From 1958m Mont Joux you cruise wood-fringed pastures to Le Bettex and St-Gervais, or you can tackle higher and more demanding exposed terrain at 2350m on Mont Joly.

Le Jaillet, Megève's third and least known area, is reached by gondola from the edge of town. The front face, leading back to the resort, has a good variety of mainly red runs and usually remains uncrowded even in high season. A six-seater chair takes you up to the 1853m summit of Christomet where you can ski down to La Giettaz. Some outstanding off-piste can be found on the wooded slopes beneath the Tête de Bonjournal, as well as runs from La Torraz into the Val d'Arly.

Megève is a popular destination for cross-country skiers, with four circuits totalling 70km, including a long, scenic track from the Mont d'Arbois cable car to Le Bettex and St-Nicolas-de-Véroce.

The resort's only terrain park is at Mont Joux, and there is a boardercross course at Rochebrune.

Learn

Both the **ESF**, **t** +33 (0)4 50 21 00 97, and the **ESI**, **t** +33 (0)4 50 58 78 88, are warmly recommended, **Ecole Freeride**, **t** +33 (0)4 50 93 03 52, and **Summits**, **t** +33 (0)4 50 93 03 52, are alternatives. New last season are **Agence de Ski a Megève**, **t** +33 (0)4 50 89 12 73, and **Evolution 2**, **t** +33 (0)4 50 58 35 41. Guiding can be arranged through the long-established **Bureau des Guides de Megève**, **t** +33 (0)4 50 21 55 11.

Children

Megève has a justified reputation for providing good childcare. The non-ski kindergarten, **Meg Accueil**, **t** +33 (0)4 50 58 77 84, situated next to the Palais des Sports, cares for children from 12 months. **Club Piou-Piou**, **t** +33 (0)4 50 58 97 65, accepts skiers from three to five years. **La Princesse**, **t** +33 (0)4 50 93 00 86, looks after skiers from two and a half years. All the ski schools offer children's classes. **Ecole Freeride**, **t** +33 (0)4 50 93 03 52, limits the class size to six.

Lunch

You can eat better on the mountain in Megève than in any other resort in France, but you will pay for the privilege. At Rochebrune, **L'Alpette**, **t** +33 (0)4 50 21 03 69, has been a lunchtime institution since 1935. **L'Auberge de La Côte 2000**, **t** +33 (0)4 50 21 31 84, is also praised. At Mont d'Arbois, **Les Mandarines**, **t** +33 (0)4 50 21 31 27, and **L'Igloo**, **t** +33 (0)4 50 93 05 84, both have good food. At Le Jaillet, **Auberge du Christomet**, **t** +33 (0)4 50 21 11 34, is warmly recommended. **Chez Ernestine**, **t** +33 (0)4 50 93 13 08, on the route from Mont d'Arbois to St Gervais via Mont Joly, is warmly praised ('an amazing steak with superb views of Mont Blanc'). **L'Idéal 1850**, T +33 (0)4 50 21 31 26, at the top of the Princesse gondola is Rothschild-owned and Michelin-rated.

Dine

Le Cintra, **t** +33 (0)4 50 21 02 60, is famed for its seafood. **Flocons de Sel**, **t** +33 (0)4 50 21 49 99, has a Michelin star. **Le Puck**, **t** +33 (0)4 50 21 06 61, a cut-price addendum to the Flocons de Sel, has gourmet fare at modest prices. **L'Alpage**, **t** +33 (0)4 50 21 30 39, has a good ambience and serves Savoyard specialities. Delightfully named **Le Sapin Chaud**, **t** +33 (0)4 50 91 08 88, is in an old wooden chalet. **Le Prieuré**, **t** +33 (0)4 50 21 01 79, and **Mirtillo**, **t** +33 (0)4 50 21 69 33, are both recommended. **Les Enfants Terribles**, **t** +33 (0)4 50 58 76 69, has now become a brasserie that is an integral part of Hotel Mont Blanc.

Party

The après ski is taken just as seriously as the skiing, with window-shopping for jewellery, antiques and designer clothing a major part of the early evening entertainment. **Club de Jazz Les Cinq Rues**, off the church square, is both an apéritif and late-night focal point. Its cosy surroundings attract some of the biggest names in jazz from both sides of the Atlantic. **Bar Tabac St-Paul** attracts the locals. The **Palo Alto** houses two popular discos. The casino, originally a 1930s bus station, also has a restaurant. **Le Pallas** is popular with a young crowd. **Bar des Alpes** is an internet café. **Wake Up** is a cocktail and tapas bar.

The **Palais des Sports** has an outdoor Olympic-size skating-rink and a pool. Electric-powered ice bumper-cars are an unusual sport on the skating-rink.

Sleep

The standard of Megève's four-star hotels and chalets is outstanding.

- ******Chalet Cashmere**, **t** +33 (0)4 50 78 27 44, *www.chalet-cashmere.fr*, is a spacious new chalet with cutting-edge style and facilities.
- ******Chalet du Mont d'Arbois**, **t** +33 (0)4 50 21 25 03, *www.chalet-montarbois.com*, used to be the Rothschild family home and is close to the Mont d'Arbois cable car. The hotel also has a separate chalet, **Le Refuge du Planay**, with four double rooms.
- ******Le Fer à Cheval**, **t** +33 (0)4 50 21 30 39, *www.feracheval-megeve.com*, is attractively decorated and serves a good English breakfast.

★★★★**Les Fermes de Marie**, **t** +33 (0)4 50 93 03 10, *www.c-h-m.com*, 10 minutes' walk from the centre, is an exquisite place to stay, based around an ancient cowshed and other farm buildings. A pool is set into rocks and the spa is one of the finest in Europe.

★★★★**Lodge Montagnard**, **t** +33 (0)4 50 54 65 36, *www.lodgemontagard.com*, is a collection of three new chalet-style properties – Le Hameau de Mavarin, l"Hotel du Hameau, and Chalet Reine des Près – all designed in traditional yet elegant chalet-style.

★★★★**Lodge Park**, **t** +33 (0)4 50 93 05 03, *www.c-h-m.com*, looks like a private club decorated in a 'hunting, shooting, fishing' style.

★★★★**Le Manège**, **t** +33 (0)4 50 21 41 09, *www.hotel-le-manege.com*, is small and chalet-style with 30 rooms.

★★★★**Hotel Mont-Blanc**, **t** +33 (0)4 50 21 20 02, *www.c-h-m.com*, perfectly placed in the centre of the pedestrian district, is one of the best small hotels in the Alps.

★★★★**Chalet Saint Georges**, **t** +33 (0)4 50 93 07 15, *www.hotel-chaletstgeorges.com*, has excellent accommodation.

★★★★**Le Chalet Saint Philippe et Son Hameau**, **t** +33 (0)4 50 91 19 30, *www.chalet-saint-philippe.com*, are four luxury chalets with hotel service.

★★★**Hotel Coin du Feu**, **t** +33 (0)4 50 21 04 94, *www.coindufeu.com*, is a delightful small hotel.

★★★**La Grange d'Arly**, **t** +33 (0)4 50 58 77 88, *www.grange-darly.com*, has the freshest food and comfortable rooms.

★★★**Au Vieux Moulin**, **t** +33 (0)4 50 21 22 29, *www.vieuxmoulin.com*, is tastefully decorated, with excellent cuisine.

★★★**Hotel Chalet d'Antoine**, **t** +33 (0)4 50 21 05 56, *www.chalet-antoine.co.uk*, is said to be comfortable and cosy. Word has it that the chef trained with Gordon Ramsay.

★★★**Le Gai Soleil**, **t** +33 (0)4 50 21 00 70, *www.le-gai-soleil.fr*, is a family-run inn with 21 bedrooms and 'wonderful' half-board food.

★★**La Chauminé**, **t** +33 (0)4 50 21 37 05, is a B&B with 11 rooms.

Les Menuires

Profile

Large purpose-built resort favoured by the budget-conscious who want to ski the giant Trois Vallées area without the high cost of staying in Méribel or Courchevel

Resort

The ugly duckling of French ski resorts from the 1960s has grown positively handsome in middle age. A swan it is not, but Les Menuires has long since matured from the low-cost concrete dormitory that it once was into a comfortable and convenient ski base that lies 450 vertical metres short of Val Thorens up the winding road from Moûtiers.'The resort

✻BEST FOR

All levels of skier and rider, families, value

ESSENTIALS

Altitude: 1850m (6,068ft)–3300m (10,827ft)

Further information: Les Menuires, **t** +33 (0)4 79 00 73 00, *www.lesmenuires.com*

Lifts in area: 165 in Trois Vallées (43 cableways, 68 chairs, 54 drags) serving 600km of piste

Lift pass: Trois Vallées adult €157–295, child 5–13yrs €112–225, both for six days

Access: Chambéry airport 2hrs, Lyon airport 2½hrs, Geneva airport 3hrs, railway station at Moûtiers 25km

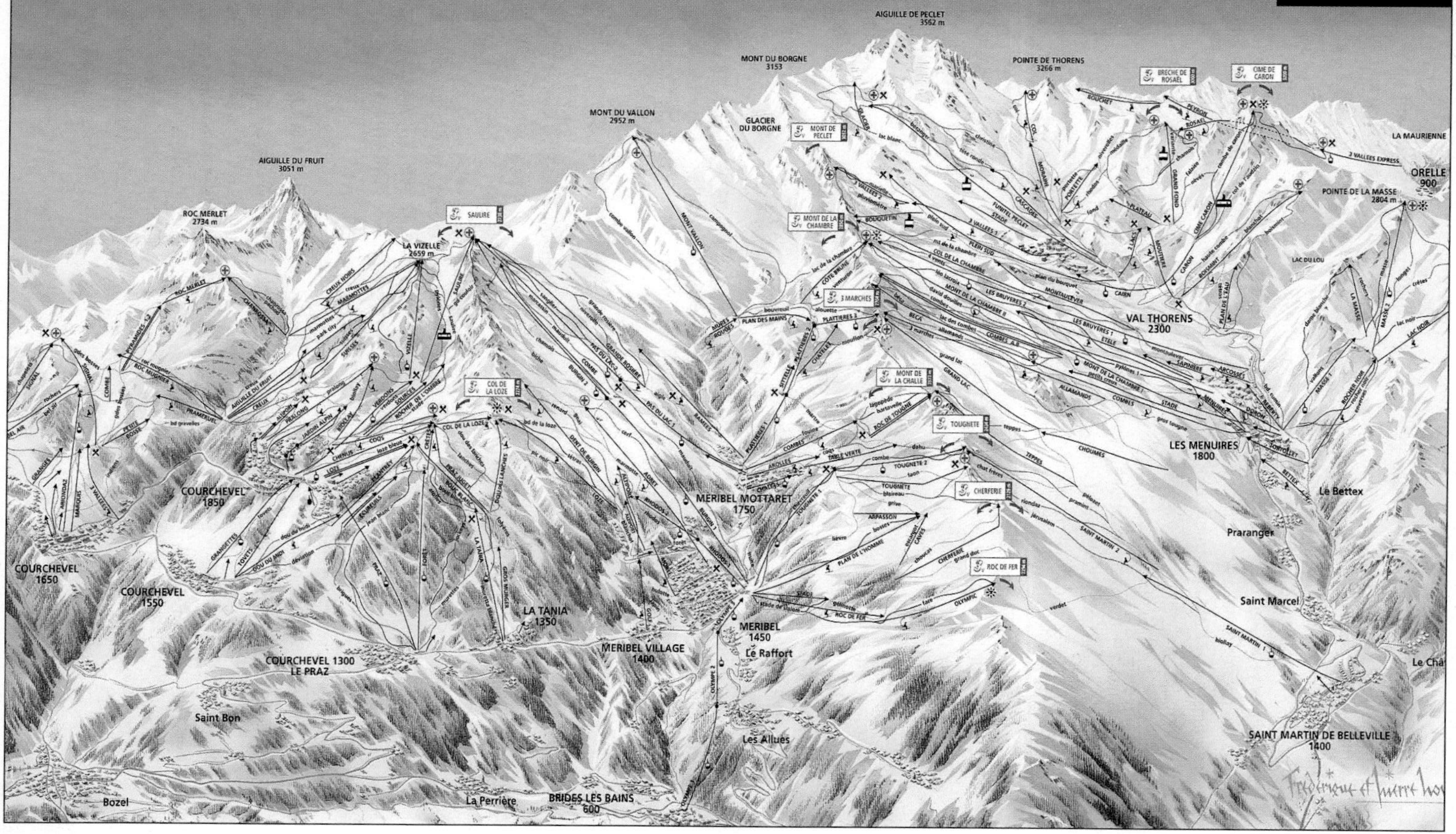

AIGUILLE DE PECLET
3562 m
MONT DU BORGNE
3153
POINTE DE THORENS
3266 m
GLACIER
DU BORGNE
MONT DU VALLON
2952 m
AIGUILLE DU FRUIT
3051 m
ROC MERLET
2734 m
LA MAURIENNE
ORELLE
900
POINTE DE LA MASSE
2804 m
LAC DU LOU
LA VIZELLE
2659 m
VAL THORENS
2300
LES MENUIRES
1800
Le Bettex
Praranger
Saint Marcel
Le Chât
SAINT MARTIN DE BELLEVILLE
1400
MERIBEL MOTTARET
1750
MERIBEL
1450
Le Raffort
MERIBEL VILLAGE
1400
Les Allues
LA TANIA
1350
COURCHEVEL
1850
COURCHEVEL
1650
COURCHEVEL
1550
COURCHEVEL 1300
LE PRAZ
Saint Bon
Bozel
La Perrière
BRIDES LES BAINS
600

was not as ugly as many people have reported,' said a reader.

The original eyesore of La Croisette had a makeover for the Albertville Olympics (the slalom events took place here) and then a few years ago the worst *résidence* was bulldozed to make way for a gleaming new MGM apartment block that has completely changed the aspect of the resort. The construction of a church also gave it physical – if not spiritual – soul by providing a focal point for the real village that Les Menuires had finally become.

Much of the new development is concentrated on the pleasant satellites of Reberty, Les Bruyères and Preyerand, slightly higher up the hill, which have really become a resort in their own right, with restaurants, shops and bars (but no pharmacy – the only one is to be found in La Croisette).

Inevitably the downside of this grand metamorphosis is that Les Menuires is no longer the bargain basement it once was. However, accommodation prices remain significantly lower than in the more fashionable big-name resorts of the Trois Vallées. Val Thorens, St-Martin-de-Belleville and Méribel are easily reached on skis. A trip to the lower reaches of Courchevel is more of an expedition – a full day out with scarcely time to grab a quick lunch before beginning the journey home. Missing the last lift connections involves an expensive taxi ride.

Mountain

The skiing takes place on both sides of the valley. Les Menuires has its own challenging and usually uncrowded ski area on the 2805m Pointe de la Masse, reached from the village by gondola and chair. Runs down the front face include the infamous black Dame Blanche, which can be tricky in icy conditions. The summit is the starting point for several off-piste itineraries towards the Lac du Lou and Val Thorens, as well as down the valley towards St-Martin.

On the other side of Les Menuires an assortment of gondolas and chairs take you up to Roc des Trois Marches and Mont de la Chambre above the Méribel Valley. The Les Granges six-seater chair has replaced two old draglifts here.

The enormous area of open slopes leading back down to Les Menuires provides the sunniest and some of the most enjoyable skiing in the Trois Vallées. 'We managed to ski for the whole week on blue runs, without having to ski the same piste twice,' said a reporter. 'Although busy on some days, lifts rarely had large queues,' said another. Riders have a new terrain park and a snowcross course in the Combes-Becca sector.

Learn

The **ESF**, **t** +33 (0)4 79 00 61 43, is the only ski school in Les Menuires. Most – but not all – instructors speak reasonable English.

Children

The nursery in the **Piou-Piou Club**, **t** +33 (0)4 79 00 63 79, cares for non-skiers from three months at La Croisette, and those from two and a half years can go to the **Village des Piou-Piou**, **t** +33 (0)4 79 00 69 50, in Bruyères. The **ESF**, **t** +33 (0)4 79 00 61 43, gives lessons from three years.

Lunch

Le Grand Lac, **t** +33 (0)4 79 08 25 78, is a gourmet restaurant at the bottom of Les Granges chair. **Chalet 2000**, **t** +33 (0)4 79 00 60 57, at Reberty, is warmly recommended. **Chalet des Neiges**, **t** +33 (0)4 79 00 60 55, above St-Martin, has good food and a sunny terrace, and **Quatres Vents**, **t** +33 (0)4 79 00 64 44, at Les Bruyères, maintains a high standard.

Dine

Eateries include **La Marmite du Géant**, **t** +33 (0)4 79 00 74 75, and **Les Sonnailles**, **t** +33 (0)4 79 00 74 28, both in Les Bruyères. **La Trattoria**, **t** +33 (0)4 79 00 74 23, in La Croisette, is recommended, and **La Ferme de Reberty**, **t** +33 (0)4 79 00 77 01, 'provide a really good meal'.

Party

après ski in Les Menuires is fairly muted, with families staying in their apartments. 'If you're looking for a busy nightlife, this is not the place to go,' said a reporter. The **Tilbury**, **L'Oisans** and **Crazy Bar** are popular watering holes. **Le New Pop** at La Croisette is a late-night venue, and **Le Leeberty** at Les Bruyères is said to be 'a great place for partying'. Night-time tubing takes place on two 200m-long pistes equipped with a moving carpet. Swimming and skating are the other activities.

Sleep

Les Menuires is mainly apartment territory. All can be booked through the reservations office, **t** +33 (0)4 79 00 79 79.

Les Menuires:

****Chalet-Hotel La Kaya t** +33 (0)4 79 41 42 00, *www.hotel-kaya.com*, is Les Menuires' first four-star with a new gourmet restaurant called **K**.

Reberty/Les Bruyères:

****Les Montagnettes 3 Vallées**, **t** +33 (0)4 79 00 20 51, *www.montagnettes.com*, is a collection of spacious chalets and apartments.

****MGM Hameau des Marmottes**, **t** +44 (0)870 750 6820, *www.ernalow.co.uk*, are extremely comfortable apartments.

****Les Alpages de Reberty**, **t** +33 (0)4 79 01 35 35, is a smart Pierre et Vacances complex.

***Les Bruyères**, **t** +33 (0)4 79 00 75 10, *www.latitudeshotels.com*, offers some good-value accommodation.

***Hôtel Le Menuire**, **t** +33 (0)4 79 00 60 33, *www.le-menuire.fr*, has family-sized rooms with satellite TV.

***L'Ours Blanc**, **t** +33 (0)4 79 00 61 66, *www.hotel-ours-blanc.com*, has a lounge with an open fireplace and a rustically decorated bar.

Chalet 2000, **t** +33 (0)4 79 00 60 57, *www.hotel-chalet2000.fr*, has double, triple and quadruple rooms.

Méribel

Profile

Sprawling chalet-style resort that acts as the most central and convenient base for fully exploring the giant Trois Vallées

*BEST FOR

Beginners and intermediates, families, big ski area, luxury chalets

ESSENTIALS

Altitude: 1400m (4,593ft)–2952m (9,685ft)
Further information: **t** +33 (0)4 79 08 60 01, *www.meribel.net*
Lifts in area: 165 in Trois Vallées (43 cable-ways, 68 chairs, 54 drags) serving 600km of piste
Lift pass: Trois Vallées adult €157–295, child 5–13yrs €112–225, both for six days
Access: Chambéry airport 2hrs, Lyon airport 2½hrs, Geneva airport 3hrs, Eurostar at Moûtiers, 18km

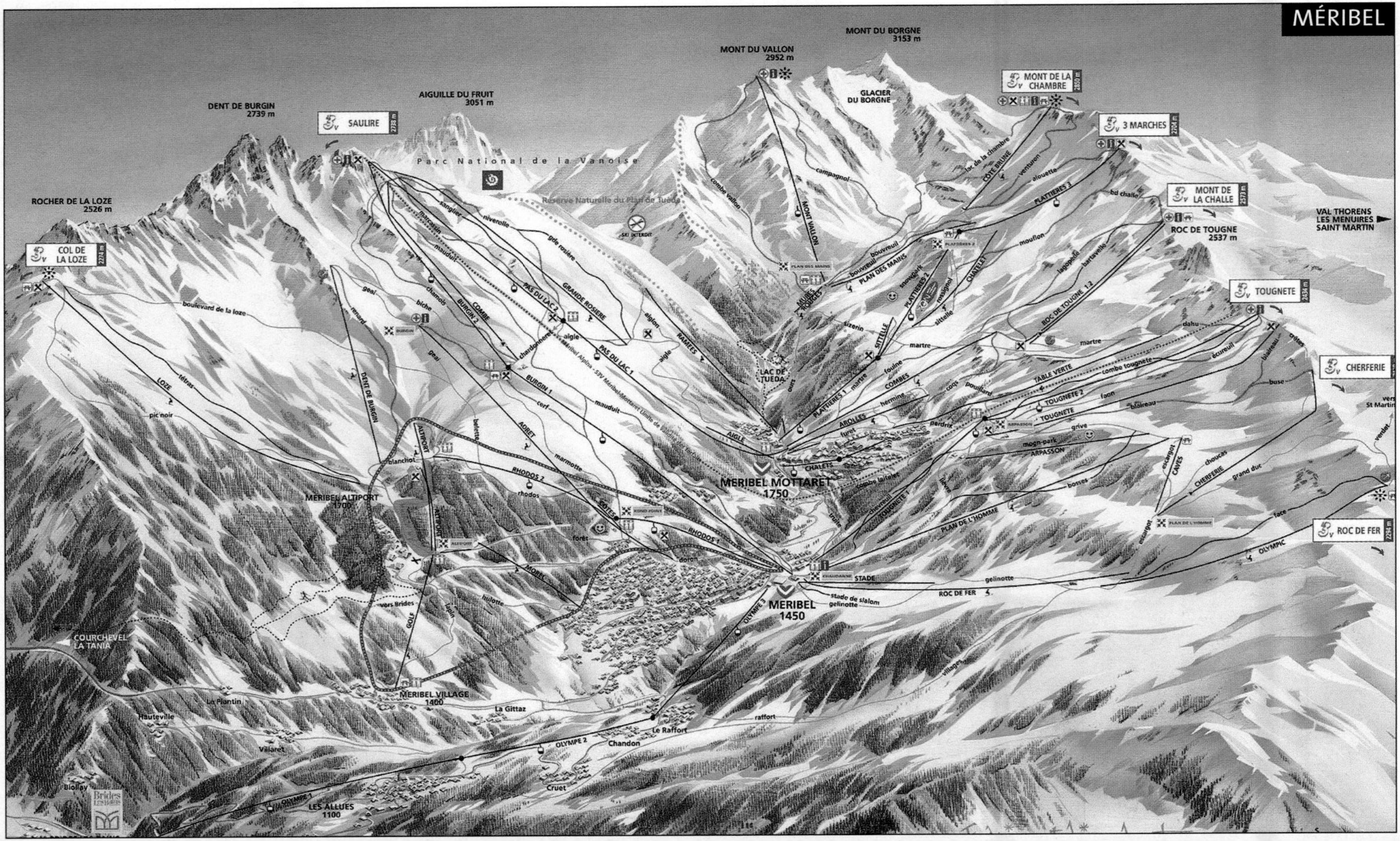

MÉRIBEL

MONT DU BORGNE
3153 m

MONT DU VALLON
2952 m

GLACIER
DU BORGNE

AIGUILLE DU FRUIT
3051 m

DENT DE BURGIN
2739 m

SAULIRE
2738 m

ROCHER DE LA LOZE
2526 m

COL DE
LA LOZE
2274 m

MONT DE LA
CHAMBRE
2850 m

3 MARCHES
2704 m

MONT DE
LA CHALLE
2573 m

ROC DE TOUGNE
2537 m

VAL THORENS
LES MENUIRES
SAINT MARTIN

TOUGNETE
2434 m

CHERFERIE

ROC DE FER
2294 m

Parc National de la Vanoise

Reserve Naturelle du Plan de Tueda

SKI INTERDIT

MERIBEL MOTTARET
1750

MERIBEL
1450

MERIBEL ALTIPORT
1700

MERIBEL VILLAGE
1400

LES ALLUES
1100

COURCHEVEL
LA TANIA

LAC DE
TUEDA

MONT VALLON
PLAN DES MAINS
PLATTIERES 1
PLATTIERES 2
PLATTIERES 3
ROC DE TOUGNE 1.2
TOUGNETE
TOUGNETE 2
TABLE VERTE
ARPASSON
CHERFERIE
CAVES
PLAN DE L'HOMME
ROC DE FER
OLYMPIC
STADE
CHALETS
AROLLES
COMBES
SITTELLE
CHATELET
COTE BRUNE
RAMEES
AIGLE
PAS DU LAC 1
PAS DU LAC 2
GRANDE ROSIERE
COMBE
BURGIN 1
BURGIN 2
DENT DE BURGIN
LOZE
ADRET
RHODOS 1
RHODOS 2
ALTIPORT
MOREL
COTES
GOLF
OLYMPE 1
OLYMPE 2
OLYMPE 3

La Plantin
Hauteville
Villaret
Biollay
La Gittaz
Le Raffort
Chandon
Cruet

Brides-les-Bains

For a totally hassle free experience...

For 23 years Meriski has been operating in the picture postcard resort of Méribel and is proud to be considered "The Méribel Specialists." Whether you are holidaying as a couple, with a group of friends or as a family, our portfolio of ten authentic chalets, offers a perfect balance of accommodation. Meriski offers a highly personalised service which is extended to children of all ages. With a range of facilities available including our own dedicated crèche and a complimentary mini-bus service.

...TRUST MERISKI TO MAKE A DIFFERENCE!

MERISKI
THE MÉRIBEL SPECIALISTS

For more information or a copy of this seasons brochure call (01285) 648518, visit www.meriski.co.uk, or email sales@meriski.co.uk

Major Resorts - Great Prices

SkiCollection

Only 4 Star Ski Apartments

Resorts throughout the French Alps include Meribel, Val d'Isere, Tignes, Les Arcs, La Plagne, Courchevel, Val Thorens, Les Menuires, Chamonix, Alpe d'Huez, Flaine...

Accommodation only or self-drive package deals

www.skicollection.co.uk

0844 576 0175

ABTA W5537

Méribel, France

Parallel Lines Ski and Snowboard School in Méribel is a British Ski School using only top British instructors.

Whether you're a beginner or advanced, skier or snowboarder, adult or child, we can help to take your enjoyment of the mountains to the next level.

www.parallel-lines.com UK Booking Office: 01702 589580
French Office: +33 479 003221 email: info@parallel-lines.com

Resort

Méribel vies with Val d'Isère for the title of the most popular resort in Europe for English-speaking skiers and snowboarders. It was founded in the late 1930s by British skier Colonel Peter Lindsay who, like other international racers, had boycotted St Anton in Austria and was looking for a new resort when he stumbled on the scenic Les Allues Valley.

The first lift was installed after the Second World War when Lindsay began developing the area in conjunction with French racer Emile Allais. He decreed that all buildings must be made of stone and wood with slate roofs in order to blend into their beautiful mountain environment.

Méribel today has grown into a ski city that he would not begin to recognize. It stretches in different *quartiers* up the mountain from Méribel Village at 1400m to the top of Méribel Mottaret at 1800m. But, miraculously, his building regulations have been vigorously adhered to and, with the exception of the original buildings of Mottaret, Méribel avoided the concrete architectural horrors of the 1960s. The main village is connected to the valley by a long gondola that climbs from the spa resort of Brides-les-Bains.

Heart of the resort is Méribel Les Allues at 1450m, which houses most of the shops, restaurants, and the lift hub of La Chaudanne. The bi-weekly street market provides colour. Other communities are situated off the dead-end road leading to the Altiport and on the edge of the wooded pistes leading into the resort. Confusingly, Méribel Village is not the main village but a more recently built satellite situated a 2km drive away from Les Allues , but linked by chairlift into the ski area.

Méribel Mottaret is a higher satellite situated at 1750m on the road above Méribel Les Allues, and is a convenient base for anyone wanting doorstep skiing and the best snow-cover. The different sectors of town are served by a ski-bus. Some walking is inevitable. Before booking accommodation – particularly for families with young children – it's important to find out where your hotel or chalet is located.

From Méribel a mighty network of lifts links Courchevel, La Tania, Les Menuires and Val Thorens to form one of the world's greatest intermediate playgrounds. However, so many English-speakers congregate here during the winter months that you could be forgiven for thinking that this was some sloping suburb of southwest London rather than a top French ski resort.

Mountain

You need a whole season to explore every corner of the Trois Vallées, and Méribel is the best place to begin. From the Chaudanne lift centre at Les Allues and from Méribel Mottaret higher up the valley, lifts rise on either side. To the east, gondolas take you up to 2738m at Saulire for a choice of descents towards Courchevel and La Tania. The mountainside back down to the resort is crisscrossed with mainly blues, benign reds and an assortment of chairs. To the west, more gondolas and chairs rise to the long ridge that separates the valleys of Les Allues and Belleville. From the top you can ski towards Les Menuires, St-Martin-de-Belleville and Val Thorens. Alternatively you can explore the dozens of lifts and runs down to Méribel Les Allues and Méribel Mottaret.

Accomplished skiers and riders head for the more challenging terrain off the Mont de la Chambre, Mont Vallon and the Col du Fruit at the head of the valley. The sheer volume of skiers funnelling into both 1450 and Mottaret at peak times means that some queuing is inevitable, but the lift system is extremely efficient.

One of the greatest assets of the Trois Vallées is that anyone who can ski parallel can travel far afield without ever leaving blue runs, while better skiers can reach the same destination almost entirely on reds. The seemingly endless range of runs has produced a whole generation of skiers who never go anywhere else.

Méribel has good nursery slopes with easy green runs around the Altiport and back to the resort. The resort has two terrain parks: the 1200m Moon Park and the Snowpark des Plattières at Mottaret.

Learn

The **ESF**, **t** +33 (0)4 79 08 60 31, has 400 teachers and the standard of instruction varies enormously. Ian and Susan Saunders are BASI instructors who work for the ESF and run **Ski Principles**, **t** +33 (0)4 79 00 52 71. **New Generation**, **t** +33 (0)4 79 01 03 18, is British-run and much praised by reporters. **Magic in Motion**, **t** +33 (0)4 79 08 53 36, is the other mainstream option. **Parallel Lines**, **t** +44 (0)1702 589 580, is an all-British ski school. **Absolute Ski**, **t** +33 (0)668 51 74 94, is a small school with local instructors. **Ski Academy**, **t** +33 (0)4 79 08 11 99, teaches skiing and snowboarding and is geared towards English-speaking clients. **Snow Systems**, **t** +33 (0)4 79 00 40 22, is a young ski school, specializing in private lessons, small groups, and off-piste. **Snow d'light**, **t** +33 (0)4 79 22 03 45, organizes mini group lessons for adults and children. Off-piste guiding is through the **Bureau des Guides**, **t** +33 (0)4 79 00 30 38.

Children

Les Saturnins, **t** +33 (0)4 79 08 66 90, is the non-ski kindergarten for children aged 18 months to three years. **Les P'tits Loups** ski kindergarten cares for children aged three to five years at **La Chaudanne**, **t** +33 (0)4 79 08 60 31, and at **Mottaret**, **t** +33 (0)4 79 00 49 49. The British ski school, **Parallel Lines**, **t** +44 (0)1702 589 580, has BASI instructors and small classes. **Snow Systems**, **t** +33 (0)4 79 00 40 22, receives praise.

Lunch

Eating on the mountain is iniquitously expensive anywhere in the Trois Vallées. **Les Castors**, **t** +33 (0)4 79 08 52 79, is an old favourite at the foot of the Truite run in Méribel. **Les Rhododendrons**, **t** +33 (0)4 79 00 50 92, at the top of the Rhodos gondola and **Restaurant Le Rond Point**, **t** +33 (0)4 79 00 37 51, are both recommended. **Bibi Phoque**, **t** +33 (0)4 79 00 30 93, at Chaudanne, has reasonably priced pancakes. The **Altiport Hotel**, **t** +33 (0)4 79 00 52 32, has a sunny terrace. **Chalet de Togniat**, **t** +33 (0)4 79 00 45 11, at the top of the Combes chair out of Mottaret, is off the beaten track.

Dine

Most visitors here eat in their chalets, which accounts for the low number of good restaurants in proportion to the size of the resort. **Chez Kiki**, **t** +33 (0)4 79 08 66 68, specializes in meat cooked over an open fire. **La Taverne**, **t** +33 (0)4 79 00 32 45, in Hôtel Le Roc, offers pizzas and Savoyarde cuisine. **Le Refuge**, **t** +33 (0)4 79 08 61 97, has a warm atmosphere, and **Le Croix Jean-Claude**, **t** +33 (0)4 79 00 61 05, is good value, with excellent food and wine. **Cactus Café**, **t** +33 (0)4 79 00 53 67, has reasonably priced Tex-Mex, said to be the 'best value in the Trois Vallées'.

In Mottaret, **Côte Brune**, **t** +33 (0)4 9 00 40 97, is an old favourite. Try **Au Temps Perdu**, **t** +33 (0)4 79 00 36 64, for a wide choice of crêpes, or **Pizzeria du Mottaret**, t +33 (0)4 79 00 40 50. **Le Ty Sable, t** +33 (0)4 79 00 43 32, is also recommended.

Party

'I just can't see how people get away with charging €8 for a beer – as a bar owner I would feel embarrassed charging that,' complained a reader. **Jack's Bar** and **Le Rond Point** in Méribel are busy in the late afternoon as the lifts close. **Le Saint Amour** was said to be 'friendly, with a laid-back ambiance and reasonable prices'. **Les Enfants Terribles** wine bar has plenty of atmosphere. **Scott's** is an internet café with good bar food. **Le Loft**, located above the ice rink, and **Dick's Tea Bar**, are the late-night discos.

In Mottaret, **Le Rastro** is famous for its Tuesday rock parties, and **Zig Zig**, beside it, is popular as the lifts close. **Downtown Bar** has a pool table and occasional live music. The **Piano Bar** in Hôtel Mont Vallon caters for an older age group. **Le Privilege** is the disco. In Méribel Village, **Le Lodge du Village** has live après ski music on Tuesdays and Thursdays.

Sleep

★★★★**Hotel Le Grand Cœur, t** +33 (0)4 79 08 60 03, *www.legrandcoeur.com*, was one of Méribel's first hotels and remains its finest. Excellent food and service.

★★★★**Hotel Le Mont Vallon, t** +33 (0)4 79 00 44 00, *www.hotel-montvallon.com*, is a stylish hotel in Mottaret, with family rooms, a pool and fitness centre. 'Very expensive but the staff were fantastic and the food delicious,' said a reader.

★★★★**Chalet Les Brames, t** +44 (0)20 7384 3854, *www.descent.co.uk*, set above Les Allues, is the most sumptuous chalet here. It sleeps 15 and has a huge open-plan living room, gym, cinema and outdoor hot tub.

★★★★**Chalet Moguls, t** +44 (0)1264 738 257, *www.belvedereproperties.net*, is a charming home-from-home set in the exclusive Belvedere sector.

★★★**Chalet-Hotel Marie Blanche, t** +33 (0)4 79 08 65 55, *www.marieblanche.com*, has wood-panelled bedrooms and a restaurant serving traditional Savoyard dishes.

★★★**Hotel Le Yeti, t** +33 (0)4 79 00 51 15, *www.hotel-yeti.com*, has large, south-facing bedrooms and an attractive lounge with log fire.

Montgenèvre

Profile

Sole French component of the otherwise-Italian Milky Way circuit, an unpretentious French border town with lots of charm and a new road tunnel bypass

Resort

Montgenèvre, the ancient village on the Italian frontier, is the only French component of the otherwise all-Italian

*BEST FOR

Big ski area, beginners and intermediates, families

ESSENTIALS

Altitude: 1860m (6,102ft)–2800m (9,186ft)
Further information: t +33 (0)4 92 21 52 52, *www.montgenevre.com*
Lifts in area: 78 in Milky Way (6 cableways, 39 chairs, 33 drags) serving 400km of piste
Lift pass: Milky Way (covers Montgenèvre, Sestriere, Sauze d'Oulx and other smaller resorts) adult and child €200, both for six days; children under 6yrs free
Access: Turin airport 1¼hrs

Milky Way ski area. The village is now free from lorries and heavy traffic, thanks to an underground tunnel that opened in 2006. The unspoilt rural town features tumbledown stone houses and a weekly market selling local produce. Reporters were impressed by the friendliness of the resort. However, the otherwise family-friendly Milky Way region now Les Allues has a single lift pass tariff for both adults and children.

Mountain

Skiing takes place on both sides of this road leading to the frontier and a piste bridge now links the two. Montgenèvre's own area, beneath 2680m Le Chalvet, holds considerable charm and challenge, with runs for all standards leading back down to the village and across the border to Clavière. Snow-cannon were added for the Turin Olympics.

On the other side of the road, a gondola and a quad-chair provide direct access towards the Monti della Luna and the long runs to Cesana Torinese. Montgenèvre has a terrain park with a half-pipe in the Gondrans area. Reporters complain that the region has too many draglifts, but these are now slowly decreasing in number.

Learn

'An ideal resort in which to learn,' said a reader. The **ESF**, **t** +33 (0)4 92 21 90 46, and **Apeak**, **t** +33 (0)4 92 24 49 97, are the alternatives.

Children

'The resort is very safe for kids,' commented a reporter, 'especially in the evening. All in all, a great family resort.' **Halte Garderie**, **t** +33 (0)4 92 21 52 50, is for six months to six years, **Club Piou-Piou**, **t** +33 (0)4 92 21 90 46, introduces three- to five-year-olds to skiing, and **Apeak** runs a children's programme ('they were great').

Lunch

Try **Les Chalmettes**, **t** +33 (0)4 92 21 93 04, **Les Anges**, **t** +33 (0)6 14 61 97 52, and **La Bergerie**, **t** +33 (0)4 92 21 81 06.

Dine

Le Jamy, **t** +33 (0)4 92 21 92 62, has the best food and is renowned for its fondues. **La Ca' del Sol**, **t** +33 (0)4 92 21 87 08, and **Pizzeria Le Transalpin**, **t** +33 (0)6 74 06 31 77, and **Le Refuge**, **t** +33 (0)4 92 21 92 97, are recommended. **Le Napoleon**, **t** +33 (0)4 79 21 94 60, is a warmly recommended pizzeria, and **Le Capitaine**, **t** +33 (0)4 92 21 89 84, is the only Italian eatery.

Party

'You can go to Ibiza if you want wild nightlife, but we still managed to get in at 3am so can't be that bad,' said a reporter. **Le Graal Café** attracts a young crowd, **La Ca' del Sol** is a resort meeting place, and **Le Blue Night** is the disco. Montgenèvre has a natural skating rink at the bottom of the slopes and a reader recommends the dedicated toboggan runs: 'Buy a cheap sledge and after the lifts have closed you can have a great time on the lower green slopes – scores of people every night.'

Sleep

★★★★**Chalet Blanc**, **t** +33 (0)4 92 44 27 02, *www.hotellechaletblanc.com*, is the resort's first luxury boutique hotel, with a gourmet restaurant with Australian chef, and a delightful spa.

★★★**Hôtel Napoléon**, t +33 (0)4 92 21 92 04, is the original inn.

★★★**Hôtel Valérie**, t +33 (0)4 92 21 90 02, *www.hotel-montgenevre.com*, near the church, is comfortable.

★★**Hôtel Alpis Cottia**, t +33 (0)4 92 21 90 14, facing the slopes, is reasonably priced.

Le Pot de Miel, t +33 (0)4 92 21 93 55, is a traditional chalet with 10 rooms.

Morzine and Les Gets

Profile

Traditional resorts in the giant Portes du Soleil region, which straddles the French border with Switzerland. Morzine is a bustling market town, while Les Gets is a traditional Savoyard village

Resort

Morzine has been a winter sports resort since before the First World War, and during the mid-1920s it established a reputation as an important international holiday centre. Wealthy guests arrived to spend the winter at the comfortable Grand Hotel, which boasted central heating and fine cuisine. They passed their days ice-skating on the frozen lake and skiing on the rolling summer pastures of Pléney.

The first cable car was installed in 1934, but the Second World War put a stop to further development. It wasn't until 1960 that the winter sports industry began to eclipse the cattle and sheep farming which, together with forestry, still forms part of the local economy.

The catalyst for this was Jean Vuarnet, a young *Morzinois*, who was packed off to the USA that February with the expectations of the entire town on his shoulders. He came home from the eighth Winter Olympics in Squaw Valley clutching the gold medal for the downhill.

As a reward he was given the task of creating the more snow-sure satellite of Avoriaz on the clifftop above the town, and of linking this new purpose-built village and Morzine to other resorts in the region – not only in France but also across the border with Switzerland.

The task proved every bit as difficult as beating Hanspeter Lanig of Germany and fellow Frenchman Guy Perillat down the mountain in California. But, with a winning combination of guile and charm, he finally persuaded the villages to bury differences, which in some cases stretched back centuries, and create the Portes du Soleil.

The first link was built in 1968 and the single lift pass – now electronic – was introduced in 1974. The ski area is named after a mountain pass above Les Crosets, on the Swiss side of the frontier, which catches the first rays of sunlight each morning. Ironically, Vuarnet is already

✱ BEST FOR

High-mileage cruisers, families, village ambience (Les Gets)

ESSENTIALS

Altitude: 1000m (3,280ft)–2466m (8,090ft)
Further information: **Morzine t** +33 (0)4 50 74 72 72, *www.morzine-avoriaz.com*; **Les Gets t** +33 (0)4 50 75 80 80, *www.lesgets.com*
Lifts in area: 195 in Portes du Soleil area (13 cableways, 80 chairs, 102 drags) serving 650km of piste
Lift pass: Portes du Soleil (covers 12 resorts) adult €189, child 5–16yrs €127, both for six days
Access: Geneva airport 1½hrs, railway stations at Thonon les Bains 31km, Cluses 25km

better remembered for his sunglasses than his sunny ski area, which now has 195 lifts and 650km of piste.

Not every farmer was converted to harvesting the lucrative annual snow crop, and the attractive town of Morzine continues to be what it always was – a regional agricultural centre with a life that exists outside tourism.

The town sits in a wooded basin marked by the confluence of several mountain streams and covers a large area on both sides of the river gorge. The principal street runs from the village centre up to the foot of Le Pléney, where many of the hotels are located. The various sectors of the town, and the lift stations, are linked by a road-train and free buses. 'A lovely, typically French town with real character and great shops, restaurants and little hotels,' enthused a reporter.

Morzine's low altitude should make snow cover in town vulnerable in mild winters. However, it benefits from the fridge effect of its vicinity to Mont Blanc and conditions have been reliable in recent years.

Morzine is linked across 1550m Pléney to the traditional dairy-farming village of Les Gets, a community that dates back to the 12th century. The two holiday bases are only 6km apart by road, but contrastingly different. Les Gets is a pleasing mix of old Savoyard chalets and more modern wooden and stone buildings constructed in keeping with their beautiful alpine surroundings. 'The village is pretty and I can recommend it for non-skiers too,' said a reporter. This is a family resort with a relaxed atmosphere and good links into the Portes du Soleil.

Mountain

A cable car from the hamlet of Les Prodains, reached by free ski-bus from Morzine, provides the quickest and most direct link to Avoriaz. Alternatively, a gondola from Morzine takes you up to Super-Morzine, where you can work your way up through the lift system to Avoriaz, or over to the pretty little goat-farming hamlet of Les Lindarets for access to Châtel and other resorts in the Portes du Soleil. The blue runs above Super-Morzine provide plenty of confidence-building cruising terrain.

From the other side of Morzine, linked by a free road-train, a side-by-side gondola and cable car rise to Pléney. Blue, red and black runs served by a sequence of chairlifts all lead back over the undulating pastureland to the town. You can also drop off the backside of the ridge and follow a long, gentle blue run down into Les Gets.

Skiing takes place on the wooded slopes on both sides of the Les Gets valley, which is crisscrossed with further lifts that extend to 1850m Le Ranfoilly and 1665m La Rosta at the far end. On the north-western side of Les Gets, a gondola and a chair lead up to Mont Chéry. This is the location for dedicated slalom and snowcross courses, as well as a terrain park. Morzine has a large floodlit area with skiing, tubing and big-air that remains open until 10pm. Off-piste is extensive. We particularly enjoy the Combe d'Angolon, a spectacular powder bowl accessed from the top of the Chamossière chair.

Anyone who can ski parallel can complete the Portes du Soleil circuit in a day, which takes you to most but not all the resorts. However, most of the time is spent on lifts rather than going downhill. It makes more sense to explore fully one sector at a time.

Learn

In Morzine, the **ESF**, **t** +33 (0)4 50 79 13 13, has a sound reputation for teaching

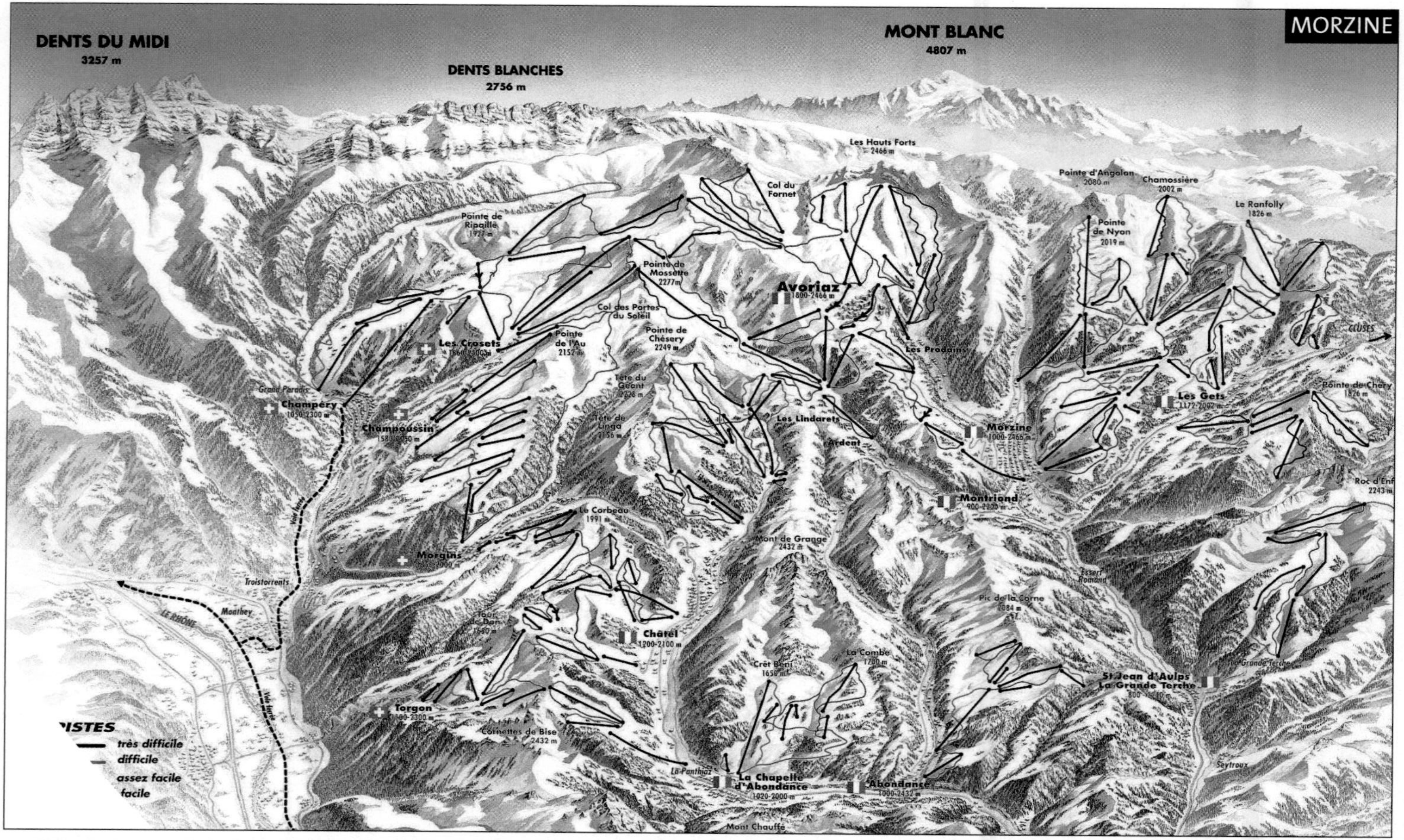

DENTS DU MIDI
3257 m

DENTS BLANCHES
2756 m

MONT BLANC
4807 m

Les Hauts Forts
2466 m

Col du Fornet

Pointe d'Angolon
2080 m

Chamossière
2002 m

Le Ranfolly
1826 m

Pointe de Nyon
2019 m

Pointe de Ripaille
1927 m

Pointe de Mossette
2277 m

Avoriaz
1800-2466 m

Col des Portes du Soleil

Pointe de Chésery
2249 m

Les Crosets

Pointe de l'Au
2152 m

Les Prodains

CLUSES

Grand Paradis

Champéry
1050-2300 m

Tête du Géant

Tête de Linga
2156 m

Les Lindarets

Les Gets

Pointe de Chéry
1826 m

Champoussin

Ardent

Morzine
1000-2466 m

Montriond

Roc d'Enfer
2243 m

Le Corbeau
1991 m

Morgins

Mont de Grange
2432 m

Troistorrents

Monthey

LE RHÔNE

Essert Romand

Pic de la Corne

Tour de Don

Châtel
1200-2100 m

Voie ferrée

La Combe

Crêt Béni
1650 m

St Jean d'Aulps
La Grande Terche

Le Grande Terche

Torgon

Cornettes de Bise
2432 m

Seytroux

La Panthiaz

La Chapelle d'Abondance
1020-2000 m

Abondance

Mont Chauffé

PISTES
très difficile
difficile
assez facile
facile

• Fine Skiing • Great Value

Resorts within 1 hour of Geneva airport include Les Gets - Portes du Soleil, Samoëns and other Grand Massif resorts, Saint-Gervais, Chamonix, Combloux, Megeve, Le Grand Bornand and 25 more in the rest of the Alps.

Accommodation only or self-drive package deals.

peakretreats.co.uk

0844 576 0173

ABTA W5537

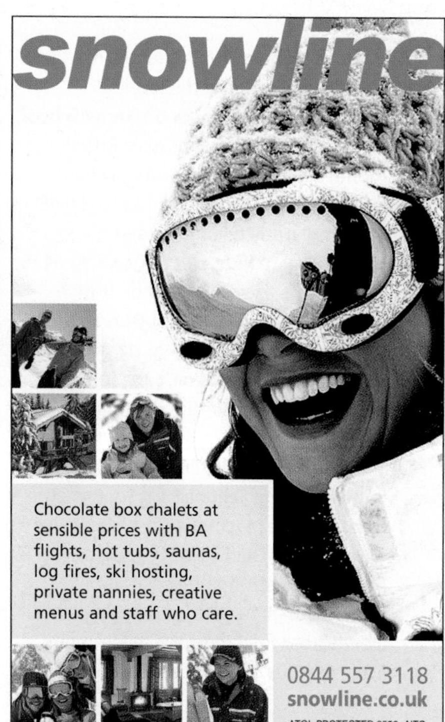

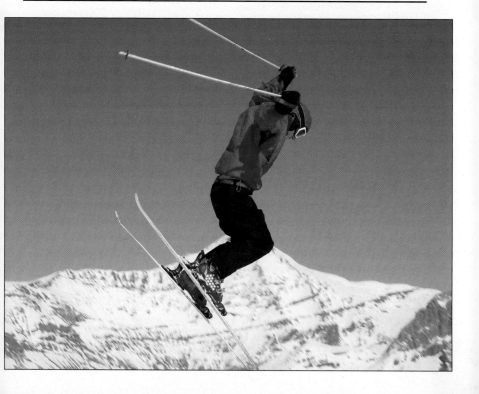

modern technique in a friendly manner ('well organized and the level of instruction was very good'). **Snow School**, **t** +33 (0)4 86 68 88 40, is new. **British Alpine Ski and Snowboarding School**, **t** +33 (0)4 50 74 78 59, or **t** +44 (0)871 780 1500, is warmly recommended. **SE2SA/Easy to Ride**, **t** +33 (0)4 50 79 05 16, has limited-size classes ('their British instructors were brilliant'). **Bureau de la Montagne**, **t** +33 (0)4 50 79 03 55, and **Maison de la Montagne**, **t** +33 (0)4 50 75 96 65, are the mountain guiding companies.

In Les Gets, the **British Alpine Ski and Snowboarding School**, **t** +33 (0)4 50 79 85 42, and **t** +44 (0)1485 572 596, receive equal praise. The **ESF**, **t** +33 (0)4 50 75 80 03, has a strong presence. **360 International**, **t** +33 (0)4 50 79 80 31, has a dedicated following. We recommend **Ecole Ski Plus**, **t** +33 (0)4 50 75 86 01.

Children

Morzine's L'Outa, **t** +33 (0)4 50 79 26 00, accepts little ones from three months to six years and was recommended by reporters. **Le Club des Piou-Piou**, **t** +33 (0)4 50 79 13 13, provides daycare with ski lessons for children from three to 12 years.

In Les Gets, which has the French government's *P'tits Montagnards* award for childcare, **Les Fripouilles**, **t** +33 (0)4 50 79 84 84, welcomes children from six months. The **ESF Jardins des Neiges Piou Piou**, **t** +33 (0)4 50 75 80 03, takes children from three to five years for a sensible mix of lessons and play. The **ESF Club des P'tits Montagnys**, **t** +33 (0)4 50 75 80 03, cares for non-skiers aged four to 12 years. **Ile des Enfants** ski school, **t** +33 (0)4 50 75 84 47, gives lessons from three years.

Lunch

Try **Les Crêtes de Zorre**, **t** +33 (0)4 50 79 24 73, at Super-Morzine, **Les Mines d'Or**, **t** +33 (0)4 50 79 03 60, in the Vallée de la Manche, and the **Belvédère**, **t** +33 (0)4 50 79 81 52, a welcoming mountain hut at Mont Chéry. In the same area is **La Grande Ourse**, **t** +33 (0)6 79 42 58 86, which received great praise: 'Probably the finest mountain food with definitely the greatest view anywhere in the skiing world. Anyone in the area must go there – we've never found anywhere better.' Another good eatery is **La Paika**, **t** +33 04 50 92 85 22, on the blue run back to La Turche. **Chez Nannon**, **t** +33 (0)4 50 79 21 15, is a romantic hut on a blue piste beneath the Pointe de Nyon.

Dine

In Morzine, **Le Tremplin**, **t** +33 (0)4 50 79 12 31, is rated by reporters. **L'Etale**, **t** +33 (0)4 50 79 09 29, serves regional cuisine in a mountain ambience, and **La Grange**, **t** +33 (0)4 50 75 96 40, is for a special occasion. **La Chamade**, **t** +33 (0)4 50 79 13 91, receives mixed reports: 'most delightful', and 'not so nice any more'. **Le Matafan**, **t** +33 (0)4 50 79 27 79, is said to be 'absolutely the best place for dinner'. **Le Mas de la Coutettaz**, **t** +33 (0)4 50 79 08 26, provides chalet-style communal dining in a centuries-old dining room. **L'Auberge de la Combe à Zorre**, **t** +33 (0)4 50 79 15 06, is warmly recommended.

In Les Gets, **Le Flambeau**, **t** +33 (0)4 50 79 80 66, and **Le Tourbillon**, **t** +33 (0)4 50 79 70 34, are both recommended, along with **Le Vieux Chêne**, **t** +33 (0)4 50 79 71 93, and **Le Peau de Vache**, **t** +33 (0)4 50 75 86 64.

Party

'A lovely lively resort,' said a reporter, and 'We were not interested in partying all night so the low key night life was fine by us,' said another. **Le Paradis du Laury's** is a popular disco. **L'Opéra**, the other late-night venue, becomes a teens-only haunt one evening each week during the school holidays. The **Cavern Bar** has a young and funky atmosphere and the **Boudha Café** is recommended for people-watching.

In Les Gets, the leisure centre has a pool and a range of other facilities. **Bar Bush** and **Le Boomerang** are popular. For dancing, the **Iglu** is a small but fun nightclub.

Sleep

Morzine has a plentiful supply of hotels in each price bracket. Les Gets has a mix of chalets and hotels.

Morzine:

*****Hôtel Les Airelles, t** +33 (0)4 50 74 71 21, *www.les-airelles.com*, has been refurbished with comfortable rooms ('good food and spotlessly clean and warm').

*****Hôtel Le Dahu, t** +33 (0)4 50 75 92 92, *www.dahu.com*, an old favourite, has tastefully decorated rooms and duplex family suites, along with delicious food.

*****Hôtel Neige Roc, t** +33 (0)4 50 79 03 21, *www.neige-roc.com*, at Les Prodains, is convenient for the cable car to Avoriaz.

*****Hôtel Le Tremplin, t** +33 (0)4 50 79 12 31, *www.hotel-tremplin.com*, at the foot of the slopes, has a great view of the night-skiing and was highly rated: 'a pleasure to stay here. Breakfast is fab with amazing coffee, croissants, meats and cheese.'

****Chalet-Hotel Fleur des Neiges, t** +33 (0)4 50 79 01 23, *www.chalethotelfleurdesneiges.com*, is rustic, has a heated pool, and a restaurant serving French country cuisine.

Le Mas de la Coutettaz, t +33 (0)4 50 79 08 26, *www.thefarmhouse.co.uk*, is an 18th-century manor house with eight delightful bedrooms.

Le Bel'Alpe, t + 33 (0)4 50 79 05 50, is said to be welcoming and cosy, with helpful staff and excellent food.

Les Gets:

******La Ferme de Moudon, t** +44 (0)20 7384 3854, *www.descent.co.uk*, is a 17th-century chalet three minutes' drive from the village centre.

******La Ferme de Montagne, t** +33 (0)4 50 75 36 79, *www.fermedemontagne.com*, is a luxuriously renovated farmhouse set above the village.

*****Chalet-Hotel Les Alpages, t** +33 (0)4 50 75 80 88, *www.hotel-alpages.com*, has a pool and spa.

*****Chalet-Hotel Crychar, t** +33 (0)4 50 75 80 50, *www.crychar.com*, on the piste, has cosy bedrooms and a restaurant with a log fire and home-cooked food.

*****Chalet-Hotel La Marmotte, t** +33 (0)4 50 75 80 33, *www.hotelmarmotte.com*, is a 1930s chalet on the edge of the village. Facilities include a pool, spa and crèche.

*****Hotel Mont-Chéry, t** +33 (0)4 50 75 80 75, *www.hotelmontchery.com*, in the town centre, has a pool, and a restaurant serving inventive cuisine.

*****Hotel Nagano, t** +33 (0)4 50 79 71 46, *www.hotel-nagano.com*, has a pool and is across the road from the ice rink.

****Alpen Sport Hôtel, t** +33 (0)4 50 75 80 55, *www.alpensport-hotel.com*, has five simple chalets in its grounds sleeping from four to 17 people.

Le Boomerang II, t +33 (0)4 50 79 80 65, *www.leboomerang2.com*, is a little piece of Australian outback in the French Alps.

La Plagne

🏆 BEST SKI SCHOOL 2009 (OXYGÈNE)

✱ BEST FOR

All levels of skier and rider, families, big ski area, off-piste

ESSENTIALS

Altitude: 1250m (4,100ft)–3250m (10,660ft)
Further information: t +33 (0)4 79 09 79 79, *www.la-plagne.com*
Lifts in area: 141 in Paradiski (1 mountain railway, 16 cableways, 66 chairs, 58 drags) serving 425km of piste
Lift pass: Paradiski (covers La Plagne/ Les Arcs area and one day in each of Val d'Isère/Tignes, Pralognan-La-Vanoise, Les Saisies) adult €237, child 6–13yrs €178, both for six days
Access: Chambéry airport 1½hrs, Geneva airport 2½hrs, Lyon airport 2½hrs, Eurostar station at Bourg-St-Maurice

Profile

The giant ski area is made up of seven purpose-built and three traditional villages set at different altitudes above the valley town of Aime. The skiing is linked by cable car to Les Arcs and together they form Paradiski, one of the largest ski circuits in the world. Alpine charm is in short supply in a couple of the higher villages

Resort

La Plagne tries and often succeeds in being all things to all people. The lower villages of Montchavin-Les Coches, Plagne Montalbert and Champagny en Vanoise have varying degrees of rustic farmland appeal, while the six higher holiday centres major in ski convenience. On paper, La Plagne is the perfect ski destination with a long vertical drop, snow-sure, high-altitude runs, ski in, ski out hotels and apartments, and a sophisticated lift system. Runs below the tree-line are delightful ('lift system absolutely superb – no queuing at all and more than enough terrain for a week'). However, the endless acres of exposed and often bland snowfields higher up, and the architecture of some of the dormitory villages, are not to everyone's taste.

Paradiski – its combined ski area with Les Arcs – is so vast that even an experienced skier will be hard put to travel from one end to the other and back in a single day. The double-decker Vanoise Express, which spans the Ponturin gorge that separates the two resorts, cost €16 million to build. Last season it was out of action, but it is scheduled to reopen in December 2008. However, both La Plagne and Les Arcs are so enormous in their own right that only a small proportion of visitors to either make use of it. Unless you plan more than two trips to Les Arcs during a one-week stay it is more economical to pay the daily supplement. The main beneficiaries are skiers who choose to stay in Montchavin or Les Coches. Instead of hiking up through the lift system on the La Plagne side, they can explore the equally rewarding terrain above Vallandry and Arc 1800. An eight-seater chair across the Ponturin Valley shortens the journey from Belle-Plagne and Plagne-Bellecôte to Peisey-Vallandry to just 20 minutes.

The original high-altitude resort of Plagne-Centre (1970m) is outwardly a monument to the alpine architectural atrocities of the 1960s but it has undergone a complete makeover down the years and functions well as a holiday centre. Aime-la-Plagne (2100m) resembles a battleship stranded on a white mountainside. Belle-Plagne (2050m) is easier on the eye with a pleasant village

- SELF-CATERING SKI HOLIDAYS
- FRENCH ALPS & PYRENEES
  - > Accommodation to suit all budgets and styles
  - > Smart apartments to simple studios
  - > Top resorts and traditional villages

020 7371 6111
www.lagrange-holidays.co.uk

LAGRANGE

ABTA
ABTA No.V554X

SKI SCHOOL
Oxygène
SKI SHOP

Skiing in
La Plagne
alpes-france

Galerie Mercure - BP 46 - 73214 La Plagne cedex
Tel. +33 479090399 - Fax +33 479092055

info@oxygene-ski.com

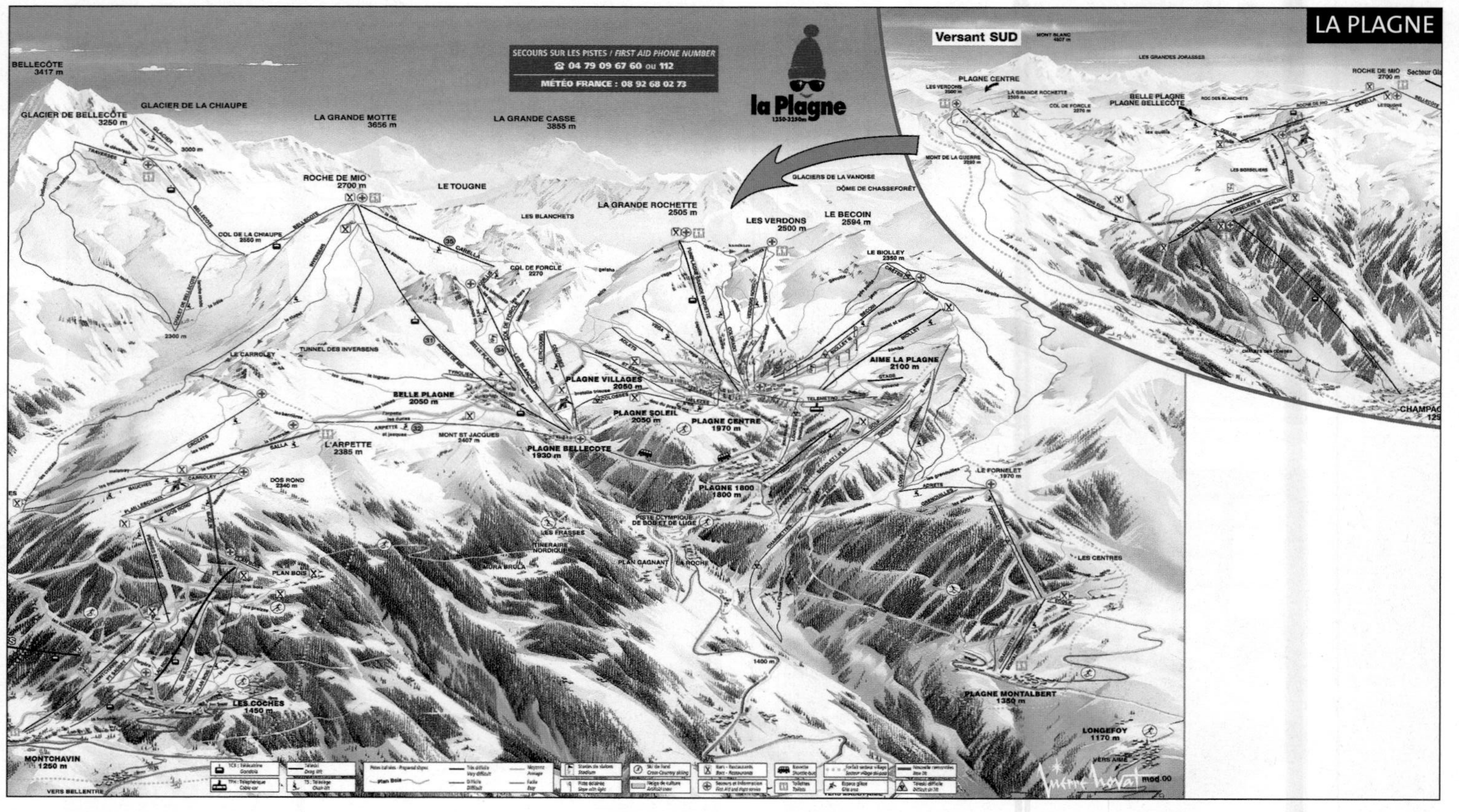

LA PLAGNE
Versant SUD
SECOURS SUR LES PISTES / FIRST AID PHONE NUMBER
☎ 04 79 09 67 60 ou 112
MÉTÉO FRANCE : 08 92 68 02 73
la Plagne
1250-3250m
BELLECÔTE
3417 m
GLACIER DE BELLECÔTE
3250 m
GLACIER DE LA CHIAUPE
LA GRANDE MOTTE
3656 m
LA GRANDE CASSE
3855 m
ROCHE DE MIO
2700 m
LE TOUGNE
LES BLANCHETS
LA GRANDE ROCHETTE
2505 m
LES VERDONS
2500 m
LE BECOIN
2594 m
GLACIERS DE LA VANOISE
DÔME DE CHASSEFORÊT
LE BIOLLEY
2350 m
COL DE LA CHIAUPE
2550 m
COL DE FORCLE
2270
TUNNEL DES INVERSENS
LE CARROLEY
PLAGNE VILLAGES
2050 m
BELLE PLAGNE
2050 m
PLAGNE SOLEIL
2050 m
PLAGNE CENTRE
1970 m
AIME LA PLAGNE
2100 m
L'ARPETTE
2385 m
MONT ST JACQUES
2407 m
PLAGNE BELLECOTE
1930 m
DOS ROND
2340 m
PLAGNE 1800
1800 m
LE FORNELET
1970 m
PISTE OLYMPIQUE
DE BOB ET DE LUGE
LES FRASSES
ITINÉRAIRE NORDIQUE
MURA BRULA
PLAN GAGNANT
LA ROCHE
PLAN BOIS
LES CENTRES
LES COCHES
1450 m
PLAGNE MONTALBERT
1350 m
LONGEFOY
1170 m
MONTCHAVIN
1250 m
VERS BELLENTRE
1400 m
2300 m
3000 m
PLAGNE CENTRE
BELLE PLAGNE
PLAGNE BELLECÔTE
ROCHE DE MIO
2700 m
MONT DE LA GUERRE
LES GRANDES JORASSES
MONT BLANC
CHAMPAG
mod.00

centre. Plagne-Bellecôte (1930m) is high-rise and plain. Plagne-Villages (2050m), Plagne-Soleil (2050m) and Plagne-1800 are much more agreeable wood-clad complexes built in sympathy with their glorious scenic surroundings.

Lower down the mountain, Montchavin and Champagny-en-Vanoise are rich in cowshed kitsch. These are old farming villages that have long since been won over to tourism, but they make excellent and attractive bases from which to explore the region.

Mountain

Wide-open motorway skiing above the treeline and gladed trails through the forest below it are the main features of the ski area. These are coupled with gentle beginner pistes and some truly outstanding off-piste, if you know where to find it. You need a guide to discover the long, sweeping descent from the Glacier de Bellecôte down to Les Bauches, as well as the challenging Cul du Nant run from the back of the glacier into the Champagny-le-Haut valley.

The disadvantage of staying in the lower and much more pleasing villages used to be the inordinate amount of time spent working your way up through the lift system before doing much actual skiing. But now high-speed lifts take you all the way up to the high-altitude area in just 30 minutes from both Champagny and Montchavin-Les Coches.

We favour basing yourself in Plagne-Villages or Plagne-Soleil, the two villages that come closest to marrying charm with convenience. From here it is easy to reach the open skiing from the Roche de Mio and the Glacier de Bellecôte.

Scenic routes wind down through the forest to Montchavin-Les Coches, Champagny and Plagne-Montalbert. Queues are not generally a feature of La Plagne, although one reporter disagreed: 'The only problem with La Plagne is the crowds. It was very depressing looking down at the spiralling mass of humanity and knowing when you joined them you would have a 20- to 30-minute wait at the lifts.' The old, slow Arpette chair out of Plagne-Bellecôte that was a notorious bottleneck has been upgraded to an eight-person chair. Terrain parks are located at Plagne-Bellecôte, Montchavin-Les Coches and Champagny. Plagne Centre has the Pro Snowpark.

Learn

The **ESF**, Plagne-Centre, **t** +33 (0)4 79 09 00 40, Plagne-Villages, **t** +33 (0)4 79 09 04 40, has around 500 instructors working from branches in each of the 10 villages.

In Plagne-Centre, **Oxygène**, **t** +33 (0)4 79 09 03 99, receives rave reviews: 'Much the best lessons we have ever had.'

Evolution 2, Montchavin, **t** +33 (0)4 79 07 81 85, and in Les Coches, **t** +33 (0)4 79 04 20 83, is recommended. In Plagne-1800, **Reflex**, **t** +33 (0)4 79 09 16 07, is a small independent school. In Belle-Plagne, **El Pro**, **t** +33 (0)4 79 09 01 33, is the alternative to the ESF. **Antenne Handicap**, **t** +33 (0)4 79 09 13 80, in Aime-la-Plagne, teaches disabled skiers.

Children

Most villages have both non-ski and ski kindergartens. In Plagne-Centre, **Les P'tits Bonnets**, **t** +33 (0)4 79 09 00 83, cares for infants from 10 weeks to three years, but prior booking is recommended.

In Montchavin, **Le Chat Bleu**, **t** +33 (0)4 79 07 82 82, provides daycare. At Plagne-Montalbert, **Les Bambins**, **t** +33 (0)4 79 09 77 24, looks after children from 18 months to six years. In Champagny, **Les Cabris**, **t** +33 (0)4 79 55 06 40, cares for children from two years.

At Belle-Plagne the **ESF Nursery, t** +33 (0)4 79 09 06 68, cares for children from 18 months. At Plagne-Village, the **ESF Nursery, t** +33 (0)4 79 09 04 40, accepts children from two years. In Aime-la-Plagne, **La Garderie des Lutins, t** +33 (0)4 79 09 04 75, takes children from two years. At Plagne-Bellecôte, **La Garderie Mini-club, t** +33 (0)4 79 09 05 91, cares for children from two years.

The **ESF, t** +33 (0)4 79 09 00 40, runs ski kindergartens in Plagne-Montalbert, Champagny, Plagne-Centre, Plagne-Villages, Plagne-Soleil, Aime-la-Plagne, Plagne-Bellecôte, Belle-Plagne and Plagne-1800.

Lunch

You can eat well particularly if you are prepared to wait until the midday–2pm rush is over. Try **Au Bon Vieux Temps, t** +33 (0)4 79 09 20 57, below Aime-la-Plagne. **Le Forperet, t** +33 (0)4 79 55 51 27, is on the piste down to Plagne-Montalbert. **Pappagone, t** +33 (0)4 79 55 18 87, next to the Roche de Mio gondola at Belle-Plagne, is recommended for its pizzas. **Auberge de Montagne chez Pat du Sauget, t** +33 (0)4 79 07 83 51, is just above the Vanoise Express cable car station. Nearby **Le Joli Bois, t** +33 (0)6 81 19 96 77, has 'great lasagne, but skip the crêpes'. **Le Petit Chaperon Rouge, t** +33 (0)4 79 09 09 39, above 1800 is an old farmhouse. **La Rossa, t** +33 (0)4 79 08 28 03, is at the top of the Champagny gondola. **Les Borseliers, t** +33 (0)6 07 54 96 19, in Champagny is known for *tartiflette* and other rustic Savoyard dishes. **Les Verdons, t** +33 (0)6 21 54 39 24, is a large wooden chalet offering excellent local cuisine.

Dine

In Montchavin, **La Boule de Neige, t** +33 (0)4 79 07 83 30, and **La Ferme de César, t** +33 (0)4 79 07 85 31, are both recommended.

In Plagne-Centre, try **La Métairie, t** +33 (0)4 79 09 11 08, and **Le Refuge, t** +33 (0)4 79 09 00 13. In Belle-Plagne, **Le Matafan, t** +33 (0)4 79 09 09 19, was rated 'great' for food. **La Cloche, t** +33 (0)4 79 09 28 24, is really nice and welcoming with excellent food for all tastes. **Le Loup Blanc, t** +33 (0)4 79 09 13 61, in Plagne-1800 ('excellent local specialities') has reasonable prices. **La Grolle, t** +33 (0)4 79 07 69 84, in Plagne-Centre, was considered to be 'very good'. In Aime-la-Plagne, **Le Montana, t** +33 (0)4 79 05 28, is a great place for dinner.

Party

'Not the spot for wild après ski,' said a reporter. Bars such as **Monica's Pub** in Plagne-Soleil ('bands and DJs in the evening') and **La Mine** in Plagne-1800 ('good beer and live music') are busy after skiing, as are **La Tête Inn** and **Le Cheyenne Café** in Belle-Plagne. Most of the action later on lies in Plagne-Centre at **Scotty's Pub** ('run by Brits and a popular hangout for resort staff') and **Le No'blem** café/bar ('a younger crowd looking for a good night out with DJs playing a mixture of indie, hip hop and rock'). The best places in Plagne-Bellecôte are the **Saloon** and **Le Cosy Bar** (the latter open until 4am). Champagny has **Le Galaxy** disco, and high-decibel **Oxygène** in rural Montchavin keeps the cows awake until the early hours.

Sleep

Aime-la-Plagne:

****MGM Les Hauts Bois apartments,** t +44 (0)20 7584 2841, are among the most luxurious in the resort. Residents have use of a stylish pool, sauna and steam room.

Belle-Plagne:

****Chalethotel Les Deux Domaines, t +44 (0)871 310 1000, *www.esprit-holidays.co.uk* was built last season, offering 'unexpected luxury in La Plagne'.

****Les Montagnettes apartments, t +33 (0)4 79 55 12 00, are spacious, convenient and extremely comfortable, with very friendly staff.

****Les Balcons de Belle-Plagne, t +33 (0)4 79 55 76 76, apartments received mixed reports. 'The food was of an extremely high standard, but there is no real focus and meeting point – just three stools around a cramped little bar in the corner of the dining room.'

***Hotel Carlina, t +33 (0)4 79 09 78 46, *www.carlina-belleplagne.com*, is a charming small hotel made from all-natural materials, with 30 rooms and a good restaurant.

**Hotel Mercure, t +33 (0)4 79 09 12 09, *www.mercure.com*, formerly the Eldorado is 'simple but satisfactory'.

Champagny en Vanoise:

****Les Chalets du Bouquetin, t +33 (0)4 79 55 01 13, *www.bouquetin.com*, are traditional chalets in the heart of the village.

Plagne-Centre:

***Paladien Terra Nova, t +33 (0)4 79 55 79 00, *www.hotels-altitude.com*, has 'a great location and good food, though a bit impersonal'.

Summit View, t +44 (0)844 557 3118, *www.snowline.co.uk*, is a complex of eight supremely luxurious chalets on the edge of the piste.

Plagne-Soleil:

****MGM Les Granges du Soleil Hotel and Apartments, t +44 (0)870 750 6820, have a restaurant, pool and spa.

Plagne-Village:

****Résidence Aspen, t +33 (0)4 79 55 75 75, receives glowing reports.

Risoul

Profile

This convenient little resort is good value for money and is usually free of lift queues. There is little choice of nightlife, but Risoul now tends to attract students and school groups, who have added to the liveliness of the place

Resort

Risoul shares its substantial ski area with Vars 1850, and they jointly market themselves as the Domaine de la Forêt Blanche. Risoul was purpose-built in the still ski boom years of the 1970s as a budget-conscious, no-frills family ski resort, looking for a French rather than an international market.

Its continued popularity at home and abroad is largely dependent on its reputation for low prices and reliable snow. When resorts elsewhere are suffering from a lack of cover at the beginning or towards the end of the season, Risoul usually has metres of the stuff from before Christmas until after Easter.

*BEST FOR

Purpose-built convenience, large ski area, value

ESSENTIALS

Altitude: 1850m (6,068ft)–2750m (9,020ft)

Further information: t +33 (0)4 92 46 02 60, *www.risoul.com*

Lifts in area: 53 (2 cableways, 15 chairs, 36 drags) serving 180km of piste

Lift pass: Forêt Blanche (covers Risoul and Vars) adult €131–149.50, child 5–11yrs €123–128, both for six days

Access: Grenoble airport 2½hrs, Marseille airport 3½hrs, railway station at Montdauphin-Guillestre 17km

The resort used to be extremely popular with the British, but the clientele has changed in recent years. Visitors from Eastern Europe now outnumber the British among the 30 per cent of skiers and riders who are not French. 'Not a resort I would rush back to, but if you are with a gang of mates in your 20s I think it would suit,' suggested a reporter.

The downside of choosing Risoul is the airport transfer from Grenoble or Marseille, which in adverse winter weather conditions can be considerably longer than advertised. The silver lining of its isolated position is the absence of day-trippers and weekenders.

Accommodation is in appealing wood and stone apartment complexes, although the small shopping area suffers from a profusion of billboards and a lack of proper pavements. Other activities include snowmobiling, guided snowshoe excursions, parapente, winter horse-riding, and skating on the large natural ice rink.

Mountain

Lifts rise from the village to 2571m Razi for connections to Vars-Ste-Marie and Vars-Les-Claux, while a six-seater chair takes you up to the second smaller ski area of Peyrefolle. The third sector of L'Homme de Pierre is reached by a sequence of draglifts – despite major improvements to the life system in recent years, the region still suffers from a predominance of these.

Risoul has a wide diversity of terrain for all standards. The green runs around the base area provide some of the best novice terrain in France, while more confident skiers will find that they can go far afield without ever being forced to stray from blue runs ('lots of wide blues and reds, on some of which you could point your skis straight and go like the wind').

Experts will enjoy the ridge run reached by the Chabrières drag from the Col de Crevoux. This takes you to starting point for the KL speed ski track, where a number of world records have been set over the years. Other descents from different points along the cornice are of sufficient gradient to test the nerve of even the most accomplished. The long runs down to Vars-Ste-Marie from 2580m La Mayt are usually uncrowded and provide perfect cruising terrain.

Vars also has its own ski area on 2273m Peynier on the far side of the town but reached on skis from Vars-Les-Claux. The black Ecureil, which follows the fall-line down the wooded slopes from the top, is one of the most enjoyable in the region. However, most of the 10 black runs are graded more for their lack of grooming than their gradient.

After a big dump, Risoul and Vars offer some outstanding off-piste opportunities between the trees. A natural half-pipe in the back bowl off the Col de Valbelle is an attraction for both skiers and riders. The Surfland terrain park on l'Homme de Pierre has a super-pipe and lots of jumps and rails, as well as a dedicated area for board novices.

Learn

The **ESF**, **t** +33 (0)4 92 46 19 22, and the rival **ESI**, **t** +33 (0)4 92 46 20 83, both have a sound reputation.

Children

Risoul has the French government's *P'tits Montagnards* award for good childcare. The **Garderie**, **t** +33 (0)4 92 46 02 60, cares for children from six months to six years. **Les Pitchouns**, **t** +33 (0)4 92 46 29 37, takes children from six months to six years.

Lunch

Serious lunchers are on the wrong mountain. Try **Le Vallon**, **t** +33 (0)4 92 46 05 75, and **Le Tetras**, **t** +33 (0)4 92 46 09 83, or descend to the resort.

Dine

'Not really the place for a foodie,' commented a reporter. **La Dalle en Pente**, **t** +33 (0)4 92 46 05 40, has traditional mountain cuisine including fondue, raclette and *pierrade*. **Le Plante de Baton**, **t** +33 (0)4 92 46 06 38, is also recommended. **La Cherine**, **t** +33 (0)4 92 46 01 80, under Les Mélèzes apartments, has good food at reasonable prices. **Snowboard Café**, **t** +33 (0)4 92 46 18 65, has cheap daily specials.

Party

Nightlife is limited to a few bars and the late-night **Le Morgan** disco, which is described as both lively and good fun. The resort centre can be extremely noisy and we advise families to choose accommodation in quieter locations.

Sleep

Most visitors opt to stay in self-catering apartments.

★★★★**Les Balcons de Sirius**, **t** +33 (0)4 92 46 03 47, *www.sara-residences.com*, are excellent, spacious and very well priced.

★★**Au Bon Logis**, **t** +33 (0)4 92 45 14 47, *www.aubonlogis.fr*, is in the hamlet of Gaudissard, 10 minutes from Risoul.

★★**La Bonne Auberge**, **t** +33 (0)4 92 45 02 40, *www.labonneauberge-risoul.com*, is a chalet-style hotel that has been run by the same family for 30 years.

★★**Le Chardon Bleu**, **t** +33 (0)4 92 46 07 27, *http://lechardonbleu.free.fr*, is a clean and modern hotel overlooking the piste.

La Rosière

Profile

The French half of an intermediate ski area shared with La Thuile in Italy's Aosta Valley. A quiet village with uncrowded slopes

Resort

La Rosière is an important resort in the Haute Tarentaise above the valley town of Bourg-St-Maurice. It provides an easy winter link – on skis – to the Aosta Valley in Italy where it shares its ski area with La Thuile. Most probably the Carthaginian general Hannibal came this way in 247 BC en route to Rome. The current lift system would have no problem in ferrying his 26,000 men across the Petit-St-Bernard Pass by detachable quad-chair, but 38 war elephants might be quite another matter.

The lift company – it also owns Val d'Isère's mountain transport – is spending €33 million on improving facilities. First steps have been a remodelling of the base area and two new six-person lifts to provide swift mountain access.

A new centre in Les Eucherts contains sports shops, ski school offices and a

✻ BEST FOR

Intermediates, families, big ski area

ESSENTIALS

Altitude: 1200m (3,937ft)–2650m (8,694ft)
Further information: **t** +33 (0)4 79 06 80 51, *www.larosiere.net*
Lifts in area: 37 (1 cableway, 17 chairs, 19 drags) serving 150km of piste
Lift pass: area (includes La Thuile) adult €161.20, child 5–12yrs €112.80, both for six days
Access: Geneva and Lyon airports 2½hrs, railway station at Bourg-St-Maurice 30mins

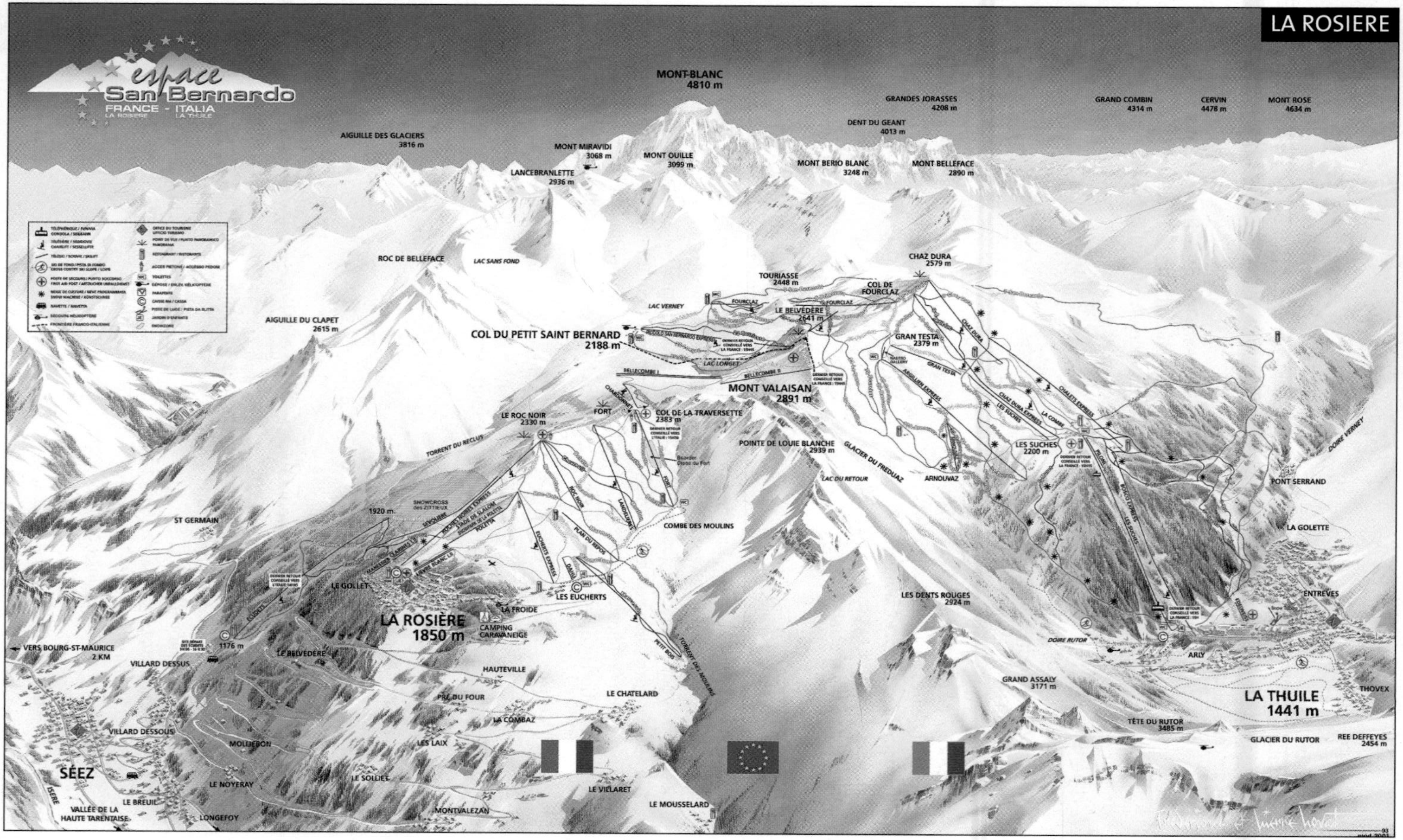

espace San Bernardo
FRANCE - ITALIA
LA ROSIERE LA THUILE

MONT-BLANC 4810 m
GRANDES JORASSES 4208 m
GRAND COMBIN 4314 m
CERVIN 4478 m
MONT ROSE 4634 m
DENT DU GEANT 4013 m
AIGUILLE DES GLACIERS 3816 m
MONT MIRAVIDI 3068 m
MONT OUILLE 3099 m
MONT BERIO BLANC 3248 m
MONT BELLEFACE 2890 m
LANCEBRANLETTE 2936 m
ROC DE BELLEFACE
LAC SANS FOND
CHAZ DURA 2579 m
TOURIASSE 2448 m
COL DE FOURCLAZ
LAC VERNEY
FOURCLAZ
LE BELVEDERE 2641 m
AIGUILLE DU CLAPET 2615 m
COL DU PETIT SAINT BERNARD 2188 m
GRAN TESTA 2379 m
LAC LONGET
BELLECOMBE I
BELLECOMBE II
MONT VALAISAN 2891 m
CHAZ DURA
GRAN TESTA
ARGUERN EXPRESS
CHALETS EXPRESS
CHAZ DURA EXPRESS
LES SUCHES
LA COMBE
LE ROC NOIR 2330 m
FORT
CHARDONNET
COL DE LA TRAVERSETTE 2383 m
TORRENT DU RECLUS
POINTE DE LOUIE BLANCHE 2939 m
GLACIER DU FREDUAZ
LAC DU RETOUR
ARNOUVAZ
LES SUCHES 2200 m
PILONE
BOSCO EXPRESS
DOIRE VERNEY
PONT SERRAND
LA GOLETTE
SNOWCROSS des ZITTIEUX
1920 m
SEVOLIERE
ROCHES NOIRES EXPRESS
STADE DE SLALOM
ROC NOIR
LANDELIERES
EUCHERTS EXPRESS
PLAN DU REPOS
DAHU
COMBE DES MOULINS
ST GERMAIN
LE GOLLET
LES EUCHERTS
LA FROIDE
LA ROSIÈRE 1850 m
CAMPING CARAVANEIGE
PETIT BOIS
TORRENT DES MOULINS
LES DENTS ROUGES 2924 m
ENTREVES
DOIRE RUTOR
ARLY
VERS BOURG-ST-MAURICE 2 KM
1176 m
VILLARD DESSUS
LE BELVEDERE
HAUTEVILLE
LE CHATELARD
PRE DU FOUR
LA COMBAZ
GRAND ASSALY 3171 m
LA THUILE 1441 m
THOVEX
TÊTE DU RUTOR 3485 m
GLACIER DU RUTOR
REE DEFFEYES 2454 m
VILLARD DESSOUS
MOLLIEBON
LES LAIX
SÉEZ
LE NOYERAY
LE SOLLIET
LE VILLARET
LE MOUSSELARD
ISERE
LE BREUIL
VALLÉE DE LA HAUTE TARENTAISE
LONGEFOY
MONTVALEZAN

sports complex with ice-skating rink and bowling alley.

Mountain

The skiing is on wide, open slopes beneath the ridge that marks the frontier with Italy and is best suited to adventurous intermediates ('no lift queues and at times we had pistes all to ourselves'). The 500m-long terrain park is reached by the Poletta drag.

Learn

The **ESF**, **t** +33 (0)4 79 06 86 21, has a worthy reputation and most instructors speak good English. The other choices are **ESI**, **t** +33 (0)4 79 06 81 26, and **Evolution 2**, **t** +33 (0)4 79 40 19 80, which offers freefall parachuting as well as the usual ski and board tuition. You can learn to snowkite with **FlyMountains Snowkiting School**, **t** +33 (0)6 29 48 02 18.

Children

'Very family orientated,' was how one reporter put it. We have good reports of **Evolution 2**, **t** + 33 (0)4 79 40 19 80. The **ESF**, **t** +33 (0)4 79 06 86 21, is said to be 'excellent'. **Le Club des Galopines** cares for skiers and non-skiers from 18 months and **Club Loisirs** from three years, both **t** +33 (0)4 79 06 89 67.

Lunch

Try **La Traversette**, **t** +33 (0)6 11 70 51 07, **Le Plan du Repos**, **t** +33 (0)4 79 06 87 92, and **L'Ancolie**, **t** +33 (0)4 79 06 86 71 ('our favourite') at Les Eucherts.

Dine

Le Relais du Petit-St-Bernard, **t** +33 (0)4 79 40 19 38, **L'Ancolie**, **t** +33 (0)4 79 06 86 71, and **Le Génépi**, **t** +33 (0)4 79 07 52 09, are recommended. **Le Turia**, **t** +33 (0)4 79 06 13 65, has fine cuisine at a good price.

Party

Nightlife is quiet, but you can find some action if you look in the right places ('the three main bars offer live music and pool, not to mention toffee vodka'). **Le P'tit Relais** and **Le Petit Danois** ('the best for chilling with excellent bar staff, music and live footie') are busy as the lifts close. **Clay's** is a piano-bar, **L'Arpin's** is a karaoke bar, and **Le Pub** provides the late-night action.

Sleep

★★★★**Les Granges de La Rosière**, **t** +44 (0)20 7584 2841, *www.ernalow.co.uk*, are smart MGM apartments.

★★★★**Chalet Matsuzaka**, **t** +33 (0)4 79 07 53 13, *www.chaletmatsuzaka.com*, is new. It has 10 spacious bedrooms with Japanese-style outside baths and saunas.

★★★**Le Ruitor**, **t** +(0)4 79 06 82 07, *www.leruitor.com*, is 'cosy and comfortable, 350m from the lifts – but there is a free shuttle service'.

★★★**Le Roc Noir**, **t** +33 (0)4 79 40 19 08, is being completely renovated for the 2008–9 season.

★★**Le Relais du Petit-St-Bernard**, **t** +33 (0)4 79 06 80 48, *www.petit-saint-bernard.com*, is well placed at the foot of the slopes.

★★**Le Solaret**, **t** +33 (0)4 79 06 80 47, *www.hotelsolaret.com*, is family-run.

Sainte-Foy

***BEST FOR**

Off-piste, mountain restaurants

ESSENTIALS

Altitude: 1550m (5,084ft)–2620m (8,596ft)

Further information: t +33 (0)4 79 06 95 19, *www.saintefoy.net*

Lifts in resort: 4 (4 chairs) serving 31km of piste

Lift pass: adult €131, student €102, child 7–11yrs €96, for six days

Access: Chambéry airport 1hr, Geneva and Lyon airports 2hrs, railway station at Bourg-St-Maurice 20km

Profile

Burgeoning *station de ski* above an old village in the Haute Tarentaise, with lots of new chalets. A resort renowned for its superb powder skiing

Resort

Sainte-Foy *station* is the purpose-built ski base above the old village of Sainte-Foy on the road up to Tignes and Val d'Isère from Bourg-St-Maurice. In recent years it has been the centre of a speculative building boom, with a large development of attractive traditional-style chalets. Resort developer MGM is banking on the premise that the amount of new accommodation will force the French authorities to allow more lifts to be built. So far it appears to have worked – it now has one extra lift. 'We have watched this little resort develop over the years,' said a reporter; 'the character has definitely changed, but the development has been very tasteful.'

Mountain

Sainte-Foy is a ski secret that has been long known to Val and Tignes habitués, who come here for the superb powder. Three quad-chairs take you up to 2612m Col de l'Aiguille, starting point for a choice of red or black pistes, while the second chair serves less demanding tree-lined terrain. The Marquise six-person chair that opened two years ago effectively doubled the resort's lift-accessed terrain.

The best reason to come here is for the exceptionally rewarding off-piste itineraries. These include the 1700m descent of the north face of Fogliettaz and a long powder run to the farming hamlet of Le Monal. 'Didn't queue for a lift once. Didn't do the same line twice and still have over half the off-piste areas left for next time,' commented a reporter.

Learn

The **ESF**, **t** +33 (0)4 79 06 96 76, receives rave reviews from reporters. 'The learner area and terrain is excellent,' said a reporter.'

Children

Les P'tits Trappeurs, **t** +33 (0)4 79 06 97 92, accepts children from three to 11 years. 'The instructors were fantastic and the kids can't wait to go back,' said a reporter.

Lunch

Try **Les Brevettes**, **t** +33 (0)6 76 35 21 70, and **Chez Léon**, **t** + 33 (0)6 09 57 23 88, at the top of the first chair, and **Maison à Colonnes**, **t** +33 (0)4 79 06 94 80, at the bottom of the lifts. **Chez Mérie**, **t** +33 (0)4 79 06 90 16, at Le Miroir serves hearty peasant fare.

Dine

La Bergerie, **t** +33 (0)4 79 06 25 51, is a gastronomic restaurant at the foot of the

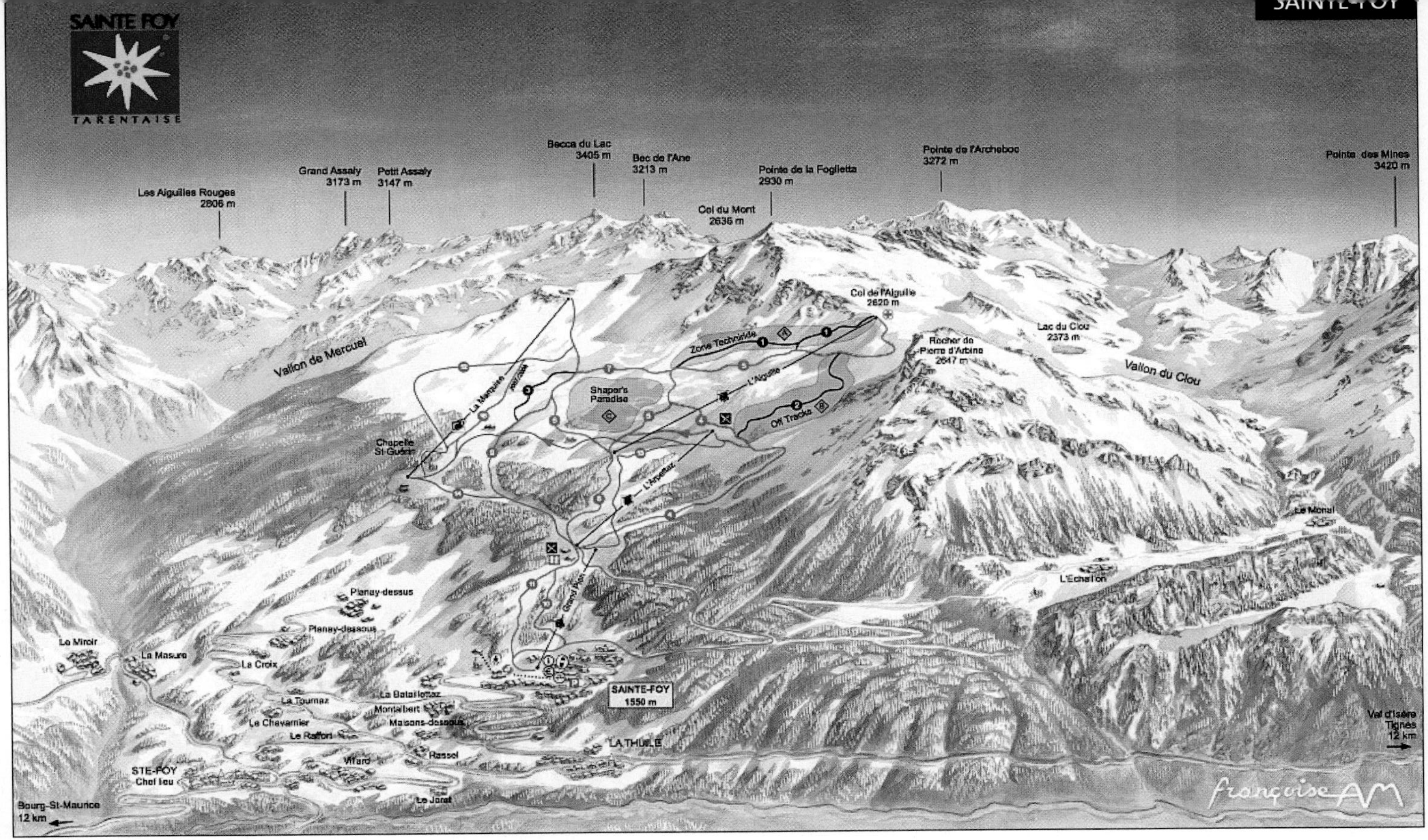

SAINTE FOY
TARENTAISE
Les Aiguilles Rouges 2806 m
Grand Assaly 3173 m
Petit Assaly 3147 m
Becca du Lac 3405 m
Bec de l'Ane 3213 m
Col du Mont 2636 m
Pointe de la Foglietta 2930 m
Pointe de l'Archeboc 3272 m
Pointe des Mines 3420 m
Col de l'Aiguille 2620 m
Lac du Clou 2373 m
Rocher de Pierre d'Arbine 2647 m
Vallon du Clou
Vallon de Mercuel
Zone Technoride
L'Aiguille
Off Tracks
Shaper's Paradise
La Marquise
L'Arpettaz
Grand Plan
Chapelle St-Guérin
Le Monal
L'Echaillon
Planay-dessus
Planay-dessous
Le Miroir
La Masure
La Croix
La Tournaz
Le Chevallier
Le Raffort
La Bataillettaz
Montalbert
Maisons-dessous
Rassel
Vilard
Le Joret
STE-FOY Chef lieu
SAINTE-FOY 1550 m
LA THUILE
Bourg-St-Maurice 12 km
Val d'Isère Tignes 12 km
françoise AM

piste. **Maison à Colonnes**, **t** +33 (0)4 79 06 94 80, is recommended, along with **La Grange** in Hôtel Le Monal, **t** +33 (0)4 79 06 97 30, and **La Bequa**, **t** +33 (0)4 79 06 90 51.

Party

The resort is quiet in the evening, with a choice of **Le Pitchouli** for a drink after skiing, **L'Iceberg** for music, and the **bar** of Hôtel Le Monal.

Sleep

★★★★**Les Fermes de Sainte-Foy**, **t** +33 (0)4 50 233 10 96, is an MGM hotel complex of three- and four-room apartments opening this season.

★★★★**Yellow Stone Chalet**, **t** +44 (0)20 7384 3854, *www.descent.co.uk*, is run as a catered chalet for 15 people. It has an indoor pool, sauna and hot tub.

★★**Auberge sur la Montagne**, **t** +33 (0)4 79 06 95 83, *www.auberge-montagne.co.uk*, in the hamlet of La Thuile, is warmly recommended.

★★**Hôtel Le Monal**, **t** +33 (0)4 79 06 90 07, *www.le-monal.com*, is in the old village.

St-Gervais

Profile

Traditional spa town with modestly priced accommodation, linked by gondola and piste into the giant Megève ski area, 4km from a TGV train station and autoroute exit

Resort

This attractive small spa town has been a resort ever since the first tourists arrived here to take the waters in 1806. It lies at the head of a dramatic river gorge midway between Chamonix and Megève, and serves as the gateway to the two important ski areas. '"Wow!" pretty much sums up our experience of our accommodation, the skiing and St Gervais in general,' said a reporter, and 'As the better-known resorts get busier it was such a pleasure to come across St Gervais with its fabulous facilities and quieter pistes – I just can't believe that it took me 20 years before I tried it.' 'The town centre was really nice, traditional and compact rather than the horrid concrete sprawl that so many resorts have become,' said another.

*BEST FOR

Big ski area, town facilities, airport access

ESSENTIALS

Altitude: 860m (2,821ft)–2350m (7,708ft)
Further information: **t** +33 (0)4 50 47 76 08, *www.st-gervais.net*
Lifts in area: 110 in Evasion Mont Blanc (13 cableways, 38 chairs, 59 drags) serving 445km of piste. 729km in Mont Blanc ski area
Lift pass: Ski Pass Mont Blanc (covers all local resorts including Chamonix, Courmayeur, Les Houches) adult €166, child 4–15yrs €133, both for six days
Access: Geneva airport 45mins, TGV railway station at Sallanches 4km, regular buses to resort

Mountain

The main skiing to the east of the town, reached by a fast, 20-person gondola from the outskirts, is linked across the slopes of Mont d'Arbois to Megève. The area has a terrain park and a half-pipe. 'For me as a boarder the icing on the cake was that there were only a handful of draglifts. I can heartily enthuse about the snowfield just off Mont Joly, which is incredible and huge,' said a reporter. On the other side of town, the venerable Mont Blanc Tramway, a rack-and-pinion railway dating back to 1904, takes you to the top of the neighbouring ski area of Les Houches.

Learn

Lessons are provided by the **ESF St-Gervais/Le Bettex**, **t** +33 (0)4 50 47 76 21, **ESF St-Nicholas-de-Véroce**, **t** +33 (0)4 50 93 21 61, and the **Mont Blanc Ecole de Ski**, **t** +33 (0)4 50 93 16 78, at Bettex.

Children

Garderie des Neiges, **t** +33 (0)4 50 93 14 81, cares for children from six months to six years in Le Bettex. **Halte-Garderie**, **t** +33 (0)4 50 93 23 90, is for two to six years in St-Nicolas-de-Véroce. The two **ESF** branches provide lessons from four years.

Lunch

Try **Hôtel-Restaurant L'Igloo**, **t** +33 (0)4 50 93 05 84, at Mont d'Arbois and **Le Prarion**, **t** +33 (0)4 50 54 41 99, above Les Houches.

Dine

St-Gervais itself has some 35 restaurants. For crêpes try **4 Epices**, **t** +33 (0)4 50 47 76 08, and for pizzas **L'Eterle**, **t** +33 (0)4 50 93 64 30. **Le Four**, **t** +33 (0)4 50 93 14 16, and **A. Robinson**, **t** +33 (0)4 50 93 59 00, serve local specialities.

Party

This is not a party town but there is a good selection of bars, including the **Nulles Bar** and the **Yucatan Bar**, both of which which were recommended by readers. a skating rink, the casino and **La Nuit des Temps** disco. The town is a world class spa centre, with myriad treatments available.

Sleep

*****Hôtel-Restaurant Le Carlina**, **t** +33 (0)4 50 93 41 10, *www.carlina-hotel.com*, is ski in, ski out with a traditional restaurant and an indoor pool.

*****Hôtel-Restaurant L'Igloo** **t** +33 (0)4 50 93 05 84, *www.ligloo.com*, is a chalet-style hotel set on the piste.

Chalet Roches, **t** +44 (0)20 7096 1666, *www.pistepursuits.com*, is said to be 'beautiful, spacious and very well furnished, as well as having every facility you could wish for. More importantly, the food was truly fabulous.'

La Maison du Vernay, **t** +33 (0)4 50 47 07 55, *www.lamaisonduvernay.com*, is a little B&B with five wood-panelled bedrooms, each with a different flower theme.

St-Martin-de-Belleville

Profile

Offbeat and attractive village in the huge Trois Vallées area. Excellent accommodation and restaurants but limited après ski

Resort

St-Martin-de-Belleville is a charming old village situated before Les Menuires on the road up from Moûtiers. It has an entirely different and more relaxed rural atmosphere than any of the better-known purpose-built resorts in the Trois Vallées. Most of the ancient stone and wood barns have been converted into chalets,

✱ BEST FOR

Intermediates and experts, big ski area, rural ambience, ski gourmets

ESSENTIALS

Altitude: 1450m (4,757ft)–3300m (10,827ft)
Further information: t +33 (0)4 79 00 20 00, *www.st-martin-de-belleville.com*
Lifts in area: 165 in Trois Vallées (43 cableways, 68 chairs, 54 drags) serving 600km of piste
Lift pass: Trois Vallées adult €157–295, child 5–13yrs €112–225, both for six days
Access: Chambéry airport 1½hrs, Lyon airport 2½hrs, Geneva airport 3hrs, Eurostar at Moûtiers 20km away

but farmhouse cheese is still made here, and you can still buy fresh milk by the pail.

Mountain

St-Martin's only fault used to lie in the inordinate amount of time that it took to link into the rest of the skiing in the Trois Vallées. But all that changed with the construction of a gondola and a fast chair that swiftly convey you up to the Tougnette Ridge for runs down to Les Menuires, or over the far side towards Méribel. In fresh powder conditions the runs from the ridge back to St-Martin are some of the best in the region – glorious acres of undulating pastures followed by tree-skiing.

Learn

The **ESF**, **t** +33 (0)4 79 00 24 78, has a branch here. **Compagnie des Guides**, **t** +33 (0)4 79 01 04, organizes 15 off-piste excursions. 'The beginner area is tiny and the only pistes are blue ones, which have narrow and steep sections. Our novice boarders found this a problem,' noted a reporter.

Children

Piou-Piou, **t** +33 (0)4 79 08 91 15, cares for both non-skiing and skiing children from two-and-a-half years. Not all the staff speak English.

Lunch

Le Corbeley, **t** +33 (0)4 79 08 95 31, has a sunny terrace and good food, while **L'Etoile des Neiges**, **t** +33 (0)4 79 08 92 80, is a lunchtime favourite.

Dine

L'Eterlou, **t** +33 (0)4 79 08 94 07, is recommended, and **Le Montagnard**, **t** +33 (0)4 79 01 08 40, is in an old hayloft and superb for an evening out. **La Voûte**, **t** +33 (0)4 79 08 91 48, serves good pizzas. **L'Etoile des Neiges**, **t** +33 (0)4 79 08 92 80, uses fresh produce for its local specialities. Chef René Meilleur's **La Bouitte**, **t** +33 (0)4 79 08 96 77, at nearby St-Marcel, has fabulous starters, two much-deserved Michelin rosettes and an intimate farmhouse atmosphere.

Party

'A bonnie wee place with a few nice pubs and restaurants, but don't expect raucous nightlife. The emphasis here is on good-humoured charm,' said a reporter. St-Martin has a few bars, including **Pourquoi Pas** piano-bar ('the karaoke was a good laugh'), **Le Jokker** and **Brewski's**, but is quiet by night.

Sleep

★★★**Hôtel St-Martin**, **t** +33 (0)4 79 00 88 00, *www.hotelsaintmartin.com*, has rooms that have all been individually decorated.

★★★**Alp'Hôtel t** +33 (0)4 79 08 92 82, *www.alphotel.fr*, is comfortable and traditional.

★★★**Hôtel Edelweiss, t** +33 (0)4 79 08 96 67, *www.hotel-edelweiss73.com*, has 16 cosy rooms and a good restaurant.

La Bouitte, t +33 (0)4 79 08 96 77, *www.labouitte.com*, in the nearby hamlet of St-Marcel, has five delightfully rustic suites tucked away in the eaves up ladders and in other corners of the farmhouse. It also has an outdoor hot tub and a small spa.

Samoëns

🏆 BEST SMALL RESORT 2009
🏆 BEST RESORT RESTAURANT 2009 (HOTEL NEIGE ET ROC)

Profile

Charming little resort linked to Flaine, with high quality hotels and restaurants

Resort

Samoëns shares its ski area with purpose-built Flaine and it is contrastingly different in character. This is one of France's *monuments historiques*, an ancient little town surrounded by magnificent mountains. It just happens also to act as a gateway to the giant 73-lift Grand Massif ski area.

The downside is that it is not a ski-in, ski-out resort and because of its low altitude you cannot necessarily expect snow-covered roofs and trees. You have to catch a cable car from the outskirts of town up to the slopes at the start of the day, and back down again at the end of it. Anyone who wants maximum skiing time should opt for the purpose-built satellite of Samoëns 1600 – staying up here is a much less architecturally attractive option, but it dispenses with the daily cable car commute.

However, if your vision of the perfect ski holidays extends beyond a racing tuck, it's a truly rewarding place to stay with a fine medieval centre and a leisurely take on life. In particular this is a good place for families that have already notched up a number of ski holidays and don't need crèches or nannies.

✱ BEST FOR

Relaxed skiers and riders, families, foodies

ESSENTIALS

Altitude: 720m (5,840ft)–2480m (8,134ft)
Further information: t +33 (0)4 92 24 98 98, *www.serre-chevalier.com*
Lifts in area: 73 in Le Grand Massif (7 cableways, 28 chairs, 38 drags) serving 265km of piste
Lift pass: Grand Massif (covers Les Carroz, Flaine, Morillon, Samoëns, Sixt) adult €187.20, youth 12–15yrs €147, child 5–11yrs €135, all for six days
Access: Geneva airport 1hr, railway station at Cluses 25km, frequent bus service to resort

Mountain

Samoëns has its own small ski area beneath the 2120m Tête des Saix. It offers a generous nursery slope, a handful of enjoyable cruisers, and one steep and usually bumpy black. However, the chairs up to the Tête are annoying slow, so leave this for the end of the day.

The best skiing in the region is further afield, much of it in the Flaine sector. No week here is complete without a visit to the quaint 9th-century village of Sixt-Fer-à-Cheval reached by the 14km blue Cascades run.

Samoëns 1600 has a small terrain park and there are others in the Grand Massif including the Jam Park Pro above Flaine.

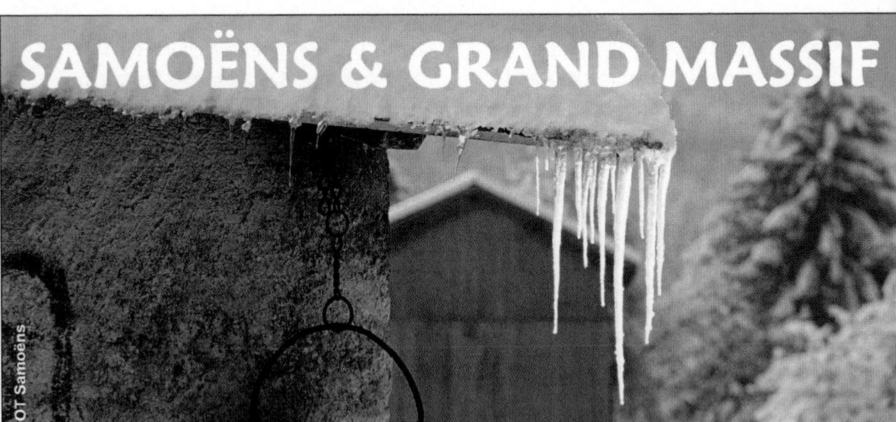

A great selection of accommodation

Great value packages including Eurotunnel or just accommodation only.
Ski school, lift passes, ski/board equipment hire,
airport transfers arranged.

peakretreats.co.uk

0844 576 0173

ABTA
W5537

Learn

The resort has a choice of four schools and tuition is reasonably priced – half the cost of a big-name resort such as Méribel. The **ESF**, **t** +33 (0)4 50 34 43 12, has a sound reputation. The others are **Zig Zag**, **t** +(0)6 86 66 07 21, **International**, **t** +33 (0)450 53 38 92, and **Ski Sessions**, **t** +33 (0)6 62 10 59 24.

Children

Les Loupiots, **t** +33 (0)4 50 34 13 96, cares for children aged six months to six years and arranges ski lessons for older ones. The schools all provide lessons for children. **Zig Zag**'s Esprit de Glisse course mixes skiing with snowboarding and blading.

Lunch

Refuge L'Igloo, **t** +33 (0)4 50 90 14 31, at La Vieille on the ridge above Morillon, is the best bet on this side of the mountain. It has a large sun terrace but can get 'hopelessly overcrowded, with subsequent loss of service'. **Le Chalet des Molliets**, **t** +33 (0)4 50 90 05 09, above Les Carroz is a good alternative.

Dine

Hotel Neige et Roc, **t** +33 (0)4 50 34 40 72, is famed for its trout and freshwater crayfish and is 'everything that a French country restaurant should be'. **La Table de Fifine**, **t** +33 (0)4 50 34 10 29, is renowned for its foie gras and fondues. **Le Monde à L'Envers**, **t** +33 (0)4 50 34 19 36, is warmly recommended. **Muscade et Basilic**, **t** +33 (0)4 50 53 65 22, is 'quite posh, but very welcoming. In Sixt, **Le Grenier à Babou**, **t** +33 (0)4 50 34 12 51, is famous for its pancakes and local specialities.

Sleep

*****Hotel Neige et Roc**, **t** +33 (0)4 50 34 40 72, *www.neigeetroc.com*, has cosy rooms and the separate Ferme des Fontany, an 18th-century chalet for 10 people ('lots of character, silk curtains and handmade quilts').

*****Chalet Arnica**, **t** +44 (0)870 770 0408, *www.peakretreats.co.uk*, is a self-catering free-standing chalet for 12, a short drive from the lift.

*****Chalet La Remise**, **t** +44 (0)870 770 0408, *www.peakretreats.co.uk*, is a new self-catering chalet for 12 with a spacious high-spec kitchen.

Serre Chevalier

Profile

The collective name for a dozen linked villages that share a large ski area with the ancient garrison town of Briançon. Attractive tree-lined slopes and varied off-piste

Resort

Serre Chevalier is not a single resort, but the collective marketing name adopted by a dozen villages that line the main Grenoble–Briançon road between the high mountain pass of the Col du Lauteret and the ancient town, close to the frontier with Italy. Accommodation and the main lifts are centred on Briançon, the quite separate villages of Chantemerle, Villeneuve-Le Bez, and the sleepy little spa resort of Monêtier-Les-Bains.

Where you choose to stay is dependent on your holiday priorities. The old walled

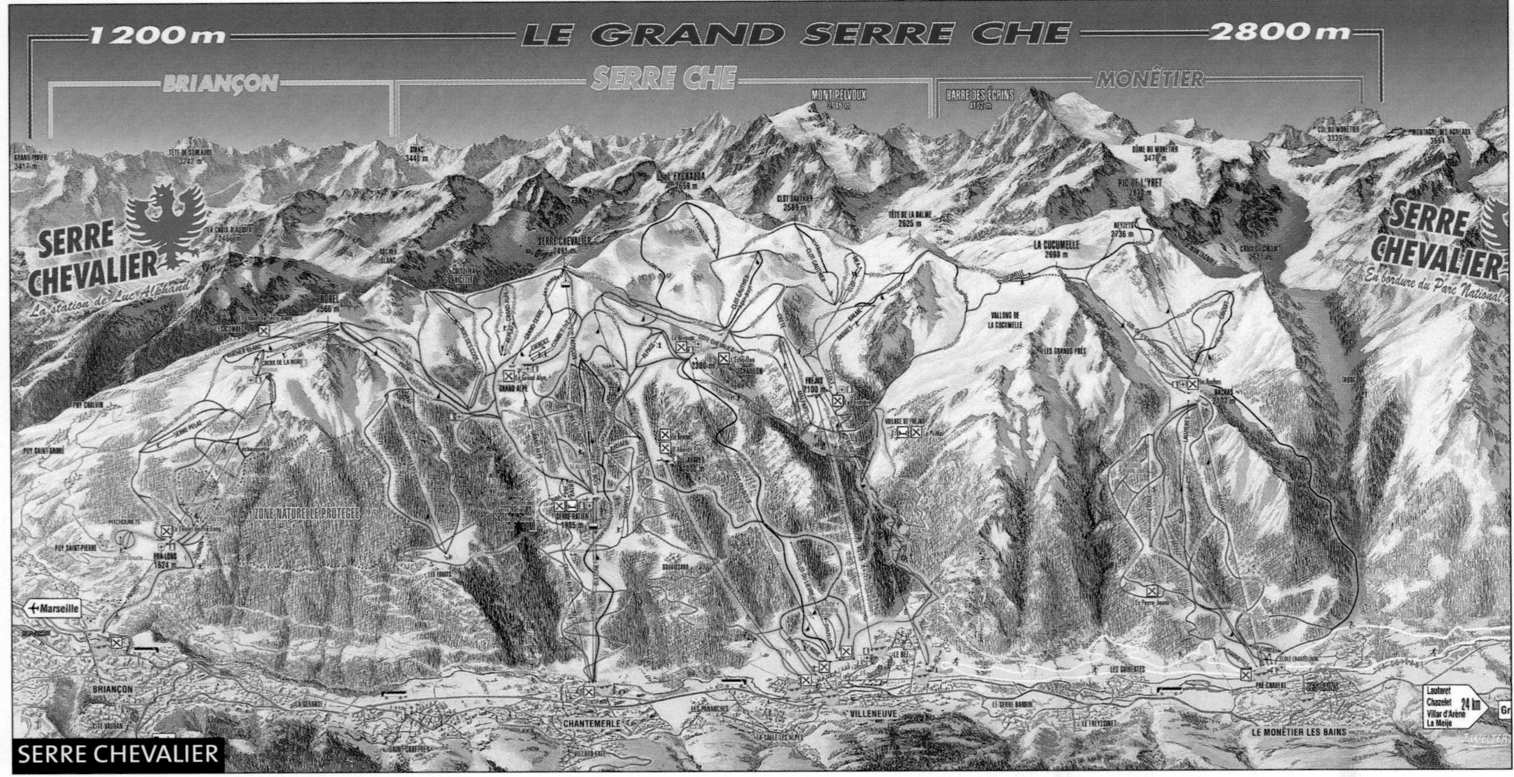

1200m
LE GRAND SERRE CHE
2800m
BRIANÇON
SERRE CHE
MONÊTIER
MONT PELVOUX
3946 m
BARRE DES ÉCRINS
4102 m
SINAC
3440 m
DÔME DU MONETIER
3479 m
PIC DE L'YRET
LA CUCUMELLE
2698 m
TÊTE DE LA BALME
2625 m
CLOT GAUTHIER
2589 m
SERRE CHEVALIER
2491 m
PROREL
2566 m
SERRE CHEVALIER
La station de Luc Alphand
SERRE CHEVALIER
En bordure du Parc National
VALLONS DE
LA CUCUMELLE
LES GRANDS PRÉS
GRAND ALPE
FREJUS
2100 m
VILLAGE DE FRÉJUS
ZONE NATURELLE PROTÉGÉE
PUY CHALVIN
PUY SAINT-ANDRÉ
PUY SAINT-PIERRE
PRA LONG
1624 m
Marseille
BRIANÇON
CHANTEMERLE
VILLENEUVE
LES GUIBERTES
LE MONÊTIER LES BAINS
Lautaret
Chazelet
Villar d'Arène
La Meije
24 km
SERRE CHEVALIER

*BEST FOR

All standards of skier and rider, big ski area, value

ESSENTIALS

Altitude: 1200m (3,936)–2800m (9,184ft)
Further information: **t** +33 (0)4 92 24 98 98, *www.serre-chevalier.com*
Lifts in area: 62 (9 cableways, 21 chairs, 32 drags) serving 250km of piste
Lift pass: Grande Serre Che (covers all centres as well as 1 day in each of Alpe d'Huez, Les Deux Alpes, La Grave, Montgenèvre, Puy-St-Vincent) adult €181, child 6–12yrs €140, both for six days
Access: Turin airport 1½hrs, Grenoble airport 2hrs, Lyon airport 3hrs, railway station at Briançon, regular bus service to villages

town has considerable charm and a wonderful choice of restaurants. But, while it is directly linked to the mountain, it lacks the atmosphere of a ski resort.

Chantemerle is the nearest village to Briançon, Villeneuve and the rustic hamlet of Le Bez beside it is the most convenient and charming village base with the most central access to the skiing that is spread along the wall of the valley.

Monêtier-Les-Bains (also known as Serre Chevalier 1500) is a picturesque spa village that has been a resort since Victorian times. The baths are well worth a visit, but you must book – even to use the outdoor thermal pool, which is for soaking in rather than swimming.

The giant Milky Way area, venue for the most recent Winter Olympics, is a short drive away. La Grave and Les Deux Alpes can both be reached across the Col de Lauteret. Puy-St-Vincent, near Briançon, is also worth a visit.

Mountain

Lots of new lifts have been introduced in recent years as Serre Che continues to compete with its rivals further north in the Alpine chain. The Clot Gautier chair above Villeneuve has been upgraded to a six-pack, as has the one from Aravet 2000 to Plateau Rouge. The Croix de la Nore quad-chair replaced an old draglift and last season the first stage of the four-person Grande Alpe gondola was upgraded to a 16-person one.

The linked runs that stretch for more than 19km down the southern side of the valley provide a playground that will test the most advanced skier and rider. But at the same time there is an easy route down to the valley from each lift. Of the different sectors, Monêtier is the most appealing and usually the least crowded. This is the best end of the circuit for accomplished skiers and riders, although the link with Villeneuve can sometimes suddenly close in bad weather and you may be forced to take the bus home if staying in Chantemerle or Briançon.

Isolée is an exciting black, which starts on the ridge from L'Eychauda at 2659m and plunges down towards Echaillon. Tabuc is a long black run through the woods with a couple of steep and narrow pitches. The Casse du Bœuf, a sweeping ridge through the trees back to Villeneuve, is one of our favourite runs.

This is considered one of the most friendly resorts in France for riders. The snowpark at Villeneuve has three tables and three boxes. The half-pipe at l'Aravet in Villeneuve is open until 9pm Tuesday to Friday during the French holidays. Chantermerle has a snowcross course with seven bends.

Learn

The **ESF** has branches in Chantemerle, **t** +33 (0)4 92 24 17 41, and Villeneuve, **t** +33 (0)4 92 24 71 99, offering excellent tuition in a friendly environment. In Chantemerle, **Evasion**, **t** +(0)4 92 24 02 419, and **Génération Snow**, **t** +33 (0)4 92 24 21 51, are recommended.

In Villeneuve, **Buissonnière ESI, t** +33 (0)4 92 24 78 66, is highly recommend by reporters: 'Brilliant – I can honestly say I learnt 10 times more because of the personal service.' **Altitude, t** +33 (0)6 08 02 51 82, provides the alternative. In Monêtier, British-owned **EurekaSki, t** +33 (0)6 79 46 24 84, is run by BASI instructors and has an excellent reputation ('our teenagers had a fantastic time going off-piste, doing jumps and leaping off ledges').

Children

This year the resort has received the coveted *Famille Plus* label, awarded for exceptional child facilities. In Chantemerle, **Les Poussins, t** +33 (0)4 92 24 03 43, accepts children from eight months. In Villeneuve, **Les Schtroumpfs, t** +33 (0)4 92 24 70 95, cares for children from six months. **Les Petit Aigles, t** +33 (0)4 92 24 29 31, takes non-skiers from three years.

In Monêtier, **Les Eterlous, t** +33 (0)4 92 24 45 75, accepts children from six months (18 months during French school holidays). The **ESF Jardin des Neiges**, in Briançon, **t** +33 (0)4 92 20 30 57, Chantemerle, **t** +33 (0)4 92 24 17 41, Villeneuve, **t** +33 (0)4 92 24 71 99, and Monêtier, **t** +33 (0)4 92 24 42 66, provides a mix of tuition and play for children from three years. **Buissonnière ESI, t** +33 (0)4 92 24 78 66, is highly praised. 'The instructor was excellent with the children, with primary focus on their enjoyment.' In Chantemerle, **Génération Snow, t** +33 (0)4 92 24 21 51, offers lessons to children aged seven to 11 years.

Lunch

Above Chantemerle, **Café Soleil, t** +33 (0)4 92 24 17 39, has carefully prepared food and a great atmosphere. **La Bergerie du Grand Alpe, t** +33 (0)681 34 34 14, serves local mountain cuisine.

Above Villeneuve, the **Pi Maï, t** +33 (0)4 92 24 83 63, has much charm, good food and attentive service as you sit by a roaring log fire. Remote **L'Echaillon, t** +33 (0)4 92 24 05 15, is also recommended. **D'Abord-L'Aravet 2000, t** +33 (0)4 92 24 97 67, is good value and has breathtaking views. **Le Bivouac de la Casse, t** + 33 (0)4 92 24 87 72, is at the top of the Casse du Bœuf chair.

Above Monêtier, **Peyra Juana, t** +33 (0)681 11 40 26, is a mountain hut with some of the best food in the ski area ('very good, although we had to queue for 20 minutes for a table'). **Le Bachas, t** +33 (0)4 92 24 50 66, is also praised. **Le Troll, t** +33 (0)4 92 24 28 47, just below Café de Soleil, was said to have good food and good service.

Dine

In Briançon, **Le Passé Simple, t** +33 (0)4 92 21 37 43, specializes in cuisine from the 17th century. **Restaurant La Caponnière, t** +33 (0)4 92 20 36 77, is warmly recommended ('excellent dinner – very French').

In Chantemerle, **Le Loup Blanc, t** +33 (0)4 92 24 14 27, was praised by reporters, and **Le Petit Chalet, t** +33 (0)4 92 24 05 79, was recommended as 'the gastronomic highlight of the week'. In Villeneuve, **La Pastorale, t** +33 (0)4 92 24 75 47, is well regarded. **Le Bidule, t** +33 (0)4 92 24 77 80, in the hamlet of Le Bez, has a warm atmosphere and enticing seafood and fish dishes. In Monêtier, **L'Antidote, t** +33 (0)4 92 4 40 02, in the Alliey Hotel is run by local celebrity chef Stéphane Froidevaux and has a Michelin star. **Chalet Auberge des Amis, t** +33 (0)4 92 24 43 27, is also recommended.

Party

This is not a party resort ('nightlife very limited'), with local bars and the occasional very Gallic disco. **Le QG** in Chantemerle, **Le Bab Bam** and **La Baïta** in Villeneuve are the main focal points. **Le Lièvre Blanc** in Villeneuve is a riders' hangout with weekly live music. **Bar l'Alpen** is said to have a good atmosphere, as does the **Bar Le Que Tal**. In Chantemerle, the **Altiforme** fitness centre offers massage and beauty treatments. Villeneuve has a pool and fitness centre. **Les Bains de Monêtier** is a thermal spa with with bath-temperature spring water.

Sleep

Most of Serre Chevalier's lodging is in apartments, and all accommodation can be booked through **Serre Chevalier Reservations**, **t** +33 (0)4 92 24 98 80.

Briançon:

******Chez Bear**, **t** +33 (0)4 92 21 11 70, *www.chezbear.com*, in the hamlet of Belvoir just outside Briançon, is the area's most luxurious chalet and sleeps up to 12.

*****Hôtel Le Vauban**, **t** +33 (0)4 92 21 12 11, *www.hotel-vauban.fr*, has a restaurant that uses fresh local produce.

*****Parc Hôtel**, **t** +33 (0)4 92 20 37 47, *www.monalisahotels.com*, is 300m from the gondola. Its restaurant serves Alsace cuisine.

Chantemerle 1350:

*****Hôtel Plein Sud**, **t** +33 (0)4 92 24 17 01, *www.hotelpleinsud.com*, is 250m from the lifts and has a pool.

****Grand Hôtel**, **t** +33 (0)4 92 24 15 16, *www.hotel-serrechevalier.com*, is more modest than its name, with a restaurant serving traditional mountain cuisine.

Villeneuve:

*****Hôtel du Mont Thabor**, **t** +33 (0)4 92 24 74 41, *www.mont-thabor.com*, has a pool and a games room.

****Chalet-Hôtel Le Pi Maï**, **t** +33 (0)4 92 24 83 63, *www.lepimai.com*, is in an isolated position up the mountain at 1985m with a warm ambience and good food.

Monêtier:

******Hôtel Les Glaciers Bonnabel**, **t** +33 (0)4 92 24 42 21, *www.hotel-bonnabel.com*, is on the Col de Lauteret outside the town centre.

*****Auberge du Choucas**, **t** +33 (0)4 92 24 42 73, *www.aubergeduchoucas.com*, is an ancient inn with a renowned restaurant with a vaulted ceiling. It serves delicious food.

****Alliey & Spa Hotel de Charme**, **t** +33 (0)4 92 24 44 20, *www.alliey.com*, has an impressive wine cellar and two pools, and children are warmly welcomed.

****Les Colchiques**, **t** +33 (0)4 92 24 42 42, *www.les-colchiques.com*, has rooms for two to six people, and good home-cooked food.

Hôtel Rif Blanc, **t** +33 (0)4 92 24 41 35, *www.hotelrifblanc.com*, is 'run as a home-from-home by English owners. Great food, small but newly decorated rooms and great showers.'

La Tania

Profile

Attractive low-level Trois Vallées alternative to the much more expensive Courchevel and Méribel

*BEST FOR

Big ski area, families, budget prices (for the area)

ESSENTIALS

Altitude: 1350m (4,429ft)–3300m (10,825ft)
Further information: t +33 (0)4 79 08 40 40, *www.latania.com*
Lifts in area: 165 in Trois Vallées (43 cableways, 68 chairs, 54 drags) serving 600km of piste
Lift pass: Trois Vallées adult €157–295, child 5–13yrs €112–225, both for six days
Access: Chambéry airport 2hrs, Lyon airport 2½hrs, Geneva airport 3hrs, Eurostar at Moûtiers, 25km

Resort

La Tania was originally built as a dormitory for the 1992 Albertville Olympics. But the village, situated a couple of kilometres from Le Praz (Courchevel 1300) quickly evolved into a pleasant little family resort in its own right. It has the skiing of Courchevel and Méribel but without the high prices. Architecture is in traditional mountain style and Le Forêt, a collection of attractive Scandinavian-style chalets set in the woods above the village, contributes to the cosy mountain ambience. 'If you want a relatively cheap holiday with great skiing and a beautiful village, then La Tania is most definitely for you,' said a reader.

Mountain

A jumbo gondola provides main mountain access and allows skiers to download when village snow-cover is limited. Lifts and pistes link to Courchevel 1850 as well as to Méribel via the Col de la Loze. When the light is flat, La Tania's own tree-lined skiing is the best place to be in the Trois Vallées.

Learn

The resort has a branch of the **ESF**, **t** +33 (0)4 79 08 80 39, as well as **Magic Snowsports Academy**, **t** +33 (0)4 79 01 07 85, and **Olivier Brané**, **t** +33 (0)4 79 08 24 21, an independent instructor who specializes in Trois Vallées tours.

Children

'Very well suited to children and parents,' said a reporter. **La Maison des Enfants**, **t** +33 (0)4 79 08 40 40, is for non-skiers from three years. Several tour operators have their own crèches.

Lunch

Le Bouc Blanc, **t** +33 (0)4 79 08 80 26, at the top of La Tania gondola, provides tasty omelettes and good service. **Le Ski Lodge**, **t** +33 (0)4 79 08 81 49, in the village, offers great value for money.

Dine

La Tania has a handful of restaurants including **Le Farçon**, **t** +33 (0)4 79 08 80 34, which has a Michelin rosette, serves gastronomic dishes. **La Taiga**, **t** +33 (0)4 79 08 80 33, and **La Ferme de La Tania**, **t** +33 (0)4 79 08 23 25, both offer inexpensive Savoyard specialities.

Party

'La Tania did not seem to have a raging night life, but plenty of places to eat and drink,' said a reporter. **Le Ski Lodge** is the main resort rendezvous.

Sleep

★★★★**Chalet Titania**, **t** +44 (0)870 754 4444, *www.leski.com*, is in Le Forêt area and has a crèche on the ground floor. Other chalets include one for 22 with a crèche and the other for 19 next door.

★★★**Hôtel Montana, t** +33 (0)4 79 08 80 08, in the village centre, is modern with a pool; the staff are very helpful and friendly, and the food is reasonable, if a little limited.

★★**Hôtel Le Télémark, t** +33 (0)4 79 08 80 32, *www.hoteltelemark.com*, is a rustic-style building set in the forest, with 12 rooms ranging from doubles to those sleeping seven.

* BEST FOR

Guaranteed snow-cover, all levels of skier and rider, off-piste, families

ESSENTIALS

Altitude: 2100m (6,888ft)–3456m (11,335ft)
Further information: **t** +33 (0)4 79 40 04 40, *www.tignes.net*
Lifts in area: 90 in Espace Killy (2 funiculars, 8 cableways, 45 chairs, 35 drags) serving 300km of piste
Lift pass: Espace Killy (Val and Tignes) adult €202.50, child 5–13yrs €162, both for six days
Access: Chambéry airport 2hrs, Grenoble airport 2hrs, Lyon airport 2½hrs, Geneva airport 3hrs, railway station at Bourg-St-Maurice 26km

Tignes

Profile

Part of the large well-linked Espace Killy ski area, shared with neighbouring Val d'Isère. Glacier skiing for most of the year and a reliable snow record. Convenient, but not suitable for those seeking traditional alpine village ambience

Resort

This is France's most snow-sure resort, extremely popular with the French and a cosmopolitan melting pot of other nationalities. It remains open for skiing for 10 months of the year and is a mandatory summer destination for national ski teams in training – and for all those who can't last from season to season without snow beneath their feet. The glacier used to be open 365 days a year, but the combination of damage from global warming and a falling interest in summer skiing has caused the resort to 'rest' from mid-May until mid-June and again from early September until October. During the summer months 13 lifts serve 20km of high-altitude pistes with a respectable vertical drop of 750m.

Tignes is divided into four main areas, with the main village also divided into quartiers. The resort lies at the head of the Haute Tarentaise, a 40-minute drive up the valley from Bourg-St-Maurice, and is connected by lifts and pistes to Val d'Isère. Together they form a 90-lift area with 300km of piste that is known as L'Espace Killy and has few equals for the diversity of its skiing and riding.

The main resort, built at 2100m, was a monument to the architectural horrors of the 1960s, a concrete jungle completely out of keeping with its beautiful setting beneath the twin peaks of La Grande Motte and La Grande Casse. However, huge investment in recent years has transformed Tignes into a much more aesthetically pleasing place. New buildings have been constructed in a sympathetic mountain style and the older beasts are either being reclad or torn down one by one for redevelopment.

Tignes itself divides into Le Lavachet with its high-rise apartment blocks, and the more agreeable and convenient Tignes-le-Lac on the edge of a small lake. Le Lac has undergone a complete makeover in recent years, and a tunnel acts as a bypass for through traffic to

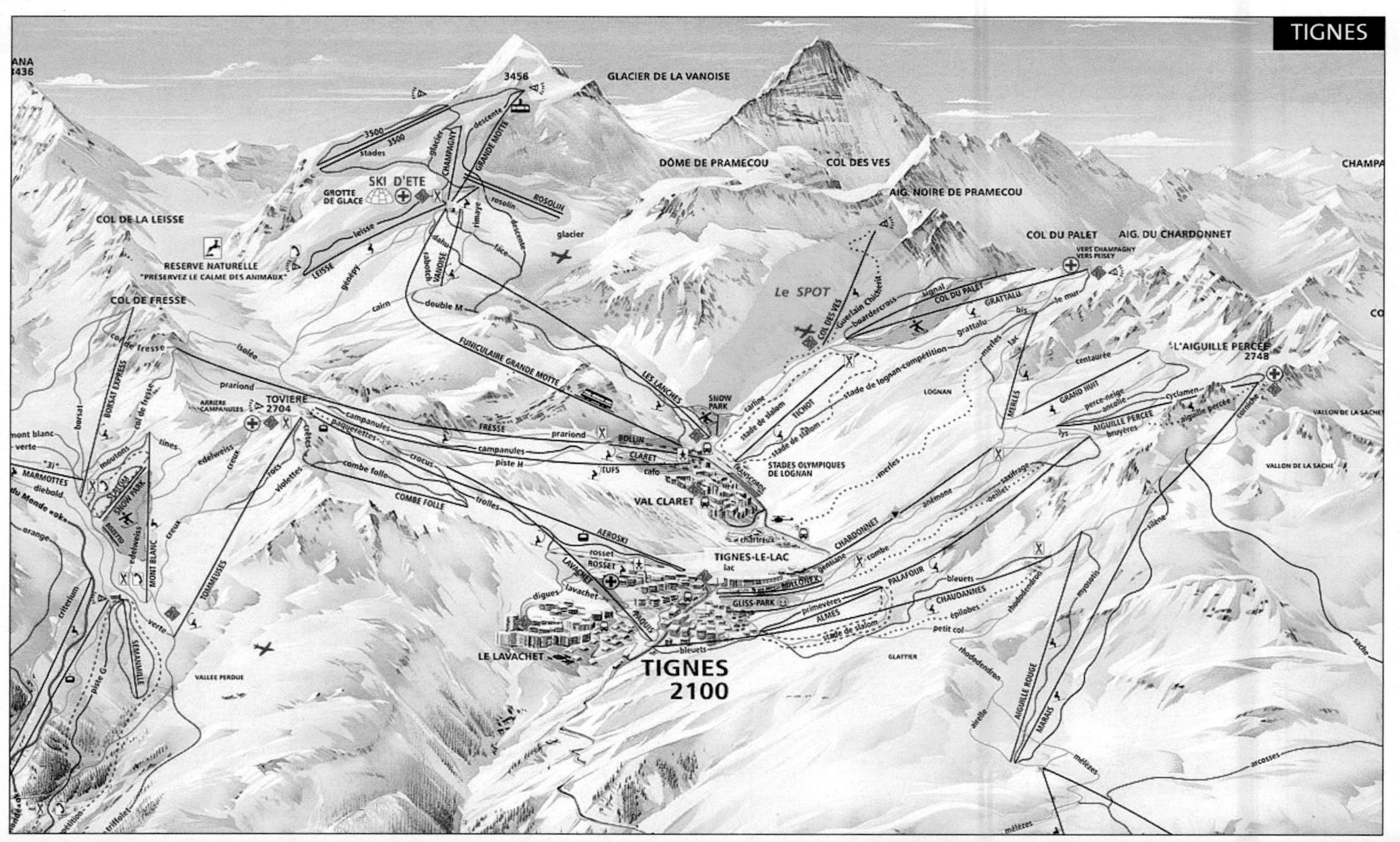
GLACIER DE LA VANOISE
3456
DÔME DE PRAMECOU
COL DES VES
AIG. NOIRE DE PRAMECOU
COL DU PALET
AIG. DU CHARDONNET
VERS CHAMPAGNY
VERS PEISEY
COL DE LA LEISSE
SKI D'ETE
GROTTE DE GLACE
RESERVE NATURELLE
"PRESERVEZ LE CALME DES ANIMAUX"
COL DE FRESSE
Le SPOT
L'AIGUILLE PERCEE
2748
TOVIERE
2704
ARRIERE CAMPANULES
SNOW PARK
STADES OLYMPIQUES DE LOGNAN
VAL CLARET
TIGNES-LE-LAC
LE LAVACHET
TIGNES
2100
VALLON DE LA SACHE
VALLEE PERDUE
GLATTIER
LOGNAN
FUNICULAIRE GRANDE MOTTE
LES LANCHES
GRANDE MOTTE
CHAMPAGNY
ROSOLIN
LEISSE
VANOISE
COL DU PALET
GRATTALU
COL DES VES
TICHOT
MERLES
GRAND HUIT
AIGUILLE PERCEE
CHARDONNET
PALAFOUR
CHAUDANNES
ALMES
MILLONEX
GLISS-PARK
AEROSKI
ROSSET
LAVACHET
PAQUIS
FRESSE
BOLLIN
CLARET
COMBE FOLLE
TOMMEUSES
BORSAT EXPRESS
MONT BLANC
SEMANMILLE
AIGUILLE ROUGE
MARAIS
MARMOTTES
TUFS
3500
stades
glacier
descente
rimaye
rosolin
face
dahu
rabotch
double M
cairn
génépy
leisse
glacier
Guerlain Chicherit
boardercross
signal
grattalu
bis
le mur
lac
merles
centaurée
perce-neige
ancolie
cyclamen
aiguille percée
corniche
bruyères
lys
stade de lognan-compétition
carline
stade de slalom
merles
anémone
taxifrage
oeillet
silène
sache
gentiane
combe
bleuets
rhododendron
myosotis
épilobes
petit col
primevères
stade de slalom
mélèzes
arcosses
airelle
charvet
cafo
piste H
campanules
pariond
paquerettes
crocus
combe folle
trolles
crêtes
rocs
violettes
creux
edelweiss
tines
isolée
col de fresse
borsat
moutons
mont blanc
verte
"31"
diebold
orange
criterium
piste G
verte
rosset
digues
lavachet
bleuets
lac

NOVEMBER SKI CLINICS IN TIGNES

Improve your skiing before the season even begins!

Snow guru Pat Zimmer and the Top Ski team invite you to join them this November on the Tignes glacier.

www.leski.com/november
Call 01484 548996
clinics@leski.com

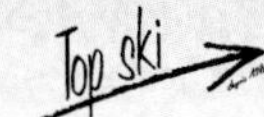

- Intensive tuition with video feedback
- Small groups for quality learning
- Smart accommodation with outdoor hot tub
- 3 or 7 day clinics – mini-breaks, weekends or weeks
- From £529 to £1219 including flight, transfer, breakfast, 3-course dinner, wine, ski passes and all tuition

---

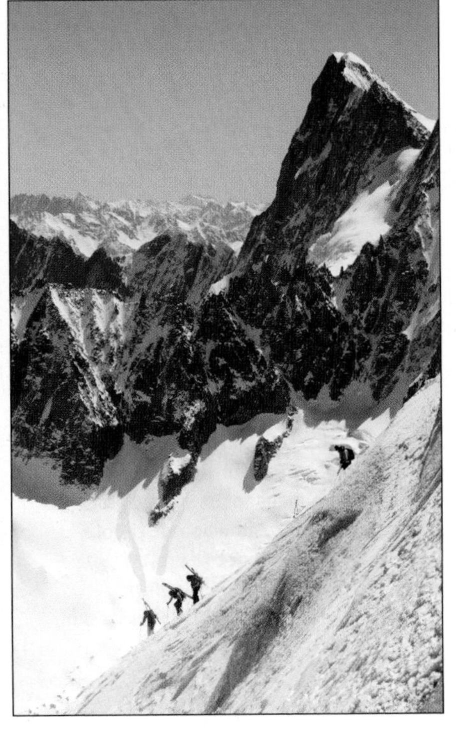

Major Resorts - Great Prices

Only 4 Star Ski Apartments

Resorts throughout the French Alps include Meribel, Val d'Isere, Tignes, Les Arcs, La Plagne, Courchevel, Val Thorens, Les Menuires, Chamonix, Alpe d'Huez, Flaine...

Accommodation only or self-drive package deals

www.skicollection.co.uk

0844 576 0175

ABTA W5537

the principal lift station still higher up at Val Claret.

This is the most convenient base for the skiing, with immediate access to the underground funicular and the link lift to Val d'Isère. The lower villages of Tignes-les-Boisses and the valley farming community of Tignes-les-Brévières provide a much more attractive, rural environment, with tree-lined pistes back to the resort and no high rise blocks. They are well linked into the lift system, and cannon-assisted snow-cover usually remains sufficient in late April. However, it is a long way up through the lift system to reach La Grande Motte and Val d'Isère. Significant plans are now taking shape for the redevelopment of Tignes-les-Boisses, including the rerouting of the road, real estate and replacement lifts.

'Downside of the area is the almost total domination of English. In many places you would be hard pushed to hear any French spoken,' complained a reader.

Mountain

The focal point is the 3656m Grande Motte, reached from Val Claret by an efficient but claustrophobic funicular or by a long two-stage quad-chair. The train takes six minutes to reach the Panoramic mountain restaurant; from there a cable car takes you to 3456m for the start of some spectacular glacial terrain. You need a local guide to explore the considerable powder opportunities such as the magnificent North Face leading through the *séracs*. Wide pistes for all standards lead back down to Val Claret. From mid-November until the lifts close in May this involves a vertical drop of 1400m. The terrain off to the sides appears benign but is dotted with crevasses and great care should be taken. A number of steep chutes, including the infamous Couloir Deux, can be reached from the funicular.

From Val Claret and the main village of Tignes, other lifts lead up to the Col du Palet, where you can ski off-piste with a guide all the way to Les Arcs and linked La Plagne. The route off the back of the col is prone to avalanche and should only be attempted with a guide. Lifts also bring you up to the 2748m Aiguille Percée, the unusual rock formation that appears on almost every postcard of Tignes. The black La Sache run, which leads from here all the way to Tignes-les-Brévières at 1500m, is wonderful when groomed but otherwise offers a long mogul run for bump enthusiasts.

The terrain park at Tignes-le-Lac has a beginner half-pipe as well as an expert one, a snowcross course and assorted obstacles. There is a summer terrain park on the glacier and Tignes has two dedicated freeride zones – each known as Le Spot (' a fantastic area for relatively safe off-piste without having to stray far off the beaten track. Every resort should have an area like this').

Learn

The **ESF Tignes le Lac**, **t** +33 (0)4 79 06 30 28, and **ESF Val Claret**, **t** + 33 (0)4 79 06 31 28, are both praised by reporters. **Ecole Henri Authier**, **t** +33 (0)4 79 06 36 38, is another alternative. **The Development Centre**, **t** + 33 (0)6 15 55 31 56, which started over the hill in Val, is a newcomer here this year ('tuition superb and I would highly recommend them to anyone wishing to improve their technique and confidence'). **Evolution 2**, **t** +33 (0)4 79 40 09 04, is a large school that receives mixed reviews. **Snow Fun**, **t** +33 (0)4 79 06 46 10, is commended for its small classes. **British Alpine Ski & Snowboard School**, **t** +33 (0)6 79 51 24 05, or **t** +44 (0)1485 572 596, specializes in teaching English-speaking pupils. **British School Progression**

Ski, **t** +44 (0)20 8123 3001, opens here this season.

ESI, **t** +33 (0)4 79 06 36 15, and **333**, **t** +33 (0)4 79 06 20 88, at **Val Claret**, are the ski and snowboard alternatives. **Snocool**, **t** +33 (0)4 79 40 08 58, **Surf Feeling**, **t** +33 (0)4 79 06 53 63, and **Kébra Surfing**, **t** +33 (0)4 79 06 43 37, are the dedicated schools. **Tetra Hors Piste**, **t** +33 (0)4 79 41 97 07, at Le Lac, specializes in off-piste. **Alliance Snowboarding**, **t** +33 (0)6 77 57 78 60 or in UK **t** 0844 484 9390, were rated 'professional, enthusiastic and spoke English'. **Bureau des Guides**, **t** +33 (0)4 79 06 42 76, offers guiding.

Children

Les Marmottons at Tignes-le-Lac, **t** +33 (0)4 79 06 51 67, and at Val Claret, **t** +33 (0)4 79 06 37 12, accept children from three and a half years. We have excellent reports of the **ESF**, **t** +33 (0)4 79 06 30 28, offers lessons from four years, and the **ESI**, **t** +33 (0)4 79 06 36 15, from five years. **Evolution 2**, **t** +33 (0)4 79 06 43 78, accepts children from three years and provides free helmets.

Lunch

Upstairs at L'Arbina, **t** +33 (0)4 79 06 34 78, in Le Lac, is a gastronomic experience with a good-value *formule* skier menu. Specialities include *rognons de veau* and *coquilles St-Jacques*; book in advance. **Le Panoramic**, **t** +33 (0)4 79 06 60 11, at the top of the Grande Motte funicular, has a good restaurant as well as a large self-service. **La Pignatta**, **t** +33 (0)4 79 06 32 97, in Val Claret, has good pizzas, pasta and a sunny terrace. Nearby **Le Dahu**, **t** +33 (0)4 79 06 50 98, offers a friendly welcome. In Tignes-les-Boisses the newly refurbished **Hôtel Le Marais**, **t** +33 (0)4 79 06 40 06, has a welcoming restaurant, conservatory and terrace with good-quality local dishes. **Auberge des Trois Oursons**, **t** +33 (0)4 79 06 35 66, in Val Claret, is recommended for 'very good atmosphere – the *pierre chaud* and raclette were both excellent'. Booking is advisable. Reporters' favourite next to the main slope in Tignes-les-Brévières is **La Bouida**, **t** +33 (0)4 79 06 48 36.

Dine

In Val Claret, **Le Caveau**, **t** +33 (0)4 79 06 52 32, has very good food and very reasonable prices. For Savoyard setting and food, try **Grattalu**, **t** +33 (0)4 79 06 30 78, and **Brasserie du Petit Savoyard**, **t** +33 (0)4 79 06 36 23. **Daffy's Café**, **t** +33 (0)4 79 06 38 75, is a popular Tex-Mex. **Le Ski d'Or**, **t** +33 (0)4 79 06 51 60, offers gourmet cuisine, and **Myako**, **t** +33 (0)4 79 06 34 79, is a sushi restaurant. **La Pizzeria 2000**, **t** +33 (0)4 79 06 38 49, has great pizzas, fondue and raclette.

In Le Lac, **Upstairs at L'Arbina**, **t** +33 (0)4 79 06 34 78, continues to be the best gourmet restaurant in the area.

Le Clin d'Œil, **t** +33 (0)4 79 06 59 10, is small and intimate. **Le Brasero**, **t** +33 (0)4 79 06 30 60, serves meat dishes.

Le Grenier, **t** +33 (0)4 79 06 37 79, is a typical Savoyard restaurant.

Party

In Val Claret, **Crowded House** lives up to its name. The **Fish Tank** is also popular. **Move Café** has live music. **Grizzly's Bar**, decorated with fur rugs and carved bears, has lots of character. **Melting Pot** and **Blue Girl** are the late-night venues.

In Le Lac, try **Loop Bar**, **L'Embuscade**, **Grotte du Yeti**, the **Red Lion** and **Alpaka**. **Angel Bar** is a popular internet café. **Red Z Winter** and **Jack's** are the nightclubs.

In Lavachet, **Harri's Bar** has become **Scotties** – run by Mark Warner. **TC's** is ever popular. Tignes-les-Brévières has three bars, including the **Underground**.

One reporter recommends horse-riding in the snow, organized by Evolution 2. 'We got a lot of envious looks from skiers as we galloped off into the distance.'

Sleep

Le Lac:

★★★★**Les Suites de Montana**, t +33 (0)4 79 40 01 44, are sumptuously decorated apartments ('perfect – lovely food, heated outdoor pool and best of all direct access on/off the slopes').

★★★**Hôtel Alpaka Lodge**, t +33 (0)4 79 06 45 30, *www.alpaka.com*, is comfortable. Its bar offers an unbelievable array of cocktails.

★★★**Les Campanules**, t +33 (0)4 79 06 34 36, *www.campanules.com*, is chalet-style and family-run ('warm, homely and extremely comfortable').

★★★**Hôtel Le Lévanna**, t +33 (0)4 79 06 32 94, *www.levanna.com*, is a welcoming family hotel.

★★**Hôtel L'Arbina**, t +33 (0)4 79 06 34 78, *www.arbina.net*, is well positioned and has a wonderful restaurant.

Val Claret:

★★★★**L'Ecrin des Neiges**, t +44 (0)870 750 6820, *www.ernalow.co.uk*, are comfortable apartments, with a mini spa complex and pool.

★★★★**Hôtel Le Ski d'Or**, t +33 (0)4 79 06 51 60, has a gastronomic restaurant, thalasso spa and gym.

★★**Hotel La Vanoise**, t +33 (0)4 79 06 31 90, *www.hotelvanoise.com*, has doorstep skiing and inviting rooms.

Val d'Isère

🏆 BEST SKI SCHOOL 2009 (OXYGÈNE)
🏆 BEST SKI SHOP 2009 (SNOWBERRY)

Profile

High-altitude resort, linked with Tignes. Excellent snow record and some of the best off-piste in Europe with a modern lift system and busy nightlife, but light on gourmet restaurants

Resort

Val d'Isère is the setting for the 2009 Alpine Skiing World Championships. It combines with neighbouring Tignes to form one of the principal winter playgrounds of Europe. More British skiers come here than to any other resort in the world, and they amount to 36 per cent of the population during the winter months. Fortunately the French also favour it, and provide counterbalance.

* BEST FOR

Complete beginners, strong intermediates and experts, off-piste, luxury chalets, snow reliability

ESSENTIALS

Altitude: 1850m (6,068ft)–3456m (11,335ft)
Further information: t +33 (0)4 79 06 06 60, *www.valdisere.com*
Lifts in area: 90 in Espace Killy (2 funiculars, 8 cableways, 45 chairs, 35 drags) serving 300km of piste
Lift pass: Espace Killy (Val and Tignes) adult €202.50, child 5–13yrs €162, both for six days
Access: Chambéry airport 2hrs, Lyon airport 2½hrs, Geneva airport 2½hrs, Grenoble airport 2½hrs, railway station at Bourg-St-Maurice 30km

Val is a cultural and social melting pot for dedicated skiers and riders from all over the world, who are drawn by the high, rugged mountains at the head of the beautiful Tarentaise Valley. The village, which stretches along the road from purpose-built La Daille to the farming outpost of Le Fornet, has smartened up its appearance in recent years and can now be described as attractive. Wide pavements have been created where there was previously none. Mature trees have been transplanted to line the main commercial area, and the worst of the concrete edifices of the 1960s have been reclad in soothing wood.

Focal point is Val Village, a cluster of 'old' buildings housing smart boutiques. This was created for the 1992 Winter Olympics around the 11th-century church and the handful of genuine old farmhouses dating back to when the settlement was a hunting lodge for the Ducs de Savoie.

Val has grown in all directions in recent years, and even the central area is now divided into different *quartiers*. Of the two satellites, La Daille has purpose-built ski convenience but little character.
By contrast, burgeoning Le Fornet is becoming an increasingly attractive place in which to base yourself, although it's a long walk home to both from the nightlife that is entirely confined to the centre.

The *Train Rouge*, the resort's free bus service, runs with startling efficiency every few minutes during the day from one end of the resort to the other. Buses between Val and Tignes are neither as frequent nor as cheap as you might expect. Parking is difficult, but having a car is useful for visiting Sainte-Foy or for trips to Paradiski and La Rosière.

Val's biggest plus point is its altitude and geographical situation, which create a snow-sure microclimate. You can ski here from early December until early May and book a holiday in the certainty that you will not find green fields on arrival. The piste-skiing is good, but to its ardent followers it is the easily accessible deep snow terrain that beckons. This is a high-mountain area that carries an ever-present risk of avalanche and should always be treated with the utmost respect. Fatal accidents – they happen each winter – are usually caused by inexperienced or ignorant skiers and riders ignoring warnings and venturing off-piste when it's not safe to do so on the principle that 'it can't happen to me'.
It can.

The ski area often takes a full day to fully reopen after a serious dump, and wise skiers head off for a day in the more sheltered and secure powder of Sainte-Foy. Conversely, the snowmaking facilities are world-class and even the Pissaillas Glacier has been fitted out, ensuring good snow in early season as well as for summer skiing in July.

Mountain

No fewer than eight entry points give access to the mountain, thus ensuring that even during high-season weeks, when French families are on holiday, queuing is never a serious problem.

The most convenient and quickest way into the system is to catch either the Funival underground funicular from La Daille or the 30-person jumbo gondola that also rises to the top of Bellevarde from near the pool at the foot of the nursery slopes.

From here a network of pistes and lifts fan out towards the Rocher du Charvet in one direction and towards Tignes in the other. The Tommeuse chair provides a efficient link to 2704m Tovière, starting point for a choice of runs down to Tignes.

Bellevarde is also the start of the OK downhill course (named after two of Val's Olympic champions, Henri Oreiller and

espace killy
le plus bel espace de ski du monde
DE LA GALISE 3343
Gde AIGUILLE ROUSSE 3482
Pte DU MONTET 3488
OUILLE NOIRE
MEAN MARTIN 3330
Pte DE LA SANA 3436
LA GRANDE MOTTE 3656
LA GRANDE CASSE 3852
GLACIER DE LA VANOISE
DÔME DE PRAMECOU
COL DES VES
AIG. NOIRE DE PRAMECOU
COL DU PALET
AIG. DU CHARDONNE
L'AIGUILL
GLACIER DES SOURCES DE L'ISERE
AIG. PERS
SIGNAL DE L'ISERAN 3241
GLACIER DE PISSAILLAS
REFUGE DU PRARIOND
SKI D'ETE
COL DE L'ISERAN 2762
ARCELLE
REF. DES FOURS
GORGES DE MALPASSET
RESERVE NATURELLE
PONT ST CHARLES
ROCHER DU CHARVET
COL DE LA LEISSE
RESERVE NATURELLE "PRESERVEZ LE CALME DES ANIMAUX"
COL DE FRESSE
SKI D'ETE
GROTTE DE GLACE
Le SPOT
LE MANCHET
SOLAISE 2560
ROCHER DE BELLEVARDE 2827
TOVIERE 2704
STADES OLYMPIQUES DE LOGNAN
VAL CLARET
TIGNES-LE-LAC
LE FORNET 1930
LE CHATELARD
FACE OLYMPIQUE DE BELLEVARDE
LE LAVACHET
TIGNES 2100
LE JOSERAY
VAL D'ISERE 1850
LE LAISINANT
LE DÔME 3026
LE CRÊT
LA DAILLE 1785
RECULAZ
LAC DU CHEVRIL
TIGNES LES BOISSES 1850
LE VILLARET DU NIAL
LE CHEVRIL
Val d'Isère
TIGNES
Pierre Novat
mod 83 © 04

Val d'Isère

COURCHEVEL AND LA TANIA

- 29 superbly placed chalets
- Genuine, friendly service
- Delicious food and wine
- Sunday flights to Chambéry

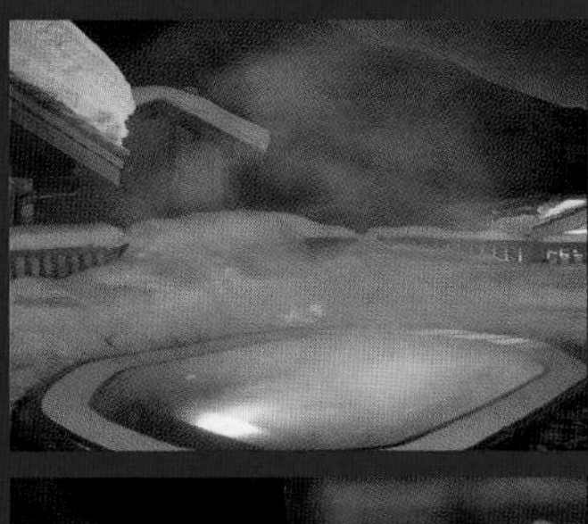

WWW.LESKI.COM

Brand new website with videos and online booking

For more information call 01484 548996

INDEPENDENT CHALET SPECIALISTS FOR 25 YEARS

www.leski.com

Jean-Claude Killy), which brings you over some moderately demanding but wonderfully enjoyable terrain all the way to the Funival station at La Daille.

From the other side of the nursery area in Val, a choice of cable car or a detachable chair takes you up Solaise and on towards Le Fornet. Solaise is the setting for a new and formidable women's downhill course for the 2009 Alpine Skiing World Championships. From the top of the Manchet chair, the long red Mattis run brings you down to the hamlet of Le Laisanant. A chairlift allows you to continue on to Le Fornet without having to take a bus. The high summer ski area at the top of Le Fornet has guaranteed snow-cover, thanks to the snowmaking infrastructure.

Dramatic improvements to the lifts at this end of Espace Killy means that you can now ski from Le Fornet to the far corners of Tignes in a single morning. It is important to note that the official piste grading in Val is markedly stiffer than you will find elsewhere. For blue, read red. Intermediates should treat runs that are marked black with considerable caution until they know what is involved.

The nursery slopes in the middle of the village are both good and free, but their position, just off the main descent from Solaise, means that fast-moving traffic often needs to be negotiated when going to and from the novice lift.

Val's *tour de force* lies in its potential for serious off-piste. Try the Face du Charvet, a steep powder classic accessed from the Grand Pré chair. Danaïdes, reached from the Solaise Express chair, brings you steeply down through the forest above the town.

No good skier or rider should miss a day trip to Bonneval-sur-Arc, an attractive little village in the neighbouring Haute Maurienne. The itinerary starts with a 20-minute hike from the top of Le Fornet, followed by a choice of sweeping powder descents over the far side of the ridge. The return journey is best accomplished by a pre-arranged four-minute helicopter ride for €90 per person. The alternative is a five-hour taxi journey.

Espace Killy is popular with freeriders who will find lots of natural gullies and cliffs. La Daille terrain park has a half-pipe and a host of obstacles, as well as two snowcross courses. Riders and twin-tippers also congregate on the Grande Motte above Tignes. The Marmottes chair on Bellevarde becomes a six-seater from December 2008.

Learn

Val has a dozen ski schools as well as 20 independent individual private instructors. Choosing the right one for your requirements is no easy task.

The **ESF**, **t** +33 (0)4 79 06 02 34, has a strong presence and offers cutting-edge tuition. It now employs an increasing number of native English-speaking instructors and is rated 'brilliant' by one reporter. We strongly recommend **Oxygène**, **t** +33 (0)4 79 41 99 58, for its skilled and sympathetic tuition, and **Top Ski**, **t** +33 (0)4 79 06 14 80, a cult school run by ex-French racer Pat Zimmer, which specializes in teaching and guiding off-piste as well as giving regular lessons and telemark instruction.

The Development Centre, **t** + 33 (0)6 15 55 31 56, run by British instructors, is singled out for its superb tuition 'highly rated', and 'brilliant' were two of the comments, along with 'Colin Tanner transformed our attitude towards skiing blacks and bumps'. British-run **Progression Ski**, **t** +33 (0)621 93 93 80, receives good reports ('we made brilliant progress in the space of one lesson, wonderful with kids of all ages, excellent value for money'). **Mountain Masters**, **t** +33 (0)4 79 06 05 14,

SKI SCHOOL
Oxygène
SKI SHOP

Skiing in Val d'Isere

ALPES-FRANCE

Galerie des Cimes - BP 110 - 73700 Val d'Isere
Tel. +33 479419958 - Fax +33 479419381

valdisere@oxygene-ski.com

création Contours 05 34 60 50 68

and **Alpine Experience**, **t** +33 (0)4 79 06 28 81, also have enormous experience in teaching and guiding off-piste.

The other schools include **Snow Fun**, **t** +33 (0)4 79 06 22 24, **Ski Concept**, **t** +33 (0)4 79 40 19 19, **Ogier**, **t** +33 (0)4 50 479 06 18 93, **Misty Fly**, **t** +33 (0)4 79 40 08 74, **Tetra Hors Piste**, **t** +33 (0)4 79 41 97 07, and **Val Glisse**, **t** +33 (0)4 79 06 00 72. Guiding can be arranged through the **Bureau des Guides**, **t** +33 (0)4 79 06 94 03, and ski schools.

Children

For tuition, we recommend **Oxygène**, **t** +33 (0)4 79 41 99 58, and **Evolution 2**, **t** +33 (0)4 79 41 16 72. **Le Village des Enfants**, **t** +33 (0)4 79 40 09 81, cares for children from three to eight years with a mix of play and ski lessons. **Le Petit Poucet**, **t** +33 (0)4 79 06 13 97, collects and delivers children from three years from wherever they are staying. The main ski schools all run courses for children.

Lunch

Le Signal, **t** +33 (0)4 79 06 03 38, at the top of the Le Fornet cable car, has excellent food and good service, all upstairs. Downstairs there is a competent self-service. **L'Edelweiss**, **t** +33 (0)6 10 28 70 64, on the blue Mangard piste above Le Fornet, is a mountain hut with a log fire and good meat and fish. **La Fruitière**, **t** +33 (0)4 79 06 07 17, situated on the OK run, is rather overpriced but has excellent spaghetti bolognese and lamb dishes. The name means 'dairy' and the building is suitably decorated with milk churns. **Le Trifollet**, **t** +33 (0)4 79 41 96 99, and **Les Tufs**, **t** +33 (0)4 79 06 25 01, are friendly pizza-and-steak alternatives. 'I especially single out Les Tufs for its mind-blowing buffet,' said a reporter. **Bananas**, **t** +33 (0)4 79 06 04 23, at the foot of Bellevarde, has good burgers and Tex-Mex, but better bacon and eggs. The best gourmet lunch in the region is at **L'Arbina**, **t** +33 (0)4 79 06 34 78, in Tignes-le-Lac. Specialities include *rognons de veau* and *coquilles St-Jacques*.

Dine

La Table de Neige, **t** +33 (0)4 79 06 12 13, in the Tsanteleina hotel is recommended. **La Grande Ourse**, **t** + 33 (0)4 79 06 00 19, by the nursery slopes, heads the list. **Le Blizzard**, **t** +33 (0)4 79 06 02 07, in the hotel of the same name, has reasonable food in a good atmosphere. For traditional Savoyarde cuisine try **l'Etable d'Alain**, **t** +33 (0)4 79 06 13 02, **La Luge**, **t** +33 (0)4 79 06 69 39, **l'Arolay**, **t** +33 (0)4 79 06 11 68, or **La Vielle Maison**, **t** +33 (0)4 79 06 11 76. **Le 1789**, **t** +33 (0)4 79 06 17 89, offers a warm welcome. **Taverne d'Alsace**, **t** +33 (0)4 79 06 48 49, provides traditional French cuisine at reasonable prices. **L'Atelier d'Edmond**, **t** +33 (0)4 79 00 00 82, in Le Fornet, has a good fixed-price menu.

Party

Dick's Tea Bar remains one of the most celebrated discos in the Alps. A new contender for Val's hottest après scene opens this winter – the **Doudoune Club**, set at the foot of the slopes is a bar, restaurant and nightclub rolled into one. Other alternatives are **Le Graal** nightclub, **Café Face**, **Le Petit Danois** and the **Pacific Bar**. There's also **Le Pub** and the **Saloon Bar** beneath the **Hotel Brussel's**. British teens gather downstairs at **Bananas**. However 'Val is extortionate for drinks – £5 for a pint of lager at Moris Bar,' complained a reader.

NOVEMBER SKI CLINICS IN TIGNES

Improve your skiing before the season even begins!

Snow guru Pat Zimmer and the Top Ski team invite you to join them this November on the Tignes glacier.

www.leski.com/november
Call 01484 548996
clinics@leski.com

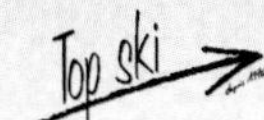

- Intensive tuition with video feedback
- Small groups for quality learning
- Smart accommodation with outdoor hot tub
- 3 or 7 day clinics – mini-breaks, weekends or weeks
- From £529 to £1219 including flight, transfer, breakfast, 3-course dinner, wine, ski passes and all tuition

Personalised skiing holidays in Val d'Isere from the resort specialists.

Insider knowledge of Val d'Isere. Centrally located apartments, chalets and hotels.

Flexible dates available.

+44 (0) 1481 236 800
info@skivaldisere.co.uk

www.skivaldisere.co.uk

Val d'Isère, Méribel & Zermatt

Traditional chalets with a contemporary twist...

Hot tubs, saunas, masseurs, wifi & private cinemas. BA & bmi flights on Sunday morning, ski hosting, fine cuisine & imaginative wine list. Childcare & exemplary VIP service.

08701 123 119
www.vip-chalets.com

ATOL 3356 AITO

VIP

Sleep

Val d'Isère is primarily a chalet resort but has a few decent hotels.

★★★★*deluxe* **Hôtel Les Barmes de l'Ours**, **t** +33 (0)4 79 41 37 00, *www.hotel-les-barmes.com*, is stylish and comfortable, but overpriced.

★★★★*deluxe* **Eagle's Nest** and **Big Yeti**, **t** +44 (0)20 8682 5050, *www.scottdunn.com*, are extraordinarily smart chalets in the Les Carats quartier.

★★★★**Hotel Le Blizzard, t** +33 (0)4 79 06 02 07, *www.hotelblizzard.com*, has a fine bar area and restaurant, but the bedrooms are disappointing.

★★★★**Hotel Christiania, t** +33 (0)4 79 06 08 25, *www.hotel-christiania.com*, has plenty of atmosphere.

★★★★**Hotel l'Aigle des Neiges**, **t** +33 (0)4 79 06 18 88, *www.latitudes-hotels.com*, was formerly Les Latitudes in the heart of the old village. It has been refurbished in contemporary style.

★★★★**Aspen Lodge**, **t** +44 (0)20 8875 1957, *www.vip-chalets.com*, is an extremely comfortable catered apartment block on the main street.

★★★★**Le Savoie**, **t** +33 (0)4 79 00 01 15, *www.lesavoie.com*, is a smart new luxury hotel that opened last season.

★★★**Hotel La Savoyarde**, **t** +33 (0)4 79 06 01 55, *www.la-savoyarde.com*, has a strong following and is conveniently located. 'Great food,' said a reporter.

★★★**Hotel Le Tsanteleina**, **t** +33 (0)4 79 06 12 13, *www.tsanteleina.com*, enjoys a strong British following and is thoroughly recommended.

A number of sumptuous private homes as well as more basic apartments are also available to let by the week through British-owned **Mountain Rooms and Chalets**, **t** +33 (0)4 79 41 17 43, *www.mrooms.com*

Val d'Isère Agence, t +33 (0)4 79 06 73 50, *www.valdisere-agence.com*, also lets accommodation.

Val Thorens

Profile

The highest ski village in Western Europe, with guaranteed snow-cover from November until May; part of the giant Trois Vallées area

Resort

This high *station de ski* in the Trois Vallées has grown in a generation from a bland and soulless lift-station-with-apartments into a rather charming village at the end of the 37km road up from Moûtiers. It sits surrounded by a horseshoe of peaks at the end of the Belleville Valley, with links across the 2850m Mont de la Chambre towards Méribel and Courchevel beyond. However, there is sufficient skiing for all levels to deter most one-week visitors from venturing far from home.

* BEST FOR

All standards of skier and rider, big ski area, off-piste

ESSENTIALS

Altitude: 2300m (7,544ft)–3300m (10,827ft)
Further information: **t** +33 (0)4 79 00 08 08, *www.valthorens.com*
Lifts in area: 165 in Trois Vallées (43 cableways, 68 chairs, 54 drags) serving 600km of piste
Lift pass: Trois Vallées adult €157–295, child 5–13yrs €112–225, both for six days
Access: Chambéry airport 2hrs, Lyon airport 2½hrs, Geneva airport 3hrs, Eurostar at Moûtiers 37km

These days, the Trois Vallées is a misnomer, because the lift system stretches over the 3200m Cime de Caron all the way down to Orelle in the Maurienne Valley. The 3 Vallées Express gondola from here provides a convenient back door into the system. Italians can reach Orelle via the Fréjus Tunnel in two hours from Turin or in less than an hour from Sestriere and the resorts of the Milky Way.

New hotels and *résidences* have been designed more in keeping with their mountain environment than the original buildings. Val Thorens is a strictly pedestrian resort – you are allowed in to unload but must then park in one of the car parks on the edge of town.

On a sunny day after a fresh snowfall, few places are more inviting than Val Thorens. But when the weather closes in you quickly realize why the locals never chose to build a farming community at this altitude. In flat light the tree-less pistes lack any point of reference. 'If you go in January, be prepared for seriously cold weather; we had -25C as a midday temperature in January,' warned a reporter.

Mountain

A chairlift and the swift Bouquetin gondola provide the link to the Col de Chambre and the long run down to Méribel-Mottaret. Pistes lead from the village to the Péclet Funitel gondola, which takes you up to the glacier and to a network of fast chairs and gondolas that crisscross the mountainside below the ridge separating the Belleville and Maurienne valleys.

A gondola and a cable car, reached by a blue piste below the resort, rise to the 3200m Cime de Caron. This is the starting point for the Combe de Caron, one of the most testing black runs in the area. Wonderful long continuations lead down through 1400m vertical to Les Menuires. For other even longer off-piste runs, like the scenic Itinéraire du Lou, you need the services of a local guide. Both the four-person Cairn and Caron gondolas have doubled capacity to eight persons this season.

From the far side of the Cime de Caron, two chairlifts take you up to the 2300m Sommet des Pistes, which accesses two high-altitude runs down the Glacier de la Pointe Renod and a snowcross course. Val Thorens' main snow park is on the 2 Lacs piste just above the resort. It has a 110m half-pipe and an assortment of rails and other obstacles. Val Thorens has France's only toboggan course with a 700m vertical drop, reached by the Péclet gondola.

Learn

There is the usual **ESF**, **t** +33 (0)4 79 00 02 86, but reporters favour **Ski Cool**, **t** +33 (0)4 79 00 04 92 ('absolutely fantastic'), **Free School Attitude**, **t** +33 (0)4 79 01 42 05, and **Ecole de ski Prosneige**, **t** +33 (0)4 79 01 07 00. A number of other little schools offer specialist courses and guiding.

Children

The **ESF**, **t** +33 (0)4 79 00 02 86, at Village Le Montana and Le Village Roc, cares for children from three months, with lessons from three years. As well as children's tuition, **Prosneige**, **t** +33 (0)4 79 01 07 00, also offers teen classes. **New Generation Sports Centre** has a children's fun park with trampoline, bouncy castles and ball pools.

VAL THORENS

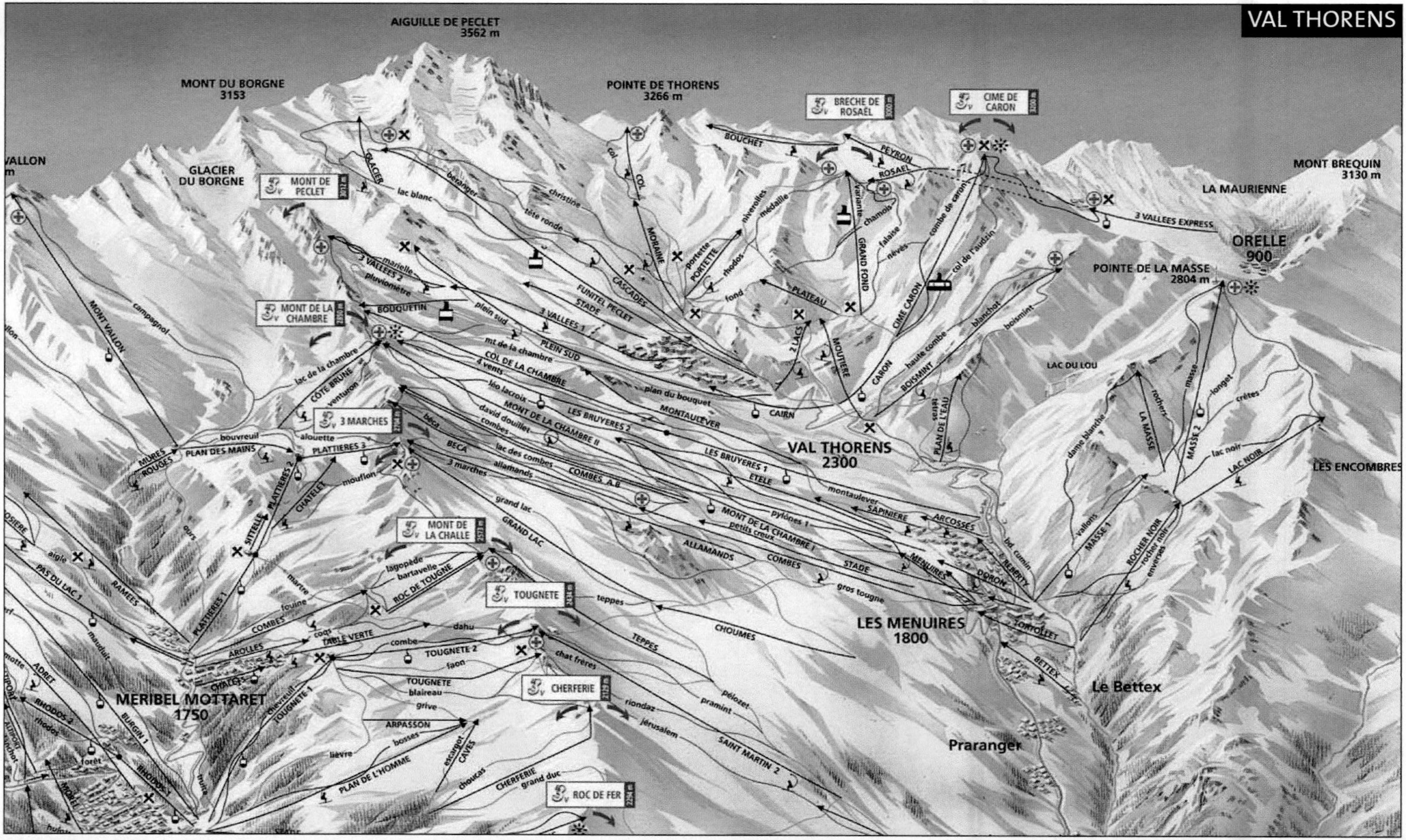

AIGUILLE DE PECLET
3562 m

MONT DU BORGNE
3153

POINTE DE THORENS
3266 m

BRECHE DE ROSAËL 3000 m

CIME DE CARON 3200 m

MONT BREQUIN
3130 m

LA MAURIENNE

GLACIER DU BORGNE

MONT DE PECLET 3012 m

MONT DE LA CHAMBRE 2850 m

3 MARCHES 2704 m

MONT DE LA CHALLE 2573 m

TOUGNETE 2434 m

CHERFERIE 2116 m

ROC DE FER 2294 m

ORELLE
900

POINTE DE LA MASSE
2804 m

LAC DU LOU

VAL THORENS
2300

LES MENUIRES
1800

LES ENCOMBRES

Le Bettex

Praranger

MERIBEL MOTTARET
1750

VALLON

GLACIER · lac blanc · beranger · christine · tête ronde · COL · col · MORAINE · CASCADES · FUNITEL PECLET · STADE · portette · PORTETTE · rhodos · niverolles · médaille · BOUCHET · PEYRON · ROSAËL · variante · chamois · GRAND FOND · falaise · névés · combe de caron · col de l'audzin · CIME CARON · 3 VALLEES EXPRESS · 3 VALLEES 2 · marielle · pluviomètre · BOUQUETIN · plein sud · 3 VALLEES 1 · PLEIN SUD · mt de la chambre · COL DE LA CHAMBRE · 4 vents · fond · PLATEAU · 2 LACS · MOUTIERE · CARON · haute combe · blanchot · boismint · BOISMINT · PLAN DE L'EAU · tétras · masse · longet · crêtes · rochers · LA MASSE · MASSE 2 · dame blanche · lac noir · LAC NOIR · MONT VALLON · campagnol · lac de la chambre · CÔTE BRUNE · venturon · léo lacroix · MONT DE LA CHAMBRE II · david douillet · combes · LES BRUYERES 2 · plan du bouquet · MONTAULEVER · CAIRN · bouvreuil · alouette · PLAN DES MAINS · MURES ROUGES · PLATTIERES 3 · PLATTIERES 2 · béca · BECA · lac des combes · allamands · COMBES A.B · 3 marches · LES BRUYERES 1 · ETELE · montaulever · SAPINIERE · ARCOSSES · mouflon · CHATELET · SITELLE · grand lac · GRAND LAC · pylônes 1 · MONT DE LA CHAMBRE I · petits creux · ALLAMANDS · COMBES · STADE · MENUIRES · DORON · bd. cumin · REBERTY · vallons · MASSE 1 · ROCHER NOIR · rocher noir · enverses · ours · aigle · PAS DU LAC 1 · RAMEES · ROSIERE · PLATTIERES 1 · martre · fouine · lagopède · bartavelle · ROC DE TOUGNE · COMBES · coqs · TABLE VERTE · dahu · combe · teppes · TEPPES · CHOUMES · gros tougne · TORTOLLET · BETTEX · AROLLES · CHALETS · TOUGNETE 2 · faon · chat frères · TOUGNETE · blaireau · grive · ARPASSON · bosses · escargot · CAVES · lièvre · PLAN DE L'HOMME · choucas · CHERFERIE · grand duc · riondaz · jérusalem · pélozet · pramint · SAINT MARTIN 2 · chevreuil · TOUGNETE 1 · truite · ADRET · motte · RHODOS 2 · rhodos · BURGIN 1 · mauduit · forêt · RHODOS 1 · MOREL

Lunch

'Main complaint is the cost,' said a reporter, 'we were spending between £20 and £30 a day on a basic lunch of one course and a soft drink.' Another added 'The prices are not just high, but astronomical – two cokes and two coffees were 26 euros, a plate of chips 7 euros.' However, **Chalet des Deux Lacs**, **t** +33 (0)4 79 00 28 54, was said to be 'a fantastic mountain retreat with open fire and a very reasonably priced menu'. Try **La Chaumière**, **t** +33 (0)4 79 00 01 13, **Chalet Les 2 Ours**, **t** +33 (0)4 79 01 14 09, and **Chalet Caribou**, **t** +33 (0)6 11 18 06 71. **L'Oxalys**, **t** +33 (0)4 79 00 12 00, offers the kind of full-blown gastro lunch that precludes afternoon skiing. In fine weather, its terrace is a delightful place for lunch. **Etape 3200**, **t** +33 (0)6 07 31 04 14, at the top of the Cime de Caron, has great views.

Dine

Celebrity chef Jean Sulspice's **L'Oxalys**, **t** +33 (0)4 79 00 12 00, and **La Table du Roy**, **t** +33 (0)4 79 00 04 78, in the Hôtel Le Fitz Roy, are the most gastronomic establishments in town – during high season you need to book in advance. **Auberge du Sherpa**, **t** +33 (0)4 79 00 00 70, in Hôtel du Sherpa and **Le Bellevillois**, **t** + 33 (0)4 79 00 04 33, in Hotel Le Val Thorens are both recommended. **La Cabane**, **t** +33 (0)4 79 00 83 84, is an old-style chalet with a warm atmosphere. **La Grange de Pierrette**, **t** +33 (0)4 79 00 00 88, is also praised along with **Le Panoramic**, **t** +33 (0)4 79 00 04 77, in Hôtel Le Bel Horizon. **Le Blanchot**, **t** +33 (0)4 79 00 05 91, is a small wine bar. **Le John's**, **t** +33 (0)4 79 00 05 15, is an American diner with the best spare ribs in the Alps.

Party

'In one bar we paid £8.15 for a pint of Guinness and the local brew is about a fiver a pint, although happy hours can be found for half that price,' said a reporter. Popular bars include **Le Tango**, **Ski Rock Café**, the **Viking Pub** and the **Frog and Roast Beef**, and the **Rhum Box Café**. **Le Malaysia** and the **Underground** are the late-night venues. 'The après ski was pretty much non-existent during our week – we couldn't find any live music at all,' said a reader. **New Generation** sports centre, **t** +33 (0)4 79 00 00 76, offers over 20 sports including tennis and swimming. A new leisure centre offers bowling, pool halls, an internet café and bar.

Sleep

★★★★*deluxe* **Résidence L'Oxalys**, **t** +33 (0)4 79 00 12 29, *www.loxalys.com*, is a chalet complex with 25 apartments and the famous Michelin-starred restaurant.

★★★★**Le Fitz Roy**, **t** +33 (0)4 79 00 04 78, *www.hotelfitzroy.com*, is a chalet-style hotel with pool and fitness centre.

★★★**Le Val Thorens**, **t** +33 (0)4 79 00 04 33, *www.levalthorens.com*, has three restaurants and a lounge with fireplace.

★★★**Le Sherpa**, **t** +33 (0)4 79 00 00 70, *www.lesherpa.com*, is good value for money and offers good food.

★★★**Le Portillo**, **t** +33 (0)4 79 00 00 88, *www.leportillo.com*, has a gourmet restaurant.

★★★**Le Bel Horizon**, **t** +33 (0)4 79 00 06 08, *www.belhorizon.com*, is good for families.

★★**Le Val Chavière**, **t** +33 (0)4 79 00 00 33, *www.hotel-valthorens.com*, is reasonably priced ('comfortable with superb piste access').

Vaujany

Profile

Rural farming village with direct links into extensive Alpe d'Huez ski area

Resort

In the late 1980s, Vaujany became unexpectedly wealthy through land sold for France's largest hydro-electric scheme. The villagers swapped tractors for piste-bashers, and converted cowsheds to chalets after Vaujany became a ski resort by building a giant cable car linking into the giant Alpe d'Huez ski area.

An escalator connects the lift area with accommodation at the top of this steep village. So far during its 20-year history as a ski resort Vaujany has managed to entirely retain its rural charm, but a considerable amount of new building has been agreed over the next few years and this may well change the character of this delightful village. 'I am loathe to tell you about this hidden jewel. This place is perfect,' was one glowing comment, and 'What a fantastic little resort with a huge ski area,' was another.

* BEST FOR

All standards, off-piste enthusiasts, families, big ski area, value

ESSENTIALS

Altitude: 1250m (4,101ft)–3330m (10,922ft)
Further information: t +33 (0)4 76 80 72 37, *www.vaujany.com*
Lifts in area: 81 (16 cableways, 25 chairs, 40 drags) serving 237km of piste
Lift pass: area (covers linked resorts, 2 days in Les Deux Alpes, 1 day in La Grave, the Milky Way, Puy-St-Vincent and Serre Chevalier) adult €203, child 5–15yrs €145, both for six days
Access: Grenoble airport 1½hrs, Lyon airport 2hrs

Mountain

Vaujany's hayricks-to-riches story explains the presence of a 160-person cable car in this picturesque but no longer sleepy village. The second stage goes up to Dôme des Petites Rousses at 2800m giving direct access to Alpe d'Huez and lifts going up to the 3330m Pic Blanc. A gondola also connects the village to Montfrais, Vaujany's own ski area with good nursery slopes, intermediate runs, and some delightful off-piste.

Learn

The **ESF**, **t** +33 (0)4 76 80 71 80, receives mixed reports: 'Very small classes and English-speaking instructors,' on one hand and 'Average of 15 children to a group; English reluctantly spoken and sporadically'. **Le Massif**, **t** +33 (0)6 07 97 38 11, **Christelle Morin**, **t** +33 (0)6 83 14 05 74, and **V.O. Coaching**, **t** +33 (0)6 60 27 60 32, also provide lessons.

Children

La Garderie, **t** +33 (0)4 76 80 77 53, offers daycare for children aged six months to five years, and British tour operator Ski Peak provides a native English-speaking nanny. 'The *garderie* was superb, very professional and welcoming.' The snow garden has been extended, with a new magic carpet lift. The **ESF**, **t** +33 (0)4 76 80 71 80, runs all English-speaking classes during school holidays.

Lunch

Les Airelles, **t** +33 (0)4 76 80 79 78, at the top of the Montfrais nursery slope, is a family favourite. **Auberge de L'Alpette**, **t** +33 (0)4 76 80 70 00, has wonderful omelettes and salads.

Ski Peak

Quality accommodation with catered chalets including the award winning Saskia, the Hotel Rissiou and the prestigious 5 star Oisans apartments. Outstanding cuisine and a personal service, good childcare and excellent travel arrangements into Grenoble airport.

T: 01428 608070
F: 01428 608071
W: www.skipeak.com

AITO
THE ASSOCIATION OF INDEPENDENT TOUR OPERATORS

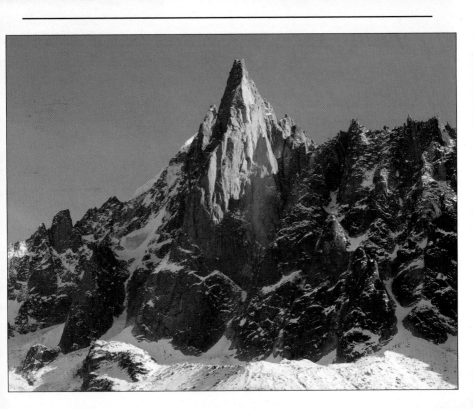

VAUJANY

MASSIF DU MONT BLANC
L'ETENDARD 3470
PIC BAYLE
PIC DE LA PYRAMIDE
PIC BLANC 3330
AIGUILLES D'ARVES
GLACIER DE SARENNE
GLACIER DE BARBARATE
GLACIER DES ROUSSES
CLOCHER DE MACLE 2800
DÔME DES PETITES ROUSSES 2800
COL DU COUARD
2700
LAC BLANC
GROTTE DE GLACE
PLAT DES MARMOTTES 2300
MINE DE L'HERPIE
GORGES DE SARENNE
L'ALPETTE 2050
MONTFRAIS 1650
SIGNAL DE L'HOMME 2176
2100
SIGNAL 2115
LA VILLETTE
OZ EN OISANS STATION 1350
ALPE D'HUEZ 1860
Connexion Auris
AURIS EN OISANS 1600
VAUJANY 1250
LE BESSEY
L'ENVERSIN D'OZ
VILLARD RECULAS 1480
HUEZ 1500
LE ROSAY
LA GARDE
LE CHATELARD
MARONNE
OZ EN OISANS VILLAGE
SARDONNE
LAC DU VERNEY
ALLEMONT
BOURG D'OISANS GRENOBLE AURIS VILLAGES
BOURG D'OISANS GRENOBLE
Frédérique et Pierre Novat
mod.200

Dine

Hôtel Rissiou, t +33 (0)4 76 80 71 00, has fine food and wine. **La Remise, t** + 33 (0)4 76 80 77 11, has great pizzas and fondues. **Table de la Fare, t** +33 (0)4 76 11 03 95, is by the lift station and offers very good cuisine.

Party

The **Swallow Bar** is the mandatory resort meeting place for teenagers and early-20s, as is **l'Etendard bar**. **Arsen's Internet Café** is also popular. The skating rink and a giant pool with flumes provide the après ski entertainment.

Sleep

Accommodation is in apartments and a couple of hotels, and in comfortable chalets in Vaujany and in the neighbouring hamlet of La Villette.

★★★★**Chalet Saskia, t** +44 (0)1428 608 070, *www.skipeak.com*, is a charming stand-alone chalet at the lower end of the village, with exquisite food.

★★★**Résidence La Perle L'Oisans, t** +44 (0)1428 608 070, *www.skipeak.com*, at the higher level of the village, has spacious and convenient apartments.

★★**Hôtel du Rissiou, t** +33 (0)4 76 80 71 00, *www.skipeak.com*, offers the best hotel accommodation in the village.

★★**Les Cimes, t** +33 (0)4 76 79 86 50, has small but pleasant rooms.

06

The Top Resorts: Italy

Arabba

***BEST FOR**

Challenging skiing, small village atmosphere

ESSENTIALS

Altitude: 1446m (4,743ft)–3269m (10,722ft)
Further information: **t** +39 0436 79130, *www.infodolomiti.it*
Lifts in area: 28 (7 cableways, 16 chairs, 5 drags) serving 54km of piste in Arabba-Marmolada area. 450 lifts serving 1220km of piste in Dolomiti Superski
Lift pass: Dolomiti Superski adult €184–209, child 8–16yrs €129–147, both for six days
Access: Verona airport 3hrs, Venice airport 2hrs, railway stations at Belluno 75km, Brunico 45km

Profile

Best base for the steepest pistes in the otherwise intermediate Sella Ronda ski area. Small village with limited nightlife, unsuitable for non-skiers

Resort

Arabba guards the gateway to the 3342m Marmolada and is the best place in the Sella Ronda for committed skiers and riders.

Mountain

The village's reputation as a base for serious skiers is built on the steep north-facing slopes of 2478m Porta Vescovo. Two cableways serve a choice of challenging black runs, as well as much gentler alternatives leading back to the resort. The Marmolada tour takes you down to the town of Malga Ciapela. A three-stage cable car rises to Punta Rocca at 3269m for a glorious 12km descent all the way back to Malga Ciapela.

Learn

The choice lies between **Arabba Ski School, t** +39 0436 79160, and **Rocca-Marmolada, t** +39 0437 722 060.

Children

Snow White Village, t +39 0437 722 277, run by the Arabba Ski School, accepts kids from two years of age on weekdays.

Lunch

Rifugio Capanna Bill, t +39 0437 722 100, near Malga Ciapela, offers homemade pasta and grilled meat. **Miky's Grill, t** +39 0436 79119, in the Hotel Mesdi, offers simple lunchtime fare. **Rifugio Plan Boé, t** +39 0436 79339, on the anti-clockwise route, has a suitably rustic atmosphere. **Bec de Roces, t** +39 0436 79193, has a self-service area and an upstairs pizzeria.

Dine

Pizzeria 7 Sass, t +39 0436 780 135, is recommended. **Al Tablé, t** +39 0436 79302, specializes in local game. **Al Forte, t** +39 0436 79329, is housed in a late 19th-century Austro–Hungarian fort and has live music on Thursdays. **Ru de Mont, t** +39 0436 780 020, in the satellite village of Renaz, has good pizzas.

Party

Nightlife is muted. **Peter's Bar**, the Sporthotel's **Bacchus Cellar Bar**, and **La Treina** are the main bars.

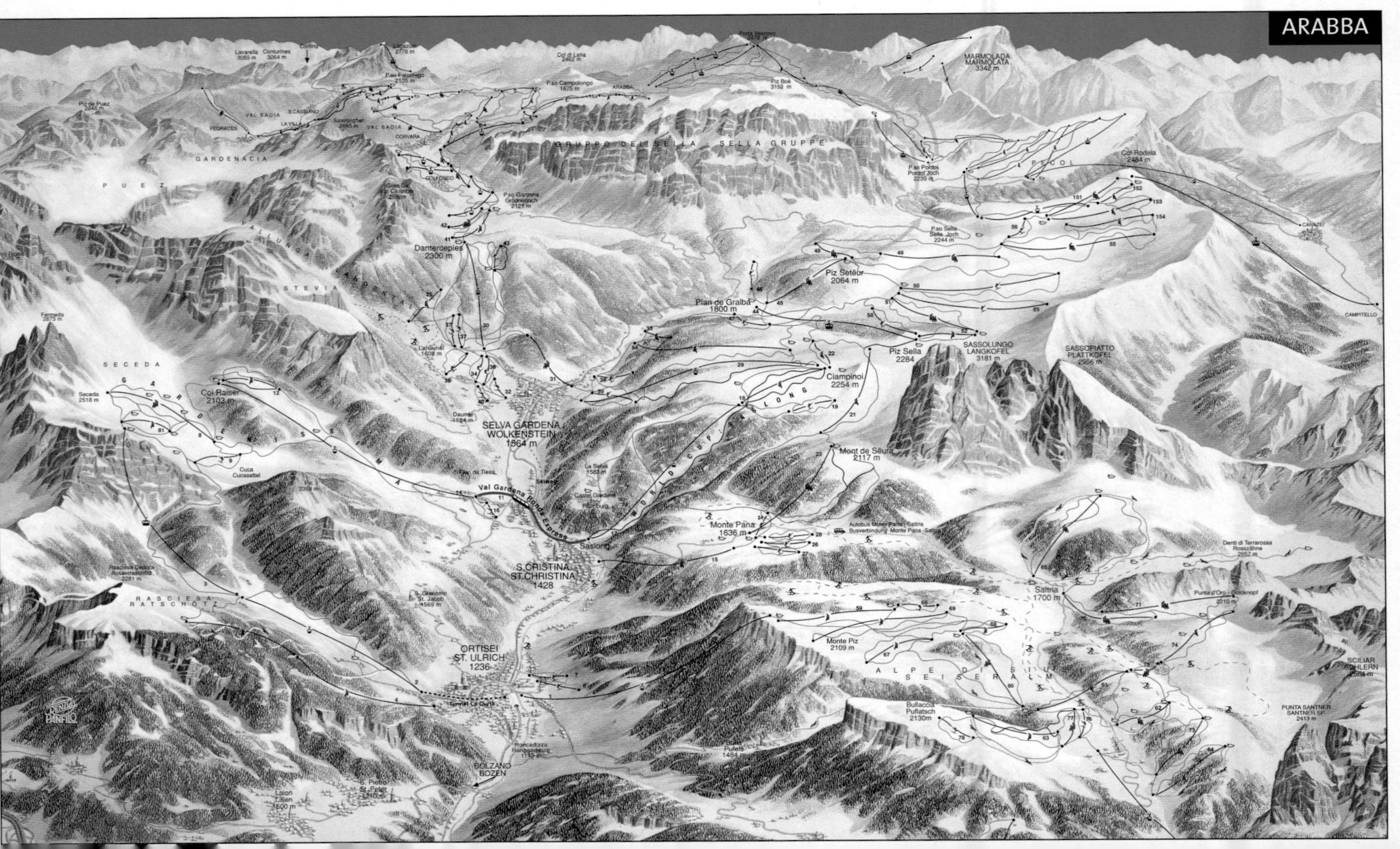

MARMOLADA
MARMOLATA
3342 m
Piz Boè
3152 m
GRUPPO DEL SELLA SELLA GRUPPE
ARABBA
P.so Campolongo
1875 m
Col di Lana
2462 m
Lavarella
3055 m
Conturines
3064 m
Cortina
P.so Falzarego
2105 m
Piz de Puez
2846 m
VAL BADIA
S.CASSIANO
LA VILLA
PEDRACES
CORVARA
GARDENACIA
PUEZ
P.so Pordoi
Pordoi Joch
2239 m
Col Rodela
2484 m
PECOL
CANAZEI
CAMPITELLO
P.so Gardena
Grödnerjoch
2121 m
P.so Sella
Sella Joch
2244 m
Danterceples
2300 m
VALLUNGA
STEVIA
Piz Setëur
2064 m
Plan de Gralba
1800 m
Piz Sella
2284
SASSOLUNGO
LANGKOFEL
3181 m
SASSOPIATTO
PLATTKOFEL
2956 m
Ciampinoi
2254 m
LONG
Mont de Sëura
2117 m
WORLD CUP
Fermeda
2873 m
SECEDA
Seceda
2518 m
Col Raiser
2103 m
GARDENA
SISMA
Cuca
Cucasattel
Daunei
1684 m
SELVA GARDENA
WOLKENSTEIN
1564 m
Val Gardena Ronda Express
Saslong
Monte Pana
1636 m
Autobus Monte Pana - Saltria
Busverbindung Monte Pana - Saltria
S.CRISTINA
ST.CHRISTINA
1428
Rasciesa Dedora
Ausserraschötz
2281 m
RASCIESA
RATSCHOTZ
S. Giacomo
St. Jacob
1569 m
ORTISEI
ST. ULRICH
1236
Tunnel La Curta
Roncadizza
Runggaditsch
BOLZANO
BOZEN
S. Pietro
St. Peter
Laion
Lajen
1600 m
Pufels
1484
Denti di Terrarossa
Rosszähne
2657 m
Saltria
1700 m
Punta d'Oro
2210 m
Monte Piz
2109 m
ALPE DI SIUSI
SEISER ALM
Bullaccia
Puflatsch
2130m
SCILIAR
SCHLERN
2564 m
PUNTA SANTNER
SANTNER SP.
2413 m
RENZO PANFILO

Sleep

★★★★**Sporthotel Arabba**, t +39 0436 79321, *www.sporthotelarabba.com*, has a large pool and a spa offering a full range of treatments.

★★★★**Hotel Grifone**, t +39 0436 780 034, *www.hotelgrifone.com*, is situated outside town on Passo Campolongo.

★★★**Hotel Portavescovo**, t +39 0436 79159, *www.portavescovo.it*, has a children's playroom, pool and gym.

★★★**Hotel Evaldo**, t +39 0436 79109, *www.hotelevaldo.it*, is traditional, with an attractive pool, wellness area and nearby self-catering apartments.

★★★**Hotel Garni Royal**, t +39 0436 79293, *www.royal-arabba.it*, has good-sized bedrooms, sauna, steam-room, and a hot tub, and is warmly recommended.

★★★**Hotel Mesdi**, t +39 0436 79119, *www.hotelmesdi.com*, has an impressive wellness area.

★★★**Hotel Olympia**, t +39 0436 79135, *www.hotel-olympia.com*, contains apartments and a restaurant.

★★★**Hotel Alpenrose**, t +39 0436 750 076, *www.alpenrosearabba.it*, is a comfortable family-run hotel with excellent food and a pleasant, homely atmosphere.

Chalet Barbara t +39 0436 780 155, is an all-wood B&B furnished in cosy alpine style.

Bormio

Profile

Historic spa town with lots of atmosphere and a small high-altitude ski area. A wide choice of ski and snowboard tuition

Resort

Bormio is a large town dating back to Roman times, with a charming pedestrianized centre and a somewhat limited ski area. It has far more of an authentic Italian atmosphere than many comparable resorts, and is best suited to couples and families.

Mountain

'I would thoroughly recommend Bormio to anyone,' said a reporter, 'especially intermediates, as all runs bar a couple are medium reds.' The resort's greatest plus point is its high altitude, which allows skiing to continue until after Easter. New lifts are an enduring legacy of the successful 2005 Alpine Skiing World Championships. The main mountain access is by a two-stage cable car from the edge of town that takes you up to the Cima Bianca top station via Bormio 2000, a mid-station with a family hotel and a shopping mall. A gondola and quad-chair offer an alternative route. The long descents provide ideal cruising territory for intermediates.

A day trip to nearby San Colombano is recommended, with barely a soul to be seen on beautifully manicured pistes both above and below the tree line.

***BEST FOR**
Families, authentic Italian ambience

ESSENTIALS

Altitude: 1225m (4,018ft)–3012m (9,879ft)
Further information: t +39 0342 903 300, *wwwbormioski.it*, *www.valtellina.it*
Lifts in area: 17 (3 cableways, 7 chairs, 7 drags) serving 40km of piste
Lift pass: 4 Valleys (covers Bormio, Santa Caterina, Le Motte and Oga) adult €162–191.50, child from 6yrs €114–133, both for six days
Access: Bergamo and Milan airports 3hrs

Learn

Of the seven ski schools, **Bormio Alta Valtellina**, **t** +39 0342 911 020, is highly recommended for its friendly, English-speaking instructors.

Children

The ski schools take children from four years, while the crèche at the **Scuola Sci Contea**, **t** +39 0342 911 605, accepts children from three years.

Lunch

Try **La Rocca**, **t** +39 0342 905 083, an old-fashioned hut on the main trail down to Bormio 2000, and **Rododendri Chalet**, **t** +39 0342 905 034, just above 2000.

Dine

La Rasiga, **t** +39 0342 901 541, is a stylishly converted sawmill. **Vecchia Combo**, **t** +39 0342 901 568, **Al Filo**, **t** +39 0342 904 771, **Osteria de I Magci**, **t** +39 0342 910 456, and **Kuerc**, **t** +39 0342 904 738, are also recommended.

Party

Plenty of après ski but **King's Disco** is a relic from the 70s and is to be avoided. **Braulio** is a microbrewery and a wine bar. **Lord Byron** attracts a young crowd. **Gordy's Pub** and **Sotto-Sotto** are popular alternatives. **The Rezia Hotel** has a jazz café, and **Shangri-la** has a good choice of cocktails.

Sleep

★★★★**Hotel Baita dei Pini**, **t** +39 0342 904 346, *www.baitadeipini.com*, is an excellent hotel 400m from the gondola.
★★★★**Hotel Palace**, **t** +39 0342 903 131, *www.palacebormio.it*, has recently been renovated and is close to the centre.
★★★★**Hotel Posta**, **t** +39 0342 904 753, *www.hotelposta.bormio.it*, is a former staging inn with an attractive interior.
★★★★ **Hotel Rezia**, **t** +39 0342 904 721, *www.reziahotel.it*, is in the pedestrianized centre. Its restaurant serves local Valtellina dishes.
★★★**Hotel Funivia**, **t** +39 0342 903 242, *www.hotelfunivia.it*, is close to the lifts and has spacious bedrooms.
★★★**Hotel Nevada**, **t** +39 0342 910 888, *www.anzibormio.com*, is at the foot of the Bormio 2000 cable car and has comfortable rooms.

Canazei

Profile

An attractive little town that acts as a mass-market base for skiers and riders wanting to explore the Sella Ronda. The Fassa valley has less crowded skiing and rural villages

Resort

Canazei and adjoining Campitello are the only resorts in the 20km Val di Fassa

***BEST FOR**

High-speed cruisers, night-owls, value

ESSENTIALS

Altitude: 1450m (4,756ft)–2950m (9,676ft)

Further information: t +39 0462 609500, *www.fassa.com*

Lifts in area: 55 (11 cableways, 28 chairs, 16 drags) serving 120km of pistes. 450 lifts serving 1220km of piste in Dolomiti Superski

Lift pass: Dolomiti Superski adult €184–209, child 8–16yrs €129–147, both for six days

Access: Verona airport 2 1/2hrs, Venice airport 2 3/4hrs, railway station at Bolzano 1hr

that link into the Sella Ronda circuit, and forms the core of the Dolomiti Superski, the world's largest area lift pass. The valley has been heavily developed for tourism, but with its backdrop of high mountain peaks and heavily wooded lower slopes it is by no means unattractive.

It takes around three hours to complete the 40km circuit that links Canazei with Selva Gardena, Arabba and Corvara – the principal compass points. It can be skied in either direction. You take 13 lifts clockwise and 15 lifts anti-clockwise. How much time is spent actually skiing depends on your level of proficiency. In planning your day you must also allow for possible lift queues. It makes sense to start before 10am and to reach the last of the four main passes by 3.30pm. The lifts close at 5pm – or earlier in bad weather conditions. Skimap Sella Ronda, available from lift stations and tourist offices, clearly indicates the route and the signposting is good. However, the number of variations and tangential links to other ski areas off the main circuit can be tempting but sometimes confusing.

Other villages in the Val di Fassa, including Alba, Pozza, Moena and Vigo, have their own small ski areas. The Ciampac (Alba) and Buffaure Pozzo di Fassa) ski areas have recently linked up and now tend to attract a more international clientèle than they used to.

Canazei itself is a clutch of narrow cobbled lanes flanked by old barns, modern hotels, a good choice of restaurants and a surprisingly wide selection of shops. Visitors are reliant on the ski or postbus for reaching the lifts from most of the accommodation, but services throughout the valley are efficient. If one of the main access lifts is crowded, you can always stay on the bus and travel to the next.

Mountain

A modern gondola on the edge of Canazei provides the only means of access to the mid-station at Pecol. The seven-minute journey leaves you with a choice of chair or a 100-person cable car for formal entry into the Sella Ronda. An intermediate can ski back down to Canazei for most of the season now that the south-facing slopes have snow cannons.

Campitello 1448m (4,749ft) acts as an alternative access point. A cable car takes you up to Col Rodella, from where you either work your way through a sequence of chairlifts to Passo Sella and Val Gardena beyond, or ski down a pleasant and long intermediate run to Plan de Frataces to catch the connection to Passo Pordoi and the anti-clockwise route to Arabba.

Passo Pordoi, midway between Canazei and Arabba, has some of the steepest off-piste in the Dolomites and is accessed by the ancient Sass Pordoi cable car. But this is a variation of the Sella Ronda strictly reserved for truly accomplished skiers.

From the top, you can either return down a very challenging itinerary run to Passo Pordoi, or follow the difficult Val Lasties to Canazei. Alternatively, you can – with a guide – explore the Val Mesdi.

This cuts across the Sella, the giant rounded stump of a mountain at the heart of the famous ski circuit, and brings you down to Colfosco. All these off-piste descents require good snow and stable weather conditions as well as a level of expertise not necessarily required elsewhere in the Sella Ronda.

Canazei- and Pozza-based skiers also have the chance to explore Sella Brunech, the lesser-known ski area on the far side of the Fassa Valley, reached by a cable car from Alba and a gondola from Passa. This is a pleasant and generally quiet intermediate playground that is augmented by other lifts on Ciampedie on the other side of the valley at Vigo.

The further reaches of the valley have other ski opportunities beginning from Carezza and Passo Costalunga as well as from Ronchi above Moena. From here it is possible to delve on skis still further to Passo San Pellegrino and also into the intricate lift system of the Val Fiemme. Not all links are seamless, and the occasional bus journey is necessary.

Learn

None of the teaching establishments in the valley stands out for its cutting-edge tuition, but an increasing number of instructors now speak fluent English. The schools are **Canazei-Marmolada, t** +39 0462 601 211, **Campitello t** +39 0462 750 350, **Moena-Dolomiti, t** +39 0462 573 770, **Vajolet Pozza di Fassa, t** +39 0462 763 309, and **Vigo di Fassa-Passo Costalunga, t** +39 0462 763 125.

Children

Baby Park Ciampedie in Vigo (at the top of the cable car), run by the Vigo di Fassa school, and **Babylandia-Alpe di Lusia** (at the top of the Lusia cable car), run by the Moena-Dolomiti school, offer daycare and lessons

Park Bimbo Neve, t +39 0462 763 309, in Pozza is operated by the Vajolet Pozza di Fassa ski school for children over three years. **Kinderland e Fantaski, t** +39 0462 601 211, is run by the Canazei-Marmolada ski school and offers daycare for three years and over, and lessons for the over-fours. **Tananai Snow Kinder Park, t** +39 335 560 7671, at the top of the Ciampac cable car in Alba di Canazei, offers daycare. **Snowkinder Cima Uomo, t** +43 347 160 9670, at Passo San Pellegrino, has an unsupervized play area.

Lunch

The mountainside is dotted with privately owned huts, and from midday onwards enticing aromas signal the start of lunch, which the Italians see as an essential component of the skiing day. Try **Rifugio Maria, t** +39 0462 601 178, on top of Sass Pordoi, which specializes in Trentino cuisine. From its sun terrace it offers some of the best views in the Dolomites. **Refuge Frederich August, t** +39 0462 750 133, is on the Col Rodella.

Baita Checco, t +39 335 656 3512, above Viga, and **Bellavista, t** +39 0462 763 200, 30m from the base cable car station at Viga are both worthy lunch spots. **Tobia del Giagher, t** +39 0462 602 385, above Alba, and **Buffaure, t** +39 0462 764 101, on the piste above Pozza, are also recommended.

Dine

'Fantastic food both on the mountain and in the village,' said a reporter. In Canazei most of the best evening restaurants are in hotels. **La Cacciattora, t** +39 0462 601 411, has fresh fish shipped in every day. **La Perla's, t** +39 0462 602 453, signature dish is *pappardelle* with a game sauce. **Wine & Dine** in Hotel Croce Biana, **t** +39 0462 601 111, is famed for its bison steaks and wine list. In Canazei, **El Pael**, **t** +39 0462 601 433, is a good choice.

In Campitello, **La Cantinetta**, **t** +39 0462 750 405, is renowned for its pizza and polenta with mushrooms and venison. In Pozza, **Al Crocefisso**, **t** +39 0462 764 260, is known for its roast lamb shanks and *porcini* dumplings. Try the house *antipasto* and grilled venison cutlets at **Al Vecchio Mulino**, **t** +39 0462 764 477, cosy **El Filo**, **t** +39 0462 763 210, and pizzeria **Le Giare**, **t** +39 0462 764 696. In Vigo, **Hotel Andes**, **t** +39 0462 764 575, has fresh pasta dishes and a pizzeria called Il Pavone. In Moena, **Malga Panna**, **t** +39 0462 573 489, is one of the truly outstanding restaurants in the region. Dishes include rabbit ravioli with rosemary. Also worth trying are **Foresta**, **t** +39 0462 573 260, **Tyrol**, **t** +39 0462 573 760, and **Rifugio Fuchiade**, **t** +39 0462 574 281, on Passo San Pellegrino.

Party

Nightlife centres around bars in the valley, including **Frogs** in Alba, **La Stua dei Ladins**, **Rosengarten**, the new Paradis après ski, La Montanara, Bar **Esso**, **Husky Pub** and **Lieber Augustin** in Canazei, with **da Giulio** and **Ton Tin Pub** in Campitello, **Miro** and **Ta Mongo** in Pozzo, **Matisse** and **Nibada** in Moena. Dancing takes place at **Speckkeller** in Canazei, **La Cantinetta** in Campitello, and **Kusk La Locanda** in Moena. The **Snow Tube** in Alba is fun evening entertainment.

Sleep

Canazei:

★★★★**Hotel Astoria**, **t** +39 0462 601 302, *www.hotel-astoria.net*, has been run by the same family since the Second World War and provides comfortable rooms and good food.

★★★★**Hotel Croce Bianca & Spa Vivenes**, **t** +39 0462 60111, *www.hotelcrocebianca.com*, has been in the same family since 1869 and houses an impressive spa and the popular Husky Pub.

★★★★**Hotel La Perla**, **t** +39 0462 602 453, *www.hotellaperla.net*, is popular with British guests and has a wellness area.

★★★★**Hotel La Cacciatora**, **t** +39 0462 601 411, *www.lacacciatora.it*, is in Alba just 100m from the Ciampac cable car and has been completely renovated.

Campitello:

★★★★**Hotel Medil**, **t** +39 0462 750 088, *www.hotelmedil.it*, offers the smartest accommodation, and has a bar with live music.

★★★**Hotel Alpi**, **t** +39 0462 750 400, *www.hotelalpi.it*, is located 400m from the cable car and has a ski bus-stop outside the door.

Hotel Panorama, **t** +39 0462 750 112, *www.panoramahotel.it*, is at the far end of the village near the nursery slope.

Moena:

★★★★**Garden Hotel**, **t** +39 0462 573 314, *www.hotelgarden-moena.it*, has an indoor pool and a piano bar.

Pozzo and Vigo di Fassa:

★★★★**Alpen Hotel Corona Sport & Wellness**, **t** +39 0462 764 211, *www.alpenhotelcorona.com*, in Vigo, is impressive and was used by former Olympic slalom champion Alberto Tomba as his training base.

★★★★**Hotel Ladinia**, **t** +39 0462 764 201, *www.hotelladinia.com*, in Pozzo, is recommended.

Cervinia

***BEST FOR**

Beginners, intermediate runs, long runs, guaranteed snow-cover

ESSENTIALS

Altitude: 2050m (6,726ft)–3883m (12,740ft)
Further information: t +39 0166 949 136, *www.montecervino.it*
Lifts in area: 57 with Zermatt (1 funicular, 23 cableways, 22 chairs, 12 drags) serving 200km of piste in Cervinia, 350km with Zermatt
Lift pass: area (covers Cervinia, Valtournenche, Zermatt) adult €240, child 9–13yrs €120 both for six days
Access: Turin, Milan and Bergamo airports 2hrs, railway station at Châtillon 27km, regular buses to resort

Profile

High-altitude resort with guaranteed snow-cover during a long season. It is linked to Valtournenche in Italy and Zermatt in Switzerland and shares a lift pass

Resort

Cervinia is a high-altitude resort with fabulous long runs and virtually guaranteed snow conditions throughout the winter – last season it had some of the best in Europe. It's somewhere Italy should be proud of. Il Duce, Benito Mussolini, felt exactly the same and decreed in the 1930s that the then-embryo resort should change its name from the Swiss–German-sounding Breuil to Cervinia to reflect the Italianate glory of the mountain above it. Unfortunately most of us think of the Matterhorn rather than Il Cervino when we view the angular peak that adorns more postcards than any other in the world. From the Italian side, the peak first climbed by Edward Whymper in 1865 looks unremarkable.

The nucleus of pre-Second World War buildings reflect the austere imperial style of the time, but all that was a long time ago. Cervinia today is a modern ski resort with a hotchpotch of mainly unenterprising architecture created over the past half-century by those who believe that this is Italy's greatest ski resort.

Actually, it is not. It's a wonderfully ski-friendly playground, dictated by the easy gradient of its seemingly never-ending slopes. These allow beginners and wobbly intermediates to gain enormous confidence in the extensive high-mountain area. At the same time boy- and girl-racers will enjoy the length of the perfectly groomed runs – and if they are bored by the benign gradient, they can always cross the Klein Matterhorn for the more severe pistes of Zermatt.

Valtournenche is an old village 9km by road from Cervinia, but linked into the same ski area.

Mountain

Cervinia's biggest asset is altitude. At 2050m, with slopes rising to 3883m, it is one of Europe's most snow-sure resorts, set against a superb glacial backdrop. It's a place where long runs right down to village level are virtually guaranteed from the beginning of December until early May. Summer skiing continues on the glacier throughout the year. Nine lifts serve 21km of prepared piste with an enormous out-of-season vertical drop of 1000m in the right conditions. A terrain park, with a super-pipe and a half-pipe, is open from the end of June until the beginning of September.

The link to Zermatt and the joint lift pass are of benefit to both parties.

However, don't make the mistake of thinking that by staying in Cervinia you can fully enjoy Zermatt on the cheap – the distances are too great to be able to do more than sample what the Swiss have to offer.

Beginners and lower intermediates will find themselves content with the 24 lifts on the Italian side that extend down to Valtournenche at 1524m. If they want to visit Switzerland during their stay they can invest in a one-day supplement to the local lift pass. It is important to allow plenty of time to make the long journey back up the Klein Matterhorn and over to Italy at the end of the day. The high-altitude link is prone to sudden rupture in adverse weather conditions. The taxi journey from one resort to the other takes six hours – it's better to bivouac for the night in a B&B.

The 2006/7 season saw the building of a new six-pack, and three quads replaced draglifts and an old double-chair. A gondola and parallel cable car take skiers up from Cervinia to the mid-mountain hub of 2559m Plan Maison. The base station is an annoying walk up from much of the accommodation. The new chairlift from Cretaz to Plan Torrette has reduced queues for mountain access and is a useful alternative to the gondola/cable car to Plan Maison.

From Plan Maison a network of modern multiple chairs, a gondola and finally a cable car bring you up to the summer ski area of Plateau Rosa at 3480m. From here you can ski down the Theodulgletscher to Trockener Steg in Switzerland, or return to Cervinia on the 8km Ventina (no.7 on the resort's piste map). This is one of the classic runs of the Alps. For the second- or third-week skier fresh from the nursery slopes, the easy gradient should present no problems. Its completion will give an enormous sense of achievement. For the advanced skier or rider, a couple of these at the start of the day when pistes are deserted should reduce the fittest legs to lasagne. If you are still hungry, try the descent from the Plateau Rosa to Valtournenche – it's more than twice as long.

The lack of gradient throughout the ski area on the Italian side can be irksome for strong skiers. They will quickly discover that Cervinia has no steep piste skiing at all, just kilometre upon kilometre of blue and red cruising runs. However, it is ideal for novices who can explore the entire mountain after just a week on skis.

In powder conditions there's plenty of good off-piste to be discovered on the shoulder above Cieloalto. Local guides can provide access from the lift system to an enormous number of enjoyable high-altitude descents that can be exceedingly demanding. Heli-skiing is also possible on the Monte Rosa.

The terrain park served by the Fornet chair has a half-pipe and a snowcross course.

Learn

The choice of schools here lies between the traditional **Cervino**, **t** +39 0166 949 034, **Breuil**, **t** +39 0166 940 960, and newer **Matterhorn Cervinia**, **t** +39 0166 949 523. **Valtournenche** has its own ski school, **t** +39 0166 92515. Mountain guides from the local bureau in Cervinia are much more reasonably priced than their Swiss counterparts, but have equal expertise on the border peaks. Go with **Guide del Cervino**, **t** +39 0166 948 169, or **Heliski Cervinia**, **t** +39 0166 949 267.

Children

Mini Club Biancaneve, **t** +39 0166 940 201, is a non-ski kindergarten taking children from newborn to 10 years old. Children must be accompanied by an

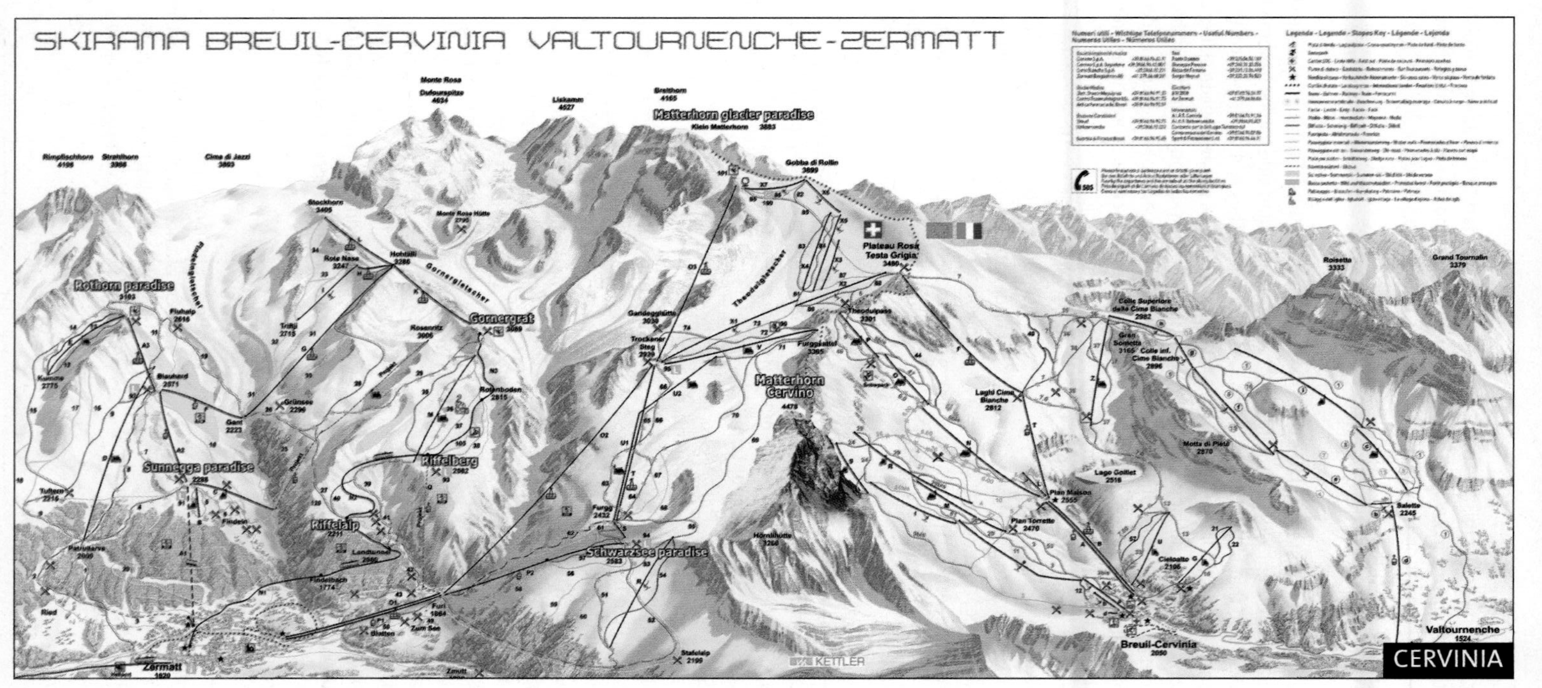

SKIRAMA BREUIL-CERVINIA VALTOURNENCHE-ZERMATT
Monte Rosa
Dufourspitze
4634
Liskamm
4527
Breithorn
4165
Matterhorn glacier paradise
Klein Matterhorn 3883
Rimpfischhorn 4199
Strahlhorn 4190
Cima di Jazzi 3803
Gobba di Rollin 3899
Stockhorn 3405
Monte Rosa Hütte 2795
Rote Nase 3247
Hohtälli 3286
Gornergletscher
Findelngletscher
Theodulgletscher
Rothorn paradise
3103
Fluhalp 2616
Gornergrat 3089
Trifji 2715
Rosenritz 3005
Gandegghütte 3030
Trockener Steg 2939
Plateau Rosa Testa Grigia 3480
Theodulpass 3301
Furggsattel 3365
Matterhorn Cervino 4478
Kumme 2775
Blauherd 2571
Grünsee 2296
Gant 2223
Rotenboden 2815
Riffelberg 2582
Sunnegga paradise 2288
Tufteren 2215
Findeln
Riffelalp 2211
Landtunnel
Furgg 2432
Schwarzsee paradise 2583
Hörnlihütte 3260
Patrullarve 2000
Findelbach 1774
Furi 1864
Zum See
Blatten
Ried
Zermatt 1620
Zmutt
Stafelalp 2199
KETTLER
Colle Superiore delle Cime Bianche 2982
Gran Sometta 3165
Colle inf. Cime Bianche 2896
Laghi Cime Bianche 2812
Roisetta 3333
Grand Tournalin 3379
Motta di Pletè 2970
Lago Goillet 2516
Plan Maison 2555
Plan Torrette 2470
Cieloalto 2196
Salette 2245
Breuil-Cervinia 2050
Valtournenche 1524
CERVINIA

adult. All the ski schools run classes and ski kindergartens for children from four or five years.

Lunch

Chalet Etoile, **t** +39 0166 940 220, near the Rocce Nere chairlift, is the best restaurant on the mountain, renowned for its spaghetti with lobster. **Ventina**, **t** +39 338 664 2596, on the way down from Plateau Rosa, offers home cooking. **Bontadini**, **t** +39 335 250 312, on the slope of the same name, also received good reviews. **Le Pousset**, **t** +39 339 694 6228, below Laghi Cime Bianche, serves local specialities, as does **Baita Cretaz**, **t** +39 0166 949 914, on the nursery slopes.

Dine

The **Hermitage**, **t** +39 0166 948 998, has outstanding international cuisine served in an elegant dining room. **Le Bistrot de l'Abbé**, **t** +39 0166 949 060, is smaller and more rustic, but a worthy runner-up. **La Nicchia**, **t** +39 0166 949 842, is smart, with rich food. **La Tana**, **t** +39 0166 949 098, is singled out for its game and mushrooms dishes. The **Copa Pan**, **t** +39 0166 949 140, is expensive, with rustic décor, and is rated for its food. **La Maison de Saussure**, **t** +39 0166 948 259, is a good choice for typical Valdostana specialities in wood-panelled surroundings. Eat tasty pizzas at **Al Solito Posto**, **t** +39 0166 949 126, and at **Matterhorn**, **t** +39 0166 948 518. **Maison Jean Bich di Pers da Mario**, **t** +39 0166 949 436, near the golf club, is warmly recommended.

Party

Nightlife is more muted than you might expect in an Italian resort of this calibre. **La Bricole**, at the bottom of run no.3, has a popular happy hour in the late afternoon. **Lino's Bar**, beside the ice rink, is everyone's favourite when the lifts close. Cocktails in the **Hotel Edelweiss** are ingenious and intoxicating. **Lo Yeti**, the **Copa Pan**, and **Hostellerie des Guides** are popular, as well as the infamous and ever-crowded **Dragon Bar.**

Sleep

★★★★**Hotel Hermitage**, **t** +39 0166 948 998, *www.hotelhermitage.com*, situated on the edge of town, has the relaxed atmosphere of a country house.

★★★★**Petit Palais**, **t** +39 0166 940 067, is a tour operator-managed hotel. It is recommended by some readers but receives mixed reviews for its half-board cuisine.

★★★★**Hotel Punta Maquignaz**, **t** +39 0166 949 145, *www.puntamaquignaz.com*, is an attractive hotel close to the draglifts.

★★★★**Sertorelli Sport Hotel, t** +39 0166 949 797, *www.sertorelli-cervinia.it*, maintains a consistently high standard.

★★★**Hotel Breuil**, **t** +39 0166 949 537, is reported to be clean, spacious and very acceptable.

★★★★**Hotel Furggen**, **t** +39 0166 948 928, *www.meublefurggen.com*, is a little basic, but clean and comfortable.

★★★**Albergo Grandes Murailles**, **t** +39 0166 932 702, *www.hotelgmurailles.com*, is a homely little hotel in Valtournenche village centre, with 16 large rooms decorated with warm rugs and wrought-iron beds.

★★★**Hotel Jumeaux**, **t** +39 0166 949 044, *www.hotel-jumeaux.com*, is pleasant, and furnished with antiques and period prints.

★★★**Hotel Mignon**, **t** +39 066 949 344, *www.mignoncervinia.com*, is centrally placed and cosy, with a good restaurant.

★★★**Les Neiges d'Antan**, **t** +39 0166 948 775, *www.lesneigesdantan.it*, is a few minutes' drive from the lifts by hotel bus. Downstairs the decoration is traditional, while upstairs the bedrooms and bathrooms have been tastefully renovated.

★★**Hotel Al Piolet**, **t** +39 0166 949 161, *www.hotelalpiolet.com*, is good value with large rooms, and copious food.

Champoluc

Profile

A linked circuit of unspoilt ski villages in a rustic corner of the Val d'Aosta. Plenty of intermediate skiing in Champoluc and Gressoney as well as truly rugged off-piste above Alagna

Resort

Champoluc, a wonderful, virtually unheard-of resort, and the linked villages of Gressoney-La-Trinité, Stafal and Alagna, form an area known as Monterosa Ski at the northeastern end of the wide Aosta Valley beneath the towering peak of Monte Rosa. 'The village is quiet compared to many of the large resorts, but for us this was the attraction,' said a reader.

Champoluc and Gressoney are best suited to families, while Alagna is more of a raw mountain experience, a glacial high-altitude ski area that rivals Argentière for its demanding off-piste opportunities. Catch it while you can – every season this resort that is so revered by powderhounds is becoming increasingly commercial.

However, most of Monterosa Ski is given over to easy blue and gentle red pistes that are well connected by a predominantly modern lift system. It is worth noting that, while the different resorts appear close on the map and are easily reached on skis from one to the other, the journey by road between any two of them is at least two hours.

Champoluc dates from the 15th century and still has some lovely old houses. It has expanded along the riverbank in recent years with a blossoming of modern hotels and restaurants, but fortunately it has managed to retain its village atmosphere, and offers excellent accommodation at a reasonable rate.

Gressoney-La-Trinité and larger Gressoney-St-Jean in the neighbouring valley are also mountain communities that have jumped in the course of a single generation from farming and forestry to feeding foreigners. Stafal is a modern purpose-built outpost above Gressoney-La-Trinité. Alagna, which lies in Piedmont just beyond the Aosta Valley, is even more rustic with little wooden houses with built-in hay frames.

✻BEST FOR

Small village atmosphere, beginners, intermediates, and challenging powder runs (Alagna)

ESSENTIALS

Altitude: 1212m (3,976ft)–2971m (9,747ft)
Further information: **t** +39 125 303 111, Alagna only: **t** +44 (0)8701 622 273, *www.monterosa-ski.com*
Lifts in area: 24 (8 cableways, 16 chairs) serving 180km of piste
Lift pass: Aosta Valley (includes Courmayeur, La Thuile, La Rosière, Champoluc-Gressoney-Alagna) adult €199, child 6–12yrs €99.50, both for six days
Access: Turin airport 1½hrs

Mountain

Wherever you choose to stay, you must contend with one of the worst lift maps in Europe; finding your way around relies more on luck than map-reading skills. All

The ski holiday specialists to the acclaimed Monterosa ski area, including the three resorts of Champoluc, Gressoney and Alagna

Holidays of any duration for families, groups and individuals

•••

Ski weekends and short breaks

•••

Our own British ski school and nursery

•••

Choice of departure and arrival airports

•••

Quality hotels and apartments

•••

Swift minibus transfers

Roger Walker Travel

tr
he

the real holiday experience

See our comprehensive website
at www.ski–2.com
call us on 01962 713330
or email us at
sales@ski–2.com

G8818
W3334

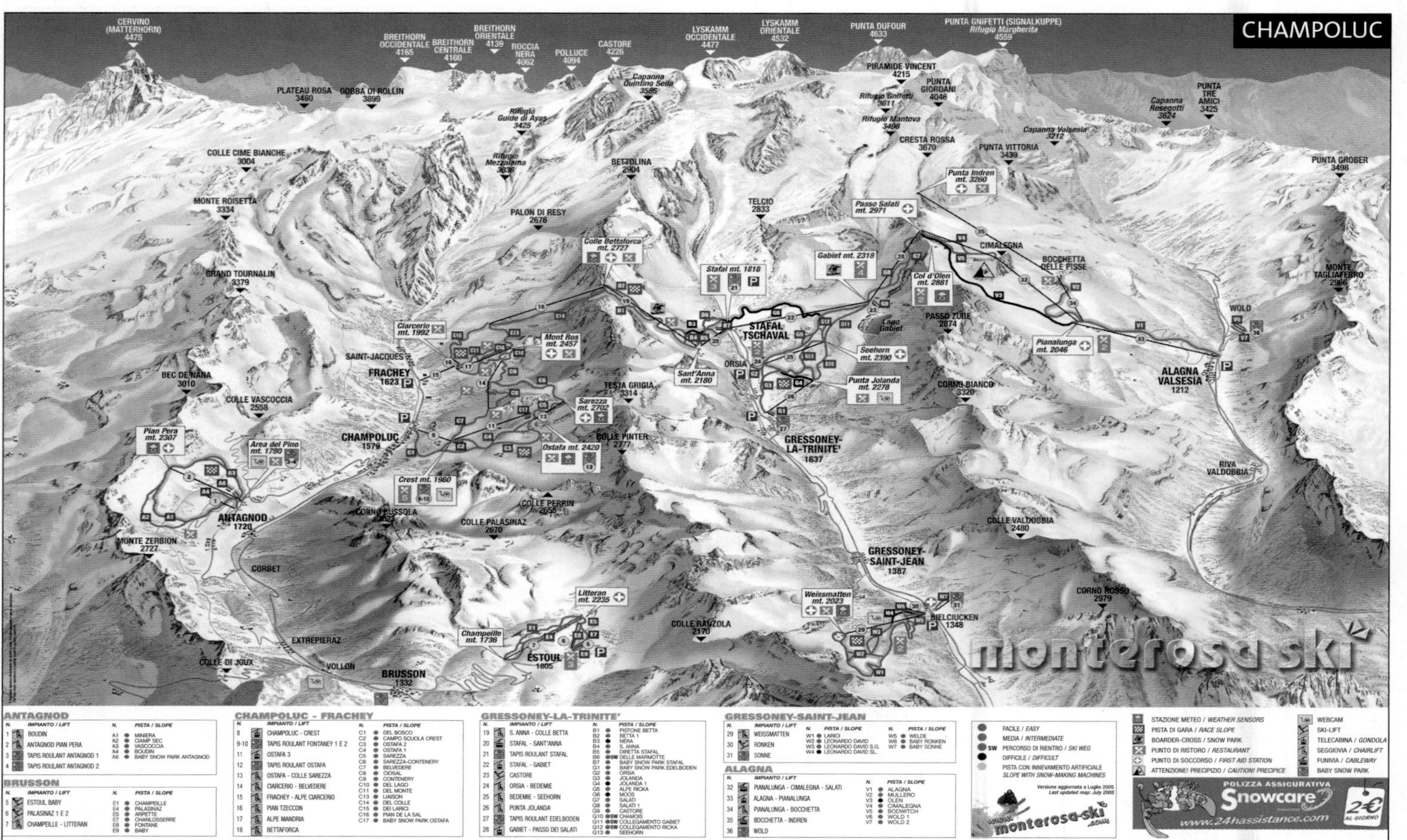
CHAMPOLUC
CERVINO (MATTERHORN) 4475
BREITHORN OCCIDENTALE 4165
BREITHORN CENTRALE 4160
BREITHORN ORIENTALE 4139
ROCCIA NERA 4062
POLLUCE 4094
CASTORE 4226
LYSKAMM OCCIDENTALE 4477
LYSKAMM ORIENTALE 4532
PUNTA DUFOUR 4633
PUNTA GNIFETTI (SIGNALKUPPE) Rifugio Margherita 4559
PIRAMIDE VINCENT 4215
PUNTA GIORDANI 4046
PUNTA TRE AMICI 3425
Capanna Resegotti 3624
PLATEAU ROSA 3480
GOBBA DI ROLLIN 3899
Capanna Quintino Sella 3585
Rifugio Gnifetti 3611
Rifugio Guide di Ayas 3425
Rifugio Mantova 3498
Capanna Valsesia 3212
COLLE CIME BIANCHE 3004
Rifugio Mezzalama 3036
BETTOLINA 2904
CRESTA ROSSA 3670
PUNTA VITTORIA 3439
PUNTA GROBER 3498
MONTE ROISETTA 3334
PALON DI RESY 2676
TELCIO 2833
Punta Indren mt. 3260
Passo Salati mt. 2971
CIMALEGNA
BOCCHETTA DELLE PISSE
MONTE TAGLIAFERRO 2966
GRAND TOURNALIN 3379
Colle Bettaforca mt. 2727
Gabiet mt. 2318
Stafal mt. 1818
Col d'Olen mt. 2881
WOLD
STAFAL TSCHAVAL
Lago Gabiet
PASSO ZUBE 2874
Ciarcerio mt. 1992
Mont Ros mt. 2457
SAINT-JACQUES
Seehorn mt. 2390
Pianalunga mt. 2046
ALAGNA VALSESIA 1212
BEC DE NANA 3010
FRACHEY 1623
ORSIA
Sant'Anna mt. 2180
TESTA GRIGIA 3314
Punta Jolanda mt. 2278
CORNO BIANCO 3320
COLLE VASCOCCIA 2558
Sarezza mt. 2702
Pian Pera mt. 2307
CHAMPOLUC 1579
COLLE PINTER 2777
GRESSONEY-LA-TRINITE' 1637
Area del Pino mt. 1780
Ostafa mt. 2420
RIVA VALDOBBIA
Crest mt. 1980
COLLE PERRIN 2655
ANTAGNOD 1720
CORNO BUSSOLA 3023
COLLE PALASINAZ 2670
COLLE VALDOBBIA 2480
MONTE ZERBION 2727
GRESSONEY-SAINT-JEAN 1387
CORBET
Litteran mt. 2235
Weissmatten mt. 2023
CORNO ROSSO 2979
BIELCIUCKEN 1348
Champeille mt. 1736
COLLE RANZOLA 2170
EXTREPIERAZ
ESTOUL 1805
monterosa ski
COLLE DI JOUX
VOLLON
BRUSSON 1332
ANTAGNOD
N. IMPIANTO / LIFT
1 BOUDIN
2 ANTAGNOD PIAN PERA
3 TAPIS ROULANT ANTAGNOD 1
4 TAPIS ROULANT ANTAGNOD 2
N. PISTA / SLOPE
A1 MINIERA
A2 CIAMP SEC
A3 VASCOCCIA
A4 BOUDIN
A6 BABY SNOW PARK ANTAGNOD
BRUSSON
N. IMPIANTO / LIFT
5 ESTOUL BABY
6 PALASINAZ 1 E 2
7 CHAMPEILLE - LITTERAN
N. PISTA / SLOPE
E1 CHAMPEILLE
E4 PALASINAZ
E5 ARPETTE
E7 CHANLOSSERRE
E8 FONTANE
E9 BABY
CHAMPOLUC - FRACHEY
N. IMPIANTO / LIFT
8 CHAMPOLUC - CREST
9-10 TAPIS ROULANT FONTANEY 1 E 2
11 OSTAFA 3
12 TAPIS ROULANT OSTAFA
13 OSTAFA - COLLE SAREZZA
14 CIARCERIO - BELVEDERE
15 FRACHEY - ALPE CIARCERIO
16 PIAN TZECCON
17 ALPE MANDRIA
18 BETTAFORCA
N. PISTA / SLOPE
C1 DEL BOSCO
C2 CAMPO SCUOLA CREST
C3 OSTAFA 2
C4 OSTAFA 1
C5 SAREZZA
C6 SAREZZA-CONTENERY
C7 BELVEDERE
C8 CIOSAL
C9 CONTENERY
C10 DEL LAGO
C11 DEL MONTE
C13 LIAISON
C14 DEL COLLE
C15 DEI LARICI
C16 PIAN DE LA SAL
C17 BABY SNOW PARK OSTAFA
GRESSONEY-LA-TRINITE'
N. IMPIANTO / LIFT
19 S. ANNA - COLLE BETTA
20 STAFAL - SANT'ANNA
21 TAPIS ROULANT STAFAL
22 STAFAL - GABIET
23 CASTORE
24 ORSIA - BEDEMIE
25 BEDEMIE - SEEHORN
26 PUNTA JOLANDA
27 TAPIS ROULANT EDELBODEN
28 GABIET - PASSO DEI SALATI
N. PISTA / SLOPE
B1 PISTONE BETTA
B2 BETTA 1
B3 NERA
B4 S. ANNA
B5 DIRETTA STAFAL
B6 SW DELLE MARMOTTE
B7 BABY SNOW PARK STAFAL
G1 BABY SNOW PARK EDELBODEN
G2 ORSIA
G3 JOLANDA
G4 JOLANDA 1
G5 ALPE RICKA
G6 MOOS
G7 SALATI
G8 SALATI 1
G9 CASTORE
G10 SW CHAMOIS
G11 SW COLLEGAMENTO GABIET
G12 SW COLLEGAMENTO RICKA
G13 SEEHORN
GRESSONEY-SAINT-JEAN
N. IMPIANTO / LIFT
29 WEISSMATTEN
30 RONKEN
31 SONNE
N. PISTA / SLOPE
W1 LARICI
W2 LEONARDO DAVID
W3 LEONARDO DAVID S.G.
W4 LEONARDO DAVID SL.
W5 WELDE
W6 BABY RONKEN
W7 BABY SONNE
ALAGNA
N. IMPIANTO / LIFT
32 PIANALUNGA - CIMALEGNA - SALATI
33 ALAGNA - PIANALUNGA
34 PIANALUNGA - BOCCHETTA
35 BOCCHETTA - INDREN
36 WOLD
N. PISTA / SLOPE
V1 ALAGNA
V2 MULLERO
V3 OLEN
V4 CIMALEGNA
V5 BODWITCH
V6 WOLD 1
V7 WOLD 2
FACILE / EASY
MEDIA / INTERMEDIATE
SW PERCORSO DI RIENTRO / SKI WEG
DIFFICILE / DIFFICULT
PISTA CON INNEVAMENTO ARTIFICIALE
SLOPE WITH SNOW-MAKING MACHINES
Versione aggiornata a Luglio 2005
Last updated map: July 2005
www.monterosa-ski.com
STAZIONE METEO / WEATHER SENSORS
PISTA DI GARA / RACE SLOPE
BOARDER-CROSS / SNOW PARK
PUNTO DI RISTORO / RESTAURANT
PUNTO DI SOCCORSO / FIRST AID STATION
ATTENZIONE! PRECIPIZIO / CAUTION! PRECIPICE
WEBCAM
SKI-LIFT
TELECABINA / GONDOLA
SEGGIOVIA / CHAIRLIFT
FUNIVIA / CABLEWAY
BABY SNOW PARK
POLIZZA ASSICURATIVA
Snowcare
www.24hassistance.com
2€
AL GIORNO

lifts eventually lead you to Stafal, the focal point of the ski area, where you turn west for 2971m Monte Bettaforca and Champoluc beyond. East takes you to Passo del Salati and to Alagna. 'Compared to other nearby resorts, it was completely empty some days. You just cruise along and look round and there's no one else there,' enthused a reader.

Both Gressoney and Champoluc offer intermediate cruising, and the beauty of the area is that you feel you are going somewhere each day. Each resort has a dedicated novice area.

The area suits all standards, although more accomplished skiers and riders are advised to stay in – or within easy reach of – Alagna. Given good snow conditions this whole area provides some extraordinary freeriding and *couloir* skiing, and heli-skiing is also possible. However, avalanche danger is ever present and this should not be attempted without a local guide.

'The only problem was that there was no snowpark or a half-pipe. Luckily it made up for this with the best off-piste in Europe,' said a snowboarder.

Learn

The schools are **Gressoney-St-Jean**, **t** +39 0125 355 291, **Gressoney Monte Rosa**, **t** +39 0125 366 015, **Alagna**, **t** +39 0163 922 961, **Antagnod**, **t** +39 0125 306 641, **Brusson**, **t** +39 340 541 0632, and **Champoluc**, **t** +39 0125 307 194. All are generally good, but English is by no means widely spoken. **Ski 2**, **t** +44 (0)1962 713 330, has its own well-organized British ski school in Champoluc with BASI instructors . Mountain guiding is with **Champoluc**, **t** +39 346 244 1219, **Gressoney**, **t** +39 0125 366 280 and **Alagna**, **t** +39 0163 91310.

Children

Ski 2, **t** +44 (0)1962 713 330, runs a crèche with British-qualified nannies for its clients in Champoluc, close to Hotel Relais des Glaciers. It accepts children from three months to skiing age, seven days a week. The operator also runs its own ski school with BASI instructors for five hours a day for kids aged four to 12 years. **Champoluc** ski school, **t** +39 0125 307 194, takes children from five years.

At Stafal, **Hotel Monboso**, **t** +39 0125 366 302, cares for children from four to eight years. In Gressoney, skiers over six years must join the adult classes. **Alagna** ski school, **t** +39 0163 922 961, accepts children from three years.

Lunch

Try **Albergo del Ponte**, **t** +39 0125 366 180, a mountain hut with rooms above Gabiet that serves delicious pasta. **Rifugio Guglielmina**, **t** +39 0163 91444, between the Alagna and Gressoney valleys, has good food and even better views. **The Belvedere**, **t** +39 349 491 5130 (at the top of lift 12), has excellent views and traditional cooking. **Bar Ostafa**, **t** +39 339 818 0709, at the top of the gondola that has replaced chairs 8 and 9, is known for its homemade pasta.

Dine

In Champoluc, **Le Sapin**, **t** +39 0125 307 598, has good food at reasonable prices. **Favre**, **t** +39 0125 307 131, features local game. **Hotel Villa Anna Maria**, **t** +39 0125 307 128, has reasonable mountain food and an exceptional wine list. At Frachey, **Le Petit Coq**, **t** +39 0125 307 997, is elegant-rustic, and there is great food at **Casa Nostra**, **t** +39 0125 307 566. In Gressoney-St-Jean, **Lo Stambecco**, **t** +39 0125 355 201, has fine grilled steaks and lamb. In Stafal, **Capanna Carla**, **t** +39 0125 366 130, serves regional cuisine at reasonable prices in a warm atmosphere. In Alagna, **Fum D'ss**, **t** +39 0163 922 923, has local game with polenta. **Ristorante Unione**, **t** +39 0163 922 930, and **Stolemberg**, **t** +39 0163 923 201, are recommended.

Party

The nightlife is what you make it. For families and serious skiers this usually means an early bath and bed. Bars such as **Hirsch Stube** and the **Petit Bar** in Gressoney provide some entertainment. **Disco Gram Parsons** is in Hotel California.

Sleep

Champoluc:

★★★★**Hotel Breithorn**, **t** +39 0125 308 734, *www.breithornhotel.com*, is smart-rustic with a good spa. 'An excellent standard of accommodation,' said a reporter.

★★★★**Hotellerie de Mascognaz**, **t** +39 0125 308 734, *www.hotelleriedemascognaz.com*, was once the village school and is now a rustic yet very comfortable little hotel with just six bedrooms.

★★★★**Relais des Glaciers**, **t** +39 0125 308 721, *www.hotelrelaisdesglaciers.com*, is traditional and has a wellness centre.

★★★**Hotel Villa Anna Maria**, **t** +39 30125 307 128, *www.hotelvillaannamaria.com*, has 20 individually decorated bedrooms.

★★★**Hotel Castor**, **t** +39 0125 307 117, *www.hotelcastor.eu*, is run by a local Englishman and is warmly recommended.

★★★**Hotel California**, **t** +39 0125 307 977, *www.hotelcalifornia.vda.it*, is decorated with 1960s music memorabilia. Choose the Bob Dylan room or The Doors room.

★★★**Hotel de Champoluc**, **t** +39 0125 308 088, *www.hoteldechampoluc.net*, is recommended: 'Great hotel – food of a very high standard, staff helpful and pleasant.'

★★**Hotel Favre**, **t** +39 0125 307 131, *www.tako.it*, is small and well managed with friendly staff.

★★★**Le Rocher Hotel**, **t** +39 +39 0125 308 711, *www.lerocherhotel.com*, has great food, comfortable rooms, and helpful staff.

Alagna:

★★★★**Hotel Cristallo**, **t** +39 0163 91285, *www.hotelcristalloalagna.com*, is in the centre near the 16th-century church.

★★★**Pensione Genzianella**, **t** +39 0163 923 921, *www.monterosa4000.it*, has recently been refurbished.

★★★**Albergo Monte Rosa**, **t** +39 0163 923 209, *www.albergomonterosa.com*, was built in 1908 and is still run by the same family.

★★★**Hotel Mirella**, **t** +39 0163 922 965, is a B&B with rooms over a cake shop.

Gressoney Valley:

★★★★**Hotel Monboso**, **t** +39 0125 366 302, *www.igrandiviaggi.it*, at Stafal, is recommended.

★★★**Hotel Gasthaus Lysjoch**, **t** +39 0125 366 150, *www.hotellysjoch.com*, in Gressoney-La-Trinité, is a cosily old-fashioned Tyrolean-style chalet.

★★★**Hotel La Gran Baita**, **t** +39 0125 356 441, near Gressoney-Weissmatten, is a lovingly restored ancient Walser house.

★★★**Hotel Lo Scoiàttolo**, **t** +39 0125 366 313, *www.htlscoiattolo.com*, in Gressoney-La-Trinité, is comfortable with a warm ambience.

Cortina d'Ampezzo

***BEST FOR**

All levels of skier and rider, sophisto-cats and ski gourmets

ESSENTIALS

Altitude: 1224m (4,015ft)–3243m (10,640ft)
Further information: t +39 0436 866 252, *www.cortina.dolomiti.it*
Lifts in area: 36 (5 cableways, 24 chairs, 7 drags) serving 170km of piste. 450 lifts serving 1220km of piste in Dolomiti Superski
Lift pass: Dolomiti Superski adult €176–220, child 8–16yrs €123–154, both for six days
Access: Treviso airport 1½hrs, Venice airport 2hrs, railway station at Calalzo-Pieve di Cadore 35km

Profile

Italy's top ski town is rich in old-world charm and reigns supreme in a beautiful setting against the backdrop of the craggy peaks of the Dolomites

Resort

Italy's smartest winter destination, dominated by its magnificent green and white bell tower and a glittering confection of grand 19th-century mansions, sits in splendid linguistic defiance of its neighbours, a two-hour drive from Venice.

Despite being variously occupied over the centuries by foreign invaders that have included Bavaria, France, Austria, Italy, Germany, and even the Americans in 1945, Cortina has stubbornly maintained a spiritual independence of its own. While the residents of surrounding towns and villages primarily speak Italian or German, the native Cortinese cling to their ancient Ladino language to converse among themselves.

The town is surrounded by soaring cathedrals of dolomitic limestone that rise to over 3000m. These distinctive mountains, named after French geologist Deodat de Dolomieu, turn a surreal shade of pink in the final rays of the setting sun. Encroaching twilight is the signal for Cortina to come out to play. A colony of fur coats and designer skiwear gathers noisily in the Piazza Venezia at the start of the evening *passeggiata*.

The actual business of skiing plays second fiddle to the social sport of seeing and being seen in the elegant boutiques and antique shops that line the Corso Italia, the pedestrianized main street. Much later, the perpetual party atmosphere is transferred to intimate wine bars, expensive restaurants and a smattering of softly lit nightclubs.

The skiing has plenty of appeal for all standards, but the resort has failed to make a regular investment in its high-speed mountain transport. However, three detachable chairs have been added in the past few seasons – one in each of the Cristallo, Faloria and Tofana areas, and this season sees the opening of a new lift connecting the Cinque Torre and Lagazuoi ski areas.

Cortina Adrenalin Center, t +39 0436 860 808, offers alternative snow sports such as bobsleigh, snowrafting and ice-climbing. Adrenalin Park behind the bob run has zip-wires with 40 platforms in the trees and is open in the evening.

Mountain

The main skiing is divided into the two separate ski areas of Faloria/Cristallo and Tofana, which can both be reached by cable cars from either side of town.

A busy ski bus service provides a link to the lifts, but skiing convenience is not a strong feature in Cortina. These two are supplemented by a diverse handful of smaller, unconnected areas as well as a direct link into the Sella Ronda via another cable car at Passo Falzarego, a 20-minute free bus ride away.

Tofana, the 3243m highest point in the ski area, provides spectacular views. Two chairs from the second stage of the cable-car give access to a collection of blue and red runs. An easy black run links into the more demanding Socrepes sector, which can otherwise be reached by a blue run from the top of the first cable car stage.

The bottom of Socrepes is devoted to a benign and scenic nursery area, served by four chairs and three draglifts, that curiously resembles a sloping Kensington Gardens. These beginner runs can be reached by bus from the town at Lacedel on the outskirts and at the top of the nursery area at Pocol, 6km from Cortina.

Faloria, reached by a cable car, which spans a cliff face on the other side of Cortina, has plenty of intermediate appeal. You can work your way along the mountainside through a sequence of chairlifts and blue/red runs down to the road at Rio Gere. A modern chairlift on the far side brings you up to Son Forca and one of the most dramatic runs in the Dolomites. The steep black Staunies, and the fast red Padeon that it becomes in the lower stages, is sandwiched dramatically between two mighty pillars of rock.

Cinque Torri, on the road up to Passo Falzareggo, is the pick of the smaller ski areas. The lifts here are modern, and at peak times Cinque Torri offers some of the best and usually least crowded skiing in the region. This season sees the opening of a link between here and Passo Falzareggo, the base station for the cable car that takes you up to Lagazuoi at 2800m for the scenic Hidden Valley run down to Armentarola and a link into the Sella Ronda.

The old lift climbs a cliff-face dotted with windows into a rabbit warren of First World War tunnels that connected gun emplacements and observation posts. These can be explored with a guide in summer, but not in winter.

With skiers arriving from both sides of the pass, the queue for the cable car can last an hour. But the reward is an 8km red rollercoaster that takes you down past a spectacular frozen turquoise waterfall to Armentarola. You have to return to Passo Falzareggo and to Cortina by bus.

Learn

Azzurra, **t** +39 0436 2694, and **Ski Snowboard Cortina**, **t** +39 0436 2911, are both recommended by reporters. The others are **Cristallo-Cortina**, **t** +39 0436 870 073, **Dolomiti-Cortina**, **t** +39 0436 862 264, and **Happy Ski**, **t** +39 335 622 0229. **Scuola Fondo Ski Cortina**, **t** +39 0436 2911, and **Fondo Morotto**, **t** +39 0436 862 201, are both based at the Fiames Nordic Centre and teach cross-country.

Children

As in most resorts, specialist childcare facilities are minimal because the Italians tend to take granny with them on holiday. **Gulliver Park Kindergarten**, **t** +39 340 055 8399, in the Pocol sector, cares for children aged up to 11 years. Four other games parks cater for children, including **Adrenaline Park**, **t** +39 +39 0436 860 808, which is in a wood of 3000 sq m with 39 platforms fixed onto the larchs and as many suspended crossings. Babysitting is available with **Facciamo un Nido**, **t** +39 0436 861 776.

Lunch

Rifugio Averau, t +39 0436 4660, in Cinque Torri, heads the list and is famous for its homemade pasta including *pappardelle con funghi*. Don't confine your choice to one type of pasta – on request, three are served on a single plate. **Rifugio Duca d'Aosta, t** +39 0436 2780, in the Tofana/Socrepes sector, is also recommended along with nearby **Rifugio Pomedes, t** +39 0436 862 061.

Dinner

Dine at Michelin-starred **Tivoli, t** +39 0436 866 400, in an intimate atmosphere enhanced by panelled walls decorated with copper pans and a wood-burning stove in one corner. **El Toula, t** +39 0436 3339, is a converted three-storey hay barn with a rustic atmosphere. **Leone e Anna, t** +39 0436 2768, is a tiny, romantic Sardinian restaurant that has been pleasing the palates of Cortina for over 30 years. **Meloncino al Camineto, t** + 39 0436 4432, has a traditional ambience and good quality food. **Zanvor, t** +39 0436 860 789, and **La Tavernetta, t** +39 0436 868 102, are both recommended. Half a dozen good pizzerias abound, as well as **Vienna, t** +39 0436 866 944, which has a wide choice of pizzas.

Party

Party in the early evening at one of six wine bars – the best known is **Enoteca**. The others are **Villa Sandi**, **Brio Divino**, **Pane Vino e San Daniele**, **El Becalen** and the new **La Suite**. **DOK-LP26** is a curious mixture of *prosciutteria* and cocktail bar with live music. It is owned by the millionaire Italian builder who constructed most of Val d'Isère and the new village in Les Arcs. The **VIP Club Piano Bar** at the Hotel Europa and the **BLV Room** liven up after midnight, along with the **Limbo** and the **Bilbo Club**. **Disco Belvedere** at Pocol has a youthful following.

Sleep

- ★★★★★**Hotel Cristallo t** +39 0436 4281, *www.cristallo.it*, is situated a five-minute uphill walk from the centre. Rooms are decorated in Gustavian style with hand-painted woodwork and delicate frescoes.
- ★★★★★**Miramonti Majestic Grand, t** +39 0436 4201, *www.miramontimajestic.it*, 2km out of town, is an imposing *fin-de-siècle* palace. It has wellness centre and a large indoor pool.
- ★★★★**Hotel Ancora, t** +39 0436 3261, *www.hotelancoracortina.com*, situated in the heart of the Corso Italia, is convenient for the nightlife. Its Terrazza Viennese is a resort meeting place.
- ★★★★**Hotel de la Poste, t** +39 0436 4271, *www.delaposte.it*, in the pedestrianized centre, is an old coaching inn and another resort rendezvous that has been run for generations by the Manaigo family. Some of the rooms are rather small, but the bathrooms are large.
- ★★★★**Parc Hotel Victoria, t** +39 0436 3246, *www.hotelvictoriacortina.com*, has a solid reputation and is conveniently situated at the beginning of the Corso Italia.
- ★★★★**Hotel Ambra, t** +39 0436 867 344, *www.hotelambracortina.it*, is an ancient building close to the clock tower, which has been refurbished as a 25-room boutique hotel.
- ★★★**Hotel Aquila, t** +39 0436 2618, *www.aquilacortina.com*, at the far end of the Corso Italia, is family-run and friendly with an indoor pool.
- ★★★**Hotel Menardi, t** +39 0436 2400, *www.hotelmenardi.it*, is a mid-19th-century farmhouse. Its original

decoration incorporates the Menardi family's memorabilia.

★★★**Hotel Olimpia**, t +39 0436 868 524, *www.hotelolimpiacortina.com*, is a reasonably priced, central B&B.

Corvara

Profile

Attractive, sophisticated village with great hotels and superb restaurants that acts as a convenient base for exploring the Sella Ronda

Resort

Corvara is a sprawling but sophisticated village that makes one of the most convenient bases from which to explore the Sella Ronda. It has on-mountain links towards Arabba in one direction and Selva in the other, while off the circuit, you can ski to Colfosco, La Villa, San Cassiano, Armentarola and Pedraces.

Mountain

The modern Boè gondola takes you towards Arabba on the clockwise circuit of the Sella Ronda. It is also the most efficient means of reaching Corvara's own ski area as well as the extensive sunny slopes that it shares with San Cassiano, Armentarola, La Villa and Pedraces.

From near the gondola base, a quad-chair takes you on the anti-clockwise route towards Colfosco and Selva. The slopes around Corvara are perfect for intermediates. However, many of the lifts away from the circuit are frustratingly slow.

Learn

Corvara-Ladinia, t +39 0471 836 126, and **Colfosco**, t +39 0471 836 218, are schools with good reputations. **La Villa**, t +39 0471 847 258, and **Pedraces**, t +39 0471 839 648, are the other schools in the area.

Children

Skikinderland, t +39 0471 836 126, cares for children from two years, and **Skiminiclub**, t +39 847 715, is in Pedraces.

Lunch

Try **Capanna Nera/Neger Hütte**, t +39 0471 836 138, at the bottom of the Pralongia piste. **Baita La Marmotta**, t +39 0471 836 125, and **Punta Trieste**, t +39 0471 836 643, both on Pralongia, and **Mesoles**, t +39 0471 836 023, near Colfosco, are recommended.

Dine

Stua di Michil, t +39 0471 831 000, is the Michelin-starred restaurant in Hotel La Perla. The 16th-century **Stüa dl'Jagher**, t +39 0471 836 085, in Hotel Sassongher has the atmosphere of the hunting lodge it once was. **La Tambra**, t +39 0471 836 281 specializes in Mediterranean cuisine.

✻ BEST FOR

High-mileage intermediates, ski gourmets, comfort-seekers

ESSENTIALS

Altitude: 1324m (4,369ft)–2778m (9,167ft)

Further information: t +39 0471 836 176, *www.altabadia.org*

Lifts in area: 51 in Alta Badia (9 cableways, 29 chairs, 13 drags) serving 130km of piste; 450 lifts in Dolomiti Superski area

Lift pass: Dolomiti Superski adult €168–191, child 8–16yrs €118–134, both for six days

Access: Verona airport 2½hrs

Hotel Alisander, **t** +39 0471 836 055, is renowned for fresh fish. **Stüa Ladina**, **t** +39 0471 836 083, in the Sporthotel Panorama provides local cuisine.

Party

Grillkeller Adler and the **Veranda Keller** are noisy. Piano bars in Hotel Sassongher, **La Perla**, and **Table** are more sophisticated. Popular **Posta Zirm Taverna** is the late spot.

Sleep

★★★★**La Perla**, **t** +39 0471 831 000, *www.hotel-laperla.it*, has walls adorned with carved angels and floors covered with Oriental rugs. 'If you want a hotel where the staff know your name before you've even said hello this is the place,' said a reporter.

★★★★**Posta Zirm Hotel**, **t** +39 0471 836 175, *www.postazirm.com*, has a spa and pool designed to feng shui principles.

★★★★**Hotel Sassongher**, **t** +39 0471 836 085, *www.sassongher.it*, is traditional with a sound reputation.

★★★**La Plaza**, **t** +39 0471 836 011, *www.laplaza.it*, is recommended.

★★★**Hotel Gran Ciasa t**, +39 0471 836 138, *www.granciasa.com*, in Colfosco, is recommended.

Courmayeur

Profile

Lovely old town on the Italian side of the Mont Blanc Tunnel, with dramatic scenery, but limited piste skiing. Superb restaurants both on and off the slopes and a lively nightlife

*BEST FOR

Intermediates and experts, romantics, serious lunchers, night-owls

ESSENTIALS

Altitude: 1200m (3,937ft)–2624m (8,609ft)
Further information **t** +39 0165 842 060, *www.aiat-monte-bianco.com*
Lifts in area: 17 (6 cableways, 8 chairs, 3 drags) serving 100km of piste
Lift pass: Aosta Valley (includes Courmayeur, La Thuile, La Rosière and Champoluc-Gressoney-Alagna) adult €195, child 6–12yrs €97.50, both for six days
Access: Geneva airport 1½hrs, Turin airport 1½hrs, Milan Malpensa 2hrs, Bergamo 3hrs. Railway station at Pré-St-Didier 5km, regular buses from station

Resort

Courmayeur is a charming and relatively small resort, a pretty village with nice shops – although more for window-shopping than spending, unless you have a large bank balance.

This is one of the great ski and climbing villages of the Alps, an ancient community situated just below the Italian end of the Mont Blanc Tunnel at the foot of the mightiest mountain in Western Europe. Like nearby Chamonix, its proximity by autoroute to Geneva airport makes it popular with weekenders from other countries, while Italians from Milan and Turin arrive in high numbers on Friday evenings.

Despite being no more than a 20-minute drive from Chamonix, Courmayeur has an entirely different weather pattern, thanks to the towering intervening presence of Mont Blanc. The snow is not always as good on the Italian side, but Courmayeur gets much more sunshine during the course of the winter.

The heart of the old village is the cobbled and pedestrianized Via Roma, lined with boutiques, bars, delicatessens and expensive interior decoration and antique shops. Steep and narrow cobbled

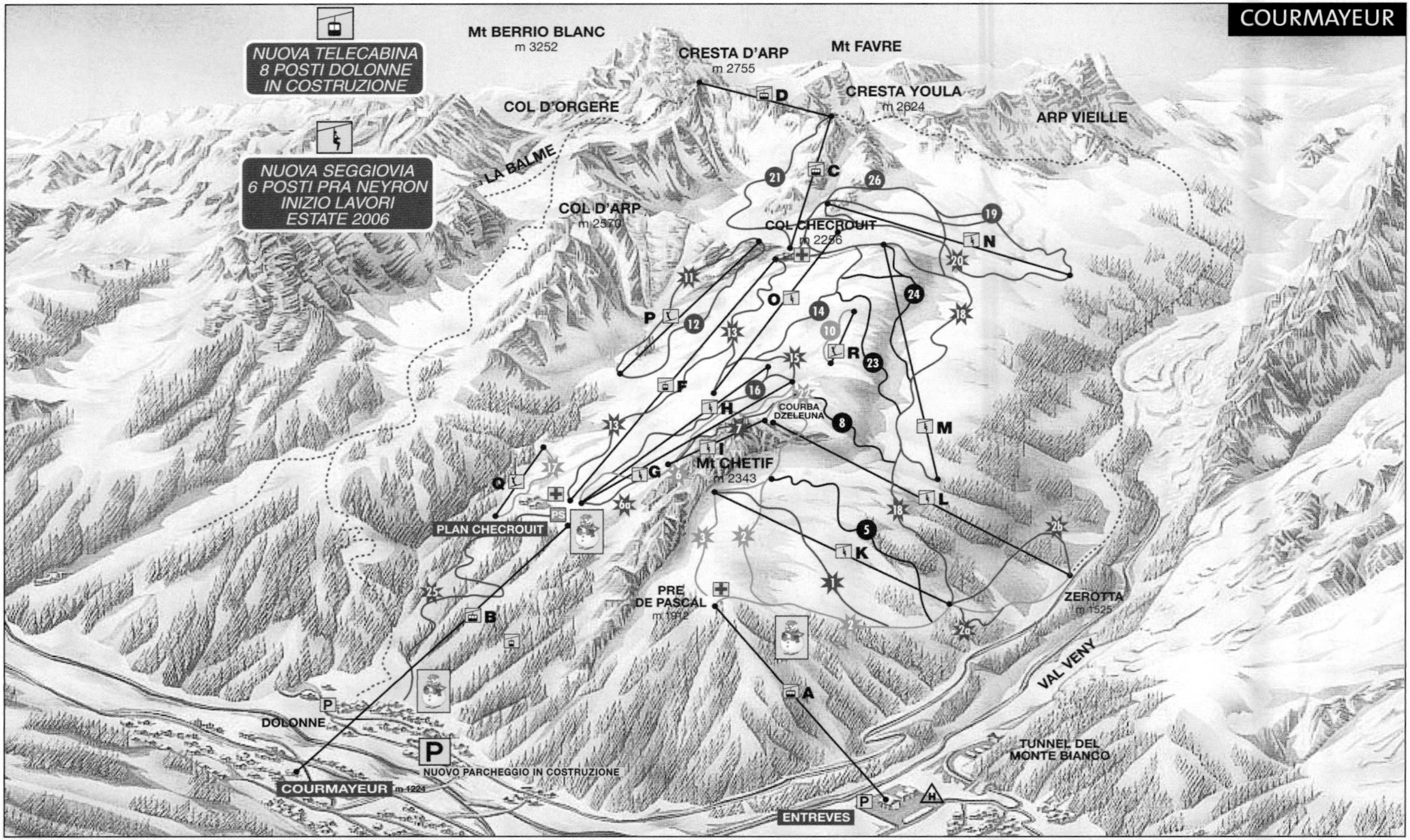

COURMAYEUR

NUOVA TELECABINA
8 POSTI DOLONNE
IN COSTRUZIONE

NUOVA SEGGIOVIA
6 POSTI PRA NEYRON
INIZIO LAVORI
ESTATE 2006

Mt BERRIO BLANC
m 3252
CRESTA D'ARP
m 2755
Mt FAVRE
CRESTA YOULA
m 2624
ARP VIEILLE
COL D'ORGERE
LA BALME
COL D'ARP
m 2570
COL CHECROUIT
m 2256
COURBA DZELEUNA
Mt CHETIF
m 2343
PLAN CHECROUIT
PRE DE PASCAL
m 1912
ZEROTTA
m 1525
VAL VENY
TUNNEL DEL MONTE BIANCO
DOLONNE
NUOVO PARCHEGGIO IN COSTRUZIONE
COURMAYEUR m 1224
ENTREVES

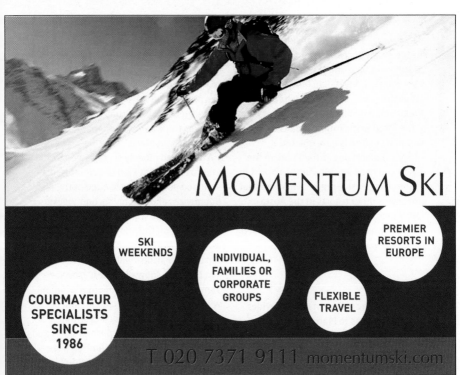

MOMENTUM SKI

SKI WEEKENDS

PREMIER RESORTS IN EUROPE

INDIVIDUAL, FAMILIES OR CORPORATE GROUPS

COURMAYEUR SPECIALISTS SINCE 1986

FLEXIBLE TRAVEL

T 020 7371 9111 momentumski.com

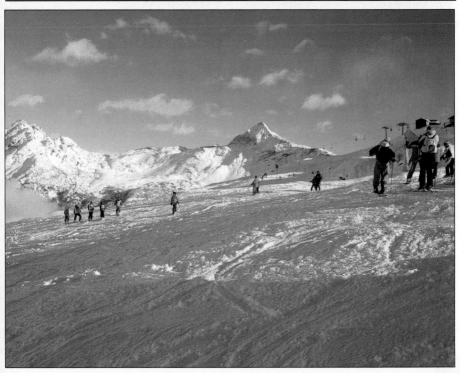

alleyways lead off on either side. Eating is the alternative occupation to skiing, with Courmayeur boasting the best mountain restaurants of any Italian resort as well a delightful choice of evening eateries. A relatively new highway to the entrance of the Mont Blanc Tunnel means that National Road 26 is now quieter.

To get the best out of the skiing in the region you need a car. It's best to invest in the more expensive regional lift pass that also covers other resorts in the Aosta Valley such as Pila, Champoluc and Gressoney, as well as La Thuile and linked La Rosière in France.

Mountain

A cable car from Courmayeur provides mountain access to Plan Chécrouit, the main hub of this moderately compact ski area facing Mont Blanc. It can also be reached by the Val Veny cable car from Entrèves, close to the Mont Blanc Tunnel. A gondola also provides direct access to Plan Chécrouit from the hamlet of Dolonne. You can ski back down a blue piste and a ski bus links Dolonne to Courmayeur. However, at the end of the day most skiers still find it more convenient to download by cable car directly to Courmayeur. Skis and boots can be left at Plan Chécrouit. The lift queues are surprisingly short at peak times.

From Plan Chécrouit, a small network of lifts takes you up to Col Chécrouit at 2256m. Two ancient cable cars rise to higher Cresta Youla and Cresta d'Arp. The latter is the 2755m starting point for some outstanding off-piste runs that take you down through 1500m of vertical to Dolonne, or through the scenic Vallon de Youla to the village of La Balme at the foot of the Petit-St-Bernard pass. These itinerary runs require no special technical skills, but it's easy to get lost and the risk of avalanche is ever-present. It makes sense to ski them with a local guide.

Other lifts from Plan Chécrouit bring you to the shoulder of 2343m Mont Chétif for the pick of Courmayeur's piste skiing – mainly red and black runs leading down towards the Val Veny, with magnificient views of Mont Blanc.

A dedicated nursery slope served by the Chiecco draglift at Plan Chécrouit is in a secluded position on the edge of the piste. But novices and wobbly second-weekers must otherwise contend with heavy traffic converging on the mid-mountain station. More easy slopes are to be found at the top of the Maison Vieille chairlift.

In the right snow conditions, the Val Veny slopes offer hours of entertainment, with a few surprisingly challenging pistes such as the black Pista dell'Orso and Diretta. However, accomplished skiers and riders will soon tire of the limited piste skiing available from Plan Chécrouit. They should head to the other side of Courmayeur to ride the three-stage Mont Blanc cable car at La Palud, near the village of Entrèves. This takes you all the way up to Punta Helbronner at 3462m, where you can descend the Vallée Blanche to Chamonix – without having to negotiate the infamous ice-steps on the French side.

A number of descents of varying difficulty and danger are possible on the Italian side of Mont Blanc and you are strongly recommended to use a local guide. Spectacular heli-skiing is also possible, with a number of fixed drops above the Val Veny.

There is a snowcross course served by the Plan de la Grabba chair and a rail park by the Le Greye drag above Plan Chécrouit. Val Ferret, at the foot of the Grandes Jorasses a few minutes' drive from Courmayeur, is the setting for 20km of spectacular cross-country trails.

Learn

Monte Bianco, **t** +39 0165 842 477, and **Courmayeur**, **t** +39 0165 848 254, are the main schools. Both have a sound reputation for teaching modern technique. However, not all instructors are fluent English-speakers. **Interski**, **t** +44 (0)1623 456 333, is a British tour operator with its own school. Guiding is available from **Società delle Guide Alpine di Courmayeur**, **t** +39 0165 842 064, **High Performance Mountain**, **t** +39 335 634 2771, **Guide Alpine del Monte Bianco**, **t** +39 347 435 0182, **Sirdar Montagne et Aventure**, **t** +39 346 578 9776, and heli-skiing with **Air Vallée**, **t** +39 0165 869 814.

Children

Kinderheim, **t** +39 0165 842 477, at Plan Chécrouit, cares for children from newborn to 12 years with an alternative pick-up and drop-off point at the foot of the cable car. Both Italian ski schools give lessons to children from four years upwards ('the ski instructor had a great way with the kids, gave them confidence and good technical skills').

Lunch

The mountain huts and restaurants are excellent, with all budgets catered for. **Rifugio Maison Vieille**, **t** +39 337 230 979, serves grilled meat and fine pasta. 'I recommend either booking or going early as it does get busy – but the food is worth it,' said a reader. **Hotel Christiania**, **t** +39 0165 843 572, at Plan Chécrouit, is a gastronomic delight. **Chiecco**, **t** +39 338 700 3035, is warmly recommended ('fantastic home-cooked food and very friendly service'). **La Grolla**, **t** +39 0165 869 095, on the Val Veny side, has lots of atmosphere and fine cuisine. On the Mont Blanc side, **Rifugio Pavillon**, **t** +39 0165 844 090, at the top of the first stage of the cable car, has a sunny terrace and great food. **Rifugio Torino**, **t** +39 0165 844 034, at the second stage, is also recommended.

Dine

Pierre Alexis 1877, **t** +39 0165 843 517, is still the top eaterie in town and has a particularly extensive wine list. **Cadran Solaire**, **t** +39 0165 844 609, is a close contender for cuisine and atmosphere. **Mont Fréty**, **t** +39 0165 841 786, and **La Terrazza**, **t** +33 0165 843 330, are also recommended. **La Maison de Filippo**, **t** +39 0165 869 797, in the suburb of Entrèves, is an exercise in unparalleled gluttony; it offers a fixed-price menu of more than 30 courses.

Party

Bar Roma and **Bar Americano** have 'good atmosphere, music and free food'. **Cadran Solaire** attracts the smart crowd. **Les Privé**, **Bar Posta** and **Bar delle Guide** both have lots of atmosphere. Poppy's is rated: 'The food was good and inexpensive, and there was music or football on most nights.' **I Maquis** in Entrèves is the best nightspot. **Jimmy Night Café** and **Planet** are the others.

Sleep

- ★★★★**Auberge de la Maison**, **t** +39 0165 869 811, *www.aubergemaison.it*, in the hamlet of Entrèves, is friendly and has attractive rooms.
- ★★★★**Gran Baita**, **t** +39 0165 844 040, *www.sogliahotels.com*, is comfortable, but set outside the town.
- ★★★★**Hotel Les Jumeaux**, **t** +39 0165 846 796, is in a great location next to the cable car.

★★★★**Hotel Pavillon**, t +39 0165 846 120, *www.pavillon.it*, has a pool and sauna.

★★★★**Royal e Golf**, t +39 0165 831 611, *www.royalegolf.com*, is close to the centre.

★★★**Hotel Courmayeur**, t +39 0165 846 732, *www.hotelcourmayeur.com*, has an open fire in the sitting room and is rated 'very friendly, with good food '.

★★★**Bouton d'Or**, t +39 0165 846 729, *www.hotelboutondor.com*, is a firm favourite: 'In a good location with clean, comfortable rooms.'

★★★**Hotel Dolonne**, t +39 0165 846 674, *www.hoteldolonne.com*, is a family hotel in the hamlet of the same name. It has some interesting antiques and log fires. 'I would have assessed it as a two-star rather than three-star, it was however clean and the food acceptable.'

★★★**Hotel Meublé Laurent**, t +39 0165 846 687, *www.meublelaurent.com*, has recently been renovated. The rooms are cosy and traditional.

★★★**Hotel Walser**, t +39 0165 844 824, *www.walserhotel.com*, is praised: 'Great food, great rooms and very friendly staff. I can't fault it on anything.'

Kronplatz

Profile

A ski area rather than a single resort in the South Tyrol that has the most sophisticated network of gondolas in the world, but is largely unknown in Britain

Resort

Kronplatz has a remarkable 19 modern gondolas and is one of the great secrets of the South Tyrol. It is the top Italian ski resort for Germans, but has remained virtually unknown in the UK. It is now linked (with a short bus ride) into the main Alta Badia lift system, with connections into the Sella Ronda.

The dome-shaped mountain, also known as Plan de Corones, is a ski area rather than a single centre. Accommodation is in the nearby town of Bruneck (Brunico) and in a dozen small villages around the mountain base. Only San Vigilio di Marebbe is Italian- and Ladino-speaking. One reporter stayed in Olang: 'Five minutes from the main lifts and the bus arrived every 10 minutes. The lift system is the best I have experienced in Europe.'

* BEST FOR

Intermediate skiers and snowboarders in search of high mileage

ESSENTIALS

Altitude: 900m (2,953ft)–2275m (7,464ft)
Further information: t +39 0474 555 447, *www.kronplatz.com*
Lifts in area: 31 (19 cableways, 6 chairs, 6 drags) serving 105km of piste; 450 lifts serving 1220km of piste in Dolomiti Superski area
Lift pass: Dolomiti Superski adult €184–254, child 8–16yrs €129–178, both for six days
Access: Innsbruck airport 1¾hrs, railway station at Bruneck 10mins

Mountain

Kronplatz has the somewhat unfair reputation of being a 'ski factory'. Its collection of super-lifts allows enormous numbers of skiers to reach the dome-shaped summit and descend on all sides. If you have the energy, you can clock up a remarkable mileage here in a single day. Most of the descents are undemanding, but the black Sylvester and the Herrneg rollercoaster provide challenge. Mountain access by gondola is from Olang, Bruneck/Reischach, San Vigilio or San Martino in Badia/Picculin.

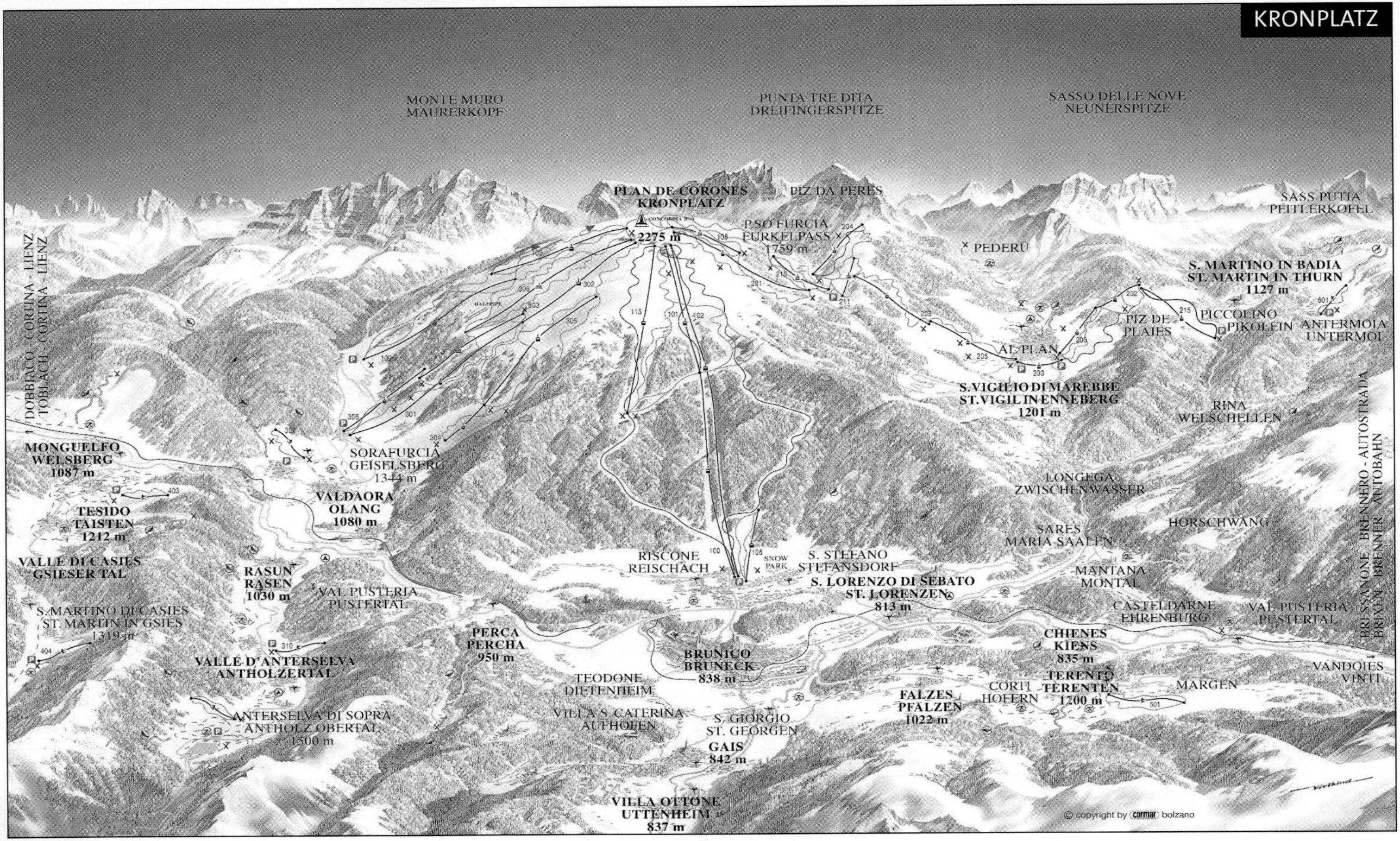

MONTE MURO
MAURERKOPF
PUNTA TRE DITA
DREIFINGERSPITZE
SASSO DELLE NOVE
NEUNERSPITZE
PLAN DE CORONES
KRONPLATZ
2275 m
PIZ DA PERES
SASS PUTIA
PEITLERKOFEL
P.SO FURCIA
FURKELPASS
1759 m
PEDERU
S. MARTINO IN BADIA
ST. MARTIN IN THURN
1127 m
PIZ DE
PLAIES
PICCOLINO
PIKOLEIN
ANTERMOIA
UNTERMOI
AL PLAN
S.VIGILIO DI MAREBBE
ST.VIGIL IN ENNEBERG
1201 m
RINA
WELSCHELLEN
DOBBIACO - CORTINA - LIENZ
TOBLACH - CORTINA - LIENZ
MONGUELFO
WELSBERG
1087 m
SORAFURCIA
GEISELSBERG
1344 m
VALDAORA
OLANG
1080 m
TESIDO
TAISTEN
1212 m
VALLE DI CASIES
GSIESER TAL
RASUN
RASEN
1030 m
VAL PUSTERIA
PUSTERTAL
S.MARTINO DI CASIES
ST. MARTIN IN GSIES
1319 m
RISCONE
REISCHACH
SNOW PARK
S. STEFANO
STEFANSDORF
S. LORENZO DI SEBATO
ST. LORENZEN
813 m
LONGEGA
ZWISCHENWASSER
SARES
MARIA SAALEN
HORSCHWANG
MANTANA
MONTAL
CASTELDARNE
EHRENBURG
VAL PUSTERIA
PUSTERTAL
BRESSANONE - BRENNERO - AUTOSTRADA
BRIXEN - BRENNER - AUTOBAHN
PERCA
PERCHA
950 m
BRUNICO
BRUNECK
838 m
CHIENES
KIENS
835 m
VANDOIES
VINTL
VALLE D'ANTERSELVA
ANTHOLZERTAL
TEODONE
DIETENHEIM
TERENTO
TERENTEN
1200 m
CORTI
HOFERN
MARGEN
FALZES
PFALZEN
1022 m
ANTERSELVA DI SOPRA
ANTHOLZ OBERTAL
1500 m
VILLA S. CATERINA
AUFHOFEN
S. GIORGIO
ST. GEORGEN
GAIS
842 m
VILLA OTTONE
UTTENHEIM
837 m

© copyright by cormar bolzano

Learn

Valdaora/Rasen, t +39 0474 592 091, teaches new technique in a friendly manner. The other schools are **Kronplatz/Plan de Corones, t** +39 0474 548 474, **San Vigilio, t** +39 0474 501 049, **Sporting Al Plan, t** +39 0474 501 448, and **Cima, t** +39 0474 497 216.

Children

'Excellent skiing for all the family,' said a reader. The resort has seven nursery slopes and a mountain restaurant especially designed for children. **Croniworld, t** +39 0474 548 474, is on the summit and cares for children from three to eight years. Olang–Rasen and St Vigilio villages both have kindergartens.

Lunch

Herzlalm, t +39 0474 550 723, is a rustic hut with waiter service, reached by the Pramstall piste. **Bergfreunder Hütte, t** +39 0474 548 049, by the valley station of the Gipfelbahn, is recommended. **Berggasthof Graziani, t** +39 0474 501 158, on piste no.12 has a welcoming atmosphere and traditional cuisine. **Oberegger Alm, t** +39 347 522 0122, a 17th-century farmhouse on the run down to Olang, is renowned for its dumplings and *Speck* and cabbage salad.

Dine

In Olang, **Pizzeria Petrus, t** +39 0474 496 202, and **Christl, t** +39 0474 498 212, are praised. In San Vigilio, **Fana Ladina, t** +39 0474 501 175, specializes in Ladino cuisine. In Bruneck, **Weisses Lamm, t** +39 0474 411 350, is a traditional inn.

Party

In Reischach, German-style après ski begins before the lifts close at the **Tenne**, **Igli Bar Gigger, K1**. Olang has a similar scene at **Ski Toni** and **Skistadl**. Lively **Igloo** is in San Vigilio. Bruneck has a more cosmopolitan choice of bars and discos.

Sleep

Bruneck:

- ******Hotel Petrus, t** +39 0474 548 263, *www.hotelpetrus.com*, has a warm atmosphere.
- ******Royal Hotel Hinterhuber, t** +39 0474 541 000, *www.royal-hinterhuber.com*, is traditional.

Olang:

- ******Hotel Mirabell**, t +39 0474 496 191, *www.mirabell.it*, has a first-rate spa.
- ******Hotel Post, t** +39 0474 496 127, *www.post-tolderhof.com*, has comfortable rooms and a separate six-bedroom Art Nouveau villa.

San Vigilio:

- ******Parc Hotel Posta, t** +39 0474 501 010,*www.parchotel-posta.com*, is family-friendly.
- ******Wellness Hotel Almhof Call, t** +39 0474 501 043, *www.almhof-call.com*, has a pool built into the rocks.

Livigno

Profile

Most remote and one of the cheapest of all Alpine resorts. The town's duty-free status encourages an alcohol-fuelled nightlife

***BEST FOR**

First-timers, value, nightlife

ESSENTIALS

Altitude: 1816m (5,956ft)–2800m (9,184ft)
Further information: t +39 0342 052 200, *www.livigno.eu*
Lifts in area: 31 (4 cableways, 14 chairs, 13 drags) serving 105km of piste
Lift pass: adult €144–170.50, child under 15yrs €101.50–118, both for six days
Access: Zurich airport 5hrs, Bergamo and Milan airports 4hrs, railway station at Tirano 2½hrs

Resort

Duty-free Livigno is the cheapest and also the most inaccessible of all mainstream resorts in the Alps. Its fiscal privileges date back to 1600 and were confirmed by Napoleon in 1805 and the EC in 1960. The resort can compete comfortably on price with Andorra, although the Pyrenean principality has the edge on skiing and accessibility. It's a tedious transfer from any airport. 'Get a good book, charge up the iPod or catch up on sleep, because it's a long trip from Bergamo,' warned a reporter.

Nevertheless, Livigno is a great beginner area for anyone who wants to discover skiing or snowboarding without huge financial commitment.

The village is divided into the four hamlets of Santa Maria, San Antonio, San Rocco and Trepalle. Of these, San Antonio is the main resort rendezvous, with the majority of hotels, bars and restaurants. A reporter summed it up: 'A picturesque resort with adequate skiing. The locals are friendly and the après ski is in plentiful supply.'

Mountain

On southeast-facing Carosello, a gondola rises to 3000m and five chairs, including the new Federia, serve undulating slopes above the tree-line. The area is ideally suited to beginners, who take their first slide on skis on a dozen nursery drags on Carosello. Intermediates will enjoy the steeper slopes on Monte Sponda and Il Mottolino, but advanced skiers will probably find too little to keep them busy for a week.

Readers remark on the general lack of lift queues and well groomed slopes. However, the resort attracts plenty of visitors over Christmas and New Year; expect lift queues and crowded mountain restaurants during these peak periods. It's better to go down to the village for lunch.

Learn

Ski classes here were said to be good fun, with quality instructors speaking excellent English. The schools are **Top Club Mottolino**, t +39 0342 970 822, **New Ski School Livigno**, t +39 0342 997 801, **Azzura Livigno**, t +39 0342 996 683, **Inverno/Estate**, t +39 0342 996 276, and **Livigno Italy**, t +39 0342 996 767. **Madness**, t +39 0342 997 792, is the specialist snowboard school. **Scuola Italiana Sci Fondo Livigno 2000**, t +39 0342 996 367, is the cross-country school.

Children

Peribimbi, t +39 0342 970 711, cares for non-skiers from 18 months to three years. **Miniclub Dau di Livigno**, T +39 0342 978 050, and **Miniclub & Babyclub**, t +39 0342 970 822 both accept babies. **M'eating Point**, t +39 0342 999 7408, takes children from three years. The ski schools provide lessons from four years.

Lunch

Try **La Costaccia**, t +39 0342 997 264, for its outdoor barbecue. **Tea da Borch**, t +39 0342 997 016, below **Carosello**, is recommended. **Camanel di Planon, t** +39 0342 970 025, above the main restaurant at the top of Teola lift, is a must. **Tea al Planei, t** +39 335 286 743, at Mottolino, and **Tea del Vidal, t** +39 0342 996 129, at Nottolino cableway base, are both rated.

Dine

'The restaurants are great and reasonably priced,' noted a reader. The Michelin-rated **La Pioda, t** +39 0342 997 610, is close to San Rocco church. **La Rusticana, t** +39 0342 996 047, is renowned for its pizzas. **Park Chalet Village, t** +39 0342 970 176, has lots of atmosphere and is good value. **Bellavista, t** +39 0342 997 334, is a must for genuine Italian food. Here and at **Ristorante Pizzeria Mario's, t** +39 0342 997 551, you should book early if you want to go on Friday or Saturday night.

Party

Early 20s really have a ball here – drinks are very good value, with plenty of lively bars, but also lots of quiet places to choose from. A reporter recommended the **Carosello** bar for music and dancing – 'sample the Bombadino, Livigno's traditional drink of hot advocaat, whisky and cream'. **Tea del Vidal** is 'a must', **Tea Borsch** is 'very wild' and **Galli's is** a busy bar. **Kokodi** and **Il Cielo** provide the late-night entertainment.

Sleep

★★★★**Hotel Amerikan, t** +39 0342 992 100, *www.amerikan.it*, has a wellness centre.

★★★★**Hotel Concordia Lungolivigno, t** +39 0342 990 100, *www.lungolivigno.com*, has attractive rooms.

★★★★**Hotel Intermonti, t** +39 0342 972 100, *www.valfin.it*, is in four chalets on the hillside.

★★★★**Hotel Spöl Charme and Relax, t** +39 0342 996 105, *www.hotelspol.it*, is in the town centre with a good spa.

★★★**Hotel Compagnoni, t** +39 0342 996 100, is at the heart of the resort – stay here for a real treat.

★★★**Hotel Europa, t** +39 0342 996 278, *www.europalivigno.it*, is directly on the bus route. Although the rooms are a little dated, the food is good and the staff are friendly.

★★★**Hotel Villaggio San Carlo, t** +39 0342 972 999, *www.valfin.it*, is set in seven chalets linked by internal corridors.

★★**Garni Sporting, t** +39 0342 996 665, *www.bormolinihotels.com* ('fab – the people were so friendly and the food delicious with lots of choice').

★★**Hotel San Giovanni, t** + 39 0342 970 515, *www.stgiovanni.com* ('so sweet, and the food was great'), is a family-run establishment at the foot of the slopes.

Madonna di Campiglio

Profile

Smart, traditional resort with good snowboarding. Excellent hotels, good restaurants and lively nightlife

Resort

Madonna has a traditional charm and village ambience, a real gem that attracts a curious combination of older skiers and young snowboarders who return here year after year – one in search of easy cruising and bodily comforts, the other for some of the best riding in Italy. Style is important: bring your best skiwear and also your fur coat – every woman seems to wear one at night.

The first chairlift opened for business here in 1948 and it has been a popular place with an international clientèle since the 1960s. By Italian standards, it is an expensive resort.

The village fathers have solved the problem of the through-traffic that used to plague the resort. A bypass has returned it to the congenial little mountain community that it used to be. New buildings blend well with the old.

Its wealthy guests demand, and get, a high standard of hotels. You can eat well here and, for those who live life in the fast lane, the nightlife is livelier than in most other Italian resorts. For one week each January the resort becomes the winter quarters of the Ferrari Formula One Team as they swap the pit lane for the piste. Kimi Raikkonen snowboards and former maestro Michael Schumacher even has a 45-degree black run named after him.

The resort is situated in the Brenta Dolomites, well to the west of the Sella Ronda, and is not included in the giant Dolomiti Superski lift pass. It is reached by a 75km serpentine climb from the Brenner–Verona *autostrada* through galleried tunnels and past spectacular drops.

Along with Cortina d'Ampezzo, Madonna attracts more glitterati than any other resorts in Italy. Like Cortina, not all its smart visitors venture on to the slopes. Shopping and eating out have both been raised to an art form, while skating on the scenic little lake provides alternative activity.

'If you're looking for relaxed skiing and civilized evenings (as opposed to expert terrain and wild partying) then Madonna is definitely worth a visit,' was how one reporter summed it up.

* BEST FOR

Sophisto-cats, intermediate skiers, snowboarders

ESSENTIALS

Altitude: 1520m (4,987ft)–2505m (8,219ft)
Further information: **t** +39 0465 447 501, *www.campiglio.it*
Lifts in area: 22 (5 cableways, 12 chairs, 5 drags) serving 60km of piste; 120 lifts including Marilleva/Folgarida, serving 340km of piste
Lift pass: Super Skirama Dolomiti (includes Madonna di Campiglio, Marilleva/Folgarida, Peio, Monte Bondone, Pinzolo, Paganella, Folgaria Lavarone and Passo Tonale) adult €176–199, child 8–17yrs, €142–160, both for six days
Access: Verona airport 2½hrs, regular bus from railway station at Trento 80km

Mountain

Madonna is officially rated the top resort in Italy for piste-grooming. This makes it popular with its slightly older than average clientèle, who revel in some of the most flattering slopes of the Dolomites. What at first sight appear to be three entirely separate ski areas covering the slopes on three sides of the village are in fact cunningly linked at valley level. The link is created by a snow-cannon-maintained piste that winds from one area to the other beneath a series of road bridges. 'An excellent, cleverly-linked modern lift system with queues a rarity,' said a reader.

The first area, Cinque Laghi, is reached on a new cable car from the centre of the village. This takes you up to a *rifugio* of the same name, starting point for an easy blue run that brings you to the Patascoss quad-chair. The 3-Tre piste from the top has a couple of sharp bends and dramatic changes in gradient. On the lower half of the mountain this red run turns a wicked shade of black as it becomes the notorious Canalone Miramonti, which used to be used as a World Cup course. The bottom half can also be reached by a double chairlift. The run is floodlit for night skiing.

From the northern end of town, a modern 12-person gondola takes you up to Pradalago at 2100m, the largest of the three ski areas. It is linked to the neighbouring resorts of Marilleva and Folgarida. Direct return to the resort is by the always challenging Amazzonia black, which crosses beneath the gondola. Less accomplished skiers and riders take the blue Pradalago Facile run, which follows a much gentler line around the shoulder. Two quad-chairs and a couple of drags access a pleasant mixture of easy and intermediate runs on Pradalago. Skiers heading for Marilleva and Folgarida, in the larger Skirama area, follow the red Genziana piste down to Malga Vigo.

The third area of Monte Spinale/Grostè is on the opposite side of the valley and is reached by a two-stage gondola from the east side of town. At 2443m this is the high point of the ski area. Cima Grostè and Corna Rossa, two short red pistes at the top, are served by a new six-person chair. The linked area of Monte Spinale can also be reached by gondola from the resort. *Spinale direttissima*, beneath the gondola, is one of the most enjoyable black runs in the resort.

The first terrain park was created here as long ago as 1993, and committed riders from all over the country gather each winter in the current park in the Grostè area.

Learn

The eight schools here all compete vigorously with one another for customers, but none stands out as being better than any of the rest. In general, the standard of teaching in Italian resorts does not reflect the enormous advances in equipment that has led to basic changes in technique. The schools are **Adamello Brenta, t** +39 0465 443 412, **Campo Carlo Magno, t** +39 0465 443 222, **5 Laghi, t** +39 0465 441 650, which is recommended, but only for the higher level, **Des Alpes, t** +39 0465 442 850, **Nazionale, t** +39 0465 443 243, **Professional Snowboarding, t** +39 0465 443 251, **Rainalter, t** +39 0465 443 300 ('a fantastic instructor'), and **Snowboard Zebra, t** +39 0465 442 080.

Children

All the ski schools offer lessons for children and some of them also have kindergartens.

Lunch

Chalet Fiat, t +39 0465 441 507, in 5 Laghi makes a startling change from the standard chalet-style mountain eatery. Snow-white upholstery and matching tablecloths, stripped wood floors and giant works of art on the walls complement the distinctly unalpine cuisine. You can even stay overnight in one of the all-white bedrooms with sheepskin throws. Try **Cascina Zeledria, t** +39 0465 440 303, just above the woods on Pradalago below Piste no.7. Artini, the owner, is a well-known local chef specializing in regional Trentino dishes. If you are lucky, you will get a tow by snowmobile back up to the piste. **Giorgio Graffer, t** +39 0465 441 358, on the blue run down from the top of Grostè, is a classic mountain refuge with homemade local dishes. **Rifugio Malga Montagnoli, t** +39 0465 443 355, at the bottom of Marchi black run on Monte Spinale, is one of the better self-service mountain restaurants in the area. **Rifugio Stoppani al Grostè, t** +39 0465 440 115, has been completely renovated.

Dine

Gallo Cedrone, **t** +39 0465 440 564, a gorgeous new eatery in Hotel Bertelli, has the top table in town ('feels a bit like you're eating in a stable – albeit a rather smart one with stripped wooden floors and beams, white linen tablecloths, smart charcoal and rust upholstery, and beaten silver candlesticks). **Da Alfiero**, **t** +39 0465 440 117, is known for its homemade spaghetti dishes and for lamb cutlets in balsamic vinegar with asparagus. **Al Sottobosco**, **t** +39 0465 440 737, is a kilometre from town, but worth the journey for its *pappardelle al mirtilli e funghi porcini* (pasta with blueberries and porcini mushrooms). **Artini**, **t** +39 0465 440 122, is famed for its risotto and its chocolate crêpes. **Osteria Al Sarca**, **t** +39 0465 440 287, has wonderful homemade salami, grilled alpine trout, and *panna cotta* with woodland fruits. **Antico Focolare**, **t** +39 0465 441 686, has a warm ambience and serves typical Trentino dishes including venison and polenta with gorgonzola and mushrooms. **La Locanda degli Artisti**, **t** +39 0465 442 980, has lots of atmosphere and good food at low prices. **Le Roi**, **t** +39 0465 443 075, and **Belvedere**, **t** +39 0465 440 396, are both warmly recommended. You can take a ride by snowcat at night to eat in **Cascina Zeledria**, **t** +39 0465 440 303, or at four other cowsheds that have been converted into mountain restaurants – **Malga Montagnoli**, **t** +39 0465 443 355, **Boch**, **t** +39 0465 440 465, **Malga Ritorto**, **t** +39 0465 442 470, and **Rifugio Stoppani**, **t** +39 0465 440 115.

Party

Ober 1 Bar at the foot of the Schumacher piste serves cocktails every day and sushi on Thursday. **Bar Suisse**, **La Cantina del Suisse** and the **Franz-Josef Stube** are the main après ski haunts. Try the **Maturi Bar** for *prosecco* and little snacks. **Bacchus Enotoca** is rated for its wines and the **Ferrari Lounge** has good prices.

Sleep

****__Alpen Suite Hotel__**, **t** +39 0465 440 100, *www.alpensuitehotel.it*, has 28 one-bedroom suites, each with its own sitting room.

****__Garni de Sogno__**, **t** +39 0465 441 033, *www.garnidelsogno.it*, offers 16 rooms, of which nine are individually decorated suites in soft colours and local woods such as larch and spruce.

****__Hotel Bertelli__**, **t** +39 0465 441 013, *www.hotelbertelli.it*, dates back to the 1930s and is traditional family hotel that was completely rebuilt in 1999. It is situated 50m from the Pradalago cable car.

****__Biohotel Hermitage__**, **t** +39 0465 441 558, *www.biohotelhermitage.it*, has been in the Maffei family for over 100 years and has been refurbished as an eco hotel. It is situated over a kilometre from the resort but operates a bus service to the lifts and shops. The accommodation, food and quality of service are second to none and the leisure facilities equally impressive.

****__Hotel Dahu__**, **t** +39 0465 440 242, *www.hoteldahu.it*, was rated 'a lovely hotel in an excellent position – Pradalago blue no. 10 takes you back directly to the hotel. Staff very friendly.'

****__Hotel Relais Club des Alpes__**, **t** +39 0465 446 238, *www.igrandiviaggi.it*, is also in a ski in, ski out position in the middle of the resort.

****__Hotel Lorenzetti__**, **t** +39 0465 441 404, *www.hotellorenzetti.com*, is on the edge of the piste and on the outskirts of the village.

****__Savoia Palace Hotel__** **t** +39 0465 441 004, *www.savoiapalace.com*, 50m from the 5 Laghi cable car, is a favourite with British visitors.

★★★★**Spinale Hotel**, **t** +39 0465 441 116, *www.spinalehotelcampiglio.it*, is close to the resort centre and skiing ('rooms are headache of colour and pattern, but the five suites are delightfully simple').

★★★★**Hotel Carlo Magno Zeledria**, **t** +39 0465 441 010, *www.hotelcarlomagno.com*, which has been run by the same family since 1947, is a lovely place, newly refurbished, with its own wellness centre and games room for kids. It is a little outside the town (2km), and the food is excellent but expensive.

★★★★**Hotel Bellavista t** +39 0465 441 034, *www.bellavistacampiglio.it*, has been upgraded to four-star and has a friendly atmosphere.

★★★**Grazia Hotel Plaza**, **t** +39 0465 443 100, *www.hotelgraziaeplaza.it*, is comfortable and conveniently located in the village centre.

Hotel Montana, **t** +39(0465)442 335, is said to be the best and friendliest *garni* in town.

Ortisei

Profile

The lowest and one of the most attractive of the Val Gardena villages, with links into both the Sella Ronda and the scenic Alpe de Suisi ski areas

Resort

Ortisei in the Val Gardena is a pretty alternative to nearby Selva. You can enjoy the skiing of the Sella Ronda, but also have direct access to the more secluded Alpe di Siusi. Pastel-painted and ornately frescoed buildings flank the main street and central piazza. Escalators and walkways provide easy access to the lifts.

*BEST FOR

Italian ambience, high-mileage skiers and riders

ESSENTIALS

Altitude: 1236m (4,055ft)–2949m (9,676ft)
Further information: t +39 0471 777 777, *www.valgardena.it*
Lifts in area: 83 (1 funicular, 9 cableways, 45 chairs, 28 drags) serving 175km of piste; 450 lifts serving 1220km of piste in Dolomiti Superski
Lift pass: Dolomiti Superski adult €167–209, child 8–16yrs €117–147, both for six days
Access: Verona airport 2hrs, railway station at Bolzano 1hr

Mountain

A long gondola, followed by a cable car, takes you up over a dramatic cliff-face to 2518m Seceda. From here, you can either return to the village, or continue to Pla da Tieja above Santa Cristina. This is the terminal for the underground funicular that effectively links Ortisei into the Sella Ronda and beyond.

On the southern edge of Ortisei, reached by a pedestrian bridge, a gondola acts as the gateway to the Alpe di Siusi. From the top station, you can reach the Alpe di Siusi plateau, where a few modern hotels have sprung up in recent years.

Learn

Ortisei, **t** +39 0471 796 153, and **Saslong**, **t** +39 0471 786 258, provide adequate instruction.

Children

Ortisei Ski School Miniclub cares for children from two years. **Hotel Cavallino Bianco Miniclub**, **t** +39 0471 783 333, takes children from one month to 12 years.

Lunch

Try **Sofie Hütte, t** +39 335 527 1240, at Seceda, and **Hotel Col Raiser, t** +39 0471 796 302, above Plan da Tieja. On the Alpe di Siusi side, stop at the **Sanon Hütte, t** +39 0471 727 002, or **Mont Seuc, t** +39 0471 727 881, at the top of the gondola.

Dine

Anna Stuben, t +39 0471 796 315, in the Hotel Gardena-Grödnerhof, serves local specialities. **Tubladel, t** +39 0471 796 879, is in a converted hay barn. **La Rosticceria, t** +39 335 617 4467, is renowned for its grilled meat and fish. **Concordia, t** +39 0471 796 276, makes its own smoked game and ham. **Vedl Mulin, t** +39 0471 796 089, is a popular pizzeria.

Party

Seceda and **Siglu**, at the Cavallino Bianco, are the main après ski rendezvous.

Sleep

★★★★★**Hotel Gardena-Grödnerhof, t** +39 0471 796315, *www.gardena.it*, has wood-panelled rooms, and an excellent spa.

★★★★**Hotel Adler, t** +39 0471 775 050, *www.hotel-adler.com*, has an impressive spa.

★★★★**Hotel Cavallino Bianco t** +39 0471 783 333, *www.cavallino-bianco.com*, was recently refurbished and has some of the most comprehensive child facilities of any ski resort.

★★★★**Hotel Hell, t** +39 0471 796 785, *www.hotelhell*, is situated in a heavenly ski in, ski out position.

★★★**Hotel Arnaria, t** +39 0471 796 649, *www.arnaria.com*, is a family-run pension.

★★★**Hotel Digon, t** +39 0471 797 266, *www.hoteldigon.com*, has recently been renovated.

Passo Tonale

Profile

Good-value village with snowsure skiing from late October until early May, as well as year-round summer skiing on the Presena Glacier

Resort

Passo Tonale is situated at the western end of the Val di Sole and its high altitude makes it one of the most snowsure resorts in Italy. Some 11 new lifts have transformed mountain access in recent years. National ski teams train here, and it has a strong international following.

Lift queues are not a problem here. 'Christmas week the après ski was practically non-existent, but on the bright side, there were no lift queues,' said a reporter, and 'there were no lift queues to speak of even though it was the New Year holiday period,' added another.

* BEST FOR

Intermediates, families, reliable snow cover

ESSENTIALS

Altitude: 1883m (6,178ft)–3069m (10,069ft)
Further information: **t** +39 0364 903 838, *www.valdisole.net*
Lifts in area: 30 (3 cableways, 19 chairs, 8 drags) serving 100km of piste
Lift pass: Super Skirama Dolomiti (includes Madonna di Campiglio, Marilleva/Folgarida, Peio, Monte Bondone, Pinzolo, Andalo/Paganella, Folgaria Lavarone and Passo Tonale/Ponte di Legno/Temu) adult €176–199, child from 8yrs €142–160, both for six days
Access: Bergamo airport 2hrs, Verona airport 2½hrs, railway stations at Edolo or Malè 30mins

Mountain

Passo Tonale has plenty of beginner and intermediate terrain ('plenty of skiing, though a bit limited for the better skiers'), with access by cable car to Passo Paradiso, where a chair and three drags bring you to the 3069m summit. From here, long runs lead back to the village over high-altitude terrain. On the other side of the main road, the south-facing slopes are served by a sequence of chairs and drags over undulating pastures. One chair takes you to the old smuggling route of Passo Contrabbandieri at 2681m. The resort is linked by two-stage gondola to the village of Ponte di Legno, with an 8km slope connecting the two resorts.

Learn

Tonale-Presena, **t** +39 0364 903 991, **Pontedilegno-Tonale**, **t** +39 0364 903 943, and **Castellaccio**, **t** +39 0364 900 302, have good reputations. **6punto9**, **t** +39 347 070 2699, is the snowboarding specialist.

Children

Miniclub, **t** +39 0364 900 501, in Hotel Miramonti cares for non-resident children from newborn to three years, and daycare for older children if they are hotel guests. **Fantaski**, **t** +39 0364 903 991, is the ski kindergarten.

Lunch

Capanna Presena, **t** +39 0463 758 299, at the top of the cable car, is recommended, as are **Rifugio Valbiolo**, **t** +39 0364 900 016, **Rifugio Negritella**, **t** +39 0364 900 661, and **Rifugio Bleis**, **t** +39 335 708 4266.

Dine

'The prices in bars and restaurants are around half of what you would expect to pay in say Les Arcs or Tignes,' said a reader. Try **Ristorante Rododendro**, **t** +39 0364 900 259, and **Serodine**, **t** +39 0364 903 724. Reporters praised pizzeria **Antares**, **t** +39 0364 903 789, and **Il Focalare**, **t** +39 0364 903 790. Others include **Mirandola**, **t** +39 0364 903 933, **Dahu**, **t** +39 0364 903 864, and **Ristorante Faita**, **t** +39 0364 91522.

Party

The resort is friendly and unpretentious. Try the **Umbrella Bar** or the Magic Pub after skiing. **Nico's Bar** is a popular resort rendezous. **Disco-Pub Miramonti** and **Heaven** are usually crowded and **Bar Paninoteca Cantuccio** stays open until 4am. **El Bait** is a 'great little bar with a good atmosphere'.

Sleep

****Grand Hotel Miramonti**, **t** +39 0364 900 501, *www.miramonti.com*, is the best hotel in town.

***Hotel Eden**, t +39 0364 03946, is on the main road through Tonale and four minutes walk from the lifts. Reporters found the hotel to be 'basic but the food was good and plentiful'.

***Hotel La Mirandola**, **t** +39 0364 903 933, is in old hospice up the mountain with snowmobile transport until 2am.

***Hotel Orchidea**, **t** +39 0364 903 935, *www.hotelorchidea.net*, is a comfortable family-run establishment.

***Hotel Panorama Edelweiss**, **t** +39 0364 903 789, *www.panoramaedelweiss.com*, offers good food.

***Sporthotel Vittoria**, **t** +39 0364 91348, is rated 'much better than any other three-star I have stayed in' by a reporter,

'The food was plentiful, lots of choice and the prices very good.'

*****Hotel La Torretta**, t +39 0364 903978, *www.hotellatorretta.com*, is in a perfect location and has mouth-watering pizzas.

San Cassiano

Profile

Small, sophisticated village that shares its unchallenging ski area with larger La Villa. Both are renowned for their designer hotels and gourmet restaurants

Resort

San Cassiano is a quiet, sophisticated village just off the main Sella Ronda circuit. Larger La Villa shares its immediate ski area, which is linked to Armentarola and Corvara. They make an attractive holiday base, but San Cassiano's links to and from the Sella Ronda are frustratingly slow.

***BEST FOR**
Comfort-lovers, ski gourmets, intermediates

ESSENTIALS

Altitude: 1537m (5,043ft)–2949m (9,676ft)
Further information: t +39 0471 849 422, *www.altabadia.org*
Lifts in area: 52 in Alta Badia (9 cableways, 29 chairs, 14 drags) serving 130km of piste; 450 lifts in Dolomiti Superski
Lift pass: Dolomiti Superski adult €184–254, child 8–16yrs €129–178, both for six days
Access: Verona airport 2½hrs

Mountain

Mountain access from San Cassiano and La Villa is by gondola and, even during peak season, queues are rare. In San Cassiano the lift station is a 10-minute walk from the centre, but the main hotels operate a courtesy minibus service. The immediate ski area consists of gentle pistes above and below the tree-line that are ideally suited to beginners and to intermediates who want the feeling of 'going somewhere' each day.

Learn

The choice lies between ski schools **San Cassiano**, **t** +39 0471 849491, **La Villa**, **t** +39 0471 847258, **Pedraces**, **t** +39 0471 839648, and **Dolomites**, **t** +39 0471 844018.

Children

La Villa ski school runs a kindergarten and miniclub. **Dolomites** ski school has a playground on Piz La Villa. **Casa Bimbo**, **t** +39 0471 838 096, in Pedraces, cares for babies and children up to 11 years.

Lunch

Try **Rifugio Scotoni**, **t** +39 0471 847330, above Armentarola, for barbecued meat in a warm ambience. Also recommended is the nearby **Capanna Alpina**, **t** +39 0471 847 330. **Malga Saraghes**, **t** +39 335 789 7164, above San Cassiano, has outstanding homemade pasta.

Dine

In San Cassiano, **St Hubertus**, **t** +39 0471 849 500, and **La Siriola**, **t** +39 0471 849 445, have Michelin stars. In La Villa, **Ciastel Colz**, **t** +39 0471 847 511, serves South Tyrol cuisine with gourmet flair.

Civetta 3218 m
Marmolada 3342 m
Sassolungo - Langkofel 3181 m
Porta Vescovo
PASSO PORDOI
PORDOI - PASS
2239 m
ALBA
CANAZEI
CAMPITELLO
Piz Sella
Ciampinoi
PASSO SELLA
SELLA - PASS
2242 m
PLAN DE GRALBA
SELVA VALGARDENA
WOLKENSTEIN
1566 m
PASSO GARDENA
GRÖDNERJOCH
2121 m
CAPRILE
BELLUNO
ARABBA
PASSO CAMPOLONGO
CAMPOLONGO - PASS
1875 m
COLFOSCO
1645 m
CORVARA
1568 m
COL PRADAT
Col Alt
PASSO FALZAREGO
FALZAREGO - PASS
2105 m
PASSO VALPAROLA
VALPAROLA - PASS
2168 m
LAGAZUOI
2778 m
ALTA BADIA
LA VILLA
1433 m
PEDRACES
1324 m
CENTRO FONDO
LANGLAUFZENTRUM
ARMENTAROLA
SAN CASSIANO
1537 m
S.LEONARDO
1371 m
SAN CASSIANO

The ski holiday specialists to San Cassiano, part of the fabulous Dolomiti ski area

Holidays of any duration for families, groups and individuals

•••

Ski weekends and short breaks

•••

Choice of departure and arrival airports

•••

Quality hand-picked hotels

•••

Swift minibus transfers

Roger Walker Travel

tr he

the real holiday experience

See our comprehensive website
at www.ski–2.com
call us on 01962 713330
or email us at
sales@ski–2.com

G8818
W3334

Party

The **Rosa Alpina** and **Siriola** both have wine bars. **Franz de la Vedla** and **Hug's** bar are both popular meeting places. In La Villa, the evening action is centred around **Durni's Pub** and **La Bercia**.

Sleep

San Cassiano:

- ****Rosa Alpina**, t +39 0471 849 500, *www.rosaalpina.it*, epitomizes the new wave of first-rate hotels being established in the Dolomites.
- ****Dolomiti Wellness Hotel Fanes**, t +39 0471 849 470, *www.hotelfanes.it*, offers good child reductions.
- ***Hotel Conturines-Posta** t +39 0471 849 464, *www.conturines.it*, is family-run.

La Villa:

- ****Ciastel Colz**, t +39 0471 84 7511, *www.colz.siriolagroup.it*, is a magnificently restored early 16th-century castle with four bedrooms.
- ***La Majun**, t +39 0471 847 030, *www.lamajun.it*, has quirky interior design and a pool lined with flagstones.
- ***Hotel La Villa**, t +39 0471 847 035, *www.hotel-lavilla.it*, has a small wellness area.

Sauze d'Oulx

Profile

Important value-for-money component of the giant Milky Way ski area with intermediate skiing and riding, decent restaurants and wild nightlife. Suits 20- and 30-somethings in search of piste and party

Resort

Sauze d'Oulx has a longstanding reputation as one of the party capitals of the snow, a place where pub culture takes precedence. However, we are beginning to see signs of it becoming a more family-friendly environment. 'Sauze is a friendly resort with lots of shops and bars to choose from, mostly child-friendly, without an imposing booze culture,' said a reporter.

Sauze is one of the main resorts of the 78-lift Milky Way/Vialattea circuit that straddles the border with France and provides a mighty 400km of groomed runs. Some of the best skiing in the region

*** BEST FOR**
High-mileage cruising, party-goers

ESSENTIALS

Altitude: 1509m (4,951ft)–2507m (8,225ft)
Further information: t +39 0122 858 009, *www.montagnedoc.it*
Lifts in area: 78 in Milky Way (6 cableways, 39 chairs, 33 drags) serving 400km of piste
Lift pass: Vialattea (covers Montgenèvre, Sestriere, Sauze d'Oulx and other smaller resorts) adult and child €155–175 for six days. Child under 8yrs free
Access: Turin airport 1hr, railway station at Oulx 5km, regular buses to resort

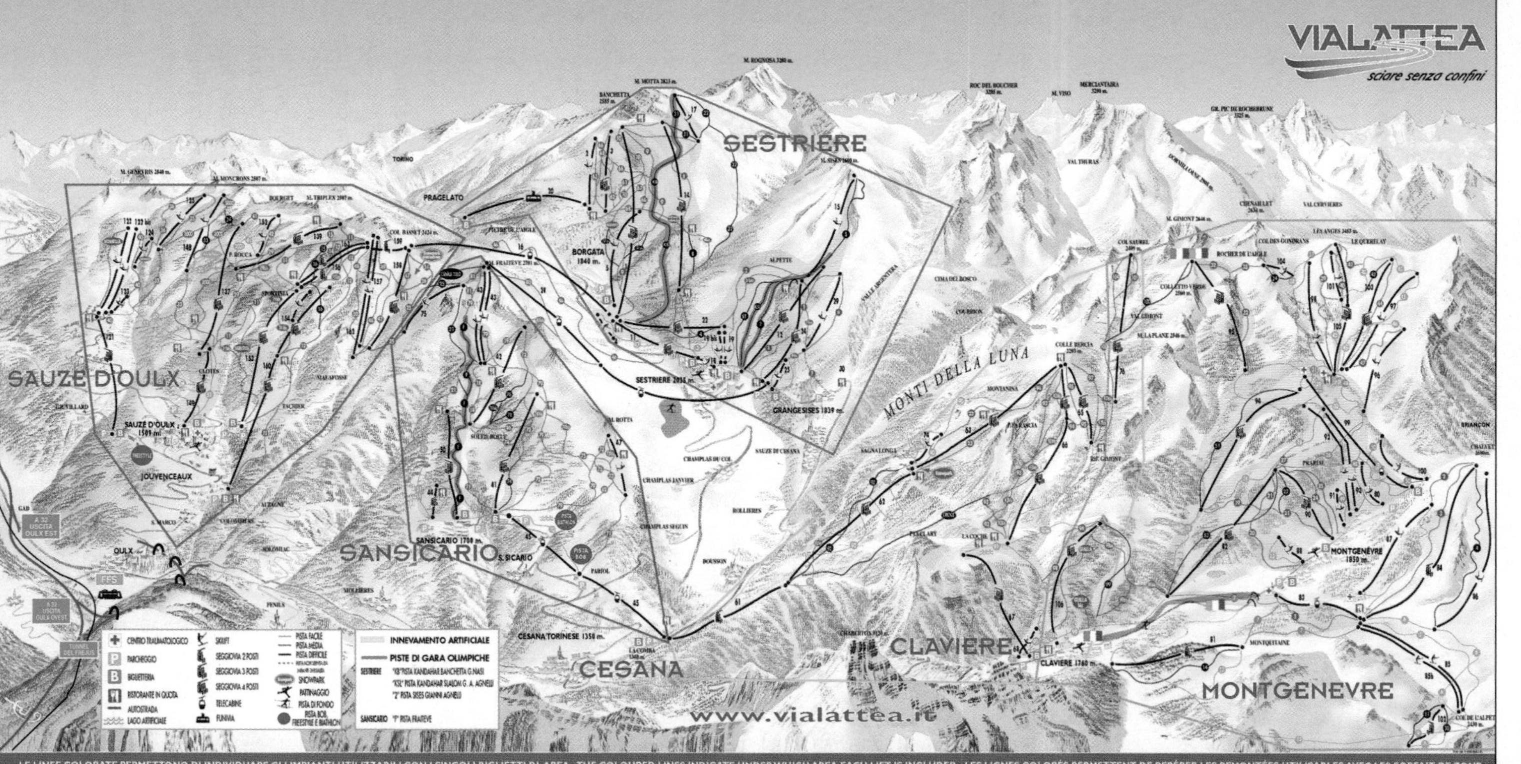
VIALATTEA
sciare senza confini
SAUZE D'OULX
SESTRIERE
SANSICARIO
CESANA
CLAVIERE
MONTGENEVRE
MONTI DELLA LUNA
PRAGELATO
BORGATA 1840 m.
SESTRIERE 2035 m.
GRANGESISES 1839 m.
SAUZE D'OULX 1509 m.
JOUVENCEAUX
OULX
SANSICARIO 1700 m.
CESANA TORINESE 1350 m.
CLAVIERE 1760 m.
MONTGENÈVRE 1850 m.
www.vialattea.it
CENTRO TRAUMATOLOGICO
PARCHEGGIO
BIGLIETTERIA
RISTORANTE IN QUOTA
AUTOSTRADA
LAGO ARTIFICIALE
SKILIFT
SEGGIOVIA 2 POSTI
SEGGIOVIA 3 POSTI
SEGGIOVIA 4 POSTI
TELECABINE
FUNIVIA
PISTA FACILE
PISTA MEDIA
PISTA DIFFICILE
SNOWPARK
PATTINAGGIO
PISTA DI FONDO
PISTA BOB, FREESTYLE E BIATHLON
INNEVAMENTO ARTIFICIALE
PISTE DI GARA OLIMPICHE
SESTRIERE "KB" PISTA KANDAHAR BANCHETTA G.NASI
"KSL" PISTA KANDAHAR SLALOM G. A. AGNELLI
"2" PISTA SISES GIANNI AGNELLI
SANSICARIO "F" PISTA FRAITEVE
LE LINEE COLORATE PERMETTONO DI INDIVIDUARE GLI IMPIANTI UTILIZZABILI CON I SINGOLI BIGLIETTI DI AREA - THE COLOURED LINES INDICATE UNDER WHICH AREA EACH LIFT IS INCLUDED - LES LIGNES COLORÉS PERMETTENT DE REPÉRER LES REMONTÉES UTILISABLES AVEC LES FORFAIT DE ZONE.

is found here. Snow cover has not been reliable in recent seasons.

The original medieval town has considerable charm but the more recent buildings adjacent to the slopes are far from sympathetic to their beautiful mountain environment. Skiing here inevitably involves a lot of walking, and the resort bus service is not included in the weekly lift pass.

Mountain

From the village, a sequence of chairlifts take you up to the mid-mountain hub of Sportinia for access to Cesana and Sestriere. Other lifts rise from the village to Clotes and the open slopes of Pian della Rocca, as well as to the secluded and nearly always uncrowded sector beneath 2540m Mont Genevris. On busy high-season weekends, this is where you will find the locals. The Sauze d'Oulx slopes face west and north, and the majority of them are below the tree-line. Sportinia is in effect a higher satellite with hotels, restaurants, and good nursery slopes.

The resort quite wrongly has a 'novice' label attached to it. In fact, the majority of the runs are graded intermediate, and it is an excellent playground for accomplished skiers and riders looking for high mileage. Some of the best skiing is found between Sportinia and Sansicario. Good skiers will also want to journey on across the Monti della Luna to Montgenèvre in France. The gondola linking Sestriere with Monte Fraiteve also allows for a swift return from Sestriere to Sauze.

Learn

Scuola Sauze d'Oulx, **t** +39 0122 858 084, has an excellent reputation for teaching up-to-date technique. The others are **Sauze Project**, **t** +39 0122 858 942, and **Sauze Sportinia**, **t** +39 0122 850 218, ('instructors excellent with good English'). **Guide Alpine Valsusa**, **t** +39 335 398 984, and **Eliskiing Valsusa**, **t** +39 335 398 984, are the off-piste specialists.

Children

All the ski schools offer children's lessons from four years old.

Lunch

Chalet Il Capricorno, **t** +39 0122 850 273, at the top of the Clotes piste, is renowned for chef Maria Rosa Sacchi's handmade ravioli and is much the best restaurant on the mountain. **Ciao Pais**, **t** +39 0122 850 280, at Clotes, is recommended. **Capanna Kind**, **t** +39 0122 850 206, and **La Tana dell'Orso**, **t** +39 0122 850 226, at Sportinia, are favourites with reporters.

Dine

'We ate great food ranging from steak to pasta for about 30 euros per person, which included a lot of wine and beer,' said a reader. **Del Borgo**, **t** +39 0122 850 329, has warm atmosphere and good food. **La Griglia**, **t** +39 0122 850 344, is also recommended.

Party

'Although it advertises itself as a lively resort, this is no Ibiza,' said a reporter. The **New Scotch Bar** at the foot of the slopes is a resort institution. **Wine Bar Gran Trun** and **Village Café** have live bands. **The Grotto**, the bar of Hotel Derby, and the **Cotton Club** are ever-popular. **Osteria dei Vagabondi** has live music. **Schuss Disco**, **Gina-Il Bandito**, **Paddy McGinty's** ('highly recommended') and **Queen's Lounge** are the late-night venues.

Sleep

★★★★**Il Capricorno, t** +39 0122 850 273, is a comfortable boutique hotel in an isolated position on the Clotes piste.

★★★★**Hotel Relais des Alpes, t** +39 0122 859 747, *www.gestioniabc.it*, in the resort centre, is said to be 'very clean and hospitable and the bedrooms were a good size'.

★★★★**Grand Hotel Besson, t** +39 0122 859 785, was rated as very good value for money by readers.

★★★★**Grand Hotel La Torre, t** +39 0122 859 812, *www.grandhotellatorre.it*, is one of Sauze's most comfortable establishments, although there are mixed reports of the half-board food.

★★★**Gran Baita, t** +39 0122 850 183, was praised highly for its cleanliness and pleasant staff.

★★★**Hotel Miravalle, t** +39 0122 858 530, *www.gestioniabc.it*, has been recently refurbished and has excellent cuisine.

★★★**Hotel Sauze t** +39 0122 850 285, *www.gestioniabc.it*, has been completely revamped but does receive criticism for the thinness of the walls.

★★★**Hotel Splendid, t** +39 0122 850 172, *www.gestioniabc.it*, is in a quiet position. 'Nice hotel, friendly staff but disappointing food,' said a reporter.

★★★**Hotel Stella Alpina, t** +39 0122 858 731, *www.stellalpinahotel.it*, is slope-side with a good atmosphere but it can be a bit noisy in the evening.

★★★**Parc Hotel Gran Bosco, t** +39 0122 850 166, *www.sauzedoulx.org/granbosco*, 1km out of town, offers a courtesy bus; the food is good and the staff are friendly.

★★**Hotel Florida Prata, t** +39 0122 859 826, *www.hotelfloridaprata.it*, was rated 'small and friendly. Overall a little dated in appearance, but it is clean, quiet, and nothing is too much trouble.'

★★**La Fontaine, t** +39 0122 850 293, *www.lafontaine.it*, is a steep 20-minute walk out of town, but was rated excellent for its genuinely friendly and helpful staff.

★★**Hotel Hermitage, t** +39 0122 850 385, *www.sauzedoulx.org/hermitage*, on the piste at Clote, is clean and comfortable.

★★**Albergo Martin, t** +39 0122 858 246, *www.hotelmartin.com*, was said to be 'perfect – the food was stunning and the bar lovely'.

★★**Hotel Meublé Gran Trun, t** +39 0122 850 016, *www.gestionabc.it*, has simple rustic-style rooms above a wine bar.

★★**Hotel Miosotis, t** +39 0122 850 288, *www.gestioniabc.it*, is conveniently situated for lifts to Clotes and Sportinia.

★★**Hotel Monte Genevris, t** +39 0122 858 086, was said to have good food and to be generally warm and clean, but some residents could be noisy at 5am.

★**Hotel Orso Bianco, t** +39 0122 850 226, has just 12 rooms. 'We couldn't fault it – especially the food and drink, which was wonderful,' said a reader.

Chalet Faure t +39 0122 859 760, *www.chaletfaure.it*, is full of atmosphere, with some split-level bedrooms and a small spa.

Rifugio Ciao Pais, t +39 0122 850 280, *www.ciaopais.it*, is an inn and restaurant up the mountain that is highly rated for its food.

Selva Gardena

Profile

One of the best-known resorts of the vast Sella Ronda ski area. The resort has good family facilities and some enticing mountain restaurants

SELVA GARDENA

Lavarella 3055 m
Conturines 3064 m
Cortina
Lagazuoi 2778 m
Col di Lana 2462 m
Porta Vescovo
MARMOLADA MARMOLATA 3342 m
P.so Falzarego 2105 m
Piz de Puez
VAL BADIA
S.CASSIANO
LA VILLA
PEDRACES
Sassongher 2665 m
CORVARA
P.so Campolongo 1875 m
ARABBA
Piz Boè 3152 m
GARDENACIA
GRUPPO DEL SELLA SELLA GRUPPE
P.so Pordoi Pordoi Joch 2239 m
Col Rodela 2484 m
P U E Z
P.so Gardena Grödnerjoch 2121 m
P.so Sella Sella Joch 2244 m
CANAZEI
Dantercepies 2300 m
Piz Setëur 2064 m
STEVIA
Plan de Gralba 1800 m
CAMPITELLO
Piz Sella 2284
SASSOLUNGO LANGKOFEL 3181 m
SASSOPIATTO PLATTKOFEL 2956 m
Larciunei 1608 m
SECEDA
Ciampinoi 2254 m
Seceda 2518 m
Col Raiser 2103 m
SELVA GARDENA WOLKENSTEIN 1564 m
Cuca Cucasattel
Mont de Sëura 2117 m
Val Gardena Ronda Express
Monte Pana 1636 m
Autobus Monte Pana - Saltria
Busverbindung Monte Pana - Saltria
Saslong
Danti di Terrarossa Roßzähne 2657 m
S.CRISTINA ST.CHRISTINA 1428
RASCIESA RATSCHOTZ
Saltria 1700 m
Punta d'Oro - Goldknopf 2210 m
Monte Piz 2109 m
ORTISEI ST. ULRICH 1236
ALPE DI SIUSI SEISER ALM
SCILIAR SCHLERN
Bullaccia Puflatsch 2130m
PUNTA SANTNER SANTNER SP. 2413 m
Pufels 1484 m
BOLZANO BOZEN

＊BEST FOR

Beginners, high-mileage intermediates, families, serious lunchers

ESSENTIALS

Altitude: 1563m (5,128ft)–1800m (5,905ft)
Further information: **t** +39 0471 777 900, *www.valgardena.it*
Lifts in area: 84 in Selva Val Gardena (1 funicular, 9 cableways, 46 chairs, 29 drags) serving 176km of piste. 450 lifts serving 1220km of piste in Dolomiti Superski
Lift pass: Dolomiti Superski adult €184–254, child 8–16yrs €129–178, both for six days
Access: Innsbruck airport 2hrs, Verona airport 2½hrs

Resort

Selva, also known as Wolkenstein, is a rather bland resort that stretches without a heart along the busy road between Bolzano and Corvara and links almost seamlessly to the neighbouring villages of Santa Cristina and Ortisei. However, the high number of hotel beds and rental chalets, coupled with direct access into the Sella Ronda, make it a popular and convenient base from which to explore the core of the Dolomites.

Selva is the setting each December for the Val Gardena Downhill, traditionally one of the earliest European venues of the season for the Men's World Cup. Britain's Konrad Bartelski famously took second place on the podium here back in 1981. This does much to publicize Selva but gives a false impression that the skiing here is demanding. In fact the area is best suited to beginners, intermediates and families looking for a bustling resort with a moderate amount of nightlife and plenty of alternative activities.

Mountain

Selva is one of the four compass points of the Sella Ronda, the 40km circuit around the Gruppo Selle massif. It takes around two hours of lifts to complete in either direction, plus or minus the joker factor of any queues. You take 13 lifts on the clockwise route and 15 lifts on the anti-clockwise. The amount of time spent actually skiing can be remarkably short – depending on your level of proficiency. You really don't need to be an accomplished skier to complete it; anyone who has skied for three weeks should be able to achieve it, but you do need a moderate level of fitness.

Skiers travelling clockwise from Selva take a chairlift followed by a long gondola up to 2300m Dantercepies to begin the long descent towards Colfosco and Corvara beyond. Anti-clockwise skiers and riders take the Ciaminoi gondola for the easy piste down to Plan de Gralba in the direction of Passo Pordoi and Arabba. You can also leave the circuit to explore the Val di Fassa.

The Ciaminoi downhill course – it is an intermediate piste when not prepared for racing – brings you down to Santa Cristina and the terminal for the Val Gardena Ronda Express, an underground funicular that gives skiers direct access to Ortisei's ski area. Ciaminoi and the adjoining Mont de Seura sector – reached by a quad-chair – provide some of the most scenic and enjoyable skiing in the valley.

Nursery slopes served by half a dozen short drags just above the resort provide a near-perfect playground for the large number of beginners who come to Selva.

Learn

In Selva, the choice lies between **2000**, **t** +39 0471 773 125, and **Ski & Boarders' Factory**, **t** +39 0471 794 257. We have mixed reports of both. In Santa Cristina, **CIR**, **t** +39 0471 790 184, and **Santa Cristina**, **t** +39 0471 792 045, are less internationally orientated.

Children

Casa Bimbo, **t** +39 348 870 0661, run by the Santa Cristina school, cares for children from 18 months. All the schools offer children's classes. Reporters praise the nursery slopes as 'brilliant'.

Lunch

'The mountain restaurants were much cleaner and cheaper, with better food than their French counterparts,' said a reporter. **L'Medel**, **t** +39 0471 795 235, on the piste of the same name, is decorated with local mountain antiques. **Piz Sella**, **t** +39 0471 794 115, is a wood-panelled restaurant with a warm atmosphere. **Rifugio Emilio Comici**, **t** +39 0471 794121, above Plan de Gralba, specializes in fresh fish. **Baita Panorama**, **t** +39 0471 795 372, on the Dantacepies piste above Selva, has good, homely fare.

Dine

Le Stuben, **t** +39 0471 795 555, in Hotel Alpenroyal, offers a choice of five dining rooms, each with a different ambience ranging from alpine hut to formal 17th-century country house. **Armin's Grillstube**, **t** +39 0471 795 347, in the Hotel Armin, has fine steaks. **Al Cervo**, **t** +39 0471 795086, and **La Bula**, **t** +39 0471 79520, are popular pizzerias. In Santa Cristina, **Bistro Susi**, **t** +39 0471 793 703, is warmly recommended, along with **Da Peppi**, **t** +39 0471 793 335.

Party

Laurinkeller is the long-established resort rendezvous. **Umbrella Bar,** in front of Hotel Wolkenstein, and **Igloo Bar** are always crowded. In Santa Cristina, **Crazy Pub**, and **Bar 2000** are the liveliest bars. **Goalies** serves a decent pint of Guinness.

Sleep

Selva:

★★★★★**Alpenroyal Sporthotel Gourmet & Relax**, **t** +39 0471 795 555, *www.alpenroyal.com*, has a giant pool housed in an all-glass conservatory. The spa offers an exhaustive range of treatments.

★★★★**Acadia Beauty & Relax**, **t** +39 0471 774 444, *www.acadia.it*, has been run by the Prinoth family for four generations.

★★★★**Granvara Sport & Wellness hotel**, **t** +39 0471 795 250, *www.granvara.com*, is in a quiet position on the edge of piste. The owner also runs the 2000 ski school.

★★★★**Sporthotel Gran Baita**, **t** +39 0471 795 210, *www.hotelgranbaita.com*, has been looking after skiers since 1953.

★★★★**Sporthotel Maciaconi**, **t** +39 0471 793 500, *www.hotelmaciaconi.com*, has a large pool, sauna and solarium.

★★★**Hotel Armin**, **t** +39 0471 795 347, *www.hotelarmin.com*, is friendly.

★★★**Hotel Ingram**, **t** +39 0471 795 118, *www.val-gardena.com/hotel/ingram*, ('a great family run hotel') was completely revamped this summer.

★★★**Albergo Gruppo Sella**, **t** +39 0471 795 182, *www.grupposella.com*, situated a couple of kilometres outside Selva at Plan de Gralba, is owned by a former Italian World Cup racer.

★★★**Hotel Wolkenstein**, **t** +39 0471 772 200, *www.wolkenstein.it*, is strong on après ski, which can last deep into the night.

★★**Pension Daniel**, **t** +39 0471 795 570, *www.pension-daniel.com*, is a small hotel set up the hill from the resort but highly recommended for home cooking and friendly atmosphere.

Santa Cristina:

★★★★**Alpenhotel Plaza**, **t** +39 0471 793 463, *www.alpenhotelplaza.com*, is a new hotel in the centre of the village.

★★★★**Hotel Diamant Port & Wellness**, **t** +39 0471 796 780, *www.hoteldiamant.it*, is set in an extensive private park.

Sestriere

***BEST FOR**

Italian atmosphere, intermediates in search of high-mileage cruising

ESSENTIALS

Altitude: 2035m, 6,675ft)–2823m, (9,262ft)
Further information: t +39 0122 755 444, *www.sestriere.it*
Lifts in area: 78 in Milky Way (6 cableways, 39 chairs, 33 drags) serving 400km of piste
Lift pass: Vialattea (covers Montgenèvre, Sestriere, Sauze d'Oulx and other smaller resorts) adult and child €155–175 for six days. Child under 8yrs free
Access: Turin airport 1½hrs, railway station at Oulx 30mins, buses to resort

Profile

A slightly austere high-altitude ski village in the Milky Way, Sestriere hosted the main alpine events in the Turin Winter Olympics

Resort

Sestriere was purpose-built as a ski resort in 1934 by the Agnelli family, which founded Fiat. Last winter it hosted with considerable success the lion's share of the alpine events in the Winter Olympics.

Sestriere is the capital of the Milky Way – or Vialattea, an alliance of villages that straddles the Italian–French frontier between Turin and Briançon. It has the highest and most challenging skiing in the region, along with a level of sophistication that is lacking in neighbouring Sauze d'Oulx. When Giovanni Agnelli originally built the resort, the high-altitude site he chose had a good snow record. However, in these times of climate change, cover is not as reliable as it used to be. The village is dominated by the twin towers of the original smart Torre and Duchi d'Aosta hotels.

Mountain

The Milky Way in general and Sestriere in particular have benefited from the 2006 Olympics. An eight-person gondola connects Cesana to Sansicario in only eight minutes instead of 30 on the old Pariol and Forte chairs. A 60-person cable car now links the ancient outlying town of Pragelato with Borgata. The overriding impression persists, however, that the ratio between skiing time and lift-riding time is far from ideal. Despite improvements, many lifts remain slow and need replacing with high speed chairs and while significant stretches of mountain are covered by snow cannon, some areas could still do with more.

The old, slow Trebials chair between Borgata and Sestriere has been upgraded to a detachable-quad. The Garnel draglift has by replaced by a chair from the Olympic Village up to Alpette, with a tunnel beneath the giant slalom piste. At Claviere, a new detachable quad-chair connects La Coche to Colle Bercia and lots more snow-cannons have been installed.

Sestriere's skiing is split into the Monte Motta and Monte Sises sectors. Both are reached by quad-chairs and offer skiing for all standards. The beginner slopes just above the village are particularly good, and Sestriere has a terrain park with a half-pipe and a snowcross course.

Best powder run in the region is the Rio Nero, which follows a river gully down to the Oulx–Cesana road from Monte Fraiteve. Heli-skiing is possible on the top of Valle d'Argentera and Val Thures.

Learn

Sestriere has four ski schools, of which **Scuola Sci Sestriere**, **t** +39 0122 77060,

VIALATTEA
sciare senza confini

SESTRIERE

SANSICARIO

CESANA

CLAVIERE

MONTGENEVRE

MONTI DELLA LUNA

M. ROGNOSA 3280 m.
M. MOTTA 2823 m.
BANCHETTA 2555 m.
ROC DEL BOUCHER 3285 m.
M. VISO
MERCIANTAIRA 3290 m.
GR. PIC DE ROCHEBRUNE 3325 m.
VAL THURAS
CHENAILLET 2634 m.
VAL CERVIERES
M. GIMONT 2646 m.
LES ANGES 2485 m.
LE QUERELAY
COL DES GONDRANS
ROCHER DE L'AIGLE
COL SAUREL 2409 m.
COLLETTO VERDE 2500 m.
VAL GIMONT
M. LA PLANE 2546 m.
COLLE BERCIA 2293 m.
TORINO
M. MONCRONS 2507 m.
BOURGET
M. TRIPLEX 2507 m.
PRAGELATO
PIETRE DE L'AIGLE
COL BASSET 2424 m.
M. FRAITEVE 2701 m.
BORGATA 1840 m.
M. SISES 2609 m.
ALPETTE
VALLE ARGENTERA
CIMA DEL BOSCO
COURBION
SESTRIERE 2035 m.
GRANGESISES 1839 m.
P. ROCCA
SPORTINIA
CLOTES
MALAFOSSE
TACHIER
SOLEIL BOEUF
M. ROTTA
CHAMPLAS DU COL
SAUZE DI CESANA
CHAMPLAS JANVIER
CHAMPLAS SEGUIN
ROLLIERES
BOUSSON
SANSICARIO 1700 m.
S. SICARIO
PARIOL
MOLLIERES
FENILS
AUTAGNE
COLOMBIERE
SOLOMIAC
CESANA TORINESE 1350 m.
LA COMBA 1360 m.
MONTANINA
P.TA RASCIA
SAGNA LONGA
RIF. GIMONT
PRAPLARY
LA COCHE
CHABERTON 3130 m.
CLAVIERE 1760 m.
PRARIAL
MONTGENEVRE 1850 m.
BRIANÇON
CHALVET 2690 m.
MONTQUITAINE
COL DE L'ALPET 2430 m.
PISTA BIATHLON
PISTA BOB

SKILIFT
SEGGIOVIA 2 POSTI
SEGGIOVIA 3 POSTI
SEGGIOVIA 4 POSTI
TELECABINE
FUNIVIA
PISTA FACILE
PISTA MEDIA
PISTA DIFFICILE
SNOWPARK
PATTINAGGIO
PISTA DI FONDO
PISTA BOB, FREESTYLE E BIATHLON

INNEVAMENTO ARTIFICIALE
PISTE DI GARA OLIMPICHE
SESTRIERE "KB" PISTA KANDAHAR BANCHETTA G.NASI
"KSL" PISTA KANDAHAR SLALOM G. A. AGNELLI
"2" PISTA SISES GIANNI AGNELLI
SANSICARIO "F" PISTA FRAITEVE

www.vialattea.it

much the largest, is praised for its fantastic teaching, with a focus on making lessons enjoyable. The others are **Borgata**, **t** +39 0122 77497, **Extrême**, **t** +39 0122 76214, and **Olimpionica**, **t** +39 0122 76116. Guiding can be arranged through **Guide Alpine Sestriere**, **t** +335 660 1940.

Children

Asilo Neve, **t** +39 0122 755 444, cares for children from two years and over. However, 'There is a lack of ski facilities for children, and I wouldn't recommend the resort to families trying to get children on their skis for the first time,' said a reporter.

Lunch

Eating on the slopes matches the best anywhere. Try **Rifugio Alpette**, **t** +39 0122 755 505, for fresh pasta, **Chisonetto**, **t** +39 0122 76094, is renowned for its polenta. **La Brua**, **t** +39 0122 76000, at Grangesises is good, **La Gargote**, **t** + 39 0122 76888, is expensive, but worth it. **Lou Brachettes**, **t** + 39 0122 77598, and **La Tana della Volpe**, **t** +39 335 362 054, at the top of the Banchetta cable car, are also recommended. Try also **Raggio di Sole**, **t** +39 0122 70170, **Valuncro**, **t** +39 0122 70286, and **Il Capret**, **t** +39 0122 70215. **Baita da Coche**, **t** +39 0122 878 629, above Claviere, received rave reviews – 'One of the best mountain eateries I have encountered. Lunch could include delights such as chicken fried in breadcrumbs with lemon, courgettes and onions, and polenta with casseroled venison.' You can also reach it in the evening by snowmobile.

Dine

'Some great places to grab food,' said a reader. **Pinky**, **t** +39 0122 76441, has wonderful food and ambience. **Ristorante Du Grand Père**, **t** +39 0122 755 970, in the hamlet of Champlas Janvier, specializes in local Piedmont dishes. **Antica Osteria**, **t** +39 0122 785 300, in Pragelato, is a converted cowshed with a vaulted ceiling. **Le Lanterne**, **t** +39 0122 795 283, in Grangesises, is recommended.

Party

'Nightlife is as lively as the guests that week make it. Some weeks are great fun and a good laugh,' commented a reporter, 'it is also around 10 euros a drink.' The **Kandahar** bar beneath the Hotel du Col is stylish and friendly. The infamous **Irish Igloo**, **Caver** and **Tabata** provide the late-night entertainment. **Barabba**, **Spotties**, **Bar Sestriere** and **Brahms Bar** are recommended.

Sleep

★★★★**Grand Hotel Sestriere**, **t** +39 0122 76476, *www.grandhotelsestriere.it*, has been recently restored with a fine spa.

★★★★**Grand Hotel Principe di Piemonte**, **t** +39 0122 7941, *www.gh-principi piemonte.it*, smart hotel with a good pool and gourmet restaurant.

★★★★**Hotel Cristallo**, **t** +39 0122 750 707, *www.newlinehotels.com*, has small rooms, a large pool and an amazing choice of food.

★★★★**Il Fraitevino**, **t** +39 0122 76022, *www.hotelilfraitevino.it*, is in the centre of town.

★★★★**Pragelato Village Resort & Spa**, **t** +39 0122 740 011, *www.pragelatoresort.it*, is a luxurious development in Pragelato, linked by cable car to Borgata.

★★★**Hotel Banchetta**, **t** +39 0122 70307, *www.sestriere2000.com*, in the satellite of Borgata, is in a peaceful position 200m from the lift.

★★★**Hotel Biancaneve**, **t** +39 0122 755 176, *www.newlinehotels.com*, is a 'no-frills hotel, with almost too much food'.

★★★**Hotel Savoy Edelweiss**, **t** +39 0122 77040, *www.hotelsavoysestriere.com*, has 29 rooms, a spa and is highly rated for its fantastic staff and proximity to the piste.

La Thuile

Profile

The Italian half of a large intermediate ski area shared with La Rosière in France, renowned for the quality of its snow and its restaurants

Resort

There is a general air of quiet charm and sophistication in La Thuile, which is situated in a remote corner of the Aosta Valley at the foot of the Petit-St-Bernard Pass to France (closed in winter). Unfortunately, not all of its new buildings are sympathetic to their beautiful mountain environment. The good snow record can sometimes provide outstanding off-piste skiing when other resorts have little to offer. The skiing is linked to La Rosière in France.

*** BEST FOR**

Uncrowded pistes, snow reliability, off-piste, value

ESSENTIALS

Altitude: 1441m (4,728ft)–2641m (8,665ft)
Further information: **t** +39 0165 884 179, *www.lathuile.it*
Lifts in area: 37 (1 cableway, 17 chairs, 19 drags) serving 150km of piste
Lift pass: Espace San Bernardo (covers La Thuile and La Rosière) adult €146–182, child 6–12yrs €62–91, both for six days
Access: Turin and Geneva airports 2hrs, railway station at Pré-St-Didier 15mins, regular buses from station

Mountain

'The skiing is fantastic and has something for all levels,' said a reporter. A cableway and a parallel chair rise over wooded terrain to the mid-mountain station of Les Sucres at 2200m. A network of further lifts climb to the French border. This is a demanding ski area, with a predominance of steep reds and the occasional black. Heli-skiing is possible on the Ruitor Glacier. La Thuile has good nursery slopes, a terrain park and half-pipe. There is a lack of queues, but some of the lifts badly need updating.

Learn

Instruction is restricted to **La Thuile Ski School**, **t** +39 0165 884 123, which was founded in 1964. Reports have been extremely favourable: 'Excellent for adults and children.'

Children

'I would thoroughly recommend this resort for a quiet family break,' said a reader. **Il Grande Albero**, **t** +39 0165 884 986, accepts children from newborn to three years. Ski school **Miniclub**, **t** +39 0165 884 123, takes children from four years.

Lunch

Rifugio Lo Riondet, **t** +39 0165 884 006, specializes in cheese dishes and game. **La Bricole**, **t** +39 0165 884 149, is in an attractive old house at the bottom of the lifts. **L'Eden**, **t** +39 0165 885 348, is

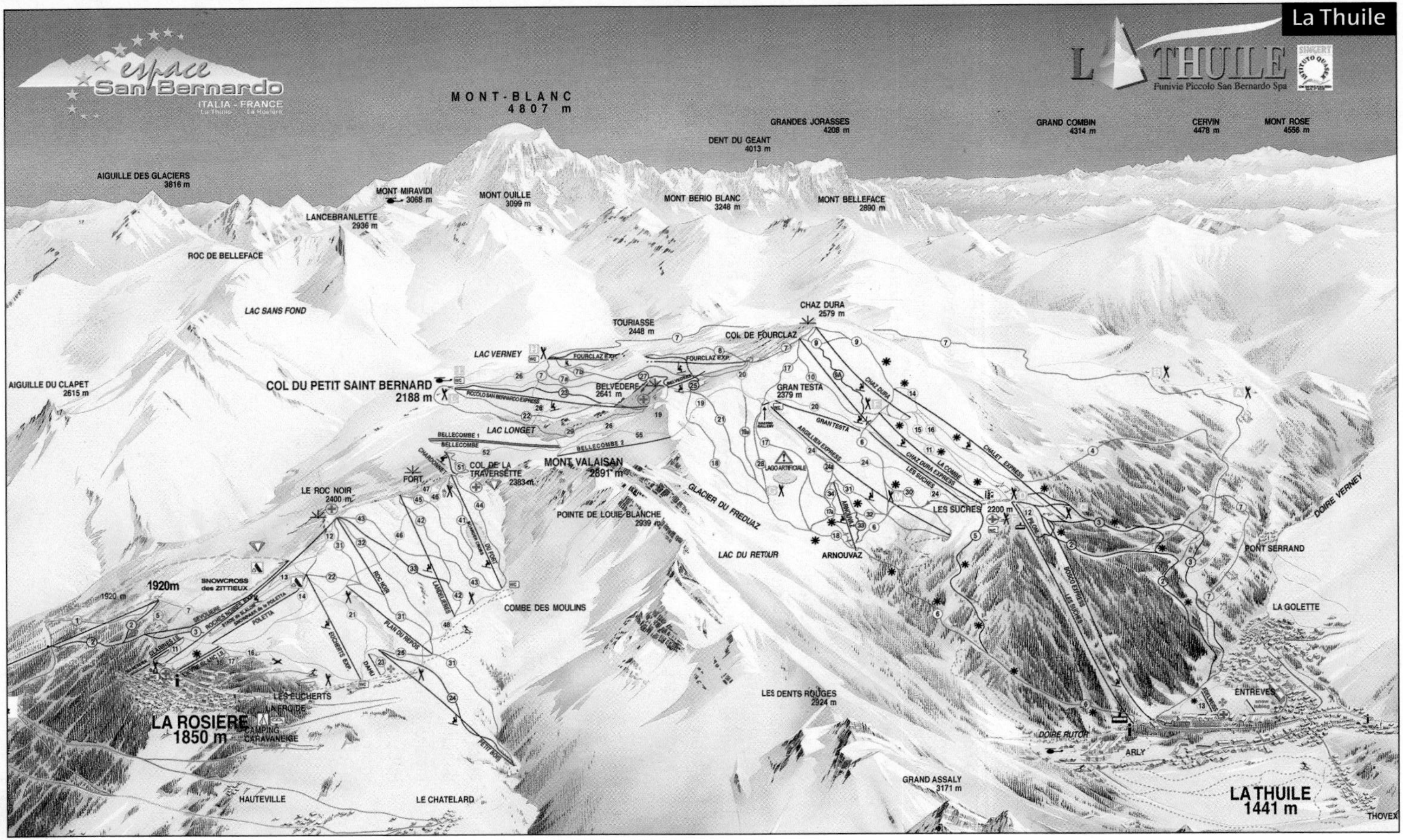
espace San Bernardo
ITALIA - FRANCE
La Thuile La Rosière
LA THUILE
Funivie Piccolo San Bernardo Spa
MONT-BLANC
4807 m
GRANDES JORASSES
4208 m
DENT DU GEANT
4013 m
GRAND COMBIN
4314 m
CERVIN
4478 m
MONT ROSE
4556 m
AIGUILLE DES GLACIERS
3816 m
MONT MIRAVIDI
3068 m
MONT OUILLE
3099 m
MONT BERIO BLANC
3248 m
MONT BELLEFACE
2890 m
LANCEBRANLETTE
2936 m
ROC DE BELLEFACE
LAC SANS FOND
CHAZ DURA
2579 m
TOURIASSE
2448 m
COL DE FOURCLAZ
LAC VERNEY
AIGUILLE DU CLAPET
2615 m
COL DU PETIT SAINT BERNARD
2188 m
BELVEDERE
2641 m
GRAN TESTA
2379 m
LAC LONGET
BELLECOMBE 1
BELLECOMBE
BELLECOMBE 2
MONT VALAISAN
2891 m
COL DE LA TRAVERSETTE
2383 m
FORT
CHARDONNET
LE ROC NOIR
2400 m
POINTE DE LOUIE BLANCHE
2939 m
GLACIER DU FREDUAZ
LAC DU RETOUR
ARNOUVAZ
LAGO ARTIFICIALE
LES SUCHES
2200 m
CHALET EXPRESS
CHAZ DURA EXPRESS
ARGILLIEN EXPRESS
FOURCLAZ EXP.
PICCOLO SAN BERNARDO EXPRESS
BOSCO EXPRESS
PILONI
DOIRE VERNEY
PONT SERRAND
LA GOLETTE
ENTREVES
DOIRE RUTOR
ARLY
LA THUILE
1441 m
THOVEX
GRAND ASSALY
3171 m
LES DENTS ROUGES
2924 m
COMBE DES MOULINS
SNOWCROSS
des ZITTIEUX
1920m
1920 m
ROC NOIR
PLAN DU REPOS
EUCHERTS EXP.
DAHU
PETIT BOIS
LES EUCHERTS
LA FROIDE
CAMPING
CARAVANEIGE
LA ROSIERE
1850 m
HAUTEVILLE
LE CHATELARD

outstanding, **Le Mélèze**, **t** +39 0165 885 553, is a self-service with good views, and **Maison Carrel**, **t** +39 334 366 0162, is a newly renovated hut. **Bar du Lac**, **t** +39 0165 843 209, at the San Bernardo Pass border, was also praised.

Dine

A La Lune, **t** +39 0165 884 964, offers Tuscan cooking and a good wine selection. **Le Rascard**, **t** +39 0165 88499, ('highlight of the week ') serves innovative cuisine including chocolate pizza. **La Fordze**, **t** +39 0165 884 800, specializes in grilled meat and game. **La Lisse**, **t** +39 0165 884 167, serves local specialities. **La Grotta**, **t** +39 0165 884 474, cooks pizzas in a wood-fired oven. **Taverna Coppa Pan**, **t** +39 0165 884 797, is praised for its food and service, and **La Bricole**, **t** +39 0165 884 149, serves excellent local food. Reporters warn, 'At weekends the Italians arrive *en masse*, and it is essential to book a table anywhere.'

Party

'The après ski is a bit thin on the ground but there are some great places if you look,' commented a reader. What there is includes **La Buvette**, **La Bricolette**, **La Cage aux Folles** and **La Bricole Disco Pub** for dancing. There is a new thermal spa in the local village of Pré-St-Didier with outdoor hot pools, an indoor waterfall, steam room, sauna and views of Mont Blanc.

Sleep

****Hotel Dora**, **t** +39 0165 883 084, *www.hoteldora.net*, has been recently restored and has a spa. It was recommended by reporters: 'Superb, and we enjoyed the restaurant food.'

****Planibel Hotel and Apartments**, **t** +39 0165 884 541, *www.tivigest.com*, is a giant complex with pool, disco, and shops. It received mixed reviews: 'overpriced for what it offers', on one hand, and 'basic, but decent value for money' on the other.

***Chalet Alpina**, **t** +39 0165 884 187, is a clean, comfortable, rustic hotel 200m from the lifts.

***Chalet Eden**, **t** +39 0165 885 050, is renowned for its food.

***Hotel du Glacier**, **t** +39 0165 884 137, is convenient and has been refurbished ('always assured of a warm welcome').

***Les Granges**, **t** +39 0165 883 048, 3km out of town, has home cooking.

Entrèves, **t** +39 0165 884 134, is a recently restored family hotel.

07 The Top Resorts: Japan

Furano

***BEST FOR**

All standards of skier and rider, culture vultures

ESSENTIALS

Altitude: 100m (329ft) – 1209m (3,966ft)
Further information: *www.skifurano.com*
Lifts in area: 10 (2 cableways, 8 chairs)
Lift pass: adults yen 25,200, children yen 19,200, both for six days.
Access: Sapporo's New Chitose Airport 2hrs 40 minutes, Asahikawa Airport 1hr with regular shuttle bus. Train station in Furano.

Profile

Major resort on the northern island of Hokkaido with international appeal

Resort

Furano, once a venue for World Cup races, has changed beyond all recognition since our first visit over 15 years ago. It now has 10 lifts including two modern cableways and a substantial vertical drop of nearly 1000m.

The ski area is much smaller than Niseko's, but has more character and is reminiscent of an American resort such as Sun Valley. The action takes place around the slopeside New Furano Prince Hotel, which owns the resort. An interesting craft village next door provides shopping opportunities and still more can be found in the traditional little city of Furano, which lies a 10-minute drive away. The town has a wide choice of low-cost Japanese restaurants as well as some noisy karaoke bars.

Mountain

Furano has hosted 10 World Cup races and, by Hokkaido standards, is a sophisticated ski area with a mile-long cable car and a modern six-person gondola at its core.

Throughout the long winter, chilly Siberian winds blow in across the Okhotsk Sea and dump up to 15m of powder on the wooded slopes above the resort. The pisted area is divided into two sectors: Furano, reached by the cable car, which is a short push from the hotel, has the more demanding slopes. Kitanomine, linked by pistes to Furano, is powered by the gondola and has a wide choice of easy reds and long cruising blues. There is extensive and enjoyable night-skiing served by a quad-chair from the Furano base.

The biggest drawback to the resort is that off-piste skiing is normally forbidden and this is firmly enforced by an enthusiastic ski patrol. Such draconian vigilance proves to be a source of extreme frustration for overseas visitors who can view perfect powder fields from the lifts, but not ski them without risking their lift pass. One small consolation, for reasons that defy logical explanation, is that a single off-piste run is opened for just 10 minutes each morning and afternoon. However, back-country skiing is allowed at your own risk in the national park off the back of the resort. For the moment you have obtain a daily permit, which involves a certain amount of bureaucracy.

We believe that the rules, both in the national park and in the resort itself, will soon soften, as Furano attracts more and more overseas visitors. The rival Hokkaido resort of Rusutsu has already set the benchmark by permitting off-piste for the first time last season. Verbier ski guru Warren Smith, who is running his Ski Academy courses in Furano in conjunction with Inghams this winter, has managed to obtain exclusive permission to take his clients under the ropes.

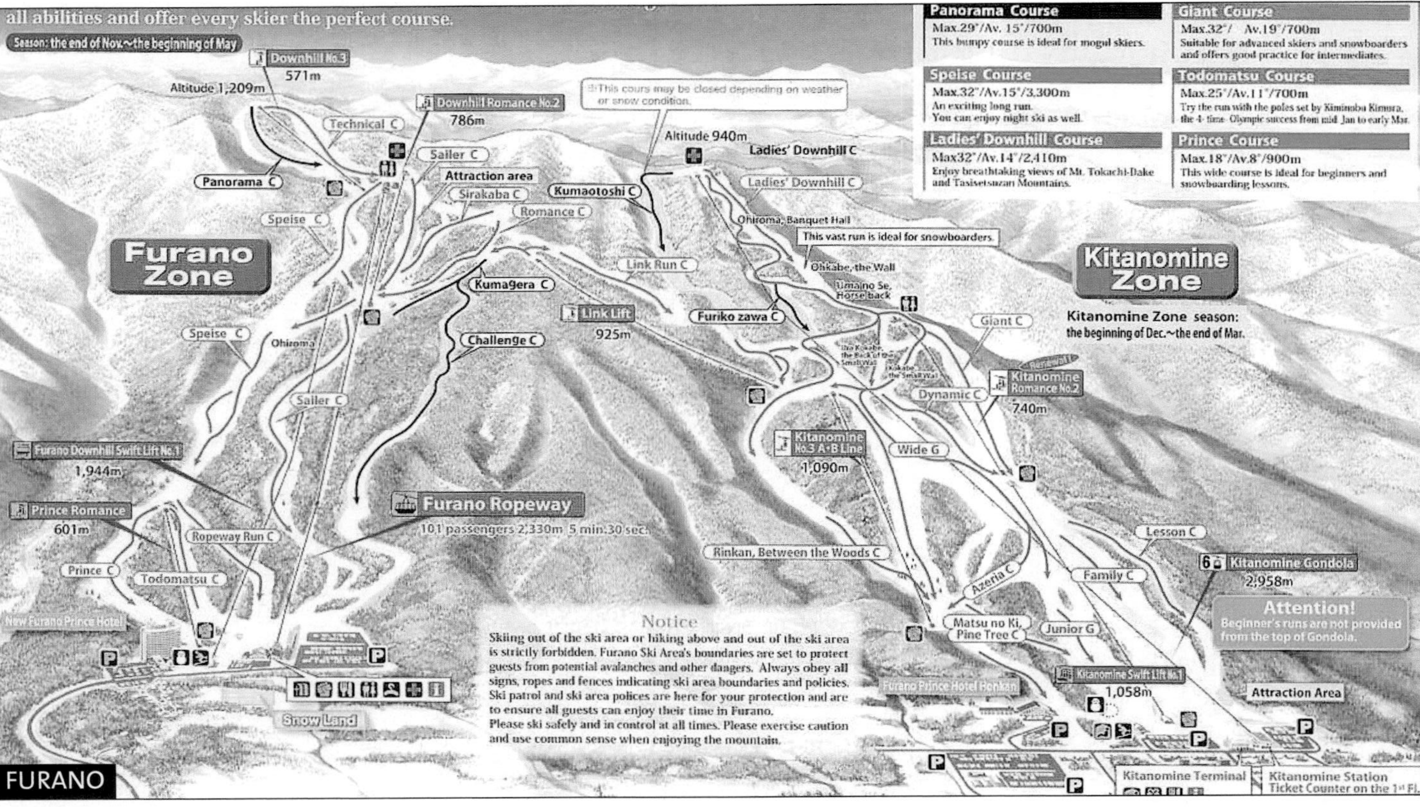

all abilities and offer every skier the perfect course.
Season: the end of Nov.~the beginning of May
Panorama Course
Max.29°/Av. 15°/700m
This bumpy course is ideal for mogul skiers.
Giant Course
Max.32°/ Av.19°/700m
Suitable for advanced skiers and snowboarders and offers good practice for intermediates.
Speise Course
Max.32°/Av.15°/3,300m
An exciting long run.
You can enjoy night ski as well.
Todomatsu Course
Max.25°/Av.11°/700m
Try the run with the poles set by Kiminobu Kimura, the 4- time Olympic success from mid Jan to early Mar.
Ladies' Downhill Course
Max32°/Av.14°/2,410m
Enjoy breathtaking views of Mt. Tokachi-Dake and Tasisetsuzan Mountains.
Prince Course
Max.18°/Av.8°/900m
This wide course is ideal for beginners and snowboarding lessons.
Downhill No.3
571m
Altitude 1,209m
Downhill Romance No.2
786m
This cours may be closed depending on weather or snow condition.
Altitude 940m
Ladies' Downhill C
Technical C
Sailer C
Attraction area
Panorama C
Sirakaba C
Kumaotoshi C
Ladies' Downhill C
Romance C
Speise C
Ohiroma, Banquet Hall
This vast run is ideal for snowboarders.
Furano Zone
Link Run C
Ohkabe, the Wall
Kitanomine Zone
Kumagera C
Umaino Se, Horse back
Link Lift
925m
Furiko zawa C
Giant C
Kitanomine Zone season:
the beginning of Dec.~the end of Mar.
Speise C
Ohiroma
Challenge C
Kitanomine Romance No.2
740m
Sailer C
Dynamic C
Kitanomine No.3 A·B Line
1,090m
Wide G
Furano Downhill Swift Lift No.1
1,944m
Furano Ropeway
101 passengers 2,330m 5 min.30 sec.
Prince Romance
601m
Ropeway Run C
Lesson C
Rinkan, Between the Woods C
Kitanomine Gondola
2,958m
Prince C
Todomatsu C
Azeria C
Family C
Attention!
Beginner's runs are not provided from the top of Gondola.
New Furano Prince Hotel
Notice
Skiing out of the ski area or hiking above and out of the ski area is strictly forbidden. Furano Ski Area's boundaries are set to protect guests from potential avalanches and other dangers. Always obey all signs, ropes and fences indicating ski area boundaries and policies. Ski patrol and ski area polices are here for your protection and are to ensure all guests can enjoy their time in Furano.
Please ski safely and in control at all times. Please exercise caution and use common sense when enjoying the mountain.
Matsu no Ki, Pine Tree C
Junior G
Kitanomine Swift Lift No.1
1,058m
Furano Prince Hotel Honkan
Attraction Area
Snow Land
Kitanomine Terminal
Kitanomine Station
Ticket Counter on the 1st Fl.
FURANO

For accomplished skiers and riders no visit is complete without a trip to nearby Mountain Asahidake. This 2290m live volcano offers outstanding off-piste opportunities, reached by a cable car that is primarily used in summer. The Ainu, the local indigenous people, so much admired the rugged beauty of the mountain that they called it the Garden of the Gods. From the top of the cable car you hike for 15 minutes (or the more adventurous for two-and-a-half hours) to reach some truly spectacular descents. Ungroomed runs take you down through stands of springy bamboo and gnarled birch trees, their branches bowed under great balls of frozen snow. You pass vents from which clouds of steam rise hundreds of feet into the air and streams of bath water temperature.

Learn

Furano has two ski schools offering a full range of tuition, but only a limited number of instructors speak English. **Kitanomine**, **t** +81 (0)167 22 4907, has a sound reputation and **Furano Prince Hotel School**, **t** +81 (0)167 22 1111, is run by Kiminobu Kimura who competed in four Olympics. **Hokkaido Powder Guides**, **t** +81 (0)80 3492 0433, provide English-speaking off-piste guides.

Children

Furano doesn't have a crèche, but the New Furano Prince Hotel can arrange babysitting. Both schools offer skiing and snowboarding lessons for kids.

Lunch

A beautifully presented bowl of noodles or rice with fish, meat, or vegetables cooked freshly to order costs £5, including a beer or soft drink. 'For that kind of money In Courchevel, you'd be lucky to get a portion of tired chips,' commented one reporter. Down Hill is a welcoming log cabin at the top of the ski area ('great noodles with a curry sauce'). Nishike Chinese Restaurant is at the Furano base area and specializes in Szechuan cuisine: 'You have to try the *gomoku yakisoba* [fried noodles].' Azalea, in the Furano Prince Hotel at the Kitanomine base area, is warmly praised.

Dine

Expect to pay as little as £10 for dinner. A seven-course banquet in a smart restaurant including all the beer, wine or sake that you can drink costs just £25. Half-board hotel meals are served buffet-style with an enormous amount of choice. Sushi and sashimi top the menu, but beef, chicken and vegetarian dishes are widely available, along with pasta and even pizza.

Party

Uta Dorobo is a popular karaoke bar with an all-you-can-drink party plan. 'This translates as Song Robber and, believe me, it was just that,' said a reporter. 'Avoid the folklorique evening unless you're into beat-the-clock flower arranging with simultaneous poetry,' said another. Après ski in Japan goes hand-in-hand with scrubbed skin, sushi and sake. **Dream House Kingyo** has dancing. **Kizutuku Mori no Midori** is a blues bar with DJ. **Furano Bar Bocco** is a pub popular with the locals. **Soh's Bar** is a log-and-stone cabin in the woods near the New Furano Prince Hotel.

Unusual après ski entertainment is to strip off your ski clothes and plunge into an open-air hot spring in a clearing in the forest. Relaxing in a natural pool of hot water surrounded by banks of snow proves an idyllic seat from which to contemplate an Eastern culture that is equally refreshing. However, the water is too hot and the surroundings too cold to be able to really relax. If you have cold feet about shedding your clothes on the snow and in public, the cosier alternative is in a sex-segregated indoor *onsen* bathhouse.

Sleep

For all accommodation, visit *www.skifurano.com*.

★★★★**New Furano Prince Hotel, t** +81 (0) 167 22 1111, is the flagship hotel on the edge of the piste at the Furano base.

★★★★**Furano Prince Hotel, t** +81 (0)167 23 4111, is located on the Kitanomine side of the resort.

★★★★**New Furano Hotel, t** +81 (0)167 2411, is situated closed to the gondola station and renowned for its seafood.

★★★★**Hotel Naturawald Furano, t** +81 (0)167 22 1211, is located by the Kitanomine Swift Lift. It has a newly renovated *onsen* and traditional Japanese restaurant.

Niseko

🏆 BEST MOUNTAIN RESTAURANT 2009 (NORTHERN RESORT)

Profile

The largest and best-known Hokkaido resort, three separate ski villages that share a joint ski area and an international lift pass

✻BEST FOR

All standards of skier and rider, powderhounds, ski gourmets

ESSENTIALS

Altitude: 300m (984ft)–1200m (3,937ft)
Further information: *www.nisekosnow.net/*, *www.niseko.ne.jp*
Lifts in area: 38 (3 cableways, 35 chairs)
Lift pass: adult yen 27,600, senior 13–15yrs yen 19,800, child 7–12yrs yen 15,600, all for six days.
Access: Sapporo airport 2hrs

Resort

Extraordinarily reliable snow-cover, coupled with surprisingly low prices, have made Hokkaido the 'hot' destination for British and other overseas skiers and riders in search of new horizons.

Reduced JAL airfares from Heathrow to Osaka have encouraged Inghams and Crystal to wiggle their toes in Japanese snow; despite fuel surcharges, others followed last season. This says much about overpriced and overcrowded European resorts.

Basic Japanese holiday packages are comparable to those in a top-range French, Swiss or North American resort. But the in-resort prices are much lower. What you get for your money is considerably more and the food is sensational – there's not a ubiquitous overcooked burger or a cheese fondue in sight. Expect to pay around £5 for a substantial mountain lunch of rice or noodles and fresh fish, pork or beef, washed down with beer, sake or a soft drink.

The only real drawback is the time it takes to get here from London: two flights totalling nearly 15 hours and a two-hour transfer to your resort from Sapporo, the quaint capital of Hokkaido, leave no change out of a 24 hour total journey time. You lose a day on the plane,

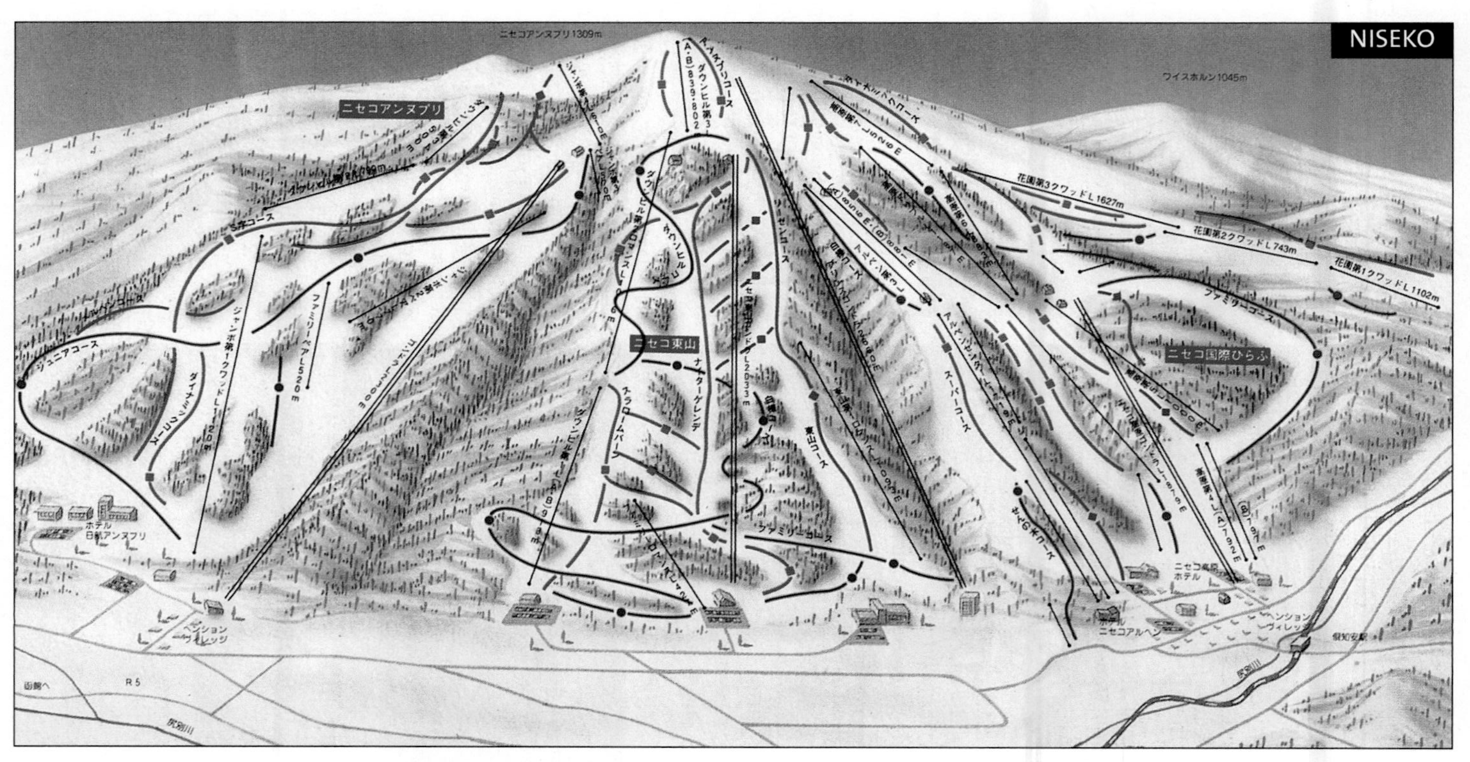
NISEKO
ニセコアンヌプリ1309m
ワイスホルン1045m
ニセコアンヌプリ
ニセコ東山
ニセコ国際ひらふ
花園第3クワッドL1627m
花園第2クワッドL743m
花園第1クワッドL1102m
ファミリーコース
スーパーコース
東山コース
ファミリーコース
ナイターゲレンデ
スラロームバーン
S字コース
ジュニアコース
ダイナミックコース
ファミリーペアL520m
ジャンボ第1クワッドL1120m
ホテル日航アンヌプリ
ペンションヴィレッジ
ホテルニセコアルペン
ニセコ高原ホテル
ペンションヴィレッジ
倶知安駅
函館へ
R5
尻別川

but of course you get it back at the end, and the whole experience for jaded ski palates is wonderfully refreshing – and that's before you even start on the Japanese *onsen* routine of bathing naked in steaming indoor and outdoor pools.

The wooded mountainsides of Hokkaido attract the best powder in Japan. This is caused by snow clouds blown all the way from Siberia, striking the rounded cone of the dormant volcano of Mount Yotei, the Fuji of the North.

Niseko United is not a Japanese football team, but a Trois Vallées-style trio of separately owned resorts on the same mountain, with a shared ski area, including 38 lifts. The problem is deciding where in Niseko to base yourself – Annupuri, Hirafu or Higashiyama. We prefer Hirafu, which has much the best ski resort atmosphere, with lots of après ski in quaint wooden houses dotted around the village. However, the better hotels are at the other bases.

Two other nearby small resorts, Moiwa and Chisenupuri, require separate lift tickets, but are havens of tranquillity on peak holiday weekends when Niseko can get crowded.

Wherever you decide to base yourself, do not ski Japan without a detour to at least one of the cities – ideally both vibrant Tokyo and cultured Kyoto, as contrasts.

Mountain

Skiing started in Niseko in 1911 when the Japanese army took to bamboo planks that looked more like ice-skates. Skiing for pleasure started in 1945 when an Austrian visited the resort and introduced the sorts of skis that were then available in the Alps. The area attracts a phenomenal 15 metres of snow each winter.

The pistes on 1308m Mount Annupuri suit all standards, with broad trails reminiscent of Whistler and much more exotic off-piste among the widely spaced birch trees and bamboos. The resort attracts an eclectic mixture of novices, families and diehard powderhounds in search of a heady cultural cocktail of snow and sushi.

The Australians have long since discovered that Hokkaido has much better snow than home and have invested heavily in the region. Lifts that have been built by Australian enterprise are high-speed detachable quads, but a few ancient single-seater chairs that are almost extinct in the Alps are still alive and well in Japan

Skiing on-piste can be a noisy business, with repetitive instructions on how to use the lifts, as well as Japanese pop music blaring out from speakers mounted on pylons.

A 20-minute hike up from the top lift gives access to glorious off-piste runs down through the National Park. Off-piste skiing is permitted apart from in areas on the lift map that are marked 'Strictly off limits'. In fact, few Japanese skiers ever leave the marked trails. They leave the steep 'n' deep to foreigners and the much more adventurous domestic snowboarders. The area has a half-pipe and three terrain parks.

The night-skiing is on some of the world's most extensive floodlit slopes, which are largely empty.

Australian-run **Inski**, **t** +81 (0)136 22 4199, and **Niseko Powder Boards & Skis**, **t** + 81 (0) 901 384 5772, rent out demo powder skis and boards.

To see a virtual tour of Niseko, visit *www.nisekomap.com*

Learn

Instructors from the Niseko ski schools offer morning and afternoon group and private lessons and appear to be technically sound. Hirafu in particular has several English-speaking instructors and guides. The schools are (English-speaking listed first) **Niseko Pro Powder**, **t** +81 (0) 90 7973 4104, **Niseko International Snowsports**, **t** +81 (0)136 21 6688, **Niseko Village**, **t** +81 (0)136 44111, at the Hilton Hotel, **Niseko An'nupuri Ski School**, **t** +81 (0)136 58 3225, at Hotel Nikko, **Niseko Grand Hirafu**, **t** +81 (0)136 22 0921, and **Mother Goose Snowboard School**, **t** +81 (0)136 22 0291.

Children

Hirafu Kids is Hirafu's first custom-designed child minding facility for six month- to six-year-olds with English-speaking staff. **Hotel Nikko Annupuri** has a crèche for children up to three years with English-speaking staff, and a children's ski school from three years. **Hotel Niseko Alpen**, **t** +81 (0)136 22 1105, cares for children aged two to six years for mornings and afternoons.

Lunch

Lunch is also quite different from what you are used to in the Alps or Rockies. For a start it's much cheaper, and you eat hot soup or a choice of noodle dishes accompanied by beer or hot sake for around £4.50–6 per head. Up on the slopes, **Bouyouso** is a basic mountain eatery serving various noodles and tempura at low prices. It was once a private house, built 47 years ago before there was even a resort here. However, **Niseko Northern Resort**, **t** +81 (0)136 583311, has the best lunchtime food.

Dine

In Hirafu, **Niseko Cuisine**, **t** +81 (0)136 556 885, offers in-house gourmet catering, **Kamimura**, **t** +81 (0)136 212 288, formerly of Tetsuya's in Sydney, offers an eight-course *degustation* menu, and **Syokusai Hirafu** in Hotel Niseko Alpen is for sushi. In An'nupuri, **Azeria** in Hotel Nikko Annupuri, is traditional Japanese. **Shi Shi**, next to the Prince Hotel, is Chinese. **148 Niseko**, **t** +81 (0)136 50 2800, has New World cuisine from the founder of 148 Hiroo in Tokyo. In Niseko Village, the **Hilton Hotel**, **t** +81 (0)136 44 1111, has a Teppanyaki restaurant, sushi counter and Yotei buffet.

Party

Wild Bill's bar in Hirafu is full of life with a diverse crowd from international wine lovers to locals. The contrastingly cool **Gyu+aka Fridge Bar** has jazz and a Cuban look – benches covered in colourful rugs, distressed walls, and a wonky wooden bar balanced on beer barrels. The new **Ice Bar** is inside an igloo.

Nightlife from the Hilton Hotel is less convenient than from the Niseko Alpen, although it's only a 10-minute bus ride to Hirafu until 12.15am – after that it's a taxi for about £8.50.

Almost everywhere you stay you will find the traditional Japanese *onsen*.

Sleep

An'nupuri:

Niseko Northern Resort, **t** +81 (0)136 58 3311, *www.niseko-northern.com/lang/english.php*, was formerly the Nikko An'nupuri. It is smaller and has more character than many of the other hotels and is ski in, ski out. The recently renovated rooms (with double beds – a rarity in Japan outside the major cities) are attractive. Apart from skiing, there is a small *onsen,* and in-room Shiatsu massage (about £20) is available.

Niseko Village:

Niseko Village Hilton Hotel, **t** +81 (0)136 44 1111, *www.hiltonhotels.co,jp/niseko*, is enormous and has a chairlift starting just outside. It is a resort in its own right, with limited doorstep night-skiing, a choice of restaurants, karaoke and an *onsen*.

Hirafu:

Hotel Niseko Alpen, t +81 (0)136 22 1105, *www.niseko-alpen.jp*, is ski in, ski out and well positioned for the nightlife. Rooms are small but the all-you-can-eat sushi in the evening is a bonus.

The Niseko Company, t +81 (0)136 21 7272, *www.thenisekocompany.com*, has luxury western chalets with large rooms and modern facilities.

Rusutsu

Profile

Hokkaido's largest single ski resort, with easy piste skiing and superb powder runs between the trees, based around one huge hotel

Resort

The resort is situated at the base of Mount Yotei, the Mount Fuji of Hokkaido, and from November until April an almost continuous band of snow clouds sweeps in across the seas from Siberia and this is the first mountain that they hit. The amount of powder is phenomenal – they routinely expect around 15m of snow each winter. The downside is that uninterrupted blue sky days are in short supply, but the skiing is below the treeline so visibility remains acceptable. The pistes are wide and perfectly groomed, while the off-piste is steep and set mainly between the trees.

Reduced international air fares to Japan last year helped to put Hokkaido firmly on the world ski map. Of course, the Australians have known about it for years, but for Europeans a visit here is an unexpected treat, with reasonably priced restaurants both on and off the mountain (expect to pay around £5 for lunch with beer or a soft drink).

Rusutsu, a 90-minute drive from New Chitose Airport at Sapporo, is one of the dozen main resorts on Japan's North Island (it has 137 in all). Importantly, since the 2007–8 season – thanks largely to the huge influx of overseas skiers and riders during recent years – off-piste through the trees is now legal.

The resort is centred around one truly enormous hotel. Rusutsu Resort Hotel sleeps 3,000 people in a massive choice of bedrooms, including suites and log cabins. A monorail runs the half-mile length of the comfortable Disney-style complex, which includes a fairground carousel and a mock Bavarian village, with 12 restaurants and shops as well as a fountain that 'dances' to the Blue Danube.

*BEST FOR

All standards, powderhounds, families, guaranteed snow cover

ESSENTIALS

Altitude: 366m (1,200ft)–994m (3,261ft)
Further information: t +81 (0)136 46 3111, *www.rusutsu.co.jp*
Lifts in area: 19 (4 cableways, 15 chairs) serving 42km of piste
Lift pass: adult £89, child £73, both for five days
Access: Sapporo New Chitose airport 1½hrs

Mountain

The main skiing takes place on the wooded slopes of Mount Isola and East Mountain, reached by a gondola that climbs up from the village. From last season a new double chair conveys guests directly to the gondola base station from

RUSUTSU RESORT
GELANDE GUIDE
HOKKAIDO NO.1
Sapporo
Niseko
New chitose airport
RUSUTSU RESORT
TRIPLE Mt.COURSE GUIDE

	Mt. Isola	East Mt.	West Mt.
EXPERT	◆◆ISOLA-A ◆◆RUSUTSU No.1	◆◆SUPER EAST	◆◆TIGER
ADVANCED	◆HEAVENLY SPIRIT ◆HEAVENLY CANYON	◆ACROSS-A ◆ACROSS-B	◆GIANT ◆SKY ◆NATURAL
INTERMEDIATE	■ISOLA-B ■ISOLA-C ■ISOLA-D ■STEAMBOAT-A ■STEAMBOAT-B ■ISOLA GRAND ■HEAVENLY VIEW ■HEAVENLY RIDGE-A ■HEAVENLY RIDGE-B ■HEAVENLY TRAIL	■EAST MUJU ■EAST TIGNES	■DYNAMIC ■ELITE ■BANBI ■NIGHTER
BEGINNER	●FURIKOZAWA ●ISOLA TOP BYPASS ●ISOLA-D BYPASS ●ISOLA GRAND BYPASS	●EASY TRAIL ●FUBORU ●JOINT	●RAINBOW ●FAMILY ●WHITE LOVER

Mt. Isola 994 meters above sea level
East Mt. 868 meters above sea level
West Mt. 715 meters above sea level
Mt.YOTEI 1,898 meters above sea level
NISEKO
Lake TOYA
HEAVENLY VIEW
HEAVENLY RIDGE-B
HEAVENLY RIDGE-A
HEAVENLY SPIRIT
HEAVENLY CANYON
HEAVENLY TRAIL
ISOLA No.4 QUAD
ISOLA No.3 QUAD
ISOLA No.5 PAIR
ISOLA TOP BYPASS
STEAMBOAT-B
ISOLA No.1 QUAD
STEAMBOAT-A
RUSUTSU No.1
ISOLA-A
ISOLA-B
ISOLA GRAND BYPASS
ISOLA No.2 QUAD
ISOLA-C
ISOLA GRAND
ISOLA GONDOLA
ISOLA-D BYPASS
ISOLA-D
ACROSS-B
ACROSS No.2 PAIR
ACROSS No.1 PAIR
JOINT
FUBORU
FURIKOZAWA
ACROSS-A
SUPER EAST
EAST TIGNES
EAST No.2 PAIR
EAST MUJU
EAST No.2 GONDOLA
EAST QUAD
EASY TRAIL
EAST No.1 PAIR
EAST Mt. CENTER STATION
SNOWMOBILE LAND
EAST No.1 GONDOLA
TOWER PAIR
CAFETERIA "STEAMBOAT"
Mt.ISOLA BASE STATION
PARKING ENTRANCE
CROSS-COUNTRY COURSE
DOG-SLED COURSE
SNOW-RAFTING COURSE
ORIENTEERING
RUSUTSU TOWER
TUBING PARK
KIDS PARK
SNOWBOARD PARK
GIANT
WEST GONDOLA
NIGHTER
SKY
WEST No.2 QUAD
BANBI
DYNAMIC
WEST PAIR
RAINBOW
TIGER
NATURAL
WEST TIGER PAIR
ELITE
WHITE LOVER
WEST No.1 QUAD
FAMILY
RUSUTSU

the high-rise Rusutsu Tower, without the need to take the monorail to the main hotel complex.

Most of the pisted terrain is intermediate, but runs such as Isola-A and Super East offer considerably greater pitch. The beauty of the off-piste is that it is all easily reached from the lifts with barely any hiking required, and the birch and bamboo are naturally well spaced. You just choose your line and go.

The second ski area of West Mountain is situated behind the hotel and has a family ski area and a terrain park with a 100m half-pipe.

You can hire a snowcat for £35 (for the whole cat) to climb the mountain before the lifts open and make fresh tracks at sunrise.

Learn

Rusutsu has its own **Ski and Board School**, which operates for two hours each morning, except Saturday. Technique is sound, and the number and quality of English-speaking instructors have greatly improved over the past few years.

Children

Childcare is available in the main building during the morning and afternoon, but lunch is not provided and parents must pick up their offspring and take them to a restaurant.

Lunch

Steamboat is a basic self-service on the mountain with simple food – the *ramen* noodles with pork are wholeheartedly recommended.

Dinner

The hotel has 12 different restaurants ranging from fast food to Japanese, Chinese, Italian, German and French establishments. 'We particularly enjoyed **Kakashi** sushi restaurant, but it was important to sit at the European-style tables rather than on the floor. Squatting for dinner after a day in the powder is not my cup of tea, green or otherwise,' said a reporter.

Party

Alternatives include night-skiing, dog-sledding and tubing. After skiing, most Japanese head for the hotel's *onsen*. The hotel also has a pool, gym, massage room, and games room. After dinner activity is limited to a couple of bars and karaoke.

Sleep

Rusutsu Resort Hotel, information and reservations, **t** +81 (0)136 46 3111, *www.rusutsu.co.jp/english/stay_here.html*, offers a variety of accommodation options. The North and South Wings house the main western-style hotel rooms. 'Each has two large single beds; it is perfectly comfortable, but not overtly luxurious,' commented a reporter. Rusutsu Tower contains larger suites, some arranged over two floors. There are also atmospheric log cabins made from imported Finnish logs to traditional Canadian design, each with a fireplace.

08

The Top Resorts: Scandinavia

Åre, Sweden

***BEST FOR**

All levels of skier and rider, alternative snow sports

ESSENTIALS

Altitude: 384m (1,259ft)–1420m (4,659ft)
Further information: **t** +46 (0)1771 84 0000, *www.skistar.com/are*
Lifts in area: 40 (1 funicular, 3 cable-ways, 5 chairs, 31 drags) serving 100km of piste
Lift pass: adult SEK1560, child 8–15yrs SEK1265, both for six days
Access: Östersund/Frösö airport (via Stockholm/Arlanda airport) 1hr, Trondheim airport 2hrs, railway station in resort

Profile

Scandinavia's only truly world-class downhill ski resort, suited to all standards of skier and snowboarder, as well as families who are not on a strict budget

Resort

Åre is an excellent resort, with very friendly people who speak perfect English. It is the only world-class resort in Scandinavia, with skiing that matches many resorts in the Alps for the length of its runs, the gradient and the extent of the terrain. It was the setting for the World Skiing Championships in 2007 and a new downhill course was created. The skiing is spread across different villages that are linked on-mountain and by ski bus.

Mountain

A detachable-quad and a six-seater chair take skiers from the valley to the top station in under four minutes. From here a network of lifts crisscrosses the mountainside both above and below the treeline. A tow behind a snowcat brings experienced skiers and riders to the 1420m summit of Åreskutan, starting point for a rewarding off-piste descent. The Olympia lift has been replaced by Scandinavia's first 'chondola' – a combination of chair and gondola, which has greatly eased mountain access at peak times. Slopes are open for night skiing until 8pm for much of the season. Cross-country skiing is also a popular pastime, with 56km of trails along the shores of the lake.

Learn

Beginners are well served by the **Åre** ski school, **t** +46 (0)771 84 0000, which enjoys a sound reputation and is staffed entirely by fluent English-speakers.

Children

'Åre Björnen is definitely for families,' said a reporter, 'a nice nursery slope with some gentle blues, very well staffed, very child-friendly – lots of happy kids.' The village crèche, **t** +46 (0)771 84 0000, cares for non-skiing children from three to five years. The ski school kindergarten offers tuition from three years.

Lunch

Try **Ullådalsstugan**, **t** +46 (0)647 53171, and **Hummelstugan**, **t** +46 (0)647 53284. You can buy reindeer burgers from **Lapps** in front of their teepees at Stendalen.

Dine

'Like eating in London or any major French resort,' said a reporter. Local specialities include smoked moose and smoked reindeer ('both divine'), *char*, which is similar to salmon, but more

ÅRE

RESTAURANGER

A	Hamrestugan	G	Rautjoxa Värdshus	M	720 Food Station
B	Linbanecafét	H	Café Olympia	N	Timmerstugan
C	Tegetornet	I	Vm-Grillen	O	Hyddan
D	Lillåstugan	J	Stormköket	P	Black Sheep Pub & Bistro
E	Ullådalsstugan	K	Toppstugan	Q	Tott
F	Buustamons Fjällgård	L	Hummelstugan	S	Carins Krog

DUVEDSOMRÅDET
TEGEFJÄLLSOMRÅDET
ULLÅDALSOMRÅDET
RÖDKULLEOMRÅDET
ÅREOMRÅDET
BJÖRNENOMRÅDET

- SVÅR NEDFART
- MEDELSVÅR NEDFART
- LÄTT NEDFART
- MYCKET LÄTT NEDFART
- SKIDVÄGAR
- EJ PREPARERAD OCH EJ BEVAKAD NEDFART
- SKIDSPÅR
- LÅGFARTSOMRÅDE
- LAVINFREKVENTA OMRÅDEN
- KVÄLLSBELYSNING
- HÅLLPLATS SKIDBUSS
- SAMLINGSPLATS SKIDSKOLA
- SKIDUTHYRNING/ SKIDSERVICE
- PARKERING
- LIFTNUMMER
- FÖRSÄLJNING SKIPASS / SKIDSKOLA
- RULLBAND
- TOALETTER
- MAT & DRYCK
- SKÄRMFLYG
- VÄRMESTUGA
- TURISTBYRÅ

	LIFTAR	LÄNGD	FALLHÖJD
1.	BYLIFTEN -gratis	290	28
2.	HAMRELIFTEN	986	238
4.	DUVEDS LINBANA	1.570	358
5.	DALLIFTEN	210	40
6.	TORPLIFTEN	180	35
7.	LERÅLIFTEN	1.002	227
8.	ENGLANDSLIFTEN	1.116	190
9.	GUNNILLIFTEN	1.613	293

	LIFTAR	LÄNGD	FALLHÖJD
10.	MINI TEGE -gratis	180	25
11.	TEGEFJÄLLSLIFTEN	1.150	275
12.	FJÄLLVALLSLIFTEN	1.040	140
14.	ULLÅDALSLIFTEN	1.171	208
15.	ULLÅDALSLIFTEN 2	840	155
16.	RÖDHAKELIFTEN -gratis	130	20
17.	LILLVITA	430	75
18.	LILLRÖDA	400	70

	LIFTAR	LÄNGD	FALLHÖJD
19.	RÖDKULLELIFTEN 1	1.245	282
20.	RÖDKULLELIFTEN 2	1.245	282
21.	BRÄCKELIFTEN	828	168
22.	VM8:AN	1.490	454
23.	OLYMPIAGONDOLEN	1.610	447
24.	STENDALSLIFTEN	581	137
25.	NEDRE TVÄRÅVALVSL.	900	262
26.	NEDRE TVÄRÅVALVSL. 2	844	257

	LIFTAR	LÄNGD	FALLHÖJD
27.	ÖVRE TVÄRÅVALVSLIFTEN	496	80
28.	TUSENMETERSLIFTEN	856	257
29.	KABINBANAN	2.900	853
30.	WORLDCUPLIFTEN	843	331
31.	VM6:AN	1.100	340
32.	HUMMELLIFTEN	616	218
33.	BERGBANAN	790	193
37.	TOTTLIFTEN	1.474	320

	LIFTAR
38.	HÖGÅSLIFTEN
39.	SADELLIFTEN
40.	BJÖRNLIFTEN
41.	LOKATTLIFTEN
42.	VARGLIFTEN
43.	RENENLIFTEN -gratis
44.	FÖRBERGSLIFTEN
45.	NALLELIFTEN

delicate, and lingenberry ketchup. **Villa Tottebo**, **t** +46 (0)647 50620, is an old hunting lodge specializing in reindeer steaks. **Liten Krog**, **t** +46 (0)647 52200, is recommended for its reasonably priced pizzas. **Easy Kitchen**, **t** +46 (0)647 12000, in **Holiday Club Åre**, features stir-fry dishes, pizzas and salads. **Carins Krog**, **t** +46 (0)647 10450, outside the village, serves reindeer tartare. Readers enjoyed **Broken**, **t** +46 (0)647 50633, for its atmosphere, and **Twins**, **t** +46 (0)647 50450, for its steaks, fish, cool décor and open fire. A reporter recommended eating in. 'Sweden is not that expensive by modern British prices. If you self-cater, the supermarket is excellent, with a great range of really, really good food.'

Party

Åre Björnen is not the place for heady nightlife, but Åre Village has plenty of restaurants and bars. **Skiers' Bar** at Hotel Diplomat, **Fjällgården**, stuffed full of people dancing on tables at 4pm, and **Wersēns Bar** are packed when the lifts close. **Bygget** at Arefjällby is one of the best nightspots. Another popular nightclub, **Country Club**, is located in Hotel Diplomat Åregården.

Sleep

Accommodation can be booked through a central office, **t** +46 (0)771 84 0000, *www.skistar.com/are*.

Luxury:

******Hotel Diplomat Åregården**, **t** +46 (0)647 17800, *www.diplomathotel.com*, is close to the lifts and receives high praise. 'One of the best hotels I have ever stayed in – well fitted, friendly, sociable, and handy for all of the town; restaurant stunningly good,' enthused a reporter.

*****Totthotell**, **t** +46 (0)647 15000, *www.totthotell.com*, has minimalist modern bedrooms and apartments, and a huge spa with 17 treatment rooms.

Moderate:

Diplomat Ski Lodge, **t** +46 (0)647 17800, *www.diplomathotel.com*, is recently refurbished, within walking distance of the lifts, and has a large number of family rooms.

Holiday Club Åre, **t** +46 (0)647 12000, *www.holidayclub.se*, is one of the biggest ski hotels in Sweden, with four restaurants, bowling, and an adventure pool with 67m of winding waterslide.

Hotel Fjällgården, **t** +46 (0)647 14500, is slope-side, with a good restaurant and a buzzing atmosphere.

Geilo, Norway

Profile

Traditional resort with impressive cross-country skiing and limited but relaxed downhill skiing for beginners to intermediates. A general sense of remoteness that you would rarely find in the Alps

Resort

The first known British visitor to the area around the Hallingskarvet mountains was in 1867, when Lord Garvagh of Portman Square, author of *The Pilgrim of Scandinavia*, arrived in what is now Geilo. When the Bergen railway line launched in 1909, the village began to

✻ BEST FOR

Beginners and low intermediates, families, cross-country

ESSENTIALS

Altitude: 800m (2,624ft)–1178m (3,864ft)
Further information: t +47 3209 5900, *www.geilo.no*
Lifts in area: 20 (6 chairs, 14 drags) serving 34km of piste
Lift pass: Kr1,135–1,350, child 7–15yrs Kr850–1,010, both for six days
Access: Fagernes airport 2hrs, Oslo airport 4½hrs

grow around the small railway station that marked the halfway point in the wilderness between Oslo and Bergen. More hotels were built the same year, including the Dr Holms Høyfjellshotell, which to this day remains the focal point of the resort.

However, the idea of Geilo as a modern ski centre didn't really catch on until one of Norway's first slalom races was held here in 1935. The first chairlift opened in 1954, the resort's first ski school in the 1950s, and since then Geilo hasn't looked back.

Geilo today is one of the best family resorts in Scandinavia, a village well known to avid cross-country skiers as one of the centres of the famous Hardangervidda Plateau, with a total of 220km of loipe in the immediate area of the resort. Geilo is also known as the European capital of kite-surfing and is a past host of the world championships.

Mountain

With a vertical drop of only 373m, the resort is best suited to beginners, low intermediates and families. The two main ski areas – Geilohovda and Geilolia/Kikut – are inconveniently situated on either side of a fjord, with the resort situated in the centre.

Most of the skiing is at the larger Geilohovda area at the foot of the famous Hardangervidda, which is Northern Europe's largest mountain plateau. But smaller Geilolia is the location for the Troll Club and the ski-school. The area links by chairlift to the Kikut ski area. There are three terrain parks with jumps and rails. The one in the Geilolia area has been upgraded with lights for night-skiing.

Learn

Per Bye, **t** +47 3209 0650 ('recommended – its instructors speak good English'), and **Geilolia**, **t** +47 3209 0000, are two excellent schools. 'This is a top resort for novice instruction,' enthused one reporter, 'no arrogant show-off instructors here – just honest, nice and well qualified people who actually want you to get better.'

Children

The much-praised **Trollklubben**, **t** +47 3209 5518, in the Geilolia area, offers excellent childcare in a warm, friendly environment, and cares for children from newborn to seven years. The **Ski School** at Vestlia is said to be friendly, though skiing in the Vestlia area is limited for better intermediates. The resort holds a weekly treasure hunt on green runs.

Lunch

'Food on the slopes was expensive and not great quality, but the hotel seemed to turn a blind eye to those taking food for a packed lunch, and the restaurants tolerated picnickers,' advised a reporter. There are six cafés and kiosks up the mountain serving basic fare – although alcohol is not available until after 3pm. The sun terrace of the **Dr Holms Hotel**, **t** +47 3209 5940, is the more sophisticated lunchtime rendezvous.

Dine

The rustic-style **Hallingstuene**, **t** +47 3209 1250, specializes in game. **Peppe's Pizza**, **t** +47 3209 1815, is the cheaper alternative.

Party

Geilo is not the place to find wild après-ski, although **Jegerbaren** and **Lille Bla** are both popular. The recently refurbished **Recepten Pub** in the Dr Holms Hotel and the **Pianobaren** in the Highland have plenty of ambience. **Highdance** is the sole disco. The **Icefestival**, which is the world's only music festival with all instruments made from ice, takes place at the end of January each year.

Sleep

All accommodation can be booked through the following central number, **t** +47 3209 5940.

Luxury:

Dr Holms Hotel, **t** +47 3209 5700, *www.drholms.no*, has been the focal point of the resort for 100 years and has a spa and a new bowling-with-dinner experience.

Moderate/Budget:

Bardøla Hyttegrend, **t** +47 3209 4100, are 22 log cabins set in the woods, each with four bedrooms and a cosy sitting room. It is a well-run family-friendly hotel – the food and service are excellent.

Geilolia Hyttetun, **t** +47 3209 0000, are 30 well-equipped chalets right next to the Geilolia ski centre.

Lia Fjellstue, **t** +47 3208 7400, *www.liafjellstue.no*, is in Skurdalen, 14km from Geilo, with magnificent views of Hardangervidda. There are eight new luxury suites and traditional Norwegian food is served.

Park Inn Highland, **t** +47 3209 6100, *www.highland.no*, is recommended for its clean, comfortable rooms, friendly staff, great food and pool.

Vestlia Resort, **t** +47 3208 7200, *www.vestlia.no*, in the Vestlia ski area, has excellent food.

Ustedalen Hotel, **t** +47 3209 6700, *www.usterdalen.no*, is a comfortable family-run establishment 700m from the resort centre. It also has three log-cabin-style apartments for up to 10 people.

Hemsedal, Norway

Profile

Best downhill skiing in Norway, suited to all standards of skier as well as families. Has an excellent terrain park for snowboarders and twin-tip skiers

Resort

Hemsedal has the most challenging downhill skiing in Norway. The resort is divided into the self-contained Skisenter at the base of the mountain and the original community of Hemsedal two

*** BEST FOR**

All levels of skier, snowboarders

ESSENTIALS

Altitude: 650m (2,133ft)–1497m (4,911ft)
Further information: t +47 3205 5030, *www.hemsedal.com*
Lifts in area: 22 (6 chairs, 16 drags) serving 43km of piste
Lift pass: Kr1,455, child 7–15yrs Kr1,190, both for six days
Access: Oslo airport 3½hrs

miles away. Plans are on the drawing board to link the two by gondola. For the present they are connected by free ski bus. 'Geared to car drivers and very pedestrian-unfriendly. Bus service is a joke,' complained a reporter.

Mountain

The skiing is suited to all standards, with some genuinely steeper terrain served by an eight-seater chair, including the Hjallerløypa run, which deserves its double-black classification. Reidarskaret is a challenging off-piste itinerary that evolves from a precipitous *couloir*. You are advised to take a guide, who will arrange for a taxi to bring you back to the resort. However, there is also plenty of benign terrain for novices and intermediates. Night-skiing until 9pm is possible four days a week until mid-March.

The resort has two terrain parks. The 600m main park, considered to be one of the best in Europe, has two half-pipes and a quarter-pipe. The recently extended second one in the Trollskogen area is aimed at new riders.

Learn

Hemsedal Ski School, t +47 3205 5067, has a good reputation ('very American in style, lessons fun, small classes and well organized'). **Solheisen Ski and Snowboard School, t** +47 4130 5094, is an alternative learning centre at Solheisen, a 10-minute drive away. Its three lifts are included in the Hemsedal lift pass.

Children

A large new children's area with five easy runs makes this one of the best resorts in Scandinavia for kids. Ski passes and helmet rental are free for under-sevens. The **Trollia** crèche, **t** +47 3205 5320, beside the slopes cares for childen from six months.

Lunch

Try **Harahorn, t** +47 3206 2380, mid-mountain. Cafés at Hemsedal Village include **Kremen Kafe, t** +47 3206 0237, and **Kafe Kakaotwo, t** +47 9509 5811.

Dine

The restaurant at **Hotel Skarsnuten, t** +47 3206 1700, serves gourmet food. **Skogstad Hotel, t** +47 3205 5000, **Peppes Pizza, t** +47 3205 9557, and the **Hemsedal Café, t** +47 3205 5410, are recommended.

Party

Skistua, Hemsen and Garasjen are the main meeting places. The **Skogstad Piano Bar** and **Hemsedal Café** are also always crowded.

Sleep

For accommodation contact **Hemsedal Booking, t** +47 3205 5060.

Luxury:

Skarsnuten Hotel, t +47 3206 1700, *www.skarsnutenhotel.no*, is at 1000m, linked by chair to the Mountain Village.

Skogstad Hotell, t +47 3205 5000, *www.skogstadhotell.no*, in Hemsedal village, has a nightclub and pool and is the centre for nightlife in the village.

Good:

Hemsedal Hotell, t +47 3205 5400, *www.hemsedalhotell.no*, is situated at Tuv, midway between Hemsedal and the lifts.

Flaget Farm, t +47 3206 2400, is where you spend the night in a wigwam-style home used by Sami herdsmen. You bathe in a hot tub and sleep on reindeer skins around a central oven. Dinner is served around an open fire.

Hemsedal Alpine Lodge, **t** +47 3205 5060, *www.skistar.com/hemsedal*, opens this season and is slopeside.

Levi, Finland

Profile

Offbeat resort in the Arctic Circle with a long snow-sure season and a wide choice of non-skiing activities, but lively après-ski

Resort

Finland's only truly international ski resort usually has snow from mid-October until mid-May, which explains why Rossignol has one of its four worldwide equipment test centres here.

Levi is situated in magical surroundings in a pine forest 161km from Rovaniemi, the capital of Finnish Lapland.

From November to January the sun fails to make it over the horizon, and, when not pitch dark, the resort is bathed in soft twilight. Some 15 runs are floodlit from 10am to 8pm by sodium lamps, which give the winter landscape a surreal tint. By night, the Northern Lights dance across the sky. After New Year the hours of daylight increase, and in spring the ski area is open without lights until 8pm.

Apart from skiing, other activities include 230km of cross-country skiing, a visit to a Lapp farm for reindeer rides, snowmobiling, dog-sledding and ice-diving.

***BEST FOR**

Beginners, low intermediates, families, reindeer- and dog-sledding

ESSENTIALS

Altitude: 400m (1,312ft)–531m (1,742ft)
Further information: **t** +358 (0)207 960 200, *www.levi.fi*
Lifts in area: 26 (2 cableway, 23 drags) serving 45km of piste
Lift pass: adult €73–146, child under 12yrs €44–88, both for six days
Access: Kittilä airport 10mins

Mountain

This is a modest ski area with short runs down all sides of the dome-shaped mountain, best-suited to beginners, low intermediates and families. 'If you are looking for challenging skiing on blacks, then this is not the resort for you,' said a reader. 'If however, you are looking for cruising on picturesque, uncrowded slopes, then this is the place.' A modern gondola acts as the backbone of the 26-lift system. A gondola and chairlift have replaced two of the longest draglifts. Huge investment in the village means that the number of rental beds is expected to double by 2009. The resort has a super-pipe and a separate terrain park with half-pipe, super-pipe and snowcross course.

Learn

Levi Ski School, **t** +358 (0)207 960 211, has an excellent reputation, and lessons include the use of lifts.

Children

Tenavatokka, **t** +358 (0)207 960 212, cares for skiing and non-skiing kids from newborn to six years. Adjoining **Children's Land** has three baby-lifts. Children under seven wearing helmets can ski free.

Lunch

Try **Alpine Cafe, t** +358 (0)207 960 280, **Draivi, t** +358 (0)207 960 283, **Horizont, t** +358 (0)207 960 285, **Sivakka, t** +358 (0)207 960 287, **Cafe Tanja, t** +358 (0)207 960 281, and **Luvattumaa, t** +358 (0)40740 0925.

Dine

Most guests eat in their hotels, where reindeer rules the menu. **Fun Action Fondue, t** +358 (0)400 503 278, is what it says it is. **Levin Gastro, t** +358 (0)16 644 884, is a gourmet experience. **Levin Bistro, t** +358 (0)16 644 125, is a pizzeria.

Party

'If anyone tells you the Finns don't know how to do après-ski – they are lying,' said a reader; 'the bar on the slopes opens at 3pm, and you can guarantee that people will be dancing on the tables by 4pm.'

The **Seika** nightclub and **Joiku Karaoke Bar** are both in Hotelli Levitunturi, while **Disco Beige** is the alternative.

Sleep

Accommodation can be booked through a central office, **t** +358 (0)16 639 3300.

Luxury:

Hotel K5 Levi, t +358 (0)16 639 1100, *www.k5levi.fi*, has 35 no-smoking rooms, minimalist decoration and private saunas or hot-tubs in each room.

Hotelli Levitunturi, t +358 (0)16 646 301, *www.hotellilevitunturi.fi*, has a pool, five restaurants, a nightclub and a sports hall with tennis, badminton and basketball courts.

Moderate:

Hotel Hullu Poro, t +358 (0)16 651 0100, *www.hulluporo.fi*, meaning 'crazy reindeer', has a newer extension with comfortable rooms – some with private saunas. The food is said to be great, with even the heartiest appetite satisfied.

09

The Top Resorts: Spain

Baqueira-Beret

*BEST FOR

All levels of skier and rider, ski gourmets, party-goers, comfort-seekers

ESSENTIALS

Altitude: 1500m (4,920ft)–2510m (8,235ft)
Further information: **t** +34 973 63 90 00, *www.baqueira.es*
Lifts in area: 26 (1 gondola, 20 chairs, 5 drags) serving 104km of piste
Lift pass: adult €208, child 6–11yrs €132, both for six days
Access: Toulouse airport 2hrs

Profile

Spain's smartest resort, set amid dramatic Pyrenean scenery and patronized by the Spanish Royal Family. A wide choice of restaurants and an exhausting nightlife

Resort

Seaside and sangria rather than slalom and snow are more familiarly associated with Spanish holidays, but the country does in fact offer surprisingly good skiing.

For years, Baqueira-Beret in the Pyrenees has remained Europe's best-kept ski secret, shared by a small but knowledgeable band of international skiers who have found a truly viable alternative to the over-commercialized resorts of the Alps. The trouble with nearly all such so-called 'alternatives' to the big-name resorts is that they usually lack either the variety of terrain or the sophisticated infrastructure of the Alps – or both.

Not so Baqueira in the Val d'Aran, a cross-cultural pocket of the Pyrenees where Spanish, Catalan and Aranese are all spoken. French is also widely understood.

As a holiday destination it has serious chic status. The Spanish monarch has a majestic home here. King Juan Carlos no longer skis, but his children and their families visit most weekends during the season. Even Victoria Beckham and her children have stayed here.

For the past 44 years since the resort opened above the ancient town of Vielha, Baqueira has been content to offer its slopes to a predominantly Spanish market. However, it is now actively seeking an international image as the ski area expands into neighbouring valleys.

Three new hotels including a five-star are scheduled to open this winter just below the resort, reached by a new stage of the gondola. Baqueira seems set to realize a major international profile. For those of us who have quietly enjoyed its skiing over the years, this is a shame – but in today's competitive market ski resorts must evolve or die. The window between unspoilt mountainsides and commercial exploitation is unfortunately an all too narrow one.

Pretty it is not. The original purpose-built edifices of the 1980s are made of functional concrete. However, more recent additions are in a much more pleasing style, in keeping with the resort's dramatically beautiful setting on the road that leads up to the high Bonaigua Pass.

Anyone not used to the Spanish way of doing things needs to understand the timetable in order to survive. For indigenous guests, skiing is an activity you rarely contemplate before 10.30am. Lunch is at 2pm or even 3pm, followed by a last run to the base area. Rioja and tapas last until 7pm when the bars empty and everyone goes to bed. The Spanish summer siesta habit remains unbroken in winter. Dinner *en famille* is at 10pm or 11pm for grown-ups, and the nightclubs start to warm up around 2am.

Mountain

Statistics tell you the resort has 26 lifts, 104km of piste and a 1000m vertical drop, but that's only a small part of the story. The skiing truly suits all standards, with plenty of easy cruising terrain as well as steeper slopes for advanced intermediates. Easily accessible off-piste in the Bonaigua and Beret sectors rivals the best of Switzerland and France. You can even heliski here at a modest price.

The newly extended gondola provides the main means of mountain access and doorstep skiing from the trio of new hotels. It takes skiers up to the mid-mountain station at 1800m. The Spanish are slow to ski each morning and rush-hour queues are almost unheard-of. The moderately extensive ski area covers four linked mountains that offer a substantial vertical drop of 1000m. Most is given over to comfortable cruising terrain, but there are all sorts of variants, with some sharp little drop-offs at the edges of runs, and plentiful off-piste opportunities with a guide. Where Goats Tumble, Baqueira's most infamous *couloir*, can test even experienced powderhounds to the full. There is a terrain park with half-pipe.

Learn

Baqueira Ski School, t +34 973 63 90 10, has 300 ski instructors, but don't expect many of them to speak fluent English. **Ski Miquel, t** +44 (0)1457 821 200, runs its own BASI ski school with British instructors. There is a new beginners' area at the top of the second gondola station.

Children

Baqueira has **Snowparks** for kids of three months to three years, opposite the Bosque ski lift at **1800, t** +34 606 54 41 32, opposite the control tower in **Beret**, **t** +34 606 54 41 34, and next to Hotel Montarto at **1500, t** +34 973 64 54 48.

Lunch

Lunch at **Restaurante Salad Bar 2200**, **t** +34 973 63 90 90, is more interesting than its name – it serves a variety of grilled-to-order meats along with the lettuce leaves. **Cap del Port, t** +34 973 25 00 82, a gothic folly, offers *haute cuisine* 200m from Bonaigua village. **Restaurant 1800, t** +34 973 64 52 02, is at the foot of the Baqueira Plain chair and serves Aranese and Catalan cuisine. The cut-price alternative is to settle for £7-a-head tapas and Rioja back in town at **Tamarro's, t** +34 973 64 43 22.

Dine

Gastronomically we rate it among the top 10 ski resorts in the world for *haute cuisine* at sensible prices – with a couple of dozen restaurants quite literally fit for a king. **La Pleta, t** +34 973 64 55 50, in the hotel of the same name, has the best table in the resort itself. **Esquiro, t** +34 973 64 54 30, specializes in hearty Aranese dishes. **La Borda Lobato, t** +34 973 64 57 08, majors in roast suckling pig and whole baby lamb carved at the table. **Urtau, t** +34 973 64 18 15, in nearby Arties, is warmly recommended for its variety of duck dishes and crêpes. **Casa Irene, t** +34 973 64 43 64, in Arties, has excellent fresh fish and grilled meat.

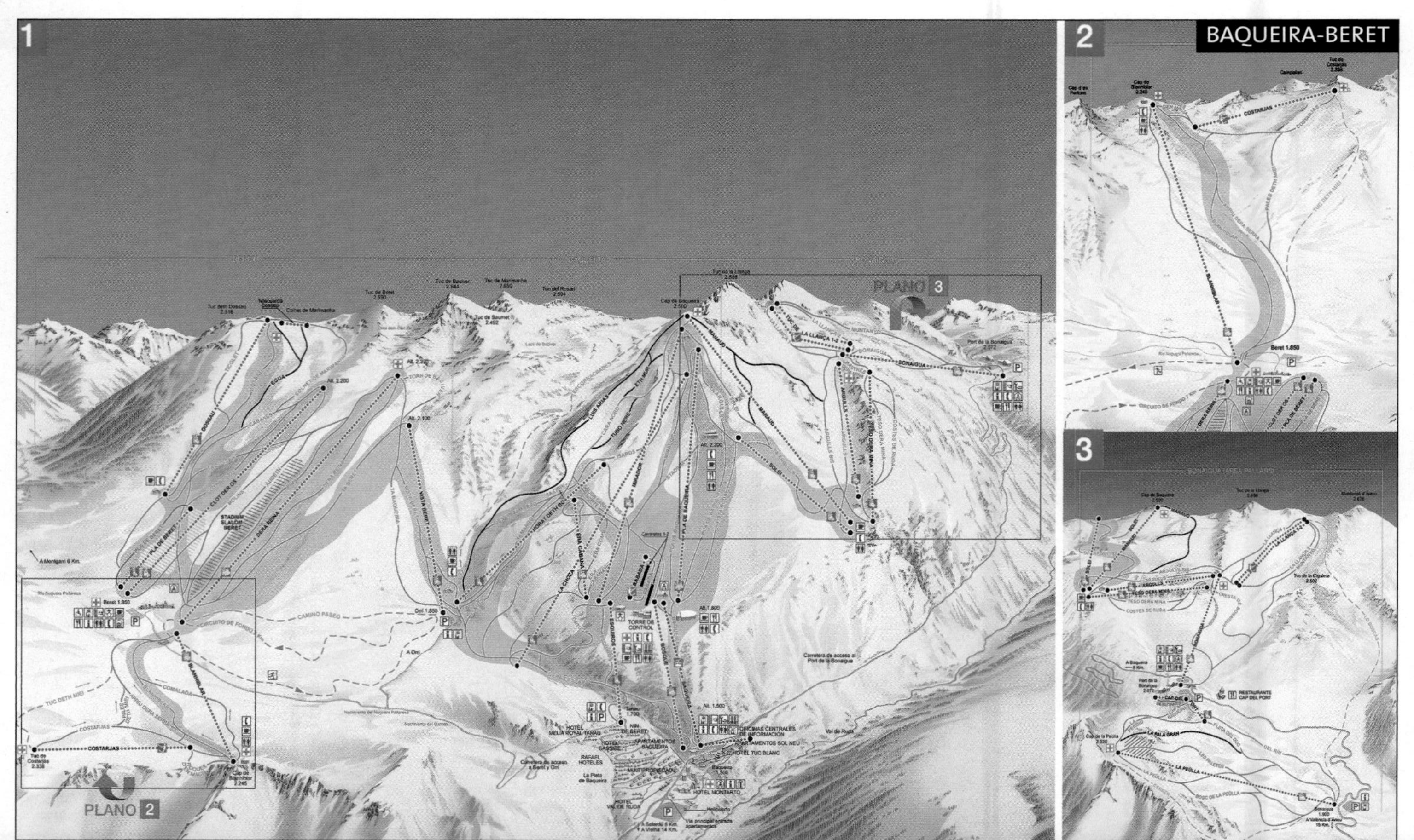

BAQUEIRA-BERET
1
2
3
PLANO 2
PLANO 3
Cap de Baqueira 2.500
Tuc de la Llança 2.659
Port de la Bonaigua 2.072
Beret 1.850
Orri 1.850
Baqueira 1.500
Alt. 2.200
Alt. 2.100
Alt. 1.800
Alt. 1.500
TORRE DE CONTROL
OFICINAS CENTRALES DE INFORMACIÓN
APARTAMENTOS SOL NEU
HOTEL TUC BLANC
HOTEL MONTARTO
HOTEL MELIÁ ROYAL TANAU
RAFAEL HOTELES
APARTAMENTOS BAQUEIRA
Carretera de acceso al Port de la Bonaigua
Val de Ruda
CAMINO PASEO
CIRCUITO DE FONDO
COSTARJAS
BLANHIBLAR
VISTA BERET
PLA DE BAQUEIRA
MANAUD
BONAIGUA
ARGULLS
TESO DERA MINA
SOLEI
LA CHOZA
ERA CABANA
ESQUIROS
BOSQUE
MIRADOR
RESTAURANTE CAP DEL PORT
LA PALA GRAN
LA PEÜLLA

Party

Nightlife starts late in Spain. **Tiffany's** is the popular nightclub, along with **Pacha**. Others include **Tuc Nere** and **Vielha Dance Club** in Vielha.

Sleep

Three more hotels including the five-star AC Baqueira are scheduled to open this winter.

★★★★★**Rafaelhoteles La Pleta**, **t** +34 973 64 55 50, *www.rafaelhoteles.com*, with its bell tower and Aranese design, has a pool and a shuttle service to the lift ('a truly outstanding modern hotel with a fine spa and the best gastronomic cuisine in the resort').

★★★★★**Melia Royal Tanau Boutique Hotel**, **t** +34 973 64 44 46, *www.solmelia.com*, has a chairlift that transports skiers to the slopes.

★★★★**Eira Stylehotel**, **t** +34 973 645 446 , *www.eirahotel.com*, is a new addition in the Tanau area, 40m from the chairlift, and has just 10 double rooms.

★★★★**Parador de Arties**, **t** +34 973 64 08 01, *www.paradores-spain.com*, is in the hamlet of Arties 7km from Baqueira. The interior features traditional mountain design with wooden beams in all the bedrooms.

★★★★**Hotel Casa Irene**, **t** +34 973 64 43 64, *www.innsofspain.com*, is also in Arties and has a good restaurant serving local specialities. The rooms are spacious and decorated in keeping with the hotel's rustic setting.

★★★★**Hotel Chalet Bassibe**, **t** +34 973 64 51 52, *www.valderuda-bassibe.com*, is up at Baqueira 1700 and has 36 bedrooms.

★★★★**Hotel Montarto**, **t** +34 973 63 90 01, *www.montarto.com*, is centrally located and boasts two restaurants and a pool, and offers children's entertainment.

★★★**Hotel Orri**, t +34 973 64 60 86, *www.husa.es*, located in the small village of Tredós 2km from Baqueira, has 30 rooms and offers free transport to the slopes.

★★★**Hotel Tuc Blanc**, **t** +34 973 64 43 50, *www.hoteltucblanc.com*, is conveniently set at the foot of the slopes.

10

The Top Resorts: Switzerland

Andermatt

***BEST FOR**
Dedicated steep 'n' deep artists, Swiss charm

ESSENTIALS
Altitude: 1444m (4,736ft)–2963m (9,719ft)
Further information: t +41 (0)41 887 1454, *www.andermatt.ch*
Lifts in area: 24in Gottard–Oberalp (1 funicular, 2 cableways, 8 chairs, 12 drags) serving 140km of piste
Lift pass: Gottard–Oberalp (covers Andermatt, Oberalp, Sedrun and Disentis) adult CHF239, youth 13–17yrs CHF180, child 6–12yrs CHF119
Access: Zurich airport 1½hrs, railway station in resort

Profile

Quaint and picturesque non-mainstream resort that is the reserve of serious skiers and riders looking for steep pistes and plenty of challenging powder runs

Resort

Andermatt has a low profile as an international resort, but all that may be about to change. Outside Switzerland it is known only to that dedicated three per cent of skiers whose enjoyment of the sport lies mainly in exploring ungroomed slopes well away from the resort. Its isolated position in the Urseren Valley by the Gotthard pass and road tunnel makes it an unlikely winter destination.

However, a wealthy Egyptian businessman has announced plans to build a year-round resort here of a kind never before seen in the Alps. It will include 800 hotel rooms, a golf course, and a pool with a sandy beach.

Samih Sawiris, the entrepreneur behind the giant El Gouna resort on the Red Sea, has the backing of most of the villagers. However, lengthy planning and environmental hurdles have to be overcome before the idea becomes reality.

The Swiss government adopted Andermatt over many years as a major training centre for its alpine troops, who are never likely to fight a war against any of its neighbours. These days, the army presence is much more muted and the military authorities have expressed a willingness to hand over 600,000 square metres of land for Sawaris' scheme.

The small village centre is attractive with pleasant cobbled streets and a smattering of hotels, bars and shops.

Mountain

The Gemstock is the main ski area, reached from Andermatt by a two-stage cable car that takes you up to the top of the Gurschengletscher at 2963m. From here a famous Bernard Russi-designed run brings you all the way back down to Andermatt. Another marginally easier piste takes you down the St Anna glacier to the mid-mountain station, Gurschen. Off-piste opportunities with a local guide are legion.

The separate ski area of Gütsch, reached by a two-stage chairlift on the other side of the resort and by a train that goes up to the 2044m Oberalppass, is overall less challenging but still has some demanding slopes. Two other areas, Hospental and Realp, provide further advanced and intermediate terrain.

Learn

Snowsports School Andermatt, t +41 (0)41 887 1240, is the only ski learning academy. **Snowlimit, t** +41 (0)41 887 0614, teaches snowboarding. **Bergschule Uri**, t +41 (0)41 872 0900, **Bergschule Montanara**, t +41 (0)41 878 1259, and **Alpina Sport**, t +41 (0)41 887 1788 all provide guiding.

Children

Snowsports School Andermatt accepts children from four and a half years.

Lunch

Try **Bergrestaurant Gurschen**, t +41 (0)41 887 1618, for wholesome fare at reasonable prices, and **Bergrestaurant Nätschen-Gütsch**, t +41 (0)41 887 1352.

The **Bahnhofbuffet**, t +41 (0)41 888 0050, is recommended. **Tre Passi**, t +41 (0)41 887 0088, is good for venison and wild boar. **Postillion**, t + 41 (0)41 887 1044, and **Spycher**, t +41 (0)41 887 1753, are also praised. In Hospental, try **Zum Dörfli**, t +41 (0)41 887 0132.

Party

Baroko Music Bar and **Pinte** are the liveliest spots. Others to try are **Ochsen**, **Barry Bar**, **Piccadilly Pub** and **Bar La Curva**.

Sleep

*****Activ Kronen Hotel Andermatt**, t +41 (0)41 887 0088, *www.kronenhotel.ch*, is a family-run hotel.

*****Drei Könige & Post**, t +41 (0)41 887 0001, *www.3koenige.ch*, is a quiet hotel in the town centre with a wellness centre.

*****Monopol-Metropol**, t +41 (0)41 887 1575, *www.monopol-andermatt.ch*, has simple rooms, some with kitchenettes.

*****Hotel Sonne**, t +41 (0)41 887 1226, *www.hotelsonneandermatt.ch*, is two minutes' walk from the Gemsstock cable car.

Hotel Schweizerhof, t +41 (0)41 887 1189, *www.schweizerhof-andermatt.ch*, is central and its restaurant specializes in Italian cooking and fondues.

Crans-Montana

Profile

Large town with smart hotels and elegant boutiques. Suits epicurean intermediates in search of certain snow, and is one of the best resorts for snowboarders

Resort

Skiing began in 1911 in Crans and the adjoining village of Montana when British pioneer Sir Arnold Lunn organized the first genuine downhill in skiing history. He chose this scenic little resort, partly because of its long vertical drop from the Plaine Morte glacier. More importantly, his father Henry had been running golf

* BEST FOR

Intermediates, snowboarders, shoppers, ski gourmets

ESSENTIALS

Altitude: 1500m (4,920ft)–3000m (9,840ft)
Further information: t +41 (0)27 485 0404, *www.crans-montana.ch*
Lifts in area: 33 (6 cableways, 6 chairs, 21 drags) serving 140km of piste
Lift pass: area adult CHF301, youth 16–19yrs CHF256, child 6–15yrs CHF181, all for six days
Access: Sion airport 30mins, Geneva airport 1½hrs, railway station at Sierre 15km, bus to resort

holidays for the previous five years and had already established the necessary local contacts.

Crans-Montana had already built a reputation from the 1890s as a centre for tuberculosis clinics. During the early days, invalid and sportsman sat uneasily side by side in the resort's cafés and restaurants. Today a large proportion of the hotels still offer health treatments, with dietary restaurants and doctors on hand to prescribe treatments, much to the bemusement of young snowboarders who congregate here for some of the best riding facilities in Switzerland.

Crans, Montana and neighbouring Aminona are in an enviable position on a sunny plateau above the Rhone Valley dotted with larches and lakes. However, they have grown together in an urban sprawl along several kilometres of main road that is often clogged with traffic. The fresh alpine air, for which it originally won acclaim, carries more than a healthy share of carbon monoxide. A funicular from the valley town of Sierre takes only 12 minutes to reach Crans and has done much to alleviate the traffic problem, particularly at weekends.

Mountain

Crans Montana is a pleasant family ski area that suits intermediates who are happy to take a few cruising runs amid spectacular scenery before settling down to a long lunch on a sunny terrace. 'We did get a little bored of the runs by the end of the week but overall a great resort for intermediate skiers,' said a reporter. It also has good nursery slopes, but advanced skiers will soon tire of the lack of challenging gradients. The only officially graded black run is a bumpy fall-line pitch under the Toula chair that does not really justify its colour. Possible itinerary routes from the Plaine-Morte glacier include an enjoyable run down to the lake at Zeuzier. By walking through tunnels – a torch is needed – and skiing down a summer road, you can reach the ski area of the neighbouring purpose-built resort of Anzère. Novice skiers get a carefree introduction to the sport on nursery slopes served by three draglifts on the golf course at Crans.

Crans-Montana and Amonina have terrain parks, and there is a half-pipe at Cry d'Err.

Learn

'A difficult place for complete beginners,' advised a reporter. **Swiss Snowsports School** in Crans, **t** +41 (0)27 485 9370, and Montana, **t** +41 (0)27 481 1480, both have worthy reputations. **Ski & Sky**, **t** +41 (0)27 485 4250, is a much-praised alternative. **Stoked**, **t** +41 (0)27 480 2421, teaches skiing and snowboarding. **Air Glacier**, **t** +41 (0)27 329 1415, and **Helicopter Services**, **t** +41 (0)27 327 3060, offer heli-skiing.

Children

'An excellent all-round family resort,' said a reader. **Fleurs des Champs** kindergarten, **t** +41 (0)27 481 2367, next to Hotel Eldorado in Montana, accepts children from three months to seven years on weekdays only and is recommended. **Zig-Zag**, **t** +41 (0)27 481 2205, also in Montana, takes children from 18 months. The **Jardin des Neiges**, **t** +41 (0)27 481 1480, is at the Grand Signal mid-station, and **Crans Ski School** kindergarten, **t** +41 (0)27 485 9370, is beside the tubing slope.

Lunch

The resort has 13 mountain eateries, including the delightful but expensive

Merbé, **t** +41 (0)27 481 2297, and **Plumachit**, **t** +41 (0)27 481 2532, which has great atmosphere and food at better prices. **Cabane des Violettes**, **t** +41 (0)27 481 3919, is a genuine touring hut providing simple meals.

Dine

In Crans, try **Nouvelle Rôtisserie**, **t** +41 (0)27 481 1885, and **La Bergerie du Cervin**, **t** +41 (0)27 481 2180, which specializes in raclette, fondue and other cheesy dishes. In Montana, **Hostellerie du Pas-de-l'Ours**, **t** +41 (0)27 485 9333 has atmosphere and good food. **La Diligence t** +41 (0)27 485 9985 is renowned for its Middle Eastern cuisine, and **Au Gréni**, **t** +41 (0)27 481 2443, a Roger Moore favourite, serves gourmet fare at film star prices. **Rhapsodie**, **t** +41 (0)27 481 1155 is new.

Party

'Après ski is a bit tame compared to some Austrian resorts we have visited,' said a reporter. Bars include **Punch Bar Cubain**, which has salsa and samba music. **Monk's Bar** and **Amadeus** are popular, and **New Pub** is on the edge of the lake. Teenagers flock to **Montana's Number Two** for late drinking. **Absolut** and **Le Barocke** are the discos, while **Sporting Club** has dancing.

Sleep

Crans:

★★★★★**Hostellerie du Pas de l'Ours**, **t** +41 (0)27 485 9334, *www.relais chateaux.com*, is stylish.

★★★★★**Hotel Royal**, **t** +41 (0)27 481 3931, *www.hotel-royal.ch*, has a wellness centre with a good pool.

★★★★★**Grand Hotel du Golf**, **t** +41 (0)27 481 4242, *www.grand-hotel-du-golf.ch*, is elegant and discreet.

★★★**Hotel Mont-Blanc**, **t** +41 (0)27 481 3143, on a hill above Crans, has striking views and 13 spacious bedrooms.

Montana:

★★★**Hotel St-George**, **t** +41 (0)27 481 2414, *www.hotel-st-george.ch*, offers good food and service but small rooms.

★★★**Hotel de la Prairie**, **t** +41 (0)27 481 4421, is chalet-style with lovely views from the breakfast table.

Davos

Profile

Glorious pistes amid spectacular scenery in the place where alpine skiing began over a century ago. The large town shares its Parsenn ski area with Klosters. Good for snowboarders; suits all standards of skier

Resort

Davos is a large spa town that has a life beyond skiing. Each winter it receives worldwide exposure when global movers

*** BEST FOR**

Sophisto-cats, intermediates and experts, off-piste

ESSENTIALS

Altitude: 1560m (5,117ft)–2844m (9,328ft)
Further information: **t** +41 (0)81 415 21 96, *www.davos.ch*
Lifts in area: 56 in Davos/Klosters area (3 funiculars, 12 cableways, 9 chairs, 36 drags) serving 305km of piste
Lift pass: adult CHF285, youth 13–17yrs CHF200, child 6–12yrs CHF100, all for six days
Access: Zurich airport 2½hrs, railway station in Davos Dorf and Davos Platz

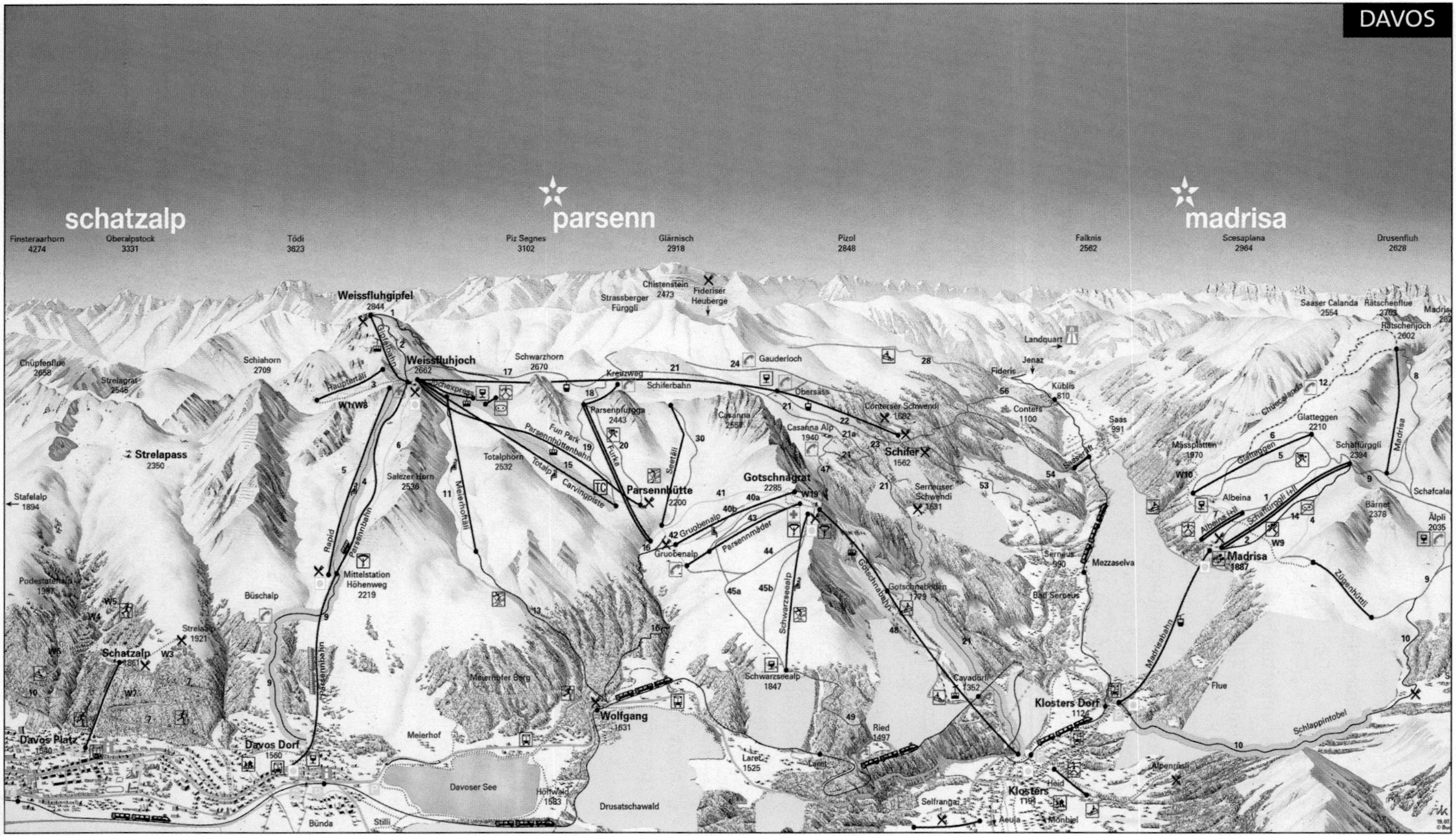

schatzalp
parsenn
madrisa

Finsteraarhorn 4274
Oberalpstock 3331
Tödi 3623
Piz Segnes 3102
Glärnisch 2918
Pizol 2848
Falknis 2562
Scesaplana 2964
Drusenfluh 2628

Weissfluhgipfel 2844
Weissfluhjoch 2662
Chistenstein 2473
Strassberger Fürggli
Fideriser Heuberge
Saaser Calanda 2554
Rätschenflue 2703
Rätschenjoch 2602
Chüpfenflue 2658
Strelagrat 2546
Schiahorn 2709
Schwarzhorn 2670
Gauderloch
Landquart
Jenaz
Fideris
Küblis 810
Conters 1100
Saas 991
Kreuzweg
Schiferbahn
Obersäss
Conterser Schwendi 1682
Parsennfurgga 2443
Casanna 2558
Casanna Alp 1940
Glatteggen 2210
Schaffürggli 2394
Mässplatten 1970
Strelapass 2350
Totalphorn 2532
Salezer Horn 2536
Meierhoftäli
Fun Park
Parsennhüttenbahn
Totalp
Carvingpiste
Furka
Seetäli
Parsennhütte 2200
Gotschnagrat 2285
Schifer 1562
Serneuser Schwendi 1631
Albeina
Bärnet 2378
Schafcalanda
Älpli 2035
Stafelalp 1894
Podestatenalp 1987
Büschalp
Mittelstation Höhenweg 2219
Rapid
Parsennbahn
Gipfelbahn
Hauptertäli
Gruobenalp
Parsennmäder
Schwarzseealp 1847
Gotschnaboden 1779
Gotschnabahn
Serneus 990
Mezzaselva
Bad Serneus
Madrisa 1887
Madrisabahn
Zügenhüttli
Flue
Schlappintobel
Strelaalp 1921
Schatzalp 1861
Meierhofer Berg
Wolfgang 1631
Cavadürli 1352
Klosters Dorf 1124
Davos Platz 1540
Davos Dorf 1560
Meierhof
Davoser See
Hohwald 1583
Drusatschawald
Laret 1525
Ried 1497
Selfranga
Klosters 1191
Heid
Alpenrösli
Aeuja
Monbiel
Bünda
Stilli

and shakers gather for the World Economic Forum. While the likes of Gordon Brown, George Bush and Bill Gates are airing their predictions in the conference centre, skiers and riders are just as importantly engaged on the mighty mountain above.

The Parsenn is one of Europe's classic ski areas, where the sport first developed in the early 1880s when a local businessman imported a pair of the new 'Norwegian snowshoes' from Oslo. They quickly became the teenage rage, and a local carpenter busily carved copies. A British woman resident who had lived in Norway showed them how to turn the planks. The trend soon caught the attention of the large foreign community in Switzerland's top sanatorium resort for victims of tuberculosis.

It might have ended there but for the man who was about to become Britain's first ski writer. Sir Arthur Conan Doyle, who created Sherlock Holmes, had brought his terminally ill wife to Davos in the hope of a cure for TB. During the many months of her treatment he became hooked on skiing. He wrote about his experiences in *Strand* magazine and encouraged a whole generation of well-to-do Brits to come out and try it for themselves.

Nearly half a century slipped by before the first mountain railway was built, and then, in 1934, a local man came up with the invention of the draglift within weeks of a similar contraption being designed in Alpe d'Huez in France. Davos never looked back. As antibiotics put the sanatorium business into decline, winter sports became increasingly big business.

The town – the highest in Western Europe – is by no means attractive. Large hotels that are urban rather than alpine in construction and character straggle along the roadside for a couple of kilometres from the railway half of Davos Dorf to Davos Platz. Where you stay is of crucial important to ski convenience. Of the two sectors, Davos Dorf is best for skiing, while Davos Platz has most of the shops, restaurants and nightlife. Regular buses run the loop of the one-way system, but it can be a long walk home to Davos Dorf late at night.

Mountain

The Parsenn is the largest and the most famous – but not the only – ski area. Jakobshorn, reached from Davos Platz, is popular with snowboarders. It has two half-pipes, a snowcross course, and night-riding every Friday. The outlying areas of Pischa and Rinerhorn are both worth visiting when the Parsenn is crowded during peak weeks.

However, the Parsenn is the main course. Take the first stage of the Parsennbahn funicular from Davos Dorf, followed by the six-person chair to the Weissfluhjoch, for the start of the first run of the day. The alternative slow second stage of the train has yet to be refurbished and should be avoided. From Weissfluhjoch a short cable car also takes you up a further 180m vertical to the 2844m Weissfluhgipfel, the highest point in the area. A network of lifts and mainly intermediate runs stretches across the mountainside to Klosters. All the different lift companies in the area are now amalgamated, and one electronic pass serves the whole region.

From the Weissfluhgipfel you can ski 12km with a 2000m vertical drop down to the farming hamlets of Küblis and Serneus, from where you can return to Klosters and then to Davos by train. Anyone who can ski parallel can do it, and in mid-season, when the snow is at its best, it's a great way to end the day.

This is not an ideal resort for complete beginners. Madrisa is too far away (suitable only for Klosters-based skiers). The Bolgen beginner slopes at the bottom of the Jakobshorn are the best bet. Bünda in Davos Dorf is steeper. At the other end of the scale of expertise, the best black run starts from the top of the Parsenn and descends through the Meierhofer Tälli to the hamlet of Wolfgang between Klosters and Davos. Still more demanding itinerary routes on the other side of the Parsenn take you down to Klosters.

In the right snow conditions, off-piste opportunities abound, and this is a great area for ski touring. Conan Doyle wrote vividly of crossing the Maienfeld Furka Pass to Arosa, and you can follow in his tracks if you are prepared for a four-hour climb and a three-hour train journey home again. Davos is also big on cross-country skiing, with 75km of trails at Jakobshorn as well as in the Dischma and Sertig valleys. Shopping is a major après ski activity, with a wide range of outlets as befits a rich town of this international calibre.

Learn

Swiss Snowsportschool, **t** +41 (0)81 416 2454, offers ski and board. **New Trend**, **t** +41 (0)81 413 2040, specializes in off-piste tours with emphasis on the use of safety equipment. **Top Secret Ski & Board Freestyle School**, **t** +41 (0)81 413 4043, and the British-run **White Heat**, **t** +44 (0)20 8989 3281, also concentrate on off-piste instruction.

Children

Swiss Snowsportschool, **t** +41 (0)81 416 2454, is praised for its children's classes from three years on Bolgen and Bünda, with lunch and lifts included in the price, and a Bobo Wonderland playground in both areas. **New Trend**, **t** +41 (0)81 413 2040, accepts children from four years. Pischa has a supervised children's play area, **t** +41 (0)79 660 3168, with a heated playhouse, a snow-tubing run and trampolining.

Lunch

Chalet Güggel, **t** +41 (0)81 413 5148, is a welcoming mountain hut on Jakobshorn with giant daybeds covered with sheep's fleeces and the best *Rösti* in the region. **Hotel Kulm**, **t** +41 (0)81 417 0707, built in 1864 in the hamlet of Wolfgang, is a favourite of Prince Charles. **Bruhin's Weissfluhgipfel**, **t** +41 (0)81 417 6644, is praised.

Dine

The **Magic Mountain**, **t** +41 (0)81 415 3747, in the Waldhotel Davos, and the **Stübli**, **t** +41 (0)81 410 1717, in Hotel Flüela, are the gourmet choices. Also try **Zauberberg**, **t** +41 (0)81 415 4201, in Hotel Europe. The **Goldener Drachen**, **t** +41 (0)81 414 9797, is a Chinese eatery in the Hotel Bahnhof Terminus, and **The Pöstli**, **t** +41 (0)81 415 4500, in the Morosani Posthotel, serves light Swiss cuisine and fish dishes.

Party

Popular bars include **Chämi** and **Ex-Bar**. **Café Cioccolino** and **Kaffee Klatsch** in Davos Platz, and **Café Weber** in Davos Dorf, are traditional coffee houses with mouthwatering cakes. Skating on Europe's largest natural ice rink at Davos Dorf attracts a large après ski crowd. Swiss league and international ice hockey matches are staged at the Sports Centre. The **Cabanna Club** is the late-night venue. Riders hang out in the disco of the **Hotel Bolgenschanze**.

Sleep

★★★★★**Hotel Steigenberger Belvédère**, t +41 (0)81 415 6000, *www.davos.steigenberger.ch*, above Platz, is traditional.

★★★★**Arabella Sheraton Hotel Waldhuus**, t +41 (0)81 415 3747, *www.sheraton.com/waldhuus*, in Platz, is chalet-style and family-friendly.

★★★★**Arabella Sheraton Seehof**, t +41 (0)81 415 9444, *www.sheraton.com/seehof*, has the fastest internet connection in Switzerland – Bill Gates stays here.

★★★★**Hotel Flüela**, t +41 (0)81 410 1717, *www.fluela.ch*, opposite Dorf railway station, has a spa, pool and piano bar.

★★★★**Hotel Sunstar Park, t** +41 (0)81 413 1414, *www.sunstar.ch/davos*, receives much repeat booking – the guest book reveals people who have been back eight times.

★★★★**Turmhotel Victoria**, t +41 (0)81 417 5300, *www.victoria-davos.ch*, in Dorf, is recommended for its health centre and good food.

★★★★**Waldhotel Davos**, t +41 (0)81 415 1515, *www.waldhotel-davos.ch*, is a traditional hotel in Platz, with helpful, friendly staff, and excellent cuisine.

★★★**ArtHaus Hotel**, t +41 (0)81 410 0510, *www.arthaushotel.ch*, is inspired by the owner's art collection. All the rooms are individually decorated.

★★★**Chalet–Hotel Larix**, t +41 (0)81 413 1188, *www.hotel-larix.ch*, is an attractive chalet-style hotel run by a British couple. Bedrooms are all individually designed.

Hotel Dischma, t +41 (0)81 410 1250, *www.dischma.ch*, is a small, family-run hotel, one bus stop from the Parsennbahn, providing excellent food.

Engelberg

Profile

High-altitude snow-sure resort in Central Switzerland within easy reach of Zurich and Luzern that is popular with snowboarders and younger skiers

Resort

Engelberg, above the beautiful lakeside city of Luzern, is better known in Calcutta or Mumbai than it is in London or New York, since in recent years it has become a location for Bollywood movies. Thousands of Indian fans flock here each summer to tread in the footsteps of their heroes on the flower-decked lower slopes of the 3238m Titlis.

In winter, Engelberg puts away its poppadoms and returns to the familiar guise of traditional ski resort that it first adopted before and immediately after the Second World War when it was one of the most fashionable ski centres in Europe. Engelberg has seen renewed success in recent years – thanks to new lifts, a good snow record, and a concerted effort to attract young snowboarders and freeriders.

Mountain

Beginners and families with small children head for the sunny slopes of Brunni, reached by a cable car followed by fixed-grip chair from just above the town.

The main Titlis ski area on the other side of town is reached by a modern gondola or a parallel, high-season combination of funicular and cable car. The second stage of the gondola rises over sheer cliffs to

***BEST FOR**

Reliable snow-cover, intermediates, off-piste, airport access

ESSENTIALS

Altitude: 1020m (3,346ft)–3028m (9,934ft)
Further information: t +41 (0)41 639 7777, *www.engelberg.ch*
Lifts in area: 25 (1 funicular, 9 gondolas, 8 chairs, 7 drags) serving 82km of piste
Lift pass: adult CHF260, youth 16–19yrs CHF182, child 6–15yrs CHF104, both for six days
Access: Zurich airport 2hrs, railway station in resort

Trübsee at 1800m where a chairlift conveys you over the frozen lake towards Jochstock at 2564m and the terrain park. Alternatively, you continue on up by cable car towards the summit of Titlis. The last stage is completed in the Rotair revolving cable car with panoramic views. Off-piste itineraries include the Laub, a powder bowl with a leg-burning 1120m vertical drop.

Learn

The excellent **Skischule Engelberg-Titlis**, **t** +41 (0)41 639 5454, has the monopoly. **Snowboard School Engelberg**, **t** +41 (0)41 639 5455, and **Boardlocal Snowboard Engelberg**, **t** +41 (0)41 637 0000, are for riders.

Children

Skischule Engelberg-Titlis, **t** +41 (0)41 639 54 54, accepts skiers from three years. **Hotel Edelweiss**, **t** +41 (0)41 639 7878, and **Hotel Ramada**, **t** +41 (0)41 639 5858, both have crèches.

Lunch

Titlis-Stübli, **t** +41 (0)41 639 5080, has high-altitude gourmet cuisine, **Untertrübsee**, **t** +41 (0)41 637 1226, and **Ritz**, **t** +41 (0)41 637 2212, at Gerschnialp, are both rated for standard cheesy mountain fare. **Brunnihütte**, **t** +41 (0)41 637 3732, at Brunni, has good home cooking. **Skihütte Stand**, **t** + 41 (0)639 50 80, is an excellent new eatery.

Dine

Spannort, **t** +41 (0)41 637 2626, is traditionally Swiss. **Hess**, **t** +41 (0)41 639 5087, serves French cuisine. **Alpenclub**, **t** +41 (0)41 637 1243, is warmly recommended.

Party

Head for **The Spindle** disco, **The Yucatan** restaurant and music club, or the smarter **Hotel Eden**.

Sleep

★★★★**Ramada Hotel Regina Titlis**, **t** +41 (0)41 639 5858, *www.ramada-treff.ch*, is a modern hotel with a pool.

★★★★**Hotel Waldegg**, **t** +41 (0)41 637 1822, *www.waldegg-engelberg.ch*, is set well above the town and houses one of the resort's leading restaurants.

★★★**Hotel Europe Europaischer Hof**, **t** +41 (0)41 639 7575, *www.hoteleurope.ch*, is in a 1905 Art Nouveau building.

★★★**Hotel Spannort**, **t** +41 (0)41 637 2626, *www.spannort.ch*, is family-run.

★★★**Hotel Terrace**, **t** +41 (0)41 639 6666, *www.terrace.ch*, was built in 1904 above the town.

The **Iglu-Village**, *www.iglu-dorf.com*, at Trubsee, is an alternative place to spend the night.

Grindelwald

***BEST FOR**
Mountain scenery, intermediates, off-piste

ESSENTIALS

Altitude 943m (3094ft)–2501m (8,206ft)
Further information: t +41 (0)33 854 1212, *www.grindelwald.ch*
Lifts in area: **Lifts in area**: 43 in Jungfrau Region (4 funiculars/railways, 15 cableways, 12 chairs, 11 drags) serving 213km of piste
Lift pass: Jungfrau (covers Grindelwald, Mürren, Wengen) adult CHF188.80, youth 16–19yrs CHF151.40, child 6–19yrs CHF94.40, all for six days
Access: Zurich airport 2hrs, Geneva airport 3hrs, railway station in resort

Profile

Busy and sophisticated village beneath the mighty Eiger that attracts a cosmopolitan crowd to its large ski area

Resort

Grindelwald is one of the world's oldest and most cosmopolitan ski resorts. The first British ski pioneers came to this corner of the Bernese Oberland in the 1880s. They were drawn by the awesome beauty of the Eiger, the Schreckhorn and the Wetterhorn that tower above it – and by the rack-and-pinion mountain railway that not only provided easy access but acted as the first ski lift. Despite its network of cableways, chair- and draglifts the railway still today forms the backbone of the lift system in the linked Jungfrau Region that Grindelwald shares with Wengen and Mürren.

Visitors from all over the world – and Japan in particular – come here to ride the train that rises though the north face of the Eiger to the 3454m Jungfraujoch, the highest station in Europe. Trains run with typical Swiss precision to a printed timetable. Some reporters complained that rail is an annoyingly slow. Others offered praise: 'A charming and civilized alternative to being stuffed inside a sweaty gondola cabin.'

A reporter summed up the resort as 'beautiful, comfortable and friendly, ideal for those who enjoy good food and service'. Another added: 'We found Grindelwald to be quiet and charming.'

Mountain

Grindelwald has its own ski area of First that is reached by gondola from the village. It takes you up to the sunny mid-mountain station of Bort and Schreckfeld. On the latter, two chairs provide high-altitude intermediate. A chair continues up to Oberjoch at 2501m. Most of the skiing is easy intermediate, but a long black run from the top of the former Egg draglift follows the line of the gondola all the way back to the resort and is of considerable challenge.

However, the main ski area is Kleine Scheidegg beneath the north face of the Eiger. Grindelwald shares these intermediate slopes with Wengen, and a train runs from the base station at Grund up the mountain and over the shoulder to Wengen on the far side. Halts along the way provide access to runs on both sides. From Kleine Scheidegg itself, on top of the shoulder, a further train or a draglift brings you up to the Eigergletscher, the high point of the joint ski area and starting point for two notorious black runs – Blackrock and Oh God. Off-piste opportunities abound, with high-altitude drops possible on the surrounding glaciers and peaks by helicopter and fixed-wing

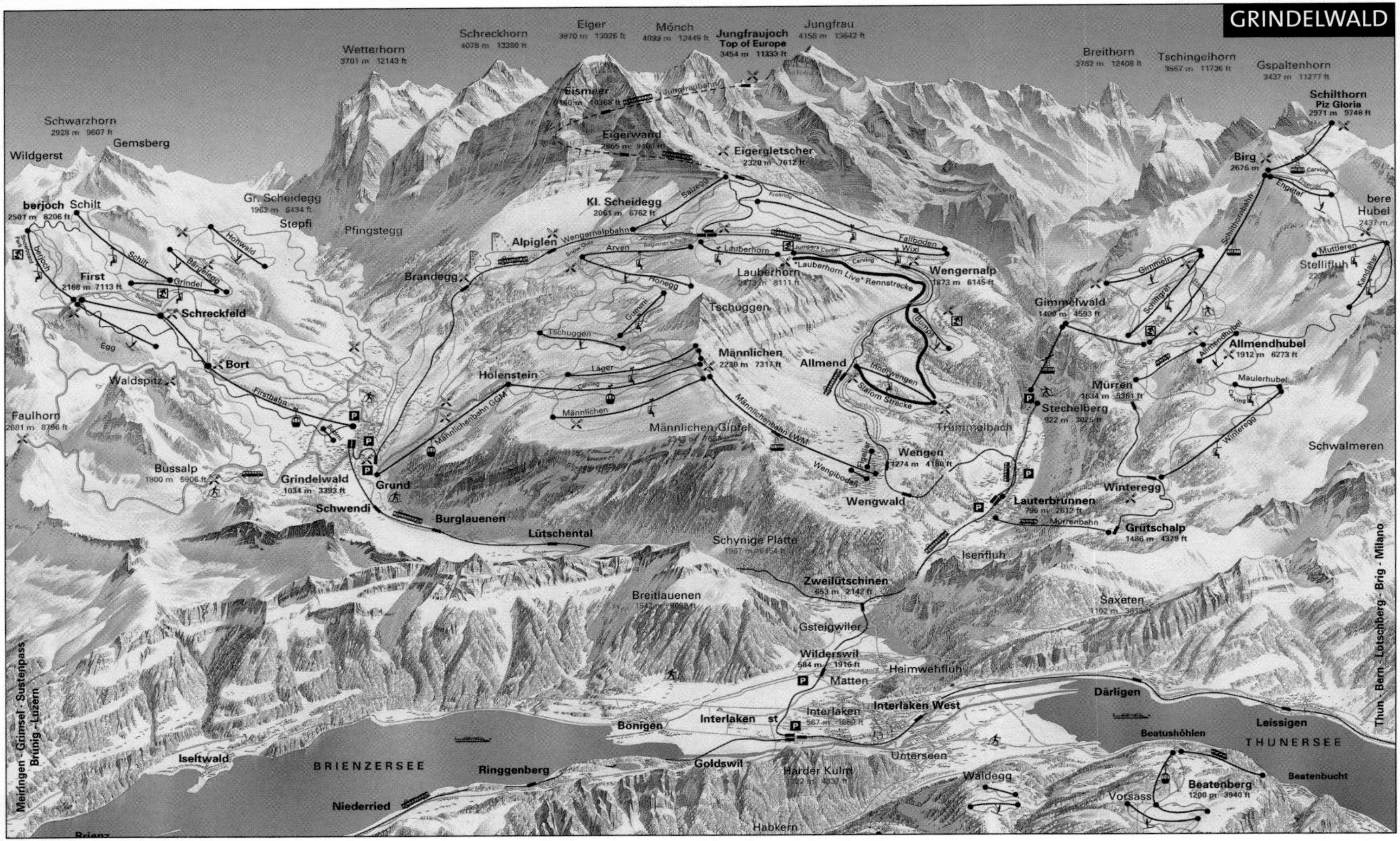

GRINDELWALD

Schwarzhorn 2928 m 9607 ft
Wetterhorn 3701 m 12143 ft
Schreckhorn 4078 m 13380 ft
Eiger 3970 m 13026 ft
Mönch 4099 m 13449 ft
Jungfraujoch Top of Europe 3454 m 11333 ft
Jungfrau 4158 m 13642 ft
Breithorn 3782 m 12408 ft
Tschingelhorn 3567 m 11736 ft
Gspaltenhorn 3437 m 11277 ft
Schilthorn Piz Gloria 2971 m 9748 ft
Wildgerst
Gemsberg
Eigerwand 2865 m
Eigergletscher 2320 m 7612 ft
Birg 2676 m
Gr. Scheidegg 1962 m 6434 ft
Stepfi
Pfingstegg
Kl. Scheidegg 2061 m 6762 ft
berjoch 2501 m 8206 ft
Schilt
First 2168 m 7113 ft
Schreckfeld
Bort
Waldspitz
Faulhorn 2681 m 8796 ft
Bussalp 1800 m 5906 ft
Grindelwald 1034 m 3393 ft
Grund
Schwendi
Burglauenen
Lütschental
Alpiglen
Brandegg
Holenstein
Männlichen 2230 m 7317 ft
Männlichen Gipfel
Lauberhorn 2473 m 8111 ft
"Lauberhorn Live" Rennstrecke
Tschuggen
Wengernalp 1873 m 6145 ft
Allmend
Wengen 1274 m 4180 ft
Wengwald
Trümmelbach
Gimmelwald 1400 m 4593 ft
Mürren 1634 m 5361 ft
Allmendhubel 1912 m 6273 ft
Stechelberg 922 m 3025 ft
Lauterbrunnen 796 m 2612 ft
Grütschalp 1486 m 4379 ft
Winteregg
Schwalmeren
Stellifluh
bere Hubel 2437 m
Schynige Platte 1967 m 6454 ft
Isenfluh
Zweilütschinen 653 m 2142 ft
Breitlauenen
Saxeten 1102 m
Gsteigwiler
Wilderswil 584 m 1916 ft
Heimwehfluh
Matten
Interlaken 567 m
Interlaken West
Interlaken Ost
Bönigen
Unterseen
Därligen
Leissigen
THUNERSEE
Beatushöhlen
Beatenbucht
Beatenberg 1200 m 3940 ft
Vorsass
Waldegg
Harder Kulm
Habkern
Goldswil
Ringgenberg
BRIENZERSEE
Iseltwald
Niederried
Brienz
Meiringen - Grimsel - Sustenpass
Brünig - Luzern
Thun - Bern - Lötschberg - Brig - Milano

aircraft. This is high alpine terrain and a guide should be used at all times.

A gondola also rises from Grund to the 2230m Männlichen ridge that separates the two resorts. From here you can work your way through a sequence of chairlifts and easy pistes to the Lauberhorn, starting point for one of the classic World Cup downhill courses. Grindelwald has a terrain park at Bargelegg.

Learn

The **Swiss Ski & Snowboard School, t** +41 (0)33 854 1280, now operates for four hours a day (two hours before lunch and two after) and received praise: 'I can honestly say the standard of teaching is excellent. My technique and confidence improved in leaps and bounds.' The other schools are **Offizielle Private Buri Sport, t** +41 (0)33 853 3353, **Kleine Scheidegg, t** +41 (0)33 855 1445, **Privat-Ski.ch, t** +41 (0)79 445 0322, and **Felix Skischule, t** +41 (0)33 853 1288. Guiding is through **Swiss Snowsports and Mountaineering School Grindelwald, t** +41 (0)33 854 1280.

Children

Kinderclub Bodmi, t +41 (0)33 853 5200, cares for non-skiing children from three years in its play area by the nursery slopes. **Kinderhort Sunshine, t** +41 (0)79 592 0209, accepts children from one month old at Männlichen. **Kinderhort Murmeli, t** +41 (0)33 853 0440, at First accepts children from six months, **Snowli Kinderclub and Kids Club, t** +41 (0)33 854 1280, cares for skiers and non-skiers from three years. **Felix Skischule** takes skiers from three years and non-skiers from three months. Pinocchio is a new children's ski lift at Männlichen.

Lunch

Brandegg on Kleine Scheidegg, t +41 (0)33 853 1057, is world-renowned for its apple fritters. **Jagerstübli, t** +41 (0)33 853 1131, below Männlichen, is a farmhouse with a cosy atmosphere. **Hotel Aspen, t** +41 (0)33 854 4000, above Grund, is sunny and welcoming. **Berghaus Bort, t** +41 (0)33 853 3651, in the First area, has 'a beautiful sunny terrace'. Inside is minimalist, and the cuisine is traditional with a difference. **Hotel Wetterhorn, t** +41 (0)33 853 1218, on the way down to Grindelwald, is recommended.

Dine

Adlerstube, t +41 (0)33 854 7777, in the Hotel Sunstar, is family-friendly, with a large play area. **La Marmite, t** +41 (0)33 853 3553, in Hotel Kirchbühl, and **The Derby-Bahnhof, t** +41 (0)33 854 5461, are recommended, as is **Schmitte, t** +41 (0)33 853 2202, in Hotel Schweizerhof. **Kreuz & Post's Challi-Stübli, t** +41 (0)33 854 5492, and **Gade, t** +41 (0)33 854 1020, in Hotel Eigerblick, are also praised. Reporters recommended the French restaurant at **Hotel Belvedere, t** +41 (0)33 854 5757, for its 'fabulous food and splendid wine list'.

Party

'Nightlife is very limited,' said one reporter. However another commented, 'The absence of loud mouthed larger louts is a bonus. There are plenty of great places to eat, good shopping and superb scenery.' **Challi-Bar** ('a must'), **Cava-Bar** and **Espresso** are resort meeting places. **Gepsi-Bar** in Hotel Eiger has live music ('a very good R&B pianist') and attracts a 30-plus clientele. **Mescalero** and the **Plaza** are the late-night venues.

Sleep

*******Grand Regina Alpin WellFit Hotel**, **t** +41 (0)33 854 8600, *www.grandregina.ch*, is decorated with antiques, and has a good pool and comprehensive spa.

******Hotel Belvedere**, **t** +41 (0)33 854 5454, *www.belvedere-grindelwald.ch*, dates back to 1907 and has recently been completely refurbished. It has a saltwater whirlpool and is renowned for its cuisine.

******Romantik Hotel Schweizerhof**, **t** +41 (0)33 853 2202, *www.hotel-schweizerhof.com*, was built in 1892 and retains its traditional character.

******Hotel Eiger**, **t** +41 (0)33 854 3131, *www.eiger-grindelwald.ch*, is unprepossessing, but has an unusual spa called the Selfness Centre, decorated in minimalist Zen style and offering a range of treatments and workshops.

******Hotel Kreuz & Post**, **t** (0)33 854 5492, *www.kreuz-post.ch*, has a wellness centre and serves good food.

******Hotel Spinne**, **t** +41 (0)33 854 8888, *www.spinne.ch*, contains three restaurants and a disco.

******Sunstar-Hotel**, **t** +41 (0)33 854 7777, *www.sunstar.ch/grindelwald*, opposite the First gondola, has a spa, and sleeps 400.

*****Hotel Alpenhof**, **t** +41 (0)33 853 5270, *www.alpenhof.ch*, is a pleasant and well-run family hotel.

*****Hotel Bodmi**, **t** +41 (0)33 853 1220, *www.bodmi.ch*, has friendly staff, offers excellent food and is on the nursery slopes .

*****Hotel Derby**, **t** +41 (0)33 854 5461, *www.derby-grindelwald.ch*, is family-run and in the town centre. 'A delightful hotel, the staff are charming, there's an ample buffet breakfast and lovely five-course dinner,' said a reporter.

*****Chalet-Hotel Gletschergarten**, **t** +41 (0)33 853 1721, *www.hotel-gletschergarten.ch*, is close to the piste, with wood-panelled public rooms and suites, and comfortable modern bedrooms.

*****Hotel Hirschen**, **t** +41 (0)33 854 8484, *www.hirschen-grindelwald.ch*, has been in the same family since 1870 and is known for its cooking.

****Hotel Tschuggen**, **t** +41 (0)33, 853 1781, *www.tschuggen-grindelwald.ch*, is a chalet-style hotel and 'a quiet, small, family-friendly hotel right in the centre'.

Gstaad

Profile

Quaint village with an exclusive hotel and smart chalets that were once the haunt of celebrities. Year-round skiing available on Les Diablerets Glacier

Resort

This was once the winter home of the rich and the famous. In the 1970s you could easily find yourself sharing a

* BEST FOR

Wealthy sophisto-cats, ski gourmets, beginners and intermediates

ESSENTIALS

Altitude: 1050m (3,445ft)–2979m (9,744ft)
Further information: **t** +41 (0)33 748 8181, *www.gstaad.ch*
Lifts in area: 62 (18 cableways, 18 chairs, 28 drags) serving 250km of piste
Lift pass: regional Top Card adult CHF285, youth 16–19yrs accompanied by parent CHF186, child 10–15yrs CHF139, all for six days
Access: Geneva airport 1½hrs, railway station in resort

chairlift with Liz Taylor, Richard Burton, Julie Andrews or Roger Moore. But times – and more significantly climates – change. By the standards of 21st-century ski resorts, the skiing is limited in challenge. Nearly half of it is graded as easy. Uncertain snow-cover at this low altitude (more than adequate cover last season was the exception rather than the rule) has driven the next generation of celebrities to seek fresh pastures.

The village understandably argues that the volume of skiing covered by the regional lift pass compensates for the absence of demanding gradient. Nearby Les Diablerets glacier, which has a top height of 2979m, always provides limited skiing even in the driest winters. 'Slopes uncrowded, straight onto lifts, good food,' was how one reporter summed it up.

Mountain

Gstaad's own skiing takes place in the separate Wispile and Eggli areas on either side of the village with a top height of less than 2000m. The mainly easy blue runs here and on the other nearby pastures offer limited challenge – and limited snow-cover for much of the winter. There are ski buses to the surrounding villages of Rougemont, Saanenmöser and Schönried. St Stephan, Zweisimmen, Lauenen, Gsteig, Saanen and Château d'Oex are all included in the regional lift pass. Two chairs at St Stephan and the Chalberhöni speed up the journey.

Terrain parks are located on Hornberg above Saanenmöser, at the Glacier 3000, and at Rinderberg above Zweisimmen. More than 160km of cross-country tracks line the valley floor.

Learn

The choice lies between **Gstaad Snowsports**, **t** +41 (0)33 744 1865, **Snowsports Saanenland**, **t** +41 (0)33 744 3665, and **Alpinzentrum Gstaad Snowsports**, **t** +41 (0)33 744 1044.

Children

All the ski schools offer lessons, and lift passes are free to children under 10 years. Babysitting is available through the tourist office.

Lunch

Try the rustic **Chemistube**, **t** +41 (0)33 722 2240, at the Lengebrand mid-station above St Stephan, **Gobeli**, **t** +42 (0)33 722 1219, at Rinderberg, **Kübelialp**, **t** +41 (0)33 744 9898, near the mid-station at Saanersloch, **Berghaus Rellerli**, **t** +41 (0)33 748 8722, above Schönried, and **Berghaus Wasserngrat**, **t** +41 (0)33 748 9622, at Wasserngrat.

Dine

In Gstaad, Robert Speth, former *Gault-Millau* Swiss Chef of the Year 2005, presides over the kitchen in the **Chesery**, **t** +41 (0)33 744 2451, built in 1962 by the Aga Khan. **Rooster Bar**, **t** +41 (0)79 481 6561, in Reusch, serves Austrian food. **By Dalsass** in the 16th-century Gault-Millau-awarded **Chlösterli**, **t** +41 (0)33 748 7979, is warmly recommended. **Hüsy**, **t** +41 (0)33 722 1056, in Blankenburg, specializes in fresh fish. Another Gault-Millau-awarded restaurant, Erich Baumer's **Sonnenhof**, **t** +41 (0)33 744 1023, in Saanen, has great food and a warm ambience.

Party

In Gstaad, the Palace Hotel's **GreenGo** nightclub is the place to see and be seen. The locals meet at **Richi's Pub**. Other haunts include **Hush**, **Stall-Bar Chlösterli**, **La Cave** and **Rialto Bar**. The **Piano Bar** in the Chesery Hotel said to have very good live music and a great atmosphere.

Sleep

*******Palace Hotel**, **t** +41 (0)33 748 5000, *www.palace.ch*, made famous by Peter Sellers in *The Pink Panther*, looks likes a fairytale castle.

*******Grand Hotel Park**, **t** +41 (0)33 748 9800, *www.grandhotelpark.ch*, is the opulent alternative.

******Hotel Bernerhof**, **t** +41 (0)33 748 8844, *www.wanderhotel.ch*, is conveniently close to the railway station.

******Hotel Christiania**, **t** +41 (0)33 744 5121, *www.christiania.ch*, has individually designed bedrooms.

****Hotel Olden**, **t** +41 (0)33 744 3444, *www.hotelolden.com*, is family-run and cosy.

Posthotel Rössli, **t** +41 (0)33 748 4242, *www.posthotelroessli.ch*, is in the village centre and has pine-panelled rooms and a restaurant serving traditional local fare.

Klosters

Profile

Attractive traditional resort that shares the Parsenn ski area with Davos. Well-groomed slopes for intermediates and tough off-piste, along with memorable mountain restaurants

* BEST FOR

All levels of skier and rider, Swiss charm

ESSENTIALS

Altitude: 1192m (3,911ft)–2844m (9,328ft)
Further information: **t** +41 (0)81 415 2196, *www.klosters.ch*
Lifts in area: 56 in Davos/Klosters area (3 funiculars, 12 cableways, 9 chairs, 36 drags) serving 305km of piste
Lift pass: adult CHF285, youth 13–17yrs CHF200, child 6–12yrs CHF100, all for six days
Access: Zurich airport 2½hrs, railway stations in Klosters Dorf and Klosters Platz

Resort

Despite its high international profile largely created by Prince Charles and his sons, Klosters clings tenaciously to its roots as a typical Swiss alpine village that combines tourism with the more serious business of farming. Unlike Davos, its much larger and more cosmopolitan sister, which shares the Parsenn ski area, Klosters entertains fame and embraces fortune but has never knowingly sought either. Of course, this unassuming air is exactly what attracts members of the British royal family, and the wealthy bankers from Zurich's Bahnhofstrasse who form an important part of its upmarket clientele. The farming community has been welcoming tourists ever since the first British skiers showed up here in 1904, drawn by the steeper ski slopes at this end of the Parsenn. However, not all reporters are unanimous in their praise: 'Klosters is worth a visit for the off-piste skiing, but be prepared for lifeless evenings and an empty wallet,' said one.

Like Davos, the resort is divided into two sectors. Klosters Platz around the main railway station is the village centre, with most of the hotels, shops, restaurants and access to the Parsenn. Klosters Dorf, also on the railway line but a couple of kilometres away, is a more remote

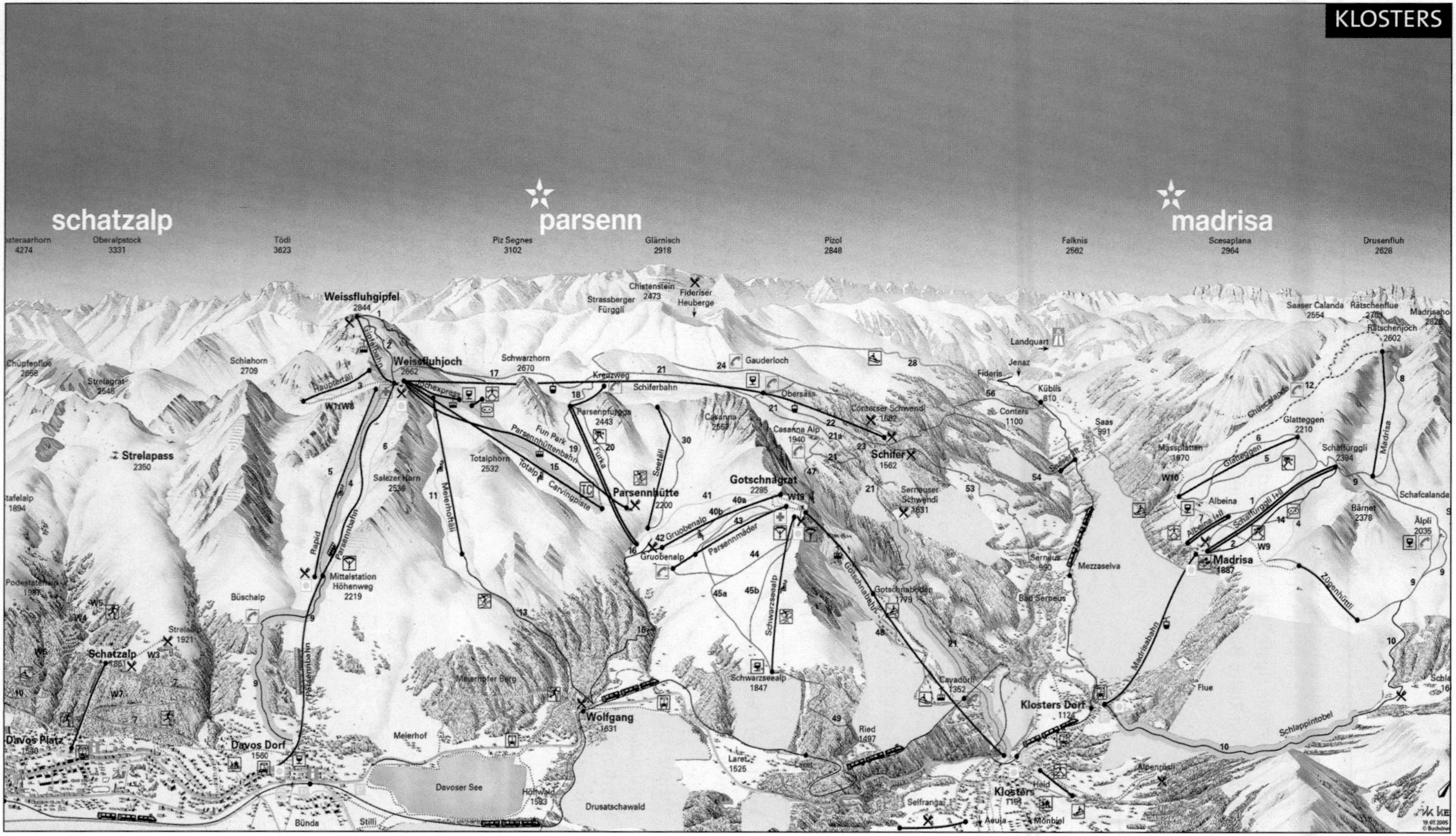

schatzalp

parsenn

madrisa

Oberalpstock 3331
Tödi 3623
Piz Segnes 3102
Glärnisch 2918
Pizol 2848
Falknis 2562
Scesaplana 2964
Drusenfluh 2628

Weissfluhgipfel 2844
Weissfluhjoch 2662
Schwarzhorn 2670
Strassberger Fürggli
Chistenstein 2473
Fideriser Heuberge
Saaser Calanda 2554
Rätschenfluе 2703
Rätschenjoch 2602
Landquart
Fideris
Jenaz
Küblis 810
Conters 1100
Saas 991
Gauderloch
Kreuzweg
Schiferbahn
Obersäss
Conterser Schwendi 1682
Schifer 1562
Casanna 2563
Casanna Alp 1940
Parsenpfurgga 2443
Fun Park
Parsennhüttenbahn
Furka
Totalp
Carvingpiste
Sneтälli
Parsennhütte 2200
Totalphorn 2532
Salezer Horn 2536
Meierhoftälli
Schiahorn 2709
Strelagrat 2548
Chüpfenflue 2658
Haupttälli
Strelapass 2350
Stafelalp 1894
Podestatenalp 1987
Rapid
Parsennbahn
Mittelstation Höhenweg 2219
Büschalp
Strelapass 1921
Schatzalp 1861
Davos Platz 1540
Davos Dorf 1560
Meierhof
Bünda
Stilli
Davoser See
Höhwald 1583
Drusatschawald
Wolfgang 1631
Gotschnagrat 2285
Gruobenalp
Parsennmäder
Schwarzseealp 1847
Gotschnabahn
Gotschnaboden 1779
Serneuser Schwendi 1631
Serneus 990
Bad Serneus
Mezzaselva
Laret 1525
Ried 1497
Cavadürli 1352
Klosters Dorf 1124
Klosters 1191
Selfranga
Aeuja
Mönbiel
Alpenrösli
Heid
Madrisabahn
Flue
Schlappintobel
Madrisa 1887
Albeina
Massplatten 1970
Glatteggen 2210
Glatteggen
Chüecalanda
Schaffürggli 2394
Schaffürggli
Madrisa
Schafcalanda
Bärnet 2378
Älpli 2035
Zügenhütti

Upmarket. Downhill.

DESCENT
INTERNATIONAL

THE MOST EXCLUSIVE ALPINE CHALETS. BEST SERVED CHILLED

+44 (0)20 7384 3854 sales@descent.co.uk www.descent.co.uk

outpost around the base of the Madrisa gondola. A regular bus service connects the two. Trains between Klosters and Davos are included in the regional lift pass and guest card.

Mountain

'The lift system is poor. It is slow and disjointed,' complained a reporter. There is much walking and waiting.' Klosters' own area, Madrisa, is inconveniently placed outside the town centre but it has some good beginner slopes. From here, a renovated gondola followed by two more lifts brings you to the start of Prince Charles' favourite run – follow the piste to the Alpi hut, then fork left on to the steep black No.10 on the map. A long path by a dramatic gully brings you back to the gondola base. From the top of Madrisa you can also ski, with a guide, to Gargellen in Austria.

However, for most skiers and riders the Parsenn is the main course. Mountain access from Klosters Platz is by the two-stage Gotschna cable car. By far the most challenging pistes and itinerary routes are to be found at this end of the Parsenn. Several spectacular and demanding off-piste runs such as the usually mogulled Drostobel lead back down through the trees to Klosters.

A network of lifts and pistes takes you across the Parsenn to the Weissfluhjoch above Davos and the still higher 2844m Weissfluhgipfel. From here you can ski 12km through 2000m of vertical down to the outlying villages of Küblis and Serneus. It is a fine way to end the day, with a drink at bottom before catching the train back up the valley to Klosters.

Snowboarders find a frustrating number of flats in the centre of the Parsenn. They tend to congregate is the separate Davos ski areas of Jakobshorn, which has a terrain park, two half-pipes and a snowcross course. Another possibility for boarders is the snowpark by the Selfranglift in Klosters.

Learn

Saas Ski and Snowboard School, **t** +41 (0)81 420 2233, has mainly young instructors with fluent English. However, the **Swiss Ski and Snowboard School Klosters**, **t** +41 (0)81 410 2828, is now the biggest school in town. **Boardriding Klosters**, **t** +41 (0)81 420 2662, and **Duty Boardsport**, **t** +41 (0)81 422 6660, are the boarding specialists. Guiding is with **Adventure Skiing**, **t** +41 (0)81 422 4825, **Berger Jürg**, **t** +41 (0)81 422 3636, and through the ski schools.

Children

Kids Land, **t** +41 (0)81 410 2170, at Madrisa, is for non-skiers from two years, while the **Snow Garden**, **t** +41 (0)81 410 2828, based in the Sports Centre at Klosters Platz, is for skiers over four years.

Lunch

Berghaus Erika, **t** +41 (0)81 422 1117, in the hamlet of Schlappin on the black run down from Madrisa, is warmly recommended for its *Rösti*. Reporters complain that the famous Schwendi Houses, rustic huts on the Parsenn that have long been a mainstay of the Klosters lunchtime scene, are now overpriced. The best bet is the **Schwendi Ski und Berghaus**, **t** +41 (0)81 422 1289. **Gotschna**, **t** +41 (0)81 422 1428, at Serneus, is a welcome sight after the long run down. **Schifer Berghaus**, **t** +41 (0)81 332 1533, has good food and a cheerful atmosphere.

Dine

Celebrity chef Armin Amrein has taken over the Gault-Millau-awarded restaurant in the **Hotel Walserhof**, **t** +41 (0)81 410 2929, which is the top dining spot in town. In high season you must book well in advance. **Chesa Grischuna**, **t** +41 (0)81 422 2222, maintains a high standard. The **Wynegg**, **t** +41 (0)81 422 1340, serves wholesome mountain fare in pleasant surroundings.

Party

'Almost nowhere to eat or party,' complained a reporter. However, the **Cresta Bar** and the **Gotschnabar** are the latest après ski meeting points. **Steinbock Bar**, **Chesa Grischuna** and The **Piano Bar** in the Silvretta Parkhotel are usually lively. Later on, **Casa Antica**, set over three floors, is the hotspot. Try also the **Rössli Bar**.

Sleep

****Hotel Alpina**, **t** +41 (0)81 410 2424, *www.alpina-klosters.ch*, is a well-located hotel with a small pool and a restaurant serving 'creative cooking'.

****Chesa Grischuna**, **t** +41 (0)81 422 2222, *www.chesagrischuna.ch*, has been welcoming guests since 1938, and retains its rustic style.

****Eugenia**, **t** +44 (0)20 7384 3854, *www.descent.co.uk*, is a handsome villa with vast bedrooms, oak-panelled walls, beautiful marble and stripped wood floors, and impressive pillared fireplaces.

****Hotel Pardenn**, **t** +41 (0)81 423 2020, *www.pardenn.ch*, is central yet quiet, with a pool and a restaurant that has vegetarian options.

****Hotel Vereina**, **t** +41 (0)81 410 2727, *www.vereinahotel.ch*, has more suites than bedrooms, a huge pool and an exquisite basement spa.

****Hotel Walserhof**, **t** +41 (0)81 410 2929, *www.walserhof.ch*, has an excellent restaurant and royal patronage.

****Silvretta Parkhotel**, **t** +41 (0)81 423 3435, *www.silvretta.ch*, has large rooms, a wellness centre and children's Flipper Club.

***Hotel Rustico**, **t** +41 (0)81 410 2288, *www.the-rusticohotel.com*, has bedrooms that are individually decorated. Its restaurant serves Asian fusion food.

Hotel Wynegg, **t** +41 (0)81 422 1340, is a cosy old hotel run along the lines of a large chalet for its mainly British guests.

Laax

Profile

One of Switzerland's largest and most snowsure ski areas. Big vertical drop, good choice of hotels and mountain restaurants, popular with snowboarders, not the best resort for non-skiers

Resorts

Flims in the Graubunden has been a spa resort since the 1880s, and a ski resort together with Laax since 1962 when the

*** BEST FOR**

High mileage skiers and riders, families

ESSENTIALS

Altitude: 1100m (3,609ft)–3018m (9,902ft)
Further information: **t** +41 (0)81 927 7001, *www.laax.com*
Lifts in area: 227 (11 cableways, 8 chairs, 8 drags) serving 220km of piste
Lift pass: CHF314, child 6–17yrs CHF105–210, both for six days
Access: Friedrichshafen and Zurich airports 1½hrs, 30mins by bus to railway station at Chur

glacier above was first developed for skiing. Together with the picturesque farming village of Falera they form what is now marketed as Laax, one of the largest ski circuits in the Alps.

Flims is made up of the two quite separate hamlets of Flims Dorf, which is the more ski-convenient option, and Flims Waldhaus, more isolated from the ski area, but offering a better choice of hotels. Laax is also a bus ride away from the lifts but has Laax Murschetg, a more ski-friendly satellite, built around the base-station. Murschetg has become a serious destination for snowboarders, who congregate at the Riders' Palace hotel. Falera is a much smaller and more rural community, but with a direct lift link into the ski area. A shuttle bus connects all the accommodation and base stations.

Mountain

The skiing takes place on the 3018m Voralb Glacier and on the slopes of four other interconnected peaks. Much of it is above the tree-line and suited to skiers of all standards, but particularly intermediates in search of long cruising runs. There is also plenty of steeper terrain, divided by bands of rock and steep gullies in the Siala and Cassons sectors. A long itinerary from the glacier descends 2000m to the remote hamlet of Ruschein Ladir. ' The long black off the back of the little glacier at the top of the resort is superb, and there is some good ungroomed itinerary terrain,' advised a reader.

The top of the glacier is the starting point for the annual Weisse Schuss, a 14km pro-am downhill race that ends in Flims Dorf. The undulating FIS downhill course from Crap Sogn Gion down to Laax-Murschetg provides plenty of scope for boy and girl racers, but no great technical difficulty when not prepared for racing. A more challenging descent is the Platt'Alva itinerary from Nagens or the black Sattel from Voralb down to Alp Ruschein and Ladir.

Laax attracts a high percentage of snowboarders and freeriderss, who gather at the terrain parks and half-pipes at Crap Sogn Gion. Several annual events now take place in the resort, including the Burton European Open, the Orage European Freeski Open by Swatch, and the British Freeski and Snowboard Championships.

Learn

The mainstream **Ski School**, t +41 (0)81 927 7171, and **Snowboard Fahrschule**, t +41 (0)81 927 7155, have branches in Flims, Laax and Falera.

Other schools in Flims Dorf are **Alpine Action Unlimited**, t +41 (0)81 936 7474, **EuroBoard**, t +41 (0)81 281 8183, **EuroSki**, t +41 (0)79 683 5642, **Rock and Snow**, t +41 (0)78 679 7153, **Roland Tuchschmid**, t +41 (0)79 742 6677, **Touchdown**, t +41 (0)78 830 5960, and **Yetis**, t +41 (0)79 635 3767.

Other schools in Flims Waldhaus are **Mountain Fantasy**, t +41 (0)81 936 7077, and **Swissraft**, t +41 (0)81 911 5250. In Laax **Inspiraziun Grischun**, t +41 (0)76 391 6894, is recommended.

Children

Ski School, t +41 (0)81 927 7171, runs a kindergarten for children from two years, with ski lessons from four years. **Waldhaus Flims Mountain Resort & Spa**, t +41 (0)81 928 4848, and **Hotel Adula**, t +41 (0)81 928 2828, both run crèches for guests. In Flims Dorf, **Annina Hägler**, t +41 (0)79 791 5221, runs a non-ski kindergarten.

Lunch

Try **Startgels Alpenrose, t** +41 (0)81 911 5848, **Naraus Enzian, t** +41 (0)81 911 5878, **Segneshütte, t** +41 (0)81 927 9925, and **Cassonsgrat Edelweiss, t** +41 (0)81 911 5898. **Capalari, t** +41 (0)81 927 7334, at Crap Sogn Gion, is recommended. **Elephant, t** +41 (0)81 927 7390, at Crap Masegn, and **Tegia Larnags, t** +41 (0)81 927 9910, are the gourmet choices. **La Vacca, t** +41 (0)81 927 9962, is a canvas teepee with a huge central open fire and decorated with cowskin rugs. It serves wholesome steaks with baked potatoes.

Dine

Recommended restaurants include **La Clav, t** +41 (0)81 928 2828, in Hotel Adula, **Clavau Vegl, t** +41 (0)81 911 3644, in Flims Dorf, for regional specialities. **Pizzeria Pomodoro, t** +41 (0)81 911 1062, and **Pizzeria La Dolce Vita, t** +41 (0)81 928 1440, in Flims Waldhaus, are also singled out. In Laax, **Romana, t** +41 (0)81 921 5055, specializes in Balkan cuisine, and **Riva, t** +41 (0)81 921 5353, has good cheese dishes. **Casa Seeli, t** +41 (0)81 921 3048, in Falera, is praised.

Party

In Flims Dorf, **Iglu Music Bar** and **Legna Bar** are the main rendezvous. Living-room Flims is less frenetic. In Flims Waldhaus, **Bellavista Bistro Bar** is popular. In Laax, **Casa Veglia** is the disco favourite with occasional live concerts. **Riders Palace Club and Lobby** at the **DesignHotel Riders Palace** is where the youth of Laax congregate for drinks at the bar, parties and international live gigs.

Sleep

All accommodation and services can be booked on, **t** +41 (0)81 927 7777, *www.laax.com*

Flims:

★★★★★**Waldhaus Flims Mountain Resort & Spa, t** +41 (0)81 928 4848, *www.parkhotel-waldhaus.ch*, is a giant hotel complex set in five buildings linked by underground walkways. It has recently been renovated and has some attractive suites, as well as the excellent Jugendstil Pavillon spa.

★★★★**Hotel Adula, t** +41 (0)81 928 2828, *www.adula.ch*, in Flims Dorf, has good children's facilities and La Mira spa.

★★★**Albana Sporthotel, t** +41 (0)81 927 2333, *www.albana-flims.ch*, is convenient for the slopes.

★★★★**Sunstar Hotel Surselva, t** +41 (0)81 928 1800, *www.sunstar.ch/flims*, in Waldhaus, has a pool and wellness centre. Children under 16 years pay only CHF1 per year of age per night.

★★★**Ayurveda-Wohlfühlhotel Fidazerhof, t** +41 (0)81 920 9010, in Fidaz, has minimalist-design rooms and a spa offering Ayurvedic treatments.

Laax:

★★★★**Rockresort, t** +41 (0)81 927 9000, *www.rockresort.com*, is a new luxury complex with rooms and apartments right at the base station.

★★★**Hotel Posta Veglia, t** +41 (0)81 921 4466, *www.poestlilaax.ch*, has attractive panelled rooms.

★★★**Hotel La Siala, t** +41 (0)81 927 2222, *www.lasiala.ch*, in the farming hamlet of Falera, has an indoor pool.

★★★**Riders Palace DesignHotel, t** +41 (0)81 927 9700, *www.riderspalace.com*, is an unusual blend of cutting-edge designer hotel and backpacker hostel.

Mürren

***BEST FOR**

Mountain scenery, intermediates and advanced skiers and riders

ESSENTIALS

Altitude: 1650m (5,412ft)–2971m (9,748ft)
Further information: t +41 (0)33 856 8686, *www.wengen-muerren.ch*
Lifts in area: 43 in Jungfrau Region (4 funiculars/mountain railways, 15 cableways, 12 chairs, 11 drags) serving 213km of piste
Lift pass: Jungfrau (covers Grindelwald, Mürren, Wengen) adult CHF188.80, youth 16–19yrs CHF151.40, child 6–19yrs CHF94.40, all for six days
Access: Zurich airport 3hrs, Geneva airport 4hrs, railway station in resort

Profile

Chocolate-box-pretty, car-free village with some steep skiing. This is not the ideal resort for beginners

Resort

Back in 1911, entrepreneurial lawn tennis equipment salesman Henry Lunn launched a new career for himself as the first ski package tour operator in this delightful Swiss village above Lauterbrunnen in the Bernese Oberland.

He persuaded the Jungfrau Railway to keep the line open during the winter, rented the Palace Hotel and asked the 'right' sort of Englishmen – those who had been privately educated – to come and join him. He never actually skied himself. His son Sir Arnold, founder of modern ski racing – and, in turn, his son Peter – continued the association. Sir Arnold's Kandahar Ski Club made its home here in 1922, and a strong relationship with Britain has continued until the present day.

The car-free village is the perfect example of a quaint Swiss alpine community, with Heidi-esque chalets and dramatic views of the Eiger, the Mönsch and the Jungfrau. The village is perched on a balcony 550m above the valley and is reached either by a cable car from Lauterbrunnen or from Stechelberg and Gimmelwald. Mürren shares its lift pass with Wengen and Grindelwald, which can be reached by train. However, distances are great and the trains are slow. Most Mürren-based skiers tend to remain in their own 12-lift territory dominated by the 2970m Schilthorn.

Mountain

'Your assessment of Mürren is very accurate – incredibly beautiful, but after a few days you'll find you have skied pretty much everything,' said a reader. The skiing here suits all standards – but, despite the vociferous protestations of committed Mürrenites, there is not much of it. A chairlift from the edge of the village and a drag above serve undulating intermediate runs on the 2145m Schiltgrat. A funicular from the village gives access to a nursery slope at Allmendhubel and further reds as well as an easy blue back to the village. The Winteregg sector, reached by train from Mürren or by piste and chair from Allmendhubel, has easy, open pistes. In good snow conditions it is possible to ski all the way down to Lauterbrunnen.

Serious skiers and riders take the cable car from the village up to Birg and then the final stage to the Piz Gloria revolving restaurant on the 2970m summit of the Schilthorn. The black descent is one of the classic runs of the Alps and starting point for the annual pro-am Inferno Race, which goes down to Winteregg or even Lauterbrunnen when conditions permit. The top section can become heavily mogulled later in the day. The Muttlern

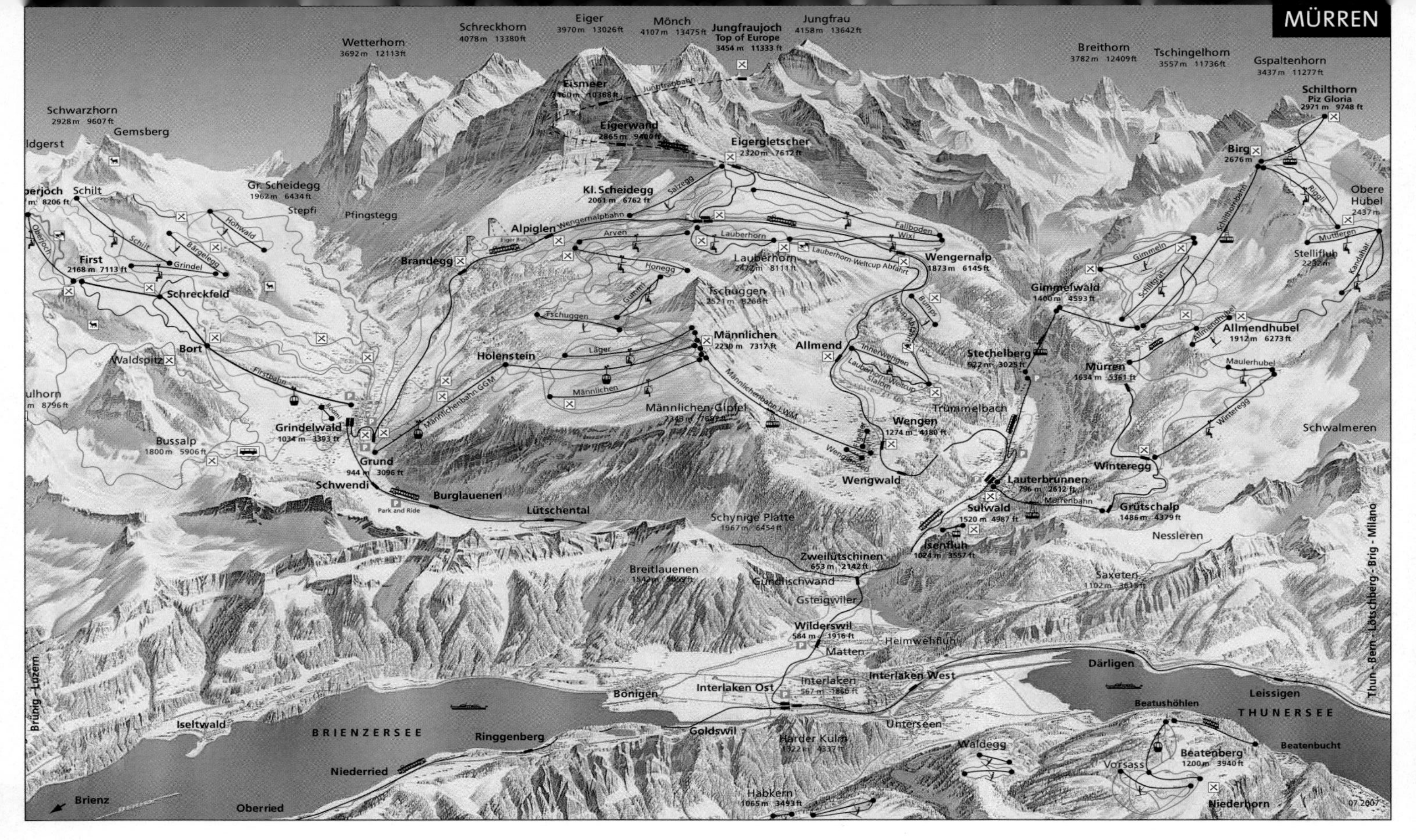
MÜRREN
Schwarzhorn
2928 m 9607 ft
Gemsberg
Wetterhorn
3692 m 12113 ft
Schreckhorn
4078 m 13380 ft
Eiger
3970 m 13026 ft
Mönch
4107 m 13475 ft
Jungfraujoch
Top of Europe
3454 m 11333 ft
Jungfrau
4158 m 13642 ft
Breithorn
3782 m 12409 ft
Tschingelhorn
3557 m 11736 ft
Gspaltenhorn
3437 m 11277 ft
Schilthorn
Piz Gloria
2971 m 9748 ft
Eismeer
Eigerwand
2865 m 9400 ft
Eigergletscher
2320 m 7612 ft
Jungfraubahn
Birg
2676 m
Schilthornbahn
Riggli
Obere
Hubel
2437 m
Muttleren
Stellifluh
Kandahar
Gimmeln
Schiltgrat
Schilt
Gr. Scheidegg
1962 m 6434 ft
Stepfi
Pfingstegg
Kl. Scheidegg
2061 m 6762 ft
Salzegg
Alpiglen
Wengernalpbahn
Arven
Lauberhorn
Fallboden
Wixi
Lauberhorn-Weltcup Abfahrt
Wengernalp
1873 m 6145 ft
Hohwald
Bärgelegg
Grindel
First
2168 m 7113 ft
Schreckfeld
Brandegg
Honegg
Gummi
Tschuggen
2521 m 8268 ft
Bumps
Gimmelwald
1400 m 4593 ft
Allmendhubel
1912 m 6273 ft
Maulerhubel
Bort
Waldspitz
Firstbahn
Holenstein
Läger
Männlichen
2230 m 7317 ft
Allmend
Innerwengen
Lauberhorn-Weltcup Slalom
Stechelberg
922 m 3025 ft
Mürren
1634 m 5361 ft
Männlichenbahn GGM
Männlichen-Gipfel
Männlichenbahn LWM
Trümmelbach
Winteregg
Schwalmeren
Grindelwald
1034 m 3393 ft
Bodmi
Bussalp
1800 m 5906 ft
Grund
944 m 3096 ft
Wengen
1274 m 4180 ft
Wengwald
Schwendi
Burglauenen
Park and Ride
Lütschental
Lauterbrunnen
796 m 2612 ft
Mürrenbahn
Grütschalp
1486 m 4379 ft
Sulwald
1520 m 4987 ft
Schynige Platte
1967 m 6454 ft
Isenfluh
1024 m 3557 ft
Nessleren
Zweilütschinen
653 m 2142 ft
Breitlauenen
Gündlischwand
Gsteigwiler
Saxeten
Wilderswil
584 m 1916 ft
Heimwehfluh
Matten
Interlaken West
Interlaken
567 m 1860 ft
Interlaken Ost
Bönigen
Unterseen
Därligen
Leissigen
Beatushöhlen
THUNERSEE
Thun - Bern - Lötschberg - Brig - Milano
Brünig - Luzern
Iseltwald
BRIENZERSEE
Ringgenberg
Goldswil
Harder Kulm
1322 m 4337 ft
Waldegg
Beatenberg
1200 m 3940 ft
Vorsass
Beatenbucht
Niederried
Brienz
Oberried
Habkern
1065 m 3493 ft
Niederhorn
07.2007

and Kandahar chairs beneath Obere Hubel allow further skiing without having to descend to the cable car.

Off-piste opportunities abound, but it is essential to take a guide. Tschingelchrachen off the Schilthornbahn is steep and technically demanding, but prone to avalanche. Others include Hidden Valley from the summit of the Maulerhubel to Grutsch, and the Blumental.

Learn

The **Swiss Ski and Snowboard School**, **t** +41 (0)33 855 1247, has no competition, but the level of instruction is surprisingly high. Group ski lessons are limited to two hours each morning from Monday to Saturday. Snowboard group lessons are afternoon-only, from Monday to Friday.

Children

Children Paradise, t +41 (0)33 856 8686, behind Hotel Jungfrau, cares for non-skiing children from two to five years with free nappies and a pick-up service from hotels on request.

Lunch

The revolving **Piz Gloria, t** +41 (0)33 826 0007, on the summit of the Schilthorn, was made famous in the 1968 Bond film *On Her Majesty's Secret Service*, and is worth a visit even if the views are more spectacular than the cuisine. The **Schilthornhütte, t** +41 (0)78 788 5767, on the way down, serves simple mountain fare. **Gimmelen, t** +41 (0)33 855 1366, is renowned for its cheesy dishes and *Apfelküchen*. **Sonnenberg, t** + 41 (0)33 855 1127, is praised for its *Rösti*. **Suppenalp, t** +41 (0)33 855 1726, has a sunny terrace and good food.

Dine

Hotel Eiger Stübli, t + 41 (0)33 856 5454, **Hotel Alpenruh, t** +41 (0)3356 8800, and the **Eiger Guesthouse, t** +41 (0)33 856 5460, are all recommended, along with **Hotel Edelweiss, t** +41 (0)33 856 5600, and the **Stägerstübli, t** +42 (0)33 855 1316, and **Café Bistro Tinu, t** +41 (0)33 855 8695.

Party

The **Ballon Bar** in the Alpin Palace, The **Pub** in the Eiger Guesthouse and the **Tächi Bar** in Hotel Eiger are the main meeting places. The **Blüemlichäller** disco in the Hotel Blumental and The **Inferno** disco in the Alpin Palace are crowded in high season.

Sleep

★★★★**Alpin Palace, t** +41 (0)33 856 9999, *www.muerren.ch/palace*, dates back to the Edwardian days of Henry Lunn.

★★★★**Hotel Eiger, t** +41 (0)33 856 5454, *www.hoteleiger.com*, across the road from the railway station, is the only hotel with its own indoor pool.

★★★**Hotel Alpenruh, t** +41 (0)33 856 8800, *www.hotelschilthorn.ch*, at the Schilthornbahn end of the village, has a good restaurant and great views.

★★★**Hotel Blumental, t** +41 (0)33 855 1826, *www.muerren.ch/blumental*, has been recently renovated.

★★★**Hotel Edelweiss, t** +41 (0)33 856 5600, *www.edelweiss-muerren.ch*, is friendly and well positioned, with excellent views and food.

★★★**Hotel Jungfrau, t** +41 (0)33 856 6464, *www.hoteljungfrau.ch*, is a friendly place, with an annexe called Haus Mönch across the road.

★**Eiger Guesthouse, t** +41 (0)33 856 5460, has Swiss-Scottish owners, low prices and a relaxed atmosphere.

Saas-Fee

✱ BEST FOR

Beginners, low intermediates, families, and ski tourers.

ESSENTIALS

Altitude: 1800m (5,905ft)–3600m (11,810ft)
Further information: t +41 (0)27 958 1858, *www.saas-fee.ch*
Lifts in area: 22 (1 funicular, 7 cableways, 1 chair, 13 drags) serving 100km of piste
Lift pass: Saastal (covers Saas-Fee, Saas-Grund, Saas-Almagell, Saaso-Bahlen, and ski bus) CHF352, child 10–16yrs CHF189, both for six days
Access: Geneva airport 4hrs, Sion airport 1½hrs, railway station at Visp or Brig, half-hourly bus connection

Profile

Traditional village offering glacier skiing 11 months of the year. Popular resort for freeriders

Resort

Saas-Fee is an ancient village in a superb high-altitude setting, surrounded by a horseshoe of no fewer than 13 peaks of 4000m. Blackened chalets interspersed with modern hotels, fashion boutiques and ski shops line its narrow, car-free streets. Its high altitude allows skiing on the glacier from the beginning of July through to the start of the winter season in November.

Despite its year-round tourism, Saas-Fee somehow manages to maintain an innocent charm often lacking in major resorts. The handful of powerful village families who still run it have been known to favour image over commercial gain. You can still buy fresh milk by the pail, the lift system is modern and efficient, and it has some of the best nursery slopes in Switzerland.

However such alpine bliss has its drawbacks. The glacial terrain is as hostile as it is beautiful. Much of the mountainside is littered by giant *séracs* and wide crevasses that beckon anyone who is foolish enough to leave the marked piste without a local guide. Such treacherous topography means that the pistes themselves are inevitably limited in scope, and reporters complain that for a resort of this size there is simply not enough skiing or riding for a whole week.

The separate outlying hamlets of Saas-Almagell and Saas-Grund provide a little more variety. Saas-Fee also has a whole mountain, served by a gondola, that is reserved for tobogganing. Cars must be left in car parks on the outskirts of the resort and transport is confined to electric ski buses and taxis.

'I thought that as the resort was listed as beginner- and intermediate-friendly the skiing would not be that challenging or varied. However it was more challenging than I expected, and the toboggan run was great too,' said a reader. 'Saas-Fee is a highly European-orientated resort, catering significantly more for German- and French-speaking visitors than English,' added another.

Mountain

'If you are expecting comfortable, modern lifts, watch out. It's three lifts to the top of the mountain, and you stand packed like a sardine the whole time,' said a reader. Access is indeed by cable cars from either end of the resort, which take you to the mid-mountain station of Morenia. A further cable car continues to 3000m Felskinn, starting point for the Metro-Alpin, the world's highest underground funicular. This brings you up to Allalin at 3500m, just below the highest point of the ski area. A gondola from the village, followed by a cable car and a sequence of draglifts, provides a slower alternative passage to the top of the mountain. Despite the full range of colour codings, neither of the main routes back down offers serious challenge.

A network of other lifts – mainly draglifts because of the itinerant nature of the glacier – give access to more short runs. The separate Plattjen sector, reached by gondola from the village, provides more intermediate skiing. Saas-Fee has a big freestyle park with half-pipe, rails and kickers served by the Mittaghorn drag reached from Morenia. There is also a second smaller freestyle park in the summer ski area.

'The ski areas are not well linked and you will find yourself lugging skis or taking the bus around the resort,' complained a reporter.

Learn

'There is little room for advancement from beginner to intermediate, and as a beginner you may find yourself completely confined to the nursery slopes for the duration of your visit,' noted a reader. In the past, the overtly staid **Swiss Ski and Snowboard School**, **t** +41 (0)27 957 2348, has had the monopoly for skiing, but the **Eskimo Ski and Snowboard School**, **t** +41 (0)27 957 4904, now has a ski division which is warmly recommended. In the past, the established Swiss school has been heavily criticized for being old-fashioned and not keeping abreast of modern technique. However, the standard of teaching is said to be much improved, and most instructors speak good English. **Warren Smith Ski Academy**, **t** +44 (0)1442 832 629, runs courses here in summer.

Children

Ferien-Kinderparadies, **t** +41 (0)27 957 457, offers daycare for children aged one month to six years.

Lunch

'The huts on the mountain are charming and a nice change from cafeteria style,' said a reader. The **Metro-Alpin** revolving restaurant, **t** +41 (0)957 1771, at Mittelallalin, has great views and average food. Try also **Meeting Point Morenia**, **t** +41 (0)957 1881, **Längfluh**, **t** +41 (0)957 2132, and the **Gletschergrotte**, **t** +41 (0)957 2160. Many skiers return to the village for lunch.

Dine

Vernissage, **t** +41 (0) 27 958 1904, a restaurant and après ski complex, was recently opened by avant-garde Zermatt artist and designe, Heinz Julen. **Steakhouse Chüestall**, **t** +41 958 9160, is new. **Cäsar Ritz**, **t** +41 (0)27 958 1900, in the Ferienart Resort & Spa, and the Michelin-rated **Fletschhorn Waldhotel**, **t** +41 (0)27 957 2131, are warmly recommended. **Boccalino**, **t** +41 (0)27 957 1731, and **Don Ciccio**, **t** +41 (0)27 957 4020, are good pizzerias.

Party

'Saas Fee's strong point is the quiet village not ruined by discos,' said a reporter. However others tell a different story: 'We had always regarded Saas-Fee as a quiet resort at night. Unfortunately, we discovered that the main road can become rather noisy due to late opening hours at several of the resort bars.' Try the **Whisky Bar** in the Metropol. Other busy places include **Alpen-Pub**, **Happy Bar**, **Metro-Bar**, **Nesti's Ski-Bar** and **Hozwurm**. Later on the action switches to **Vernissage**, **John's Pub** and **Popcorn the Snowboard Point** in Hotel Dom, and **Poison**.

Sleep

- ★★★★★**Ferienart Resort & Spa**, **t** +41 (0)27 958 1900, *www.ferienart.ch*, has six restaurants and a new health and fitness centre.
- ★★★★**Hotel du Glacier**, **t** +41 (0)27 958 1600, *www.duglacier.ch*, has comfortable rooms and a lovely little spa.
- ★★★★**Romantik Hotel Beau-Site**, **t** +41 (0)27 958 1560, *www.beausite.org*, was considered to be an excellent hotel in all respects, with first class facilities, high quality food and welcoming staff.
- ★★★★**Allalin Relais du Silence**, **t** +41 (0)27 957 1815, *www.silencehotel.com*, is in a peaceful setting and has lots of atmosphere.
- ★★★★**Hotel Metropol**, **t** +41 (0)27 957 1001, *www.metropol-saas-fee.ch*, is run on feng shui principles with bio- and Finnish saunas, as well as a billiard lounge.
- ★★★★**Hotel Schweizerhof**, **t** + 41 (0)27 958 7575, *www.schweizerhof-saasfee.ch*, has waterfall in the lounge and the reception rooms are decorated in Belle Epoque style.
- ★★★**Fletschhorn Waldhotel**, **t** +41 (0)27 957 2131, *www.fletschhorn.ch*, set in the woods above Saas-Fee, houses a modern art gallery and an outstanding wine cellar.
- ★★★**Unique Hotel Dom**, **t** +41 (0)27 957 5101, *www.uniquedom.com*, is a central snowboarders' rendezvous, with a state-of-the-art Sony sound system in every room.

St Moritz

Profile

One of the world's most famous resorts, with beautiful scenery, good skiing, and a wide range of other winter sports

Resort

The first home of winter sports in the Alps has been an important spa town since the Middle Ages and has never knowingly lost an opportunity to market itself internationally. The brand name, synonymous with wealth and high-living, is protected by trademark in 50 countries around the world. As long ago as 1519, Pope Leo X was offering full absolution for every Christian who visited the healing mineral springs.

Reliable summer weather in the Engadine Valley brought summer visitors, but it wasn't until 1864 that hotelier Johannes Badrutt hit upon the idea of creating a winter season. That September he overheard four Englishmen lamenting the fact that they must soon return to

*BEST FOR

All levels of skier and rider, wealthy sophisto-cats, ski gourmets, non-skiers

ESSENTIALS

Altitude: 1800m (5,904ft)–3303m (10,834ft)
Further information: **t** +41 (0)81 837 3333, *www.stmoritz.ch*
Lifts in area: 56 (1 funicular, 10 cable-ways, 18 chairs, 27 drags) serving 350km of piste
Lift pass: Upper Engadine (covers Celerina, Pontresina, St Moritz, Sils Maria, Maloja, Silvaplana, Zuoz) adult HF348, youth 13–17yrs CHF233, child 6–12yrs CHF118, all for six days
Access: Zurich airport 3–4hrs, railway station in resort

ST MORITZ

Piz Güglia
Piz Julier
3380 m
Piz d'Agnel
Tschima da Flix
Piz d'Err
Piz Mitgel
Corn de Tinizong
Piz Ela
Julierpass
Piz Suvretta
Piz Bever
Piz Grisch
Piz Glüna
Piz Saluver
Piz Nair, 3057 m
Fuorcla Grischa
Lej da la Pêsch
Piz Schlattain
Albulapass
Fuorcla Schlattain
2840 m
Val Suvretta
Val Schlattain
Chamanna Saluver
Las Trais Fluors
Munt da San Murezzan, 2659 m
Chamanna
Alpina
Corviglia, 2486 m
Glüna
el paradiso
Trutz
Snowpark
Sass Runzöl
Marguns, 2278 m
Alp Giop
Alp Nova
Signal
Chasellas
Salastrains
2040 m
1928 + 1948
Alp Saluver
Telefon
Suvretta
Alp Laret
Chantarella, 2005 m
Maloja
Silvaplana
Julierpass
St. Moritz Dorf, 1856 m
St. Moritz Bad, 1772 m
Celerina, 1720 m
Samedan
Zuoz
Pontresina
04/04

London for the winter and would be back again the following July. He suggested they return in January and wagered that if they experienced fewer sunny days in winter than in summer he would pay for their accommodation. Johannes was on a statistical winner – and the rest is history.

They skated on the frozen lake and tobogganed on a steep slope that was to become the Cresta Run. Today it remains the most macho and dangerous of all winter sports. The private and still British-run St Moritz Tobogganing Club maintains a sexist men-only stance as it has done for more than 100 years.

Socially well-connected beginners can launch themselves head-first down the ice on a heavy metal skeleton toboggan four mornings a week from Christmas to the end of February. They achieve speeds of around 100kph.

The Cresta should not be confused with the bobsleigh. St Moritz has the world's one remaining natural ice run which is rebuilt each winter with nine serpentine bends snaking down to Celerina. Skating and curling are also important activities that take place on the frozen lake. Not all alternative sports involve sliding – golf, polo, horse-racing, show jumping, greyhound-racing and even cricket are played and watched by St Moritz's hedonistic clientèle.

First, you need some essential orientation. St Moritz divides into Dorf and Bad, which are 3km apart. Together with Celerina, they provide direct access to the main Corviglia ski area.

St Moritz Dorf, on the shore of the lake, is the smart one that is home to most of the major hotels, restaurants, shops and clubs. Generally less expensive, but also less attractive, St Moritz Bad has a number of hotels dominated by the giant five-star Grand Hotel des Bains Kempinski. The Suvretta House, one of the resort's most luxurious hotels, lies in splendid isolation at the extreme edge of the ski area in neither Bad nor Dorf.

Celerina is situated 3km from Dorf at the bottom of the Cresta. It makes a charming and more intimate base. Samedan, slightly further along the valley, has its own beginner lift, while hamlets such as La Punt provide further accommodation.

'The streets are packed with millionaires and trophy wives,' said a reader, 'The smell of success and money hangs in the air.' Surprisingly for a place with such an impeccable pedigree, the architecture is far from aesthetically pleasing. The beauty of the place lies not in the views of the resort itself, but in the views from it.

Mountain

Corviglia is the core of the skiing, reached by funicular from Dorf and by cable car from Bad. A modern gondola provides the link from Celerina, while the Suvretta has its own chairlift. A 100-person cable car continues on up to Piz Nair at 3057m.

Corvatsch, on the other side of the valley and reached by bus, is of greater interest to advanced skiers and riders. It is reached from Sils Maria, Silvaplana and Surlej.

The third main area, made up of Diavolezza and Lagalb, rises to a snowsure 3000m and is reached from St Moritz by bus or train. The two mountains offer some of the best expert skiing in the region. The 10km descent, with a guide from Diavolezza down the glacier to Morteratsch, is spectacular.

Zuoz is a little village at the far end of the Engadine Valley that is far removed from the sophistication of its famous neighbours. This is where you will find local families and freeriders when the big-name resorts are crowded.

The high prices restrict the number of young riders who can afford to come to

St Moritz, but those who do find some outstanding terrain. Diavolezza is another great place for freeriding. The terrain park at Corviglia is accessed by the Munt da San Murezzan chair.

Cross-country skiing is as popular as the downhill variety, with tracks through the pine forest and along the shores of the lake. The annual pro-am 42km Engadine Marathon attracts thousands of langlaufers and is a highlight of the European cross-country calendar.

Learn

'Unsuitable for complete beginners,' warned a reporter. **Swiss Snowsports School**, **t** +41 (0)81 830 0101, and **Suvretta**, **t** +41 (0)81 836 3600, are both recommended, along with **Engadin Snow and Fun School**, **t** +41 (0)81 837 5353, in Celerina. A high number of the resort's wealthy guests book private guides, which has resulted in the establishment of a number of specialist organizations: **Private Ski Instructor Association St Moritz/Engadin**, **t** +41 (0)81 852 1885, **AAA**, **t** +41 (0)81 832 2233, **Bergsteigerschule Pontresina**, **t** +41 (0)81 838 8333, and the **St Moritz Experience**, **t** +41 (0)81 833 7714. **Heli Bernina t**, +41 (0)81 851 1818, and **Air Grischa Helicopter**, **t** +41 (0)81 852 3535, can arrange heli-skiing.

Children

Hotel Schweizerhof, **t** +41 (0)81 837 0707, has daycare for children over three years, as does **Badrutt Palace Hotel**, **t** +41 (0)81 837 1000. **Suvretta House Hotel**, **t** +41 (0)81 836 3636, has a kindergarten for small guests from 12 months old, and a children's restaurant. **Kempi Kids Club**, **t** +41 (0)81 838 3838, in the Grand Hotel des Bains Kempinski, officially takes children from three years, although it will also care for guests' babies. All the ski schools take children from four years.

Lunch

On Corviglia, **Mathis Food Affairs**, **t** +41 (0)81 833 6355, has a justified reputation as the best (and most expensive) high-altitude lunching experience in the Alps. Owner Reto Mathis serves caviar and truffle-rich dishes in a stately style. **Chasellas**, **t** +41 (0)81 833 3854, **Trutz**, **t** +41 (0)81 833 7030, and **Chamanna**, **t** +41 (0)79 682 5080, are all owned by the Suvretta House Hotel and are recommended warmly along with **Salastrains**, **t** +41 (0)81 833 3867. **El Paradiso**, **t** +41 (0)81 833 40 02, on the outer limits of the ski area, has been refurbished in lavish style with candelabra on the open-air bar, sheepskin-covered benches, and a montage of magnums of Champagne on the terrace. It is a true contender for best eateryhere.

On Corvatsch, our favourite is **Alpetta**, **t** +41 (0)81 828 86 30, a mountain hut renowned for its game dishes. It is stuffed with cowbells, antlers and other mountain eclectica. Dorigo, the owner, is on hand to tell wildly improbable stories of how he either shot your lunch or ran it over in his Range Rover.

At Diavolezza, try **Berghaus Diavolezza**, **t** +41 (0)81 839 39 00, at 3000m – it claims the highest Jacuzzi in the world. At Lagalb, eat high-altitude *Rösti* in the **Röstizzeria**, **t** +41 (0)81 839 39 20.

Dine

Chesa Veglia, **t** +41 (0)81 837 2800, serves Engadine specialities and fine pizzas. **Jöhri's Talvo** at Champfér, **t** +41 (0)81 833 4455, is renowned for its local venison and game. **Nobu**, **t** +41 (0)81 837 2624, has opened in Badrutt's Palace Hotel for gourmet sushi and other Japanese cuisine, and the **Sunny Bar** at the Kulm,

t +41 (0) 81 836 8000 also serves sushi. **Trutz**, **t** + 41 (0)81 836 3737, is open for evening fondue and raclette. The **Grischuna** at the Hotel Monopol, **t** +41 (0)81 837 0404 is warmly recommended. **Engiadina**, **t** +41 (0)81 833 3265 is recommended for fondue and steaks.

Party

Hanselmann's in St Moritz Dorf is a 100-year-old coffee house serving coffee, pastries and delectable ice cream. Moroccan-themed **King's Club**, **t** +41 (0)81 837 1000, is the top nightclub. **Diamond** has a lounge, restaurant and club. **Vivai**, **Cascade**, and **Cava** in the Hotel Steffani are highly rated. **Devil's Place** bar at Hotel Waldhaus am See has the world's biggest range of malt whisky and receives a mention in the *Guinness Book of Records*. The **Stübli** at the Schweizerhof has late-night dancing on tables, and after 10pm is 'so crowded that you could not possibly fall off'. The **Muli Bar** hosts country and western music, **Bobby's Bar** is for the under-20s.

Sleep

★★★★★**Badrutt's Palace Hotel**, **t** + 41 (0)81 837 1100, *www.badruttspalace.com*, with its landmark tower, is the most famous establishment, housing seven restaurants and the King's Club.

★★★★★**Grand Hotel des Bains Kempinski**, **t** +41 (0)81 838 3838, *www.kempinski-stmoritz.ch*, in St Moritz Bad, has an impressive spa, a kids' club, the smartest wine bar in town, and a casino.

★★★★★**Kulm Hotel**, **t** +41 (0)81 836 8000, *www.kulmhotel-stmoritz.ch*, is the customary choice of Cresta riders.

★★★★★**Hotel Carlton**, **t** +41 (0)81 836 7000, *www.carlton-stmoritz.ch*, rumoured to have been built as a summer residence by Tsar Nicholas II in 1913, has reopened as the resort's first luxury boutique hotel after extensive renovation. Its rooms have the best views in the resort.

★★★★★**Suvretta House**, **t** +41 (0)81 836 3636, *www.suvrettahouse.ch*, has a spa, skating-rink, kids club, nursery slope, its own ski lift and a ski school.

★★★★**Hotel Schweizerhof**, **t** +41 (0)81 837 0707, *www.schweizerhofstmoritz.ch*, is renowned for its Acla and Clavadatsch restaurants and its basement Hofkeller.

★★★★**Hotel Steffani**, **t** +41 (0)81 836 9696, *www.steffani.ch*, is a traditional family-owned hotel in the centre of town with the resort's oldest restaurant. It is now a Best Western.

★★★**Hotel Waldhaus am See**, **t** +41 (0)81 836 6060, *www.waldhaus-am-see.ch*, is comfortable, and famous for its whisky collection, but situated a brisk walk from the town centre.

★★★**Hotel Arte**, **t** +41 (0)81 837 5858, in St Moritz Dorf, has nationally themed bedrooms including Engadine, Japanese, Venetian and Mexican.

★★★**Hotel Languard**, **t** +41 (0)81 833 31 71, *www.languard-stmoritz.ch,* is a comfortable family-run hotel.

Verbier

🏆 BEST SKI RESORT 2009
🏆 BEST MOUNTAIN RESTAURANT 2009: L'Olympic
🏆 BEST APRES-SKI VENUE 2009: Le Farinet/Casbah

Profile

Switzerland's overall most challenging skiing both on and off-piste. Some excellent chalet accommodation, and a magnet for party-goers and freeriders

Mont Collon 3637 m.
Pigne d'Arolla 3796 m.
Mont Blanc de Cheilon 3870 m.
La Ruinette 3875 m.
Rosablanche 3336 m.
Mont-Fort 3330 m.
Grand Combin 4314 m.
Petit Combin 3672 m.
Mont Vélan 3734 m.
Super St-Bernard 2800 m.
Italie
Hospice 2469 m.
4 Vallées
Grande Dixence
Col des Gentianes 2950 m.
Bec des Rosses 3222 m.
Mont Rogneux 3084 m.
Mont-Gelé 3023 m.
Greppon Blanc 2700 m.
L'Etygeon
Lac de Cleuson
Mont-Rouge 2491 m.
Combatzeline 2238 m.
Tortin 2050 m.
Chassoure 2740 m.
Attelas 2727 m.
La Chaux 2260 m.
2482 m.
Six Blanc 2245 m.
Bourg-St-Pierre
La Breya 2188 m.
La Fouly 1600 m.
Vichères 1423 m.
Orsières
Champex-Lac 1470 m.
Etherolla 2450 m.
Plan-du-Fou 2430 m.
Lourtier
Champsec
EVOLÈNE
Included in Prinze skipass
SIVIEZ 1730 M.
Col des Mines
Les Ruinettes 2200 m.
Versegères
Dent de Nendaz 2463 m.
Vallon d'Arbi
BRUSON 1060 M.
Tracouet 2200 m.
LE CHÂBLE 821 M.
Hérémence
Croix de Coeur 2174 m.
Savoleyres 2354 m.
THYON 2000 2100 M.
Prarion 1768 m.
LES MASSES 1515 M.
VERBIER 1500 M.
LES COLLONS 1800 M.
Sembrancher
Pierre-Avoi 2473 m.
VEYSONNAZ 1400 M.
Martigny 10 km
NENDAZ 1400 M.
MAYENS-DE-L'OURS 1470 M.
LA TZOUMAZ Mayens-de-Riddes 1500 M.
Vex
Aproz
Riddes
Sion

Ski Verbier
The Verbier Specialists

020 7401 1101 www.skiverbier.com

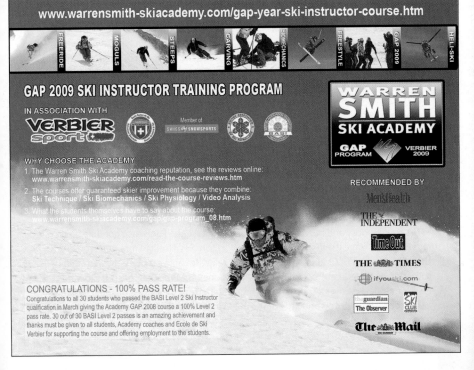

www.warrensmith-skiacademy.com/gap-year-ski-instructor-course.htm

FREERIDE MOGULS STEEPS CARVING BIOMECHANICS FREESTYLE GAP 2009 HELI-SKI

GAP 2009 SKI INSTRUCTOR TRAINING PROGRAM

IN ASSOCIATION WITH
VERBIER sport
Member of SWISS SNOWSPORTS

WARREN SMITH SKI ACADEMY
GAP PROGRAM VERBIER 2009

WHY CHOOSE THE ACADEMY
1. The Warren Smith Ski Academy coaching reputation, see the reviews online: www.warrensmith-skiacademy.com/read-the-course-reviews.htm
2. The courses offer guaranteed skier improvement because they combine: Ski Technique / Ski Biomechanics / Ski Physiology / Video Analysis
3. What the students themselves have to say about the course: www.warrensmith-skiacademy.com/gap/gap-program_08.htm

RECOMMENDED BY
Men'sHealth
THE INDEPENDENT
TimeOut
THE TIMES
ifyouski.com
the guardian The Observer
SKI CLUB
The Mail on Sunday

CONGRATULATIONS - 100% PASS RATE!
Congratulations to all 30 students who passed the BASI Level 2 Ski Instructor qualification in March giving the Academy GAP 2008 course a 100% Level 2 pass rate. 30 out of 30 BASI Level 2 passes is an amazing achievement and thanks must be given to all students, Academy coaches and Ecole de Ski Verbier for supporting the course and offering employment to the students.

Resort

Verbier may lack the Edwardian pedigree of Davos or the aristocratic authority of the Bernese Oberland, but it has the panache and the high mountain terrain to attract the cream of international skiers and riders.

The first lift, a Heath Robinson petrol-driven affair that pulled a sledge 200 vertical metres, wasn't opened until 1946. In those austere times, British and, indeed, German skiers were still otherwise engaged. Another 11 years passed before the Attelas cable car was built, and only then could Verbier properly describe itself as a ski resort.

Verbier today is a thriving modern ski town with an improved lift system and some extraordinarily challenging pistes as well as a clutch of stomach-churningly steep *couloirs* and limitless powder terrain.

It is a hugely popular weekend destination for wealthy Swiss from Geneva and avid skiers from London – many of whom rent apartments for the season and commute on Friday and Sunday evenings. As a result, the nightlife is rivalled by few other resorts in the Alps.

Verbier is linked by lift and electronic pass to neighbouring Nendaz, Veysonnaz and Thyon. Together they form the Four Valleys, an uneasy alliance that should not be compared to the French Trois Vallées. In practice few Verbier-based skiers bother to journey into the far corners of the area because of the primitive link lifts. More importantly, the pick of the slopes are found close to home on Mont-Fort and Mont-Gelé.

'The town is busy and buzzy,' said a reporter. The village itself, situated above the valley town of Le Châble, is a pleasing collection of chalets centred around the Place Centrale. Just over a thousand of the 12,000 beds are in hotels and little of the accommodation offers doorstep skiing. You can learn to ski or ride here and enjoy some easy intermediate runs ('the on-piste skiing is surprisingly average and unchallenging'), but overall the resort best suits skiers and riders looking for steep slopes and endless nightlife.

*BEST FOR

Strong intermediates and experts, cosmopolitan sophistication, party-goers

ESSENTIALS

Altitude: 1500m (4,920ft)–3330m (10,925ft)
Further information: t +41 (0)27 775 3888, *www.verbier.ch*
Lifts in area: 89 in Four Valleys (16 cableways, 24 chairs, 46 drags) serving 412km of piste
Lift pass: Four Valleys (covers Bruson, Nendaz, Thyon, Verbier, Veysonnaz) adult CHF331, youth 15–18yrs CHF265, child 6–15yrs CHF166.50, all for six days
Access: Geneva airport 2–3hrs, railway station at Le Châble 12mins by car or 10mins by cableway

Mountain

Access to Verbier's main ski area is from Médran, a bus ride or a short walk from the Place Centrale. From here two gondolas rise to the 2200m mid-mountain hub of Les Ruinettes. A gondola also comes up from Le Châble and day-visitors are encouraged to use this rather than drive up to the resort.

A lift now links Les Ruinettes to 2260m La Chaux, where the Jumbo cable car rises to 2950m Col des Gentianes and finally to Mont-Fort, the top of the ski area at 3330m. This allows skiers arriving at Le Châble station to reach Mont-Fort in 50 minutes.

The alternative route from Les Ruinettes is to take the Funispace gondola up to 2740m Les Attelas. From here, you either take the cable car up to the demanding slopes of Mont-Gelé, descend towards Les Ruinettes, or continue on into the Lac des Vaux sector. The black piste from the top of Mont-Fort demands considerable concentration, particularly in icy conditions. Verbier is also famous for its ski itineraries, which are patrolled but not groomed. Most notorious of these is Tortin, a steep, wide slope that is often dangerous to access because of exposed rocks at the top.

'Steeps, *couloirs* and huge moguls can be found around every corner,' said a reader. Consequently the standard of skier and rider here is high. Within hours of a fresh snowfall you will find tracks on even the most impossible-looking slopes, and runs such as Stairway to Heaven and Hidden Valley give the appearance of having been pisted. The north face of Mont-Fort, with its B52 and Poubelle variants, is routinely skied, despite its hair-raising entry.

Not all the skiing is so radical. Les Ruinettes offers plenty of easier blue runs, as does the resort's second ski area of Savoleyres, reached by gondola from the other side of town. The skiing here has been improved with a detachable eight-person gondola starting in La Tzomaz and going to the top of Savoleyres. It benefits from sunny, south-facing slopes towards Verbier and longer, better runs down its back side to La Tzoumaz.

Novices make their first turns on a short nursery slope on the golf course and at Les Esserts. You can learn to ski in Verbier, but there are easier places in the Alps to do so. Verbier is a major centre for freeriding. There is a giant terrain park at La Chaux, with separate snowcross and freestyle sectors and a picnic area at the base.

Learn

Verbier has a wide choice of ski schools, all with good reputations. **Powder Extreme, t** +41 (0)76 479 8761, specializes in off-piste, with excellent guiding and instruction. British-run **Altitude, t** +41 (0)27 771 6006, is highly rated. 'The best lessons I have ever had,' said one reporter. British-run **Warren Smith Ski Academy, t** +44 (0)1442 832 629, is 'truly outstanding. Warren is one of the architects of modern ski technique,' said one reader. **European Snowsports, t** +41 (0)27 771 62 22 ('very good and they all speak English'), offers courses for just six skiers, including off-piste and women-only clinics. **Verbier Sport +, t** +41 (0)27 775 3363, is the official resort Swiss ski school. **Adrénaline, t** +41 (0)27 771 7459, **No Limits, t** +41 (0)27 771 5556, and **Swiss Snowboard School, t** +41 (0)775 3366, are the remaining competition. **Bureau des Guides** at Verbier Sport + and **La Fantastique, t** +41 (0)27 771 4141 ('fun but not cheap'), are the mountain-guiding companies. **Eagle Hélicoptère, t** +41 (0)27 327 3060, and **Air Glacier, t** +41 (0)27 329 1415, are the heli-skiing operations.

Children

Kids' Club, t +41 (0)27 775 3363, for skiers over four years, is run by Verbier Sport + at the Moulins nursery site, which has its own lift and restaurant. **Les Schtroumpfs, t** +41 (0)27 771 6585, also at Moulins, offers daycare for little ones aged three months to four years.

Lunch

L'Olympique, t +41 (0)27 771 2615, is the gourmet choice, set in an unremarkable building at the top of the Funiscape lift. Apart from excellent and imaginitive cuisine, it also has walls decorated with Winter Olympics memorabilia and photos of its celebrity clientele. **Cabane Mont-Fort, t** +41 (0)27 771 1384, is a popular mountain refuge off the La Chaux piste, and **Cabane de Tortin, t** +41 (0)27 288 1153, serves heart-warming food. **Chez Dany, t** +41 (0)27 771 2524, in the woods below the Ruinettes chair, is a resort institution. **Vieux-Verbier, t** +41 (0)27 771 1668, at Médran, is cosy and well positioned. On Savoleyres, **Marlénaz**, **t** +41 (0)27 771 5441, is off-piste and has a good sun terrace, **Marmotte**, **t** +41 (0)27 771 6834, specializes in *Rösti*, and **Le Sonalon**, **t** +41 (0)27 771 7271, is popular. **Chez Simon**, **t** +41 (0)27 306 8055, is atmospheric and non-smoking. **Le Carrefour**, **t** +41 (0)27 771 7010, has a sunny terrace, **Namasté**, **t** +41 (0)27 771 5773, is an atmospheric old cabin on the piste at Savoleyres, and **Au Mayen**, **t** +41 (0)27 771 1894, serves local specialities.

Dine

Caveau, **t** +41 (0)27 771 2226, has raclette and fondues. The restaurant in **Hotel Montpelier**, **t** +41 (0)27 771 6131, offers outstanding cuisine. **La Table d'Adrien**, **t** +41 (0)27 771 6200, in Chalet d'Adrien, specializes in French-international cuisine. **Chez Martin**, **t** +41 (0)27 771 2252, and **Al Capone**, **t** +41 (0)27 771 6774, serve pizzas. **Netsu**, **t** +41 (0)27 771 6272, is Japanese, **La Grange**, **t** +41 (0)27 771 6431, has French cuisine and is rated by *Gault-Millau*.

Party

'Verbier rocks!' was how one reporter put it, and 'The nightlife can keep you up till dawn,' said another. This is a party town, especially at weekends when wealthy players from London and Geneva hit town. **Le Farinet** in the Place Centrale is the most popular venue as the lifts close. Young skiers and snowboarders crush into the glass-sided terrace bar with live music, 30-somethings chill out inside over a bottle of wine in leather armchairs, while downstairs is the late-night alternative – Moroccan-themed **Casbah**, which hosts some world-class DJs. **Offshore** with its pink VW Beetle centrepiece is a great place for après ski drinks, and **Fer à Cheval** are both busy by mid-afternoon. Resort staff flock to **Pub Mont-Fort** for its cheap drinks. Later on, sophisticated **Crock No Name** provides the warm-up act for the nightclubs. London- and Manhattan-priced **Farm Club** has long been the traditional favourite, but newcomer, **The Coco Club** (ex-Tara's), has now overtaken it as the smartest place in town.

Accommodation

★★★★★**Le Chalet d'Adrien**, t +41 (0)27 771 6200, *www.chalet-adrien.com*, in Savoleyres, is small with individually decorated rooms, two restaurants and a spa.

★★★★**The Lodge**, *www.virgin.com/limitededition*, is Virgin Limited Edition's first ski chalet. It features nine rooms and suites and a kids' bunkroom for up to six children. The luxurious property comes complete with private pool plus indoor and outdoor spa areas.

★★★★**Hotel Montpelier**, **t** +41 (0)27 771 6131, *www.hotelmontpelier.ch*, has a shuttle bus to the lifts. Its bedrooms are attractive and there's an indoor pool.

★★★★**Chalet Cheyenne**, **t** +44 (0)20 7385 8050, *www.skiverbier.com*, is a comfortable chalet built from ancient timbers and offering delicious cuisine.

★★★★**Hotel Nevai**, **t** +41 (0)27 771 6121, is the resort's newest attraction, with cutting-edge style, a spa, and a convenient position in town ('minimalist rooms, questionable service, but great public areas').

★★★★**Hotel Vanessa**, **t** +41 (0)27 27 775 2800, *www.hotelvanessa.ch*, is convenient and family-friendly, with good food.

★★★**Hotel Bristol**, **t** +41 (0)27 27 771 6577, *www.bristol-verbier.ch*, is conveniently positioned and houses a disco in the basement.

★★★**Le Mazot**, **t** +41 (0)27 27 775 2121, owned by former ski racer Serge Tacchini, is small and pleasant.

*****Hotel Phenix**, **t** +41 (0)27 27 771 6844, *www.hotelphenix.pagesjaunes.ch*, is comfortable and central.

****Hotel Garbo**, **t** +41 (0)27 771 6272, *www.hotelgarbo.com*, has two restaurants – French and sushi – and is well positioned.

The Bunker, **t** +41 (0)27 771 6602, *www.thebunker.ch*, next to the sports centre, attracts a large number of young people to its good-value dormitory accommodation.

Villars

Profile

An underrated area easily reached from Geneva. Its low altitude means snow-cover is uncertain, but Les Diablerets glacier is open all year

Resort

Villars is one of the original resorts in the Alps that first attracted British skiers in the 1960s, largely because it was then one of the few places in Switzerland where foreigners could buy property in their own right without serious restriction. Snow-cover would be uncertain for much of the season, were it not for the 3209m Diablerets Glacier which offers year-round skiing. The skiing here is ideal for unadventurous intermediates and families, who come here in large numbers to enjoy gentle slopes and magnificent scenery above the Rhône Valley in the beautiful Vaudois Mountains.

The resort shares its ski area with Les Diablerets, a large village with mainly chalet accommodation.

* BEST FOR

Beginners, intermediates, families, airport access

ESSENTIALS

Altitude: 1300m (4,265ft)–2113m (6,932ft)
Further information: Villars: **t** +41 (0)24 495 3232, *www.villars.ch*; Les Diablerets: **t** +41 (0)24 492 3358, *www.diablerets.ch*
Lifts in area: 42 (6 cableways, 11 chairs, 25 drags) serving 125km of piste
Lift pass: Villars-Gryon-Diablerets Glacier 3000 adult CHF163, child 9–15yrs CHF106, both for six days
Access: Geneva airport 1½hrs, railway station in resort

Mountain

Mountain access from Villars is by an eight-seater gondola, which takes six minutes to go up the mountain. The base station includes an escalator and direct access from the pistes. The old rack-and-pinion mountain railway still goes to Roc d'Orsay and to the mid-mountain station of Bretaye at 1806m. A gondola from the outlying hamlet of Barboleusaz provides a third means of mountain access.

From Bretaye, a sequence of lifts and pistes leads across Les Chaux des Conches into the Diablerets sector, with a choice of runs down from 1949m Meilleret and 1727m Les Mazots to Vers L'Eglise and Les Diablerets itself. From here a gondola climbs the gentle pastureland to Isenau for some easy blue and slightly more challenging red runs. A bus takes you to Col du Pillon for the gondola up to the glacier, which can also be reached by cable car and chair from Reusch near Gstaad. The long run from the top takes you down the Combe d'Audon to Oldenalp at 1840m, from where you can ride two chairs back up again in order to descend by cable car to Cold du Pillon and a bus back to Les Diablerets for the homeward journey to Villars. Terrain parks are at Bretaye and Les Chaux.

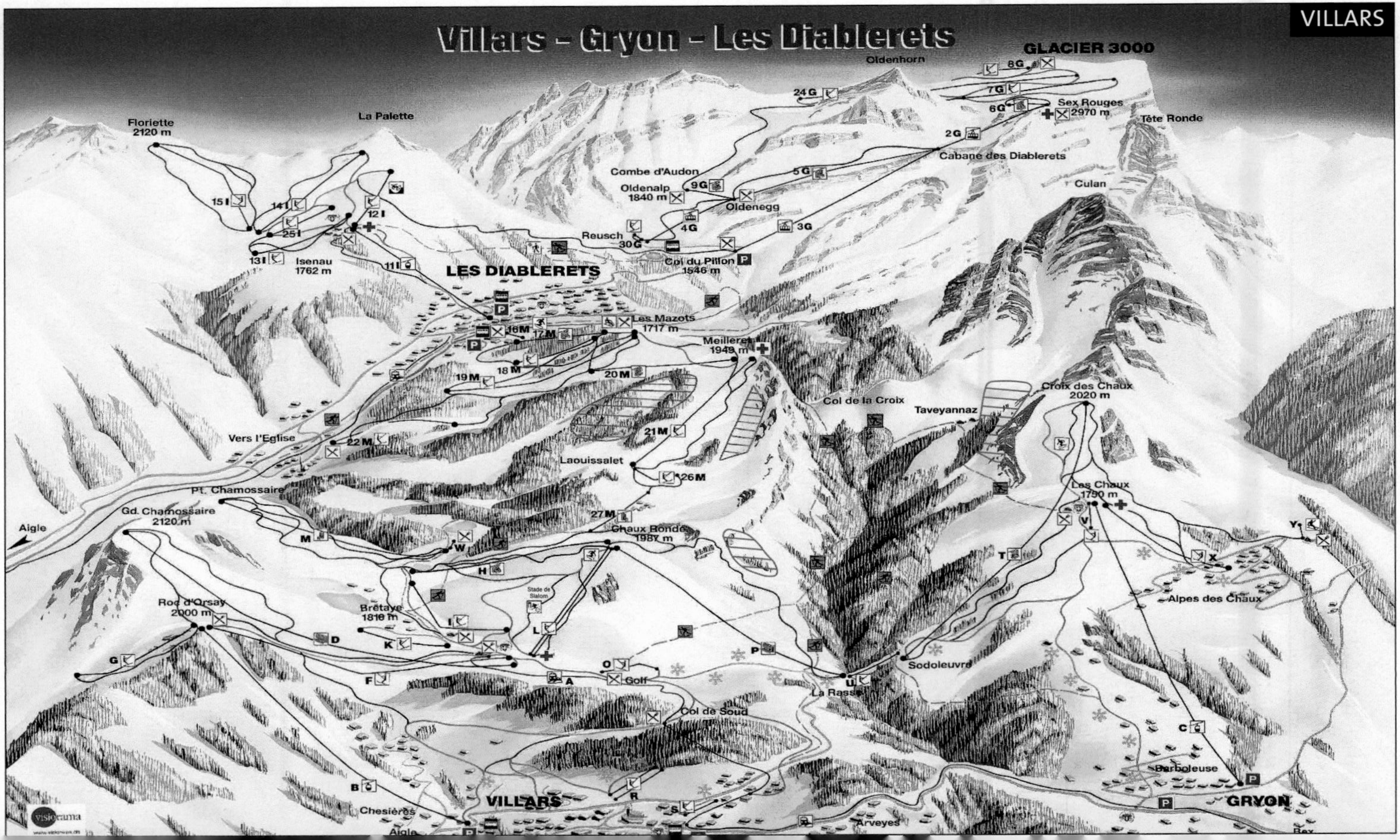

Villars - Gryon - Les Diablerets

GLACIER 3000
Oldenhorn
8G
7G
24G
6G
Sex Rouges
2970 m
Tête Ronde
2G
Cabane des Diablerets
Floriette
2120 m
La Palette
Combe d'Audon
5G
Oldenalp
1840 m
9G
Oldenegg
Culan
15 I
14 I
12 I
25 I
4G
3G
Reusch
30G
Col du Pillon
1546 m
13 I
Isenau
1762 m
11 I
LES DIABLERETS
Les Mazots
1717 m
16M
17M
Meilleret
1949 m
18M
20M
19M
Col de la Croix
Croix des Chaux
2020 m
Taveyannaz
Vers l'Eglise
22M
21M
Laouissalet
26M
Pt. Chamossaire
Les Chaux
1750 m
Gd. Chamossaire
2120 m
27M
Chaux Ronde
1987 m
V
Y
Aigle
M
W
T
X
H
Stade de Slalom
Alpes des Chaux
Roc d'Orsay
2000 m
Bretaye
1810 m
I
L
D
K
P
G
O
Sodoleuvre
F
A
Golf
U
La Rasse
Col de Soud
C
Barboleuse
B
R
VILLARS
S
GRYON
Chesières
Arveyes
Aigle
Bex
visiorama

Learn

Villars Ski School, **t** +41 (0)24 495 4545 ('they were brilliant'), uses the graduated length method of teaching. **Riderschool**, **t** +41 (0)24 495 1600, is the dedicated boarder academy. **Gryon**, **t** +41 (0)24 498 2434, is warmly recommended. **Swiss Ski and Snowboard School**, **t** +41 (0)24 495 2210, is the traditional option, **Handicapt Sports & Loisirs**, **t** +41 (0)24 498 1028, is a sit-ski learning centre with a worldwide reputation. Off-piste guiding is available through **Villars Expérience**, **t** +41 (0)24 495 4138, and the ski schools. **Swiss Ski and Snowboard School**, **t** +41 (0)24 492 2002, is where to learn in Les Diablerets.

Children

Snowli – the Swiss school's kindergarten – and **Villars Ski School** both teach children from three years at Bretaye. **La Trottinette**, **t** +41 (0)24 495 8888, down in the village, cares for non-skiers from two months to six years. In Les Diablerets, the **Swiss Ski and Snowboard School** has a kindergarten from four years. **Hotel Le Chamois**, **t** +41 (0)24 492 2653, has an in-house kindergarten, and **Diablodocus Park** is part of the ski and snowboard school, offering lessons and childcare. Lift passes are free for all children under nine years.

Lunch

Try **Hotel du Lac de Bretaye**, **t** +41 24 495 2192, and **Les Mazots at Meilleret**, **t** +41 24 492 1023. **Le Col de Bretaye**, **t** +41 (0)24 495 2194, and **Les Chaux**, **t** +41 (0)24 498 1187, are both recommended, and **Lake Chevonnes**, **t** +41 (0)24 495 2131, is in a lovely lakeside setting at Bretaye. The new **Roc** restaurant, **t** +41 (0)24 495 2814, serves pizzas and fresh pasta; it faces the new gondola top station and has DJ and terrace.

Dine

Les Ecovets, **t** +41 (0)24 495 2378, specializes in regional dishes. **Le Vieux Villars**, **t** +41 (0)24 495 2525, is renowned for its fondue and raclette. **Le Soleil**, **t** +41 (0)24 495 4530, is a new gourmet restaurant. **Pasta & Basta**, **t** +41 (0)24 495 1818, in Chesières, **Le Sporting**, **t** +41 (0)24 1313, in Villars, and **L'Escale**, **t** +41 (0)24 498 1215, at Gryon below Les Chaux, are cheaper alternatives. In Les Diablerets, **Auberge de la Poste**, **t** +41 (0)24 492 3124, and **Café des Diablerets**, **t** +41 (0)24 492 0909, serve regional specialities. **Le Soleil**, **t** +41 24 495 4530, is a new gourmet restaurant.

Party

Après ski includes live rock and pool at **Café Central** in Villars or **Harambee Café** in Barboleuse, and drinking at **Charlie's Bar**, **L'Alchimiste**, **Murphy's Wine Bar** and the **Jazz or Blues Bar** in Villars. Dance the night away at **El Gringo** in Villars. Les Diablerets' nightlife is quiet and centres around a few bars and discos, including **La Diabletine** bar and internet café, **Maroccan Bar**, which is new, **Atomix Bar**, **B'Bar** disco in **Mon Abri**, and **Pote Saloon**, the other disco. **Les Vioz** is a good place for a *vin chaud* after the last run down.

Sleep

Villars:

★★★★★**Grand Hotel du Parc**, **t** +41 (0)24 492 2828, *www.parcvillars.ch*, contains a choice of gastronomic and regional restaurants. It is currently undergoing a major makeover.

★★★★★**Chalet Royalp Hotel & Spa**, **t** +41 (0)24 495 9090, *www.royalp.ch*, opens this season and has a 1200sq meter spa, two kids' play area, and a 15-seat cinema.

★★★★Eurotel Victoria, t +41 (0)24 492 3131, *www.forum.ch/eurotel-victoria-villars*, is in the village centre and has spacious rooms.

★★★★Hotel du Golf, t +41 (0)24 492 3838, *www.hotel-golf.ch*, is central, with attractive rooms and a wellness area.

★★★★Hotel La Renardière, t +41 (0)24 495 2592, *www.larenardiere.ch*, has a home-from-home ambience and lovely wood-panelled bedrooms.

★★★Hotel Alpe Fleurie, t +41 (0)24 492 3464, is a chalet-style hotel in the resort centre.

★★★Hotel Ecureuil, t +41 (0)24 492 3737, *www.hotel-ecureuil.ch*, has been run by the same family for over 50 years and is child-friendly.

Les Diablerets:

★★★★Eurotel-Victoria, t +41 (0)24 492 3721, *www.eurotel-victoria.ch*, is the biggest hotel, with very pleasant staff, good food, large, modern rooms and an indoor pool.

★★★★Hotel des Diablerets, t +41 (0)24 492 0909, *www.diablerets.com*, is traditional and close to the slopes.

★★★Hotel Le Chamois, t +41 (0)24 492 0202, *www.hotelchamois.ch*, is at the heart of the village, family-friendly, with its own kindergarten.

Wengen

Profile

A car-free traditional resort with a large intermediate ski area linked to Grindelwald. Recommended for beginners and intermediates, as well as off-piste skiers

✱ BEST FOR

Alpine charm, intermediates, dramatic scenery

ESSENTIALS

Altitude: 1274m (4,180ft)–2320m (7,612ft)

Further information: **t** +41 (0)33 855 1414, *www.wengen-muerren.ch*

Lifts in area: 43 in Jungfrau Region (4 funiculars/mountain railways, 15 cableways, 12 chairs, 11 drags) serving 213km of piste

Lift pass: Jungfrau (covers Grindelwald, Mürren, Wengen) adult CHF188.80, youth 16–19yrs CHF151.40, child 6–19yrs CHF94.40, all for six days

Access: Zurich airport 3hrs, Geneva airport 4hrs, railway station in resort

Resort

Wengen is one of the Edwardian cradles of modern skiing. Foreign – mainly British – visitors first arrived here in the late 19th century to gaze at the mighty peaks of the Eiger, Mönsch and Jungfrau – and they came by train. The Jungfraubahn, the rack-and-pinion railway in the beautiful Bernese Oberland, was one of the engineering feats of the new Iron Age, climbing eventually through the granite heart of the Eiger to the 3454m Jungfraujoch, the highest railway station in Europe. It is now a UNESCO World Natural Heritage site that attracts tourists throughout the year from all over the world and notably the Far East.

From 1911, the rail company took the commercial decision to keep the network open in winter, and sports-minded visitors quickly discovered that it could be used as a ski lift. Not all of these hardy tweed-clad pioneers approved of such easy uphill transport. They believed it offended the principle of 'no pain, no gain' and detracted from the achievement of skiing downhill. But in February 1925 the Downhill Only Club was formed in Wengen by British skiers to race against their Kandahar rivals encamped at Mürren

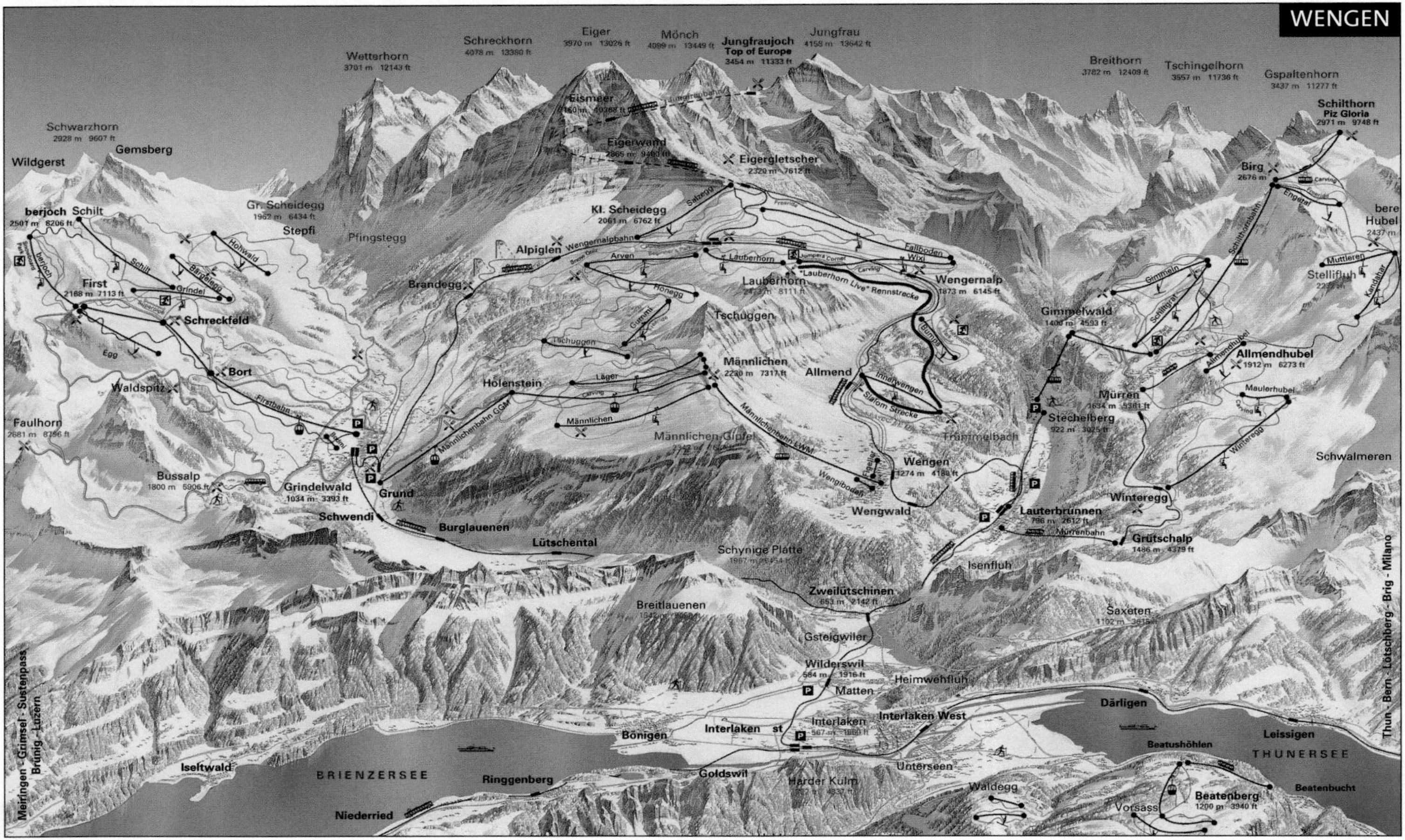

WENGEN

Schwarzhorn
2928 m 9607 ft
Wildgerst
Gemsberg
Wetterhorn
3701 m 12143 ft
Schreckhorn
4078 m 13380 ft
Eiger
3970 m 13026 ft
Mönch
4099 m 13449 ft
Jungfraujoch
Top of Europe
3454 m 11333 ft
Jungfrau
4158 m 13642 ft
Breithorn
3782 m 12409 ft
Tschingelhorn
3557 m 11736 ft
Gspaltenhorn
3437 m 11277 ft
Schilthorn
Piz Gloria
2971 m 9748 ft
Eismeer
Eigerwand
Eigergletscher
2320 m 7612 ft
Birg
2676 m
berjoch
2501 m 8206 ft
Schilt
Gr. Scheidegg
1962 m 6434 ft
Stepfi
Pfingstegg
Kl. Scheidegg
2061 m 6762 ft
Alpiglen
Wengernalpbahn
Arven
Lauberhorn
Jumpers Corner
Fallboden
Wixi
Engetal
Schilthornbahn
bere
Hubel
Muttleren
Stellifluh
Kandahar
First
2168 m 7113 ft
Schreckfeld
Grindel
Bärgelegg
Hohwald
Egg
Brandegg
Honegg
Lauberhorn
2473 m 8111 ft
"Lauberhorn Live" Rennstrecke
Wengernalp
1873 m 6145 ft
Gimmelwald
1400 m 4593 ft
Gimmeln
Schiltgrat
Tschuggen
Gummi
Bumps
Allmendhubel
1912 m 6273 ft
Bort
Männlichen
2230 m 7317 ft
Allmend
Innerwengen
Slalom Strecke
Mürren
1634 m 5361 ft
Maulerhubel
Waldspitz
Holenstein
Läger
Männlichenbahn GGM
Männlichen
Faulhorn
2681 m 8796 ft
Firstbahn
Stechelberg
922 m 3025 ft
Trümmelbach
Männlichen Gipfel
Männlichenbahn LWM
Winteregg
Schwalmeren
Bussalp
1800 m 5906 ft
Grindelwald
1034 m 3393 ft
Grund
Wengen
1274 m 4180 ft
Wengiboden
Wengwald
Schwendi
Burglauenen
Lauterbrunnen
796 m 2612 ft
Mürrenbahn
Winteregg
Grütschalp
1486 m 4379 ft
Lütschental
Schynige Platte
Isenfluh
Zweilütschinen
653 m 2142 ft
Breitlauenen
Saxeten
1102 m
Gsteigwiler
Wilderswil
584 m 1916 ft
Matten
Heimwehfluh
Därligen
Interlaken West
Interlaken
567 m 1860 ft
Interlaken Ost
Bönigen
Leissigen
Beatushöhlen
THUNERSEE
Meiringen - Grimsel - Sustenpass
Brünig - Luzern
Thun - Bern - Lötschberg - Brig - Milano
Iseltwald
BRIENZERSEE
Ringgenberg
Goldswil
Unterseen
Harder Kulm
Waldegg
Beatenberg
1200 m 3940 ft
Beatenbucht
Vorsass
Niederried

on the other side of the Lauterbrunnen Valley. Both clubs are happily alive, active, and as big rivals as ever in the 21st century.

Today the railway connecting the three resorts of Wengen, Grindelwald and Mürren still acts as the backbone of the shared Jungfrau ski region, along with a network of conventional ski lifts.

Car-free Wengen sits on a sunny ledge nearly 500m above Lauterbrunnen and is reachable only by rail. Electric taxis and a few licensed motor vehicles provide the in-resort transport. The main street stretches back from the station to a modest collection of hotels, shops, restaurants, a giant skating rink and family-friendly nursery slopes. Hotels and private homes line the steep mountainside above.

In recent years, Wengen has lost some of its faded Edwardian ambience in favour of the high-tech demands of a modern ski resort. Nevertheless it remains a tranquil alpine backwater best suited to intermediate piste skiers and riders looking for distance over challenging gradient against one of the world's most spectacular mountain backdrops.

Sadly, the failure of the Swiss Ski School to offer afternoon group lessons makes it an inconvenient destination for families with small children.

Mountain

'One of the most breathtaking places I have skied in,' said one reporter. 'One of the most picturesque resorts in the world,' said another, and, 'The only place I have found where I can truly relax and enjoy my skiing.'

Certainly the commute up to the main skiing at Kleine Scheidegg is unquestionably more relaxing and scenic than the daily grind into Manhattan or London. Swiss trains run to a precise timetable, with halts along the way. From Kleine Scheidegg you can drop back towards Wengen or take a run down the far side to Grindelwald. Trains also continue down to Grindelwald as well as up to the 2320m Eigergletscher. This is the highest point from which you can ski. The train then disappears behind the rock face and takes foot passengers on to the Jungfraujoch. Don't miss this excursion (the final section is not included in the lift pass), which stops at the famous window in the north face of the Eiger. From here mountain guides have launched dramatic rescue operations to save climbers stranded on the treacherous Eigerwand.

Alternative mountain access from Wengen is provided by a cable car that rises to the 2230m Männlichen ridge separating the Lauterbrunnen and Grindelwald valleys. From here, a network of pistes and lifts brings you over to Kleine Scheidegg and the Eigergletscher. Long runs also continue down to the rail station at Grund near Grindelwald.

Each January, Wengen is the setting for the Lauberhorn, the longest – as well as one of the most celebrated and testing – downhill races in the World Cup Calendar. When not prepared for racing, the course which begins at the top of the Wixi chair, provides a glorious 4.5km red descent back to Wengen.

Advanced skiers and riders will find that even the handful of runs marked black on the piste map lack real challenge; however, the opportunities for lift-accessible off-piste are enormous. The dramatic White Hare, which begins from the foot of the Eigerwand and is reached from Eigergletscher, is a favourite.

Wengen has a terrain park with a variety of jumps and obstacles, served by the Bumps T-bar. Mürren is included in the lift pass and linked by train but not by piste. A day trip is viable, but distances are great and the trains are slow.

Learn

Swiss Ski and Snowboard School, **t** +41 (0)33 856 2022, gives three-hour morning group lessons from Sunday to Friday, as well as private lessons at any time. **Privat Ski and Snowboard School**, **t** +41 (0)33 855 5005, offers private tuition from young English-speaking instructors. **Swiss Snowsports School Kleine Scheidegg**, **t** +41 (0)33 855 1547, is based up the mountain.

Children

Swiss Ski and Snowboard School, **t** +41 (0)33 856 2022, runs morning-only group lessons, which makes life difficult for parents with small skiers who consequently never get the chance to explore far afield. Both the **Swiss**, **t** +41 (0)33 856 2022, and **Privat** ski schools, **t** +41 (0)33 855 5005, offer private afternoon lessons. However these constitute an expensive form of childcare. **Playhouse Wengen**, **t** +41 (0)79 817 5849, is a good alternative choice for non-skiers from 18 months to seven years. **Kinderhort Sunshine Männlichen**, **t** +41 79 632 8178, accepts babies from four weeks at the top of Männlichen.

Lunch

Hotel Jungfrau, **t** +41 (0)33 855 1622, at Wengernalp, has outstanding views from the terrace and the best food on the mountain. **Brandegg**, **t** +41 (0)33 853 1057, is famous for its apple fritters. **Kleine Scheidegg Bahnhof**, **t** +41 (0)33 828 7828, is a hotel and good restaurant as well as a station. **Mary's Café**, **t** +41 (0)33 855 2775, at the foot of the Lauberhorn race course, has 'excellent French cooking' and wholesome and reasonably priced mountain fare. Try also **Allmend**, **t** +41 (0)33 855 5800, for cheese fondue, **Eigergletscher**, **t** +41 (0)33 828 7888, and **Männlichen**, **t** +41 (0)33 853 1068.

Dine

With a few notable exceptions, the restaurants in Wengen are almost all located in hotels. **Da Sina**, **t** +41 (0)33 855 3172, is a lively pizzeria. **Hirschenstübli**, **t** +41 (0)33 855 1544, in the **Hotel Hirschen**, is renowned for its *fondue chinoise*. **Hotel Berghaus**, **t** +41 (0)33 855 2151, has a fish restaurant, and the **Bernerhof**, **t** +41 (0)33 855 2721, serves good fondue and raclette. Local produce is cooked at Bären, **t** +41 (0)33 855 1419. Gourmets can try **Chez Meyer's** in Hotel Regina, **t** +41 (0)33 856 5858, **Caprice**, **t** +41 (0)33 856 0606, and **Schônegg**, **t** +41 (0)33 855 3422.

Party

At the end of the day, skiers and riders gather around the outdoor **Brunner Snowbar** or **Figeller Snowbar** on the home run. The last trains up the mountain are packed with families heading to Wengernalp for the 4km toboggan run back to the village. **Mary's Café** is ever popular. Later on the action moves to **Tanne Bar**, **Sina's Pub**, **Tiffany**, the **Underground** and **Crystal**.

Sleep

★★★★+**Beausite Park Hotel**, **t** +41 (0)33 856 5161, *www.parkwengen.ch*, is in a peaceful location above town. It has a leisure area with pool.

★★★★**Hotel Regina**, **t** +41 (0)33 856 5858, *www.wengen.com/regina*, is a stately old hotel housing two good restaurants, rooms from a bygone age, and one floor of modern suites.

★★★★**Hotel Sunstar**, **t** +41 (0)33 856 5111, *www.sunstar.ch/wengen*, is one of the most convenient hotels, with family duplexes and a pool. 'A model of Swiss efficiency,' enthused a reporter.

★★★**Hotel Alpenruhe Kulm**, **t** +41 (0)33 856 24 00, *www.wengen.com/hotel/alpenruhe*, is set beside the woods with lovely views.

★★★**Hotel Brunner**, **t** +41 (0)33 855 2494, *www.wengen.com/hotel/brunner*, is ski in, ski out above the village, and family-friendly.

★★★**Hotel Falken**, **t** +41 (0)33 856 5121, *www.hotelfalken.com*, is one of the resort's original Edwardian hotels and decorated with historic photographs.

★★**Hotel Bernerhof**, **t** +41 (0)33 855 2721, *www.wengen.com/hotel/bernerhof*, is said to be very friendly with good food.

Zermatt

Profile

Ancient, historic climbing town with ski area linked to Cervinia in Italy. Lashings of alpine charm and luxury accommodation

Resort

Zermatt is no stranger to change. Ever since Victorian mountaineer Edward Whymper controversially conquered the Matterhorn in 1865, with four of his companions falling to their deaths on the downward journey, Zermatt has regularly reinvented itself as a tourist destination. Most recently this has been in the form of a high-tech ski resort by building a modern lift system to replace the old network of sardine-can cable cars and draglifts that had changed precious little during the previous 40 years. At the same time is has developed a range of smart hotels and sumptuous restaurants on the mountain that have few rivals anywhere else in the world. 'This resort has it all – picturesque scenery, the best mountain restaurants and great après ski,' said a reporter.

The bustling little town, set above the valley town of Visp, attracts well-heeled skiers and snowboarders who want to combine snowsports with excellent eating and nightlife. Faithful followers include Robbie Williams, the Duchess of York, Sir Bob Geldof, Sir Paul McCartney and Nicole Kidman, along with members of Pink Floyd and Dire Straits.

The town – actually it is a large village, its size dictated by limited avalanche-safe building territory – dates back to the Middle Ages. Old blackened barns stand beside modern hotels and smart boutiques and farmers still tend to their chickens and goats within 200m of the resort centre. Transport is by high-speed electric taxis and an electric ski-bus system. These reduce noise and air pollution but can be a dangerous traffic hazard to pedestrians.

Zermatt's ski area is linked via the Klein Matterhorn to Cervinia in Italy, and the two resorts share a lift pass. Skiing continues here 365 days a year at 3900m on the border with Italy, with seven lifts and a vertical drop in summer of 1000m.

*BEST FOR

All standards of skier and rider, non-skiers, reliable snow cover, mountain restaurants

ESSENTIALS

Altitude: 1620m (5,314ft)–3899m (12,788ft)
Further information: **t** +41 (0)27 966 8100, *www.zermatt.ch*
Lifts in area: 58 with Cervinia (2 funiculars/railways, 20 cableways, 22 chairs, 14 drags) serving 313km of piste in Zermatt and 200km in Cervinia
Lift pass: International (Zermatt and Cervinia) adult CHF394, youth 17–19yrs CHF335, child 9–16yrs CHF197, all for six days
Access: Sion airport 1½hrs, Berne airport 2hrs, Geneva and Zurich airports 4hrs, railway station in resort

ZERMATT

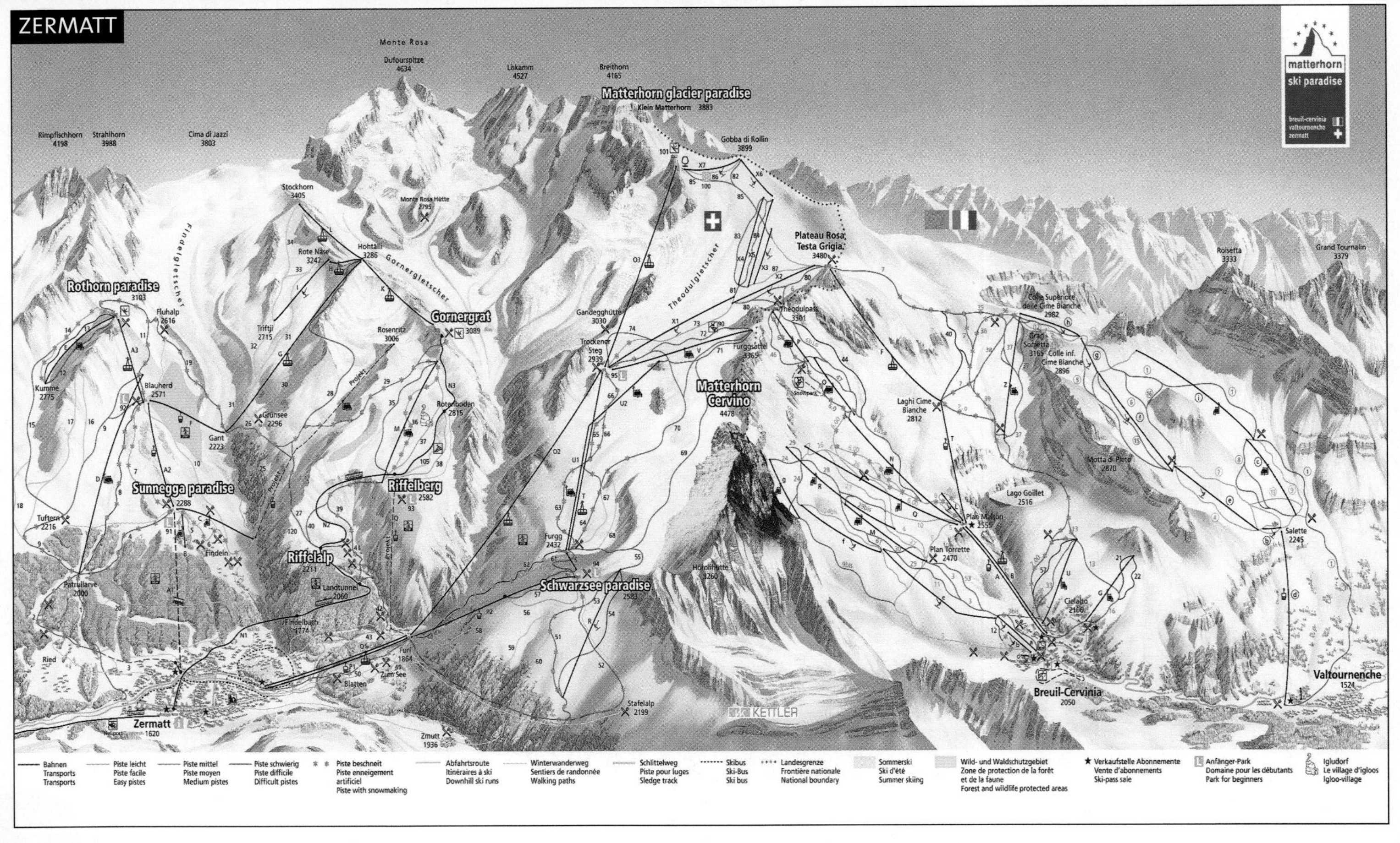

matterhorn ski paradise
breuil-cervinia
valtournenche
zermatt
Monte Rosa
Dufourspitze 4634
Liskamm 4527
Breithorn 4165
Matterhorn glacier paradise
Klein Matterhorn 3883
Gobba di Rollin 3899
Rimpfischhorn 4198
Strahlhorn 3988
Cima di Jazzi 3803
Stockhorn 3405
Monte Rosa Hütte 2795
Rote Nase 3247
Hohtälli 3286
Gornergletscher
Findelgletscher
Theodulgletscher
Plateau Rosa Testa Grigia 3480
Roisetta 3333
Grand Tournalin 3379
Rothorn paradise 3103
Fluhalp 2616
Triftji 2715
Gornergrat 3089
Rosenritz 3006
Gandegghütte 3030
Trockener Steg 2939
Theodulpass 3301
Furggsattel 3365
Colle Superiore delle Cime Bianche 2982
Grand Sometta 3165
Colle inf. Cime Bianche 2896
Kumme 2775
Blauherd 2571
Grünsee 2296
Gant 2223
Rotenboden 2815
Matterhorn Cervino 4478
Laghi Cime Bianche 2812
Motta di Plete 2870
Sunnegga paradise 2288
Riffelberg 2582
Tuftern 2216
Findeln
Riffelalp 2211
Furgg 2432
Lago Goillet 2516
Plan Maison 2555
Plan Torrette 2470
Salette 2245
Patrullarve 2000
Landtunnel 2060
Schwarzsee paradise 2583
Hörnlihütte 3260
Cielalto 2106
Findelbach 1774
Ried
Furi 1864
Blatten
Zum See
Stafelalp 2199
Zermatt 1620
Zmutt 1936
KETTLER
Breuil-Cervinia 2050
Valtournenche 1524
Projekt
Bahnen Transports Transports
Piste leicht Piste facile Easy pistes
Piste mittel Piste moyen Medium pistes
Piste schwierig Piste difficile Difficult pistes
Piste beschneit Piste enneigement artificiel Piste with snowmaking
Abfahrtsroute Itinéraires à ski Downhill ski runs
Winterwanderweg Sentiers de randonnée Walking paths
Schlittelweg Piste pour luges Sledge track
Skibus Ski-Bus Ski bus
Landesgrenze Frontière nationale National boundary
Sommerski Ski d'été Summer skiing
Wild- und Waldschutzgebiet Zone de protection de la forêt et de la faune Forest and wildlife protected areas
Verkaufstelle Abonnemente Vente d'abonnements Ski-pass sale
Anfänger-Park Domaine pour les débutants Park for beginners
Igludorf Le village d'igloos Igloo-village

The terrain park has a super-pipe and a half-pipe open from the second week of July until the end of October.

Mountain

'Superb lift system. Despite it being half term, the longest we had to wait was 15 minutes. Most of the time we just turned up at a lift and got on it,' said a reporter. The skiing divides into three linked areas on the mountain.

The focus for experienced skiers and riders is on the Trockener Steg–Klein Matterhorn–Schwarzsee sector that is linked across the Plateau Rosa to Cervinia. The Matterhorn Express gondola provides fast access to Furi and Schwarzsee. A cable car from Furi takes you up to 2939m Trockener Steg, and another continues to the Klein Matterhorn at 3820m. An eight-person gondola connects Furi to Riffelberg.

The area provides a wide range of scenic and occasionally demanding snow-sure skiing with magnificent views of the mighty Matterhorn. On sunny days, Zermatt-based skiers head over the top for the long intermediate run to Cervinia and an Italian lunch at half the price of Switzerland. Distances are huge and it is important to allow plenty of time for the return journey. Missing the last lift involves a six-hour taxi journey or an overnight stay in a B&B.

The second area of Sunnegga is reached by an underground funicular from near the town centre that takes you up to 2288m. A *chondola* – half gondola, half six-pack chair – brings you on up to Blauherd. The Sunnegga sector has some demanding pistes including the black rollercoaster Obere National FIS, as well as more benign red descents to the valley.

From 3103m Rothorn, the area links via a long scenic piste and the Gant cable car to the third sector of Gornergrat. This can also be accessed from the resort by a slow surface train that winds gently up the mountainside. Hohtälli, above Gant, and parallel Rote Nase-Stockhorn, are the starting points for some of the best advanced pistes in the resort, including the notorious Stockhorn descent to Triftji. However, these runs are often closed until mid-January because of insufficient snow.

The whole of Zermatt has enormous off-piste potential, with heli-skiing possible on the Monte Rosa and the Alphubeljoch. Snowboarding is a serious business with free-riding popular beneath Hohtälli. The winter terrain park is served by the Furggsattel lift above Trockener Steg. The downside is the snowboarding, according to a reporter: 'it's not the greatest terrain, but easily remedied by heading over to the superb Cervinia side'.

Learn

The **Swiss Ski and Snowboarding School**, **t** +41 (0)27 966 2466, used to run a tight monopoly here, which was broken some years ago by the younger and more go-ahead instructors of **Stoked the Ski and Snowboard School**, **t** +41 (0)27 967 7020. British-run **Summit Ski & Board School**, **t** +41 (0)27 967 0001, has since raised the game with over 30 instructors and a cult following that includes the Duchess of York and Sir Bob Geldof ('excellent tuition from British instructors really made a difference to my skiing'). The other schools are **Almrausch Swiss Snow Sport School**, **t** +41 (0)27 967 0808, **European Snowsport**, **t** +41 (0)27 967 6787, **Independent Swiss Snowsport Instructors**, **t** +41 (0)27 967 7067, and **Prato Borni**, **t** +(0)27 967 5115. **Alpin Center**, **t** +41 (0)27 966 2460, provides guiding, and **Air Zermatt**, **t** +41 (0)27 966 8686, heli-skiing.

Children

Summit, **t** +41 (0)27 967 0001, takes children in groups of six from six years, with New School courses for teens. Stoked's **Snowflakes Kids Club**, **t** +41 (0)27 967 4340, at the top of the Matterhorn Express at Schwarzee, cares for children from three years. **Snowli Snow Club**, **t** +41 (0)27 966 2466, run by the Swiss School, is a kindergarten for four- to six-year-olds at Riffelberg. Child-minding for children from two years is available at **Kinderclub Pumuckel**, **t** +41 (0)27 966 5000, in Hotel La Ginabelle six days a week. **Kinderparadies**, **t** +41 (0)27 967 7252, cares for infants from three months and offers babysitting until 10pm.

Lunch

No resort in the world has a more enticing – and expensive – collection of welcoming mountain huts offering gourmet fare. **Chez Vrony**, **t** +41 (0)27 967 2552, in Findeln, is renowned for its *Rösti*, spicy fish soup, and spaghetti with prawns and wild mushrooms. The ancient hamlet of **Zum See**, **t** +41 (0)27 967 2045, houses a restaurant of the same name, serving delicious, albeit pricey, cuisine such as carpaccio of tuna with olive oil and lemon juice, and Thai-style duck breast with basmati rice. **Blatten**, **t** +41 (0)27 967 2096, below Furi, has fantastic *Rösti*. Also at Furi is **Simi**, **t** +41 (0)27 967 2695, with a wood grill and serving Valais dishes at reasonable prices. **Alphittä**, **t** +41 (0)27 967 2114, at Riffelalp, is wood-panelled and offers local specialities. **Fluhalp**, **t** +41 (0)27 967 2597, en route to Gant, offers fine food and the best views of the Matterhorn. **Stafelalp**, **t** +41 (0)27 967 3062, specializes in *Rösti* and sweet omelettes. **Pizzeria Cervino**, **t** +41 (0)27 967 1812, at Trockner Steg, has 'no charm whatsoever, but the pizzas were excellent and cooked on a traditional wood-burning fire'. **Hotel Silvana** at Furi, **t** +41 (0)27 966 2800, is furthest from the cable car station and is usually uncrowded. **Hotel Schwarzsee**, **t** +41 (0)27 967 2263, is also praised for its fondue and pleasantly quiet atmosphere. Wherever you go, even in low season, it is essential to book in advance.

Dine

'Service is superb,' said a reader. **Le Mazot**, **t** +41 (0)27 966 0606, specializes in lamb cooked on an open grill. **Le Gitan**, **t** +41 (0)27 968 1940, has its own 'gypsy kebabs' and succulent giant prawns. The rustic **Schäferstube**, **t** +41 (0)27 966 7605, in Hotel Julen, serves lamb from its own flock. **Rua Thai**, **t** +41 (0)27 966 6181, in Hotel Albana Real, has authentic Thai cuisine. **Fuji of Zermatt**, **t** +41 (0) 27 966 6171, is also in the Albana Real ('genuine Japanese, fun and entertaining'). **Casa Rustica**, **t** +41 (0)27 967 4858, has meat fondues and homely fare. **Mood's**, **t** +41 (0)27 967 8484, has a glass floor and gourmet nouvelle cuisine. **Méditerranée**, **t** +41 (0)27 967 4525, provides an outstanding seafood platter. **Corbeau d'Or**, **t** +41 (0)27 966 2660, in Hotel Mirabeau has 'excellent food and wine.'

Party

'We were pleasantly surprised by prices. Beer and wine can easily be found in nice bars at less than you would pay in the major French resorts,' said a reporter. **Hennustall** is the piste-side bar on the way down from Furi. **Papperla** is always bursting at the seams at the end of the skiing day. **Elsie's Bar**, by the church, is a crowded and atmospheric place to enjoy champagne and oysters. At the Post Hotel, the **Brown Cow** is 'always buzzing and sells the local beer for 6CHF'. Upstairs in the same complex is **Papa Caesar's** bar, downstairs is **Pink** with jazz, **Le Village** plays house music, and **Le Broken** is the traditional disco. **Mood's** is quiet and sophisticated. **Arvenstube** in the Hotel Pollux is 'busy and good fun, great atmosphere'. **Schneewittchen** is another popular meeting place. **Hotel Alex** nightclub attracts a 30-plus age group. Artist Heinz Julen's **Vernissage** is full of atmosphere with an art gallery and eclectic furniture.

Sleep

'Despite the prominence of five-star hotels you can stay in Zermatt at a reasonable price by sourcing B&B hotels or apartments through the local tourist office,' advised a reporter.

*****__Grand Hotel Zermatterhof__, **t** +41 (0)27 966 6600, *www.matterhorn-group.ch*, once a favourite of Audrey Hepburn, is a glamorous hotel with recently refurbished rooms.

*****__Mont Cervin Palace__, **t** +41 (0)27 966 8888, *www.seiler-hotels.ch*, founded in 1851, has a three-storey Daniel Steiner Beauty Spa. It has some new suites, and a wine cellar housing 10,000 bottles.

*****__Riffelalp Resort 2222__, **t** +41 (0)27 966 0505, *www.zermatt.ch/riffelalp*, is a luxurious mini-resort at Gornergrat with an indoor pool as well as Europe's highest outdoor pool.

****__Hotel Alex__, **t** +41 (0)27 966 7070, *www.hotelalexzermatt.com*, an alpine-Byzantine mix, has individually designed rooms, pool and spa.

****__Hotel Alpen Resort__, **t** +41 (0)27 966 30 00, *www.alpenresort.com*, has family rooms, spa, pool, gym and indoor tennis. 'Fantastic five/six course meals and a courtesy taxi to the Klein Matterhorn lifts in the morning,' enthused a reader.

****__Hotel Ambassador__, **t** +41 (0)27 966 26 11, *www.ambassador-zermatt.ch*, is comfortable, traditional, and rated excellent by reporters.

****__Hotel Christiania__, **t** +41 (0)27 966 80 00, *www.christiania-zermatt.com*, is next to the Sunnega. 'I can't recommend the hotel highly enough – great food, great service and well located,' said a reader.

****__Hotel La Ginabelle__, **t** +41 (0)27 966 5000, *www.la.ginabelle.ch*, is family-friendly with a kids' club.

****__Seiler Hotel Monte Rosa__, **t** +41 (0)27 966 0333, the base from which Edward Whymper set off to conquer the Matterhorn, is very central.

****__Hotel Sonne__, **t** +41 (0)27 966 2066, *www.sonne.masch.com*, is family-run and chalet-style, with a wellness centre and a good restaurant.

***__Hotel Alpenroyal__, **t** +41 (0)27 966 6066, *www.alpenroyal.ch*, is warmly praised. 'An excellent location and the best food we have ever had in any hotel anywhere.'

***__Hotel Atlanta__, **t** +41 (0)27 966 3535, is highly rated: 'great value for money and the location was perfect'.

***__Hotel Biner__, **t** +41 (0)27 966 5666, *www.hotel-biner-zermatt.ch*, near the railway station, has been renovated using natural materials; facilities include a spa with huge pool.

***__Hotel Perren__, **t** +41 (0)27 966 5200, *www.hotel-perren.ch* ('this hotel has it all, and a great location'), has been welcoming guests since 1937 and has a relaxed and informal atmosphere.

Chalets Zaphir and Louise, **t** +44 (0)20 8682 5050, *www.scottdunn.com*, are luxury chalet-apartments sleeping 10. They are spread over three floors near the Papperla pub.

Chalet Zen, **t** +44 (0)20 7384 3854, *www.descent.co.uk*, one of only a handful of stand-alone chalets available to rent in Zermatt, is decorated with antique furniture, rugs and paintings.

Hotel Butterfly, **t** +41 (0)27 966 4166, *www.hotelbutterflyzermatt.com*, is comfortable, friendly and great value, just minutes from the station and lifts.

11

The Top Resorts: USA

Aspen, Colorado

🏆 BEST FAMILY RESORT 2009 (SNOWMASS)

*** BEST FOR**

Sophisto-cats, shoppers, all levels of skier and rider, ski gourmets

ESSENTIALS

Altitude: 7,945ft (2422m)–12,518ft (3815m)
Further information: t +1 970 925 1220, *www.aspensnowmass.com*
Lifts in area: 40 (2 cableways, 30 chairs, 8 drags) serving 5,285 acres of terrain
Lift pass: area (covers all 4 mountains) adult $222–390, child 7–17yrs $186–246, both for six days
Access: Aspen airport 10mins, Denver airport 3½hrs, Eagle County/Vail airport 1½hrs

Profile

One of the top resorts in North America, with skiing and snowboarding for all standards. The historic town has a wide choice of restaurants, shops and nightlife. Neighbouring Snowmass is the less expensive accommodation base

Resort

You don't have to be able to ski or even to be famous to visit America's most celebrated resort, but either helps. It has been called Hollywood-on-ice and, judging by its growing celebrity A-list of residents and regulars, Aspen still lives up to its reputation. Yet a favourable exchange rate means that prices are no higher – and often lower – than in Val d'Isère or Verbier.

Antonio Banderas and Melanie Griffiths like to spend New Year here with their children. Jack Nicholson and the *grande dame* of Wimbledon, Martina Navratilova, make regular forays to the nearby slopes from their £4 million houses. In a place where you can buy a Picasso with greater ease than a pair of socks – art galleries outnumber clothing stores by three to one – you might be forgiven for thinking that the quaint Colorado town has forfeited its place on the world stage of serious skiing in favour of fur-clad frippery. You would be wrong.

It's true that while riding the six-person gondola up Aspen Mountain you may well find yourself sharing a cabin with Mariah Carey or Michael Douglas. But celebrity presence stretches far beyond the desire to mingle with money. The reason why so many famous people make their home or take their holidays here is because they are fanatical skiers or riders who want some of the best facilities and most challenging slopes that America has to offer. 'Expectations were high. It did not fail,' said a reporter.

It is a wealthy town that was founded on money – back in the 1880s Aspen was briefly the silver-mining capital of the world. Its 14-year reign as a boom town ended in 1893 with the US adoption of the gold standard and by the early 1930s its population of 12,000 had plummeted to 350. But then came the discovery of 'white gold' and Aspen's rebirth as a ski town.

Its legacy from those early years is a collection of fine Victorian buildings including Hotel Jerome, the original inn. They have all been beautifully restored, and more recent additions are constructed in sympathetic period style and restricted in size by stringent planning laws. Property prices are some of the highest in America. In 2006 a Saudi prince sold his 15-bedroom mansion for £69 million.

Some 200 shops range from art galleries and designer boutiques like Prada to sportswear outlets and beauty salons.

No other resort in American has such a wonderful range of restaurants. This is not a place for budget skiers and riders but, as in France, with a little careful research it is possible to enjoy a holiday here without spending a fortune.

The town centre at the foot of Aspen Mountain – also known as Ajax – is relatively compact. An efficient bus service from Ruby Park (near the gondola) connects outlying hotels as well as the three other ski areas of Buttermilk, Aspen Highlands and Snowmass.

Over the years, Snowmass has suffered from an identity crisis. It's wholly owned by Aspen, but plays second fiddle to the bigger name. However, after 40 years it is now developing two multimillion dollar villages at the base of the mountain with direct lift links. The first properties have been completed. But meanwhile the original mall, destined for future redevelopment, has considerable charm and is traffic-free and child-friendly.

You can fly directly to Aspen from Denver and several other US cities, including Chicago, Salt Lake City, Atlanta and Los Angeles. The airport is only three miles from town, and Frontier Airlines began flights into it this summer.

'Fantastic is the only word to describe the time we had there. Bit of a trek and, as expected, a bit pricey but well worth the extra expense,' said a reader.

Mountain

'We experienced wide, open, groomed pistes that were virtually empty. There are waist-high moguls if you wanted them, long cruises and short steep blasts with not a patch of ice anywhere,' was how one reporter summed it up. The skiing is divided into four separate areas linked by ski bus. Furthest apart are Aspen Mountain and Snowmass (20 minutes). Each has its own character.

Buttermilk is a benign beginner and family area with lots of easy green runs served by the West Buttermilk Express and some marginally more taxing routes back to the base down the front face. The eastern side of the mountain is given over to runs marked black on the piste map, although they should present few difficulties to anyone who can ski parallel. An enormous terrain park is accessed by the Summit Express and runs from top to bottom.

Snowmass is the largest and most underrated sector, and is suited to everyone from beginner to expert. It has a vertical drop of 4,406ft (1343m), one of the longest in North America. The upper mountain is mostly for advanced skiers, with some truly steep terrain such as the Cirque headwall. Elk Camp and Big Burn have plenty of intermediate runs. From the top of Big Burn, start down Whispering Jesse and meander all the way back to the village. Cirque headwall and Dikes require considerably more skill and concentration.

This season marked the opening of the Treehouse Kids' Adventure Center at Snowmass base village. The US$17 million project is the focal point of the new base village, located at the intersection of three new lifts on Fanny Hill.

Elk Camp Meadows Beginner Area is a new dedicated novice area that will surround the entire lift from top to bottom. This area will be used by the ski school for all beginner lessons, and five-year-olds will start their day on the magic carpets at the bottom.

An eight-person gondola runs from the base of Fanny Hill to Elk Camp with a mid-station at the base of Funnel. Pipeline Park, served by the Burlingame chair, has three half-pipes and a warming yurt.

Aspen Highlands is only a nine-minute ride from downtown Aspen and its proximity means that the base area lacks soul. However, the skiing is as rugged as it

ASPEN MOUNTAIN
ASPEN
CATHEDRAL PEAK 13,943'
HAYDEN PEAK 13,561'
SUNDECK 11,200'
KRISTI, HYRUP'S AND WALSH'S SCHEDULED TO CLOSE AT 3 P.M. DAILY
OTHELLO'S RAIL RIDERS
WALSH'S
HYRUP'S
KRISTI
LUD'S LANE
NORTH STAR
GENT'S RIDGE
COPPER CUTOFF
BUCKHORN
CUTOFF
DIPSY DOODLE
SUMMIT
MIDWAY ROAD
BLONDIE'S
BLAZING STAR
PUSSYFOOT
PUMP HOUSE HILL
TOURTELOTTE PARK
BONNIE'S 10,400'
PERCY
RED'S RUN
FIS TRAIL
AJAX EXPRESS
DEER PARK
SUNRISE/SUNSET
HANGING TREE
KNOWLTON'S
SEIBERT'S
BACK OF BELL #1
BACK OF BELL #2
FACE OF BELL
RIDGE OF BELL
SHOULDER OF BELL
KEITH GLEN
GLADE #1
GLADE #2
GLADE #3
GENTLEMAN'S RIDGE
COPPER CONNECTOR
COPPER BOWL
JACKPOT
BINGO GLADES
SPAR GULCH
BEAR PAW
INTERNATIONAL
SHORT SNORT
ZAUGG DUMP
PERRY'S PROWL
LAST DOLLAR
RAYBURNS
RUTHIE'S RUN
RUTHIE'S
SUMMER ROAD
SCHILLER ROAD
SILVER QUEEN
SILVER RUSH
AZTEC
SPRING PITCH
TRAINORS
CONUNDRUM VALLEY
WHITE RIVER NATIONAL FOREST
GATED TERRAIN: TRAINORS, RAYBURNS AND BINGO GLADES ARE AREAS MANAGED ON A DAILY BASIS. GATES WILL BE OPENED AND CLOSED DEPENDING ON SNOW AND WEATHER CONDITIONS. PLEASE CHECK WITH SKI PATROL FOR STATUS.
ASPEN MOUNTAIN IS LOCATED IN THE WHITE RIVER NATIONAL FOREST AND IS UNDER PERMIT FROM THE FOREST SERVICE USDA.
CASTLE CREEK VALLEY
SKI AREA BOUNDARY
COMPROMISE MINE
BELL MOUNTAIN
NIAGRA
MAGNIFICO ROAD
SUPER 8
LIFT LINE
CORKSCREW
CORKSCREW GULLY
STRAWPILE
TOWER TEN ROAD
FRANKLIN DUMP
FIS SLALOM HILL
SHADOW MOUNTAIN
SUMMER ROAD
5TH AVENUE
NORWAY SLOPE
SCHUSS GULLY
LITTLE NELL
SILVER QUEEN GONDOLA
CLOSED AREA
THE LITTLE NELL HOTEL
AJAX TAVERN
RUBEY PARK TRANSPORTATION CENTER
TOWN OF ASPEN
TO ASPEN CROSS COUNTRY CENTER
SUNDECK
BONNIE'S 10,333'
TORTILLA FLATS
NORTH AMERICAN
GENT'S FLATS
ELEVATION TOP: 11,212 ft/3,418 m
VERTICAL RISE: 3,267 ft/996 m
TERRAIN: 673 acres/273 hectares
LONGEST RUN: 3 miles/4.83 km
LIFTS: Silver Queen Gondola, 1 high-speed quad, 1 high-speed double, 2 quads, 3 doubles
LIFT CAPACITY: 10,755 riders per hour
AVERAGE ANNUAL SNOWFALL: 300 inches/762 cm
SNOWMAKING CAPABILITIES: 210 acres/85 hectares (33% of area)
EASIEST TERRAIN: None
MORE DIFFICULT TERRAIN: 48%
MOST DIFFICULT TERRAIN: 26%
EXPERT TERRAIN: 26%
SEASON DATES: November 25, 2004 – April 10, 2005
ASPEN MOUNTAIN
Trail Map and Terrain Guide
More Difficult
Most Difficult
Expert Only
Extreme Terrain
Lifts
High-Speed Quad
High-Speed Double
Gondola
Secondary Lift
Slow Skiing
Flat Catwalk
Closed Area Do Not Enter
Ski Patrol
Restrooms
Public Lockers
Ski/Snowboard Check
Mountain Photo
Four-Mountain Sports/D&E
Handicapped Access
Ski/Snowboard School
Ticketing
Restaurant
Picnic Tables
Buses
Guest Service Center
TV 16 Live Broadcast
NASTAR
XC Skiing
Snowshoe Trails
Danger
Symbols and color codes indicate the relative skiing difficulty for slopes and trails on Aspen Mountain only. For your own protection, do not start down a trail or slope until you know its degree of difficulty and never ski/ride a CLOSED trail.

gets. Beginner and intermediate runs are found on the lower part of the mountain. Broadway and other intermediate blues provide top-to-bottom cruising, but generally this is not a place for the faint-hearted. Highland Bowl, Steeple Chase, and Olympic Bowl have awesome reputations. A series of vertiginous runs, served by the Deep Temerity lift to the skier's left of Highland Bowl, greatly adds to the area's appeal for accomplished skiers and riders.

Aspen Mountain is the 'home' hill, situated directly above the town and reached by the Silver Queen gondola.

Beginners and wobbly second-weekers are strongly discouraged from venturing on to what is billed as an experts-only mountain, with 74 per cent of runs classified as 'more' or 'most' difficult and the rest as just plain 'expert'.

Don't be deterred. In fact, any mildly confident intermediate can enjoy glorious top-to-bottom descents on beautifully groomed slopes. You don't have to ski steep, icy bumps unless that's what you want to do.

Ruthie's Run and Copper Bowl hide no surprises for anyone who can ski parallel. Walsh's and Shoulder of Bell are great in fresh powder, but get heavily bumped up between falls. Strong skiers and riders will enjoy runs such as Bear Paw, Short Snort and Zaugg Dump. Walsh's is considered the most challenging. Face of Bell leading down into Spar Gulch provides usually excellent tree-skiing.

If you rent skis, do so from branches of the resort's own **Four Mountain Sports**, **t** +1 970 923 2337. At the end of each day, your skis and poles are transported free of charge to whichever mountain you plan on skiing the next morning.

Learn

Ski and Snowboard School of Aspen/Snowmass, **t** +1 970 925 1227, has branches on all four mountains and is highly rated. 'The private lessons were fantastic.' Courses include **Too Cool For School** teen skiing. There is also **Aspen Adventures**, **t** +1 970 925 7625, and **Aspen Mountain Powder Tours**, **t** +1 970 920 0720.

Children

'Our eight and 10 year olds were in heaven,' said a reporter, and added: 'Attentive, friendly lift operators were more than happy to hoik our little one onto every lift.' Children aged 12 years and under joining ski school classes must wear helmets. **Kids' Room**, **t** +1 701 456 7888, provides childcare in town, and a **kindergarten**, **t** +1 970 925 1227, is at each mountain base. At Snowmass, **Snow Cubs**, **t** +1 970 923 0563, caters for those aged from eight weeks with lessons from as young as 18 months. **Big Burn Bears**, **t** + 1 970 923 0570, or the **Grizzlies**, **t** +1 970 923 0580, are for older children. At Buttermilk, **Powder Pandas**, **t** +1 970 923 1227, cares for 3–6 year olds.

Lunch

Buttermilk has **Bumps**, **t** +1 970 920 0991, at the base, and the **Cliffhouse**, **t** +1 970 920 0933, at the top of the Summit Express, offers a variety of wok dishes.

At Snowmass, **Gwyn's High Alpine**, **t** +1 970 923 5188, at the bottom of the High Alpine Lift, is both a self-service and a tablecloth restaurant. The sit-down restaurant has the best food on the mountain. **Sam's Knob**, **t** +1 970 925 1220, has good pasta and views. **Ullrhof**, **t** +1 970 923 5143, is recommended for elk medallions and Thai shrimp. **Up 4 Pizza**, **t** +1 970 925 1220, is fast and cheerful.

At Highlands, **Cloud Nine Alpine Bistro**, **t** +1 970 544 3063, is a small gourmet restaurant with magnificent views of the Maroon Bells; it gets crowded, so book early. This is one of those rare North American attempts at a Swiss or Austrian wayside mountain restaurant that almost comes off, but not quite.

On Aspen Mountain, **Bonnie's**, **t** +1 970 925 1220, has wonderful white bean chilli and *Apfelstrudel*. The **Tavern**, **t** +1 970 920 9333, at the foot of the Silver Queen gondola, is where to see and be seen as well as enjoy the best gourmet fare on the mountain. The **Sundeck**, **t** +1 970 920 6974, at the top of the gondola, is a welcoming self-service with unusually good food including Chinese and Indian.

Dine

Most restaurants are expensive, but if you are prepared to eat at the bar you are served the same food in smaller portions at a greatly reduced price. In Aspen, favourites include Social, t +1 970 925 9700, **L'Hostaria**, **t** +1 970 925 9022, and **Rustique Bistro**, **t** +1 970 920 2555. **Mezzaluna**, **t** +1 970 925 5882, serves pizza and other Italian cuisine. **Kenichi**, **t** + 1 970 920 2212, **Takah Sushi**, **t** +1 970 925 8588, and **Matsuhisa**, **t** +1 970 544 6628, all serve Japanese food. **Olives Aspen**, **t** + 1 970 920 7356, in the St Regis Resort, serves Mediterranean-inspired American food. **La Cocina**, **t** +1 970 925 9714, **Little Annie's**, **t** +1 970 925 1098, **Mother Lode**, **t** +1 970 925 7700, and **Wild Fig**, **t** +1 970 925 5160, are all warmly recommended. **Jimmy's**, **t** +1 970 925 6020, is said to be 'posh, but not too posh'. In Snowmass, try **Mountain Dragon**, **t** +1 970 923 3576, and **Sage Bistro**, **t** +1 970 923 0923. More affordable eateries include the **Steak Pit**, **t** +1 970 925 4459, **Su Casa**, **t** +1 970 920 1488, and **Boogies Diner**, **t** +1 970 925 6610.

Party

The **Jerome Bar** (or **J-Bar**) is a popular resort rendezvous. The **Tavern** is always crowded after skiing. **Social, Elevation, Jimmy's**, the **Mogador** and **Club Chelsea** attract a sophisticated after-dinner crowd. **Regal Watering Hole** is a cool lounge and bar. **Shooters** is a country and western saloon with live bands. The health-conscious head for the **Aspen Club and Spa** or the fabulous **Remède Spa** in the St Regis Resort. Those who have celebrity friends or pay for temporary membership gather in the exclusive **Caribou Club**. **39 Degrees** is the Sky Hotel's all-day dining room/bar, serving sushi nachos and Asian beef summer rolls. The signature cocktail is a Botox Martini, which comes with two cherries – one wrinkled and one pristine.

Sleep

'The accommodation was fantastic and much larger than a similar priced apartment in the Alps,' said a reader.

Aspen:

Luxury:

Hotel Jerome, **t** +1 970 920 1000, *www.hoteljerome.com*, is the original Victorian inn.

Hotel Lenado, **t** +1 970 925 6246, *www.hotellenado.com*, is a small, friendly B&B hotel full of rustic charm. Each of its 19 bedrooms has a carved four-poster bed. Some also have wood-burning stoves and whirlpool baths.

The Little Nell, **t** +1 970 920 4600, *www.thelittlenell.com*, is a five-star resort institution at the base of Aspen Mountain. It has now opened a second hotel at Snowmass.

St Regis Resort Aspen, **t** +1 970 920 3300, *www.stregisaspen.com*, also at the base, has received a $35-million makeover and houses the excellent Remède Spa.

The Sky Hotel, **t** +1 970 925 6760, *www.theskyhotel.com*, is the hip place to stay at the foot of Aspen Mountain, with an outdoor pool and hot tub. All suites have whirlpools and iPod music bars.

Luxury/Moderate:

The Gant, **t** +1 970 925 5000, *www.gantaspen.com*, is a condo-hotel with accommodation ranging from good to luxury. A reporter rated it 'the best skiing accommodation we've ever stayed in'.

Moderate/Budget:

Aspen Mountain Lodge, **t** + 1 970 925 7650, *www.aspenmountainlodge.com*, has a pool and a hot tub.

Hotel Durant, **t** +1 970 925 8500, *www.durantaspen.com*, is two blocks from the centre and offers free breakfast.

Innsbruck Inn, **t** +1 970 925 2980, is a favourite with budget-conscious visitors.

Limelite Lodge, **t** +1 970 925 3025, *www.limelitelodge.com*, has been rebuilt as a cutting-edge hotel with a lovely pool – and it is still good value.

St Moritz Lodge, **t** +1 970 925 3220, *www.stmoritzlodge.com*, has triple-bed dormitories and regular hotel bedrooms.

Fifth Avenue Apartments, **t** +1 615 316 6000, *www.resortquest.com*, five-minutes from the Silver Queen gondola, are spacious and reasonably priced.

Snowmass:

Moderate/Budget:

Chamonix Inn, **t** +1 970 923 3232, *www.snowmass.ski.com*, has piste-side rental units with a pool.

Crestwood Inn, **t** +1 970 923 2450, *www.snowmass.ski.com*, has three-bedroom condos and town houses.

Silvertree Hotel, **t** +1 970 923 3520, *www.silvertreehotel.com*, is Snowmass' only full-service ski in, ski out hotel.

Snowmass Club, **t** +1 970 923 5600, *www.snowmassclub.com*, is a smart condo complex.

Snowmass Inn, **t** +1 970 923 4302, *www.snowmassinn.com*, is family-owned and adjacent to the Village Mall.

Stonebridge Inn, **t** +1 970 923 2420, *www.stonebridgeinn.com*, has slope-side hotel rooms and suites.

Beaver Creek, Colorado

Profile

An upmarket choice for families, with a good snow record and an excellent ski school. Not ideal for those on a budget

Resort

Beaver Creek is Vail's rich and beautiful sister, who lives up a private road above the valley town of Avon, a 15-minute drive away along I-70. 'Couldn't believe the luxury,' said one reporter, 'Why walk when

*BEST FOR

Cosmopolitan sophistication, families, all levels of skier and rider

ESSENTIALS

Altitude: 8,100ft (2,470m)–11,440ft (3488m)
Further information: **t** +1 970 845 9090, *www.beavercreek.com*
Lifts in area: 16 (2 cableways, 14 chairs) serving 1,805 acres of terrain
Lift pass: Summit Ticket (covers Arapahoe Basin, Beaver Creek, Breckenridge, Keystone, Vail) adult $330–570, child 5–12yrs $1,264, both for six out of nine days
Access: Denver airport 2½hrs, Eagle County/Vail airport 45mins

BEAVER CREEK

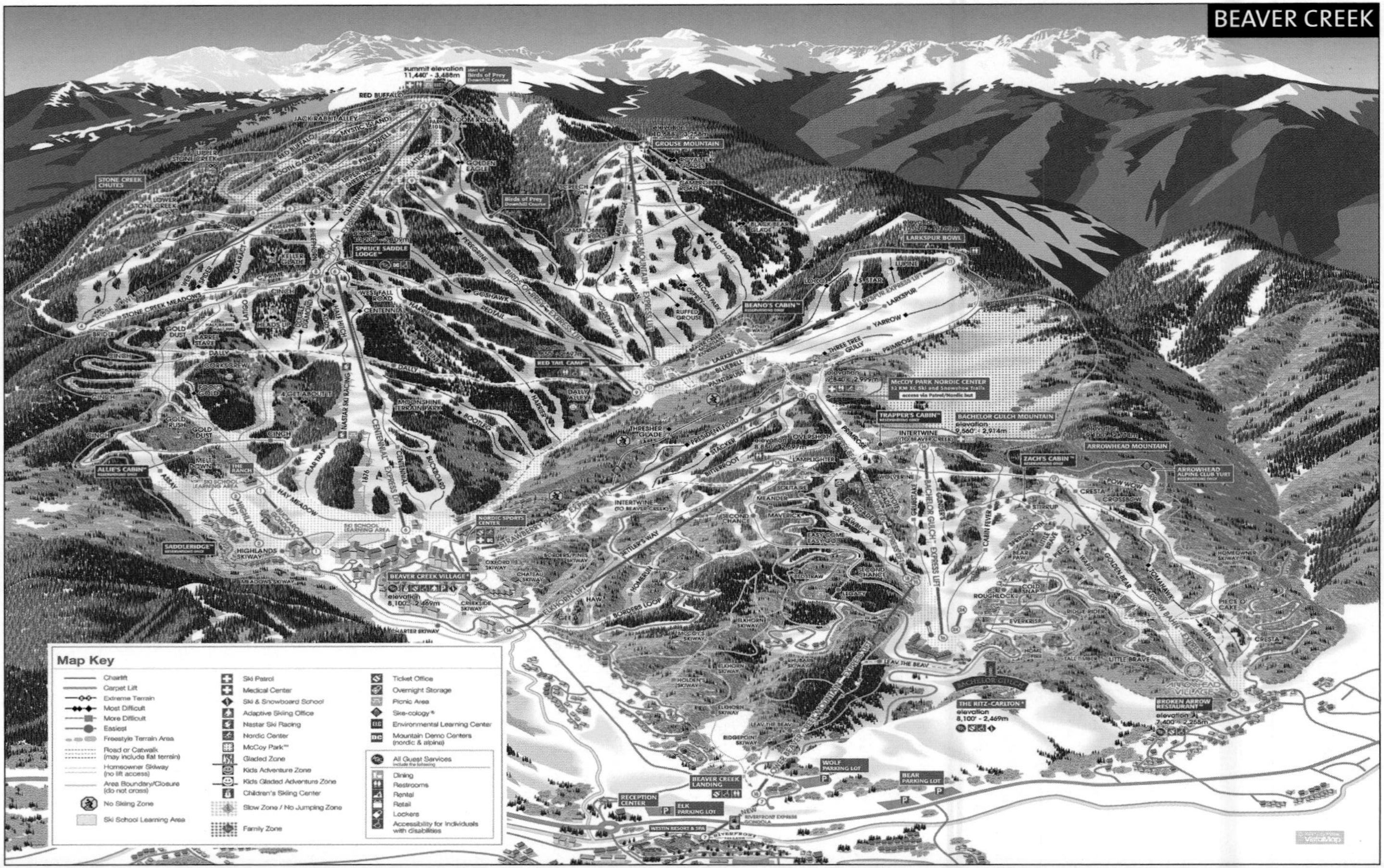

summit elevation 11,440' - 3,488m

Start of Birds of Prey Downhill Course

RED BUFFALO

GROUSE MOUNTAIN

SPRUCE SADDLE LODGE

LARKSPUR BOWL

BEANO'S CABIN

RED TAIL CAMP

McCOY PARK NORDIC CENTER

12 KM XC Ski and Snowshoe Trails

TRAPPER'S CABIN

BACHELOR GULCH MOUNTAIN

ARROWHEAD MOUNTAIN

ZACH'S CABIN

ARROWHEAD ALPINE CLUB YURT

ALLIE'S CABIN

SADDLERIDGE

NORDIC SPORTS CENTER

BEAVER CREEK VILLAGE

elevation 8,100' - 2,469m

THE RITZ-CARLTON

elevation 8,100' - 2,469m

BROKEN ARROW RESTAURANT

elevation 7,400' - 2,255m

BEAVER CREEK LANDING

RECEPTION CENTER

ELK PARKING LOT

WOLF PARKING LOT

BEAR PARKING LOT

WESTIN RESORT & SPA

RIVERFRONT EXPRESS GONDOLA

CENTENNIAL EXPRESS LIFT

GROUSE MOUNTAIN EXPRESS LIFT

BIRDS OF PREY EXPRESS LIFT

LARKSPUR EXPRESS LIFT

BACHELOR GULCH EXPRESS LIFT

ARROW BAHN EXPRESS LIFT

HIGHLANDS LIFT

ELKHORN LIFT

STRAWBERRY PARK EXPRESS LIFT

Map Key

- Chairlift
- Carpet Lift
- Extreme Terrain
- Most Difficult
- More Difficult
- Easiest
- Freestyle Terrain Area
- Road or Catwalk (may include flat terrain)
- Homeowner Skiway (no lift access)
- Area Boundary/Closure (do not cross)
- No Skiing Zone
- Ski School Learning Area
- Ski Patrol
- Medical Center
- Ski & Snowboard School
- Adaptive Skiing Office
- Nastar Ski Racing
- Nordic Center
- McCoy Park℠
- Gladed Zone
- Kids Adventure Zone
- Kids Gladed Adventure Zone
- Children's Skiing Center
- Slow Zone / No Jumping Zone
- Family Zone
- Ticket Office
- Overnight Storage
- Picnic Area
- Ske-cology®
- Environmental Learning Center
- Mountain Demo Centers (nordic & alpine)
- All Guest Services include the following:
  - Dining
  - Restrooms
  - Rental
  - Retail
  - Lockers
  - Accessibility for Individuals with disabilities

you can stand on a motorized walkway?' Both resorts are owned by the same giant corporation, but each has its own character. Beaver Creek has a much more intimate atmosphere, lots of accommodation on the edge of the piste, and is more family-orientated.

Unusually for North America, the resort is linked on-mountain to two small hamlets – Arrowhead and Bachelor Gulch – that provide alternative bed bases along with the valley town of Avon, now linked by gondola.

Focal point of the village is an open-air ice rink surrounded by designer boutiques, a plethora of art galleries where prices are only available on request, and sports shops that sell fur coats as well as ski gear. One outraged and thirsty reader protested in last year's edition of this guide that the cheapest bottle of wine in the resort's only off-licence was a bottle of 'undrinkable' Algerian *vin de table* priced at $14.99; things have not improved.

The resort's clientele is as sleekly groomed as its perfect corduroy pistes, and this air of sophistication is reflected in a wide choice of luxury hotels and giant, well-appointed condos as well as fine dining establishments. Childcare facilities here are exceptionally good.

The lift ticket allows skiers and riders to go to Vail, Breckenridge, Keystone and Arapahoe Basin. A regular subsidized shuttle runs to and from Vail but you need a car to go further afield and sample the other Vail resorts – the bus service to these has been suspended through lack of interest.

Mountain

Despite its modest size, Beaver's ski area holds plenty of interest for all standards of skier and rider, but with the emphasis on intermediates.

The Centennial Express Chair – effortlessly reached from the heart of the village by a two-stage escalator – takes you up the mid-mountain hub of Spruce Saddle with access to plenty of wide, undulating blue pistes back down to the resort and off the shoulder down Stone Creek Meadows into the Rose Bowl.

From Spruce Saddle, the Cinch Express chair brings you on up to the top of the ski area for more intermediate terrain – or the much greater demands of the Birds of Prey downhill course, one of the toughest on the World Cup Circuit. When not prepared for racing it tends to become severely mogulled between snowfalls and lives up to its double-diamond rating. When groomed it makes for a fast descent. Pick of the steep stuff is found on adjoining Grouse Mountain. Runs such as Royal Elk Glades, Bald Eagle, Falcon Park and Osprey served by the Grouse Mountain Express provide high-octane entertainment. The Rose Bowl lift also serves a range of black-diamond trails. After a major dump, powder opportunities here are exceptional. For anyone staying here, a visit to Vail's Back Bowls and Blue Sky Basin is a must, but don't ignore the powder on your doorstep – this is where you will find the locals.

The easiest terrain is served by the Bachelor Gulch Express and the Arrow Bahn Express from Arrowhead, and novices and wobbly intermediates have a chance to explore the whole mountainside.

Last season the eight-person Buckaroo Gondola opened, which was designed specifically for children.

Beaver Creek has three terrain parks that attract as many twin-tipped skiers as they do snowboarders. Park 101, situated on Upper Sheephorn, is designed for park novices. Zoom is for accomplished riders, and has a half-pipe as well as the full range of obstacles.

Learn

Beaver Creek Ski and Snowboard School, **t** +1 970 845 5300, is part of the Vail school and has an excellent reputation both for the quality of instruction and the friendliness of the teachers ('best lesson I have ever had anywhere').

Children

The ski school runs a full range of classes and is highly rated ('I really felt my children benefited hugely from the whole week of instruction – and loved every minute of it'). **Small World Play School**, **t** +1 970 845 5325, provides all-day care for children from three years.

Lunch

In a resort of such wealth, lunch should be an important part of the day – and indeed it is for property owners and other VIPs. They have access to **Beano's Cabin**, **t** +1 970 949 9090, **Zach's Cabin**, **t** +1 866 395 3185, and **Allie's Cabin**, **t** +1 970 845 5762, which all operate at lunchtime as private clubs. Public self-service restaurants tend to be overcrowded and wise skiers head back to town. **Beaver Creek Chophouse**, **t** +1 970 845 0555, on the edge of the piste, serves grilled meat and seafood. **Coyote Café**, **t** +1 970 949 5001, is a reasonably priced Mexican. **Blue Moose**, **t** +1 970 845 8666, serves gourmet pizzas.

Dine

Splendido at the Chateau, **t** +1 970 845 8808, has Russian caviar and lobsters flown in from Maine. **SaddleRidge**, **t** +1 970 845 5762, houses a museum of Western memorabilia and serves game and seafood. **Allie's**, **t** +1 970 845 5762, and **Zach's**, **t** +1 866 395 3185, are open by night to all. **Beano's Cabin**, **t** +1 970 949 9090, reached by motorized sleigh, has memorable five-course meals. **Mirabelle**, **t** +1 970 949 7728, has contemporary Belgian and French cuisine. **TraMonti**, **t** +1 970 949 5552, and **Toscanini**, **t** +1 970 845 5590, are both Italian. **Foxnut**, **t** +1 970 845 0700, has Asian fusion cuisine. **Sato Sushi**, **t** +1 970 926 7684, in the nearby town of Edwards, is popular with locals, and has outstanding cuisine.

Party

Nightlife is distinctly muted in what is essentially a family resort.

The **Coyote Café**, **Beaver Creek Chophouse** and **Dusty Boot Saloon** capture the main crowd, along with the **Beaver Creek Tavern** and **McCoy's** for live music. The **Black Family Ice Rink** is open until 10pm.

Sleep

- ★★★★★**The Charter**, **t** +1 970 949 6660, *www.thecharter.com*, at the base, houses two restaurants, a spa and indoor pool.
- ★★★★★**Park Hyatt Resort & Spa**, **t** +1 970 949 1234, *www.beavercreek.hyatt.com*, has a renowned spa and two restaurants.
- ★★★★★**Ritz-Carlton**, **t** +1 970 748 6200, *www.ritzcarlton.com*, at the base of Bachelor Gulch, is like a small village in its own right, and has a magnificent spa.
- ★★★★★**SaddleRidge**, **t** +1 970 845 5990, *www.beavercreekresortproperties.com*, consists of separate two-bedroom chalets furnished with Ralph Lauren fabrics and Western antiques.
- ★★★★**The Osprey at Beaver Creek**, **t** +1 970 845 5990, *http://vbcrp.com/vbcrp/info/osprey-at-beavercreek.aspx*, was formerly the Inn and received a $7 million refurbishment in summer 2008.

★★★★**Elkhorn Lodge**, t +1 970 845 5990, is in a ski in, ski out position on the edge of the golf course, offering extremely comfortable and spacious apartments with a helpful concierge.

Trapper's Cabin, t +1 970 845 5900, *www.trapperscabincolorado.com,is* a rustic hideaway in the trees for 10 people with dinner and breakfast provided.

★★**Comfort Inn**, t +1 970 949 5511, *www.comfortinn.com*, in Avon, is recommended for 'those on a less-than-champagne budget. Spacious quiet rooms, free continental breakfast, outdoor heated swimming pool. Ask for a mountain view room. The new (free) gondola has made getting to the lifts a snap.'

The new Westin in Avon, beside the gondola, is scheduled to open in time for this season.

Breckenridge, Colorado

Profile

Lively old mining town with a good nightlife. Large ski area with reliable snow conditions, but short runs. Snowboarding is popular. Time is needed to acclimatize at this extremely high altitude

* BEST FOR

All levels of skier and rider, mogul-hoppers, snowboarders

ESSENTIALS

Altitude: 9,600ft (2927m)–12,998ft (3962m)

Further information: t +1 970 453 5000, *www.breckenridge.com*

Lifts in area: 29 (1 cableway, 16 chairs, 12 drags) serving 2,358 acres of terrain

Lift pass: Summit Ticket (covers Arapahoe Basin, Beaver Creek, Breckenridge, Keystone, Vail) adult $296–534, child 5–12yrs $240, both for six out of nine days

Access: Denver airport 2hrs, Eagle County/Vail airport 1½hrs

Resort

Breckenridge earned its inclusion on the map of the world one day in July 1887 when miners Tom Grove and Harry Lytton stumbled across a nugget of gold that weighed an astonishing 13lb 7oz. Tom's Baby, as it was christened, was the culmination of a 10-year mining boom that created the attractive Victorian town that is now one of Colorado's top ski destinations and still the most popular American resort with British skiers.

The legacy of the boom years of the 19th century is a number of fine pastel-painted weatherboarded buildings along Main Street, the focal point of the resort with its wide range of shops and restaurants. Others have been created in a sympathetic style, while the late 20th century ski in, ski out accommodation around the ski base is more utilitarian, with few concessions to architectural frivolity. The skiing and riding is suitable for all standards but until recently the resort was best for intermediates.

The construction of the Imperial Express SuperChair, the highest lift in the northern hemisphere, opened up advanced and expert terrain that was previously only accessible to skiers and boarders prepared to hike at high altitude.

The digital i
by the IKON
from an altit

BRECKENRIDGE

Peak 10 Summit
13,643ft/4,157m

Peak 9 Summit
13,198ft/4,024m

Peak 8 Summit
12,998ft/3,963m

Peak 7 Summit
12,677ft/3,865m

Imperial Bowl

Hike To Terrain

Lake Chutes

Extreme Terrain

Whale's Tail

Peak 7 Bowl

SnowWhite

North Bowl

Imperial Express SuperChair

Horseshoe Bowl

Art's Bowle

Tele

Sadie

The End

Contest Bowl

Cucumber Bowl

Vista Haus

Ole Bucket

The Back 9

Broadway

Twin Chutes

Windows

Peak 10

Peak 9

Peak 9 Restaurant

The Burn

Stock

Kid's Castle

Bergenhof Restaurant

Beaver Run Resort

Patrol response time to hike to terrain may vary from lift serviced terrain.

Legend

- Easiest Trails
- More Difficult Trails (Intermediate)
- More Difficult Trails (Advanced Intermediate)
- Most Difficult Trails
- Most Difficult Trails (Expert Only)
- Extreme Terrain
- Terrain Parks
- Catwalks
- 8-Passenger Gondola
- 6-Passenger SuperChairs
- Quad SuperChairs
- Triple Chairlifts
- Double Chairlifts
- Surface Lifts
- Carpet Lifts

Mountain Stats

Hours of Operation	8:30 am - 4:00 pm, MST
Base Elevation	9,600 feet / 2,926 meters
Summit Elevation	12,998 feet / 3,963 meters
Vertical Rise	3,398 feet / 1,036 meters
Average Annual Snowfall	300 inches / 761 centimeters
Lift Capacity	37,880 people per hour
Total Terrain	2,358 acres / 954 hectares
Bowls	722 acres / 312 hectares
Snowmaking	540 acres / 218 hectares

The eight-person Breck Connect gondola from the town and the base of Peak 8 has increased mountain access. A terminal at Peak 7 opens in this season.

Breckenridge shares a lift pass with Keystone, Vail, Beaver Creek and Arapahoe Basin all of which are within easy reach. They are linked by a free bus service to Keystone and the local challenging ski area of A-Basin. During a week or 10-day stay here you are strongly advised to explore further afield.

Visitors arriving at Denver can reach Breckenridge in just 90 minutes but it is easy to forget the enormous change in altitude. This, combined with low humidity, can cause dehydration and headaches that are exacerbated by exercise. 'The lack of oxygen really hits you. Best bet – book a 1/2 hour oxygen therapy at the Beaver Run Spa – works wonders! Better than wasting your money on the bottled oxygen and sickness tablets at the supermarket,' advised a reporter. At this altitude, Breckenridge is always snow-sure until the end of the season. 'The notices at the bottom of the lifts said 'any exposed skin will freeze' and they were right,' complained a reader.

Mountain

'Breckenfridge' is its apt nickname. The mercury can plunge at this high altitude, and in mid-winter you need technical ski clothing to be comfortable. The skiing takes place on four side-by-side peaks in the Ten Mile Range alongside the town. Someone devoid of imagination originally named them Peaks 10, 9, 8, and 7 and no one else has so far found the courage to change them.

This season sees the opening of a whole new base area with the new Crystal Peak Lodge and Sevens restaurant at Peak 7, which is now linked into the Breck Connect gondola from the parking lots. From the town there is now the choice of taking the Quicksilver Super 6 from the base of Peak 9 or the Breck Connect.

From the top of the Quicksilver easy runs fan out to the Falcon SuperChair on Peak 10, the starting point for a network of predominantly advanced runs with some testing mogul-fields. It is also possible to ski to the Mercury and Beaver Run SuperChairs on Peak 9, which has some of the most inviting cruising in the resort, plus Gold King, a terrain park designed for learner freeriders. Peak 7 is built for cruising, with huge rollers on all seven of its trails.

The opening of the SuperConnect lift has reduced queuing by integrating the ski area efficiently. This has considerably eased access to Peak 8 from Peak 9.

The Vista Haus mid-station is the focal point for the chairlifts that serve the network of blue and black trails on the lower slopes of Peak 8. The Independence SuperChair has extended Breckenridge's boundaries into a glade area cut from the forest on the lower slopes of Peak 7 that is suited to intermediates.

Breckenridge's expert terrain, created as a result of local demand for more 'European-style off-piste', covers the wide open upper slopes on Peaks 7 and 8. The T-Bar takes snow-users into Peak 8's double-black-diamond zone, comprising Horseshoe, Contest, North and Cucumber Bowls, all of them ungroomed. To go higher, you can take the Imperial Express SuperChair, which is 12,840ft at the top. Formerly only acccessible with a hike, this chair provides easy access to double-black-diamond terrain such as Whales Tail and Art's Bowl. This also accesses the Lake Chutes, which have slopes of up to 50 degrees. With a hike you can also visit the 150 acres of terrain called Snow White.

Breckenridge was the first resort in Colorado to allow snowboarding, and remains popular with riders, who form 25 per cent of the winter clientèle. The four dedicated areas include the Freeway Terrain Park and the Breckenridge Super-Pipe, which are equally attractive to twin-tippers.

Learn

Breckenridge Ski & Ride School, t +1 970 453 3272, has an excellent reputation with a wide range of courses including those for teens and 50+.

Children

'A fantastic resort for families,' said a reader. **Breckenridge Children's Center, t** +1 970 453 3258, offers slopeside crèches for kids from two months at Peak 8 and Peak 9. Both have pagers for parents to hire, provide lunches and offer a non-skiing, outdoor snow-play programme. Advance reservations are essential during the busiest weeks.

Breckenridge Ski & Ride School accepts skiers for three years and snowboarders from five, and is praised by reporters.

Lunch

This is not a ski area for gourmets whose ideal skiing day involves a hard morning, followed by a lazy afternoon at a laden table. You can eat well in town, but good food on the mountain is harder to come by. Restaurants listed below without numbers belong to the resort, **t** +1 970 453 5000.

Ten Mile Station, at the top of the Quicksilver Chair, has a heated outdoor deck, a mining-themed food court, and a barbecue in fine weather. On Peak 8, **Border Burritos** at the Bergenhof has good-value salads and tacos. The **Vista Haus** food court at the top of the Colorado SuperChair has a great view of the Continental Divide, while the food is less spectacular.

Sevens is a new Mediterranean-style restaurant at the base of 7 which opens this season.

Dine

'The food was great with a lot of variation,' said a reader. Breckenridge has a choice of some 50 restaurants. In high season, booking is essential. **Hearthstone, t** +1 970 453 1148, is a converted Victorian brothel with loads of atmosphere and a creative Western menu. Try the granola-crusted elk chops. **South Ridge Seafood Grill, t** +1 970 547 0063, has oysters flown in daily from Chesapeake Bay. The **Blue River Bistro, t** +1 970 453 6974, and **Café Alpine, t** +1 970 453 8218, are fine dining destinations. **Steak and Rib, t** +1 970 453 0063, is recommended, and **Relish, t** +1 970 453 0989, serves regional cuisine.

Mi Casa, t +1 970 453 2071, is a good-value Mexican restaurant, and **Columbine Café, t** +1 970 547 4474, offers nutritious breakfasts. The **Red Orchid, t** +1 970 453 1881, specializes in Mandarin and Szechwan fare. **Mountain Flying Fish, t** +1 970 453 1502, and **Wasabi, t** +1 970 453 8311, are sushi restaurants. Italian eateries include **Fatty's, t** +1 970 453 9802, and **Giampetro, t** +1 970 453 3838. The **Cellar Restaurant & Wine Bar, t** +1 970 453 4777, specializes in small 'sharing' dishes. If you don't want to go out **Gourmet Cabby, t** +1 970 543 7788, will deliver food and drink from 30 restaurants to your condo, and a reporter recommended self-catering. 'The supermarkets were good; we even managed to buy organic vegetables.'

Party

This is a lively town, although we received mixed reports: 'Very little about, completely different to the Austrian scene. More family orientated,' said a reader, and 'There is life in Breckenridge after dark, but you have to hunt for it,' said another. **Mi Casa** serves mean jugs of margaritas. Try also **Breckenridge Brewery**, **Sherpa & Yeti**, **Gold Pan Saloon** (the oldest bar in the USA west of the Mississippi), **Downstairs at Eric's** and **Ullr's Sports Grille**.

Sleep

Breckenridge offers spacious rather than deluxe hotels, an assortment of condos and some restored Victorian inns.

★★★**Crystal Peak Lodge**, **t** +1 970 453 6000

★★★**Beaver Run Resort**, **t** +1 970 453 6000, *www.beaverrun.com*, is a 500-room ski-in ski-out condo complex rated 'top class, although the appearance is a little dated. The staff are friendly and take a lot of pride in customer service.' Another reader called it 'Centre Parcs on snow – absolutely everything in one place: après ski, pools, hot tubs, food – you barely had to go outside in the evening'.

★★★**Breckenridge Mountain Lodge**, **t** +1 970 453 2333, *www.breckenridgemountainlodge.com*, provides budget accommodation at the end of Main Street, offering an 'Old West bed and breakfast experience'.

★★★**Great Divide Lodge**, **t** +1 970 453 4500, *www.greatdividelodge.com*, is near Peak 9 base and is one of the only full-service hotels.

★★★**Lodge and Spa**, **t** +1 970 453 9300, *www.thelodgeatbreck.com*, is set above the town and offers a shuttle bus to the slopes.

★★★**The Mountain Thunder Lodge**, **t** +1 888 547 8092, *www.mtnthunderlodge.com*, contains comfortable studios, condos and suites below Peak 8.

The Canyons, Utah

Profile

Purpose-built resort with convenient and extensive skiing for all standards. A good choice for foodies, with gastronomic choices including a superb mountain restaurant

Resort

The Canyons is one of three side-by-side ski areas situated an easy 40-minute drive from Salt Lake City. Leave the highway at Kimball Junction and you come first to The Canyons, followed by Park City Mountain Resort and then Deer Valley. Linking all three would involve the construction of just one lift. Rivalry has so far prevented this, but the three now operate a joint adult and children's pass for foreign visitors only, sold through tour operators, with a single rate throughout the season.

The Canyons is the relative newcomer. It has developed over a decade from a small, local ski area into what is now the

*BEST FOR

All levels of skier and rider, off-piste, mountain restaurant

ESSENTIALS

Altitude: 6,800ft (2073m)–9,990ft (3045m)

Further information: **t** +1 435 649 5400, *www.thecanyons.com*

Lifts in area: 16 (2 cableways, 13 chairs, 1 drag) serving 3,500 acres of terrain

Lift pass: Utah Three Resort Pass (Deer Valley, Park City Mountain Resort, The Canyons) adult $408, child 4–12yrs $225, both for six out of seven days

Access: Salt Lake City airport 40mins

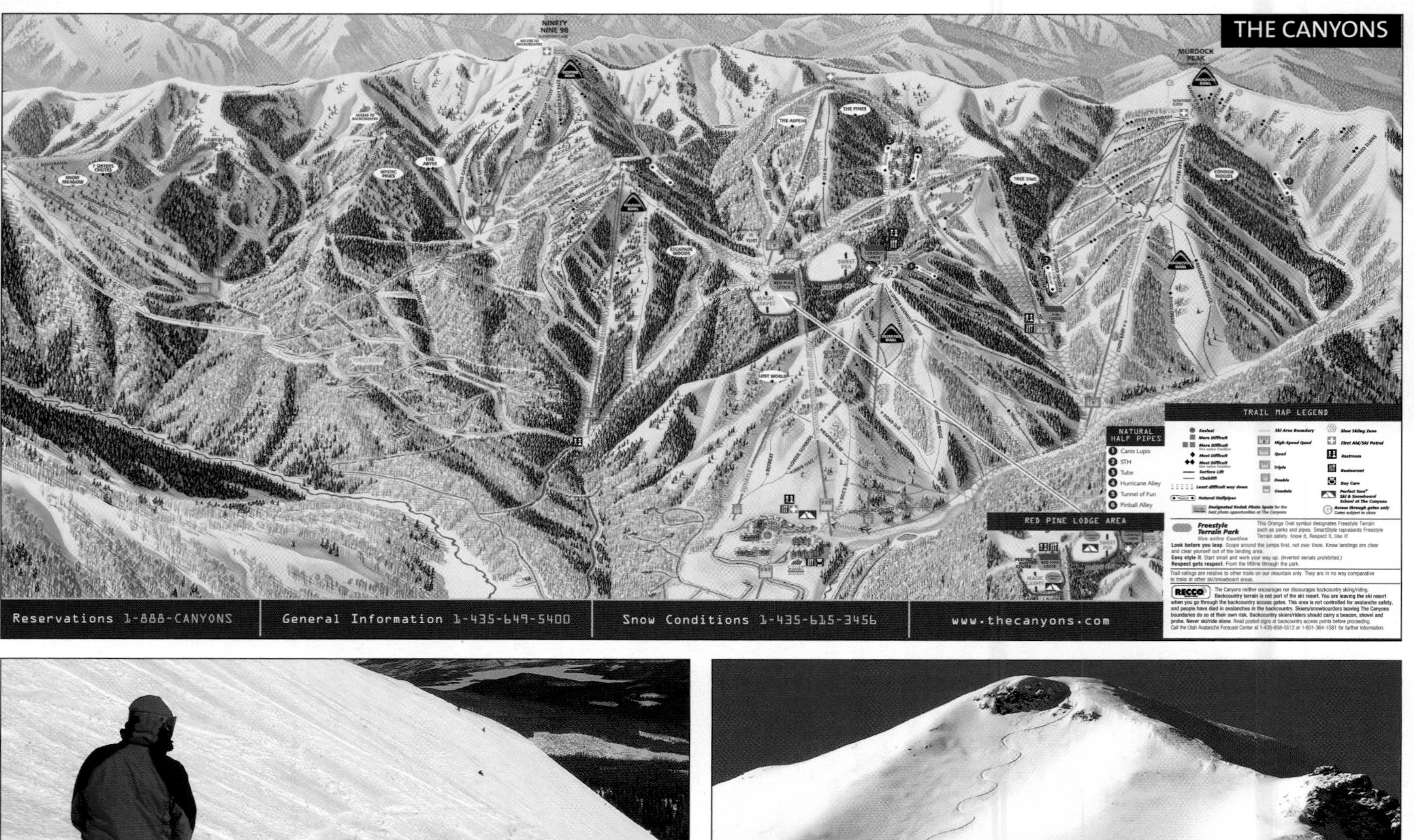
THE CANYONS
NINETY NINE 90
MURDOCK PEAK
NATURAL HALF PIPES
1 Canis Lupis
2 STH
3 Tube
4 Hurricane Alley
5 Tunnel of Fun
6 Pinball Alley
RED PINE LODGE AREA
TRAIL MAP LEGEND
Easiest
More Difficult
More Difficult
Most Difficult
Most Difficult
Surface Lift
Chairlift
Least difficult way down
Natural Halfpipes
Ski Area Boundary
High-Speed Quad
Quad
Triple
Double
Gondola
Slow Skiing Zone
First Aid/Ski Patrol
Restroom
Restaurant
Day Care
Perfect Turn® Ski & Snowboard School at The Canyons
Designated Kodak Photo Spots for the best photo opportunities at The Canyons
Access through gates only
Gates subject to close
Freestyle Terrain Park
Use extra Caution
This Orange Oval symbol designates Freestyle Terrain such as parks and pipes. SmartStyle represents Freestyle Terrain safety. Know it, Respect it, Use it!
Look before you leap. Scope around the jumps first, not over them. Know landings are clear and clear yourself out of the landing area.
Easy style it. Start small and work your way up. (Inverted aerials prohibited.)
Respect gets respect. From the liftline through the park.
Trail ratings are relative to other trails on our mountain only. They are in no way comparative to trails at other ski/snowboard areas.
RECCO
The Canyons neither encourages nor discourages backcountry skiing/riding. Backcountry terrain is not part of the ski resort. You are leaving the ski resort when you go through the backcountry access gates. This area is not controlled for avalanche safety, and people have died in avalanches in the backcountry. Skiers/snowboarders leaving The Canyons boundaries do so at their own risk. Backcountry skiers/riders should carry a beacon, shovel and probe. Never ski/ride alone. Read posted signs at backcountry access points before proceeding.
Call the Utah Avalanche Forecast Center at 1-435-658-5512 or 1-801-364-1581 for further information.
Reservations 1-888-CANYONS
General Information 1-435-649-5400
Snow Conditions 1-435-615-3456
www.thecanyons.com

fifth largest ski resort in the United States, with the facilities to attract international skiers and snowboarders. A further $400 million expansion is now under way, with a new lift opening up 200 acres of intermediate and expert terrain in the Dreamscape sector. The Utah Olympic Park, adjoining The Canyons, has a bobsleigh and luge track. It is also one of the few places in the world where beginners can try their hand at ski-jumping.

Mountain

From the rather soulless purpose-built village, the Flight of the Canyons gondola rapidly conveys skiers and riders to the Red Lodge Pine mid-station. This is the only main access lift and can be heavily oversubscribed at peak times. Lifts fan out from the top in all directions across the mainly tree-covered mountainside.

The skiing suits all standards with lots of easy cruising runs as well as some more demanding terrain reached by the Super Condor Express and the Ninety Nine 90 Express at the 9,990ft summit of the ski area. DreamCatcher, a quad-chair with a 1,600ft vertical drop, adds 200 acres of intermediate and advanced gladed runs. The Canyons has two terrain parks for beginners and experts that are accessed by the Sun Peak lift.

Kimball Junction, just outside the entrance to the resort, has a large collection of designer outlets stores with attractive prices.

Learn

The **Canyons Ski & Snowboard School**, **t** +1 435 615 3449, offers group and private tuition, and courses such as learn-to-ski packages, clinics with Olympic athletes, and telemark.

Children

The **Canyons Ski & Snowboard School** offers children's tuition, and **The Canyons Little Adventures Center**, **t** +1 435 615 8036, provides daycare for children from six weeks to four years.

Lunch

The **Lookout Cabin**, **t** +1 436 615 2892, at the top of the Golden Eagle and Short Cut chairs is an unexpected gastronomic treat ('superb food but you will need to pre book'), a European-style mountain hut with a sophisticated menu and friendly service. Other mountain eateries, **t** +1 435 649 5400, for all, include **Red Pine Lodge**, at the top of the gondola, which has pizzas and deli-sandwiches. **Sun Lodge**, at the base of the Sun Peak Express, is less crowded and majors on grilled meat. **Westgate Grill**, in the village, has lots of atmosphere and an all-American menu.

Dine

The **Cabin**, **t** +1 435 615 8060, in The Canyons Grand Hotel, is one of the best dining options in the region. Try the seafood mixed grill or the rack of venison. Join an evening excursion by snowcat to the **Viking Yurt**, **t** +1 435 615 9878, for a five-course Scandinavian dinner. The eating out is found a short drive away in Park City.

Party

Late-night bars must conform to the strictures of a private club licence in Utah, but temporary membership is easily obtained. **Doc's** at the Gondola is the main bar at The Canyons. In Park City, try **J.B. Mulligans Club and Pub**, **Wasatch Brew Pub Cantina** and the **Star Bar** at Plan B for live bands.

Sleep

All accommodation can be booked on **t** +1 800 472 6309, *www.thecanyons.com*.

Luxury:

The Canyons Grand Hotel (formerly The Grand Summit Resort) is an impressive slopeside complex, with a spa and outdoor pool.

The Miner's Club, t +1 435 615 8900, has elegant two- to four-bedroom condos ('very comfortable but isolated. You can ski to the door, but you need a courtesy car to reach the lifts').

Sundial Lodge has a roof top hot tub and pool, daycare for kids, and all the rooms – from the studios to family-sized condos – are comfortably furnished.

Budget:

Holiday Inn Express Park City, t +1 435 658 1600, *www.hiexpress.com*, is a budget-priced option at nearby Kimball Junction.

Copper Mountain, Colorado

***BEST FOR**

Families, all levels of skier and rider

ESSENTIALS

Altitude: 9,712ft (2926m)–12,313ft (3767m)
Further information: **t** +1 970 968 2882, *www.coppercolorado.com*
Lifts in area: 22 (15 chairs, 7 drags) serving 2,450 acres of terrain
Lift pass: Rocky Mountain International ticket (Copper Mountain, Steamboat and Winter Park) adult $240–358, child 6–13yrs $156–210, both for six days
Access: Denver airport 1½hrs

Profile

Car-free resort with good facilities for families with young children. The skiing suits all standards and snowboarding is a particular strength

Resort

Despite being voted for the fifth year running Summit County's favourite resort for skiing and riding, Copper Mountain is currently still one the best-kept secrets of Colorado. Copper has emerged from its $400 million makeover since it was acquired by giant resort developer Intrawest, and the car-free base is set around four lodges and plazas with a good range of shops and restaurants.

Copper is no newcomer to skiing. It first opened as a ski area back in 1972. It has one of the best snow records in Colorado and the terrain suits all standards of skier and boarder, with plenty of powder opportunities.

Mountain

Copper is a serious snowboarding destination. Kidz terrain park, located near the top of the American Flyer lift, is for novices and has a mini-pipe. Night Riders Jib Park by the Burning Stones Plaza is floodlit on Friday and Saturday evenings. Catalyst is the main park, with three distinct lines for different levels and a super-pipe. New park zones under the American Flyer lift link up with Kidz and Catalyst to form a top to bottom park run.

The mountain summit is reached in eight minutes by the Super Bee chairlift. The shape of the mountain naturally allows for one of the best-designed ski areas in the United States. The tree-lined trails become more difficult as you move towards the left of the piste map. Thus, advanced skiers and boarders tend to stick to the main face of Copper Peak, and beginners will find little beyond their capabilities on the other side of the resort. In between, the terrain is mainly intermediate. Copper Bowl and Spaulding Bowl provide some of the best off-piste skiing in Colorado, with the latter full of natural jumps and lips for riders. Free snowcat rides take you up to Tucker Mountain and its untracked powder.

Learn

Ski & Ride School, t +1 866 841 2481, ioffers a range of special courses including freestyle, Bumps Busters and Women's Wednesdays. **Over The Hill Gang, t** +1 970 968 3059, was founded here in 1976 for the over-45s and arranges guiding for different levels.

Children

Kids Jump Start, t +1 866 841 2481, at the Ski & Ride School offers lessons from three to 15 years. **Copper Freeride Camp, t** +1 866 385 0144, is a weekend course for ages 12 to 18 years. **Belly Button Bakery & Babies, t** +1 970 968 2882, accepts children from six weeks to eight years.

Lunch

Try **Double Diamond, t** +1 970 968 2880, in the Foxpine Inn, for fried fish on Fridays. The **Blue Moose, t** +1 970 968 9666, by the American Eagle lift serves New York-style pizzas and salads. **Creekside Pizza and Restaurant, t** +1 970 968 2033, is a local favourite, offering 'hand-tossed' pizzas as well as pasta and BBQs. **Alpinista Mountain Bistro, t** +1 970 968 1144, is Copper's newest restaurant.

Dine

CB Grille, t +1 970 968 3113, is a fine dining establishment. **Salsa Mountain Cantina, t** +1 970 968 6300, is for Mexican cuisine. **Imperial Palace, t** +1 970 968 6688, in the Village Square Plaza, serves low-cholesterol Chinese dishes without any MSG.

Party

'We are not big nightlife people, but even for us there was very little to do in the evening,' complained a reporter. **Endo's Adrenaline Café** sells huge sandwiches and is popular for après ski from 3pm. **Pravda** is a Russian vodka bar with the contemporary atmosphere of the Cold War Soviet era. **JJ's Rocky Mountain Tavern** in East Village has live entertainment and a 52-foot bar. **McGillycuddy's** is a Celtic-style pub. **Storm King Lounge** has pool, darts and a sushi bar, while **Zizzo Ski Bar** is the resort's newes t bar and nightclub.

Sleep

Most of the accommodation is in apartments; your main choice is between locations and then you can pick the quality you prefer. Call, **t** +1 888 219 2441, for all reservations. The **Village** at Copper is well placed for most of the dining and shopping. **East Village** is at the base of the intermediate to expert terrain, and **Union Creek** is at the base of the beginner terrain. Accommodation ranges from Platinum (with heated pool) through to Bronze, which is the most affordable.

Lewis Ranch offers some of Copper's most luxurious accommodation in four- to five-bedroom slopeside town houses.

Crested Butte, Colorado

Profile

Attractive old town set a short drive away from the ski area base. Some excellent steep and deep off-piste and a well-regarded ski school. The drawback is difficult international access

Resort

The first thing you need to know about Crested Butte is how to pronounce it. A butte (as in 'beaut-iful') is a stand-alone mountain that provides the town with a reputation for challenging skiing that stretches far beyond Colorado. The small Victorian town is no newcomer to the ski scene. Miners from Scandinavia were competing in jumping and downhill races here at least a decade before European skiers attempted their first awkward turns in the Swiss Alps. The January 1887 edition of *Outing* magazine gave graphic details of a team skiing competition that had taken place in Crested Butte the previous year.

The resort is currently undergoing a major development plan. However, its remote location has meant that until now Crested Butte has remained something of a backwater. Visitors must first fly into Denver, catch a connecting flight to Gunnison and then make a 30-minute transfer to the resort. For those coming from overseas it is not always possible to complete the journey in a single day.

Some 40 original buildings have been restored to their Victorian glory and others have been constructed in sympathetic style. Reporters warn of the need to acclimatize to the resort's high altitude. The ski area is located three miles from the town.

First phase of the $200 million reconstruction came on stream last winter with the opening at the base area of Mountaineer Square with a new hotel and condos. The old Club Med is also being turned into a hotel.

*BEST FOR

All standards of skier and rider, resort atmosphere

ESSENTIALS

Altitude: 9,100ft (2774m) –12,162ft (3707m)
Further information: t +1 970 349 2303, *www.skicb.com*
Lifts in area: 13 (12 chairs, 1 drag) serving 1,073 acres of terrain
Lift pass: adult $198–438, youth 13–17yrs $150–330, child 7–12yrs $102–222, all for six days
Access: Gunnison airport 30mins, daily service from Denver airport to Gunnison

Mountain

'A great place to ski,' said a reporter. Crested Butte has some of the steepest lift-served terrain in North America and regularly hosts ski-extreme competitions. Most, but not all, of the mountain is suited to competent skiers and riders in search of new and challenging experiences. Main mountain access from the new Mountaineer Village is by the Red Lady Express and Silver Queen lifts. The first gives access to plenty of intermediate terrain, while the second takes you up into steep double-diamond territory.

The Prospect lift carries skiers from the Prospect housing development to the top of the Goldlink and Painter Boy lifts.

Last season the East River lift was upgraded to a high-speed quad.

The resort is a favourite with snowboarders. The Canaan terrain park, served by the Paradise lift has a host of jumps and rails and a super-pipe.

Learn

Crested Butte Ski and Snowboard School, **t** +1 970 349 2252, offers workshops on turning skills, all-terrain and ski-racing.

Children

The new **Kids Base Camp**, **t** +1 970 348 2259, replaces the old daycare arrangement here. The building has been gutted and entirely redesigned for this season.

Lunch

On the mountain, **Ice Bar and Restaurant**, **t** +1 970 349 2275, offers fine dining and exotic martinis. **Andiamo** in the Paradise Warming Hut, **t** +1 970 349 2274, has sound Italian cuisine and good service.

Dine

Crested Butte has more restaurants than you could possibly visit in a week. Recommended restaurants include **Buffalo Grille & Saloon**, **t** +1 970 349 9699, for buffalo and beef steaks. The **Secret Stash**, **t** +1 970 349 6245, is a 100-year-old miners' cabin with Japanese-style seating, serving Asian BBQ wings and gourmet pizzas. **Le Bosquet Restaurant**, **t** +1 970 349 5808, offers fine dining. **Lil's Land & Sea**, **t** +1 970 349 5457, serves fresh seafood, game and sushi. **Izzy's**, **t** +1 970 349 5630, specializes in stuffed Mediterranean crêpes. The **Firehouse Grill**, **t** +1 970 349 4666, in the Plaza building, is owned and operated by local firefighters and serves pizzas, pasta and steaks. The **Last Steep**, **t** +1 970 349 7007 is the resort's newest eatery featuring affordable soups, salads and pasta.

Party

Hotspots include **Talk of the Town**, **Kochevar's** and the **Eldo**. The **Firehouse Grill** has pool tables. **Performing Arts** is the local theatre, presenting drama, music and comedies. 'The nightlife is not so hot,' was how reporters summed it up.

Sleep

******Lodge at Mountaineer Square**, **t** +970 349 222, *www.mountaineersquare.com* is a new and extremely comfortable hotel at the base area.

*****Nordic Inn**, **t** +1 970 349 5542, *www.nordicinncb.com*, is a friendly, family-run ski lodge.

The Elevation Hotel, **t** +1 970 349 2303, has been revamped and reopens this season with 260 rooms and a spa.

Purple Mountain Lodge B&B and Spa, **t** +1 970 349 5888, *www.purplemountainlodge.com*, offers five rooms, massage and a hot tub.

Deer Valley, Utah

Profile

Glitzy upmarket resort renowned for the immaculate grooming of its trails and guests alike, but with some surprisingly challenging skiing. Snowboarding is still not permitted

*** BEST FOR**

All levels of skier and rider, cosmopolitan ambience

ESSENTIALS

Altitude: 6,570ft (2003m)–9,570ft (2917m)
Further information: t +1 435 649 1000, *www.deervalley.com*
Lifts in area: 21 (1 cableway, 20 chairs) serving 1,825 acres of terrain
Lift pass: Utah Three Resort Pass (Deer Valley, Park City Mountain Resort, The Canyons) adult $408, child 4–12yrs $225, both for six out of seven days
Access: Salt Lake City airport 40mins

Resort

Deer Valley is the the furthest from Salt Lake City of a trio of major resorts (the others are Park City Mountain Resort and The Canyons) reached by a 40-minute drive to Kimball Junction. Its carefully nurtured reputation as the smartest – and most expensive – ski destination in America has done nothing to endear it to hardcore skiers, who instinctively dismiss it as a place for middle-aged lower intermediates who are only happy if every wrinkle has been surgically removed from the slopes.

In fact this is an unfair and ageist misconception: the mountain at Deer Valley offers plenty of challenge for advanced skiers – but not for snowboarders. The resort remains a founding member of the tiny clutch of destinations around the world where snowboarding continues to be banned. You don't have to be old or as rich as Croesus to ski Deer Valley, although the latter helps.

Deer Valley lies one mile to the south-east of Park City, up a winding mountain road lined with multi million-dollar homes. It's so exclusive that the staff who unload the skis from your car and carry them to the snow won't accept tips. Any visit here should include days in Park City Mountain Resort (so close that skiers illegally go under the rope from one to the other), and The Canyons on the other side of the town of Park City.

Linking all three would involve the construction of just one lift. Rivalry has so far prevented this, but the three have come a step closer by launching a joint adult and children's pass for foreign visitors that is only sold through tour operators, with a single rate throughout the season.

Mountain

Main mountain access from the car parks at Snow Park Lodge is by two parallel high-speed chairs that bring you up to Silver Lake Lodge mid-mountain hub. From here you can make your way to lots of easy cruising terrain on Flagstaff Mountain and Empire Canyon. Both Sultan and Sterling chairlifts have been upgraded to detachable quads. The 9,400ft peak of Bald Mountain, reached by the Wasatch Express lift, is the starting point for some more challenging black-diamond terrain. The Daly Chutes and Daly Bowl, accessed from Empire Canyon, are steep powder tests.

Riders may be noticeable by their absence, but twin tippers have their own Trick 'n' Turn rail park and a skiercross course on Empire Canyon.

Learn

The **Deer Valley Ski School, t** +1 435 649 1000, offers group and private lessons, as well as lessons for women on Wednesdays and for men on Thursdays.

Children

Deer Valley Children's Center, t +1 435 645 6648, cares for children from 2 months to 12 years. Deer Valley Ski

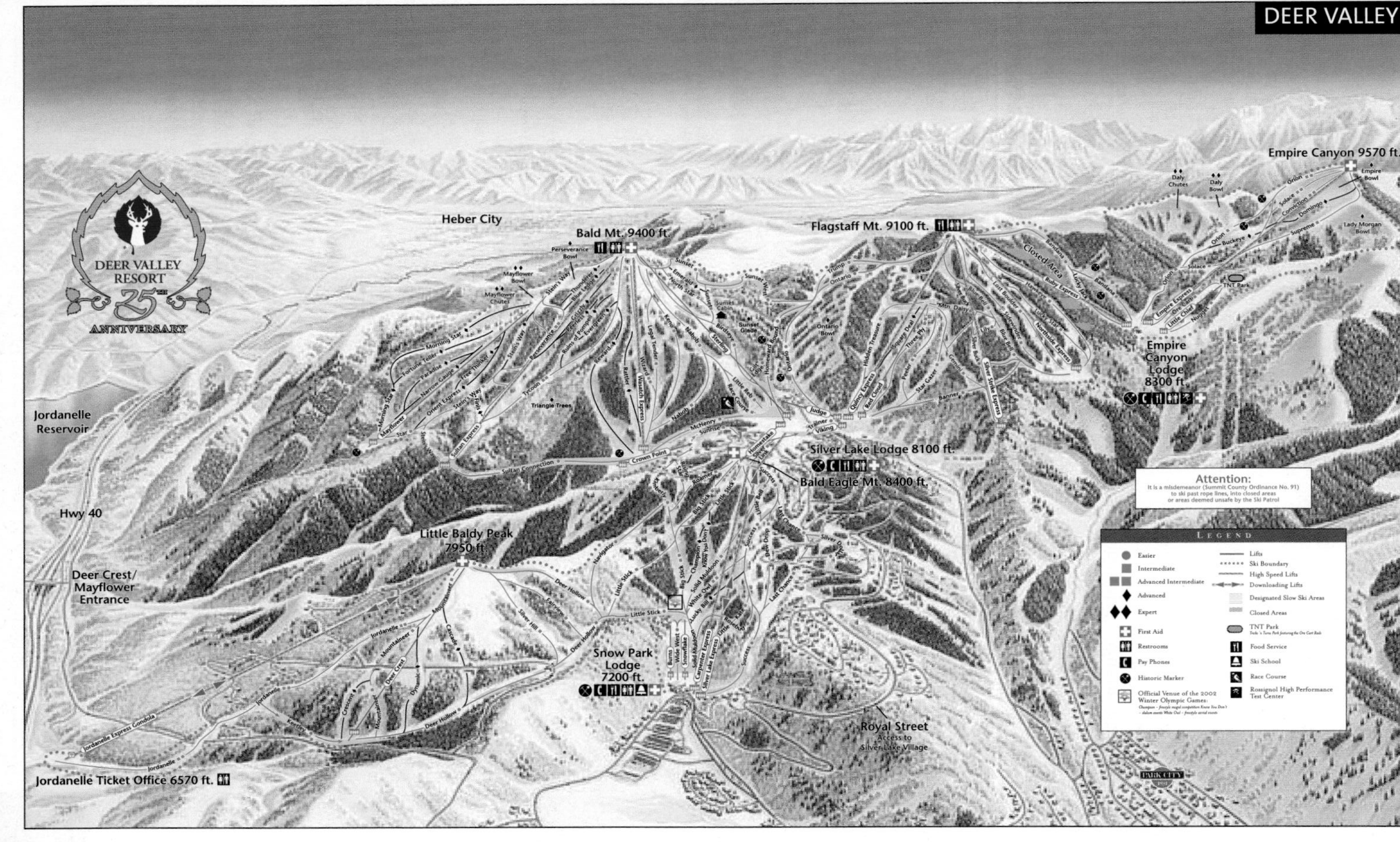
DEER VALLEY
DEER VALLEY RESORT
25TH
ANNIVERSARY
Heber City
Bald Mt. 9400 ft.
Flagstaff Mt. 9100 ft.
Empire Canyon 9570 ft.
Empire Canyon Lodge 8300 ft.
Silver Lake Lodge 8100 ft.
Bald Eagle Mt. 8400 ft.
Little Baldy Peak 7950 ft.
Snow Park Lodge 7200 ft.
Jordanelle Reservoir
Hwy 40
Deer Crest/ Mayflower Entrance
Jordanelle Ticket Office 6570 ft.
Royal Street
Access to Silver Lake Village
Closed Area
Attention:
It is a misdemeanor (Summit County Ordinance No. 91) to ski past rope lines, into closed areas or areas deemed unsafe by the Ski Patrol
LEGEND
Easier
Intermediate
Advanced Intermediate
Advanced
Expert
First Aid
Restrooms
Pay Phones
Historic Marker
Official Venue of the 2002 Winter Olympic Games
Lifts
Ski Boundary
High Speed Lifts
Downloading Lifts
Designated Slow Ski Areas
Closed Areas
TNT Park
Food Service
Ski School
Race Course
Rossignol High Performance Test Center
PARK CITY

School accepts children from four to 12 years, with clubs for different age groups and Teen Equipe lessons for 13–17-year olds.

Lunch

For restaurants listed without numbers call, **t** +1 435 649 1000.

You can arrange a private lunch for two to 15 people at **Sunset Cabin**, **t** +1 435 645 6650, tucked away off Sunset run. At **Royal Street Café** at Silver Lake Lodge try the Vermont cheddar burger or the shrimp and lobster margarita appetizer served in a margarita glass. Try **Bald Mountain Pizza** at Silver Lake Lodge, **Empire Canyon Grill**, as well as **Snow Park** for burgers and chilli.

Dine

Deer Valley has four evening restaurants: the **Seafood Buffet**, **t** +1 435 645 6632, at the Snow Park Lodge ('still good, but not as good as it used to be'), the **Mariposa**, **t** +1 435 645 6715, at Silver Lake Lodge, which offers fine dining, **Royal Street Café**, **t** +1 435 645 6724 at Silver Lake, and **Fireside Dining**, **t** +435 645 6632, in the Empire Canyon Lodge.

Party

The **Après Ski Lounge** at the Snow Park Lodge in Deer Valley is popular after skiing, but the best of the nightlife is on **Historic Main Street** in Park City, which has some 70 shops, bars and restaurants.

Sleep

The Lodges at Deer Valley, **t** +1 435 615 2600, is a condominium hotel built in Old West style with views across the Snow Park Ponds.

Goldener Hirsch Inn, **t** +1 435 649 7770, *www.goldernhirschinn.com*, is an Austrian-style hotel with a fine restaurant.

Stein Eriksen Lodge, **t** +1 435 649 3700, *www.steinlodge.com*, at Silver Lake Village has a Scandinavian ambience and is named after the legendary Norwegian who won gold at the 1954 Oslo Olympics – the 'father' of Deer Valley.

The Châteaux at Silver Lake, **t** +1 435 649 4040, is an elegant condo hotel with French country décor.

Heavenly, California/ Nevada

Profile

Quirky resort straddling the California–Nevada border, with spectacular views of Lake Tahoe as well as the desert. Suits all standards as well as party-goers and gamblers

Resort

The skiing and gambling town of South Lake Tahoe used to be famous for slow lifts and fast dealers, but all that has changed since Vail Resorts bought the adjoining 50-year-old ski resort of Heavenly nine years ago. 'Vail West', as it has been dubbed, has since been the beneficiary of the lavish annual funding that is the hallmark of America's richest resort company.

*BEST FOR

All levels of skier and rider, tree-skiing, high rollers, lakeland scenery

ESSENTIALS

Altitude: 6,565ft (2002m)–10,067ft (3068m)
Further information: t +1 775 586 7000, *www.skiheavenly.com*
Lifts in area: 28 (2 cableways, 18 chairs, 8 drags) serving 4,800 acres of terrain. Fifteen alpine resorts and eight cross-country centres at Lake Tahoe with over 100 lifts and 17,520 acres of terrain
Lift pass: Heavenly adult $260–440, child 5–12yrs $180, both for six days
Access: Reno airport 1½hrs, Sacramento airport 2hrs, San Francisco airport 4hrs

The development of a village around the base of the gondola has created an identity that it previously lacked. Tacky is slowly giving way to trendy as the budget motels and T-shirt shops along the Californian end of the strip are torn down to give way to a burgeoning Marriott hotel and apartment complex as well as 40 shops and restaurants.

Work is ongoing for the Château at Heavenly Village, a new $420 million hotel and shopping complex scheduled to open in time for the 2009–10 season.

The Big Four casinos – Caesar's, Harrah's, Harvey's and Horizon – that hug the Nevada side of the stateline with California all offer the promise of instant riches. The monotonous clunk of one-arm bandits and the frenetic cries from the craps tables ring out 24 hours a day in the clockless casinos.

Croupiers still shuffle decks faster than the eye can follow, but a modern gondola and $40 million of high-speed quads are gradually transforming mountain access.

In more serene California, quite literally on the other side of the road, gambling is forbidden and the emphasis is on snow business rather than showbusiness.

Heavenly is the largest of the 15 resorts that fringe the 72-mile shoreline of Lake Tahoe, the second largest and most beautiful alpine lake in the world behind Titicaca in Peru. Its position, straddling the frontier between two states, gives it an intriguing split personality. On the Californian side the swirling azure waters – so deep that they never freeze over – are the ever-present backdrop. In Nevada, the slopes reach down towards the arid, painted desert.

The choice of where to stay is equally contrasting. California's is more tranquil, with a peaceful waterfront and simple single-storey homes. Nevada's South Lake Tahoe has monstrous casino hotels where the ground floors are given over to 24-hour slot machines. The third choice is more skier-orientated at the small and somewhat remote Nevada base areas.

Seven resorts around the lake – Squaw Valley, Sierra-at-Tahoe, Kirkwood, Northstar, Mount Rose and Alpine Meadows – provide possible day trips.

Free shuttles operate from South Lake Tahoe to Sierra and Kirkwood. The *Tahoe Queen* paddle-steamer provides a scenic way of reaching Squaw Valley on the North Shore. However, if you want to explore the region fully, it makes sense to hire a car. However one reader, who stayed in South Lake Tahoe, disagreed: 'Save money by not hiring a car. There are daily ski buses to Heavenly and Sierra-at-Tahoe, plus buses for the other local resorts.'

Heavenly has put into action a 10-year master plan to position itself at the forefront of environmental conservation in the winter sports industry. The plan includes significant environmental enhancements including the replacement of chairlifts that are obstructing meadows and trees. The resort is also working with conservationists to help protect Lake Tahoe's water quality and 'Keep Tahoe Blue'.

'Heavenly did get busy on the weekends (but we did have 60 inches of snow in

HEAVENLY

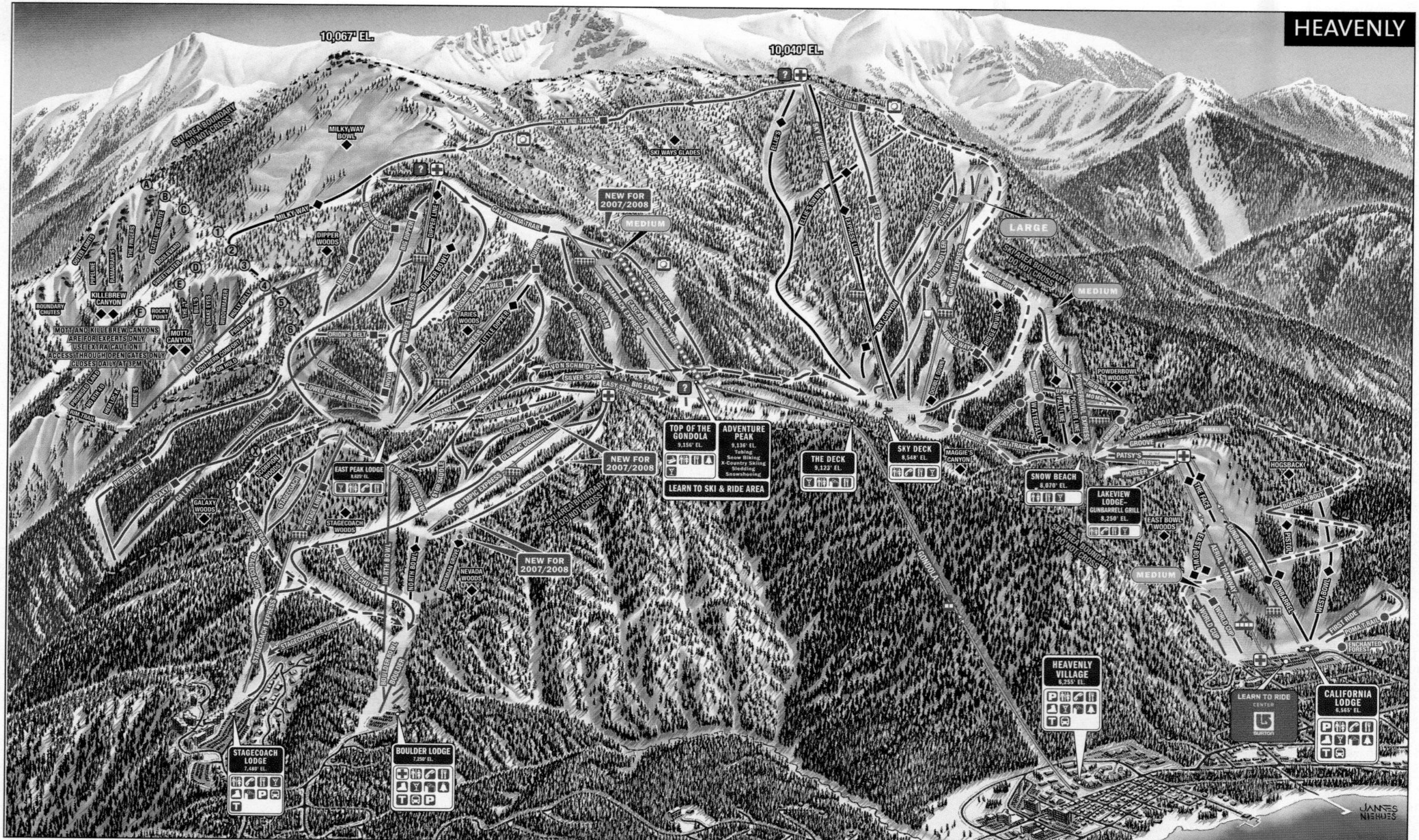

10,067' EL.

10,040' EL.

SKI AREA BOUNDARY DO NOT CROSS

MOTT AND KILLEBREW CANYONS ARE FOR EXPERTS ONLY USE EXTRA CAUTION! ACCESS THROUGH OPEN GATES ONLY CLOSES DAILY AT 3PM

NEW FOR 2007/2008

TOP OF THE GONDOLA 9,156' EL.

ADVENTURE PEAK 9,136' EL. Tubing Snow Biking X-Country Skiing Sledding Snowshoeing

LEARN TO SKI & RIDE AREA

THE DECK 9,123' EL.

SKY DECK 8,548' EL.

SNOW BEACH 6,070' EL.

LAKEVIEW LODGE– GUNBARRELL GRILL 8,250' EL.

EAST PEAK LODGE 9,425' EL.

HEAVENLY VILLAGE 6,255' EL.

LEARN TO RIDE CENTER

CALIFORNIA LODGE 6,565' EL.

STAGECOACH LODGE 7,480' EL.

BOULDER LODGE 7,250' EL.

LARGE

MEDIUM

SMALL

JAMES NIEHUES

24 hours), so every man and his dog went skiing. The weekdays were much quieter,' said a reader.

Mountain

Unfortunately the gondola, built by the cash-strapped previous owners, stretches only three-quarters of the way up the mountain to a sunny balcony at just over 9,000ft. It provides great views of the lake and easy access to some of the best glade skiing in the whole of North America. Go left for Nevada, right for California, or stay put for tubing, tobogganing and cross-country skiing.

The alternative is to start by chair or cable car from California Lodge, or on the Nevada side from Stagecoach Lodge or Boulder Lodge.

The upper Californian side is generally fast blue cruising terrain, with the more difficult runs higher up. The notorious California Face and Gun Barrel are vicious bump runs, leading down to the California base area. Most of the trails are ideally suited to intermediates – long cruisers bordered by pine trees and enhanced by the stunning view of the lake.

The Nevada Face consists mainly of blue trails, but this side of the mountain also houses the most advanced skiing and riding in Mott Canyon and Killebrew Canyon. Steep chutes are cut through the trees, with runs such as Snake Pit, Widowmaker, and the difficult Boundary Chutes. If you happen across a visionary figure here with a Mohican haircut jumping off a 30ft cliff, that *is* Glen Plake; the rebel extreme skier, who works as an ambassador for the resort.

The new Olympic Express quad opened last season, accessing the mid-mountain Nevada terrain and also providing a faster way to East Peak Lodge from both Nevada base areas. Heavenly has four terrain parks and a super-pipe.

'The black diamond runs seem to just mean "ungroomed" – they are reasonably steep but, unless you are good at moguls, very tricky,' said a reporter. However, 'Even at New Year, there were very few queues and blissfully empty pistes.'

Learn

Resort-owned **Heavenly Ski School**, **t** +1 775 586 7000, ext. 6206, has the monopoly here as in most American resorts. Quality of teaching is always a lottery. One reporter complained that his teacher was Argentinian and had only a rudimentary grasp of English.

Children

The **Daycare Center**, **t** +1 775 586 7000, ext. 6912, at the Californian Base Lodge, takes non-skiers from six weeks. Private nannies are available from the **Nanny for a Day Program**. The ski school has a **Ski/Play Program** for kids from three years. ('Kids enjoyed the ski school, although it appeared a little disorganized when dropping them off in the morning.')

Lunch

Readers complained that the mountain restaurants are like giant cafeterias: 'The mountain restaurants were universally awful with very limited indoor seating. You're much better off going down to the bases and eating there.' On the California side, try **Café Blue** at the first stop on the gondola, and **Adventure Peak Grill** at the top. **Lakeview Lodge** offers unrivalled views of Lake Tahoe, and **Sky Deck** is located at theSky Express base. On the Nevada side, **Slice of Heaven** at the Stagecoach base-lodge is Italian, while **Black Diamond Cantina** at Boulder Lodge offers Mexican fare. For information on restaurants, telephone **t** +1 775 586 7000.

Dine

Where once the ubiquitous burger ruled, you can now create your own Oriental stir-fry at **Fire and Ice**, **t** +1 530 542 6650, or dine on sushi and Hawaiian fusion cuisine at **Kalani's**, **t** +1 530 544 6100.

The casinos house a range of restaurants at competitive prices, including **Harrahs**, **t** +1 702 588 6611, with its 'All you can eat steak and seafood buffet' for $20.99. **Ciera's Steak and Chophouse** in the Montbleu, **t** +1 775 588 3515, has an upscale menu and ambience. In South Lake Tahoe, the **Summit**, **t** +1 775 588 6611, in Harrah's is one of America's top 100 restaurants. The **Naked Fish**, **t** +1 530 541 3474, offers outstanding sushi, and The **Chart House**, **t** +1 775 588 6276, is more expensive but has wonderful views. The **Red Hut**, **t** +1 775 588 7488, **Ernie's Coffee Shop**, **t** +1 530 541 2161, and **Heidi's Pancake House**, **t** +1 530 544 8113, all offer 'powder breakfasts'.

Party

Traditional après ski is limited. You must head into South Lake Tahoe and try your hand at the green baize tables. As in Las Vegas, the by-product of casino culture is a wide range of cabaret acts and pop concerts featuring famous American and occasionally international artists. A reporter recommended **Fire and Ice** as 'a great place for a drink after the slopes, with large outdoor fire pits'.

The Heavenly Flyer is an exciting zip-line ride from the top of Tamarack Express to the top of the gondola – a drop of 525ft.

Sleep

Luxury:

Tahoe Seasons Resort, **t** +1 530 541 6700, *www.tahoeseasons.com*, complex is within walking distance of the lifts at the California base.

Moderate:

Caesars Tahoe, **t** +1 702 588 3515, *www.caesars.com*, has six restaurants including the Roman Feast Buffet, and houses Club Nero Nightclub, a lagoon-style pool, and a wedding chapel.

Harrah's Lake Tahoe, **t** +1 702 588 6611, *www.harrahs.com*, is a large casino-hotel at South Lake Tahoe.

Tahoe Lakeshore Lodge & Spa, **t** +1 530 541 2180, *www.tahoelakeshorelodge.com*, on the South Shore, has a view of the lake from every room, all of which are spacious and decorated with lodgepole pine furniture.

Embassy Suites Hotel, **t** +1 530 541 4418, is close to the gondola. It has an indoor pool and a free cooked breakfast.

Harveys Resort Hotel & Casino, **t** +1 775 588 2411, *www.harrahs.com*, is located close to Heavenly's gondola base. It houses eight restaurants, 10 cocktail lounges, a health club and the ubiquitous wedding chapel.

Horizon Casino Resort, **t** +1 775 588 6211, *www.horizoncasino.com*, has a vast gaming floor. 'The place is nothing fancy, but it's a clean place to put your head,' said a reporter.

Best Western Station House Inn, **t** +1 530 542 1101, *www.stationhouseinn.com*, has a shuttle-bus to the skiing, and features some spa rooms.

Quality Inn, **t** +1 530 541 5400, *www.qualityinn.com*, is in South Lake Tahoe and reported as 'comparatively basic but it was perfectly adequate, cheap and had really hospitable staff'.

Jackson Hole, Wyoming

🏆 BEST SKI SCHOOL 2009 (JACKSON HOLE MOUNTAIN SPORTS SCHOOL)

Profile

Some of North America's most challenging trails and steepest backcountry terrain. Stay in the town of Jackson with its Wild West ambience, or for ski convenience at Teton Village. Wide range of moderate to extreme luxury accommodation

Resort

Along with powder bums from all over the world, Jackson Hole manages to draw a glitteringly wealthy clientele worthy of Switzerland's St Moritz or France's Megève, and the reason for this lies in Jackson's long history of dude ranching.

City Slickers have been answering the call of nature in the Tetons ever since 1908 when rancher Louis Joy discovered that the urban rich would pay good money for chuck-wagon fare, lumpy mattresses and saddle sores. Little and much has changed since dude-ranching was overtaken by skiing.

The mighty Tetons remain unchallenged in their wild beauty. Jackson Hole rancher Struthers Burt once wrote, 'You must search for the loveliness of America. It is not obvious, it is scattered. But when you find it, it touches you and binds you to it like a great secret oath taken in silence.' Presumably he was looking out of his window at the time.

The mountain range is captivating from the moment you step from the plane at Jackson Hole airport, where the runway is fringed by huge herds of grazing elk and the occasional enormous moose.

A 15-minute car-ride from the airport takes you to the quaint cowboy town of Jackson. The jet-lagged visitor assumes that the steep groomed trails immediately above it are his ski destination. Wrong. This mountain is the small and entirely separate resort of Snow King. Jackson Hole Ski Resort is located a further 20-minute drive away at Teton Village on the far side of the Snake River, an enticing trout stream that coils across the valley floor.

This leaves you with a dilemma as to where to base yourself. Teton Village has a range of smart spa properties and condo hotels, while Jackson town has some historic properties and budget options. But the convenience of doorstep skiing has to be weighed against the shops, restaurants and nightlife of Jackson. If you can't make up your mind, you can stay in rural tranquillity between the two. Personally we now favour Teton Village since it has expanded into a real resort rather than just a base station. The police

*** BEST FOR**

Experts, romantics, luxury hotels

ESSENTIALS

Altitude: 6,311ft (1924m)–10,135ft (3135m)
Further information: **t** +1 307 733 2292, *www.jacksonhole.com*
Lifts in area: 11 (2 cableways, 9 chairs) serving 2,500 acres
Lift pass: $360, youth 15–21yrs $295, child 14yrs and under $180, all for six out of eight days
Access: Jackson Hole airport 15mins from Jackson, 35mins from Teton Village

take a dim view on drink-driving, and if you enjoy an evening out in Jackson it makes sense to travel by bus or taxi.

Some 8,000 elk and a host of celebrities including Russell Crow, Uma Thurman, Ralph Fiennes and Jack Nicholson agree that this is the best place in the Rockies to spend all or part of the winter. The winning combination of spectacular scenery, yesteryear cowboy values and what we consider to be some of the best skiing in North America make the long journey from Europe worthwhile.

To the chagrin of purist powderhounds, Teton Village has doubled in size in recent years. The establishment of such exotic hotels as the Amangani (located between the town and village) and the slopeside Four Seasons has brought a new breed of winter visitor who is not necessarily wedded to the mountainside from first to last lift. To the astonishment of local diehards, some have even been seen carrying shopping bags at lunchtime rather than a pair of powder skis.

Focus in the quaint town of Jackson is on the main square with its archway made from hundreds of antlers naturally shed by elk in their winter reserve. Others have tried, but only Jackson – and Telluride on a smaller scale – has succeeded in welding the dusty gun-slinging charisma of a Western frontier town to the high-tech facilities of a modern ski resort.

Mountain

Jackson Hole is ambrosia for snow gourmets. You don't have to be an expert to enjoy it, but it sure helps. Some 50 per cent of the terrain is best described as 'difficult' to 'very difficult', although an increased amount of intermediate skiing can now be found off the Bridger Gondola and on Aprés Vous, the much more benign of the two adjoining mountains.

It is hard to imagine that a resort with only 11 lifts can produce such excitement, but, as one reporter put it, 'I am certain I could ski here every day for a whole season and never tire of the ever-changing and challenging terrain.'

This season sees the opening of the long awaited new cable car. The replacement for the old red sardine can which ran out of hours is twice the size, carrying 100 passengers in sleek modern cabins. At the top of the windswept peak is Corbet's Couloir, a notorious gully reached by a four-metre jump off a cornice. The less adventurous – if still of an advanced level – can head down off the longest vertical drop in the United States served by a single lift. The full range of bowls and chutes is radical in the extreme. However, in all but the most difficult snow conditions confident intermediates will have no trouble in picking out manageable descents – provided they remember that, in Jackson, expert-only double-black-diamond trails take no prisoners. The Hobacks are a series of seemingly endless off-piste itineraries that will test even the strongest legs.

The Bridger gondola provides access to the intermediate area between the two mountains as well as to the upper mountain. A 20-minute hike up the Headwall opens up Casper Bowl. A further short walk takes you out of the resort area to Granite Canyon, a magnificent mile-long powder field followed by a wilderness traverse back to base, but it is avalanche-prone and should not be attempted without a guide, transceivers and shovels. The same applies to Cody and Rock Springs Bowls off Rendezvous Mountain.

The second mountain of Après Vous is prime beginners' territory, with a beginner network of runs at the bottom served by the Teewinot quad, and slightly

JACKSON HOLE

RENDEZVOUS MOUNTAIN 10,450' (3,185 METERS)
VERTICAL RISE 4,139' (1,261 METERS)

GRAND TETON NATIONAL PARK

RENDEZVOUS BOWL
CODY BOWL
(ACCESS THROUGH GATES ONLY)
ROCK SPRINGS BOWL
CHEYENNE BOWL
BERNIE'S BOWL
LARAMIE BOWL
TENSLEEP BOWL
CIRQUE
HEADWALL
BRIDGER TETON NATIONAL FOREST

GONDOLA SUMMIT
9,095' (2,772 Meters)
BRIDGER RESTAURANT

CASPER BOWL
(ACCESS THROUGH GATES ONLY)

CRAGS
(ACCESS THROUGH GATES ONLY)

MORAN FACE
TEEWINOT FACE
SARATOGA BOWL

APRES VOUS MOUNTAIN
8,481' (2,585 Meters)

Corbet's Cabin
Corbet's Couloir
East Ridge Double Chair
Sublette Quad Chair
Thunder Quad Chair
Bridger Gondola
Casper Bowl Triple Chair
Sweetwater Triple Chair
Teewinot Quad Chair
Apres Vous Quad Chair
Union Pass Quad
Moose Creek Quad
Tram

Tensleep
Laramie Traverse
Dog Face
Expert Chutes
Flip Point
Alta Chutes
Pepi's Run
Bird In The Hand
Table Rock
Split Rock
Central Chute
Bivouac Woods
Bivouac
Cheyenne Gully
South Hoback
Middle Hoback
North Hoback
Backcountry Yurt
Lower Sublette Ridge
Rawlins Bowl
South Colter Ridge
Buffalo Bowl
North Colter Ridge
Riverton Bowl
Tower Three Chute
Hoops Gap
Paint Brush
Thunder
Elk Alley
Dicks Ditch
Amphitheater
Coombs
Cascade
Ranger
Beartooth
Casper Traverse
Greybull
Moccasin
Fremont
Shot 9
Shot 8
Shot 7
Sheridan Ridge
Avalanche
Surprise
Nez Perce
Jackson Face
Beaver Tooth
Ashley Ridge
Rock Garden
Moran Woods
Moran Traverse
Head Rush
Solitude Way
Eagle's Rest
South Pass Traverse
Gros Ventre
Cowboy Couloir
FIS
Slalom
Sundance
Werner
Moran
Upper Teewinot
Lower Teewinot
Buck Run
Secret Slope
Saratoga Bowl Traverse
Big Horn
Pathfinder
Crowheart
Symmetry
Upper Werner
NEW

Four Shadows
No Shadows
Pucker Face
Powder 8 Slope

SKI AREA MAP COVERS
2,500 ACRES
(4 SQUARE MILES)

CONDOMINIUMS

TETON VILLAGE
ELEVATION 6,311' (1,924 Meters)

SADDLEHORN NORDIC CENTER

TO JACKSON

JAMES NIEHUES

more demanding intermediate terrain at the top, served by the Après Vous quad. The recently installed Sweetwater Triple Chair provides a link to the Caspar Bowl lift from the top of the Eagle's rest chair, serving some excellent intermediate terrain and one of the two mountain eateries. The adjacent freestyle terrain park and half-pipe is as popular with twin-tippers as it is with riders.

'The skiing was as good as the reports say it is and there was excellent easy skiing close to all the steeper stuff,' said a reader.

Learn

Jackson Hole Mountain Sports School, t +1 307 739 2779, has an outstanding reputation. Courses include Learn to Turn, Mountain Masters and Race Clinics. The demanding Steep and Deep Camp provides a safe introduction to Jackson's radical terrain. **Jackson Hole Alpine and Backcountry Guide Service, t** +1 307 739 2779, offers off-piste guiding. **High Mountain Heli-skiing, t** +1 307 733 3274, is another option.

Children

The purpose-built **Kids' Ranch, t** +1 307 733 2292, has its own corral complete with magic carpet lift and playground. It offers childcare from six months to three years, and ski programmes for three- to 14-year-olds in small classes. **Annie's Nannies, t** +1 307 733 8086, and **Babysitting by the Tetons, t** +1 307 730 0754, are the childcare options for non-skiers.

Keen teens can join **Team Extreme, t** +1 307 733 2292, a demanding ski and snowboarder clinic aimed at those who have outgrown ski school.

Lunch

On-mountain lunches never used to be a strong feature, but all has changed. The slopeside terrace of the **Four Seasons Resort, t** +1 307 734 5040, is a welcome reward for a hard morning in the Hobacks. Three restaurants – **Couloir, Headwall Deli** and **Mountain Servery** – are at the top of the Bridger Gondola. The other lunchtime venues worth considering are the **Mangy Moose, t** +1 307 733 4913, and upstairs at the **Alpenhof, t** +1 307 733 3242, both at the village base.

Dine

In Teton Village, **Couloir, t** +1 307 739 2675, at the top of the gondola, serves contemporary Western dishes. The **Westbank Grill** in the Four Seasons has an international menu and cosy atmosphere. The **Mangy Moose** (*see* above) is a family favourite set in a vast barn. **GameFish, t** +1 307 732 6040, in the Snake River Lodge and Spa, focuses on fish and smoked game, and **Mizu Sushi, t** +1 307 732 2962, just outside Teton Village, is outstanding, with minimalist design and fresh fish flown in daily. **Calico, t** +1 307 733 2460, is a good-value Italian family restaurant on Teton Village Road. In Jackson, try **Nikai Sushi, t** +1 307 734 6490, and **Koshu's Wine Bar, t** +1 307 733 5283, which is popular with the locals. TRIO, **t** +1 307 734 8038, is a new bistro. Signature dishes at the **Snake River Grill, t** +1 307 733 0557, include smoked tuna carpaccio and pan-roasted Idaho trout. **Rendezvous Bistro, t** +1 307 739 1100, is run by the son of Snake River Grill's owner. Intimate **Wild Sage, t** +1 307 733 2000, at the Rusty Parrot, is the first four-diamond restaurant in Wyoming. Also try the **Teton Steakhouse, t** +1 307 733 2639. ('Do we serve vegetarians? Of course, what do you think cows are?') for huge amounts of good food.

Party

The slopeside **Peak** in the Four Seasons Resort attracts skiers at the end of the day, and has a new après ski sushi bar. **The Snake River Brewing Company** is popular with the locals. Those in search of serious drinking should head for the **Million Dollar Cowboy Bar** on Jackson's Town Square. This huge saloon has stools made from Western saddles, live music and pool tables, all of which is dominated by a stuffed grizzly. **The Stagecoach** in the nearby village of Wilson has a disco on Thursday evenings, the **Mangy Moose** in Teton Village has live entertainment three nights a week, and **The Wort** in Jackson has bluegrass on Tuesdays. A word of warning: Jackson is strict about licensing laws, which forbid anyone under 21 to go to bars; even over-21s must carry ID.

Sleep

Luxury:

Amangani, t +1 307 734 7333, *www.amangani.com*, is a veritable palace set on a bluff halfway between Teton Village and Jackson town. Rooms are minimalist, with black resin, animal hide and pale wood floors, as well as slate bathrooms and wraparound balconies.

Four Seasons Resort, t +1 307 734 5040, *www.fourseasons.com/jacksonhole*, has the best slopeside location of any hotel here. It is decorated with work by Miró and Giacometti, slate floors and animal hide upholstery. There are substantial bedrooms and suites, a kids' club, and a state-of-the-art spa.

Rusty Parrot Lodge, t +1 888 739 1749, *www.rustyparrot.com*, in Jackson, is a five-star with a welcoming atmosphere with old terracotta floors, Persian rugs and an open fire in the lobby.

Moderate:

North Colter Lodge, t +44 (0)8702 416723, *www.skiworld.ltd.uk*, is the smartest luxury rental chalet in Teton Village.

The Rock Springs Yurt, t +1 307 739 2633, provides simple accommodation for nights in the backcountry and includes dinner, breakfast and a guide.

Spring Creek Resort, t +1 307 735 8833, *www.springcreekresort.com*, is next to the Amangani and more traditional.

Snake River Lodge & Spa, t +1 307 732 6000, *www.snakeriverlodge.rockresorts.com*, is at the foot of the ski area and operated by Vail Resorts. It has a pleasant lobby and lounge area but dated rooms. The spa includes an attractive indoor-outdoor pool among the rocks.

Hotel Terra, t +1 307 732 1800, *www.hotelterrajacksonhole.com*, was new last season. The condo-hotel adheres to sustainable green construction and operation, and has two restaurants and a spa.

Teton Club, t +1 307 734 9777, *www.tetonclub.com*, is a very comfortable condo development in Teton Village with maid service and a spa.

Teton Mountain Lodge, t +1 307 734 7111, *www.tetonlodge.com*, at Teton Village offers great service, and is ideal for families. The condos contain cosy bedrooms and modern kitchens with huge fridges. It has a new rooftop spa.

Teton Village Condos, t +1 307 733 3990, are spacious, well equipped and a free bus-ride from the slopes.

The Wort Hotel, t +1 307 733 2190, *www.worthotel.com*, is an inviting stagecoach inn close to the main square in Jackson; the best-situated hotel in town.

Keystone, Colorado

***BEST FOR**

Intermediates, families, night-skiing, airport access

ESSENTIALS

Altitude: 9,300ft (2835m)–12,200ft (3719m)
Further information: **t** +1 970 496 4386 or **t** +44 (0)1708 224 773, *www.keystone.snow.com*
Lifts in area: 14 (2 cableways, 11 chairs, 1 drag) serving 81 miles (130km) of piste
Lift pass: Summit Ticket (covers Arapahoe Basin, Beaver Creek, Breckenridge, Keystone, Vail) adult $296–534, child 5–12yrs $240, both for six out of nine days
Access: Denver airport 1¼hrs

Profile

As well as easy access from an international airport, the attractive purpose-built village has the largest night-skiing operation in North America

Resort

Keystone has been a Colorado community since the 1880s, and is the only resort of that vintage that does not owe its existence to gold or silver strikes. For a while in those heady days, Old Keystone was the end of the line for the Denver, South Park (yes, of cartoon fame) and Pacific railroad. Not a lot happened here again until the 1960s, when an enterprising group of developers persuaded the US Forest Service to let them build a ski resort. Its location, only 75 miles on I-70 from Denver, made it attractive to local skiers. The establishment of what is now the largest floodlit night-skiing operation in North America appealed to city workers, who could drive out after work as well as at weekends.

In the 1990s, Keystone underwent a complete makeover, with a new resort village constructed by Canadian ski property giant developer Intrawest. The result is a friendly family resort divided into the linked 'villages' of Lakeside and River Run. It has considerable atmosphere for somewhere that has been largely purpose-built. Keystone also has a substantial amount of intermediate skiing of its own and shares a lift pass with nearby Breckenridge and Arapahoe Basin as well as Vail and Beaver Creek, which are slightly further afield. The first two are linked by a free ski-bus. Skiers or riders spending a week or more here are strongly advised to explore the other Vail resorts as well as separate Copper Mountain.

Mountain

Skiing takes place on three interlinked mountains that lie one behind the other; each is progressively more challenging.

Main mountain access to Dercum, the closest peak to the resort, is by the gondola or multiple-chair from River Run. This season sees replacement of the old six-seater gondola with a brand new eight-seater. Alternatively, start from the other end of the strung-out resort with the Argentine chair from Mountain House. The easy and intermediate cruising runs on Dercum are floodlit for night-skiing. A gondola continues across to the summit of the second mountain, North Peak, which offers slightly more challenging terrain. Pistes and a quad-chair connect to the Outback at 11,980ft, which has steeps, trees and lots of bumps. The terrain at Keystone has been considerably extended in the last few years by the opening of Bergman, Erikson and Independence Bowls. The three bowls can only be

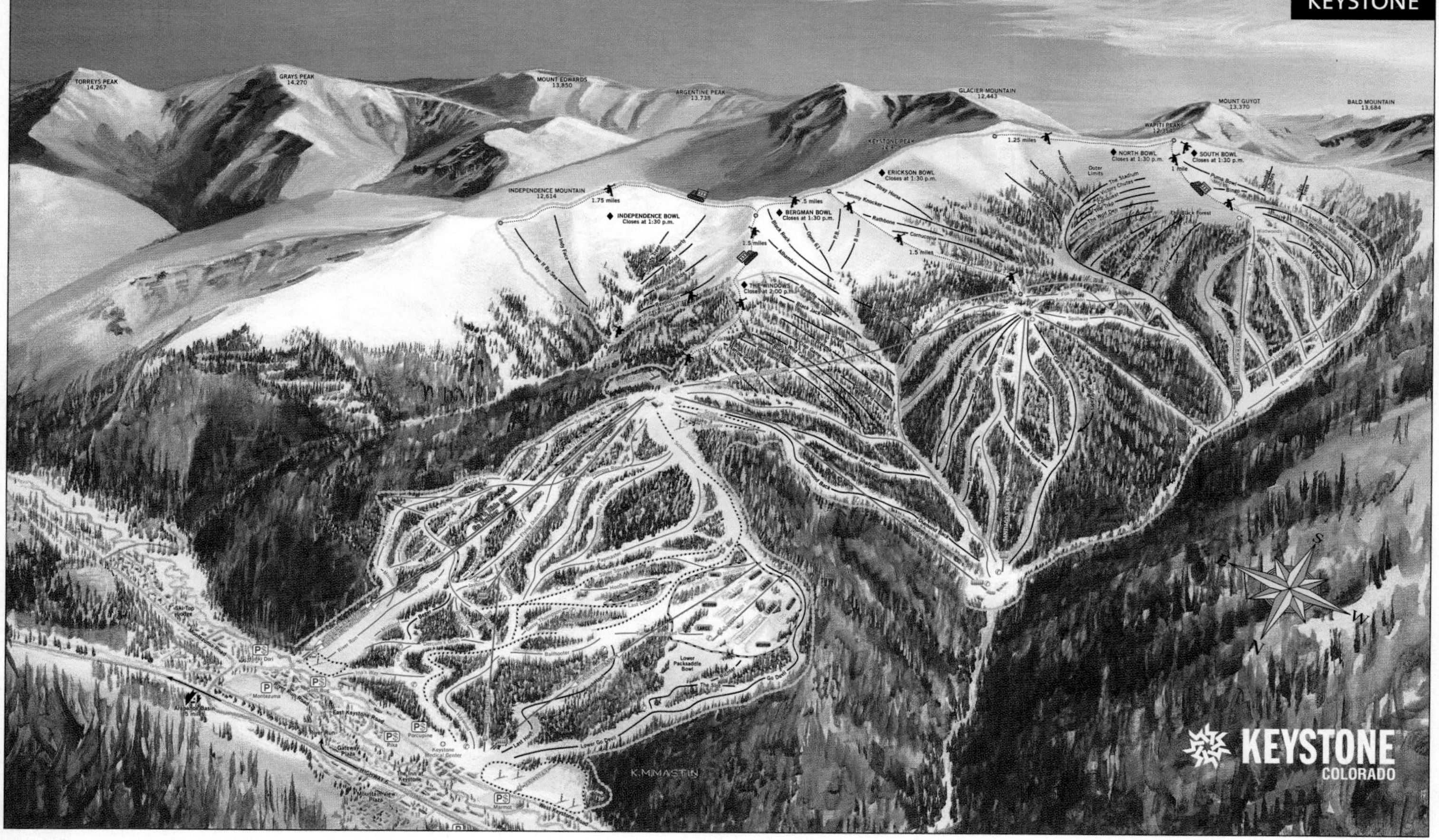

TORREYS PEAK
14,267

GRAYS PEAK
14,270

MOUNT EDWARDS
13,850

ARGENTINE PEAK
13,738

GLACIER MOUNTAIN
12,443

MOUNT GUYOT
13,370

BALD MOUNTAIN
13,684

WAPITI PEAK

KEYSTONE PEAK

INDEPENDENCE MOUNTAIN
12,614

1.75 miles

INDEPENDENCE BOWL
Closes at 1:30 p.m.

Indy Face

Two If By Sea

BERGMAN BOWL
Closes at 1:30 p.m.

.5 miles

1.5 miles

Black Rock

Open 61

Alhambra

ERICKSON BOWL
Closes at 1:30 p.m.

Stray Horse

Tommy Knocker

Rathbone

1.5 miles

THE WINDOWS
Closes at 2:00 p.m.

1.25 miles

NORTH BOWL
Closes at 1:30 p.m.

SOUTH BOWL
Closes at 1:30 p.m.

1 mile

Outer Limits

The Stadium

The Black Forest

Puma Bowl

Lower Packsaddle Bowl

Lower Go Devil

Last Hoot

Montezuma

Porcupine

Pika

Gateway Plaza

East Keystone Road

Keystone Medical Center

Marmot

Mountain View Plaza

K.MMASTIN

KEYSTONE
COLORADO

accessed by the resort's snowcat operation, which takes visitors on a half-day expedition with around 10 descents – most often in virgin powder.

Keystone's beginner and advanced terrain parks are located on the front side of Dercum Mountain in Pack Saddle Bowl.

Learn

Keystone Ski and Ride School, **t** +1 970 496 4170, offers group and private lessons.

Children

Keystone Children's Center and Snowplay Programs, **t** +1 970 496 4181, cares for babies from two months at River Run and at the Mountain House base area. Keystone has six magic carpet lifts.

Lunch

The **Alpenglow Stube**, **t** +1 800 354 4386, serves the highest *haute cuisine* in North America. The four-course lunch menu costs a modest $30.

Dine

'If you don't want to go out to eat at night you'd better choose another resort. There is only a tiny grocery store at River Run Village and at the Lakeside you have to walk nearly a mile down the unlit highway to get a few basics,' warned a reporter. However, the free on-call Ease Bus will take you anywhere you require in the resort. **Ski Tip Lodge**, **t** +1 877 625 1540, offers four-course menus. Almost as rustic is the 1930s **Keystone Ranch**, **t** +1 970 496 4386, which serves 'Colorado Frontier and fine-dining, fusion cuisine'. The **Bighorn Steakhouse**, **t** +1 970 496 2316, at Keystone Lodge in Lakeside Village, serves fine American beef. Dinner is also available at the **Alpenglow Stube**, **t** +1 800 354 4386, reached by two gondola rides to the top of North Peak.

Party

'Nightlife is non-existent,' complained a reader. **Great Northern Tavern**, **Kickapoo Tavern** and **Inxpot** provide snacks and après ski entertainment, while **Snake River Saloon** has pool and live music. **Parrot Eyes** at River Run serves tacos, margaritas and draft beer.

Sleep

All accommodation can be booked through central reservations, **t** +1 970 496 4386. Location is everything, so the closer to the slopes the higher the price. The lowest prices are in the forest at West Keystone, but only a few minutes away fom the slopes and nightlife by free shuttle bus.

River Run Condos are close to the gondola and the rates reflect this.

Inn at Keystone, **t** +1 970 496 4242, offers three-star lodging in a good position at affordable prices.

Keystone Lodge, **t** +1 970 496 2316, has smart guest rooms and loft suites.

Ski Tip Lodge, **t** +1 877 625 1540, *www.skitiplodge.com*, is an original and charming stagecoach inn. It offers B&B with a separate restaurant, and is also a bus ride from the resort.

Killington, Vermont

***BEST FOR**

Beginners, intermediates, long season

ESSENTIALS

Altitude: 1,165ft (354m)–4,241ft (1293m)
Further information: t +1 802 422 1330, *www.killington.com*
Lifts in area: 31 (3 cableways, 22 chairs, 6 drags) serving 87 miles of trails
Lift pass: adult $351–390, youth 13–18yrs $275–312, child 6–12yrs $238–264, all for six out of seven days
Access: Burlington airport 2hrs, Boston airport 3hrs

Profile

Chilly East Coast resort with phenomenal snowmaking capability and recommended ski school. Good accommodation, but the resort lacks a village centre

Resort

Killington is usually the first resort in the US, to open each November and the last to close in May or June. The reason for this has nothing to do with nature's bounty, but with the most sophisticated snowmaking system on the planet. The resort claims 250 inches of natural snow each winter but this doesn't always fall to order. Instead, cannons mounted on 'giraffe' poles can blanket 1,182 acres with sufficient artificial cover to open terrain on all seven of its peaklets without a flake of the real thing. However, the resort does usually attract its fair share of the real thing – last winter six feet of snow fell in April alone.

Arriving by car on a blue-sky day, you may notice with gloom that the only clouds in the sky hang over your destination. But that's no cloud – just a prescribed mix of crystallized air-and-water falling from hundreds of snow cannon. Not only the pistes but the surrounding forest is laden with man-made snow that is manufactured in a dozen different qualities from adhesive base layers to fluffy finishes.

Killington's main shortcoming is that it lacks a heart. 'Everything was spread out with no central focal point and very windy, which made the wind chill a big issue both day and night,' said a reader. Hotels, bars, and restaurants sprawl along the five-mile approach road from the highway. However, plans for a new Killington Village have been revived, and a number of new homes and shops are now being built. Reporters warn that it can be bitterly cold here in mid-winter ('I recommend taking good thermals and make the most of layers to keep warm'). The resort shares a lift pass with the neighbouring attractive little resort of Pico. Despite years of promises, a mountain link between the two has yet to be established.

Mountain

Killington claims to have skiing on seven mountains, but this is creative topography. The reality is one – 4,241ft Killington Peak – which has six shoulders. Together they form a naturally shaped ski area that extends for miles across a heavily wooded mountainside with a number of isolated condo-clad base areas. Snowshed, at the top of the road from the highway, is the main one with a clutch of high-speed chairs providing mountain access.

The much lower base of Skyship is served by a two-stage heated gondola that brings you up to Skye Peak 450ft

Killington VERMONT

killington peak
Elev. 4241

skye peak
Elev. 3800

snowdon mountain
Elev. 3592

ramshead mountain

bear mountain

sunrise mountain

K-1 lodge

snowshed

ramshead

bear mountain

skyeship

skye peak

SUNRISE VILLAGE CONDOS

BEAR PAW RESTAURANT

SNOWSHED POND

KILLINGTON GRAND RESORT HOTEL

MOUNTAIN GREEN CONDOS

KILLINGTON GOLF COURSE

WHIFFLETREE CONDOS

JAMES NIEHUES

below the top of the ski area. Killington suits all standards of skier and rider but the emphasis is on quantity rather than variety – so many of the gladed runs have the same pitch that it is often hard to differentiate between them. The most demanding runs are to be found on the front face of Killington Peak, reached by the K1 Express gondola and on lower Bear Mountain. Killington is popular with snowboarders and has three terrain parks with a super-pipe and a snowcross course. 'Good points were uncrowded slopes, very little waiting time at the lifts,' said a reporter.

Learn

The **Perfect Turn Ski School, t** +1 802 422 1234, uses the graduated length teaching method and has a good reputation for imparting the basics.

Children

Friendly Penguin Day Care, t +1 802 422 6222, is for kids aged six weeks to 23 months at the **Ramshead Family Center** and for up to six years at the **Grand Hotel**. Children as young as two years can join **First Tracks** for lessons, and **SnowZone** is ski or ride tuition for 13 to 18 years, **t** +1 800 923 9444, for all.

Lunch

Mountain Top Inn, t +1 802 483 6737, is traditional American. **Peak Restaurant, t** +1 802 422 6780, is a cafeteria on Killington Peak.

Dine

'Eating out can be a major task in itself as everything seems to be very spread out especially when it is cold,' advised a reporter. **Hemingway's, t** +1 802 422 3886, near the Skyship base, is good but expensive. Other eateries include the award-winning **Cascades, t** +1 802 422 3731, which has a casual atmosphere. **Casey's Caboose, t** +1 802 422 3539 is traditional American. **Kong Chow, t** +1 802 775 5244, and **Sushi Yoshi, t** +1 802 422 4241, offer Asian dishes. **Santa Fe Steakhouse, t** +1 802 422 2124, is recommended. The **Wobbly Barn, t** +1 802 422 6171, has some of the best steaks and seafood in the area ('excellent value for money'). **Ppeppers, t** +1 802 422 3177, in Killington Mall, is reminiscent of a 1940s diner and is a good place for breakfast.

Party

'Many of the bars have a free bus ride home so there is no need to have a designated driver or freeze on the walk home,' advised a reader, and 'a good range of evening entertainment to choose from,' said another. A good place to stop is **The Long Trail** pub at Snowshed Lodge. Happy hour in the bars starts at 3pm and finishes at 6pm. **Pickel Barrel** on Killington Road is the hub of the evening action, with big-name bands playing at weekends. **Mogul's Pub** ('the cheapest place to drink at $3 a pint') is also on Killington Road. The **Wobbly Barn** is where Killington's nightlife first began and still features world-class rock 'n' roll.

Sleep

Snowshed base is the best place to stay if you don't have a car.

Inn of the Six Mountains, t +1 800 228 4676, *www.sixmountains.com*, ('staff very friendly and helpful') is close to the nightlife and a short drive from the base lodges. A free taxi service is provided.

Killington Grand Resort Hotel, t +1 802 422 1330, *www.killington.com*, is a slopeside condominium-hotel.

Butternut on the Mountain, t +1 800 524 7654, *www.bestlodging.com*, is a no-smoking property with an indoor pool and games room.

Vermont Inn, t +1 888 636 8107, *www.vermontinn.com*, is an 1840s farmhouse 10 miles out of town, offering 18 individually decorated rooms, some with fireplaces or hot tubs.

Mammoth, California

Profile

Large but remote high-altitude ski area for all standards, with good sunshine and usually reliable snow cover. Particularly recommended for snowboarders

Resort

Skiing is no newcomer to the high Sierra Nevada mountain range that lies behind California's sunny coastline. Back in the 1850s, some 30 years before skiing began in Switzerland, immigrant Scandinavian miners were using Lapp hunting skis as winter transport and for weekend recreation. As winter storms sweep in from the Pacific Ocean they normally attract some 400 inches of snow each winter, resulting in a season that lasts from November until May or June. Last winter had superb cover once again in the wake of an unusually poor season in 2006–7.

Mammoth, named after the Mammoth Mining Company, which staked claim to the mountain after the discovery of gold here in 1878, has some of the best and most weather-reliable skiing in California. When it is not snowing the sun shines for an average of 300 days each year. Mammoth it is, the largest single mountain ski and ride destination in North America.

The drawback is that it is situated a long way from anywhere. The local airstrip has been rebuilt, but plans for services from Chicago and Dallas have so far failed to materialize.

Outside the main US holiday dates the resort is quiet mid-week, although young Los Angelinos think nothing of driving up for the weekend and do so in large numbers. Mammoth ski resort is situated just above the town of Mammoth Lakes and has been expanded at a cost of $830 million in recent years. The focal point is the three-year-old Village at Mammoth, which is the best place to begin and end your skiing day. The village is linked by gondola to the ski area.

A regular free shuttle bus runs to and from the ski-area bases at Main Lodge, Canyon Lodge and Juniper Springs, and there is a bus service to Mammoth Lakes. June Mountain, situated 20 miles away, shares the lift pass and has easy intermediate runs in a spectacular setting.

* BEST FOR

All levels of skier and rider, long season

ESSENTIALS

Altitude: 7,953ft, (2424m)–11,053ft (3369m)
Further information: t +1 760 934 2571, *www.mammothmountain.com*
Lifts in area: 28 (3 cableways, 23 chairs, 2 drags) serving 3,500 acres of terrain
Lift pass: area (Mammoth and June Mountain) adult $379, youth 13–18yrs $284, child 7–12yrs $190, all for six out of eight days
Access: Reno airport 3hrs, Los Angeles airport 5½hrs

MAMMOTH MOUNTAIN
CALIFORNIA
PANORAMA LOOKOUT
11,053'/3,369m
DAVE'S RUN
HUEVOS GRANDE
UPPER DRY CREEK
CLIMAX
UPPER ROAD RUNNER
HANGMAN'S HOLLOW
MJB'S
CORNICE BOWL
DROP OUT CHUTES
WIPE OUT CHUTES
SKY LINE
BEYOND THE EDGE
DRAGON'S BACK
RICOCHET
WAZOO
DRAGON'S TAIL
GOLDHILL
SOLITUDE
SANCTUARY
TRIANGLE
DRY CREEK
ROOSTER TAIL
EAST BOWL
CHRISTMAS BOWL
CHINA BOWL
SLIVER
FACE OF FIVE
CENTER BOWL
ST. ANTON
SADDLE BOWL
HAIR JUMP
GREMLIN'S GULCH
SCOTTY'S
PARANOID FLATS
PHILIPPE'S
SANTIAGO BOWL
HEMLOCK RIDGE
HEMLOCK BOWL
OUTPOST 14
WHITE BARK BOWL
SLOT
QUICKSILVER
RELIEF
ONE CHANCE
SPOOK
AVALANCHE CHUTES
CHAIR 9
RICOCHET
GOLDHILL
QUICKSILVER
HOLIDAY
HAVEN'T THE FOGGIEST
BACK FOR MORE
SHAFT
GRIZZLY
SUNSHINE
REPEAT 22
CHAIR 25
MANZANITA
VIVA
FOLLOW ME
WATERFALL
CHAIR 5
PANORAMA GONDOLA
FACE LIFT EXPRESS - 3
WEST BOWL
WORLD CUP
CHAIR 23
ST. ANTON
CHAIR 12
WHITE BARK RIDGE
PUMPKIN
SLEEPY HOLLOW
JUNIPER
WATERTANK
CHRISTMAS TREE
CHICKADEE
SWELL
REDWING
REDTAIL
HULLY GULLY
LOWER GRIZZLY
DOWNHILL
SIDE SHOW
AVALANCHE
CROSSWALK
LOST IN THE WOODS
EASY RIDER
DRY CREEK
COYOTE
McCOY STATION
ST. MORITZ
WALL
GRAVY CHUTE
GLADES
BRISTLECONE
LOGGERPOLE
PONDEROSA
NEW CRITTERS
CRITTERS
SECRET SPOT
THE ACTS
ENCORE
DOWNHILL
ROUND ROBIN
CANYON EXPRESS
ROGER'S RIDGE
KNEE DEEP
POWDER BOWL
FAR WEST
FASCINATION
TERRY'S RUN
ALBE'S RUN
BLUE OX
EAGLE LODGE
LUPIN
BRIDGES
BLUEJAY
CLOVER LEAF
GINGERBREAD
SPRING CANYON
ROLLER COASTER
UNBOUND SOUTH
X-COURSE
LOWER DRY CREEK
EASY RIDER
OLD COMEBACK TRAIL
ST. MORITZ
MAMBO
UNBOUND MAIN
FOREST TRAIL
BROADWAY
RALPHIES
BROADWAY EXPRESS - 1
CHAIR 26
ST. ANTON
DISCO PARK
COMIN' THRU
LOWER ROAD RUNNER
CANYON LODGE
SCHOOLYARD
FAMILY FUN PARK
WAY HOME
ROUND ABOUT
LITTLE BIRD
SCHOOL YARD
HANSEL
GRETEL
CHAIR 7
WALL STREET
BIG BIRD
LOST IN THE WOODS
DROP 18
STUMP ALLEY
STUMP ALLEY EXPRESS - 2
PATROLMEN'S
OVER EASY
JILL'S RUN
ST. MORITZ
FOREST TRAIL
PANORAMA GONDOLA
SESAME STREET
SESAME STREET WEST
GUS' PASTURE
MAIN LODGE
MAMBO
PHANTOM'S ESCAPE
MAMBO
MOUNTAIN CENTER
THE MILL CAFE

Mountain

The Village Gondola takes you up to Canyon Lodge, with access to some easy beginner and intermediate terrain as well as testing double-diamonds such as Grizzly, Viva, and Avalanche Chutes. However, the most challenging slopes are reached by two-stage gondola from Main Lodge that brings you up to Panorama Lookout at 11,053ft. From here and from Chair 23 you can traverse and drop into some phenomenal chutes and bowls such as Hangman's Hollow, Cornice Bowl, and Beyond the Edge. The lower half of the mountain has plenty of cruising terrain and some good novice slopes, but overall Mammoth is a mountain that will please good skiers and riders in search of testing gradients and fresh challenges. Recent improvements include a new high-speed six-pack, Cloud Nine Express. The new $6.5 million lift takes skiers from the Eagle Lodge side of the mountain up to a point near Dragon's Back in just over six minutes.

Snowboarders are particularly at home in Mammoth and the Unbound terrain parks are considered among the best in North America. Mammoth is the only area in the world to have three sizes of half-pipe: mini, super and super-duper. JM2 at June Mountain has spines, pipes and rails. To further enhance Mammoth's focus on freestyle development, the Wonderland Park at Canyon Lodge has undergone a $250,000 renovation.

Learn

Mammoth Ski and Snowboard School, **t** +1 760 934 2571, offers courses including Park and Pipe, Women Only and Mogul Camps.

Children

Small World Child Care, **t** +1 760 9340646, looks after babies and children from newborn to eight years with ski or snowboard lessons for those aged three years and older.

Lunch

Choices include the **Mill Café**, **t** +1 760 934 2571, **Mountainside Grill**, **t** +1 760 934 0601, in the Mammoth Mountain Inn, and **The Yodler Restaurant and Pub**, **t** +1 760 934 2571 x 2234. In the Village at Mammoth try **Hennessey's**, **t** +1 760 934 8444, and **Lakanuki Café**, **t** +1 760 934 7447 – the latter is a hip Hawaiian tiki bar.

Dine

Skadi, **t** +1 760 934 3902, and **Nevado's**, **t** +1 760 934 4466, offer gourmet fare. **Ocean Harvest**, **t** +1 760 934 8539, specializes in seafood. **Matsu**, **t** + 1 760 934 8277, offers an eclectic Far Eastern menu, including Thai and Chinese specialities. **Chart House**, **t** +1 760 934 4526, and **The Mogul**, **t** +1 760 934 3039, have fine steaks. **Alpenrose**, **t** +1 760 934 3077, offers cheese fondue. Other dining options in the Village include **Hennessey's**, **t** +1 760 934 8444, and **Pita Pit**, **t** +1 760 924 7482. **Restaurant LuLu**, **t** +1 760 924 8781, features seasonal Provençal cuisine. **Parallax Snowcat Dinners**, **t** +1 760 934 2571, serves sophisticated cuisine and is reached by snowcat.

Party

The Auld Dubliner is a traditional-style Irish pub with the addition of 50 TVs lining the walls. **Lakanuki** ('cheap place to eat and drink') is a tiki bar where you can try hula-dancing in your ski boots while sipping tropical drinks. **Unbound** is a cool place to buy a new snowboard or hang out after a day in the terrain park. **Canyon Lodge** regularly has live bands. The **Clocktower** in Alpenhof Lodge and **Whiskey Creek** are popular meeting places in town.

Sleep

All accommodation can be reserved on **t** +1 760 9340745.

Luxury/Moderate:

The Village Lodging, are condos that include Lincoln House, White Mountain Lodge, and Grand Sierra Lodge.

Mammoth Mountain Inn, t +1 760 934 2581, *www.mammothmountain.com*, is right at the base of the slopes.

Austria Hof Lodge, t +1 760 934 2764, *www.austriahof.com*, at the ski area base is good value, with some units containing fireplaces and hot tubs.

Juniper Springs Resort has upscale condos and town houses close to town.

Mammoth Lakes:

Alpenhof Lodge, t +1 760 934 6330, *www.alpenhof-lodge.com*, is within easy access of the skiing and the town.

Shilo Inn Suites, t +1 760 934 4500, *www.shiloinns.com*, are conveniently located on Main Street.

June Mountain:

Double Eagle Resort & Spa, t +1 760 648 7004, *www.double-eagle-resort.com*, has a full-service spa, pool and health club.

Park City, Utah

Profile

Convenient town for airport access with a wide choice of nearby resorts, attractive town with good restaurants and shopping

Resort

Park City is confusing until you understand the geography. This quaint former silver-mining town serves three side-by-side but still separate ski resorts: Park City Mountain Resort (on the edge of town), Deer Valley, and The Canyons.

The three ski areas sprawl across a five-mile stretch of mountainside and could be linked by the addition of just one lift, but rivalry has so far prevented this. A joint lift pass for foreign visitors is now sold at a fixed rate throughout the season – but you can only buy it through a tour operator before you leave home.

Historic Main Street climbs steeply through the centre of town and is lined with carefully restored Victorian buildings

*BEST FOR

All levels of skier and rider, excellent snow record, ski gourmets

ESSENTIALS

Altitude: 6,900ft (2104m)–10,000ft (3049m)

Further information: **t** +1 435 649 8111, *www.parkcitymountain.com*

Lifts in area: 15 (15 chairs) serving 3,300 acres of terrain

Lift pass: Utah Three Resort Pass (Park City Mountain Resort, Deer Valley, The Canyons) adult $300–438, child 4–12yrs $180–264, both for six out of seven days

Access: Salt Lake City airport 40mins

housing art galleries, shops and boutiques. It has a wider choice of restaurants than almost any other American ski town – and plenty of entertainment.

Back in 2002, the Mormon fathers of Salt Lake City believed that their hugely successful Winter Olympics would pave the way for a ski tourist boom to Utah's dozen main resorts, all within easy reach of the state capital – but it never quite happened.

Its remoteness – no direct flights to Europe – and largely unfounded concern over Utah's archaic alcohol licensing laws – have perhaps contributed to the fact that foreign winter tourism has not significantly increased.

But those British who venture no further than Vail and Breckenridge in Colorado miss out on some of the best skiing in the United States – with virtually guaranteed good snow-cover throughout the winter.

Park City Mountain Resort at the foot of the pistes is a moderately well-designed complex on three levels, with accommodation, shops and cafés set around a skating-rink and a car park.

'Nice (short) runs through the trees, good grooming, free bus service around the resorts was excellent and coped well with crowds, and a friendly welcome everywhere,' was how one reader summed it up.

Mountain

Main mountain access is by two detachable six-person chairs, which take 12 minutes to reach the Summit House Restaurant. Alternatively, you can ride a triple-chair from the top end of town. It's a far automated cry from the early 1960s when the first skiers travelled up on an underground mine train before being brought to the surface on a hoist lift. The Crescent high-speed quad has replaced the old Ski Team lift.

The skiing is much more varied and challenging than is indicated by the lift map. The lower half of the mountain has plenty of easy intermediate terrain, but much of it is given over to steepish gladed blacks. The top half of the mountain served by McConkey's Six-pack and the Jupiter lift is a much more serious proposition with an abundance of double-diamond chutes and bowls, and still more off-piste opportunities for those prepared to hike along Pinecone Ridge.

Anyone spending a week or more here – Park City is a sensible accommodation base – is advised to not only explore Deer Valley and The Canyons but also Snowbird and Alta, which are a 45-minute drive away.

Learn

Park City Ski & Snowboard School, **t** +1 435 649 5496, has a justifed reputation for some of the best cutting-edge technical instruction in the USA, as befits the town that is official home of the US ski team. Strong skiers and riders should try the Mountain Experience programme for exploring Jupiter Peak. Guided off-piste can be arranged through **Park City Powder Cats**, **t** +1 435 649 6596, **Ski Utah Interconnect Tour**, **t** +1 801 534 1907, and **Wasatch Powderbird Guides Heli-skiing**, **t** +1 801 742 2800.

Children

Park City Mountain Resort has no childcare facilities, but the town has three non-ski kindergartens: **Annie's Nannies**, **t** +1 435 615 1935, **Creative Beginnings**, **t** +1 435 645 7315, and **Guardian Angel**, **t** +1 435 783 2662. The ski school provides lessons from three years.

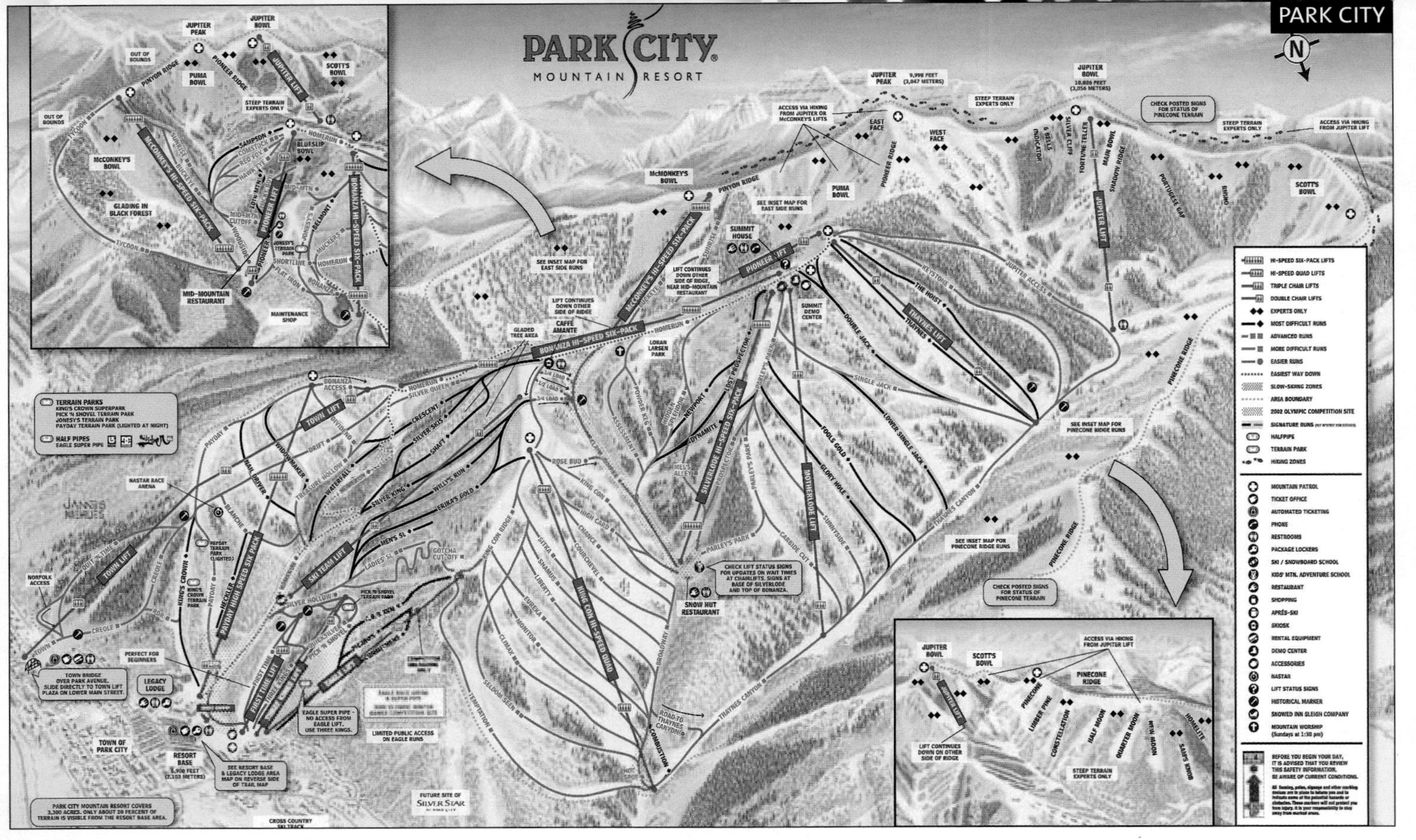
PARK CITY
MOUNTAIN RESORT
JUPITER PEAK
9,998 FEET (3,047 METERS)
JUPITER BOWL
10,026 FEET (3,056 METERS)
CHECK POSTED SIGNS FOR STATUS OF PINECONE TERRAIN
STEEP TERRAIN EXPERTS ONLY
ACCESS VIA HIKING FROM JUPITER LIFT
ACCESS VIA HIKING FROM JUPITER OR McCONKEY'S LIFTS
EAST FACE
WEST FACE
PIONEER RIDGE
INDICATOR
6 BELLS
SILVER CLIFF
FORTUNE TELLER
MAIN BOWL
SHADOW RIDGE
PORTUGESE GAP
RHINO
SCOTT'S BOWL
McMONKEY'S BOWL
PINYON RIDGE
PUMA BOWL
SEE INSET MAP FOR EAST SIDE RUNS
SUMMIT HOUSE
PIONEER LIFT
LIFT CONTINUES DOWN OTHER SIDE OF RIDGE, NEAR MID-MOUNTAIN RESTAURANT
McCONKEY'S HI-SPEED SIX-PACK
SUNRISE
BUCKEYE
HOMERUN
BONANZA HI-SPEED SIX-PACK
CAFFÉ AMANTE
GLADED TREE AREA
LORAN LARSEN PARK
SUMMIT DEMO CENTER
KEYSTONE
JUPITER ACCESS
JUPITER LIFT
THE HOIST
THAYNES LIFT
THAYNES
DOUBLE JACK
SINGLE JACK
LOWER SINGLE JACK
FOOLS GOLD
GLORY HOLE
SUNNYSIDE
MOTHERLODE LIFT
CARBIDE CUT
PARLEY'S PARK
SILVERLODE HI-SPEED SIX-PACK
LOST PROSPECTOR
PROSPECTOR
NEWPORT
HIDDEN SPLENDOR
DYNAMITE
MEL'S ALLEY
POWDER KEG
ASSESSMENT
SEE INSET MAP FOR PINECONE RIDGE RUNS
PINECONE RIDGE
THAYNES CANYON
CHECK LIFT STATUS SIGNS FOR UPDATES ON WAIT TIMES AT CHAIRLIFTS. SIGNS AT BASE OF SILVERLODE AND TOP OF BONANZA.
SNOW HUT RESTAURANT
ROSE BUD
KING CON
HIGH CARD
CHANCE
COURCHEVEL
SITKA
SHAMUS
LIBERTY
EUREKA
MONITOR
CLIMAX
SELDOM SEEN
TEMPTATION
KING CON RIDGE
KING CON HI-SPEED QUAD
BROADWAY
ROAD TO THAYNES CANYON
COMBUSTION
HOT SPOT
1/4 LOAD
1/2 LOAD
3/4 LOAD
BONANZA ACCESS
SILVER QUEEN
CRESCENT
SILVER SKIS
SHAFT
WILLY'S RUN
ERIKA'S GOLD
SILVER KING
MEN'S SL
LADIES' SL
GOTCHA CUT-OFF
SKI TEAM LIFT
TOWN LIFT
DIVIDEND
DRIFT
WIDOWMAKER
TREASURE HOLLOW
WATERFALL
NAIL DRIVER
PAYDAY
HECKLER
PAYDAY HIGH SPEED SIX PACK
PAYDAY TERRAIN PARK (LIGHTED)
KING'S CROWN
KING'S CROWN TERRAIN PARK
BLANCHE
NASTAR RACE ARENA
CREOLE
QUIT 'N TIME
NORFOLK ACCESS
TOWN
SILVER HOLLOW
PICK 'N SHOVEL TERRAIN PARK
PICK 'N SHOVEL
QUICKSILVER
FIRST TIME LIFT
FIRST TIME
THREE KINGS
PERFECT FOR BEGINNERS
LEGACY LODGE
EAGLE SUPER PIPE - NO ACCESS FROM EAGLE LIFT. USE THREE KINGS.
LIMITED PUBLIC ACCESS ON EAGLE RUNS
TOWN BRIDGE OVER PARK AVENUE. SLIDE DIRECTLY TO TOWN LIFT PLAZA ON LOWER MAIN STREET.
TOWN OF PARK CITY
RESORT BASE
6,900 FEET (2,103 METERS)
SEE RESORT BASE & LEGACY LODGE AREA MAP ON REVERSE SIDE OF TRAIL MAP
FUTURE SITE OF SILVER STAR
PARK CITY MOUNTAIN RESORT COVERS 3,300 ACRES. ONLY ABOUT 20 PERCENT OF TERRAIN IS VISIBLE FROM THE RESORT BASE AREA.
CROSS COUNTRY SKI TRACK
TERRAIN PARKS
KING'S CROWN SUPERPARK
PICK 'N SHOVEL TERRAIN PARK
JONESY'S TERRAIN PARK
PAYDAY TERRAIN PARK (LIGHTED AT NIGHT)
HALF PIPES
EAGLE SUPER PIPE
OUT OF BOUNDS
TYCOON
McCONKEY'S BOWL
GLADING IN BLACK FOREST
SAMPSON
COMSTOCK
RED FOX
HAWK EYE
10TH MTN
MID-MTN CUTOFF
MID-MTN
BLUESLIP BOWL
WOODSIDE
JONESY'S TERRAIN PARK
JONESY'S
BELMONT
MUCKERS
SHORTLINE
FLAT IRON
BONANZA
MID-MOUNTAIN RESTAURANT
MAINTENANCE SHOP
PINECONE RIDGE
PINECONE
LIMBER PINE
CONSTELLATION
HALF MOON
QUARTER MOON
NEW MOON
SAMS KNOB
HOMELITE
LIFT CONTINUES DOWN ON OTHER SIDE OF RIDGE
HI-SPEED SIX-PACK LIFTS
HI-SPEED QUAD LIFTS
TRIPLE CHAIR LIFTS
DOUBLE CHAIR LIFTS
EXPERTS ONLY
MOST DIFFICULT RUNS
ADVANCED RUNS
MORE DIFFICULT RUNS
EASIER RUNS
EASIEST WAY DOWN
SLOW-SKIING ZONES
AREA BOUNDARY
2002 OLYMPIC COMPETITION SITE
SIGNATURE RUNS
HALFPIPE
TERRAIN PARK
HIKING ZONES
MOUNTAIN PATROL
TICKET OFFICE
AUTOMATED TICKETING
PHONE
RESTROOMS
PACKAGE LOCKERS
SKI / SNOWBOARD SCHOOL
KIDS' MTN. ADVENTURE SCHOOL
RESTAURANT
SHOPPING
APRÈS-SKI
SKIOSK
RENTAL EQUIPMENT
DEMO CENTER
ACCESSORIES
NASTAR
LIFT STATUS SIGNS
HISTORICAL MARKER
SNOWED INN SLEIGH COMPANY
MOUNTAIN WORSHIP
(Sundays at 1:30 pm)
BEFORE YOU BEGIN YOUR DAY, IT IS ADVISED THAT YOU REVIEW THIS SAFETY INFORMATION. BE AWARE OF CURRENT CONDITIONS.

Lunch

Legends has grills and fresh fish. **Summit House** near the top of the Bonanza lift has pizzas, grills, and a large deck with views of Park City and beyond. **Mid-Mountain Lodge**, near the base of the Pioneer and McConkey lifts, is a modified version of an old miners' home, with pasta, pizza, and chilli. Further information on **t** +1 435 649 8111.

Dine

Chenez, t + 1 435 940 1909, is a French restaurant with an intimate ambience. Robert Redford's **Zoom, t** +1 435 649 9108, is an old favourite, with Californian cuisine. **Adolph's, t** + 1 649 7177, is Swiss American with an emphasis on veal dishes. **Blind Dog, t** +1 435 655 0800, has outstanding sushi. **Chimayo, t** +1 435 649 6222, serves southwestern cuisine. **Café Terigo, t** +1 435 645 9555, is contemporary American ('great West Coast mussels and Utah trout'). **Grappa Italian Restaurant, t** +1 435 645 0636, features traditional Tuscan dishes. **Claimjumper Steakhouse, t** +1 435 649 8051, is a carnivore's delight, and **Kampai Sushi, t** +1 435 649 0655, offers Japanese cuisine. **350 Main, t** +1 435 649 3140, has fresh seafood, while **The Riverhorse** on Main, **t** +1 435 649 3536, is hip American.

Party

This is the Mormon heartland, but contrary to popular belief it is far from 'dry'. Pocket guide to the drinking laws: restaurants willingly serve wine, but usually you have to ask to see the wine list – it won't be offered. Pubs sell beer, but the alcohol content is limited to 3.2 per cent. Bars operate as private clubs, but visitors can buy a two-week membership for a nominal fee which allows you to host up to seven guests. Hotel and airport lounges can serve drinks without a licence. Regulars can legally no longer sponsor strangers in return for a drink – but they do.

Try **Legends at The Resort** in the Legacy Lodge at the base area. **No Name Saloon** displays the local Park City Rugby Club memorabilia on its walls. **J.B. Mulligans Club and Pub** and **Wasatch Brew Pub Cantina** are popular, along with **Spur Club**. The **Star Bar** at Plan B features live bands.

Sleep

Luxury:

Hotel Park City, t +1 435 200 2000, *www.hotelparkcity.com*, is an all-suite hotel in the style of a grand national park lodge of the early 1900s, and a leading Small Hotel of the World.

Silver King, t +1 435 649 5500, *www.silverkinghotel.com*, is a smart condo-hotel one mile from Main Street.

Yarrow Resort Hotel, t +1 435 649 7000, *www.yarrowresort.com*, is a full-service hotel next to the Holiday Village Mall.

Moderate:

Angel House Inn, t +1 435 647 0338, *www.angelhouseinn.com*, has each of its nine rooms modelled on a different angel.

Lodge at Mountain Village, t +1 435 649 8111, *www.parkcitymountain.com*, is a full-service hotel at the base area.

Marriott's Summit Watch, t +1 435 647 4100, *www.marriott.com*, is conveniently located at the lower end of Main Street.

Park City Marriott, t +1 435 649 2900, *www.parkcitymarriott.com*, is situated one mile from the downtown area.

Radisson Inn, t +1 435 649 5000, *www.radisson.com*, has spacious rooms and mountain views.

Budget:

Best Western Landmark Inn, t +1 435 649 7300, *www.bwlandmarkinn.com*, is five miles out of town at Kimball Junction, but good value.

Holiday Inn Express Park City, t +1 435 658 1600, also at Kimball Junction, is another budget-priced option.

Washington School Inn Bed & Breakfast, t +1 435 649 3800, *www.washingtonschoolinn.com*, was a school until 1932, and one of the few survivors of the great fire of 1898. A dozen guest rooms and three suites are all named after former teachers. 'I slept in what used to be the dark, dreary, scary attic,' said a reader.

Snowbird and Alta, Utah

Profile

Two contrasting, though linked, resorts for accomplished skiers and riders that attract the best powder snow in the world. No snowboarding is permitted in Alta

Resort

It is hard to find two more contrastingly different resorts than Snowbird and adjoining Alta in Little Cottonwood Canyon, a 40-minute uphill drive from Salt Lake City. But, strangely, they admirably complement each other. Their alliance has a created a formidable European-style ski circuit with two villages separated by some of the most exciting and radical terrain in North America. The canyon – Brigham Young and his 143 Mormon pioneers came this way in 1847 from Nebraska to found their city beside the great salt lake – is home to Champagne Powder. These talcum-like flakes are freeze-dried in their passage above the desert from the Pacific Ocean; they land here throughout the winter in copious quantities.

This annual phenomenon persuaded Ted Johnson, who was working at the Alta Lodge at the time, to build Snowbird in the 1970s. He met Texan oilman and rancher, Dick Bass, at a party in Vail and persuaded him to finance the operation. Unfortunately as a role model they chose utilitarian concrete architecture. Cliff Lodge, with its 11-storey atrium, dominates the resort. Snowbird Center, departure point for the Aerial Tram, a dated but renovated cable car, is the official heart of the village. The open space is surrounded by shops on three levels and other nearby accommodation blocks. Snowbird is no beauty, but is extremely ski-convenient; under its maximum-tog duvet of snow it is by no means unappealing.

Little Alta, higher up the canyon, is an altogether different proposition, a handful of lodges providing simple but exclusive accommodation favoured by 'old money' Americans and new money wannabees.

✻ BEST FOR

Powderhounds, ski convenience, airport access

ESSENTIALS

Altitude: 7,740ft (2359m)–11,000ft (3352m)
Further information: **Alta t** +1 801 359 1078, *www.altaskiarea.com*; **Snowbird t** +1 801 742 2222, *www.snowbird.com*
Lifts in area: 26 (1 cableway, 18 chairs, 7 drags) serving 4,700 acres of terrain
Lift pass: Snowbird adult $318, child 7–12yrs $234, Alta adult $282, child under 12 $138, all for six days
Access: Salt Lake City airport 45mins

Both hark back to halcyon Hemingway-esque days when handsome couples in cable-knit sweaters and white polo-necks sat around the fireplace at the end of day drinking mulled wine, while wooden skis were stretched and leather lace-up boots dried in the boiler room below. Skiing started in Alta in the 1930s, and the first lodge was built in 1939.

The lifts all used to be fixed double-chairs that gave the formidable ski area an atmosphere reminiscent of St Anton in 1960. However, while retro-skiing has proved to be big business, ever-aloof Alta has been unable to ignore some of the refinements to the original invention of the wheel. Since its alliance to Snowbird after decades of bitter rivalry, a couple of detachable-quads – to the chagrin of Alta purists – have surreptitiously crept into the system.

'The locals are the most friendly and helpful you will ever meet. I highly recommend Alta for superb accommodation and fantastic skiing. People of any ability could holiday here for years and not get bored,' raved a reporter.

Mountain

The joint area is a world-class point of pilgrimage for anyone who is hooked on sliding down mountains and knows how to do it at a reasonably high level. Reports praise the lift system for its speed and good organization. The continued ban on snowboarding in Alta makes Little Cottonwood Canyon a more suitable destination for those who prefer two planks to one. The gradient of the double-diamonds and the off-piste in both resorts, backed by usually sensational snow-cover, has few rivals in North America. 'Snowbird has a European feel to it with the mountains being more sheer here than other US resorts,' commented a reader. There is a reasonable amount of lower intermediate terrain in both resorts, as well as good novice slopes. Snowbird has a super-pipe next to the Big Emma terrain park. The main terrain park is located by the Baby Thunder lift.

Main access from Snowbird is by cable car straight up to 11,000ft Hidden Peak. Importantly, there are two easy routes down from the top. Better skiers and riders will head for Upper Cirque or Silver Fox, as well as High Baldy Traverse and the steep descents of Thunder Bowl. Mineral Basin, 500 acres of prime alpine terrain, provides the gateway to Alta, reached through a manned frontier gate to deter snowboarders.

Last season the old Peruvian lift was replaced with a high-speed quad. The new top station is located below the steepest Chip's Run pitch. From here, a 600ft tunnel with a conveyor lift provides easy access for intermediates to Mineral Basin.

Main mountain access from Alta is by the Collins quad, gateway to an enormous range of intermediate and advanced runs back down the mountain and across to the Sugarloaf quad. A glance at the lift map shows a complete absence of double-black-diamond runs. Don't be deceived – it's just Alta's quirky way of doing things. They printed the first map a decade or two before such gradings were invented and see no reason for change. Some of the most demanding terrain is reached from the Supreme triple-chair, and the most challenging routes are not on the lift map – you need to ask the locals. Also try the Ski Utah Interconnect, a guided day tour from Deer Valley to Snowbird via Solitude, Brighton and Alta.

Learn

Snowbird Mountain School, **t** +1 801 933 2170, has a sound reputation and a full range of ski and snowboard courses. **Alf Engen Ski School**, **t** +1 801 359 1078, is named after America's greatest skier of the 1930s, who taught skiing here in 1945–46. Guiding is with the **Ski Utah Interconnect Tour**, **t** +1 801 534 1907, or **Wasatch Powderbird Guides Heli-skiing**, **t** +1 801 742 2800. **Alta Snowcat Skiing**, **t** +1 801 799 2271, offers guided skiing – and even boarding – in Grizzly Gulch.

Children

Camp Snowbird, **t** +1 801 933 2256, at Cliff Lodge, looks after children from six weeks to 12 years. **Mountain School**, **t** +1 801 933 2170, at Camp Snowbird, gives lessons from three years.

Alta's **Alf Engen Ski School**, **t** +1 801 359 1078, provides children's lessons. **Alta Lodge Kids' Program**, **t** +1 801 742 3500, is aimed at its four- to 10-year-old residents and provides transport to and from ski school, as well as après ski activities. **Alta Children's Center**, **t** +1 801 742 3042, offers daycare.

Lunch

The only eating places on the mountain at Snowbird are **Mid-Gad Restaurant**, **t** +1 801 933 2245, and **Creekside Café and Grill**, **t** +1 801 933 2477. Serious lunchers must return to the base where there is the choice of **The Rendezvous**, **t** +1 801 933 2222, **The Forklift**, and **The Atrium**, both **t** +1 801 933 2140.

On the slopes at Alta, the **Watson Shelter**, **t** +1 801 799 2296, at the Collins lift mid-station, offers grills and snacks. **Alf's Restaurant**, **t** +1 801 799 2295, serves lunch and snacks, while **Collins Grill**, **t** +1 801 799 2297, features French cuisine. **Albion Grill**, **t** +1 801 742 2500, is a cafeteria at Albion base area. **Alta Lodge**, **t** +1 801 742 3500, at Wildcat Base, serves breakfast, lunch and dinner.

Dine

Snowbird has 15 restaurants, including **The Aerie**, **t** +1 801 933 2160, at the top of Cliff Lodge, which serves continental cuisine. **El Chanate**, **t** +1 801 933 2025, specializes in Mexican cooking, while the **Wildflower Restaurant**, **t** +1 801 933 2230, at Iron Blosam Lodge features Mediterranean fare. **The Steak Pit**, **t** +1 801 933 2260, serves steak and seafood, but **The Lodge Bistro**, **t** +1 801 742 2300, has much the best cuisine in town.

In Alta, the **Shallow Shaft**, **t** +1 801 742 2177, is rated one of the top restaurants in the USA, but you need to book days in advance. In **Alta Lodge**, **t** +1 801 742 3500, wealthy guests from Boston and New York dine at communal tables. **Goldminer's Daughter**, **t** +1 801 742 2300, serves New Mexican fare at Alta's mountain base.

Party

At Snowbird, **Aerie Lounge & Sushi Bar**, **The Wildflower Lodge**, **Lodge Bistro Lounge** and **El Chanate Cantina** are the main meeting places. **The Tram Club** at Snowbird Center has billiards, video games, live music and 13 televisions. **The Aerie** has live jazz on Wednesdays and Saturdays.

In Alta, après ski entertainment is limited to the slopeside hot-tub or the screening of black and white ski films, followed by drinks around a roaring log fire. Guests at Alta Lodge swap tales in the **Sitzmark Club**.

Sleep

Snowbird:

Call **t** +1 801 742 2222, for all reservations.

Cliff Lodge is the smartest address, with a major spa, rooftop pool and what claims to be the world's largest collection of Oriental rugs. The Cliff Club in the west wing has 54 three-room suites furnished in Mission style.

Lodge at Snowbird, by the cable car, is the original lodge, now completely renovated, with outdoor pool and hot tub.

The Inn has simple studios, suites, and an outdoor pool.

Iron Blosam Lodge is geared towards families, with its own spa and pool.

Alta:

Alta Lodge, t +1 801 742 3500, is a lovely place that has been attracting visitors since 1939 and was renovated in 1990.

Alta Peruvian Lodge, t +1 801 742 3000, has a pool.

Alta's Rustler Lodge, t +1 801 742 2200, has a heated outdoor pool.

Goldminer's Daughter Lodge, t +1 800 453 4573, is rustic and unassuming.

Alta Chalets, t +1 866 754 2426, are seven ski in, ski out log homes and chalets ranging from four to eight bedrooms.

Squaw Valley, California

Profile

Scenic Lake Tahoe resort with good intermediate terrain as well as steep slopes. Also particularly good for snowboarding. For those with transport, the evening dining choices throughout the area are superb

*** BEST FOR**

Intermediates and advanced skiers, snowboarders

ESSENTIALS

Altitude: 6,200ft, (1890m)–9,050ft (2758m)
Further information: t +1 530 583 6985, *www.squaw.com*
Lifts in area: 32 (3 cableways, 25 chairs, 4 drags) serving 4,000 acres of terrain
Lift pass: Ski Lake Tahoe 7 Resort Pass (covers Alpine Meadows, Heavenly, Kirkwood, Northstar-at-Tahoe, Sierra-at-Tahoe, Squaw Valley, and Mount Rose) adult and child $324 for six days. Other lift pass options available
Access: Reno airport 1hr, San Francisco airport 4hrs

Resort

Squaw Valley, despite a virtual absence of lifts at the time, managed with a little help from Walt Disney to convince the Olympic Committee that it should host the 1960 Winter Olympics, the first to be televised. Jean Vuarnet of France won gold in the downhill and went on to re-invent sunglasses. Squaw Valley has never looked back. The resort sits in natural splendour on the north shore of beautiful Lake Tahoe, which is home to 15 alpine resorts and eight cross-country centres with over 100 lifts in 17,520 acres of skiable terrain. Squaw has the best of it. Its modern Intrawest-built village provides the base area it previously lacked, while no one has ever questioned the quality of the skiing.

You need a car to explore the other Lake Tahoe resorts included in the various lift pass choices. You can buy a local Squaw Valley pass, but we strongly advise the purchase of either the Lake Tahoe 7 pass (Alpine Meadows, Heavenly, Kirkwood, Northstar-at-Tahoe, Sierra-at-Tahoe, Squaw Valley and Mount Rose) or the Lake Tahoe North 7 (Squaw Valley, Homewood, Alpine Meadows, Diamond Peak, North Star-at-Tahoe, Sugar Bowl and Mount Rose). Both regional passes are the same price for adults and children and it may be financially advantageous to buy local one-day resort passes for children and teens under 19 years of age.

Tahoe City, a 10-minute drive away, is a small town providing an alternative bed base with considerable atmosphere and some appealing restaurants.

Mountain

'A top ski resort,' said a reporter, 'plenty of variety in the runs, which are well linked, well prepared and fairly quiet.' No fewer than seven lifts, including the Gold Coast Funitel gondola, give mountain access from the village, while the Squaw Valley Creek triple-chair provides an eighth way into the system. Val d'Isère in the French Alps is the only other ski destination with comparable diversity.

The lifts lead up to six peaks: Granite Chief, Snow King, KT22, Squaw Peak, Emigrant and Broken Arrow. The area is divided into three sectors, with the 32 lifts, rather than the runs, colour-graded. All the main lifts on KT22, Squaw Peak and Granite Chief are black-diamond, while those on Snow King and Emigrant are blue. Intermediates will find a huge amount of skiing – the highlight is a three-mile trail from the High Camp area to the mountain base. However, Squaw was birthplace of the American extreme skiing movement and offers a comprehensive menu of steep chutes. The most radical terrain is found off KT22, Headwall, Cornice II and Granite Chief chairlifts.

Three terrain parks and three half-pipes, as well as exciting freeride terrain, make this a serious destination for snowboarders. All are accessed by the gondola or cable car. Start in Belmont, move on to Central Park (floodlit at night), and then into the jumps and rails of Mainline Park.

Learn

Squaw Valley Ski and Snowboard School, t +1 530 581 7263, has a sound reputation. 'The turn-up-and-pay ski lessons were great value,' said a reporter, 'never more than three people in the group and the instructors were excellent'.

Children

Squaw Kids Children's Center, t +1 530 581 7166, takes children from three to 12 years. **Squaw Kids Ski & Snowboard School, t** +1 530 581 7263, gives lessons from four years.

Lunch

The resort has dozens of eateries and bars both on the mountain and in the base village. These include **Gold Coast, t** +1 530 583 6985, at the top of the Funitel in Squaw Valley, which features a barbecue, restaurants and bars on three levels. Newest addition is the **Crossroads Café**, which serves a wide selection of foods, including wraps, salads and sandwiches. **High Camp, t** +1 530 583 2555, boasts six different restaurants and bars, and the main dining room is open at night.

Dine

Dining in the area offers a huge choice of venues. Restaurants in the new village include **PlumpJack Café, t** +1 530 583 5850, which is an 'American bistro', and **Fireside Pizza Co, t** +1 530 584 6150, offering gourmet pizzas 'with a sourdough crust and farm-fresh toppings'. **High Sierra Grill, t** +1 530 584 6100, has steaks and salads, and **Mamasake Sushi Bar, t** +1 530 584 0110, is a real treat. **Zenbu Tapas Lounge, t** +1 530 583 9900, upstairs in the Olympic House, has late-night 'Asian Tapas' and dancing. **Glissandi, t** +1 530 583 6300, in the Resort at Squaw Creek, is a more expensive Italian.

Ten minutes' drive away in Truckee are **Java Sushi**, **t** +1 530 582 1144, **China Garden** Restaurant, **t** +1 530 587 7625, and **Blue Agave Mexican Restaurant**, **t** +1 530 583 8113. **Cottonwood**, **t** +1 530 587 571, has seafood and live jazz.

In Tahoe City, **Wolfdale's**, **t** +1 530 583 5700, advertises its 'Flavors of the West & Far East'. **Yama Sushi**, **t** +1 530 583 9262, is affordable and fun. **Bacchi's Inn**, **t** +1 530 583 3324, is Italian, **Christy Hill**, **t** +1 530 583 8551, overlooking the lake, serves Californian cuisine with a French influence. **Sunnyside**, **t** +1 530 583 7200, serves seafood. **Izzy's Burger Spa**, **t** +1 530 583 4111, has great views, and **Rosie's Café**, **t** +1 530 583 8504, is friendly.

Party

Bar One in the Olympic House features live music, pool and karaoke. Also in Olympic House is **Zenabu Tapas Lounge** is for late-night dining and dancing. Other post-slope options include **Le Chamois** at Village Green, and **Red Dog Bar & Grill** at Far East Center. In the Village are **PlumpJack Café** which has live music twice a week, and **Auld Dubliner pub** that was built in Ireland, dismantled, shipped over and reassembled. **High Camp** is open until 9pm with a **Snowtubing Arena and Olympic Ice Pavilion** in winter, and **Swimming Lagoon & Spa** in the spring.

Sleep

******Resort at Squaw Creek**, **t** +1 530 583 6300, *www.squawcreek.com*, is a luxury ski in, ski out complex near the base with spa, pool, ice rink, and five in-house restaurants.

******Squaw Valley Lodge**, **t** +1 530 583 5500, *www.squawvalleylodge.com*, is ski in, ski out and contains condos with kitchens and hot tubs.

******The Village at Squaw Valley**, **t** +1 530 584 1000, contains smart and well-equipped condos in the new base village. Shared facilities include a movie room, games room and billiards lounge.

PlumpJack Squaw Valley Inn, **t** +1 800 323 7666, dates back to 1959 and was upgraded in 1995 with attractively minimalist decoration and a renowned restaurant.

Olympic Village Inn, **t** +1 530 583 1576, served as the home to many of the 1960 Olympic athletes but was remodelled in 1982. It contains one-bedroom suites with kitchenettes and a shuttle-bus to the ski base.

Tahoe City and Truckee provide alternative bed bases for visiting other resorts in the area.

Steamboat, Colorado

Profile

A Wild West town set apart from the ski area base. The resort offers a good choice of restaurants. The ski area suits families and beginners, and is particularly good for snowboarders

Resort

The unlikely name of Steamboat Springs originated when three French fur trappers exploring the River Yampa at the foot of Rabbit Ears Pass in 1865 thought they heard the chugging sound of a paddle-steamer – only to discover it was

MT. WERNER
10,568'

MORNINGSIDE PARK
(see inset)

STORM PEAK
10,372'

SUNSHINE PEAK
10,384'

FRYING PAN
COWBOY COFFEE
JUMP START
HOT CAKES

FOUR POINTS HUT
9,716'

RENDEZVOUS SADDLE
RAGNAR'S FINE DINING
9,325'

THUNDERHEAD
Hazie's FINE DINING
WESTERN BBQ
9,080'

BEAR RIVER BAR & GRILL
GONDOLA BASE
GONDOLA SQUARE
INFORMATION CENTER
BASE ELEVATION: 6,900'
VERTICAL DROP: 3,668'

MAVERICKS
North America's Longest Superpipe
FREESTYLE
TERRAIN PARK

EAST FACE
NO NAMES
NORTH ST. PATS
CHRISTMAS TREE BOWL
EAST
WEST
CHUTE 3
CHUTE 2
CHUTE 1
OVER EASY
CROWTRACK
THE RIDGE
LAST CHANCE
FIRST CHANCE
BIG MEADOW
BUDDY'S RUN
CALF ROPER
MEADOW LANE
FLYING Z
FOOLS GOLD
CABIN FEVER
NASH JUNCTION
CINCH
ROYAL FLUSH
PERRY PARK
LONGHORN
MIDDLE RIB
FETCHER GLADE
DIAMOND HITCH
AMBUSH
PONY EXPRESS LIFTLINE
CHUCKWAGON
WJW
WAPITI
CHAPS
OUTLAW
CANTER
LARIAT
PONY EXPRESS
DROP OUT
VORTEX
TORNADO LANE
STORM PEAK EXPRESS
CYCLONE
TYPHOON
TRIANGLE 3
STORM PEAK NORTH
STORM PEAK SOUTH
TORNADO
FOUR POINTS
FOUR POINTS LIFTLINE
NELSON'S RUN
TWISTER
HURRICANE
CHISOLM TRAIL
RAINBOW
DUSK
SUNSET
EGO
BURGESS CREEK
SURPRISE
SO WHAT
WHY NOT
BO SKI WAY
TRAVERSE
HIGHLINE
KUIS CRUISE
SUNDOWN LIFTLINE
SHADOWS
CLOSET
DAWN
TOMAHAWK
TOMAHAWK CUT-OFF
KIT
TWILIGHT
THREE O'CLOCK
TWO O'CLOCK
ONE O'CLOCK
HIGH NOON
SUNSHINE LIFTLINE
FLINTLOCK
CUB
QUICKDRAW
PUP
BUCKSHOT
RAMROD
BABY POWDER
SUNSHINE
FAWN
SPIKE
SOUTH PEAK
DUSTER
DAYBREAK
TOWER HIGH NOON
ROLEX
WEST SIDE
BROADWAY
PRIEST CREEK
SUNDOWN EXPRESS
LIGHTS OUT
MOONLIGHT
SUNNYSIDE
VELVET
SKYLINE
WHITE OUT
B.C. LIFTLINE
NORTHER
TOWER
RUDI'S RUN
BLIZZARD
LIGHTNING
FLATOUT
FEATHER
ELKHEAD
VAGABOND
WHY NOT
BETWIXT
MOTHER NATURE
THUNDERHEAD EXPRESS
CONCENTRATION
EAGLES NEST
OOPS
TED'S RIDGE
VERTIGO
HEAVENLY DAZE
VALLEY VIEW
LOWER CONCENTRATION
ROUGH RIDER
NASTAR RACE AREA
MAVERICKS SUPERPIPE
BASHOR
TERRAIN PARK
SEE YA
SEE ME
VOO DOO
VOGUE
YOO HOO
LOWER VALLEY VIEW
GONDOLA
CHRISTIE III
CHRISTIE II
HEADWALL NORTH
HEADWALL
TENDERFOOT
STEAMBOAT
SPRINGER
SHORTCUT
GIGGLE GULCH
RIGHT-O-WAY
SKI TIME SQUARE
STEAMBOAT GRAND

*** BEST FOR**
Resort ambience, choice of restaurants

ESSENTIALS
Altitude: 6,900ft (2103m)–10,568ft (3221m)
Further information: **t** +1 970 879 6111, *www.steamboat.com*
Lifts in area: 16 (1 cableway, 15 chairs) serving 2,965 acres of terrain
Lift pass: Rocky Mountain International ticket (Copper Mountain, Steamboat and Winter Park) adult $372, youth 13–17yrs $342, child 6–12yrs $276, all for six days
Access: Steamboat/ Hayden Airport 30mins, Denver airport 3hrs

actually the sound of the bubbling local mineral springs.

A lot of water has passed under the bridge since then, and Steamboat has built a reputation as a Wild West ski town famous for its annual Cowboy Downhill, when the skills of skiing and ranching come together. After negotiating a slalom course, competitors must first lasso a mountain host and then saddle a horse, before crossing the finishing line on skis. It produces a dramatic, and often hilarious, spectacle.

The history of skiing here goes back to 1914, when a bricklayer called Carl Howelsen organized a ski carnival and won every event. He possibly failed to mention that he had already won 14 trophies for ski jumping in his native Norway. Steamboat is an area that suits all standards of skier but is particularly suited to intermediates. Steamboat resort lies three miles from the town of Steamboat Springs and both offer a choice of hotels and condos. The ski area was recently sold to Intrawest, the giant international resort developer and we are already beginning to see some major changes. Last winter over $16 million was spent on mountain improvements.

Mountain

Main mountain access is by a gondola from the base area, This is a large resort with skiing on six linked peaks in the Routt National Forest: Mounts Werner, Sunshine, Storm, Thunderhead and Christie Peaks, and Pioneer Ridge. It all adds up to 142 trails with a vertical drop of 3,688ft (1124m).

As part of the $16 million spend, the Christie Peak Express six-pack chair replaces three lifts in the base area. This cuts the ride time to the summit of Christie Peak from 15 minutes to under five and offsets the electricity used with alternative energy.

In a good winter, the off-piste opportunities at Steamboat are exceptional. The modern lift system is backed up by extensive snowmaking. The resort is popular with riders and the 66ft Mavericks super-pipe is the longest in North America.

Learn

Steamboat Ski and Snowboard School, **t** +1 970 871 5375, has a good reputation as befits a school that claims to have produced more Olympians than any other in the world. It incorporates the Billy Kid Performance Center, founded by the resort's most famous champion, which provides specialized coaching to get skiers off the 'intermediate plateau'. **Steamboat Powdercats**, **t** +1 970 871 4260, offers 10,000 acres of cat-skiing terrain only 20 minutes from the town on Buffalo Pass.

Children

The **Kids Vacation Center**, **t** +1 970 871 5375, accepts non-skiing children from six months and offers a monitoring service called Steamboat Mountain Watch. The centre arranges ski lessons for older children. 'I can't recommend the ski school highly enough. They were very friendly and made the lessons so much fun,' said a reader.

Lunch

The most sophisticated lunch option is **Hazie's, t** +1 970 871 5150, at the top of the gondola, which serves New American cuisine. **Ragnar's, t** +1 970 871 5191, at **Rendezvous Saddle**, specializes in seafood, game and beef. Try also **Gondola Pub & Grill, t** +1 970 879 4448, at Gondola Square.

Dine

At Steamboat Resort, the **Butcher Shop, t** +1 970 879 2484, has been feeding carnivores for 34 years. The **Cabin, t** +1 970 871 5550, features contemporary Colorado cuisine. **La Montana, t** +1 970 879 5800, serves Tex-Mex.

At Steamboat Springs, **Antares, t** +1 970 879 9939, **Giovanni's, t** +1 970 879 4141, and the **Steamboat Yacht Club, t** +1 970 879 4774, are all recommended. **Yama Chan's, t** +1 970 879 8862 is a great sushi restaurant. The **Cottonwood Grill, t** +1 970 879 2229, has tasty Pacific Rim cuisine.

Party

Skiers gather at the **Slopeside Grill** and **The Tugboat** in Times Square, as well as at **Mahogany Ridge** in downtown Steamboat Springs. Other popular bars include **Chaps** in the Grand Resort Hotel, **Bear River Bar & Grill, Dos Amigos** and **Levelz**.

Sleep

Steamboat Base Area:

Luxury:

Bear Claw, t +1 970 879 6100, is a smart condo complex.

Sheraton Steamboat, t +1 970 879 2220, *www.sheraton.com/steamboat*, has Western décor.

Steamboat Grand Resort & Conference Center, t +1 970 871 5500, *www.steamboatgrand.com*, has a spa and fitness centre, a themed restaurant, and 327 rooms.

Torian Plum, t +1 970 879 8811, offers comfortable suites at the base area.

Budget:

Fairfield Inn, t +1 970 870 9000, has reasonably priced rooms close to the skiing.

Steamboat Springs:

Moderate/Budget:

Alpiner Lodge, t +1 970 879 1430, is a low-cost Tyrolean-style lodge within walking distance of the shops and restaurants.

Hampton Inn & Suites, t +1 970 871 8900, *www.hamptonsteamboat.com*, is a new hotel located midway between the resort and downtown.

Harbor Hotel, t +1 970 879 1522, has simple rooms at budget prices.

Stowe, Vermont

Profile

A classic New England village surrounded by beautiful scenery. Not all of the accommodation is convenient for the slopes, and nightlife is quiet

✱ BEST FOR

New England charm and luxury lodging, all standards of skier and rider

ESSENTIALS

Altitude: 1,300ft (396m)–3,640ft (1109m)
Further information: **t** +1 802 253 3000, *www.stowe.com*
Lifts in area: 13 (2 cableways, 9 chairs, 2 drags) serving 485 acres of terrain
Lift pass: adult $204–360, child 6–12yrs $115–208, both for six days
Access: Montreal airport 2¼hrs, Boston airport 3¼hrs, Burlington 40mins

Resort

Back in February 1914, when war clouds were gathering over Europe, a librarian from Dartmouth College called Nathaniel L. Goodrich made the first recorded descent of skis down Mount Mansfield. 'It was', he said, 'a lot of fun and very satisfying. But my stops – voluntary and otherwise – were very frequent.' What he achieved was rather greater than personal satisfaction: he had set in motion the future prosperity of the charming 18th-century New England town of Stowe.

The trouble with Stowe is that the skiing takes place a full six miles from either Mount Mansfield or smaller and tamer Spruce Peak beside it. Hotels line the route, but wherever you stay is inconvenient for the skiing, the nightlife – or both. You need a car, but note that the police take a zero tolerance stance on drink-driving. However all that is set to change as Stowe Mountain Resort develops $400-million village at Spruce Peak that will acts as a bed base for both mountains. Much of the work is now complete, with Stowe Mountain Lodge and Spruce Base Camp now open.

Stowe is the most patrician of all East Coast resorts, with a pedigree going back to the 1920s and 1930s. It attracts wealthy Bostonians and New Yorkers, as well as 10 per cent of its skiers from Britain. The appeal lies in the quintessential Vermont town with its red and white weatherboarded houses set around a steepled, white church on attractive Main Street, where most of the shops and restaurants as well as some of the hotels are located.

Mountain

Stowe has three new lifts at Spruce Peak, additional trails, a new half-pipe and terrain park. As well as this, a new transfer gondola connects Spruce with Mount Mansfield.

Anyone who has mastered the basics on Spruce will quickly want to progress to the 'real' skiing, which takes place a short shuttle-bus ride away on Mount Mansfield. Two fast lifts serve nearly all the trails. An eight-person gondola up to the Cliff House Restaurant offers a choice of mainly blue runs down, while the Cliff Trail links with the main part of Mansfield. On this sector a high-speed quad carries skiers to the self-service Octagon Café & Gallery, with superb views.

The main course on the mountain is the Front Four, a choice of fall-line double-diamond runs, which are steep and often glazed with ice. It is rightly said that if, in these testing conditions, you can stand up on and ski gracefully down Starr, Liftline, National and Goat, you can ski just about any pisted trail in the world.

Learn

Stowe Ski & Snowboard School, **t** +1 802 253 3000, offers group and private lessons. If you order lift passes at least seven days ahead, you get a 15% discount, and a free ski school lesson every day, representing fantastic value.

Children

'Highly recommended for families,' said a reporter. **Cubs Daycare Center**, **t** +1 802 253 3000, accepts children from six weeks to six years.

Lunch

The **Cliff House Restaurant**, **t** +1 802 253 3000, at the Gondola Summit was recently renovated ('pricey – but worth it for the view'). **Fireside Tavern**, **t** +1 802 253 3656, at the slopeside Inn at the Mountain, serves salads, grilled sandwiches, regional specials and light appetizers at lunchtime. Another choice is **Solstice Restaurant**, **t** +1 802 253 3000, in the Stowe Mountain Lodge.

Dine

Partridge Inn, **t** +1 802 253 8000, serves seafood in a typical New England ambiance. Next door **Pie in the Sky**, **t** +1 802 253 5100, serves good-value wood-fired pizzas. **Blue Moon Café**, **t** +1 802 253 7006, features innovative cuisine based on seafood and game. **Olive's Bistro**, **t** +1 802 253 2033 ('expensive'), has eclectic Mediterranean–Pacific cuisine. **Cactus Café**, **t** +1 802 253 7770, takes an imaginative approach to Mexican cuisine. **Charlie B's**, **t** +1 802 253 7355, in the Stoweflake Mountain Resort & Spa, is said to be a 'good experience'. **Harrisons**, **t** + 1 802 253 7773, is for pasta, seafood and steaks. **Shed Restaurant & Brewery**, **t** + 1 802 253 4364, is set in a conservatory and has a kids' menu.

Party

The Midway Lodge is rated 'a nice place to finish off the day with a hot chocolate and plate of nachos'. **José's Cantina** at Midway Lodge and the **Den** at Mansfield Base Lodge are busy when the lift close. In town, the **Shed Brewery** is the liveliest place. **Rusty Nail Bar & Grille**, always busy and offering good value food, offers live weekend entertainment and pool tables. The **Matterhorn** ('good for a beer on the way down the mountain') has pool, darts and video games, as well as a sushi restaurant.

Sleep

Luxury:

Stowe Mountain Lodge, **t** +1 802 253 3000, *www.stowemountainlodge.com*, is a brand new luxury hotel with a spa.

Top Notch Resort & Spa, **t** +1 802 253 8585, *www.topnotch-resort.com*, has rooms decorated in sprigged English country house style, and a spa that is rated one of the best in the country.

The Trapp Family Lodge, **t** +1 802 253 8511, *www.trappfamily.com*, four miles out of town, is an opulent Tyrolean-style lodge containing the Mountain Kids Club and Activity Center providing activities for children. The Von Trapp Suite was once the private residence of Maria von Trapp.

Moderate:

Golden Eagle Resort, **t** +1 802 253 4811, *www.stoweagle.com*, along the road from Stowe, is friendly and offers accommodation for every budget, from comfortable rooms to large suites with fireplace and whirlpool bath.

Green Mountain Inn, **t** +1 802 253 7301, *www.greenmountaininn.com*, has been welcoming guests since 1833. It has an outdoor heated pool, two restaurants and a health club.

Honeywood Inn and Lodge, **t** +1 800 659 6289 or **t** +44 (0)800 085 7730 from the UK, *www.honeywoodinn.com*, offers B&B accommodation at the Inn with patchwork quilts, lacy pillows and curtains; the Lodge has high ceilings and four-poster beds.

Inn at the Mountain, t +1 802 253 3656, *www.stowe.com/lodging/inn.php*, is the resort's only slopeside accommodation, offering 33 rooms and suites.

Stoweflake Mountain Resort & Spa, t +1 802 253 7355, *www.stoweflake.com*, houses two restaurants, a world-class spa and state-of-the-art fitness centre.

Sun Valley, Idaho

Profile

Charming resort based around an old Idaho mining town with a laid-back atmosphere. Good intermediate skiing, great restaurants and nightlife

Resort

America's oldest and most remote ski resort is in a delightful corner of Idaho. Sun Valley, created in 1936 by Averell Harriman, chairman of the Union Pacific Railroad as an All-American answer to St Moritz, Megève and St Anton and a way of 'roughing it in luxury'.

*BEST FOR

Beginners and intermediates, cosmopolitan ambience, resort charm

ESSENTIALS

Altitude: 5,750ft (1753m)–9,150ft (2789m)
Further information: t +1 866 305 0408, *www.sunvalley.com*
Lifts in area: 17 (17 chairs) serving 2,045 acres of skiable terrain
Lift pass: adult $275–438, child under 12yrs $155–225, both for six out of seven days
Access: Sun Valley Airport 20mins

Sun Valley Lodge, made of poured concrete that was coloured to resemble wood, is the grand hotel in a rural village near the base that was constructed to house the big names of Hollywood. Ernest Hemingway wrote his earth-moving epic *For Whom The Bell Tolls* in room 206, which is kept as a museum. The room is surprisingly cramped by 21st-century ski resort standards. Sun Valley Inn is a later addition in similar style within the extensive manicured grounds. A small number of smart shops and restaurants complement the carefully maintained original resort image.

It's all good historical fun, but the real skiing that you have come all this way to experience – and it is indeed a long way across the desert from anywhere to Sun Valley – lies not on little Dollar but on Bald Mountain a mile away to the west. This is directly above the quaint but vibrant Victorian mining town of Ketchum, much the most convenient place to stay. It would be a mistake, but you could easily spend an enjoyable week here without even visiting actual Sun Valley and little Dollar Mountain – and you still may find yourself riding a chair with Tom Hanks, Sheryl Crow, Jodie Foster, Hilary Swank, Clint Eastwood, Arnold Schwarzenegger, Demi Moore and Ashton Kutcher.

Mountain

In skiing terms, Sun Valley's biggest claim to fame is that it invented the chairlift. In the heat of August in 1936 a system for shifting stems of bananas onto ships in Panama was installed. However, no allowance was made for the snowfall and sub-zero temperatures of the Rockies, and by the the start of the season it had completely ground to a halt. Lifts today are of more reliable design and Bald Mountain also has one of the world's most extensive automated snowmaking systems.

The skiing here suits all standards, but especially intermediates. Main mountain access is by quad-chair from River Run Plaza at one end of the town or from Warm Springs Day Lodge at the other. Both take you up to the Look Out restaurant where you can take a choice of routes back down or ride a triple chair to the 9,150ft summit for some challenging bowl skiing. The most demanding runs are in Easter Bowl. Snowboarding is popular, with a half-pipe on Lower Warm Springs and a new superpipe.

Learn

Sun Valley Ski and Snowboard School, **t** +1 208 622 2289, has a fine reputation and regularly employs Austrian instructors.

Children

Sun Valley Playschool, **t** +1 208 622 2288, caters for children aged six months to six years.

Lunch

For further information on restaurants listed without individual telephone numbers call, **t** +1 208 622 41110.

The Roundhouse, **t** +1 208 622 2371, at the top of the Exhibition and Cold Springs lift, offers a proper gourmet lunch in a warm atmosphere and is much the best place to lunch. **Look Out** and **Seattle Ridge Lodge** are the above average self-service alternatives, along with **River Run Plaza** and **Warm Springs Day Lodge** at the bottom of Bald Mountain. At Sun Valley, **Gretchen's**, **t** +1 208 622 2144, has pasta and salads. **Trail Creek Cabin**, **t** +1 208 622 2135, 1½ miles east of Sun Valley and reached by sleigh or on cross-country skies, features prime rib, chops and an open log fire.

Dine

In Ketchum, **Michel's Christiania**, **t** +1 208 726 3388, is a French restaurant renowned for its *truite aux amandes* and *tournedos au Stilton*. **Chandler's**, **t** +1 208 726 1776, has Hawaiian *ahi* tuna, Alaskan halibut, and local elk tenderloin. **Felix's**, **t** +1208 726 1166, has Spanish Andalusian cuisine. The **Pioneer Saloon**, **t** +1 208 726 3139 – Clint Eastwood's favourite – is cheerful, much cheaper and serves steaks. **Sushi on Second**, **t** +1 208 726 5181, is warmly recommended.

At Sun Valley, **Bald Mountain Pizza**, **t** +1 208 622 2143, has fine hand-tossed pizzas and a children' s games room. The **Ram**, **t** +1 208 622 2225, has local trout and lamb as well as fresh seafood. A relaxing and romantic way to end the day is by taking a sleigh ride to **Trail Creek Cabin**, **t** +1 208622 2135, for dinner. It was popular with the Gable–Cooper–Gardner set and later became one of the watering holes of choice for Ernest Hemingway.

Party

Whiskey Jacques' on North Main in Ketchum has dancing and live music. **Dirty Little Roddy's**, **t** +1 208 726 1611, is Ketchum's newest nightclub. The **Cellar Pub** is what it says it is. At Sun Valley, the **Boiler Room** has comedy show, live bands, and karaoke nights. **Duchin Lounge** is the piano bar in the Lodge.

Sleep

Luxury:

Sun Valley Lodge, **t** +1 208 622 4111, *www.sunvalley.com*, has a smart 'old money' atmosphere.

Sun Valley Inn, **t** +1 208 622 4111, *www.sunvalley.com*, is the slightly later addition that has been completely refurbished.

Les Saisons, **t** +1 208 727 1616, is warm and welcoming and contains condos with hickory wood floors, as well as a small spa and gym.

Thunder Spring, **t** +1 208 726 606, *www.thunderspring.com*, contains impressive condos: bedrooms have wrought iron bed frames; sitting rooms have wood floors, and kitchens are open-plan. There is a 25m heated outdoor pool, and the 40,000-sq-ft Zenergy centre houses a state-of-the-art gym, two indoor tennis courts and squash courts.

Knob Hill Inn, **t** +1 208 726 8010, *www.knobhillinn.com*, is a European-style *Relais et Chateaux* hotel.

Moderate:

Best Western Kentwood Lodge, **t** +1 208 726 4114, *www.bestwestern.com/kentwoodlodge*, is within easy reach of shops, nightlife and Bald Mountain.

Clarion Inn of Sun Valley, **t** +1 208 726 5900, *www.resortswest.net*, has spacious rooms and is centrally situated in Ketchum.

Taos, New Mexico

Profile

Quirky resort in desert surroundings with steep skiing and good ski school tuition, but banned to snowboarders

* BEST FOR

Exotic setting, steep 'n' deep, ski school

ESSENTIALS

Altitude: 9,207ft (2807m)–11,819ft (3603m)

Further information: **t** +1 505 776 2291, *www.skitaos.org*

Lifts in area: 11 (11 chairs) serving 1,294 acres of terrain

Lift pass: $378, youth 13–17yrs $318, child 7–12yrs $240, all for six days

Access: Santa Fe 1¼hrs, Albuquerque airport 2¼hrs

Resort

Even by the diverse standards of America, skiing scattered across a 2,500-mile continent, Taos, is a glorious one-off. The premier resort of New Mexico is surrounded by the magical peaks of the Sangre de Cristo mountains. Like D.H. Lawrence, Georgia O'Keeffe and Wild West frontiersman Kit Carson, who all lived here, you don't have to ski to enjoy it, but you can have a lot more fun if you do.

The original 1,000-year-old town with its adobe buildings and dominant Native American culture has been inspiring writers, artists and musicians for more than a century. The skiing – snowboarding is still not allowed here – takes place an 18-mile drive away up the road from the cactus and sage of the desert floor, among the alpine pines of the Carson National Forest. Like Jackson and Jackson Hole, you must choose between staying beside the ski hill or among the après ski action. Our advice is to opt for the latter and base yourself in the town.

Taos Ski Valley (TSV) has a distinctly European atmosphere and, although it sits on the same latitude as Rome, it usually has copious amounts of high-quality snow. It was this giant white basin that Swiss-born German Ernie Blake spotted from the window of his single-engined Cessna as he flew over the

TAOS
KACHINA PEAK
12,481
MAIN STREET
CABIN CHUTE
LIFT SHACK CHUTE
TWIN TREES CHUTE
TRESCKOW
CORNER CHUTE
TWO BUCKS
BILLY SOL
NINOS HEROES
JUAREZ
HIDALGO
HIGHLINE RIDGE
SKI PATROL
HEADQUARTERS
HIGH TRAVERSE
WEST BASIN RIDGE
STAUFFENBERG
ZDARSKY
FABIAN
OSTER
SPITFIRE
WEST BLITZ TREES
BLITZ
REFORMA
WEST BASIN
ST. BERNARD
THUNDERBIRD
HONDO
WONDER BOWL
EASY TRIP
HUNZIKER BOWL
WHEELER
WILDERNESS AREA
HIGH NOON
STAUB
SHOWOFF
HONEYSUCKLE
MOE'S
BOB'S
WALKYRIES BOWL
WALKYRIES CHUTE
CASTOR
POLLUX
BAMBI
UPPER TOTEMOFF
LOWER TOTEMOFF
MAXIE'S
WALKYRIES GLADE
SIR ARNOLD LUNN
LORELEI TREES
LONE STAR
PAPA BEAR
RUBY GULLY
EL FUNKO
LOWER PATTON
STREET CAR
LORELEI
PIERRE'S
WERNER CHUTE
ZAGAVA
LONGHORN
BONANZA
JESS'S
GUSTO
POCO
WHISTLESTOP
CAFE
PSYCHO PATH
POWDERHORN
WHITE FEATHER
LOWER STAUFFENBERG
FIRLEFANZ
TELL TREES
TELL GLADE
BAMBI GLADE
PORCUPINE
AL'S RUN
RHODA'S
SPENCER'S
INFERNO
JEAN'S GLADE
LOWER INFERNO
SNAKEDANCE
EDELWEISS
EDELWEISS GLADE
WAYNE ABBEY
SHOWDOWN
THE PHOENIX
GRILL
RESORT CENTER
SHOPS • TICKETS
CHILDREN'S
SKI SCHOOL
JAMES
NIEHUES

mountains in 1954. He took one look from the ground and moved there the following year to found the resort, which is still run by the family today.

The resort is a collection of lodges and condo buildings, that line the banks of the Rio Hondo creek, linked by bridges and walkways near the base of what at first – and at second – glance looks like an extaordinarily steep mountain.

'Don't panic,' says the sign at the bottom of Al's run, the fall-line mogul field beneath the chairlift, 'you are looking at 1/90th of Taos Ski Valley.'

Mountain

The resort insists that Taos suits all standards of skier. But, while there is some good novice terrain and excellent ski instruction, this is a place for skiers who like their mountain steep and deep, or heavily mogulled between dumps. It seems strange that such a pinnacle in the desert can offer some of the toughest double-black-diamond skiing in North America.

Oster and Stauffenberg, two of the most respected of these trails off the High Traverse, are named after the German officers who plotted against Hitler – a statement of Ernie Blake's anti-Nazi stance during the Second World War. British skier Sir Arnold Lunn, founder of slalom racing, is also remembered by his own trail. The terrain park for twin-tippers – remember, no snowboarders – is located on Maxie's run under lift no.7. It has a couple of big jumps, rails, and a quarter-pipe.

Learn

Ernie Blake Ski School, t +1 505 776 2291, ext. 1355, provides tuition with a full range of courses, and has an excellent reputation.

Children

Ernie Blake Ski School has a maximum class size of nine pupils. Little ones aged six weeks to three years are cared for by **Bebekare** and **Kinderkare**, and skiers join **Junior Elite.** Kids' nights with entertainment, and teen party nights are regularly organized.

Lunch

Rhoda's Restaurant, t +1 505 776 2291, slopeside in the Resort Centre, has an eclectic menu at affordable prices. **The Phoenix Grill,** T +1 575 776 2291, at the base of the quad-chair in Kachina Bowl, is the perfect spot for enjoying lunch and watching skiers go by. **The Whistlestop Café, t** +1 888 285 8920, at the base of no.6 lift and close to the no.2 quad, is where to get a quick pizza or soup. **The Bavarian, t** +1 505 776 8020, is mid-mountain and – despite its name – looks as if it is in Alpbach or Kitzbühel, with staff in *dirndl* dresses, carved wooden furniture, and warmth provided by a tiled fireplace oven.

Dine

Rhoda's Restaurant, t +1 505 776 2291, features steaks, prime rib, salads, pasta, chicken and seafood at affordable prices. **De la Tierra, t** +1 505 758 3502, at El Monte **Sagrado Living Resort & Spa, t** +1 505 758 3502, serves regional and seasonal American dishes and has an impressive wine list. **Doc Martin's Restaurant, t** +1 505 758 1977, at the Historic Taos Inn at Taos, is an acclaimed fine dining establishment. **Micheal's Kitchen, t** +1 505 758 4178, in Taos, serves New York steaks and Tex-Mex. **Lambert's of Taos, t** +1 505 758 1009, serves contemporary American cuisine.

Party

The **Martini Tree Bar**, upstairs at **Tenderfoot Katie's**, is the hot place for après ski action. The **Adobe Bar** at Historic Taos Inn serves 18 different tequilas, 14 margaritas and features an adobe fireplace and jazz evenings. **Thunderbird Lodge** hosts live jazz.

Sleep

Luxury:

El Monte Sagrado, t +1 505 758 3502, *www.elmontesagrado.com*, in Taos town, offers 36 elegant suites and *casitas* with décor inspired by Native American culture and local artists. The property has an exquisite spa and two restaurants.

Moderate:

St Bernard Hotel & Condos, t +1 505 776 2251, *www.stbernardtaos.com*, in TSV, is owned by Jean Mayer – director of the ski school. Rooms are normally booked out by August. The hotel has a kids' club and a bar with live music.

Snakedance Condos & Spa, t +1 505 776 1410, *www.snakedancecondos.com*, provides comfortable accommodation beside the main access lift.

Historic Taos Inn, t +1 505 758 2233, *www.taosinn.com*, is the old pub where Doc Martin dispensed medicine for 40 years. It has authentic charm and a wicked menu of margaritas.

Hotel la Fonda de Taos, t +1505 758 2211, *www.lafondataos.com*, is the oldest hotel in town and houses the Forbidden Art collection by D.H. Lawrence that was banned as obscene in Britain.

Sagebrush Inn & Conference Center, t +1 505 758 2254, *www.sagebrushinn.com*, in Taos town, is an adobe building housing an impressive collection of Indian artefacts. The inn has been hosting visitors since the 1920s.

Rio Hondo Condos, t +1 505 776 2347, *www.riohondocondos.com*, between Taos town and TSV, features *casitas* – one-bedroomed guesthouses with fireplaces and hot tubs.

Quail Inn Ridge Resort, t +1 505 776 2211, *www.quailridgeinn.com*, four miles from TSV, is in an adobe building with a desert ambience.

Telluride, Colorado

Profile

Lovely old old town with a wide choice of restaurants. Gondola to separate mountain village with further accommodation

Resort

The old mining town of Telluride, tucked away in a remote corner of the San Juan mountains, has a more colourful history and more present-day charm than any resort in North America. In 1889, Butch Cassidy and the Sundance Kid relieved the

*** BEST FOR**

Intermediate and advanced skiers, snowboarders, restaurants, luxury accommodation

ESSENTIALS

Altitude: 8,725ft (2660m)–12,247ft (3734m)
Further information: **t** +1 970 728 6900, *www.tellurideski resort.com*

Lifts in area: 16 (2 cableways, 12 chairs, 2 drags) serving 2,000 acres of terrain
Lift pass: $480, child 6–12yrs $288, both for six out of eight days
Access: Montrose airport 1¼hrs

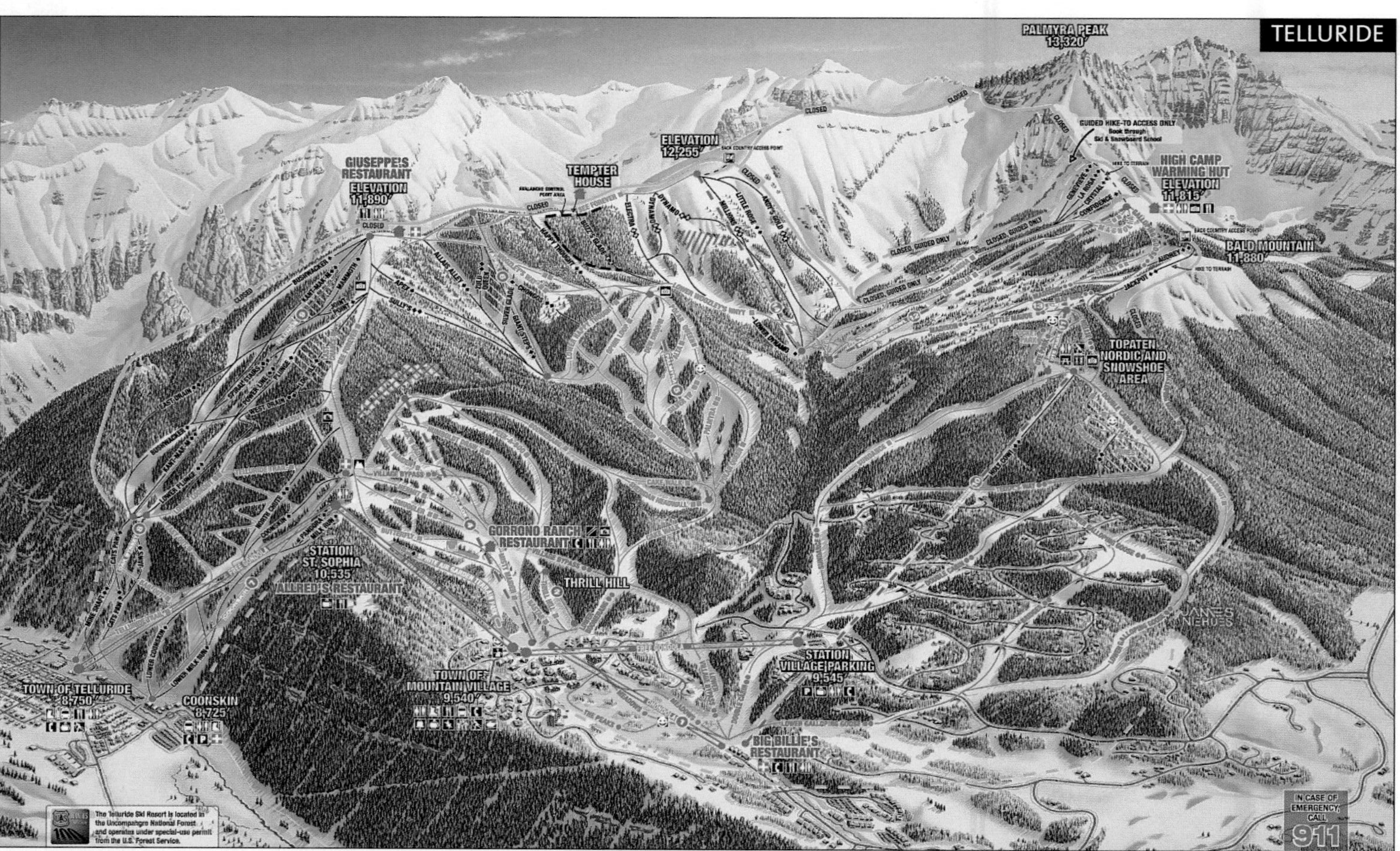
TELLURIDE
PALMYRA PEAK 13,320′
ELEVATION 12,255′
BACK COUNTRY ACCESS POINT
GUIDED HIKE-TO ACCESS ONLY
Book through Ski & Snowboard School
HIGH CAMP WARMING HUT ELEVATION 11,815′
BALD MOUNTAIN 11,880′
GIUSEPPE'S RESTAURANT ELEVATION 11,890′
TEMPTER HOUSE
AVALANCHE CONTROL POINT AREA
CLOSED
CLOSED, GUIDED ONLY
HIKE TO TERRAIN
GENEVIEVE
LA ROSA
CRYSTAL
CONFIDENCE
AUDREY
JACKPOT
ELECTRA
DYNAMO
MILLIONS
LITTLE ROSE
ANDY'S GOLD
LOWER DYNAMO
HAPPY THOUGHT
BUTZ'S GLADE
ALLAIS ALLEY
APEX
SULLY'S
ZULU QUEEN
SILVER GLADE
GIANT STEPS
BUSHWACKER
KANT-MAK-M
MAMMOTH
SPIRAL STAIRS
POWER LINE
PLUNGE
LOWER PLUNGE
EAST DRAIN
WEST DRAIN
NORTH CHUTE
COONSKIN
PANDORA
MILK RUN
LOWER MILK RUN
LOWER COONSKIN
CATS PAW
JAWS
MINE SHAFT
PALMYRA
THE PEAKS
LOWER GALLOPING GOOSE
TOPATEN NORDIC AND SNOWSHOE AREA
GORRONO RANCH RESTAURANT
STATION ST. SOPHIA 10,535′
ALLRED'S RESTAURANT
THRILL HILL
TOWN OF MOUNTAIN VILLAGE 9,540′
STATION VILLAGE PARKING 9,545′
BIG BILLIE'S RESTAURANT
TOWN OF TELLURIDE 8,750′
COONSKIN 8,725′
JAMES NIEHUES
The Telluride Ski Resort is located in the Uncompahgre National Forest and operates under special-use permit from the U.S. Forest Service.
IN CASE OF EMERGENCY, CALL 911

San Miguel Valley Bank of $24,000. Jack Dempsey washed dishes in a brothel here before finding his fists full of dollars elsewhere.

In the 1890s Telluride built a power station and became the first town in the world to be lit by alternating electrical current. At the height of the gold rush 5,000 miners crowded into a town that supported one hotel and 100 brothels. Most probably it took its name either from tellurium, a non-metallic element in gold and silver ore, or less likely from 'to hell you ride'.

The extra-wide streets, with their beautifully preserved Victorian buildings including the New Sheridan Hotel and the original courthouse, were designed so that a carter could turn a full team of oxen. Modern traffic regulations limit speed to 15mph, and cars give way to pedestrians. The old town is connected by gondola to the purpose-built Mountain Village Resort, four miles away by road. This provides a convenient – and increasingly extensive – bed base.

In the late 1980s Telluride caught the eye of Hollywood investors as it developed as a ski resort, attracting stars looking for an as yet uncommercialized Aspen. Tom Cruise has a home here, as does singer Alanis Morisette. Their presence helped to forge Telluride into one of the smartest destinations in America, with shops and restaurants of commensurate quality – and price.

The Mountain Village is reached from the old town by a gondola running 7am to midnight seven days a week. It was built in 1987 and linked in 1995, with a pedestrian centre surrounded by luxury condos and hotels, shops and restaurants. The most luxurious hotel here is The Peaks. At Mountain Village there is a further free gondola that links yet more properties. A new Four Seasons hotel and a St Regis are planned for the Mountain Village in the near future.

Mountain

The modest-sized ski area suits all standards, with plenty of easy terrain, as well as some demanding steep chutes. The gondola rises steeply from the edge of the old town and dog-legs down from the top station to Mountain Village. The backbone of the skiing is See Forever, a rolling blue run from Giuseppe's Restaurant at 11,890ft down to the village at 9,540ft. The whole area is made up of gladed runs with a good pitch for intermediate cruising. A new quad-chair was added this summer.

The sector immediately above the town is steeper with some tough fall-line options such as Kant-Mak-M, Spiral Stairs, and East and West Drain. Further challenging runs are served by the Gold Hill lift. The expansion into Prospect Bowl a few years ago greatly added to Telluride's appeal. A short hike from the top accesses Genevieve, La Rosa and Crystal – three of the steepest double-black-diamonds in the resort.

Telluride Air Garden terrain park, served by the gondola from Mountain Village, has a monster super-pipe.

Learn

Telluride's **Ski & Snowboard School**, **t** +1 970 728 7507, offers adult group and private lessons as well as women's ski courses and adaptive skiing.

Children

The **Children's Nursery**, **t** +1 970 728 7531, is part of the Ski & Snowboarding School and is for kids aged two months to three years. The ski school also offers lessons for skiers from three to 12 years, and a nightly activities programme for five to 12 year olds. **Mountain Village Nursery**, **t** +1 970 728 7533, and **Annie's Nannies**, **t** +1 970 728

2991, are the alternatives for babysitting. **The Ski & Snowboard School** provides special teen programmes.

Lunch

On-mountain dining is in a choice of five venues. **Giuseppe's**, **t** +1 970 728 7503, has a cosy atmosphere, and **Big Billie's**, **t** +1 970 728 7556, offers 'friendly family fare', **Gorrono Ranch**, **t** +1 970 728 7566, is located on a late 1800s Basque sheep herder's homestead and **That Pizza Place**, **t** +1 970 728 7499, is family-friendly and you can bake your own pizza.

Dine

Restaurants are one of Telluride's many strengths. **Rustico Ristorante**, **t** +1 970 728 4046, offers freshly made pasta, wood-fired pizzas, and one of the largest selections of Italian wines in Colorado. **Brown Dog**, **t** +1 970 728 8046, is the hippest pizza joint in town. **Honga's Lotus Petal**, **t** +1 970 728 5134, features an extensive selection of Asian cuisine. **BluePoint Grill**, **t** +1 970 728 8862, a block from the gondola base, is a hip seafood and steak house. **Harmon's**, **t** +1 970 728 3773, located in Telluride's historic train depot, serves modern American cuisine.

Up at the Mountain Village is **Allred's**, **t** +1 970 728 7474, a private club by day but open to all at night. It provides regional American dishes and fine wines. **La Piazza**, **t** +1 970 728 0737, also in Mountain Village, is authentic northern Italian.

Party

Ski to the **Crunchy Porcupine** for cocktails. In town you can sip a martini at the fashionable **Noir Bar** in the Bluepoint restaurant, adorned with leather sofas, and a leopard-print carpet. **Fly Me to the Moon Saloon** has live music.

Sleep

Telluride:

Luxury:

Camel's Garden, **t** +1 888 772 2635, *www.camelsgarden.com*, is right next to the gondola station. It has 35 rooms and a spa.

Elk Mountain Resort, **t** +1 970 252 4900, *www.elkmountainresort.com*, is a member of the *Small Luxury Hotels of the World*, and has deluxe lodge rooms as well as three-bedroom cottages.

Hotel Telluride, **t** +1 866 468 3501, *www.thehoteltelluride.com*, is a stylish boutique hotel housing a day spa.

Moderate:

The New Sheridan Hotel, **t** +1 800 200 1891, *www.newsheridan.com*, has been welcoming guests since 1891. It is decorated in Victorian style and its restaurant serves elk, ostrich and venison.

Ice House Lodge & Condos, **t** +1 800 544 3436, *www.icehouselodge.com*, is modern, smart and convenient for the gondola station. Adjoining the lodge are 16 luxury condos.

Mountain Village:

Inn at Lost Creek, **t** +1 970 728 5678, *www.innatlostcreek.com*, contains individually decorated rooms with deluxe kitchenettes.

Mountain Lodge, **t** +1 970 369 5000, *www.mountainlodgetelluride.com*, has comfortable condos, a pool and hot tub.

The Peaks Resort & Golden Door Spa, **t** +1 800 789 2220, *www.thepeaksresort.com*, is the ultimate ski in, ski out hotel. It has a sumptuous five-storey spa. As well as lovely bedrooms and suites, there is a collection of three-bedroom cabins in the grounds. One of the swimming-pools has a waterslide for kids. There is also a climbing wall, where Tom Cruise learnt the sport for *Mission Impossible 2*.

Vail, Colorado

Profile

Pedestrianized village with smart hotels and restaurants. A good choice for well-heeled families, and skiers and riders of all levels

Resort

For most visitors, Vail is the one resort that is close to perfection. A large and easily accessible mountain offers beginner and intermediate trails immediately above the village that are groomed nightly to pristine perfection. The back side is given over to thousands of acres of lift-accessed off-piste terrain that, after a fresh dump, become one the of the greatest winter playgrounds in the world.

The resort itself, built in neo-Tyrolean style, promises a pipe-dream image of a sophisticated winter wonderland borrowed from a Christmas card – and manages to deliver. Luxurious hotels are complemented by an outstanding array of restaurants and, by American standards, a busy nightlife.

The only people dissatisfied with this rose-tinted view of a snow-sure corner of Colorado are the 3 per cent of expert skiers and riders who find the gradient too tame in a destination that is more moneyed than mogulled. Chamonix or Jackson Hole it is not. This is skiing at its most comfortable, a state of affairs that would doubtless have been appreciated by eccentric Scottish Baronet 'Lord' St George Gore when he passed through present-day Vail on a hunting trip in 1855 with no skis, but accompanied by 112 horses and 50 dogs. While slaughtering 2,000 buffalo, 1,600 elk and 100 bears, he slept every night in a brass bed. The hedonistic trappings of his camp included a commode with a fur-lined seat, a library of rare books, and a silver dinner service.

Vail annually injects huge sums of cash into maintaining the resort as the premier showcase of American skiing. In a move of which the likes of Tignes in France should take note, the centre of the ugly 1970s satellite of Lionshead has been demolished as part of a $1 billion five-year redevelopment programme. Last season skiers could only view the work, which started in April 2005. The new building, the Arrabelle at Vail Square, houses 36 hotel rooms and 50 condos, along with shops, restaurants and an ice rink. It opened in January 2008 and its European-style architecture has totally transformed the base area at Lionshead.

Where you stay is important for reaching shops and restaurants, but not the slopes. The resort sprawls for seven miles along the busy I-70 freeway, if you include East Vail. The main resort, from Golden Peak to Cascade Village, is one-and-a-half miles long and anyone staying here is never far from a lift. The lodging is all linked by an

* BEST FOR

Large and varied ski area, excellent ski and snowboard tuition, families, off-piste

ESSENTIALS

Altitude: 8,120ft (2475m)–11,570 ft (3526m)
Further information: t +1 970 476 9090, *www.vail.com*
Lifts in area: 28 (1 cableway, 24 chairs, 3 drags) serving 5,289 acres of terrain
Lift pass: Colorado Ticket (covers Arapahoe Basin, Beaver Creek, Breckenridge, Keystone, Vail) adult $330–570, child 5–12yrs $264, both for six out of nine days
Access: Denver airport 2½hrs, Eagle County airport 40mins

efficient bus service. Vail shares its lift pass with Beaver Creek 10 miles to the west, as well as with Breckenridge, Keystone, and the small, high-altitude ski area of Arapahoe Basin.

'Trails are so wide and numerous that the crowds scatter. There is limitless powder and safe off-piste skiing, the grooming is flawless, and the staff are extremely friendly and helpful,' enthused a reporter. 'However, there is a lack of more modern and comfortable covered chairs and gondolas.'

Mountain

Main mountain access is by the Vistabahn Express chair from Vail Village, but five other lifts at different points along the valley offer alternative routes. As a result, lift queues are rarely a problem. From the Mid-Vail, hub lifts and pistes fan out all along the front face of the mountain, offering an extraordinarily wide range of terrain. It is essentially an intermediate paradise spiced with some vicious bump runs such as Highline, Blue Ox and the infamous Roger's Run.

The Back Bowls, accessed from the top of the mountain, are ideally suited to beginner and inexperienced deep-snow skiers, who get a chance to find their feet in a controlled and lift-served environment with a mainly modest pitch. Nevertheless, it is rewarding for advanced skiers too, with plenty of good chutes, drop-offs and tree-skiing.

Beyond the bowls lies Blue Sky Basin, Vail's most prized possession. This 645-acre area houses some truly stupendous off-piste served by the Skyline Express and Pete's Express lifts.

The Minturn Mile is an itinerary route that in the right snow conditions takes you down through some scenic and challenging terrain to the small town of Minturn; margaritas or pitchers of beer at the Saloon make a pleasant end to the outing.

Beginner areas are located at Golden Peak and at Eagle's Nest where there is also an activity centre – open in the evenings – with tubing, skating and kids' snowmobiling. The Golden Peak terrain park features a 400ft super-pipe with 18ft walls. There is also a smaller park on Bwana, which has jumps and rails.

Highline and Sourdough lifts have been replaced by high-speed quads, the latter making access to Two Elk Lodge and Blue Sky Basin faster and easier.

Learn

Vail/Beaver Creek Ski and Snowboard School, t +1 970 754 4300, has a formidable reputation as an excellent, albeit expensive, learning academy. Courses include dedicated classes for teenagers, women's clinics, terrain park and skiing for the disabled.

Children

Small World Play School, t +1 970 754 3285, is the non-ski kindergarten for children aged from eight weeks to six years. **Children's Ski and Snowboard School, t** +1 970 754 4300, at Golden Peak, and Lionshead, arranges classes for children from three to 12 years.

Lunch

Blue Moon, t +1 970 479 4530, at Eagle's Nest, has a relaxed atmosphere and specials such as smoked duck quesadilla and blackened catfish stuffed with a black bean-mango salsa. **Larkspur, t** +1 970 479 8050, in the Golden Peak base lodge, has American cooking with a rustic French influence. **Cucina Rustica, t** +1 970 476 5011, at the Lodge at Vail, has an excellent and reasonably priced buffet. **Two Elk**

The Front Side

VAIL

It is against Colorado state law to cross any rope on Vail Mountain; violators will be prosecuted. Enter bowls through open gates only. Ski with a partner. Skiing or snowboarding irresponsibly will result in the loss of privileges. SNOWCATS, SNOWMOBILES AND UNMARKED OBSTACLES MAY BE ENCOUNTERED AT ANY TIME.

MAP KEY

EXPRESS LIFT
DOWNLOADING LIFT
CHAIRLIFT
SURFACE LIFT
SURFACE LIFT (two-way travel)
CARPET LIFT
MOST DIFFICULT
MORE DIFFICULT
EASIEST
ROAD or CATWALK (may include flat terrain)
AREA BOUNDARY/CLOSURE (do not cross)
GROOMED TRAIL
SKI & SNOWBOARD SCHOOL
ADAPTIVE SKIING OFFICE
RECREATIONAL SKI RACING
FREESTYLE TERRAIN
VAIL SPORTS DEMO CENTER
BUS STOP (every 10 minutes)
CHILDREN'S SKIING CENTERS
KIDS ADVENTURE ZONE
SKE-COLOGY
BEGINNER ZONE
APRÈS SKI
FULL SERVICE RESTAURANT
KIDS SPECIALTY RESTAURANT
DINING COURT, GRILL
PICNIC AREA
QUICK EATS
OVERNIGHT STORAGE
SUNDAY SERVICES
RETAIL/RENTAL
RESTROOMS
ACCESSIBILITY for INDIVIDUA[LS] WITH DISABILITIES
SLOW ZONE

Vail Mountain facilities, operated by Vail Associates, Inc., are located within the White River National Forest and are under permit from the Forest Service, U.S.D.A.

TERRAIN PARKS

VAIL FLY ZONE TERRAIN PARK

[Nea]rly a mile long, the **Fly Zone Terrain [Par]k** at Golden Peak features the Superpipe, [free]style jumps, rails and hits, the jib park and [it]s unique log rails. It's also home to the [Hon]da Session Snowboard Invitational [in J]anuary.

VAIL FLIGHT SCHOOL TERRAIN PARK

Flight School is Ski and Snowboard School's learning park, located next to Fly Zone at Golden Peak. This new location for Flight School offers amazing views of Fly Zone, but has its own separate entrance.

VAIL AVIATOR TERRAIN PARK

[Loca]ted on Bwana trail under the gondola [at L]ionsHead, **Aviator Park** features [a co]mbination of small and medium hits, rails [and] boxes designed for freestyle progression [and] a beginner half-pipe with 13-foot walls.

VAIL SKY WAY TERRAIN PARK

Sky Way Park is located at nearly 11,000 feet on Hunky Dory trail and offers "ground low" boxes, rails and mini hits designed for those just starting out.

[Pip]es	2
[Su]perpipe	1
Length	450 feet
Walls	18 feet
[Ta]bletops	24
[Ra]ils	30, plus 12 unique hand-carved rails

© 2006 Gary [...] VistaM[...]

Lodge, **t** +1 970 476 9090, on the ridge separating the Front Face from the China Bowl and Blue Sky Basin, is a huge self-service with Oriental dishes such as sushi and stir-fry with noodles or rice as well as the ubiquitous burger 'n' fries. **Bart & Yeti's**, **t** +1 970 474 2754, at Lionshead, is all-American. **Pepi's**, **t** +1 970 476 4671, has fine *moules marinière* and *Wienerschnitzel*. **Los Amigos**, **t** +1 970 476 5847, is a long-established Mexican restaurant. 'Food on the mountain was generally good, however there are simply not enough restaurants and it becomes massively overcrowded at peak times,' said a reporter. 'The resort's advice to eat before 11.30am and after 2pm does not address the key problem: it needs more restaurants.'

Dine

Nozawa, **t** +1 970 476 9355, in the West Vail Lodge, has great sushi. **Terra Bistro**, **t** +1 970 476 6836, has an eclectic menu with Oriental–Italian fusion cuisine. **Montauk Seafood Grill**, **t** +1 970 476 2601, serves oysters flown in daily from both coasts, and Dungeness crab. **Russell's**, **t** +1 970 476 6700, offers fine steaks and seafood. **Campo de' Fiori**, **t** +1 970 476 8994, specializes in pasta and risotto. **La Tour**, **t** +1 970 476 4403, is a celebrated French restaurant. Try the seared *foie gras* and the black truffle-scented pheasant breast. **Mezzaluna**, **t** +1 970 477 4410, has modern Italian–American cuisine. **Up The Creek**, **t** +1 970 476 8141, on the banks of Gore Creek, is renowned for its fresh fish, duck and pasta. **May Palace**, **t** +1 970 476 1657, is a good Chinese restaurant. The **Lancelot**, **t** +1 970 476 5828, specializes in prime rib. The **Wildflower**, **t** +1 970 476 5011, in the Lodge at Vail, is considered one of the top restaurants in Colorado. **Pazzo's Pizzeria**, **t** +1 970 476 9026, has sensibly priced pizzas and pasta. **Game Creek Restaurant**, **t** +1 970 479 4275, is open to everyone in the evening and accessed by snowcat from the top of the gondola. It serves American–French fusion cuisine.

Party

Chill out at the **Blue Moon** bar at Eagle's Nest after tubing, ski-biking, orienteering and a choice of other activities at Adventure Ridge at the top of the Eagle Bahn gondola. **Mickey's Piano Bar** at the Lodge is the place to spot celebrities. The **Red Lion** in Bridge Street is the most popular après ski bar, with live music. The **Tap Room & Sanctuary** has dining and dancing. Numerically named **8150** is a fashionable nightclub. The **Ore House** offers happy-hour prices.

Sleep

Luxury:

The Lodge at Vail, **t** +1 970 476 5011, *www.lodgeatvail.com*, on the edge of the piste, is owned by the resort and remains one of the best addresses.

Sonnenalp Resort, **t** +1 970 476 5656, *www.sonnenalp.com*, is an elegant Bavarian-inspired hotel built in 1979 and is still one of Vail's top places to stay.

The Arrabelle at Vail Square, **t** +1 970 754 7777, *http://arrabelle.rockresorts.com/*, is Vail's latest five-star property just a few steps from the Eagle Bahn Gondola.

Vail Marriott Mountain Resort & Spa, **t** +1 970 476 4444, *www.marriott.com*, at Lionshead, makes a convenient and comfortable base.

Moderate:

Evergreen Lodge, **t** +1 970 476 7810, *www.evergreenvail.com*, located between Lionshead and Vail Village, heads the second rank.

Roost Lodge, **t** +1 970 476 5451, *www.roostlodge.com*, has been recently renovated and is a good-value place to stay in West Vail.

Vail Mountain Lodge and Spa, t +1 970 476 0700, *www.vailmountainlodge.com*, has been revamped and is highly recommended.

Antlers at Vail, t +1 970 476 2471, *www.antlersvail.com*, is a condo hotel on Gore Creek that recently underwent a $20 million refurbishment.

Winter Park, Colorado

Profile

Unsophisticated family resort with plenty of advanced skiing, reasonable prices, and a short airport transfer. Not recommended for night-owls

Resort

Winter Park is the closest major ski destination to Denver and currently in the throes of a 15-year rebuild. The municipally owned ski area has been leased to Intrawest over a 50-year period. Consequently it now shares a lift pass for foreign visitors with Copper Mountain, Intrawest's other resort in this part of Colorado.

Central to the expansion plan is the new Village at Winter Park Resort beside the base area, which will have 1,500 residential units and 24 shops and restaurants. The company has invested $70 million in the first phase, which is scheduled for completion at the start of the 2008–9 winter season.

All this augurs well for the future, but the problem for the present is that the town of Winter Park is an inconvenient two miles from the skiing. Plans to link the mountain to the town by gondola are included in the master plan but still seem to be a decade away. A regular bus service operates between the two but finishes at 10.30pm.

*** BEST FOR**

All standards, families, airport convenience

ESSENTIALS

Altitude: 9,000ft (2743m)–12,050ft (3677m)

Further information: t +1 970 726 1564, *www.skiwinterpark.com*

Lifts in area: 21 (19 chairs, 2 drags) serving 2,770 acres of terrain

Lift pass: Rocky Mountain International ticket (Copper Mountain, Steamboat and Winter Park) adult $358, child 6–13yrs $210, both for six days

Access: Denver Airport 90mins, ski train from Denver 2¼hrs

Mountain

Winter Park offers extensive terrain for all levels. The area naturally divides into two main sectors. Winter Park has beginner, intermediate and expert trails, with main access by the Zephyr Express quad. More demanding Mary-Jane features bump skiing, tree-level romps and double-diamond chutes from Vasquez Cirque. Main access is by the six-seater Summit Express. The Panoramic Express is a new $8 million six-pack that is reputedly the world's highest, taking skiers and riders up to 12,060ft (3676m) and accessing Parsenn Bowl.

Winter Park has three terrain parks and a 450ft super-pipe. Neighbouring Berthoud Pass has some superb off-piste runs from the top of the pass, but you will need a local guide and a strategically parked car to access it.

Learn

Winter Park Resort Ski & Snowboard School, **t** +1 800 729 7907, runs a full range of courses.

Children

Kids Adventure Junction Center, **t** +1 970 726 1564, provides free pagers for parents and cares for non-skiing children from eight weeks to six years. **Winter Park Kids' Ski & Snowboard School** has a friendly team of instructors.'

Lunch

Doc's Roadhouse, **t** +1 970 722 5450, at Zephyr Mountain Lodge, specializes in prime rib, **Club Car**, **t** +1 970 726 5514, at the Mary-Jane Center, and the **Dining Room** at the Lodge at Sunspot, **t** +1 970 726 1446, are the main mountain options.

Dine

'Don't expect great restaurants,' warned a reader, 'it is a bit of a one horse town.' **Untamed Steakhouse**, **t** +1 970 726 1111, is recommended. **Carlos and Maria's**, **t** +1 970 726 9674, offers good Mexican food. **Deno's Mountain Bistro**, **t** +1 970 726 5332, serving steaks and seafood, is a resort institution. **Fontenot's Cajun Café**, **t** +1 970 726 4021, features Cajun dishes. **New Hong Kong**, **t** +1 970 726 9888, offers Szechwan, Mandarin, Cantonese and Thai specials.

Party

'Places close early, by 9.30pm they are packing up around you and the fire at the bus stop is turned off at 9pm,' said a reader. The **Derailer Bar** at West Portal Station is busy as the lifts close, but Winter Park is a family destination with limited après ski entertainment. Deno's was rated: 'friendly and noisy with great food'. Try **Buckets Saloon**, **Doc's**, **Smokin' Moe's**, **Moffat Station Restaurant and Brewery**, **Randi's Irish Saloon** and **Winter Park Pub**.

Sleep

Luxury:

For further information and reservations call, **t** +1 970 726 5587.

Zephyr Mountain Lodge provides rustic contemporary style and accommodation beside the lifts.

Moderate/Budget:

Beaver Creek Condos is a comfortable complex a seven-minute drive from the slopes and five minutes from the centre.

Iron Horse Resort is the original condo complex, with an outdoor pool.

Super 8 Motel, **t** +1 970 726 8088, close to the centre, features an indoor hot tub.

Winter Park Mountain Lodge has been refurbished, and is situated three minutes by bus from the base area.

A–Z of World Resorts

Abetone, Italy

t +39 0329 4207373, *www.abetone.org*
Altitude 1390m (4,560ft)–1900m (6,233ft)
Lifts 25

Apennine resort within easy reach of Florence and Pisa.

Achenkirch, Austria

t +43 (0)5246 5321, *www.achensee.info/achenkirch*
Altitude 930m (3,050ft)–1800m (5,906ft)
Lifts 10
Tour operator Ramblers

Skiing is on the Karwendel and Rofan mountains where you can ski downhill on 20km of mainly intermediate slopes or glide along the 58km of cross-country tracks. The five-star **Posthotel Resort & Spa**, **t** +43 (0)5246 6522, *www.posthotel.at*, is situated on the Achensee lake. The hotel houses the Atrium Spa.

Adelboden and Lenk, Switzerland

Adelboden: t +41 (0)33 733 3131, *www.lenk.ch*
Altitude 1068m (3,503ft)–2357m (7,733ft)
Lifts 56 in area
Tour operators Crystal, Indigo Lodges, Kuoni, Thomson

The unspoilt village of Adelboden consists of chalets set on a sunny terrace below the Wildstrubel massif ('cared-for groomed pistes that are seldom truly busy'). Neighbouring Lenk is a spa village, and the two resorts share a 170km intermediate ski area with a selection of mountain restaurants. In Lenk, four-star **Sporthotel Wildstrubel**, **t** +42 (0)33 736 3111, *www.wildstrubel.ch*, occupies a central position and offers excellent food and leisure facilities, though the décor is a little dated.

Alagna, Italy

See Champoluc–Alagna–Gressoney, page 268
Tour operators Alpine Answers Select, J2Ski, Momentum, Original Travel, Pyrenean Mountain Tours, Ski Freshtracks, Ski Weekend

Alpbach, Austria

Page 46
Tour operators Crystal, Inghams, Made to Measure

Alpe d'Huez, France

Page 156
Tour operators Alpine Answers Select, Alpine Elements, Erna Low, Equity, Club Med, Crystal, Directski, First Choice, Inghams, Interhome, Lagrange, Made to Measure, Mark Warner, Momentum, Neilson, On the Piste, Ski Activity, Ski Arrangements, Ski Collection, Ski Expectations, Ski France, Ski Independence, Ski Miquel, Ski Solutions, Ski Supreme, Skiworld, Thomson, Tops, Wasteland

Alpendorf, Austria

See Wagrain and the Salzburger Sportwelt, page 98
Tour operator Ski Astons

Alpine Meadows, California, USA

t +1 530 583 4232, *www.skialpine.com*
Tour operator Ski Dream
Altitude 6,835ft (2083m)–8,637ft (2633m)
Lifts 14

Challenging small ski area with an excellent laid-back atmosphere next to Squaw Valley on Lake Tahoe with 2,400 acres of terrain for intermediate and advanced skiers and riders. 'Great kids' ski school, especially away from holiday weekends, which can be busy,' said a reporter.

Alta, Utah, USA

See Snowbird and Alta, page 429
Tour operators Ski All America, Ski Dream, Ski Independence

Alta Pusteria, Italy

t +39 0474 913 156, *www.three-peaks.info*
Altitude 1310m (4,298ft)–2,000m (6,562ft)
Lifts 27

Seven small alpine ski areas within the Hochpustertal, which is a popular cross-country destination. Some 200km of trails begin around the scenic village of Sesto and charming Moso in the Val di Sesto, and around the thriving Tyrolean village of Dobbiaco and the ancient historic town of San Candido in the Val Pusteria. These head southwest to the quiet Val Fiscalina, with striking views of the Tre Cime de Lavaredo (Three Peaks) en route. A popular trail also leads south from Dobbiaco to Cortina d'Ampezzo. **Berghotel Tirol**, **t** +39 0474 710386, *www.berghotel.com*, is in Sesto, and **Hotel Villa Stefania**, **t** +39 0474 913588, *www.villastefania.com*, is a small hotel with a good restaurant in San Candido.

Altenmarkt, Austria

See Wagrain and the Salzburger Sportwelt, page 98
Tour operators Interhome, Made to Measure, Sloping Off

Alyeska, Alaska, USA

t +1 907 754 1111, *www.alyeskaresort.com*
Altitude 76m (250ft)–1200m (3,939ft)
Lifts 9
Tour operators Crystal, Frontier Ski, Ski All America, Ski Dream

Alaska's steep peaks offer excellent heli- and snowcat-skiing and fabulous scenery and have made this a cult destination for ski extremists. The cable car conveniently starts inside the **Alyeska Prince Hotel**, **t** +1 907 754 1111, *www.princehotels.co.jp/alyeska-e*

Amonina, Switzerland

See Crans-Montana, page 336
Tour operator Lagrange

Andalo, Italy

t +39 0461 585 570, *www.aptdolomiti paganella.com*
Altitude 1040m (3,412ft)–2125m (6,972ft)
Lifts 18
Tour operators Equity/Rocket Ski, SkiBound

Town dating back to the 12th century with pleasant intermediate skiing. This is the place where the World Cup started.

Andermatt, Switzerland

Page 335
Tour operators McNab, Momentum, Mountain Tracks, Ski Freshtracks, Ski Safari, Ski Weekend

Anzère, Switzerland

t +41 (0)27 399 2800, *www.anzere.ch*
Altitude 1500m (4,921ft)–2420m (7,940ft)
Lifts 11
Tour operators Alpine Tours, Lagrange

Purpose-built neighbour of Crans-Montana and Aminona, with 1970s apartment buildings and a loyal Swiss following. 'Anzère is on the sunny side of the hill, very family-orientated and friendly,' said a reporter.

Aonach Mor, Scotland

See Nevis Range, page 488
Tour operator Skisafe Travel

Aosta, Italy

See Pila, page 491

Apex, BC, Canada

t +1 250 292 8222, *www.apexresort.com*
Altitude 575m (5,197ft)–2180m (7,197ft)
Lifts 4
Tour operators Frontier Ski, Ski Safari

Little-known village in the Okanagan Valley offering high-quality skiing without the crowds. The resort is 30 minutes' drive up a private road from the town of Penticton, and an hour from Kelowna airport. The varied runs include blues and easy black-diamonds on the front face, with the highest chair accessing some short and steep trails. Recommended hotels include the **Coast Inn Apex**, **t** +1 250 979 3939, **Saddleback Lodge**, **t** +1 250 292 8118, and the low-cost **Double Diamond Hostel**, **t** +1 250 292 8256.

Aprica, Italy

t +39 0342 746 113, *www.apricaonline.com*
Altitude 1181m (3,875ft)–2361m (7,746ft)
Lifts 19
Tour operators Club Europe, Tops

Pleasant family resort 170km from Milan with 50km of piste. The lifts get very busy at weekends. 'Great skiing for beginners, but do not come if you are after après ski,' said a reporter.

Arabba, Italy

Page 257
Tour operators Inghams, J2Ski, Neilson, Ski Expectations

Arapahoe Basin, Colorado, USA

t +1 970 496 7077, *www.arapahoebasin.com*
Altitude 3283m (10,780ft)–3967m (13,050ft)
Lifts 5
Tour operator Ski Activity

Arapahoe Basin (A-Basin) is a small high-altitude ski area with certain snow until May. Most of the trails suit beginners to intermediates, with the Palavicinni bump run one of the longest and steepest in North America. The nearest accommodation base is six miles away at Keystone. A-Basin shares a lift pass with Vail, Keystone, Breckenridge and Beaver Creek.

Arcalis, Andorra

See Pal-Arinsal, page 34

Les Arcs, France

Page 159

Tour operators Alpine Answers Select, Alpine Elements, Alpine Tracks, Club Med, Crystal, Directski, Equity/Rocket Ski, Erna Low, Esprit, First Choice, French Freedom, Inghams, Interhome, J2Ski, Lagrange, Made to Measure, Momentum, Neilson, On the Piste, Optimum Ski, Ski Activity, Ski Adventures, Ski Amis, Ski Arrangements, Ski Beat, Ski Collection, Ski France, Ski Independence, Ski-Line, Ski Olympic, Ski Solutions, Skiworld, Thomson, Total Ski

Ardent, France

Altitude 1260m (4,134ft)–2466m (8,090ft)
Lifts 206 in Portes du Soleil area (14 cableways, 82 chairs, 110 drags)
Tour operators The Chalet Company, Family Ski Company

Charming little village linked into Les Lindarets near Avoriaz in the Portes du Soleil ski area by a 10-person gondola. L'Escapade is recommended for après ski drinks.

Åre, Sweden

Page 321

Tour operators Mountain Leap, Neilson

Argentière, France

Page 168

Tour operators AWWT, BoardnLodge, Collineige, Crystal, Ski Freshtracks, Indigo Lodges, J2Ski, Lagrange, McNab, Mountain Retreats, Peak Retreats, Ski Hillwood, Ski Independence, White Roc

Arinsal, Andorra

See Pal–Arinsal, page 34

Tour operators Crystal, Directski, First Choice, Inghams, J2Ski, Neilson, Ski Wild, Thomson

Arosa, Switzerland

🏆 BEST SKI SPA 2009 (HOTEL TSCHUGGEN)

t +41 (0)81 378 7020, *www.arosa.ch*
Altitude 1800m (5,904ft)–2653m (8,702ft)
Lifts 13
Tour operators Altitude Inspires, Kuoni, Made to Measure, Momentum, Powder Byrne, Ski Weekend, Snowy Pockets, Switzerland Travel Centre, White Roc

This pretty village offers the all-round winter sports holiday, with skiing for beginners to intermediates. Reporters rated the pistes as 'mainly wide, varied and really good fun to ski'. Recommended hotels include five-star **Arosa Kulm**, **t** +41 (0)81 378 8888, *www.arosakulm.ch*, and **Tschuggen Grand Hotel**, **t** +41 (0)81 378 9999, *www.tschuggen.ch*, which has one of the world's most impressive destination spas. **Hotel Cristallo**, **t** +41 (0)81 378 6868, *www.cristalloarosa.ch*, has bedrooms with four-posters; attractive **Hotel Arlenwald**, **t** +41 (0)81 377 1838, *www.arlenwaldhotel.ch*, has just eight rooms and is ski in, ski out. **Stylish Hotel Eden**, **t** +41 (0)81 377 0261, *www.edenarosa.ch*, has individually decorated bedrooms with a theatrical theme. **Hotel Alpensonne**, **t** +41 (0)81 377 1547, *www.hotelalpensonne.ch*, is another good choice.

Aspen and Snowmass, Colorado, USA

Page 384

Tour operators Alpine Answers Select, American Ski Classics, AWWT, Carrier, Crystal/Crystal Finest, Directski, Elegant Resorts, Erna Low, Lotus Supertravel, Momentum, Original Travel, Seasons in Style, Ski Activity, Ski All America, Ski Dream, Ski Expectations, Ski Independence, Ski Safari, Ski Solutions, Skiworld, United Vacations, Virgin Snow

Auffach, Austria

See Niederau, page 70

Auris-en-Oisans, France

t +33 (0)4 76 80 13 52, *www.auris-en-oisans.com*
Altitude 1600m (5,249ft)–3330m (10,922ft)
Lifts 85 in linked area
Tour operator Lagrange

Purpose-built village linked into the Alpe d'Huez ski area that is well placed for day trips to Les Deux Alpes, Serre Chevalier and La Grave.

Auron, France

t +33 (0)4 93 23 02 66, *www.auron.com*
Altitude 1165m (3,822ft)–2450m (8,038ft)
Lifts 12

Traditional resort with a good atmosphere, linked to St-Etienne-de-Tinze and only 90km from Nice. The ski area provides good intermediate skiing on 130km of piste, with a decent terrain park and ice-skating rink. 'The resort is empty during the week – wonderful,' said a reader.

Aussois, France

t +33 (0)4 79 20 42 21, *www.aussois.com*
Altitude 1500m (4,921ft)–2750m (9,022ft)
Lifts 10
Tour operator Peak Retreats

Aussois is an easily accessible resort situated on a wide, sunny plateau at the foot of the 3697m Dent Parrachée in the Maurienne Valley. ('Nice small family-orientated resort you won't bump into many Brits here.') The old village with its traditional stone-and-slate houses, shared in winter by man and beasts, is built around the central *place*. The skiing is best suited to beginners and intermediates looking for easy cruising runs amid spectacular scenery. The village shares a joint lift-pass with nearby La Norma and Valfréjus. It has 35km of cross-country trails.

Autrans, France

t +33 (0)4 76 95 30 70, *www.ot-autrans.fr*
Altitude 1050m (3,445ft)–1710m (5,610ft)
Lifts 12

Small and attractive low-altitude ski area in the Vercors. **Auberge de la Croix Perrin, t** +33 (0)4 76 95 40 02, *www.aubergedelacroixperrin.com*, is a two-star hotel with eight bedrooms, set in the woods 5km from the village.

Aviemore, Scotland

See Cairngorm Mountain (Aviemore), page 463
Tour operator Skisafe Travel

Avoriaz, France

Page 163

Tour operators Chalet Snowboard, Club Med, Crystal, Directski, Erna Low, First Choice, French Freedom, Lagrange, Momentum, Neilson, On the Piste, Original Travel, rudechalets, Ski Arrangements, Ski Collection, Ski Independence, Thomson, White Roc

Axalp, Switzerland

See Meiringen, page 484

Axamer Lizum, Austria

t +43 (0)5125 9850, *www.innsbrucktourist.info*
Altitude 874m (2,867ft)–2343m (7,687ft)
Lifts 10
Tour operators Crystal, Thomson

This small modern resort offers the best skiing and snowboarding within easy reach of Innsbruck. Axamer is one of the top snowboarding destinations in Austria. There is almost no après ski, so go in a group and make your own, or go for the snow and get an early night. There are only a dozen runs, so it's not suitable for a whole week if you're reasonably experienced. 'Weekends are moderately busy, but during the week it is almost deserted. In all my years of skiing, I've never seen a resort so quiet,' said a reporter.

Bad Gastein and Bad Hofgastein, Austria

See The Gasteinertal, page 47
Tour operators Crystal, Directski, First Choice, Inghams, Made to Measure, Ski Miquel, Ski Wild

Bad Kleinkirchheim and St Oswald, Austria

t +43 (0)4240 8212, *www.badkleinkirchheim.at*
Altitude 1080m (3,543ft)–2000m (6,560ft)
Lifts 26
Tour operators Crystal, Sloping Off

Bad Kleinkirchheim (BKK) is the home resort of Austrian racing legend Franz Klammer. The 103km intermediate ski area is linked with the village of St Oswald. There are lots of wonderfully wide slopes for all standards of skier. Overall the ski area is suited to intermediates and there is an adequate amount of runs for a week's skiing. Accommodation includes five-star **Thermenhotel Ronacher, t** +43 (0)4240 282, *www.ronacher.com*, which has a good spa. The resort has four ski schools and a ski kindergarten. The old Roman baths have been transformed with a 14.5 million makeover and will offer 4,000sq m of wellness area when they open this winter.

Banff/Lake Louise, Alberta, Canada

Page 108

Tour operators Alpine Answers Select, American Ski Classics, AWWT, Crystal/Crystal Finest, Directski, Elegant Resorts, First Choice, Frontier Ski, Inghams, Lotus Supertravel, Momentum, Neilson Nonstopski, Seasons in Style, Ski Activity, Ski All America, Ski Dream, Ski Arrangements, SkiBound, Ski Independence, Ski-Line, Ski Safari, Skiworld, Thomson, Trailfinders, United Vacations, Virgin Snow

Bansko, Bulgaria

Page 146

Tour operators Balkan Holidays, Balkan Tours, Directski, First Choice, Inghams, J2Ski, Neilson, Thomson

Baqueira-Beret, Spain

Page 330

Tour operators Exsus Travel, Inghams, Ski Miquel

Bardonecchia, Italy

t +39 0122 99032, *www.bardonecchiaski.com*
Altitude 1290m (4,232ft)–2750m (9,022ft)
Lifts 24
Tour operators Crystal, Erna Low, Momentum, Neilson, Ski Arrangements, Ski High Days, Thomson, Tops

The busy market town is by the entrance to the Fréjus Tunnel and close to the resorts of Montgenèvre and Sestriere. It offers good value. 'The resort is very child-friendly and the pistes are well groomed. Many times I never saw another soul on the whole run down to the bottom,' enthused a reporter. Three ski areas offer some challenging skiing with few crowds ('some of the slopes seemed a little steeper than the map suggested'), and a choice of 11 mountain restaurants. The resort has recently added a new chairlift and an eight-seater gondola. There are four luxury hotels and six three-stars, but a reporter singles out four-star **L'Hotel Des Geneys Splendid**, **t** +39 0122 99001, *www.hoteldesgeneys.it*, for its 'very good food and accommodation'.

Barèges and La Mongie, France

Barèges, **t** +33 (0)5 62 92 16 00, *www.bareges.com;* La Mongie, **t** +33 (0)5 62 91 94 15, *www.bagneresdebigorre-lamongie.com*
Altitude 1250m (4,100ft)–2350m (7,708ft)
Lifts 43 in linked area
Tour operators Borderline, Lagrange, Pyrenean Mountain Tours

'Utterly charming,' was how one reader described Barèges, 'like Alpine ski resorts used to be 30 years ago. Cheap and cheerful and a delightful little village.' Barèges and La Mongie make up the largest ski area in the Pyrenees, sharing pistes suited to all standards on both sides of the Col du Tourmalet ('great place for a mixed party, lots of varied pistes and lots of good off-piste'). There is virtually no queuing due to a fast six-seater chair. La Mongie is the better base for complete beginners, with lots of off-piste the locals don't seem to use. The one-street spa village of Barèges has more atmosphere than its neighbour. Recommended hotels in Barèges include the two-star **Hôtel Igloo**, **t** +33 (0)5 62 92 68 10, *www.hotel-bareges.com*, which has been refurbished and has a good brasserie, and **Hôtel Alphée**, **t** +33 (0)5 62 92 68 39, offering cheap and tasty food. **Hôtel Europe**, **t** +33 (0)5 62 92 68 04, is also recommended. Accommodation in La Mongie includes three-star **Le Pourteilh**, **t** +33 (0)5 62 91 93 33, *www.hotel-pourteilh.com*, and **Résidence Le Montana**, **t** +33 (0)5 62 91 99 99.

Bariloche, Argentina

See Gran Catedral (Bariloche), page 473

Beaver Creek, Colorado, USA

Page 389

Tour operators American Ski Classics, AWWT, Carrier, Crystal Finest, Elegant Resorts, Original Travel, Seasons in Style, Ski Activity, Ski All America, Ski Dream, Ski Independence, Ski Safari, Ski Wild, United Vacations

Le Bettex, France

See St Gervais, page 224

Big Mountain, USA

t +1 406 862 2900, *www.bigmtn.com*
Altitude 1372m (4,500ft)–2134m (7,000ft)
Lifts 13
Tour operators AWWT, Ski Dream

Large ski area at Whitefish, close to the Canadian border, with 3,000 acres of mainly bowl- and tree-skiing.

Big Sky, Montana

t +1 406 995 5750, *www.bigskyresort.com*
Altitude 11,150ft (3398m)–6,800ft (2073m)
Lifts 22
Tour operators AWWT, Momentum, Ski Activity, Ski Dream, Ski Independence, Ski Safari

Uncrowded high-altitude skiing for all standards 45 miles from Bozeman and 18 miles from Yellowstone National Park. The skiing takes place on three mountains with 150 marked runs in 3,812 acres of skiable terrain. The main action is on 11,150ft Lone Mountain reached by the Lone Peak Tram. Runs from the top include the Big Couloir, a vertiginous fall-line descent that requires considerable concentration. The Gullies and the exposed south face can be almost as challenging. The lower half of the mountain, together with the adjoining peaks of Andersite and Flat Iron, provide plenty of intermediate gladed skiing. The 1,300ft terrain park is the longest in Montana and has a half-pipe. Combined with neighbouring Yellowstone Club, to which it is linked, it would arguably be one of the biggest ski resorts in the USA. Big Sky and adjoining little Moonlight Basin now share a lift pass, making a total area of 5,512 acres. Big Sky opened a new village centre in the 2007–8 season, housing new lodging, shops and restaurants. **Big Sky Snowsports School, t** +1 406 995 5743, has a sound reputation. Best hotel is **The Summit at Big Sky**. **Shoshone Condominium Hotel** has comfortable units with fireplaces. **Powder Ridge Cabins** are rustic-style with hand-hewn log finishes and three or four bedrooms. Call **t** +1 406 995 5000 for all reservations.

Big White, BC, Canada

Page 114
Tour operators American Ski Classics, AWWT, Frontier Ski, Momentum, Ski Activity, Ski All America, Ski Dream, Ski Independence, Ski Safari

Bled, Slovenia

See Bohinj, page 149
Tour operators Crystal, Balkan Holidays, Balkan Tours,Exodus, Thomson

Blue Cow, Australia

See Perisher-Blue, page 491

Bohinj, Slovenia

Page 149
Tour operators Balkan Holidays, Balkan Tours, Directski, Thomson

Bolzano, Italy

t +39 0473 279 457, *www.ortlerskiarena.com*
Altitude 1459m (4,787 ft)–2070m (6,791ft)
Lifts 74 in Ortler Skiarena

Valley town that offers accessible nearby skiing at Meran 2000, Rittner Horn and a host of other resorts. Hotel choices include **Parkhotel Laurin, t** +39 0471 311 000, *www.laurin.it*, **Hotel Kohlern, t** +39 0471 329 978, and **Park-Hotel Holzner, t** +39 0471 345 231, *www.parkhotel-holzner.com*, all with excellent restaurants.

Borca, Italy

See Macugnaga, page 482

Borgata, Italy

t +39 0122 755 449, *www.montagnedoc.it*
Altitude 1840m (6,035ft)–2823m (9,262ft)
Lifts 93 in Milky Way

Hamlet adjoining Sestriere in the Milky Way that acts as an alternative tranquil bed base.

Bormio, Italy

Page 259
Tour operators Directski, J2Ski, Ski Arrangements, Tops

Borovets, Bulgaria

Page 150
Tour operators Balkan Holidays, Balkan Tours, Crystal, Directski, First Choice, Inghams, J2Ski, Neilson, Thomson

Bottières, France

See Le Corbier, page 467

Bourg-St-Maurice, France

See Les Arcs, page 159
Tour operators Erna Low, Vanilla Ski

Brand, Austria

t +43 (0)5559 2240, *www.brand.at* or *www.brandnertal.at*
Altitude 910m (2,986ft)–2000m (6,562ft)
Lifts 14
Tour operator Ski-Line

This uncommercialized family resort used to be popular with the British in the 1960s and '70s and is bidding for a comeback. Brand is making a full-scale overhaul of its ski area and to date has added a new six-seater chair, an eight-person gondola and a spectacular cable car, as well as new pistes. The Gulmabahn cable car links the resort to neighbouring Burserberg across the dividing valley. A panoramic blue trail connects the two ski areas back beneath the lift.

This is an excellent and quiet little resort for first-timers (Keira Knightly learnt to ski here last winter), with plenty of wide open slopes, and a good choice for intermediates not wanting too much of a challenge. 'The word queue does not exist in Brand,' boasts the resort's website. There are five four-star hotels and four three-stars. Four-star **Hotel Scesaplana**, **t** +43 (0)5559 221, *www.scesaplana.at*, has been welcoming guests since 1948 and has a gourmet restaurant and spa.

Breckenridge, Colorado

Page 393
Tour operators Alpine Answers Select, Alpine Tracks, American Ski Classics, AWWT, Crystal/Crystal Finest, Erna Low, Inghams, Interhome, Ski Activity, Ski All America, Ski Dream, Ski Expectations, Ski Independence, Ski-Line, Ski Safari, Ski Solutions, Ski Wild, Skiworld, Thomson, Trailfinders, United Vacations, Virgin Snow

Briançon, France

See Serre Chevalier, page 229
Tour operator Lagrange

Brides-les-Bains, France

t +33 (0)4 79 55 20 64, *www.brides-les-bains.com*
Altitude 1400m (4,593ft)–2952m (9,685ft)
Lifts 165 in Trois Vallées
Tour operators AWWT, Crystal, Erna Low, First Choice, J2Ski, Lagrange, Peak Retreats, Ski Independence, Skiweekends

An alternative spa town choice for those wishing to ski the Trois Vallées ski area on a budget. 'Friendly and accessible' was how one reporter described it. However, another complained about accessibility. 'Gondola ride both ends of the day very tedious and limited as to where you could ski in the afternoon to make sure you caught the last one down.' The gondola links up to Méribel. The town has 21 hotels including **Grand Hôtel des Thermes**, **t** +33 (0)4 79 55 38 38. 'Village very poor for choice of eating out and only one small supermarket for self-catering,' noted a reader.

Brienz, Switzerland

See Meiringen-Hasliberg, page 484

Brighton, Utah, USA

t +1 801 532 4731, *www.brightonresort.com*
Altitude 2668m (8,755ft)–3277m (10,750ft)
Lifts 12

Utah's oldest ski area was founded in 1936 and is located 45 minutes by road from Salt Lake City. It is an attractive resort best suited to intermediates. Brighton has some of the most extensive night skiing in the country, with over 22 trails floodlit until 9pm six days per week. The **Brighton Lodge**, **t** +1 800 873 5512 ext. 236, *www.brightonresort.com*, is slopeside and friendly.

Brixen im Thale, Austria

t +43 (0)5334 8433, *www.brixenimthale.at*
Altitude 800m (2,624ft)–1829m (6,001ft)
Lifts 93 in SkiWelt
Tour operator J2Ski

Traditional Tyrolean village near Kitzbühel, linked by gondola into the SkiWelt.

Bruson, Switzerland

t +41 (0)27 776 1682, *www.verbier.ch*
Altitude 1100m (3,543ft)–2445m (8,022ft)
Lifts 89 in Four Valleys

Small, uncrowded resort near Verbier with some steep powder skiing. Bruson has a couple of hotels, and some apartments on the mountain. This is the next alpine village earmarked for development by Intrawest.

Burserberg, Austria

Village linked by cable car and piste with Brand.
Tour operator Ski-Line

Cairngorm Mountain (Aviemore), Scotland

t +44 (0)1479 810 363, *www.cairngorm mountain.com* or *www.ski.visitscotland.com*
Altitude 550m (1,804ft)–1100m (3,608ft)
Lifts 17
Tour operator Ski Norwest

Aviemore is Britain's best-known ski resort – despite the fact that it is not a ski resort at all; the action takes place on Cairngorm Mountain, 10 miles to the east. Main mountain access is by funicular, and the skiing and riding are surprisingly challenging when conditions allow. The skiing at Cairngorm can be comparable to that of an alpine resort of similar size, but booking in advance is a risky business. A reader complained, 'We were really disappointed. On arrival we were told that there was no ski hire equipment left for children. You also have to queue for 45 minutes to get served in the café. Not recommended for children, and very expensive.' Aviemore, the nearest town, is located about 120 miles north of Edinburgh and Glasgow on the A9. Recommended places to stay include the three-star **Cairngorm Hotel, t** +44 (0)1479 810233, *www.cairngorm.com*, and the **Hilton Coylumbridge Hotel, t** +44 (0)1479 810 661, *www.hilton.co.uk/coylumbridge*.

Campitello, Italy

See Canazei and the Val di Fassa, page 260
Tour operator Neilson

Campo Felice, Italy

t +39 06 943 00001, *www.campofelice.it*
Altitude 1410m (4,626ft)–2065m (6,775ft)
Lifts 14

Little resort with a good lift system and five restaurants, linked to village of Rocca di Cambio and within a one hour-drive of Rome.

Canazei, Italy

Page 260
Tour operators First Choice, Inghams, Neilson

Canillo, Andorra

See Soldeu–El Tarter, page 41
Tour operator Lagrange

The Canyons, Utah, USA

Page 397
Tour operators AWWT, Ski All America, Ski Dream, Ski Independence, Ski Safari, Skiworld, United Vacations

Cardrona, New Zealand

See Wanaka (Cardrona and Treble Cone), page 513

Les Carroz, France

t +33 (0)4 50 90 00 04, *www.lescarroz.com*
Altitude 1140m (3,740ft)–2480m (8,134ft)
Lifts 72 in Grand Massif
Tour operators Altitude Holidays, Erna Low, In Resort Services, Lagrange, Peak Retreats

One of the main resorts of the Grand Massif that is centred around Flaine. 'Your typical charming alpine village. Great for families, lots of activities, good food' and, 'a nice ordinary French village – you don't have to pay the earth for a cup of coffee' were just two of the favourable comments. **L'Igloo, t** +33 (0)4 50 90 14 31, at the top of the Morillon chair, is warmly praised as a lunch spot. The village is more architecturally appealing than Flaine and attracts families and weekend visitors. The cableway and chair are reached by efficient ski-bus from the village centre, and are within easy reach of hotels such as **Les Airelles, t** +33 (0)4 50 90 01 02, **Les Belles Pistes, t** +33 (0)4 50 90 00 17, and **Croix de Savoie, t** +33 (0)4 50 90 00 26. The old village has been renovated and apartment blocks including **MGM, t** +44 (0)20 7584 2841, have been added in keeping with the resort's style. The instruction by **Nouvelle Dimension** was 'first-rate and the children very well catered for'. One reporter recommended the large enclosed picnic area at the top of the *télécabine*, should you wish to take your own lunch and avoid the rather pricey restaurant.

Castelrotto (Kastelruth), Italy

t +39 0471 706 333, *www.castelrotto.com*.
Altitude 1060m (3,478ft)–2180m (7,152ft)
Lifts 24 in Alpe di Suisi

A village of the South Tyrol at the end of the Val Gardena near Ortisei with access to Alpe di Siusi and Sella Ronda. Nearby Zanseralm is a resort dedicated to snowshoeing. **Hotel Cavallino d'Oro**, **t** +39 0471 706337, *www.cavallino.it*, is an ancient and pretty little hotel with quaint decoration. A ski-bus takes you to Alpe di Suisi under 30 minutes away.

Cauterets, France

t +33 (0)5 62 92 50 50, *www.cauterets.com*
Altitude 1000m (3,280ft)–2350m (7,710ft)
Lifts 15
Tour operators Lagrange, Ski Collection

Small spa town 40km from Lourdes-Tarbes airport, offering skiing mainly for beginners and intermediates. 'The Cirque du Lys ski area is fantastic and there are lots of runs. They have a recently built *télécabine* from the town to the ski area and it is uncrowded.' One reporter complains of the 'very limited skiing'. A reader advises, 'English is rarely spoken or understood in shops, restaurants or bars. You'd be well advised to brush up on your French before you go.' Nearby Pont d'Espagne is a separate ski area with four lifts and 37km of cross-country trails. Recommended three-stars in Cauterets include **Hôtel Bordeaux**, **t** +33 (0)5 62 92 52 50, and **Hôtel-Résidence Aladin**, **t** +33 (0)5 62 92 60 00.

Cavalese, Italy

t +39 0462 241 199, *www.valdifiemme.info*
Altitude 860m (2,622ft)–2388m (7,833ft)
Lifts in area 45
Tour operator Thomson

Cavalese is the capital of the Val di Fiemme, a heavily wooded valley north of Trento with five separate ski areas. The spruce is prized by furniture makers and, in the 1700s, Stradivari selected the raw material here for his violins.

Fiemme is otherwise best known for its 70km cross-country race each January for 5,000 pro-am skiers. The pick of the skiing is found at Cavalese, and at Predazzo, the other main town.

The pleasant ski area is more scenic than challenging. Mainly blue and easy reds lead down summer pastureland and through the woods to Cavalese's valley floor. Predazzo is starting point for the more complex 18-lift area of Ski Center Latemar, which extends through Pampeago to Obereggen.

In Cavalese, the choice of accommodation includes four-star **Hotel Grünwald**, **t** +39 0462 340 369, *www.hotelgrunwald.it*, **Hotel La Roccia**, **t** +39 0462 231 133, *www.hotellaroccia.it*, with three-stars, **Hotel Excelsior e Molin**, **t** +39 0462 340 403, *www.excelsiorcavalese.com*, and **Orso Grigio**, **t** +39 0462 341 481, *www.hotelorsogrigio.it*. The latter is where Emperor Franz Josef used to stay in the 19th century.

In Predazzo the four-star of choice is **Hotel Ancora**, **t** +39 0462 501 651, *www.ancora.it*, which offers some of the best accommodation in the valley. Three-star **Hotel Sole**, **t** +39 0462 576 299, *www.hsole.it*, is outside the town at Bellamonte.

Celerina, Switzerland

t +41 (0)81 830 0011, *www.celerina.ch*
Altitude 1720m (5,643ft)–3057m (10,030ft)
Lifts 56 in area
Tour operators First Choice, J2Ski, Thomson

Quiet alternative to St Moritz, with old frescoed houses and access on skis to the Corviglia ski area. **Cresta Palace**, **t** +41 (0)81 836 8080, *www.crestapalace.ch*, **Chesa Rosatsch**, **t** +41 (0)81 837 0101, *www.rosatsch.ch*, the offbeat **Hotel Misani**, **t** +41 (0)81 833 3314, *www.hotelmisani.ch*, with its themed bedrooms, **Posthaus**, **t** +41 (0)81 836 3333, *www.posthaus-celerina.ch*, and **Saluver**, **t** +41 (0)81 833 1314, *www.saluver.ch*, are the hotels of choice.

Cervinia, Italy

Page 264
Tour operators Alpine Answers Select, Club Med, Crystal, Elegant Resorts, First Choice, Inghams, Interhome, Momentum, Mountain Leap, Ski Arrangements, Seasons in Style, SkiBound, Ski Solutions, Thomson

Cesana-Sansicario, Italy

t +39 0122 89202, *www.montagnadoc.it*.
Altitude 1350m (4,428ft)–2823m (9,262ft)
Lifts 92 in Milky Way

Cesana, setting for the Olympic bobsleigh and biathlon events, was given something of a face-lift for the 2006 games. The attractive 12th-century village is set on a busy road close to the Montgenèvre Pass. The lifts accessing the skiing are a long walk from the village centre. Accommodation includes **Hotel Chaberton, t** +39 0122 89147, *www.hotelchaberton.com*. Halfway up the mountain lies the purpose-built village of Sansicario – mainly apartment buildings and a shopping mall. The recommended billet is **Hotel Rio Envers, t** +39 0122 811 333.

Chamonix, France

Page 168

Tour operators Alpine Answers Select, Alpine Elements, Alpine Tracks, Alpine Weekends, Altitude Holidays, AWWT, Bigfoot Travel, Barelli Ski, BoardnLodge, Chamonix Locations, Classic Ski, Club Med, Collineige, Concept Chalets, Corporate Ski Company, Crystal, Directski, Erna Low, Esprit, First Choice, Flexiski, High Mountain Holidays, Huski, Indigo Lodges, Inghams, Interhome, J2Ski, Lagrange, Made to Measure, McNab, Momentum, Mountain Leap, Mountain Retreats, Mountain Tracks, Neilson, Original Travel, Oxford Ski Company, Peak Retreats, Pollen Brooks, rudechalets, Ski Activity, Ski Arrangements, Ski Collection, Ski Expectations, Ski France, Ski Independence, Ski-Line, Ski in Luxury, Ski Solutions, Ski Weekend, Skiweekends, Thomson, Total Ski, White Roc

Champagny-en-Vanoise, France

See La Plagne, page 212

Tour operators Alpine Tracks, Barelli Ski, Erna Low, J2Ski, Lagrange, Peak Retreats, Ski Independence

Champéry, Switzerland

t +41 (0)24 479 20 20, *www.champery.ch*
Altitude 1053m (3,455ft)–2350m (7,708ft)
Lifts 204 in Portes du Soleil
Tour operators Alpine Answers Select, Alpine Tracks, Made to Measure, Momentum, Oak Hall, Ski Independence, Ski Weekend, White Roc

Traditional village in the trans-frontier Portes du Soleil. A large cable car whisks you to the mid-mountain station at Planachaux. Alternative access is by six-seater covered chair from Grand-Paradis. In town, attractive wooden chalets, hotels, shops and restaurants line the main street, but the resort is finally beginning to modernize, with a new ice hall featuring a revamped sports centre. The resort has three ski schools. Recommended places to stay include the comfortable **Hotel Suisse, t** +41 (0)24 479 0707, **Hotel National, t** +41 (0)24 479 1130, and **Hotel Beau-Séjour, t** +41 (0)24 479 5858, *www.beausejour-champery.com*. **Auberge du Grand-Paradis, t** +41 (0)24 479 1167, *www.grandparadis.ch*, is well regarded, while **Hotel la Rose des Alpes, t** +41 (0)24 479 2303, *www.rosedesalpes.com*, is good value.

Champex-Lac, Switzerland

t +41 (0)27 783 2828, *www.champex.ch*
Altitude 1470m (4,823ft)–2188m (7,178ft)
Lifts 4

Charming small resort close to Verbier but not sharing a lift pass. The skiing is limited but never crowded, with some excellent tree-skiing. **Hotel Belvédère, t** +41 (0)27 783 1114, *www.le-belvedere.ch*, is characterful.

Champoluc, Italy

Page 268

Tour operators Alpine Answers Select, Alpine Tracks, Crystal, Indigo Lodges, J2Ski, Momentum, Ski 2, Ski Expectations

Champoussin, Switzerland

t +41 (0)244 76 83 00,
www.royalalpageclub.com
Altitude 1680m (5,512ft)–2350m (7,708ft)
Lifts 211 in Portes du Soleil

Champoussin in the Portes du Soleil is a mini-resort of modern, rustic-style buildings. Most are apartments, but the focal point is **Résidence Royal Alpage Club, t** +41 (0)244 76 83 00, a hotel containing pool, games room, disco and kindergarten.

Chamrousse, France

t +33 (0)4 76 89 92 65, *www.chamrousse.com*
Altitude 1700m (5,577ft)–2255m (7,398ft)
Lifts 24
Tour operators Crystal, Erna Low, Lagrange, Ski Collection, Ski France, Ski Independence, Wasteland

A ski-convenient collection of buildings on the mountainside a 30-minute drive from Grenoble. The resort, scene of Jean-Claude Killy's clean sweep in the 1968 Olympics, attracts a mainly French clientèle and is popular at weekends. 'A good-value resort –

apartment prices well below other French resorts. Very French – expect no English to be spoken. Good for beginners and intermediates but limited for better skier,s, said a reporter. There is a terrain park and a boardercross course. **Hôtel La Datcha**, **t** +33 (0)4 76 89 91 40, is a two-star, and family-friendly **Hôtel Le Virage**, **t** +33 (0)4 76 89 90 63, is simpler.

La Chapelle d'Abondance, France

t +33 (0)4 50 73 51 41, *www.portesdusoleil.com/station/chapelle*
Altitude 1010m (3,313ft)–1700m (5,577ft)
Lifts 207 in Portes du Soleil
Tour operators Ski Addiction, Ski La Côte

A farming village 6km from Châtel. On one side of the road two long chairs take you up to Crêt Bèni; on the other a gondola and chair take you to Châtel and Torgon. **Hôtel Les Cornettes**, **t** +33 (0)4 50 73 50 24, *www.lescornettes.com*, houses one of the area's best restaurants, and **Alti 1000**, **t** +33 (0)4 50 73 51 90, *www.valdabondance.com/alti-1000*, also has a pool. The **Fer Rouge** is the local meeting place.

Château d'Oex, Switzerland

t +41 (0)26 924 25 25, *www.chateau-doex.ch*
Altitude 1050m (3445ft)–2979m (9,744ft)
Lifts 62
Tour operators Alpine Tours, Corporate Ski Company

Small, attractive village, popular with hot-air-balloon enthusiasts, sharing Gstaad's 250km ski area. 'A beautiful traditional resort with lots of facilities,' said a reader, 'lovely, enjoyable runs with few people on them. Great for families, restaurants are good, and nightlife is not a big issue.' Accommodation includes **Gourmet-Hotel Ermitage**, **t** +41 (0)26 924 60 03, *www.gourmet-hotelermitage.ch*, and **Hotel Le Vieux Chalet**, **t** +41 (0)26 924 6879, *www.hotels-suisse.ch/le-vieux-chalet/le-vieux-chalet.htm*, which is a simple old chalet with home cooking.

Châtel, France

t +33 (0)4 50 73 22 44, *www.chatel.com*
Altitude 1200m (3,936ft)–2350m (7,708ft)
Lifts 207 in Portes du Soleil
Tour operators Alpine Tracks, Equity, First Choice, Interhome, Lagrange, Momentum, Ski Addiction, Skialot, Ski Arrangements, Ski Independence, Ski Rosie, Ski Weekend, Snowfocus, Tops

'Quite a pretty, friendly Savoyarde village, with a good selection of restaurants,' was how one reporter described the resort. The small farming village is set in the vast Portes du Soleil. Not a lot of planning has gone into development, which consists of buildings scattered up towards the Morgins Pass and Switzerland, and along the valley to the Linga lift access to Avoriaz. Reporters complain that lifts in the Super-Châtel sector are 'somewhat tired'. However, the old and slow three-man chair between Les Linderets and the Col de Dassachaux (the only direct link between Avoriaz and Châtel's Linga area) has now been replaced with a fast six-man. **Hôtel Fleur de Neige**, **t** +33 (0)4 50 73 20 10, *www.hotel-fleur-deneige.fr*, is a restaurant with rooms. **Hôtel Castellan**, **t** +33 (0)4 50 73 20 86, is renowned for its food, and **Hôtel Les Rhododendrons**, **t** +33 (0)4 50 73 24 04, has the best position. The resort is limited for nightlife. One exception is the Lion Bar ('almost entirely populated by "cloggies" – it's enormous fun from 4pm until 7pm even if you don't understand the singing').

Le Chazelet, France

t +33 (0)4 76 79 95 73, *www.lagrave-lameije.com*
Altitude 1500m (4,921ft)–2100m (6,890ft)
Lifts 1

Close to the extreme skiing at La Grave, on the north face of the Meije, are the three more moderate areas of Le Chazelet, Villar d'Arène and the Col du Lautaret, which are ideal for beginners. If you are staying in La Grave, this is the nearest place to find ski tuition.

Claviere, Italy

t +39 0122 878 856, *www.claviere.it*
Altitude 1760m (5,773ft)–2293m (7,523ft)
Lifts 92 in Milky Way
Tour operators Crystal, Equity/Rocket Ski, First Choice, Ski High Days

Set on the Franco–Italian border, the village is made up of a handful of hotels and shops. Claviere is linked into the giant Milky Way ski area, with access to the skiing above

Montgenèvre and Cesana Torinese and easy home runs. Claviere town was said to be 'a bit boring with no shops'. Accommodation includes **Grand Albergo Clavière**, **t** +39 0122 878 787, **Passero Pellegrino**, **t** +39 0122 878 914, **Hotel Pian del Sole**, **t** +39 0122 878 085, *www.hotelpiandelsole.com*, and **Savoia**, **t** +39 0122 878 803. Ski-in, ski-out **Sporthotel Sagnalonga**, **t** +39 0122 878 856, was criticized: 'Adequate, but breakfast very basic,' said a reporter. 'The evening buffet consisted of pasta and tomato all week,' added another.

La Clusaz, France

Page 172
Tour operators Alpine Tracks, Classic Ski, Crystal, Interhome, Lagrange, Ski Activity, Ski Arrangements, SkiBound, Skitopia, Ski Weekend, Snowlife

Les Coches, France

See La Plagne, page 212
Tour operators Erna Low, Lagrange, Peak Retreats, Ski Independence

Colfosco, Italy

See Corvara, page 276

El Colorado, Chile

See Valle Nevado, page 509

Compaccio (Compatsch), Italy

t +39 0471 704 122, *www.schlern.info*
Altitude 1236m (4,055ft)–2949m (9,676ft)
Lifts 24 in Alpe di Suisi
Tour operator Inntravel

Small, high-altitude hamlet above Ortisei with skiing in the Alpe di Suisi (Seiseralm) and a back-door link into Sella Ronda ski area. Ski-in, ski-out **Hotel Urthaler**, **t** +39 0471 727 919, *www.hotel-urthaler.com*, is fresh and modern.

Les Contamines-Montjoie, France

t +33 (0)4 50 47 01 58, *www.lescontamines.com*
Altitude 2500m (8,202ft)–1164m (3,818ft)
Lifts 24
Tour operators Alpine Tracks, Classic Ski, Club Europe, HF Holidays, Interhome, Lagrange, Ski Arrangements, Ski Weekend

The resort is little-known internationally, but it has a loyal following. Set a short distance from Megève, the village is based on one side of the river while the skiing is the opposite side. The lift access is an 1km uphill walk from the town centre, although a bus service provides transport. It is immediately after a fresh snowfall that Les Contamines comes into its own, offering delightful off-piste skiing. Three-star **Hôtel La Chemenaz**, **t** +33 (0)4 50 47 02 44, *www.chemenaz.com*, is said to be friendly with good food, and **Chalet-Hôtel Camille Bonaventure**, **t** +33 (0)4 50 47 23 53, *www.camillebonaventure.com*, is in the village centre and 600m from the piste.

Copper Mountain, Colorado, USA

Page 400
Tour operators American Ski Classics, AWWT, Crystal, Erna Low, Ski Activity, Ski All America, Ski Dream, SkiBound, Ski Independence, Ski Safari, Thomson, United Vacations, Virgin Snow

Le Corbier, France

t +33 (0)4 79 83 04 04, *www.le-corbier.com*
Altitude 1550m (5,085ft)–2600m (8,530ft)
Lifts 76 in area
Tour operators Equity/Rocket Ski, Interhome, Lagrange, On the Piste, Ski Collection, Ski Independence

Le Corbier is part of Les Sybelles, one of the largest ski areas in the Maurienne Valley, sharing 300km of terrain with the neighbouring resorts of Les Bottières, St-Jean d'Arves, St-Sorlin d'Arves and La Toussuire. The new Sybelles Express six-person chairlift takes skiers up from the village centre to the top of Mont Corbier in eight minutes. The skiing is ideal for beginners and lower intermediates. Most of the accommodation in Le Corbier is in apartments. It also has a couple of two-stars: **Hôtel Mont Corbier**, **t** +33 (0)4 79 56 70 27, in the centre, and **Le Grillon**, **t** +33 (0)4 79 56 72 59, 3km away.

Coronet Peak, New Zealand

See Queenstown (Coronet Peak and The Remarkables), page 494

Corrençon, France

See Villard-de-Lans, page 512

Cortina d'Ampezzo, Italy

Page 273

Tour operators Alpine Answers Select, Crystal, Elegant Resorts, Exodus, Ski Freshtracks, Inghams, J2Ski, Made to Measure, Momentum, Original Travel, Ski Arrangements, Ski Equipe, Ski Expectations, Ski Freshtracks, Ski Solutions, Ski Weekend, White Roc

Corvara, Italy

Page 276

Tour operators Momentum, Neilson, Pyrenean Mountain Tours, Seasons in Style

Courchevel, France

Page 173

Tour operators Alp Leisure, Alpine Answers Select, Alpine Elements, Altitude Holidays, Corporate Ski Company, Crystal, Descent international, Elegant Resorts, Erna Low, Esprit, Family Friendly Ski, Finlays, First Choice, Flexiski, French Freedom, Indigo Lodges, Inghams, Jeffersons, Kaluma, Lagrange, Le Ski, Lotus Supertravel, Made to Measure, Mark Warner, Momentum, Mountain Leap, Mountain Tracks, Neilson, Oxford Ski Company, Powder Byrne, Powder White, Scott Dunn Ski, Seasons in Style, Silver Ski, Ski Activity, Ski Amis, Ski Arrangements, Ski Collection, Ski Deep, Ski Expectations, Ski France, Ski Freshtracks, Ski Independence, Ski in Luxury, Ski-Line, Ski-Link, Ski Olympic, Ski Power, Ski Solutions, Ski Val, Ski Weekend, Skiworld, Thomson, Total Ski, White Roc

Courmayeur, Italy

Page 277

Tour operators Alpine Answers Select, Alpine Tracks, Alpine Weekends, Corporate Ski Company, Crystal, First Choice, Inghams, Interski, J2Ski, Mark Warner, Momentum, Mountain Leap, Ski Arrangements, Ski Expectations, Ski Solutions, Ski Weekend, Thomson, White Roc

Crans-Montana, Switzerland

Page 336

Tour operators Corporate Ski Company, Crystal, Directski, Indigo Lodges, Inghams, Interhome, Kuoni, Made to Measure, Momentum, Mountain Leap, Oxford Ski Company, Ski Solutions, Swiss Travel Service, Switzerland Travel Centre

Crested Butte, Colorado, USA

Page 402

Tour operators AWWT, Club Med, Crystal, Ski Activity, Ski Dream, Ski Safari, Thomson, United Vacations

Crest-Voland, France

See Notre-Dame-de-Bellecombe, page 489 and Les Saisies, page 499

Les Crosets, Switzerland

t +41 (0)24 477 2077, *www.lescrosets.com*
Altitude 1660m (5,445ft)–2350m (7,708ft)
Lifts 207 in Portes du Soleil

The hamlet sits at the in the heart of the Portes du Soleil and is highly rated by riders. It has its own snowboard school and terrain park. Not the most appealing of resorts, it is best suited to serious skiers and boaders who favour early nights. **Hotel Télécabine, t** +41 (0)24 479 0300, *www.hotel-telecabine.com*, is simple with good food.

Dachstein Glacier, Austria

See Wagrain and the Salzburger Sportwelt, page 98

La Daille, France

See Val d'Isère, page 240

Davos, Switzerland

Page 338

Tour operators Alpine Answers Select, Alpine Weekends, Altitude Inspires, Carrier, Corporate Ski Company, Crystal/Crytal Finest, Descent International, Exodus, Flexiski, Headwater, Inghams, Kuoni, Made to Measure, Momentum, Mountain Leap, Ski Expectations, Ski Freshtracks, Ski Independence, Ski Safari, Ski Solutions, Ski Weekend, Swiss Travel Service, Switzerland Travel Centre, White Roc

Deer Valley, Utah, USA

Page 403

Tour operators American Ski Classics, Momentum, Ski Dream, Ski Independence, Ski in Luxury, Ski Safari

Les Deux Alpes, France

Page 179

Tour operators Crystal, Erna Low, Equity/Rocket Ski, First Choice, French Freedom, Inghams, Interhome, J2Ski, Lagrange, Made to Measure, Mark Warner, McNab, Momentum, Neilson, On the Piste, Peak Retreats, Ski Activity, Ski Arrangements, Ski France, Ski Independence, Ski Solutions, Ski Supreme, Skiworld, Thomson, Tops, Wasteland

Les Diablerets, Switzerland

See Villars, page 371

Tour operators Crystal, J2Ski, Momentum, Ski Freshtracks, Sloping Off, Solo's, Swiss Travel Service, Switzerland Travel Centre, Thomson

Dienten, Austria

See Maria Alm, page 483

Tour operator Made to Measure

Dobbiaco, Italy

See Alta Pusteria, page 456

Tour operators Exodus, Headwater, Ramblers

Durango, Colorado, USA

t +1 970 247 9000, *www.durangomountainresort.com*

Altitude 2680m (8,793ft)–3299m (10,822ft)

Lifts 10

A purpose-built, alpine-style resort in southern Colorado with an old-town ambience. The skiing takes place on Purgatory Mountain. The resort makes an ideal two-centre trip with Telluride, which is two and a half hours' drive away. Snowboarders and twin-tippers are well catered for with a freestyle arena and terrain park. The **Adaptive Sports Association** is one of the best schools for disabled skiers in the USA. Hotels include **Purgatory Village Hotel, t** +1 970 385 2100, the **Inn at Durango Mountain, t** +1 970 247 9669, and **Sheraton Tamarron Resort, t** +1 970 259 2000.

Ehrwald, Austria

See Garmisch-Partenkirchen, page 472

Tour operator J2Ski

Eichenhof, Austria

See St Johann in Tirol, page 86

Ellmau, Austria

t +43 (0)5358 2301, *www.ellmau.at*

Altitude 820m (2,690ft)–1829m (6,001ft)

Lifts 93 in SkiWelt

Tour operators Crystal, Inghams, Neilson, Ramblers, Ski Wild, Thomson

Ellmau received ecstatic comments. 'My favourite place in the world,' said one reporter, and, 'Everyone was very friendly – in the village, the ski school, even in the lift queues. Relatively few boarders and a lack of serious black runs,' added another. The largest resort of the SkiWelt offers good access into the lift system and a wide choice of accommodation. **Hotel Christoph, t** +43 (0)5358 3535, *www.hotel-christoph.com*, a five-minute walk from the main lift, has spacious rooms. **Hotel Hochfilzer, t** +43 (0)5358 2501, *www.hotel-hochfilzer.com*, and **Sporthotel Ellmau, t** +43 (0)5358 3755, *www.sporthotel-ellmau.com*, are both four-stars. The deluxe **Relais & Chateaux der Bär, t** +43 (0)5358 2395, *www.hotelbaer.com*, has a spa. The **Ellmau** ski school was rated 'fantastic, with a range of fluent English-speaking, easy-going staff who are extremely capable skiers and snowboarders' and 'Ellmau Hartkaiser ski school did a fantastic job with my children'.

Encamp, Andorra

See Soldeu, page 41

Engelberg, Switzerland

Page 342

Tour operators Alpine Answers Select, Crystal, Exodus, Inntravel, Interhome, J2Ski, Kuoni, Made to Measure, Momentum, Mountain Leap, Oak Hall, Ski Independence, Ski Safari, Ski Solutions, Ski Weekend, Swiss Travel Service, Switzerland Travel Centre, White Roc

Entrèves, Italy

See Courmayeur, page 277

Espace Diamant, France

See Notre-Dame-de-Bellecombe, page 489

Espace Killy, France

See Val d'Isère page 240 and Tignes page 235

Falls Creek and Mount Hotham, Australia

Falls Creek, t +61 (0)3 5758 3224; **Mount Hotham, t** +61 (0)3 5759 4444, *www.fallscreek.com.au* or *www.hotham.com.au*
Altitude 1450m (4,757ft)–1861m (6,105ft)
Lifts 13

The major resorts in Victoria share a lift pass and are linked by a six-minute helicopter ride. Falls Creek Alpine Resort is four hours' drive from Melbourne on the edge of the Bogong High Plains. The European-style, ski in, ski out village has accommodation among the gum trees. Australia's largest snowmaking system covers the main trails, and the resort has a good terrain park.

Mount Hotham is the highest alpine resort in Victoria, with most of the skiing below the village. Dinner Plain, Mount Hotham's sister village, has good-value accommodation, 10km from the mountain, linked by free ski-bus.

Le Fayet, France

See St-Gervais, page 224

Fernie, BC, Canada

Page 115
Tour operators Alpine Answers Select, American Ski Classics, AWWT, Crystal, Frontier Ski, Inghams, Momentum, Neilson, Nonstopski, Original Travel, Ski Activity, Ski All America, Ski Dream, Ski Arrangements, Ski Independence, Ski Safari, Skiworld, Virgin Snow

Fieberbrunn, Austria

t +43 (0)5354 563330, *www.pillerseetal.at*
Altitude 800m (2,625ft)–2020m (6,627ft)
Lifts 11
Tour operators Snowscape, Thomson, Tyrolean Adventures

Small, attractive ski area near St Johann in Tirol with a reputation for good snow and a network of long, easy, tree-level runs. 'The resort is very snowboard friendly,' said a reporter, 'even the draglifts have wide tracks so no problems for boarders.' **Austria Trend Sporthotel Fontana, t** +43 (0)5354 56453, *www.austria-trend.at/fib*, and **Hotel-Pension Lindauerhof, t** +43 (0)5354 56382, are convenient while **Schloss Rosenegg, t** +43 (0)5354 56201, is a 14th-century castle with dungeons, and bedrooms reached by spiral staircase.

Filzmoos, Austria

See Wagrain and the Salzburger Sportwelt, page 98
Tour operators Inghams, Interhome

Great little village and ski area, linked to Flachau, Waidring and Altenmarkt. Relatively easy skiing with mostly blue slopes and some reds – a very good place to learn. 'Eating is reasonably priced and the food is great. Definitely recommend it for beginners to early intermediates,' said a reporter .

Finkenberg, Austria

See Mayrhofen, page 64
Tour operator Crystal

Fiss, Austria

t +43 (0)5476 62390, *www.serfaus-fiss-ladis.at*
Altitude 1427m (4,682ft)–2684m (8,806ft)
Lifts 53 in area
Tour operator Alpine Tours

Small, traditional village sharing a ski area with Ladis and Serfaus. The village centre has been retained – most of the houses were built in the 16th and 17th centuries, with stone walls, arched doorways and overhanging gabled roofs. The resort has 20 restaurants and cafés.

Flachau, Austria

See Wagrain and the Salzburger Sportwelt, page 98
Tour operators Interhome, Made to Measure, Ski Astons

Flaine, France

Page 183
Tour operators Alpine Answers Select, Altitude Holidays, Alpine Tracks, Classic Ski, Crystal, Erna Low, Inghams, In Resort Services, Lagrange, Momentum, Neilson, Ski Arrangements, Ski Collection, Ski Freshtracks, Ski Independence, Thomson

Flims, Switzerland

See Laax, page 353

Flumet, France

See Nôtre-Dame-de-Bellecombe, page 489 and Les Saisies, page 499

Folgarida, Italy

t +39 0463 901280, *www.valdisole.net*
Altitude 1300m (4,265)–2505m (8,219ft)
Lifts 47 in area
Tour operator SkiBound

Purpose-built resort linked to Marilleva, and to Madonna di Campiglio 9km away. Some 120km of linked skiing, popular with budget skiers and school groups.

La Foux d'Allos, France

See Pra-Loup, page 493
Tour operator Club Europe

Font-Romeu, France

t +33 (0)4 68 30 68 30, *www.font-romeu.fr*
Altitude 1700m (5,577ft)–2250m (7,382ft)
Lifts 26
Tour operators Lagrange, Ski Collection, Solo's

'A real Gallic feel to the town and good skiing,' said a reader. The old Pyrenean village is 90km from Perpignan with the skiing and purpose-built ski station 4km away and linked by gondola. The pistes are best suited to beginners, lower intermediates and families. Weekend queueing can be a problem. There are two dozen hotels and *pensions*, including three-star **Hôtel Carlit, t** +33 (0)4 68 30 80 30, *www.carlit-hotel.fr*, **Le Grand Tetras, t** +33 (0)4 68 30 01 20, *www.hotelgrandtetras.free.fr*, **La Montagne, t** +33 (0)4 68 30 36 44, and **Sun Valley, t** +33 (0)4 68 30 21 21, *www.hotelsunvalley.fr*. **Hôtel Lassus, t** +33 (0)4 68 30 09 75, *www.hotel-lassus.com,* is recommended.

Fulpmes, Austria

See Neustift and the Stubaital, page 68
Tour operators Crystal, J2Ski, Lagrange

Furano, Japan

Page 310
t +44 (0)20 7734 6870, *www.snowjapan.com*
Altitude 235m (771ft)–1209m (3,966ft)
Lifts 11
Tour operators Inghams, Ski Independence, Ski Safari

Galtür, Austria

t +43 (0)50990 200, *www.galtuer.com*
Altitude 1585m (5,200ft)–2300m (7,546ft)
Lifts 67 in area
Tour operators First Choice, Inghams, Lagrange, Neilson

Small resort with considerable atmosphere close to Ischgl. Galtür's pistes are at Wirl, five minutes' away by a free and frequent shuttle bus. The skiing is gentle and well suited to beginners and families, and the area is also a notable centre for ski-touring. The family-run **Flüchthorn Hotel, t** +43 (0)5444 55550, *www.fluchthorn-buentali.at*, offers a warm welcome in a central location. Four-star **Hotel Post, t** +43 (0)5444 5232, *www.hotel-post.at*, is convenient.

Gargellen, Austria

t +43 (0)5557 6303, *www.gargellen.at*
Altitude 1430m (4,692ft)–2300m (7,546ft)
Lifts 62 in area

The attractive chalet-style village in the Montafon area is close to the border with Switzerland and attacts a loyal international clientèle. The ski area is shared with 10 other villages in the area, with a total 222km of piste and 62 lifts, as well as extensive ski-touring on the Silvretta glaciers, and 100km of cross-country trails: 'some spectacular off piste,' noted a reader. The ski school is criticized. 'When I wanted the instructor to speak English to me, he simply couldn't.' Hotels in Gargellen include the four-star **Madrisa, t** +43 (0)5557 6331, *www.madrisahotel.com*, which was built as a country house at the beginning of the 20th century and opened as a hotel in the 1920s ('excellent, family-run, and very friendly. It is right by the beginner slope and you can ski back to the door'). **Hotel Heimspitze, t** +43 (0)5557 63190, *www.heimspitze.com*, is also rated. The resort has a modern eight-person gondola, and free ski buses link Gargellen with neighbouring **Gaschurn** and **St Gallenkirch**.

Garmisch-Partenkirchen, Germany

t +49 (0)8821 1806, *www.garmisch-partenkirchen.de*
Altitude 710m (2,330ft)–1330m (4,364ft)
Lifts 32 in Zugspitze

Tour operators Crystal, Momentum, Moswin's Germany

The towns of Garmisch and Partenkirchen are surrounded by striking scenery (the view from the top of Zugspitz is phenomenal) and lie beneath Austria and Germany's highest mountain. Partenkirchen is an ancient Roman town dating back to 15 BC, while Garmisch has frescoed medieval houses. The towns were linked for Hitler's 1936 Winter Olympics. The ski area is made up of five mountains and offers 15km of Germany's only glacier skiing. Although Garmisch has 18km of undemanding piste, the majority of runs are best suited to intermediates, with a terrain park featuring a super-pipe. The mountain can be accessed from three starting places, including a cable car and cog railway from Garmisch. 'Good selection of runs and easy access to all three areas. Access to Hausberg is the only fly in the ointment. The two cable cars are simply not enough for the amount of people wanting to use it. Queuing for 45 minutes is just not acceptable,' complained a reader. The glacier can also be reached from the village of Ehrwald in Austria. Hotels include five-star **Reindl's**, **t** +49 (0)8821 943 870, and the four-star **Hotel Alpina**, **t** +49 (0)8821 7830, *www.alpina-gap.de*.

Gaschurn, Austria

t +43 (0)5557 6303, *www.gargellen.at*
Altitude 1430m (4,692ft)–2300m (7,546ft)
Lifts 62 in area
Tour operator Made to Measure

The ski area is shared with 10 other villages in the area, with a total 222km of piste and 62 lifts, as well as extensive ski-touring. Free ski buses link Gaschurn with neighbouring Gargellen and St Gallenkirch.

The Gasteinertal, Austria

Page 47

Geilo, Norway

Page 323
Tour operators Alpine Tracks, Crystal, Exodus, Headwater, Inntravel, Neilson

Les Gets, France

Page 206

Tour operators Alpine Elements, Descent International, Equity/Rocket Ski, Esprit, First Choice, Lagrange, Momentum, Oxford Ski Company, Peak Retreats, Reach4theAlps, Ski Activity, Ski Expectations, Ski Famille, Ski Hillwood, Ski Independence, Ski-n-Do, Total Ski

Glencoe and Glenshee, Scotland

Glencoe t +44 (0)1855 851 226, *www.ski-glencoe.co.uk* / **Glenshee t** +44 (0)1339 41320, *www.ski-glenshee.co.uk*
Altitude 304m (1,000ft)–1109m (3637ft)
Tour operator (Glenshee) Skisafe Travel

Glencoe is the orginal UK resort and has the longest black run in Scotland, while Glenshee has the largest lift system in Britain ('The back corries at Glenshee are absolutely fantastic'). However, both are victims of the changing European weather pattern and suffer from lack of snow for much of the winter. When it does fall, both can offer good skiing and have excellent ski schools, but it is impossible to book a holiday in advance and be certain of sufficient cover. Near Glencoe, recommended accommodation is the **Macdonald Hotel**, **t** +44 (0)1855 831 539, *www.macdonaldhotel.co.uk*, and **Invercoe Highland Holiday Cottages**, **t** +44 (0)1855 811 210. Near Glenshee, recommended hotels include **Callater College Hotel**, **t** +44 (0)1339 741 275, **Braemar Lodge**, **t** +44 (0)1339 741 627, **Dalmunzie House Hotel**, **t** +44 (0)1250 885 224, and the **Spittal Hotel**, **t** +44 (0)1250 885 215.

Going, Austria

t +43 (0)5358 2438, *www.going.at*
Altitude 800m (2,624ft)–829m (6,001ft)
Lifts 93 in SkiWelt

Linked into the SkiWelt area, Going has stunning views and a good nursery slope. One of the village highlights is five-star **Hotel Stanglwirt**, **t** +43 (0)5358 2000, *www.stanglwirt.com*, which has a Lipizzaner riding school.

Golden, BC, Canada

See Kicking Horse, page 119

Gosau, Austria

See St Wolfgang, page 499

Grächen, Switzerland

t +41 (0)27 955 60 60, *www.graechen.ch*
Altitude 1615m (5,330ft)–2890m (9,537ft)
Lifts 13
Tour operator Interhome

Chalet-style village close to Saas-Fee and Zermatt. The ski area is accessed by a choice of two gondolas.

Gran Catedral (Bariloche), Argentina

t +54 (0)2944 423776, *www.bariloche.com*
Altitude 1050m (3,445ft)–2050m (6,725ft)
Lifts 32
Tour operators Andes, Ski Dream

San Carlos de Bariloche, in Patagonia, is home to Gran Catedral – Argentina's oldest and most famous ski resort – better known as Bariloche. It is a large, attractive resort not far from the Chilean border.

Sophisticated Bariloche is South America's biggest resort, boasting a modern lift system, 50 trails, a vertical drop of 1000m and the largest snowmaking system in South America. The area provides intermediate slopes with high-speed cruising and abundant off-piste. ('Complete lack of people on the slopes, which meant that we had the place more or less to ourselves.'). Hotels include the five-star **Panamericano**, *www.panamericano bariloche.com*, and four-star **Hotel Nevada**, **t** +54 (0)2944 522 778, *www.nevada.com.ar*, and **Hotel Edelweiss, t** +54 (0)2944 445 500, *www.edelweiss.com.ar*.

Le Grand Bornand, France

t +33 (0)4 50 02 78 00,
www.legrandbornand.com
Altitude 950m (3,120ft)–2100m (6,890ft)
Lifts 39
Tour operators Lagrange, Peak Retreats, Ski Arrangements, Thomson

Charming village 10 minutes' drive from La Clusaz with 90km of piste suited to all levels. The main ski station is at Le Chinaillon. The picturesque Col des Annes offers motorway cruising. From Lachat, at 2100m, the piste stretches out to the gentle slopes of Joyère. The Aiguille Mountain terrain park provides a good playground and La Clusaz is an easy drive away. The three-star hotels are **Best Western Chalet Les Saytels, t** +33 (0)4 50 02 20 16, *www.bestwestern-chaletlessaytels.com*, and chalet-style **Les Cimes, t** +33 (0)4 50 27 00 38, *www.hotel-les-cimes.com*.

Grand Targhee, Wyoming, USA

t +1 307 353 2300, *www.grandtarghee.com*
Altitude 8,000ft (2438m)–10,230ft (3118m)
Lifts 8
Tour operators AWWT, Ski Safari

Small purpose-built resort 47 miles from Jackson Hole. It boasts a wonderful snow record, which is why the main attraction is snowcat-skiing. If you can't get a space on a snowcat, the resort's 2,000-acre ski area offers challenge and plenty of powder. Prices are considerably lower than in Jackson Hole, and accommodation, **t** +1 800 827 4433 for booking office, includes **Teewinot Lodge**, **Targhee Lodge** and **Sioux Lodge Condominiums**.

Grandvalira, Andorra

See Pas de la Casa page 37 and Soldeu page 41

Grau Roig, Andorra

See Pas de la Casa, page 37

La Grave, France

Page 188
Tour operators J2Ski, Lagrange, Momentum, Peak Retreats, Ski Arrangements, Ski Weekend

Gressoney, Italy

See Champoluc–Alagna–Gressoney, page 268
Tour operators Alpine Answers Select, Alpine Tracks, Crystal, J2Ski, Momentum, Pyrenean Mountain Tours, Ski Expectations, Ski Freshtracks, Ski Weekend

Grimentz, Switzerland

🏆 MOST PROMISING RESORT 2009

t +41 (0)27 475 1493, *www.grimentz.ch*
Altitude 1553m (5,095ft)–2900m (9,514ft)
Lifts 10
Tour operators Interhome, J2Ski, Made to Measure, Ski Freshtracks

A cult resort in the beautiful Val d'Anniviers where it pays to hire a guide and ski the fabulous off-piste. At the heart of the village one of the largest collections of perfectly-preserved blackened wood *mazots* to be found in a ski resort in switzerland. The Grimentz-

Bendola area has a total 50km of surprisingly good pistes, and the shared liftpass gives access to all the ski resorts in the Val d'Anniviers – Zinal, St-Luc/Chandolin and Vercorin – covering more than 220km. **Hotel Alpina**, **t** +41 (0)27 476 1616, *www.alpinagrim.ch*, is the only three-star, but a four-star is in the pipeline. The resort crèche accepts children from two years and the ski school also offers alpine skiing, telemark and snowboarding.

Grindelwald, Switzerland

Page 344

Tour operators Altitude Inspires, Crystal, Elegant Resorts, Inghams, Interhome, J2Ski, Jeffersons, Kuoni, Made to Measure, Momentum, Powder Byrne, Seasons in Style, Ski Freshtracks, Swiss Travel Service, Switzerland Travel Centre, Thomson, White Roc

Grossarl, Austria

t +43 (0)6414 281, *www.grossarltal.info*
Altitude 920m (3,018ft)–2442m (8,012ft)
Lifts 270 in Ski Amadé area

Small village with ski area linked to Dorfgastein. Four-star **Hotel Bergzeit**, **t** +43 (0)6414 200 40, *www.hotel-bergzeit.at*, is less than 100m from the new gondola and was highly rated. 'Rooms clean and modern, the half-board food out of this world.' The bars and restaurants on the slopes were 'not too expensive, all food was tasty and beer a-plenty. I would not hesitate to recommend this resort to any intermediate,' said a reader.

Gstaad, Switzerland

Page 347

Tour operators Altitude Inspires, Corporate Ski Company, Indigo Lodges, J2Ski, Made to Measure, Momentum, Mountain Leap, Seasons in Style, Ski Expectations, Ski Weekend, Switzerland Travel Centre, White Roc

Guthega, Australia

See Perisher-Blue, page 49

Hafjell, Norway

See Lillehammer, page 482

Happo'one and Hakuba Valley, Japan

t +44 (0)20 7734 6870, *www.snowjapan.com*
Altitude 760m (2,493ft)–1830m (6,007ft)
Lifts 33

This pretty village has the biggest ski area in the Nagano Prefecture's resort-studded Hakuba Valley, and is arguably the best resort in the country. The valley lies 200km from Tokyo, to which it is linked by the bullet train. The resort has striking scenery, challenging terrain, and longer-than-average runs. Accommodation includes **Hotel Omoshiro Hasshinchi**, **t** +81 (0)261 72 6663, at the resort base. The **Hotel Lady Diana & St George's**, **t** +81 (0)261 75 3525, is also rated.

Hasliberg, Switzerland

See Meiringen-Hasliberg, page 484

Tour operator Interhome

Haus im Ennstal, Austria

t +43 (0)3686 2234, *www.haus.at*
Altitude 750m (2,460ft)–2015m (6,611ft)
Lifts 46 in area

A peaceful little farming village linked into the Schladming-Dachstein region. **Hotel Gasthof Herrschaftstaverne**, **t** +43 (0)3686 2392, *www.herrschaftstaverne.at*, has a spa, traditional **Dorfhotel Kirchenwirt**, **t** +43 (0)3686 2228, *www.kirchenwirt.net*, is in the village centre, **Gasthof Reiter**, **t** +43 (0)3686 2225, *www.gasthofreiter.at*, is lovely, and **Panoramahotel Gürtl**, **t** +43 (0)3686 2383, *www.hotel-guertl.at*, is family-run.

Heavenly, California, USA

Page 406

Tour operators American Ski Classics, AWWT, Crystal, Erna Low, Ski Activity, Ski All America, Ski Dream, SkiBound, Ski Independence, Ski Safari, Skiworld, Thomson, Tops, Trailfinders, United Vacations

Hemsedal, Norway

Page 325

Tour operators Alpine Tracks, Crystal, Neilson

Hinterthal and Hintermoos, Austria

See Hochkönig, opposite

Hintertux, Austria

See Tux im Zillertal, page 508

Hochkönig, Austria

t +43 (0)6216 2020 2727, *www.hochkoenig.at*
Altitude 802m (2,630ft)–2,012m (6,600ft)
Lifts 39
Tour operators Elevation Holidays, Club Europe, Tops

The 150km ski area is in Salzburgerland and has some 39 lifts. It includes the resorts of Maria Alm, Dienten, Hintermoos, Hinterthal, Mühlbach and Saalfelden. There are four ski schools, 50km of cross-country tracks, and almost 40 restaurants in the area.

Hochsölden, Austria

See Sölden, page 93

Hopfgarten, Austria

t +43 (0)5335 2322, *www.hopfgarten.com*
Altitude 622m (2,040ft)–1829m (6,001ft)
Lifts 93 in SkiWelt
Tour operators Contiki, First Choice

Traditional village in the SkiWelt circuit dominated by the twin yellow towers of its church. Despite its friendly atmosphere, few British are attracted to the resort; most visitors are Australians and New Zealanders. Accommodation includes **Aparthotel Hopfgarten**, **t** +43 (0)5335 3920, *www.hotel-hopfgarten.at*, and **Sporthotel Fuchs**, **t** +43 (0)5335 2420, *www.sporthotel-fuchs.at*.

Les Houches, France

Page 190
Tour operators Barelli Ski, Erna Low, French Freedom, Inghams, Interhome, Lagrange, Made to Measure, Peak Retreats, Ski Expectations, Ski France, Ski Independence, Skiweekends, Snow Safari

Huez, France

t +33 (0)4 76 11 44 44, *www.alpedhuez.com*
Altitude 1120m (3,674ft)–3330m (10,922ft)
Lifts 85 in Alpe d'Huez area

Old village below Alpe d'Huez resort and connected by cable car. **Hôtel L'Ancolie**, **t** +33 (0)4 76 11 13 13, is a renovated farmhouse with a good restaurant.

Humber Valley Resort, Newfoundland

t +0800 404 9251 (UK toll free), *www.humbervalley.com*
Altitude: 10m (33ft)–546m (1,791ft)

Newfoundland has the closest North American skiing to the UK, with a five-and-a-half hour flight and a three-and-a-half-hour time difference. The scenery is beautiful, but temperatures can be low. The resort of Humber Valley is an alternative to the over-commercialized and overpriced mainstream resorts on both sides of the Atlantic. You can buy luxury chalets here at incredibly low prices. Marble Mountain, 10 minutes' drive from Humber Valley Resort, is a small area with 35 trails, but one of the main attractions is the rough and ready cat-skiing, **t** +1 709 783 2712, a rugged experience like no other.

The restaurants at Corner Brook, Pasadena and Deer Lake provide a choice of dining. **Gitanos'**, **t** +1 709 634 4389, serves European cuisine, **Thirteen West**, **t** +1 709 634 1300, has hearty Newfoundland tucker such as seafood chowder. Humber Valley Resort has **Sully's at the Beach House** and Sunday brunch at the **Eagle's Perch**, **t** +1 709 686 8100 for both, while **Mansion Pool Dining Room** at Strawberry Hill Resort, **t** +1 877 434 0066, offers high quality food and wine. A shopping service is available for guests at Humber Valley Resort, and pizzas and burgers can be delivered.

Rural Newfoundland is not party land and nightlife is restricted to a few bars. Snowmobiling is a major resort pastime, with 746 miles (1200km) of groomed trails and guided evenings. Most visitors stay in the excellent **Humber Valley Resort chalets and apartments**, **t** +1 709 686 8100 or 0800 404 9251 (UK).

Hungerburg, Austria

See Innsbruck, page 476

Igls, Austria

t +43 (0)5125 9850, *www.innsbrucktourist.info*
Altitude 900m (2,953ft)–2247m (7,372ft)
Lifts 6
Tour operators Inghams, Lagrange, Made to Measure

Small village 5km from Innsbruck towards the Europabrücke and the Italian border. The skiing is limited, with the Olympic downhill run – of Franz Klammer fame – presenting the only real challenge. ('Apart from three elderly Austrian gentlemen we were more or less the only people on the slopes for the first half-hour – heaven.') The village is made up of traditional hotels and coffee houses ('A lovely café/bar, Fiorina'), some bracing winter walks, and the Olympic bob-run which is open to the public. **Sporthotel Igls, t** +43 (0)5123 77241, *www.sporthotel-igls.com*, has good food, and the five-star **Schlosshotel, t** +43 (0)5123 77217, *www.schlosshotel-igls.com*, is recommended, and **Hotel Batzenhäusl, t** +43 (0)5123 8618, *www.batzenhaeusl.at*, is very comfortable. 'There didn't seem to be many tourists – mainly locals and there aren't that many bars and restaurants on the mountain. Not much in the way of après ski either, said a reader.

Inneralpbach, Austria

See Alpbach, page 46

Innsbruck, Austria

t +43 (0)512 59850, *www.innsbruck.info*
Altitude 580m (1,903ft)–2334m (6,250ft)
Lifts 78 in nine ski areas
Tour operators J2Ski, Lagrange, Ramblers

A minor ski resort in its own right, but its real significance is as a base for visiting other well-known resorts of the Tyrol and the Arlberg. Hungerberg is the home ski area just outside the city, set on the steep south-facing slopes of the Hafelekar. The city's best hotel is the five-star **Europa-Tyrol, t** +43 (0)5125 9310, *www.europatyrol.com*. Four-stars include **Hotel-Restaurant Goldener Adler, t** +43 (0)5125 71111, **Hotel Penz, t** +43 (0)512 575657, *www.the-penz.com*, and **Romantikhotel Schwarzer Adler, t** +43 (0)5125 87109. **Hotel Weisses Kreuz, t** +43 (0)5125 94790, *www.weisseskreuz.at*, is a 500-year-old hotel where Mozart stayed as a child.

Interlaken, Switzerland

t +41 (0)33 826 53 00, *www.interlaken tourism.ch*
Altitude 796m (2,612ft)–2971m (9,748ft)
Lifts 41 in Jungfrau Top Ski Region
Tour operators Crystal, Kuoni, Ski Astons, Swiss Travel Service

Sophisticated, attractive town positioned between two lakes at the foot of the dramatic Eiger, Munch and Jungfrau mountains. It provides a good base for mixed groups with non-skiers who would rather stay in a bustling town than in a ski resort. From the centre it is a short train ride to Lauterbrunnen where you can catch the cable car to Mürren, or a train to Wengen and Grindelwald. The best place to stay is outwardly traditional **Grand Hotel Victoria-Jungfrau, t** +33 (0)828 2828, *www.victoria-jungfrau.ch*, which has a state-of-the-art spa and minimalist rooms in its spa wing.

Ischgl, Austria

Page 51
Tour operators Alpine Answers Select, Alpine Tracks, Crystal/Crystal Finest, First Choice, Inghams, Made to Measure, Momentum, Ski Expectations, Ski Independence, Ski Safari, Ski Solutions, Ski Wild

Isella, Italy

See Macugnaga, page 482

Isola 2000, France

t +33 (0)4 93 23 15 15, *www.isola2000.com*
Altitude 1800m (5,904ft)–2610m (8,561ft)
Lifts 22
Tour operators Crystal, Erna Low, French Freedom, Lagrange, Ski Arrangements, Ski Collection, Ski France

Purpose-built resort with 120km of piste and built by a British property company in the 1960s. Isola is the most southerly ski area in France but it is a good place to find late-season snow. Created with families in mind, there's a decent collection of shops, bars, no-frills apartments and hotels, and a large, sunny nursery area. British skiers make up a large portion of the clientèle, with many owning apartments. The ski area is limited, but varied enough for beginners, families with young children, and undemanding intermediates. 'The lift system is old, slow and badly needs upgrading,' complained a reader. However, a new gondola provides the main mountain access and two of the chairlifts have been updated for this season.

Reporters recommend the wide choice of restaurants in the resort, some of them On the Piste, for lunch. However, 'the quiet nightlife was a bit of a drag'. **La Marmotte, t** +33 (0)4 93 23 98 65, *www.lamarmot-teisola2000.com*, is recommended for lunch. **Hôtel Le Chastillon, t** +33 (0)4 93 23 26 00, *www.hotel-le-chastillon.cote.azur.fr*, ('very dated, but clean and comfortable') and **Hôtel Diva, t** + 33 (0)4 93 23 17 71, are the four-stars, while the three-stars are **Hôtel de France**, **t** +33 (0)4 93 02 17 04, and **Hôtel Pas du Loup**, **t** +33 (0)4 93 23 27 00. Chalets and apartments can be rented through *www.chaletisola.com* and *www.decolombe.com.*

Itter, Austria

t +43 (0)43 5335 2670, *www.hohe-salve.com*
Altitude 703m (2,306ft)–1829m (6,001ft)
Lifts 93 in SkiWelt

Small village with just 850 tourist beds. A fast gondola with no queues for the uphill journey, plus the longest run in the SkiWelt (8.5km), make it a quiet and good-value alternative to Söll. **Sporthotel Tirolerhof**, **t** +43 (0)5335 2690, *www.sporthotel-tirolerhof.com*, has a bowling alley.

Jackson Hole, Wyoming, USA

Page 411
Tour operators Alpine Answers Select, American Ski Classics, AWWT, Carrier, Crystal, Inghams, Lotus Supertravel, Momentum, Original Travel, Seasons in Style, Ski Activity, Ski All America, Ski Dream, Ski Freshtracks, Ski Independence, Ski Safari, Skiworld, United Vacations, Virgin Snow

Jasper, Alberta, Canada

🏆 BEST SMALL RESORT 2009
t +1 780 852 3816, *www.skimarmot.com*
Altitude 1686m (5,534ft)–2601m (8,534ft)
Lifts 8
Tour operators Crystal, Elegant Resorts, Frontier Ski, Inghams, Jasper, Neilson School Groups, Ski Activity, Ski All America, Ski Dream, SkiBound, Ski Independence, Ski Safari, Virgin Snow

Arguably the most beautiful Canadian resort – and the most northerly – is set close to the Icefields Parkway with its forests, glaciers, frozen lakes and waterfalls. The small but varied ski area is located at Marmot Basin, 20 minutes' drive out of the quaint railway-town of Jasper. 'A very good ski hill. Friendly staff and very reasonable prices,' said a reporter, 'I can recommend it without reservation but keen skiers may not find enough for a whole week.' The terrain is mainly open bowls, with steep chutes and glades cut through the trees. **Château Jasper**, **t** +1 780 852 5644, *www.decorehotels.com/chateau*, is an extremely comfortable place to stay, with a spa and several restaurants, and its rooms are gradually being revamped.

June Mountain, California, USA

See Mammoth, page 422

Kandersteg, Switzerland

t +41 (0)41 675 8080, *www.kandersteg.ch*
Altitude 1200m (3,937ft)–1920m (6,299ft)
Lifts 7
Tour operators Exodus, Headwater, HF Holidays, Inghams, Inntravel, Interhome, Kuoni

Charming village ('a true winter wonderland') in the Bernese Oberland, popular with cross-country skiers and boasting 75km of *loipe*. It also has commendable alpine skiing for beginners. 'The children loved it and I learnt to ski in fantastic scenery on uncrowded slopes,' said a reader. Hotels include the five-star **Royal Park**, **t** +41 (0)675 8888, *www.royalkandersteg.ch*, the four-star **Waldhotel Doldenhorn**, **t** +41 (0)675 8181, *www.doldenhorn-ruedihus.ch*, with a wellness centre, and sister hotel **Landgasthof Ruedihus**, **t** + 41 (0)33 675 8181, which are both full of atmosphere. Three-star **Victoria Ritter**, **t** +41 (0)675 8000, *www.hotel-victoria.ch*, is also recommended.

Kaprun, Austria

See Zell am See and Kaprun, page 102
Tour operators Crystal, Directski, Esprit, First Choice, Interhome, J2Ski, Neilson, Ski Wild, Thomson

Katschberg, Austria

t +43 (0)4734 630, *www.katschberg.at*
Altitude 1072m (3,517ft)–2220m (7,283ft)
Lifts 16
Tour operator Neilson

A small and family-friendly resort in the Upper Carinthia region, with 60km of mainly intermediate pistes. Everything is conveniently placed, with the ski schools, après ski venues and shops all located in the centre and accessible both on foot or on skis. Katschi's Kids World has a funpark with mini-jet and talking comic figures. There is night-skiing with music four days per week. A free ski-bus links the neighbouring village of Rennweg where you can find yet more traditional guest-houses, spacious apartments and small B&Bs.

Kelchsau, Austria

See Söll and the SkiWelt, page 94

Ketchum, Idaho, USA

See Sun Valley, page 440

Keystone, Colorado, USA

Page 416

Tour operators American Ski Classics, AWWT, Crystal, Erna Low, Ski Activity, Ski All America, Ski Dream, Ski Independence, Ski Safari, Solo's, Thomson, United Vacations

Kicking Horse, BC, Canada

Page 119

Tour operators Alpine Answers Select, AWWT, Bramble Ski, Crystal, Frontier Ski, Neilson, Ski All America, Ski Dream, Ski Independence, Ski Safari

Killington, Vermont, USA

Page 419

Tour operators American Ski Classics, Crystal, Directski, Inghams, Ski Activity, Ski All America, Ski Arrangements, SkiBound, Ski Dream, Ski Independence, Ski Safari, Thomson, Tops, Trailfinders, United Vacations, Virgin Snow

Kimberley, BC, Canada

t +1 250 427 4881, *www.skikimberley.com*
Altitude 1230m (4,035ft)–1981m (6,500ft)
Lifts 9
Tour operators Frontier Ski, Inghams, Ski Activity, Ski Dream, Ski Independence, Ski Safari

'If you have kids, this resort is the one for you. The three words that best describe Kimberley are quaint, quiet and quality,' enthused a reader. The log-cabin-style ski village is a five-minute drive from the Tyrolean-style town of Kimberley at the foot of the Purcell Mountains and ideal for a two-resort holiday combined with Fernie. The front face offers gentle slopes, while the Backside provides more challenge. 'The ski school is amazing,' said a reporter. There is night-skiing two nights a week on the longest floodlit trail in the country. In the rather spread-out ski village the choice of accommodation includes ski in, ski out **Polaris**, **t** +1 877 286 8828, and **Trickle Creek Residence Inn by Marriott**, **t** +1 877 282 1200.

Kirchberg, Austria

t +43 (0)5357 2000, *www.kitzbuehel-alpen.com*
Altitude 860m (2,821ft)–2000m (6,562ft)
Lifts 57
Tour operators Directski, First Choice, Interhome, Made to Measure, Neilson, Thomson

The town shares the Hahnenkamm and the Ski Safari to Pass Thurn with nearby Kitzbühel and is linked by eight-person cable car to the 1956m Gampen above Westendorf in the SkiWelt. In theory this creates a single mammoth circuit of 150 lifts and over 400km of skiing, but you still have to take a bus from Westendorf to Brixen or Hopfgarten, as well as a bus from the outskirts of Kirchberg to the new gondola. A wide piste has been created back down on the Kirchberg side. Kirchberg lacks the medieval charm of Kitzbühel but has considerable character. It has its own nursery area on the Gaisberg. **Tiroler Adler**, **t** +43 (0)5357 2327, *www.tiroler-adler.com*, is not particularly convenient but is one of the best hotels in town. **Hotel Alexander**, **t** +43 (0)5357 2222, *www.alexander.at*, and **Hotel Metzgerwirt**, **t** +43 (0)5357 2128, *www.metzgerwirt.at*, are recommended. **Restaurant Rosengarten** in **Hotel Taxacherhof**, **t** +43 (0)5357 2527, *www.taxacherhof.at*, is run by one of Austria's celebrated young chefs.

Kirkwood, California, USA

t +1 209 258 6000, *www.kirkwood.com*
Altitude 7,800ft (2377m)–9,800ft (2987m)
Lifts 10
Tour operator TBA

Lake Tahoe resort with plenty of sunny intermediate skiing. 'Superb, varied and interesting skiing, both on and off-piste, with a lovely atmosphere and generally a much higher standard of skiers/boarders,' said a reporter. New is a dedicated skier/boarder-cross course. Accommodation is offered in several buildings in the Kirkwood Valley, the newest is **Meadowstone Lodge**, offering luxury units just steps from the lifts.

Kitzbühel, Austria

Page 54

Tour operators Alpine Weekends, Crystal/Crystal Finest, Directski, Elegant Resorts, First Choice, Indigo Lodges, Inghams, Interhome, Made to Measure, Momentum, Mountain Leap, Neilson, Ski Activity, Ski Astons, Ski Wild, Sloping Off, Thomson

Kleinarl, Austria

See Wagrain and the Salzburger Sportwelt, page 98

Klosters, Switzerland

Page 349

Tour operators Altitude Inspires, Crystal Finest, Descent International, Flexiski, Indigo Lodges, Inghams, Kuoni, Made to Measure, Mountain Leap, Oxford Ski Company, Powder Byrne, Seasons in Style, Ski Expectations, Ski Freshtracks, Ski Independence, Ski Safari, Ski Solutions, Ski Weekend, Swiss Travel Service, White Roc

Kopaonik, Serbia

t +381 (0)11 318 1400, *www.tckopaonik.com*
Altitude 1780m (5,840ft)–2017m (6,617ft)
Lifts 23
Tour operators Balkan Holidays, Crystal, Ski-Line, Thomson

Located in the southern part of central Serbia, the resort is in a national park spread over part of the Kopaonik plateau. A quad-chair, built at a cost of €4.5 million and financed by the Serbian government, is part of the country's national investment plan. The lift rises 373 vertical metres (1,224 vertical ft) to a top height of 1988m (6,522ft). As well as the skiing on 60km of piste, the resort has a choice of cafés, bars and nightclubs. The accommodation is in hotels and apartments, including **Hotel Grand**, **Jat Apartments**, and **Konaci Sunny Heights Apartments**. For all reservations, **t** +381 (0)11 318 1400.

Kranjska Gora, Slovenia

t +386 (0)4588 1768, *www.kranjska-gora.si*
Altitude 810m (2,667ft)–1630m (5,348ft)
Lifts 20
Tour operators Balkan Holidays, Balkan Tours, BoardnLodge, Crystal, Directski, First Choice, Inghams, Just Slovenia, Mountain Tracks, Solo's, Thomson

Slovenia's best-known resort – but not necessarily its best. The village, set in a pretty, flat-bottomed valley between craggy wooded mountains, has much charm and a level of sophistication that puts it on a par with any similar-sized Austrian or Italian resort. The 30km of skiing served by five chairlifts and 15 drags lacks variety and challenge, but Kranjska is an ideal base for beginners to early intermediates. The ski school, the Alpine Ski Club, has an excellent reputation, and the 5km toboggan run is not to be missed. Stay at the four-star **Hotel Kompas**, *www.hoteli-kompas.si*, or at the pleasant **Hotel Lek**. **The Razor** apartments are 200m from the lifts. Accommodation can be booked centrally, **t** +386 (0)4588 1768, or via a tour operator.

Kronplatz, Italy

Page 282

Tour operator Neilson

Krvavec, Slovenia

t +386 (0)425 25 930, *www.rtc-krvavec.si*
Altitude 1450m (4,757ft)–1971m (6,466ft)
Lifts 12
Tour operator Just Slovenia

Ski area within a few minutes' drive of Ljubljana Airport. The network of runs served by chairlifts from the top of the modern access-gondola resembles a modest North American resort; in mid-winter you can even ski the whole way to the valley floor. This season a six-pack replaces an old fixed double chair. The ski area has no village, but you can stay in the **A&S Hotel Krvavec**, **t** + 386 (0)4201 9152, *www.hotel-as.com*. Some 90 per cent of the trails are covered by snow-cannon.

Kuhtai, Austria

t +41 (0)5239 5222, *www.kuehtai.co.at*
Altitude 2020m (6,627ft)–2520m (8,268ft)
Lifts 12
Tour operators Crystal, Inghams

Pretty little Tyrolean village offering 40km of piste and a lack of queues. **Jagdschloss Kühtai**, **t** +44 (0)5239 5201, five minutes from the village centre, was once a hunting lodge and is brimming with character. Four-star **Hotel Astoria**, **t** +43 (0)5239 5215, *www.hotelastoria.*

at, is considered excellent. Reporters praised the resort: 'No buses, few queues and wide, uncrowded, undemanding slopes that suit our very moderate intermediate standard to a T,' said one, and 'A great resort for families progressing from beginner to intermediate,' added another.

Kvitfjell, Norway

See Lillehammer, page 482

Laax, Switzerland

Page 353

Tour operators Alpine Answers Altitude Inspires, Select, Corporate Ski Company, J2Ski, Made to Measure, Momentum, Powder Byrne, Ski Safari, Ski Weekend, Switzerland Travel Centre, White Roc

Ladis, Austria

t +43 (0)5476 62390, *www.serfaus-fiss-ladis.at*
Altitude 1427m (4,682ft)–2684m (8,806ft)
Lifts 53 in area

Small village sharing a ski area with Fiss and much larger Serfaus.

Lake Louise, Alberta, Canada

See Banff/Lake Louise, page 108

Lake Tahoe, California, USA

See Heavenly, page 474 and Squaw Valley, page 432

Tour operators Lotus Supertravel, Thomson

Lana, Italy

See Monte San Vigilio, page 485

Lauterbrunnen, Switzerland

t +41 (0)37 856 8568, *www.wengen-muerren.ch*
Altitude 796m (2,612ft)–2971m (9,748ft)
Lifts 41 in Jungfrau Top Ski Region
Tour operators Oak Hall, Re-lax Holidays, Ski Miquel

Railway junction town near Interlaken that provides a cheap alternative to better-known Mürren and Wengen. Hotels offer a convenient, if rather characterless, base from which to explore the skiing. Mürren, reached by a cable car, is the easier to get to. Try three-star **Hotel Schützen, t** +33 (0)855 2032, *www.hotelschuetzen.com*, and **Hotel Silberhorn, t** +33 (0)856 2210, *www.silberhorn.com*, or, for an alternative to hotels, **Camping Jungfrau, t** +33 (0)856 2010, *www.camping-jungfrau.ch*, is rated. 'It has a free bus to the slopes, as well as bungalows and dormitories for families/groups. Highly recommend the facilities and friendly crew.'

Lech, Austria

Page 59

Tour operators Alpine Answers Select, Alpine Tracks, Altitude Inspires, Carrier, Crystal, Elegant Resorts, Flexiski, Inghams, Jeffersons, Kaluma, Lotus Supertravel, Made to Measure, Momentum, Mountain Leap, Original Travel, Powder Byrne, Seasons in Style, Ski Activity, Ski Expectations, Ski Independence, Ski Safari, Ski Solutions, Total Ski, White Roc

The Lecht, Scotland

t +44 (0)1975 651 440, *www.lecht.co.uk*
Altitude 643m (2,109ft)–793m (2,600ft)
Lifts 14

Scotland's smallest ski area ('a great place for kids') has a network of short lifts on both sides of the A939 Cockbridge–Tomintoul road. It lies 56 miles west of Aberdeen and about 45 miles from Glenshee and Cairngorm. The area is best suited to beginners and intermediates living within reasonable driving distance. The longest run is 900m. 'The café is really nice, with an outside balcony so you can watch your loved ones get snow in their ears and down their backs,' said a reader. The nearest accommodation is the **Allargue Arms, t** +44 (0)1975 651410, *www.allarguearmshotel.co.uk*, three miles away at Corgarff.

Las Leñas, Argentina

t +54 262 747 1100, *www.laslenas.com*
Altitude 2240m (7,349ft)–3431m (11,257ft)
Lifts 11
Tour operators AWWT, Scott Dunn Latin America, Ski Dream

The most challenging resort in South America, dependent on the weather and the operation or closure of a single lift. If there is sufficient stable snow and little enough wind to open the avalanche-prone Marte chair, then strong skiers and riders are in for the finest feast in the southern hemisphere. The lift provides the only mechanized access to some extraordinary off-piste with powder bowls and vertiginous *couloirs*. The area is exposed to avalanche danger and dotted with cliffs. A local guide is absolutely essential.

If the Marte chair is closed, Las Leñas reverts to being a treeless wilderness that is not necessarily worth the 90-minute flight from Buenos Aires to Malargue and the one-hour bus transfer. You can also fly to San Rafael, a three-hour drive from the resort. All accommodation is in hotels and lodges within a short distance of a lift. The five-star **Hotel Piscis, t** +54 262 747 1100, is the most luxurious, featuring what claims to be the highest ski-resort casino in the world. The **Aries, t** +54 262 742 7120, has its own cinema.

Lenk, Switzerland

See Adelboden and Lenk, page 456

Lenzerheide and Valbella, Switzerland

t +41 (0)81 385 1120, *www.lenzerheide.ch*
Altitude 1500m (4,920ft)–2865m (9,397ft)
Lifts 34 in area
Tour operators Kuoni, Made to Measure

Linked resorts at either end of the beautiful Heidsee with considerable charm and mainly intermediate skiing. They used to attract a high number of British families but have declined in popularity for no discernible reason. ('Excellent resort. Lift system still improving.') None of the terrain is particularly difficult, and it makes a pleasant holiday centre. Best suited to families and intermediates. Recommended hotels include the four-star **Sunstar, t** +41 (0)81 384 0121, and **Romantik Guarda Val, t** +41 (0)81 385 8585, *www.guardaval.ch*. Valbella has less charm. Both the four-star **Posthotel Valbella, t** +41 (0)81 384 1212, *www.posthotelvalbella.ch*, and the **Valbella Inn, t** +41 (0)81 384 3636, *www.valbellainn.ch*, are recommended.

Leogang, Austria

t +43 (0)6583 8234, *www.leogang-saalfelden.at*
Altitude 800m (2,625ft)–2096m (6,877ft)
Lifts 55 in area

'The thinking man's way into the Saalbach Hinterglemm Ski Circus, with most of its slopes north-facing, well covered by artificial snow, and a village untouched by mass alpine tourism,' pronounced a reader. The village is a collection of 10 farming hamlets with a modern gondola up to Berghaus Asitz at 1758m, where a quad-chair and six-seater chair link into the Saalbach-Hinterglemm area. Four-star **Hotel Salzburgerhof, t** +43 (0)6583 7310, *www.salzburgerhof.co.at*, is convenient. 'The best food in Leogang is without doubt at the **Hotel Kirchenwirt, t** +43 5475 381, *www.kirchenwirt.com*, run by the fabulous Hannes and Elisabeth Unterrainer,' said a reporter.

Lermoos, Austria

t +43 (0)5673 20000, *www.lermoos.at*
Altitude 1004m (3,294ft)– 2200m (7,218ft)
Lifts 9 in Lermoos
Tour operators Interhome, J2Ski

Small traditional village set at the base of a small ski area along the valley from a second small resort called Biberwier. A total 33km of piste, but the resorts are included in the Happy Ski Card offering skiing on the Zugspitz in Austria and at Garmisch in Germany.

Levi, Finland

Page 327
Tour operators Inghams, Neilson, Nortours

Leysin, Switzerland

t +41 (0)24 494 2244, *www.leysin.ch*
Altitude 1330m (4,363ft)–2200m (7,218)
Lifts 15
Tour operators Crystal, Mountain Tracks, Sloping Off, Switzerland Travel Centre

This village above the town of Aigle is historically associated with finishing schools, health clinics and cut-price student holidays. Today it is also one of the top resorts in Switzerland for snowboarders, with a 50km area featuring virtually no draglifts. 'Uncrowded – once or twice in January we were the only people on the piste,' said a reporter. **Garderie Arc en Ciel, t** +41 (0)24 494 1200, cares for children from newborn to seven years. It is a friendly village with an excellent ski school for teenagers.

Best-situated accommodation is the four-star **Hotel Classic-Terrasse, t** +41 (0)24 493 0606, with spacious rooms, and the simpler **Bel-Air, t** +41 (0)24 494 1339. The **Hiking Sheep, t** +41 (0)24 494 3535, is a renovated Art Deco building, now a hostel with good dormitories.

Lillehammer, Norway

t +47 612 89800, *www.lillehammerturist.no* or *www.hafjell.com*
Altitude 200m (656ft)–1050m (3,444ft)
Lifts 11
Tour operators Crystal, Directski, Exodus, Nortours, Original Travel
Cosy little town with a single main street of weatherboarded houses that was a surprising but successful choice for the 1994 Winter Olympics. The closest skiing is 15 minutes away at Hafjell. Kvitfjell, 50km from Lillehammer, has only 18km of pistes but provides more demanding terrain. 'I would recommend the resort to anyone who wants snow security late in the season,' said a reporter. **Radisson SAS Lillehammer, t** +47 612 86000, *www.lillehammerhotel.no*, **Rica Victoria, t** +47 612 50049, and **First Hotel Breiseth, t** +47 612 47777, *www.breiseth.com*, are all recommended.

Limone, Italy

t +39 0171 925280, *www.limonepiemonte.it*
Altitude 1009m (3,310ft)–2050m (6,726ft)
Lifts 22
Tour operators First Choice, Indigo Lodges

Historic town centred on Monte Baldo in the Piedmont region, 50km north of the Mediterranean coast. The 80km of piste is mainly intermediate, served by a cableway and mainly chairlifts. **Grand Hotel Principe, t** +39 0171 92 389, *www.hotel-principe-limone.it*, is the only four-star accommodation and there is a handful of three-stars. Some first-rate restaurants serve local cuisine but the après ski is limited to a few bars.

Livigno, Italy

Page 284
Tour operators Crystal, Directski, Inghams, Neilson, Ski Arrangements

Long-Zhu Erlongshan, China

t +86 (0)451 791 3640
Altitude 266m (872ft)–1371m (4,500ft)
Lifts 4

The second most important resort in the Heilongjiang province after larger Yabuli. It is situated at Bin Xian, 56km from Harbin. The ski area is currently being developed by the Beijing Long-Zhu Leisure Group, which is pumping millions into mountain facilities.

Loveland, Colorado, USA

t +1 303 571 5580, *www.skiloveland.com*
Altitude 3231m (10,600ft)– 3965m (13,010ft)
Lifts 11
Small but high ski resort that competes annually with Killington to be the first US resort to open at the end of October or in early November. It is set on the Continental Divide 53 miles west of Denver and 12 miles east of Silverthorne. The resort is a local favourite due to reliable snow-cover and low prices. 'This place is seriously high, but well worth a visit if you are in one of the other Colorado resorts and have your own transport. There is not much here other than skiing,' said a reporter. The most convenient accommodation is **Silver Mine Lodge, t** +1 877 733 2656, in Silver Plume, 10 miles from Loveland, **Georgetown Mountain Inn, t** +1 303 569 3201, at Georgetown 12 miles away, and **Peck House, t** +1 303 569 9870, in Empire 14 miles away.

Luosto, Finland

t +358 (0)16 624 367, *www.luosto.fi*
Altitude 203m (665ft)–531m (1,750ft)
Lifts 4
Tour operator Canterbury Travel

Geographically in the centre of Lapland and easily accessible from Rovaniemi airport. The seven pistes are best suited to families. Pyhä is 20km away and offers a further ten pistes and four lifts. Luosto has 74km of cross-country trails, 25km of which are floodlit. Other activities in the area include snowmobile or reindeer safaris through the forest, snowshoe hiking, and dinner in a *kota* (Sámi teepee). Don't miss a visit to Lampivaara amethyst mine, and do watch the Northern Lights through the glass-roofed Pohjan Kruunu *kota*. Stay in the village of log cottages or in **Hotel Luostotunturi**, *www.luostotunturi.com*, which houses an 'amethyst spa'.

Macugnaga, Italy

t +39 0324 65119, *www.macugnaga-online.it*
Altitude 1327m (4,353ft)–2984m (9,790ft)
Lifts 12
Tour operator J2Ski

'Great little resort for beginners and intermediates. Very friendly and really good tuition,' said a reader. The resort is made up of five villages: Borca, Isella, Pecetto, Pestarena and Staffa. They are set at the foot of the Monte Rosa, close to the Swiss border and two hours from Turin. Due to the proximity of the border, many of the buildings are Swiss in style. The dozen hotels include **Hotel Dufour**, **t** +39 0324 65529, in Staffa's main square, and **Hotel Zumstein**, **t** +39 0324 65490, *www.zumstein.macugnaga.it*. **Hotel Girasole**, **t** +39 0324 65052, has large rooms, good service and food – but no frills. Three-star **Hotel Flora**, **t** +39 0324 65910, was highly rated. 'Hospitality fantastic and we felt like we were staying with friends. Spotlessly clean and really good food.'

Madesimo, Italy

t +39 0343 53015, *www.madesimo.com*
Altitude 1530m (5,018ft)–2984m (9,790ft)
Lifts 19
Tour operators Inghams, J2Ski
Attractive old village with narrow streets and a scattering of converted farmhouses.
The resort has a considerable international following among families who want a quiet resort offering snow-sure intermediate skiing. ('Not a place for party animals. If you are looking for a relaxed holiday without any nightlife but with great skiing, this is the place.') Madesimo lies close to the Swiss border, a two-hour drive from Bergamo, and it is possible to make a day trip to St Moritz. The skiing in the Valle Spluga ski area is mostly intermediate and takes place on the usually uncrowded slopes of the Pizzo Groppera, with long trails leading into the neighbouring Valle di Lei. Mostly red runs and some challenging blacks, including the famous Canelone run.

Hotels include four-star **Emet**, **t** +39 0343 53395, family-run **Andossi**, **t** +39 0343 57000, *www.hotelandossi.com*, **Hotel Harlequin**, **t** +39 0343 53005, which is well located, and **Hotel Cascata e Crystal**, **t** +39 0343 53108, with a pool and mini-club.

Madonna di Campiglio, Italy

Page 286

Tour operators Crystal, Directski, Equity/Rocket Ski, Exodus, First Choice, Inghams, Ski Arrangements, Ski Expectations, Solo's

Mammoth, California, USA

Page 422
Tour operators American Ski Classics, AWWT, Ski Activity, Ski All America, Ski Dream, Ski Independence, Ski Safari, United Vacations, Virgin Snow

Marble Mountain, Newfoundland

t +1 709 637 7601, www.skimarble.com
Altitude 33ft (10m)–1,791ft (546m)
Marble Mountain, 10 minutes' drive from Humber Valley Resort, is a small area with 35 trails, a terrain park and half-pipe. **Marble Mountain Snow School**, **t** +1 709 637 7601, offers tuition for adults and children, and **Marble Children's Center** has a supervised play area. There is a self-service in the lodge at the base. **Marble Villa**, **t** +1 709 637 7601, at the base of Marble Mountain, is the resort's only ski in, ski out accommodation. Most visitors stay in the excellent **Humber Valley Resort chalets and apartments**, **t** +1 709 686 8100.

Maria Alm, Austria

t +43 (0)6584 7816, *www.mariaalm.at*
Altitude 800m (2,625ft)–2000m (6,562ft)
Lifts 39
Tour operators Club Europe, Equity, Tops

Beautiful village close to Zell am See dominated by a church boasting the highest spire in Salzburgerland. Maria Alm is part of the Hochkönig area, along with Dienten, Mühlbach and Saalfelden. 'It genuinely is a totally unspoilt traditional Austrian village. The area pass stretches as far as Schladming and takes in Flachau and Gastein, so skiing is almost unlimited,' said a reporter. **Sporthotel Alpenland**, **t** +43 (0)6584 7491, *www.alpenland.at*, has an indoor-outdoor pool and is conveniently close to the Natrun slopes.

Mariborsko Pohorje, Slovenia

t +386 (0)2 603 6554, *www.pohorje.org*
Altitude 325m (1,066ft)–1347m (4,419ft)
Lifts 20
Slovenia's second largest city and the modest slopes above it are home each January to the Golden Fox Trophy, one of the most

important events in the Women's World Cup calendar. The 80km of trails are backed up by snow-cannon, and low temperatures usually ensure top-to-bottom skiing. Stay at the base in the luxurious five-star **Hotel Habakuk**, **t** +386 (0)2 300 8100, *www.termemb.si*, or in the more modest three-star **Hotel Tisa**, **t** +386 (0)2 603 6100.

Marilleva, Italy

t +39 0463 901280, *www.valdisole.net*
Altitude 1300m (4,265)–2505m (8,219ft)
Lifts 47 in area
Tour operators Alpine Tours, Interhome

Purpose-built resort linked to Folgarida, and to Madonna di Campiglio which is 9km away. A total of 120km of linked skiing, popular with budget skiers and school groups.

Marmot Basin, Alberta, Canada

See Jasper, page 477

La Massana, Andorra

See Pal-Arinsal, page 34
Tour operators Directski, Exodus, First Choice, J2Ski, Neilson

Le Massif, Québec, Canada

t +1 418 632 5876, *www.lemassif.com*
Altitude 36m (118ft)–806m (2,644ft)
Lifts 5
Tour operators Frontier Ski, Ski All America, Ski Dream, Ski Safari, SkiBound

Currently under new ownership and undergoing a CD$5 million makeover to turn it into a four-seasons resort. So far the skiable terrain has inceased by 30 per cent. As a ski centre it has the unusual attribute of being upside-down: you park your car at the top of the mountain and ski all the way down to take the first lift. The resort and mountain with its 43 trails are perched on the bank of the mighty St Lawrence, a 45-minute drive from Québec City, and have one of the most enchanting views of any ski destination in the world. So steep is the angle of descent down the principal run that you feel you might tumble off the mountain and onto the ice flows of the river far below. The resort suits all standards of skier and is used as a training centre by the Canadian national team.

Mayrhofen, Austria

Page 64
Tour operators Crystal, Equity/Rocket Ski, Directski, First Choice, HF Holidays, Inghams, Neilson, Redpoint, Ski Activity, Ski Astons, Ski Wild, Snowcoach, Thomson

Megève, France

Page 191
Tour operators Alpine Answers Select, Alpine Tracks, Classic Ski, Erna Low, Indigo Lodges, Lagrange, Made to Measure, Momentum, Mountain Leap, Peak Retreats, Simon Butler Skiing, Ski Arrangements, Ski Barret-Boyce, Ski Collection, Ski Expectations, Ski Independence, Ski Solutions, Stanford Skiing, White Roc

Meiringen-Hasliberg, Switzerland

t +41 (0)33 972 5050, *www.alpenregion.ch*
Altitude 1061m (3,481ft)–2433m (7,982ft)
Lifts 22
Tour operators J2Ski, Ski Weekend

The key component of four linked villages that form the Alpen region in the Bernese Oberland, between Lucerne and Interlaken. Brienz, Axalp, Hasliberg and Meiringen offer a modest intermediate ski area set against an awesome alpine backdrop. Meiringen is known to Sherlock Holmes fans for its Reichenbach Falls, where Sir Arthur Conan Doyle's character fell to his untimely death during his final struggle with arch-villain Moriarty. The Alpen region is great for riding, with natural obstacles that form Switzerland's first 'natural snowboard park'.

In Meiringen, **Alpin Sherpa**, **t** +41 (0)33 972 5252, *www.alpinsherpa.ch*, **Parkhotel du Sauvage**, **t** +41 (0)33 971 4141, *www.sauvage.ch*, and three-star **Sporthotel Sherlock Holmes**, **t** +41 (0)33 972 9889, *www.sherlock.ch*, are recommended. In Hasliberg try **Hotel Bären**, **t** +41 (0)33 971 6022, *www.hotel-restaurant-baeren.ch*, and the **Bellevue**, **t** +41 (0)33 971 2341. In Brienz, recommended places to stay include **Hotel Brienz**, **t** +41 (0)33 951 3551, and **Grandhotel Giessbach**, **t** +41 (0)33 952 2525.

Les Menuires, France

Page 196
Tour operators Club Med, Crystal, Directski, Erna Low, Family Ski Company, First Choice,

Interhome, Lagrange, Neilson, Silver Ski, Ski Amis, Ski Arrangements, Ski Collection, Ski France, Ski Independence, Ski Olympic, Ski Supreme, Skitopia, Wasteland

Meran 2000, Italy

t +39 0473 279 457, *www.hafling.com*
Altitude 1650m (5,413ft)–2300m (7,546ft)
Lifts 7 in resort, 74 in Ortler Skiarena

South Tirol village close to Bolzano and 30 minutes' drive from the ski area. The resort is part of the Ortler Skiarena, with 13 unconnected resorts sharing one lift pass. Some 260km of piste is served by eight cableways and 66 chairs and drags. Hotels in Meran 2000 are headed by minimalistic **La Pergola Residence**, **t** +39 0473 201 435, *www.pergola-residence.it*, on a hillside outside the village. Its kitchen uses organic products straight from the farm. Other hotels include **Romantik Hotel Staffler**, **t** +39 0472 771 136, **Grand Hotel Palace**, **t** +39 0473 271 000, *www.palace.it*, **Hotel Sissi**, **t** +39 0473 231 062, *www.hotel-adria.com*, and **Castel Fragsburg**, **t** +39 0473 244 071, *www.fragsburg.com*.

Méribel, France

Page 199
Tour operators Alpine Action, Alpine Answers Select, Alpine Elements, Alp Leisure, AWWT, Belvedere Chalets, Bonne Neige, Cooltip, Crystal/Crystal Finest, Descent International, Directski, Elegant Resorts, Erna Low, Esprit, First Choice, Four Winds Meriski, Flexiski, Indigo Lodges, Inghams, J2Ski, Lagrange, Lotus Supertravel, Made to Measure, Mark Warner, Momentum, Mountain Leap, Neilson, Original Travel, Oxford Ski Company, Powder White, Purple Ski, Scott Dunn Ski, Seasons in Style, Ski Activity, Ski Amis, Ski Basics, Ski Beat, Ski Blanc, Ski Collection, Ski Cuisine, Ski Expectations, Ski France, Ski-Line, Ski in Luxury, Ski Olympic, Ski Solutions, Skiworld, Snowcoach, Snowline, Thomson, Total Ski, VIP, White Roc

Mieders, Austria

See Neustift and the Stubaital, page 68

The Milky Way, Italy

See Clavière, page 466; Montgenèvre, page 204; Sauze d'Oulx, page 500; Sestriere, page 502

Mittersill, Austria

See Kitzbühel, page 54

Moena, Italy

See Canazei and the Val di Fassa, page 260

La Molina, Spain

t +34 972 89 20 31, *www.lamolina.com*
Altitude 1700m (5,577ft)–2445m (8,022ft)
Lifts 17

Pyrenean resort with 17 lifts including a cable car and 44 mainly beginner to intermediate trails. There is a crèche and six mountain restaurants.

La Mongie, France

See Barèges and La Mongie, page 460
Tour operator Lagrange

Montafon, Austria

See Gargellen page 471, Gaschurn page 472, Schruns page 501, St Gallenkirch page 497 and Tschagguns page 507
Tour operators Alpine Tracks, Made to Measure

The Montafon Valley lies in the south of the of the Vorarlberg, in Austria's southwestern corner. Its 11 villages lie at altitudes between 600m and 1430m and are surrounded by three mountain chains with mountains as high as the Piz Buin at 3312m.

Montchavin, France

See La Plagne, page 212
Tour operators Erna Low, J2Ski, Snow Monkey Chalets

Montgenèvre, France

Page 204
Tour operators Club Europe, Crystal, Equity/Rocket Ski, French Freedom Holidays, Lagrange, Neilson, Ski Etoile, Ski France, Skitopia

Monte San Vigilio, Italy

t +39 0473 561770, *www.lana.net*
Altitude 1500m (4,921ft)–1800m (5,906ft)
Lifts 3

From the town of Lana, a cable car with real leather seats – a 1970s replacement of the original cabin built in 1912 – takes you up to a lone building in the small ski area of Monte San Vigilio. The building is **Hotel Vigilius**, **t** +39 0473 556600, *www.vigilius.it*, a true mountain hideaway oozing understated elegance. Skiing is on the gentle Vigiljoch with lifts outside the door. The more extensive resorts of Val d'Ultimo are 20 minutes' drive and Val Senales 75 minutes.

Montriond, France

t +33 (0)4 50 79 12 81, *www.portesdusoleil.com*
Altitude 950m (3,116ft)–2350m (7,708ft)
Lifts 211 in Portes du Soleil
Tour operator Reach4theAlps

A suburb of Morzine, with no real centre and a collection of simple, good-value hotels. A bus links the village to the gondola that accesses the Portes du Soleil area. The British Alpine Ski and Snowboarding School has a branch here.

Mont-Ste-Anne, Québec, Canada

t +1 800 827 4579, *www.mont-sainte-anne.com*
Altitude 175m (575ft)–800m (2,625ft)
Lifts 13
Tour operators Frontier Ski, Ski All America, Ski Dream, Ski Safari, Tops

One the best ski areas in Eastern Canada, situated a 30-minute drive from Québec City, with lots of intermediate slopes of a respectable gradient that are interspersed with much more challenging double-black-diamonds. As all destinations in Québec, occasionally the resort considers it is just too dangerously cold to open the lifts. But Canadians wrap up well and take low temperatures in their stride. On weekdays, city-dwellers pop out to catch a few runs after work. Some 17 trails are floodlit for night-skiing on the biggest illuminated vertical drop (2,000ft) in Canada. A terrain park, the Telus X-Large Park, is for experienced riders.

Chateau Mont-Ste-Anne, **t** +1 800 463 4467, is at the base area, and the **Chalets Mont-Ste-Anne**, **t** +1 800 463 4395, is a condo complex nearby.

Morgins, Switzerland

t +41 (0)24 477 2361, *www.morgins.ch*
Altitude 1350m (4,428ft)–2000m (7,710ft)
Lifts 211 in Portes du Soleil
Tour operators Ski Morgins, Ski Rosie

Laid-back resort a short distance from Châtel on the Swiss–French side of the Portes du Soleil circuit. Most of the accommodation is in chalets and apartments. The two-stars are **Hotel La Reine des Alpes**, **t** +41 (0)24 477 1143, and **Hotel Beau-Site**, **t** +41 (0)24 477 1138.

Morillon, France

t +33 (0)4 50 90 15 76, *www.ot-morillon.fr*
Altitude 700m (2,296ft)–2480m (8,134ft)
Lifts 78 in Grand Massif
Tour operators Altitude Holidays, Erna Low, In Resort Services, Lagrange, Peak Retreats

'What a delightful, very French, resort. Friendly people, smiles at the bakery, a world away from the big resorts,' enthused a reader, and 'A great place for newbie skiers,' said another. The old village in the beautiful Giffre Valley has a 16th-century church and is linked by gondola to the purpose-built satellite of Morillon 1100. Together they make a popular second-home resort for the French. Morillon has seven of its own lifts and is linked into the Grand Massif ski area, of which Flaine is the best-known resort. ('Morillon is well worth a visit and half the price.') Two-star **Hotel Le Morillon**, **t** +33 (0)4 50 90 10 32, *www.hotellemorillon.com*, has a recommended restaurant and the **Refuge d'Alpage** apartments, **t** +44 (0)20 7584 2841, are MGM-owned.

Morzine, France

Page 206
Tour operators Alpine Answers Select, Alpine Elements, Alpine Tracks, Alpine Weekends, AWWT, The Chalet Company, Chalet Snowboard, Challenge Activ, Crystal, Directski, Erna Low, First Choice, Independent Luxury Travel, Inghams, Lagrange, Momentum, Mountain Highs, Mountain Tracks, Peak Retreats, Reach4theAlps, Rudechalets, Ski Activity, Ski Arrangements, Ski Chamois, Ski Expectations, Ski Famille, Ski in Luxury, Ski Weekend, Snowline, Tgski, Thomson, Trail Alpine, White Roc

Moso, Italy

See Alta Pusteria, page 456

Mount Buller, Australia

t +61 (0)3 5777 6077, *www.mtbuller.com.au*
Altitude 1390m (4,559ft)–1804m (5,917ft)

Lifts 22
The major area for Melbourne-based skiers, located a three-and-a-half-hour (250km) drive north-east of the city. It has the largest lift capacity in the country, and there are some long cruising runs as well as some genuine black-diamond runs. The scenery is impressive, with panoramic views across the gum forests. Boutique hotel, **The Breathtaker**, **t** +61 (0)3 5777 6377, *www.breathtaker.com.au*, is Australia's first mountain spa hotel. The **Schuss Lodge**, **t** +61 (0)3 5777 6007, *www.schuss.asn.au/buller.html*, is a small hotel with great views.

Mount Hotham, Australia

See Falls Creek and Mount Hotham, page 470

Mount Hutt, New Zealand

t +64 (0)3 302 8811, *www.nzski.com*
Altitude 1403m (4,602ft)–2075m (6,808ft)
Lifts 4
See Queenstown, page 494

Mount Ruapehu, New Zealand

t +64 (0)7 892 3738, *www.mtruapehu.com*
Altitude 1605m (5,266ft)–2322m (7,616ft)
Lifts Turoa 9, Whakapapa 14
Tour operator Scott Dunn Asia Pacific

The country's largest and busiest ski area in the midst of North Island's Tongariro National Park. The lift company is investing NZ$30 million to upgrade the lift system and install snowmaking. The area comprises Whakapapa on the northwestern side of the volcano, and Turoa, on the southwestern slopes.

Mount Ruapehu is renowned for its unpredictable weather – on a good day the skiing can be excellent, but during a wet and windy white-out the visibility can be so poor that the resort is barely skiable. In bad weather the mountain can shut down for days on end. Happy Valley is New Zealand's largest beginner area, tucked away from the main slopes at Whakapapa.

Turoa shares a pass and has Australasia's biggest vertical drop (720m). Unfortunately there is no easy way to get from resort to resort on snow. Turoa is always the last resort in the country to close in early November, and offers fabulous spring skiing.

Whakapapa village, 6km from the mountain, boasts the smart and pricey **Grand Château**, **t** +64 (0)7 892 3809, *www.chateau.co.nz*, while the cheaper **Skotel**, **t** +64 (0)7 892 3719, *www.skotel.com*, is nearby. **Adventure Lodge & Motel**, **t** +64 (0)7 892 2991, *www.adventurenationalpark.co.nz*, and **Howards Lodge**, **t** +64 (0)7 892 2827, *www.howardslodge.co.nz*, are at National Park Village 22km away, but convenient for both ski fields. Lively Ohakune provides a wide choice of accommodation including **Powderhorn Chateau**, **t** +64 (0)7 385 8888.

Mühlbach, Austria

See Maria Alm, page 483

Mürren, Switzerland

Page 356
Tour operators Inghams, Kuoni, Made to Measure, Momentum, Ski Freshtracks, Ski Solutions, Swiss Travel Service, Switzerland Travel Centre

Naeba, Japan

t +44 (0)20 7734 6870, *www.snowjapan.co.uk*
Altitude 900m (2,953ft)–1800m (5,905ft)
Lifts 30
One of the busiest ski areas in Yuzawa-machi in the Niigata Prefecture, which in turn is in the northern Japanese Alps, with 24-hour skiing. It is presided over by the **Naeba Prince**, **t** +81 (0)25 789 2211, *www.princehotels.co.jp/ski/naeba*, the world's largest ski hotel – containing a shopping mall, spa, amusement centre, and over 40 restaurants. At weekends, when packed bullet trains and buses disgorge their human cargo, an absurd number of skiers floods the slopes, which are open all night – so at 4am there is some chance of finding a place to turn.

Nakiska, BC, Canada

t +1 403 256 8473, *www.skinakiska.com*
Altitude 1524m (5,003ft)–2215m (7,415ft)
Lifts 4
Tour operator Ski Dream

Small ski area 83km from Calgary and a venue for the 1988 Olympics.

Nasserein, Austria

See St Anton, page 497
Tour operators Albus Travel, Ski-Line

Nassfeld, Austria

t +43 (0)4285 8241, *www.skiarena.at* or *www.hermagor.com*
Altitude 600m (1969ft)–1500m (4,921ft)
Lifts 40
Tour operators Crystal, Interhome, Ski Wild, Sloping Off, Thomson

Carinthian resort offering mainly intermediate skiing and claiming to have the longest cable car in the Alps – the Millennium-Express covers 6000m and takes 17 minutes to climb from the valley. The resort is increasing in popularity, which means there are crowds during peak season.

The 11 four-star hotels include **Alpen Adria**, **t** +43 (0)4282 2666, *www.alpenadriahotel.at*, **Berghotel Presslauer**, **t** +43 (0)4285 209, and **Hotel Berghof**, **t** +43 (0)4285 8271, *www.berghof-nassfeld.at*. **Cube**, *www.cube-hotels.com*, is a clever hotel concept that combines function with cutting-edge design. The glass and concrete building doesn't have rooms: it has minimalist 'cube boxes'.

Nelson, BC, Canada

See Whitewater, page 513

Nendaz, Switzerland

t +41 (0)27 289 5589, *www.nendaz.ch*
Altitude 1365m (4,478ft)–3330m (10,925ft)
Lifts 89 in Four Valleys
Tour operators Crystal, Erna Low, Interhome, J2Ski, Lagrange, Ski Independence, Ted Bentley

Cheaper alternative bed-base to Verbier, with access into the Four Valleys. A free ski-bus operates between Nendaz and Siviez and a fast chair takes you up from Siviez towards Veysonnaz. **Neige Aventure Ski School**, **t** +41 (0)27 288 3131, received rave reviews ('best I've come across for young children in 35 years of skiing').

Neuberg, Austria

See Wagrain and the Salzburger Sportwelt, Page 98

Neustift (Stubai), Austria

Page 68
Tour operators Alpine Tours, Esprit, J2Ski, Made to Measure, Momentum, Original Travel

Nevis Range, Scotland

t +44 (0)1397 705 825 for snow info **t** +44 (0)1397 703 781 for tourist info, *www.nevisrange.co.uk*; or *www.ski.visitscotland.com*
Altitude 655m (2,148ft)–1221m (4,006ft)
Lifts 12
Tour operators Skisafe Travel

Scotland's premier ski resort, a compact but challenging ski area that is reached by a modern six-seater gondola. It is situated near Ben Nevis – Britain's highest peak – seven miles north of the ancient town of Fort William, which provides accommodation. You can also find B&Bs in the pretty nearby hamlet of Torlundy. In good snow conditions Nevis (sometimes known as Aonach Mor) can offer just as good skiing as its Alpine counterparts of similar size. The Braveheart chair accesses the back bowls of the Coire Dubh, which provide outstanding off-piste opportunities after a fresh snowfall. Like all Scottish resorts, Nevis Range suffers from lack of regular cover. ('If it snows, the terrain is absolutely fantastic and the views superior to any I have seen in the Alps.') A reporter warns, 'The only negative here (other than the unpredictable weather and snow) is the T-bars – very tiring for boarders.' Nineteenth-century **Inverlochy Castle**, **t** +44 (0)1397 702 177, *www.inverlochycastlehotel.com*, is a convenient and luxurious place to stay.

Niederau, Austria

Page 70
Tour operators Directski, First Choice, Inghams, Neilson, Thomson

Niseko, Japan

Page 313
Tour operators Crystal, Inghams, Ski Dream, Ski Independence, Ski Safari

La Norma, France

t +33 (0)4 79 20 31 46, *www.la-norma.com*
Altitude 1350m (4,429ft)–2750m (9,022ft)
Lifts 18
Tour operators Erna Low, Lagrange, Peak Retreats

Car-free family resort in the Maurienne Valley with wooden ski in, ski out buildings that blend into the scenery. **Hôtel-Restaurant**

l'Auberge Pastorale, t +33 (0)4 79 05 02 63, *www.auberge-pastorale.com*, is 5km away at Le Bourget, and offers traditional cuisine. Most of the other accommodation is in apartments, including **Les Chalets et Balcons de la Vanoise, t** +33 (0)4 79 20 22 18, and **Les Balcons d'Anais, t** +33 (0)4 79 20 22 31, *www.goelia.com*.

Northstar-at-Tahoe, California, USA

t +1 530 562 1010, *www.northstarattahoe.com*
Altitude 6,330ft (1929m)–8,610ft (2624m)
Lifts 17
Tour operators Ski Dream, Ski Independence, United Vacations

Notre-Dame-de-Bellecombe, France

t +33 (0)4 79 31 61 40, *www.notredamedebellecombe.com*
Altitude 1150m (3773ft)–2070m (6,791ft)
Lifts 72 in area
Tour operators Lagrange, Peak Retreats

Pretty village in the rural Val d'Arly between Megève and Albertville with a distinctive bulb-shaped bell tower that dates back from the 11th century. The ski area is linked to Flumet and Praz-sur-Arly, and more recently also connected to Les Saisies and Crest-Voland as part of the Espace Diamant area. 'The only negative point for us was the lack of *télécabines*; almost all of the lifts are drags – going right up the mountain. This was problematic for our boarders and small children who struggled to hang on,' complained a reader.

Nozawa Onsen, Japan

t +44 (0)20 7734 6870, *www.snowjapan.co.uk*
Altitude 560m (1,837ft)–1650m (5,414ft)
Lifts 29

Attractive spa village with old-world charm that is neighbour to better-known Shiga Kogen. The busy, narrow streets are marred by traffic and imbued with the aroma of sulphur from the 13 public hot-spring bathhouses. The slopes are reached by a steep uphill walk, followed by two long escalators. The ski terrain is varied, with some steep pitches and accommodation is mainly in ryokans (inns) and small hotels, with **Kameya Ryokan, t** +82 (0)269 852 124, recommended.

Oberau, Austria

See Niederau, page 70
Tour operators Inghams, Neilson, Sloping Off

Obergurgl-Hochgurgl, Austria

Page 71
Tour operators Crystal, Directski, Esprit, First Choice, Inghams, Made to Measure, Momentum, Neilson, Ski Activity, Ski Expectations, Ski Freshtracks, Ski Independence, Ski Solutions, Thomson

Oberlech, Austria

See Lech, page 59

Oberndorf, Austria

See St Johann in Tirol, page 86
Tour operators Lagrange, Ski Astons

Obertauern, Austria

Page 75
Tour operators Alpine Answers Select, Club Europe, Inghams, SkiBound, Snowscape, Thomson

Oppdal, Norway

t +47 72 40 0470, *www.oppdal.com*
Altitude 545m (1,788ft)–1300m (4,265ft)
Lifts 16

One of Norway's most northerly and largest downhill resorts, 120km south of Trondheim, with three ski areas: Stölen, Hovden and Vangslia. There is some good off-piste skiing, and 60km of cross-country trails. **Quality Hotel Oppdal, t** +47 72 40 0700, is in the village centre, **Nor Alpin Hotel, t** +47 72 40 4700, is recommended, and **Vangslia Fjelltun, t** +47 72 40 0801, contains piste-side apartments.

Orcières-Merlette, France

t +33 (0)4 92 55 89 89, *www.orcieres.com*
Altitude 1850m (6,070ft)–2725m (8,944ft)
Lifts 30
Tour operators Lagrange, Ski Collection, Ski France

Remote purpose-built and – from an architectural perspective – visually challenging resort with an almost exclusively French clientèle in the southern French Alps 45 minutes from Gap. Merlette is set just above Orcières.

Ordino, Andorra

See Pal-Arinsal page 34

Les Orres, France

t +33 (0)4 92 44 01 61, *www.lesorres.com*
Altitude 1550m (5,085ft)–2720m (8,924ft)
Lifts 23
Tour operators Lagrange, Ski Collection

'Not the prettiest village but functional and friendly. Very French, very quiet and is suited to families,' said a reporter. Set in the southern French Alps, the resort has 88km of skiing in wooded terrain. The five two-star hotels include **La Portette, t** +33 (0)4 92 44 00 02, *www.laportette.com*, at the foot of the slopes.

Ortisei, Italy

Page 290
Tour operators Inghams, Neilson, Seasons in Style

Oz-en-Oisans, France

t +33 (0)4 76 80 78 01, *www.oz-en-oisans.com*
Altitude 1350m (4,429ft)–3330m (10,922ft)
Lifts 84 in area
Tour operators Erna Low, Lagrange, Peak Retreats, Ski Activity, Skiworld

The purpose-built village of Oz Station is set above the old village of Oz-en-Oisans and provides a back door into the Alpe d'Huez lift system. The small **Hotel Le Hors Piste, t** +33 (0)4 76 79 40 25, *www.lehorspiste.com*, is the only hotel. 'Quality of accommodation is extremely high,' said a reader.

Pal, Andorra

Page 34
Tour operators Directski, J2Ski

Pamporovo, Bulgaria

t +359 (0)2987 9778, *www.bulgariatravel.org*
Altitude 1450m (4,757ft)–1925m (6,316ft)
Lifts 8
Tour operators Balkan Tours, Crystal, Directski, First Choice, Inghams, Thomson

Small resort 85km from the attractive old town of Plovdiv. Most of the accommodation is in the handful of hotels straggling between the centre and the lift station. At the top of the mountain of Snezhanka is the Bulgarian telecom tower. Pamporovo boasts an average of 272 sunny days each year, although it does not always snow on the other days. Lift queues are rare, except for a 15-minute spell in the morning when all the ski school classes set off together. Ski school instructors are said to speak 'great English'.

It is advisable to book hotels through one of the many tour operators to the resort. Reporters criticize the hotel food. **Hotel Orlovets** was built in 2005, with a pool and spa facilities. **Hotel Pamporovo** is a recommended four-star in the resort centre. **Hotel Finlandia** is of a good standard but lacks atmosphere. **Hotel Murgavets** has a spa with fitness room, massage and beauty treatments. **Hotel Snezhanka** is said to be 'very cosy' with good food. **Hotel Perelik** is basic but clean – avoid rooms above the disco that closes at 3am; the hotel also houses Pamporovo's main shopping centre. The resort's après ski is lively.

Panorama, BC, Canada

Page 122
Tour operators Alpine Tours, Frontier Ski, Inghams, Ski Activity, Ski All America, Ski Dream, Ski Independence, Ski Safari

Park City, Utah, USA

Page 425
Tour operators Alpine Answers Select, American Ski Classics, AWWT, Crystal, Momentum, Ski Activity, Ski All America, Ski Dream, Ski Independence, Ski Safari, Skiworld, Thomson, United Vacations

Paradiski, France

See Les Arcs, page 159; Peisey–Vallandry, page 491 La Plagne and page 212

La Parva, Chile

See Valle Nevado, page 509
Tour operators Andes, Scott Dunn Latin America

Pas de la Casa, Andorra

Page 37
Tour operators Crystal, Directski, First Choice, Inghams, J2Ski, Lagrange, Neilson, Thomson

Passso Tonale, Italy

Page 291

Tour operators Alpine Tours, Club Europe, Crystal, Directski, Equity/Rocket Ski, First Choice, Inghams, Neilson, Thomson, Tops

Pecetto, Italy

See Macugnaga, page 482

Peisey-Vallandry, France

t +33 (0)4 79 07 94 28, *www.peisey-vallandry.com*
Altitude 1350m (4,428ft)–3226m (10,581ft)
Lifts 144 in Paradiski
Tour operators Club Med, Erna Low, Esprit, Lagrange, Peak Retreats, Ski Collection, Ski Hiver, Snow Monkey Chalets

The delightful village of Vallandry, with its wide and well-groomed pistes, is situated just below the Vanoise Express cable car station. From this quiet little base, your biggest decision each day is whether to ski the slopes of Les Arcs or to take the link and explore La Plagne. What Vallandry offers that larger resorts cannot is a true village ambience, for the village still boasts more cows than people.

The village has over 80 chalets, some low-rise apartments, and a couple of hotels. **L'Orée des Cimes**, **t** +44 (0)20 7584 2841, is an **MGM** development, and there is a four-star **Club Med** village. 'The resort itself is quiet but the Mont Blanc bar at the Grizzly chair is good,' advised a reporter.

Pestarena, Italy

See Macugnaga, page 482

Perisher-Blue, Australia

t +61 (0)2 6459 4419, *www.perisherblue.com.au*
Altitude 1605m (5,264ft)–2034m (6,672ft)
Lifts 47

If you've conquered Zermatt, St Anton and Chamonix, don't go to Perisher expecting big things. But if you want distinctive 'rounded' alps, gum trees covered in snow and perhaps a glimpse of some of Australia's rarer mammals, then Perisher-Blue is definitely worth a look. Perisher, in New South Wales, is part of the largest ski area in Australia and is linked to Blue Cow, Guthega and Smiggins. You get there on the Koscuszo Road or, better, by train – the Skitube takes you through 10km of tunnels on a 20-minute journey to Perisher and Blue Cow from Bullocks Flat. Snowcats take you from the Perisher terminal to your lodge. 'Great beginner skiing across the front valley stretch – my personal favourite is the Early Starter chair at Blue Cow,' said a reporter.

The country's first eight-person chair was installed here. Blue Cow has a high proportion of advanced terrain, and more than half the trails are intermediate. Excelerator is the longest run in the Perisher-Blue area. Guthega has some short challenging runs and its half-pipe is rated the best in Australia. The whole area has recently been the subject of a Aus$750,000 makeover.

Perisher Valley Hotel, **t** +61 26459 4455, is said to offer the best accommodation. **Perisher Manor**, **t** +61 26457 5291, *www.perishermanor.com.au*, is ski in, ski out, and smoking is banned at **The Lodge**, **t** +61 26457 5341, *www.thelodgesmiggins.com.au*.

Peyragudes-Les Agudes, France

t +33 (0)5 62 99 69 99, *www.peyragudes.com*
Altitude 1600m (5,249ft)–2400m (7,874ft)
Lifts 14
Tour operators Lagrange, Ski Collection, Ski France

Up-and-coming resort in the Pyrenees close to Bagnères de Luchon with 60km of piste, cross-country trails, a permanent boardercross course and a snowpark. The ski area is based around two village centres – Peyresourde and Les Agudes, both at 1600m, with the two-star **Hotel Le Yeti**, t +33 (0)5 61 79 07 13, at the foot of the slopes, as well as a range of apartments and attractive chalet buildings. Apart from skiing you can also go dog-sledding, para-pente, or try the more unusual activity of airboarding – an inflatable toboggan on which you descend the slopes on your stomach.

Pila, Italy

t +39 0165 521 148, *www.pila.it*
Altitude 1750m (5,741ft)–2750m (9,022ft)
Lifts 12
Tour operators Crystal, Interhome, Interski, Momentum, Thomson

Compact ('easy to get around') but surprisingly challenging ski area with pistes of mainly intermediate level, but with lots of accessible off-piste. 'Great resort but possibly not big enough for experts,' said a reader. An impressive gondola links with the regional capital of Aosta in 18 minutes, making it feasible to commute. The old Roman town, although blighted by commercial development, has a delightful pedestrianized centre. Accommodation in Pila includes the ski in, ski out **Hotel Etoile de Neige**, **t** +39 0165 521 541, *www.etoiledeneige.it*, offering a relaxing atmosphere and good food, **Hotel Pila 2000**, **t** +39 0165 521 148, modern and efficient, with friendly staff and fantastic food, **Lion Noir**, **t** +39 0165 521 704, *www.lionnoirhotel.it*, which is very good with pleasant food and friendly staff, and **Hotel Printemps**, **t** +39 0165 521 246. In Aosta you can stay at **Hotel Europe**, **t** +39 0165 236 363.

Pitztal, Austria

t +43 (0)5414 86999 or **t** (0)5413 8288 (Pitztaler Glacier), *www.pitztal.com*
Altitude 2880m (9,446ft)–3440m (11,283ft)
Lifts 11
Tour operator J2Ski

The Pitztal region in the Tyrol is made up of four villages, with St Leonhard the main accommodation base close to the Pitztaler Glacier and Rifflsee ski area. The skiing at Rifflsee is for all standards. The glacier skiing is accessed by funicular and the highest gondola in Austria. Club Alpin offers guides to those who want to explore the Wildspitz glaciers and surroundings. The area has invested 17 million euros in improvements recently, including lodging, a new gondola and a six-seater chair. The area has a wide range of hotels, including the four-star ski in, ski out **Alpinhotel**, **t** +43 (0)5413 86361, at the glacier base station.

Plan-Peisey, France

See Les Arcs, page 159

La Plagne, France

Page 212
Tour operators Alpine Answers Select, Club Med, Crystal, Equity/Rocket Ski, Erna Low, Esprit, Family Ski Company, Finlays, First Choice, French Freedom, Inghams, J2Ski, Lagrange, Mark Warner, Momentum, Mountain Heaven, Neilson, On the Piste, Silver Ski, Ski Activity, Ski Amis, Ski Arrangements, Ski Beat, Ski Expectations, Ski Collection, Ski Freshtracks, Ski Independence, Ski-Line, Ski Olympic, Ski Solutions, Ski Supreme, Skiworld, Sloping Off, Snowline,Thomson

Plagne Montalbert, France

See La Plagne, page 212
Tour operators Erna Low, Mountain Heaven

Poiana Brasov, Romania

Page 152
Tour operators Balkan Holidays, Balkan Tours, Inghams, Neilson, Solo's, Thomson

Pont d'Espagne, France

See Cauterets, page 464

Ponte di Legno, Italy

See Passo Tonale, page 291

Pontresina, Switzerland

t +41 (0)81 838 8300, *www.pontresina.com*
Altitude 1800m (5,904ft)–2978m (9,770ft)
Lifts 56 in St Moritz area
Tour operators Interhome, Made to Measure

Midway between the Diavolezza and Corviglia ski areas of St Moritz. **Grand Hotel Kronenhof**, **t** +41 (0)81 842 0111, *www.kronenhof.com*, is a five-star, and **Saratz Hotel**, **t** +41 (0)81 839 4000, *www.saratz.ch*, is a four-star that mixes traditional with modern design. **Kochendorfer's Albris**, **t** +41 (0)81 838 8040, is a relatively inexpensive three-star. **Hotel Steinbock**, **t** +41 (0)81 842 6371, is comfortable.

Portes du Soleil, France

See Avoriaz, page 163; Champéry, page 465; Châtel, page 466; Morgins, page 486; Morzine, page 206

Portillo, Chile

t +56 2 263 0606, *www.skiportillo.com*
Altitude 2512m (8,241ft)–3348m (10,984ft)
Lifts 15
Tour operators Andes, AWWT, Crystal Finest, Lotus Supertravel, Momentum, Original Travel, Scott Dunn Latin America, Ski All America, Ski Dream, Ski Safari

Chile's oldest ski area is the best-known resort, but not necessarily the best, in South America. Its American owner runs the hotel and mountain with impeccable efficiency. Portillo lies 160km north of Santiago on the frontier with Argentina. The brilliant yellow **Hotel Portillo** sits in a deep cleft in the Andes on the shore of the beautiful Laguna de Inca surrounded by towering peaks incuding 6960m Aconcagua, the highest mountain in the southern hemisphere.

The sophisticated hotel attracts the US and Austrian national teams, who spend part of each off-season training here. Their presence is in sharp contrast to the bygone era that lingers in the lakeside dining-room, harking back to winters when Harris tweed plus-fours rather than latex cat-suits were worn at breakfast. The walls are covered in antique leather, and waiters wear bow-ties and red jackets.

The number of guests in the whole resort is limited to just 450. Free daycare and après ski activities are provided for children aged three to six years, with lessons from three years. **Tio Bob's** is the only mountain restaurant, with a daily selection of grilled meats and salads. The skiing is suited to all standards, with intermediate terrain as well as some dramatically steeper slopes. The two infamous *va et vient* lifts – multiple draglifts without pylons designed by Poma to access steep avalanche-prone slopes – tow you up the mountain at a knee-juddering 22kph. 'The only drawback is the slopes are limited in variety and size – you can cover the lot in a day,' said a reporter.

Pradollano, Spain

See Sierra Nevada, page 502

Pralognan-la-Vanoise, France

t +33 (0)4 79 08 79 08, *www.pralognan.com*
Altitude 1400m (4,593ft)–2350m (7,710ft)
Lifts 12
Tour operators Erna Low, Lagrange

Attractive family resort with good cross-country skiing and modest alpine skiing between Courchevel and La Plagne. **La Vanoise, t** +33 (0)4 79 08 70 34, *www.hoteldelavanoise.fr*, is the resort's only three-star hotel, situated in the village centre and a few steps from the nearest lift. The village also has three two-star hotels. Dog-sledding is offered in the resort.

Pra-Loup, France

t +33 (0)4 92 84 10 04, *www.praloup.com*
Altitude 1600m (5,249ft)–2500m (8,202ft)
Lifts 50 with La Foux d'Allos
Tour operators Lagrange, Ski Collection

Shares a ski area with neighbouring La Foux d'Allos, and further down the valley from La Foux is the even prettier resort of Le Seignus. The skiing takes place on two main mountains, accessed by cable car from the top of the village of 1600. Pra-Loup has a wide choice of beginner and intermediate runs, including a variety of open-bowl skiing, good tree-level runs, and extensive off-piste. Weekend queueing can be a problem. The resort is divided into the two villages of 1500 and 1600, which are linked by chair and made up of a collection of 1960s hotels and apartments. Try **Hotel Club Les Bergers, t** +33 (0)4 92 84 14 54, *www.hotel-soleil-pra-loup.cote.azur.fr*, or **Hotel Le Prieuré, t** +33 (0)4 92 84 11 43.

Pragelato, Italy

t +39 0122 740 011, *www.pragelatoresort.com*
Altitude 2035m (6,675ft)–2823m (9,262ft)
Lifts 88 in Milky Way
Tour operators Carrier, Neilson

Old village 10km by road from Sestriere given a face-lift as the ski jumping venue and an accommodation base for the Turin Winter Olympics. A cable car connects the village with Sestriere and accommodation is in the luxury **Pragelato Resort, t** +39 0122 740 011, *www.pragelatoresort.com*, which has 205 chalet-style units and a spa. **Antica Osteria, t** + 39 0122 785 300, a converted cowshed with a vaulted ceiling, is the best restaurant in the region.

Prato Nevoso, Italy

t +39 0174 334 133, *www.pratonevoso.com*
Altitude 1500m (4,921ft)–2000m (6,562ft)
Lifts 24
Tour operators Equity/Rocket Ski, Ski-Line, Sloping Off, Thomson

Resort in the Maritime Alps built in 1965 and an ideal place to learn to ski or snowboard ('a small, friendly resort'). The Board Park has a half-pipe and is floodlit at night. The areas of

Artesina, Frabosa Sporana and Prato Nevoso make up MondoleSki, with 100km of piste featuring mainly gentle runs suited to beginners and intermediates ('a good range of skiing for everyone').

'There isn't that much to do in the town if you're after nightlife,' complained a reporter. **Movida Pub**, **Baita del Verde** and **Baita del Rosso** are the nightspots. **Hotel Galassia**, **t** +39 0174 334 183, is recommended ('friendly staff, and the food was OK considering we were getting the school kids' menu').

Praz-sur-Arly, France

See Nôtre Dame-de-Bellecombe, page 489
Tour operators French Freedom, Lagrange, Ski France

Puy-St-Vincent, France

t +33 (0)4 92 23 35 80, *www.puystvincent.com*
Altitude 1400m (4,593ft)–2750m (9,022ft)
Lifts 16
Tour operators Erna Low, Lagrange, Snowbizz Vacances

A well-established resort that was extremely popular with British families in the 1970s. It is located 20km from Briançon on the edge of the Ecrins National Park. Its micro-climate usually ensures secure late-season snow-cover, along with 300 days of sunshine per year. As one reporter put it, 'Everything is in a safe family environment, where the kids can be left to play without being out of sight. The food and drink is also very cheap as ski resorts go, and the ski school and children's facilities are second to none.'

PSV 1400 is an unspoilt mountain village connected by a six-pack to PSV 1600. More recent *résidences*, a few chalets and a handful of shops and restaurants have been built on the edge of the piste, and the higher village is the better bet if you want doorstep skiing.

The 67km of piste in the small but challenging area has enough variety to suit all standards, although most runs are beginner to intermediate. From PSV 1600, two chairlifts give easy access to the main skiing, and queues are rare outside school holidays. The resort has a small terrain park that is floodlit at night, and a cross-country track.

The best of the apartments are in the **Mona Lisa** building. Three-star **Hôtel Saint Roche**, **t** +33 (0)4 92 23 32 79, is down at 1400.

Pyhä, Finland

See Luosto, page 482

Québec City, Canada

t +1 418 649 2608, *www.quebecregion.com*
Altitude Stoneham: 695ft (420m)–2,075ft (632m) / **Mont-Ste-Anne**: 575ft (175m)–2,625ft (800m)
Lifts Stoneham 8, Mont-Ste-Anne 15
Tour operators Carrier, Crystal, Frontier Ski, Virgin Snow

Romantic, beautifully preserved – and reasonably priced – Québec acts as a bed-base from which to explore the nearby ski areas, each of which is worth a day or two's exploration. A regular shuttle-bus operates between the city, Stoneham (20-minute drive) and Mont-Ste-Anne (30 minutes away). Le Massif is also 30 minutes away. The city was built in 1608 and its cobbled streets added in the 18th century. There is a wide choice of restaurants, shops, art galleries and the city is home to a thriving club scene. **Fairmont Chateau Frontenac**, **t** +1 418 692 3861, *www.fairmont.com/frontenac*, is a prominent hotel at the heart of the city, overlooking the St Lawrence River.

Queenstown (Coronet Peak, Mount Hutt and The Remarkables), New Zealand

t +64 (0)3 450 1970, *www.queenstown-nz.co.nz*
Altitude 1200m (3,937ft)–1957m (6,421ft)
Lifts 10
Tour operators Original Travel, Scott Dunn Asia Pacific

These are six resorts under the marketing umbrella of the Southern Lakelands, based around Queenstown and Wanaka.
Queenstown is a lively and picturesque lake-side town situated in the southwest of the South Island and flanked by Coronet peak and The Remarkables. The traditional but recently modernized resort is Coronet Peak, with six lifts (including a six-seater chair) providing a variety of good all-round skiing. The nursery slope claims the longest magic carpet lift (146m) in the world.

The Remarkables resort is visually exciting, but has fewer options than Coronet Peak. From Queenstown, The Remarkables range seems impossibly steep, but the ski area is in gentle bowls ideal for family skiing. Coronet peak has the most extensive snowmaking in New Zealand.

The third resort in the area is Mount Hutt, the best-known resort in the country. It's a 35-minute drive from Methven and 90 minutes from Christchurch airport and has wonderful views from the Pacific Ocean across to the heart of the Southern Alps. Mount Hutt is normally the first resort to open in Australasia each winter. Although the weather is unpredictable, the skiing is some of the best in the country for all standards. Mount Hutt has extensive terrain parks, a half-pipe, and some steep chutes. The village of Methven has a choice of accommodation.

The Remarkables Lodge, **t** +64 (0)3 442 2720, is highly rated and closest to the resort.

Radstadt, Austria

See Wagrain and the Salzburger Sportwelt, page 98

Ramsau, Austria

Tour operators HF Holidays, Inntravel

Small village near Schladming that is strong on cross-country skiing.

Rauris, Austria

t +43 (0)6544 20022, *www.rauris.net*
Altitude 950m (3,114ft)–2200m (7,253ft)
Lifts 10
Tour operators Crystal, Neilson

Old gold-mining village with beginner and family skiing in the Hohe Tauern mountains between the Gasteinertal and Zell-am-See. 'A compact village with a quiet, cosy atmosphere,' said a reader, although during February school holidays it was a different story. 'The resort could not cope with the numbers – ski bus packed to the rafters, no lockers available, and 45-minute queues for the gondola. The slopes were highly populated, so you had to have 360 degree vision to avoid collisions.' Three of the four main hotels are next to each other – **Ferienwelt Kristall**, **t** +43 (0)6544 7316, *www.ferienwelt-kristall.at*, **RauriserHof**, **t** +43 (0)6544 6213, *www.rauriserhof.at*, and **Hotel Alpina**, **t** +43 (0)6544 6562, *www.hotel-alpina-rauris.at* ('of a similar, good standard').

Reberty, France

See Les Menuires, page 196

Red Resort, BC, Canada

Page 125
Tour operators AWWT, Frontier Ski, Nonstopski, Ski Independence, Ski Safari

Reith, Austria

See Alpbach, page 46

The Remarkables, New Zealand

See Queenstown (Coronet Peak and The Remarkables), opposite

Rennweg, Austria

See Katschberg, page 477

Revelstoke Mountain Resort, BC, Canada

See page 126
Tour operators Frontier Ski, Mark Warner

Riederalp, Switzerland

t +41 (0)27 928 6050, *www.riederalp.ch*
Altitude 900m (2,953ft)–2227m (7,306ft)
Lifts 35
Tour operator Made to Measure

A quirky traditional resort in the Aletsch area reached by cable car from the valley below. The car-free resort has no roads, high street or walking paths – everything is set on the piste and is ski-in ski-out. The ski area is connected by lifts to the further resorts of Bettmeralp, Fiesch, Fiescheralp and Morel, all with their own accommodation and creating a total 99km of piste. **Wellness-Resort Alpenrose**, **t** +27 (0)928 4545, *www.artfurrer.ch*, is a traditional four-star hotel with suites and a wellness centre. **Bobo's Kinder-Club** is for children from 2½yrs.

Riksgränsen, Sweden

t +46 (0)980 400 80, *www.riksgransen.nu*
Altitude 500m (1,640ft)–909m (2,982ft)
Lifts 5
Tour operators Discover the World, Original Travel

Resort in Swedish Lapland 300km into the Arctic Circle yet just 90 minutes from Stockholm. This far north the sun doesn't set during midsummer (mid-May to mid-June), so you can ski, snowboard or heli-ski even in the early hours of the morning. **Hotel Riksgränsen, t** +46 (0)980 400 80, is the accommodation of choice, with a spa and swimming pool.

Risoul, France

Page 127
Tour operators Crystal, Erna Low, First Choice, Lagrange, Neilson, On the Piste, Ski Arrangements, Ski Collection, Thomson, Wasteland

Rittnerhorn (Corno Renon), Italy

t +39 (0)471 352 993, *www.ortlerskiarena.com*
Altitude 1530m (5,020ft)–2070m (6,791ft)
Lifts 74 in Ortler Skiarena

To the north of Bolzano is a small village, especially good for families, with 8km of piste, one gondola and three draglifts. The resort is part of the Ortler Skiarena, with 13 unconnected resorts covered by one lift pass. A total 260km of piste is served by eight cableways and 66 chair- and draglifts.

Rocca di Cambio, Italy

See Campo Felice, page 463

Rohrmoos, Austria

t +43 (0)3687 61147, *www.rohrmoos.at*
Altitude 870m (2,854ft)–1850m (6,070ft)
Lifts 46 in Schladming area
Tour operator J2Ski

Spread-out satellite of Schladming with ski in, ski out accommodation and unchallenging skiing. Try **Hotel Austria, t** +43 (0)3687 61444, **Hotel Seiterhof, t** +43 (0)3687 61194, *www.seiterhof.com*, or **Hotel Waldfrieden, t** +43 (0)3687 61487, *www.waldfrieden.at*, all of which are good value. Smarter **Hotel Schwaigerhof, t** +43 (0)3687 61422, *www.schwaigerhof.at*, is on the edge of the piste and has a pool. **Hotel Schütterhof, t** +43 (0)3687 61205, is recommended.

Rougemont, Switzerland

Tour operator Indigo Lodges

Small village close to Gstaad and sharing its ski area.

Ruka, Finland

t +358 860 0225, *www.ruka.fi*
Altitude 291m (955ft)–492m (1,614ft)
Lifts 19
Tour operator Inghams

Ruka will never be a world-class resort and it isn't even the best-known resort in Finland (Levi is), but it is a good little place for families who want an all-round wintersports experience. It has mainly beginner to intermediate pistes, with over half the slopes floodlit at night. 'Uncrowded slopes and no lift queues,' said a reporter.

Rusutsu, Japan

Page 317
Tour operators Crystal, Inghams, Ski Independence, Ski Safari

La Rosière, France

Page 219
Tour operators Crystal, Erna Low, Esprit, Lagrange, Ski Amis, Ski Arrangements, Ski Beat, Ski Collection, Ski France, Ski Independence, Ski Olympic, Thomson

Ruapehu, New Zealand

See Whakapapa and Turoa, page 487

Saalbach-Hinterglemm, Austria

Page 77
Tour operators Alpine Answers Select, BoardnLodge, Club Europe, Crystal, Directski, Equity/Rocket Ski, First Choice, Inghams, Interhome, Neilson, Ski Activity, Ski Astons, SkiBound, Ski Independence, Sloping Off, Thomson

Saalfelden, Austria

See Maria Alm, page 483

Saas-Fee, Switzerland

Page 359
Tour operators Alpine Answers Select, Crystal, Erna Low, Esprit, Inghams, J2Ski, Kuoni, Made to Measure, Momentum, Oak Hall, Ski Independence, Ski Solutions, Swiss Travel Service, Switzerland Travel Centre, Thomson, Warren Smith Ski Academy

St Anton, Austria

Page 81
Tour operators Albus Travel, Alpine Answers Select, Alpine Weekends, Altitude Inspires, Carrier, Crystal/Crystal Finest, Directski, Elegant Resorts, Esprit, First Choice, Flexiski, Inghams, Kaluma, Lotus Supertravel, Made to Measure, Mark Warner, Momentum, Mountain Leap, Neilson, Original Travel, Scott Dunn, Seasons in Style, Ski Activity, Ski Equipe, Ski Expectations, Ski Freshtracks, Ski Independence, Ski-Line, Ski in Luxury, Ski Safari, Ski Solutions, Ski Val, Ski Wild, Skiworld, Thomson, Total Ski, White Roc

St Christoph, Austria

t +43 (0)5446 22690, *www.stantona marlberg.com*
Altitude 1800m (5,90 6ft)–2811m (9,222ft)
Lifts 82 on Arlberg Ski Pass
Tour operators Elegant Resorts, Flexiski, Jeffersons, Kaluma, Made to Measure, Momentum, Neilson, Powder Byrne, Seasons in Style, Thomson

Delightful village directly linked into St Anton's ski area, providing a peaceful alternative base. It consists of a small collection of restaurants and hotels, of which the **Arlberg-Hospiz**, **t** +43 (0)5446 2611, *www.hospiz.com*, is the most famous and comfortable. St Christoph has five other hotels, as well as the Bundes Ski Academy – where future ski and snowboard instructors are trained.

St-Christophe-en-Oisans, France

Small village linked off-piste with La Grave.

St-François-Longchamp, France

See Valmorel, page 510
Tour operators Erna Low, Lagrange, Wasteland

St Gallenkirch, Austria

t +43 (0)5557 66000, *www.stgallenkirch.at*
Altitude 1430m (4,692ft)–2300m (7,546ft)
Lifts 62 in area

Part of the extensive Montafon area with its 11 villages and a total 222km of piste. The resort has a permanent GS and timed carving track. Four-star **Alpensporthotel Grandau**, **t** +43 (0)5557 6384, *www.grandau.at*, contains hotel bedrooms, a spa and apartments for up to six people.

St-Gervais, France

Page 224
Tour operators Holidays, Erna Low, French Freedom, Interhome, Lagrange, Mountain Tracks, Peak Retreats, Ski France, Snowcoach

St-Jean d'Arves, France

See Le Corbier, page 467
Tour operators First Choice, Peak Retreats, Ski France, Thomson, Wasteland

St-Jean d'Aulps, France

t +33 (0)4 50 79 65 09, *www.saintjean daulps.com*
Altitude 950m (3,117ft)–1800m (5,905ft)
Lifts 14
Tour operator Independent Luxury Travel

Attractive village in the Portes du Soleil with its own separate ski area, Le Grande Terche, providing 34km of skiing suitable for beginners to intermediates, and a crèche. The village has several bars and restaurants including **Bar National**, which also serves snacks. Ten minutes' drive away is the much larger resort of Morzine.

St Johann im Pongau, Austria

See Wagrain and the Salzburger Sportwelt page 98
Tour operator Interhome

St Johann in Tirol, Austria

Page 86
Tour operators Crystal, Directski, Ski Wild, Snowscape, Thomson

St Lary, France

t +33 (0)5 62 39 50 81, *www.saintlary.com*
Altitude 830m (2,723ft)–2515m (8,251ft)
Lifts 32
Tour operators Lagrange, Pyrenean Mountain Tours, Ski Collection

Typical Pyrenean village 80km from Lourdes, with stone-built houses and one narrow main street. The skiing is suitable for beginners to intermediates, and it takes four minutes to walk from the village centre to the cable car to St-Lary-Pla-d'Adet, a small modern ski station with some accommodation. This is linked by road and by lift to an alternative base at St-Lary-La Cabane. The fourth base area of St-Lary-Espiaube is reached by road, or on skis from Soum de Matte. The ski area is mainly treeless and lacks variety. It extends into the neighbouring Auron Valley and up the snow-sure glacier on Mont Pichaleye.

Hôtel Mercure Coralia, **t** +33 (0)5 62 99 50 00, **Hôtel La Terrasse Fleurie**, **t** +33 (0)5 62 40 76 00, *www.la-terrasse-fleurie.com*, and **Les Arches**, **t** +33 (0)5 62 49 10 10, *www.hotel-les-arches.com*, are all recommended, while **Hôtel Christiania**, **t** +33 (0)5 62 98 40 62, *www.christiania-pyrenees.com*, is a more recent addition. At Espiaube, **Hôtel La Sapinière**, **t** +33 (0)5 62 98 44 04, is reasonably good.

St-Luc, Switzerland

🏆 BEST SKI HOTEL 2009 (HOTEL BELLA TOLA)

t +41 (0)27 475 14 12, *www.st-luc.ch*
Altitude 1650m (5,413ft)–3000m (9,842ft)
Lifts 16
Tour operators Inntravel, Made to Measure

Attractive and unspoilt little resort in the Val d'Anniviers with 75km of pistes and within day-tripping distance of other resorts such as Grimentz, 15 minutes away. Highlight is the gorgeous four-star **Grand Hotel & Pension Bella Tola**, **t** +41 (0)27 475 14 44, *www.bellatola.ch*, one of the most atmospheric hotels in the Alps, with three restaurants and a small spa and swimming-pool Staying here is like taking a journey to another era – it was built in 1883 on the foundations of a Roman villa. The current owners have since given it a total makeover completely in keeping with its history.

St-Martin-de-Belleville, France

Page 225
Tour operators The Alpine Club, Alpine Tracks, Crystal, Erna Low, First Choice, Kaluma, Peak Retreats

St Michael, Austria

t +43 (0)6477 8913, *www.stmichael-lungau.at*
Altitude 1100m (3,609ft)–2411m (7,910ft)
Lifts 38
Tour operators Alpine Tours, Club Europe, Equity/Rocket Ski

Pretty, traditional village and intermediate ski area near Obertauern on the border of Salzburgerland and Carinthia. **Lifestyle-Hotel der Wastlwirt**, **t** +43 (0)6477 7155, *www.wastlwirt.at*, is a 600-year-old building that used to be a country restaurant. Today it is Austria's first 'lifestyle hotel', offering more then 50 lifestyle packages. Everyone has their own lifestyle coach, biological juices and fresh fruit are served around the clock, and once a week there's a late-night wellbeing session. You can even check out your energy on the 'bodycheck' system.

St Moritz, Switzerland

Page 361
Tour operators Alpine Answers Select, Altitude Inspires, Club Med, Corporate Ski Company, Crystal, Elegant Resorts, Flexiski, Indigo Lodges, Inghams, Interhome, Jeffersons, Kuoni, Made to Measure, Momentum, Mountain Leap, Oak Hall, Original Travel, Oxford Ski Company, Seasons in Style, Ski Independence, Ski Solutions, Ski Weekend, Switzerland Travel Centre

St-Nicholas-de-Véroce, France

See St Gervais, page 224

St-Sorlin d'Arves, France

t +33 (0)4 79 59 71 77, *www.saint sorlindarves.com* or *www.sybelles.com*
Altitude 1550m (5,085ft)–2620m (8,595ft)
Lifts 75
Tour operators Holidays, Crystal, First Choice, Lagrange, Peak Retreats, SkiBound, Ski France, Thomson, Wasteland

Quaint mountain village of Savoyard farmhouses and long-established shops built around a early 17th-century Baroque church in the Maurienne Valley. The village is part of the 310km Les Sybelles ski area linked to St-Jean, Le Corbier and La Toussuire. The skiing is best suited to intermediates and has two terrain parks and 16km of cross-country trails. Hotels in the village include two-star **La Balme**, **t** +33 (0)4 79 59 71 71, *www.hotel-balme.com*, and **Hotel Beausoleil**, **t** +33 (0)4 79 59 71 42, *www.hotel-beausoleil.com*. The village has more than a dozen restaurants and the local ski area boasts three mountain eateries. The resort is renowned for its children's facilities.

St Wolfgang, Austria

t +43 (0)6138 8003, *www.stwolfgang.at*
Altitude 550m (1,800ft)–1600m (4,763ft)
Lifts 8
Tour operators Crystal, First Choice, Inghams, Thomson

Unassuming little 16th-century village ('so quiet, it's unreal – absolutely no nightlife') at the centre of Austria's lake district. It acts as a pleasant base for those wishing to ski the modest Postalm plateau, a magnificent 35-minute drive away. 'The area is little visited by Brits,' confirmed a reader. St Wolfgang's nursery slope is just outside the village, and additional skiing is available at Gosau an hour away. Four-star **Hotel Cortisen**, **t** +43 (0) 6138 2376, *www.cortisen.at*, is warmly praised by reporters.

Ste-Foy, France

Page 222
Tour operators Alpine Answers Select, Alpine Elements, Descent, Erna Low, Lagrange, Made to Measure, Mountain Tracks, Peak Leisure, Peak Retreats, Première Neige, Ski Arrangements

Les Saisies, France

t +33 (0)4 79 38 90 30, *www.lessaisies.com*
Altitude 1650m (5,413ft)–1941m (6,368ft)
Lifts 29 in Les Saisies, 84 in Espace Diamant
Tour operators Classic Ski, Erna Low, Lagrange, Peak Retreats, Ski Collection, Ski Independence

'If you are seeking an authentic French experience I would give Les Saisies five stars,' enthused a reporter. Les Saisies sits in a delightfully scenic position on the ridge dominating the Arly and Beaufortain valleys in a beautiful area of woodland and alpine pastures 30km from Albertville. The small resort is primarily a cross-country destination with 140km of *loipe*, but it is also part of the Espace Diamant, an alpine ski area of 84 lifts covering 175km of pistes that connect with neighbouring resorts of Crest-Voland, Nôtre-Dame-de-Bellecombe and Flumet. The resort also provides a back-door entrance to Les Contamines.

'A resort geared to children', remarked a reader. Accommodation is headed by three-star **Hôtel Le Calgary**, **t** +33 (0)4 79 38 98 38, in the village centre, with a health club, pool and gourmet restaurants.

Sälen, Sweden

t +46 (0)28 018700, *www.skistar.com*
Altitude 366m (1,201ft)–620m (2,034ft)
Lifts 77

The town of Sälen, 53km from the better-known resort of Trysil, has a range of ski areas close by. These are Lindvallen, which is linked to smaller Högfjället, and the two linked resorts of Tandådalen and Hundfjället. Additional small resorts include Kläppen and Stöten. Most of the pistes are of intermediate standard, although there are over 30 black runs in the area. The Trollskogen – or Enchanted Forest – at Hundfjället is a children's trail featuring 400 trolls in theatrical stage sets with sound-effects. Lindvallen has the first ski in, ski out **McDonald's**. **Högfjälls Hotel**, **t** +46 (0)28 087000, *www.salen-hotell.se*, is comfortable and piste-side, with a spa and sushi restaurant.

Salzburger Sportwelt, Austria

See Wagrain, page 98

Samnaun, Switzerland

t +41 (0)81 868 5858, *www.samnaun.ch*
Altitude 1840m (6,035ft)–2864m (9,394ft)
Lifts 44 in Ischgl-Samnaun area

Village living off its duty-free status and with a linked ski area to Ischgl in Austria. The resort has a loyal Swiss following. Hotels include **Chasa Montana**, **t** +41 (0)81 861 9000, *www.hotelchasamontana.ch*, **Hotel Post**, **t** +41 (0)81 861 9200, and **Hotel Silvretta**, **t** +41 (0)81 861 9500, *www.hotel-silvretta.ch*.

Samoëns, France

Page 227
Tour operators Alps Accommodation, Altitude Holidays, Erna Low, In Resort Services, Interhome, Lagrange, Peak Retreats

San Candido, Italy

See Alta Pusteria, page 456

San Cassiano, Italy

Page 293
Tour operators Momentum, Mountain Sun, Powder Byrne, Seasons in Style, Ski 2

San Martino (Reinswald), Italy

t +39 0471 623 091, *www.sarntal.com* or *www.reinswald.com*
Altitude 1570m (5,151ft)–2460m (8,071ft)
Lifts 5 in resort, 74 in Ortler Skiarena

South Tirol village in the Val Sarentino, with a modern gondola and three draglifts serving 12km of piste. The resort is part of the Ortler Skiarena, with 13 small resorts sharing a lift pass, and 260km of piste served by eight cableways and 66 chair and draglifts. For the skiing of San Martino you can stay 15 minutes' drive away at the charming **Hotel Bad Schörgau, t** +39 0471 623048, *www.bad-schoergau.com*.

San Martino di Castrozza, Italy

t +39 0439 768 867, *www.sanmartino.com*
Altitude 1450m (4,757ft)–2385m (7,825ft)
Lifts 17

Resort on the eastern edge of the Trentino Dolomites, surrounded by wild forest with soaring mountain peaks above. In 1700, violin-maker Stradivari used to go into the same woods to select the spruce for his violins. Skiing started at San Martino di Castrozza in the early 1930s, and it has developed into three separate areas (two of which are linked). The resort lacks high-season queues and snow-boarders, and has the charm of a low-profile ski station, although the majority of lifts are old-fashioned and slow. Accommodation includes four-star **Hotel Savoia**, t +39 0439 68094, and three-star **Hotel-Residence Colfosco, t** +39 0439 68224.

Sansicario, Italy

See Sauze d'Oulx, page 296
Tour operator Thomson

Santa Caterina, Italy

t +39 0342 935 598, *www.valtellinaonline.com*
Altitude 1738m (5,702ft)–2725m (8,940ft)
Lifts 8
Tour operator Neilson

Quiet village, 30 minutes by bus from Bormio, ideal for families and beginners. It is set up a mountain road that is a dead end in winter when the Gavia Pass is closed. Local skiing is on the northeast-facing slopes of the Sobretta. The higher slopes are fairly steep and there are some intermediate trails through the trees. Comfortable **San Matteo Hotel, t** +39 0342 925 121, *www.hotelsmatteo.com*, has good food.

Sauze d'Oulx, Italy

Page 296
Tour operators Crystal, Directski, First Choice, Inghams, J2Ski, Momentum, Neilson, Ski Arrangements, Ski High Days, Thomson

Savognin, Switzerland

t +41 (0)81 659 16 16, *www.savognin.ch*
Altitude 1200m (3,937ft)–2715m (8,907ft)
Lifts 17

Attractive village close to St Moritz and Davos. It has a cutting-edge **Cube Hotel**, *www.cube-hotels.com* (*see* Nassfeld).

Scheffau, Austria

t +43 (0)5358 7373, *www.scheffau.com*
Altitude 752m (2,467ft)–1829m (6,001ft)
Lifts 93 in SkiWelt
Tour operators Crystal, Esprit, Neilson, xSki Astons, Ski Wild, Thomson

A quieter alternative to popular Söll. 'Not a very testing area if you are advanced, but a great range of routes if you like to explore and have a goal in mind for each day,' advised a reporter. **Hotel Alpin Scheffau, t** +43 (0)5358 85560, *www.hotelalpinscheffau.at*, is comfortable, with large quad rooms for families and a pool. Après-ski is muted apart from the Red Bull tent beside the gondola, which is crowded for a couple of hours when the lifts close.

Schladming, Austria

Page 88
Tour operators Alpine Answers Select, Crystal, Equity/Rocket Ski, Inghams, Interhome, Oak Hall, Sloping Off

Schlick 2000, Austria

See Neustift and the Stubaital, page 68
Tour operator Alpine Tours

Schönberg, Austria

See Neustift and the Stubaital, page 68

Schruns, Austria

t +43 (0)5556 721660, *www.schruns-tschagguns.at*
Altitude 700m–1300m
Lifts 11 in Schruns
Tour operator Interhome

Montafon village is one of the smaller resorts in the country, with 40km of fairly low-lying piste. The skiing is ideal for beginners and the resort it is easily accessible from Friedrichshafen airport, an hour away, and Innsbruck, 90 minutes. Ten other nearby villages of the Montafon area give access to a total 222km of piste and 62 lifts.

Seefeld, Austria

Page 91
Tour operators Crystal, Directski, Headwater, Inghams, Interhome, Lagrange, Momentum, Thomson

Seiseralm, Italy

See Ortisei, page 290

Sella Ronda, Italy

See Arabba, page 257; Canazei and the Val di Fassa, page 260; Corvara, page 276; San Cassiano, page 293; Selva Gardena, page 299

Selva Gardena, Italy

Page 299
Tour operators Alpine Answers Select, Crystal/Crystal Finest, Esprit, First Choice, Inghams, Momentum, Neilson, Ski Arrangements, Ski Expectations, Thomson, Total Ski

Serfaus-Fiss-Ladis, Austria

t +43 (0)5476 6239–71, *www.serfaus-fiss-ladis.at*
Altitude 1427m (4,682ft)–2684m (8,806ft)
Lifts 53 in area
Tour operator Alpine Tours

'Unequivocably a hidden gem,' said reporters. The smart resort attracts a mainly Austrian, German and Dutch families to its flattering slopes and luxury hotels. ('You could count on one hand how many British people we met or heard in a week.') The village is car-free with an underground railway, which runs on air cushions rather like a hovercraft. This offers four stops between the far end of the village and the lifts, and contributes to the resort's serene atmosphere. The 175km ski area, linked to the villages of Fiss and Ladis, has a terrain park and an impressive 25 mountain restaurants ('countless top quality restaurants serving decent food at decent prices'). The slopes are floodlit for night-skiing and there is a tubing park and mini snowmobile course.

Serfaus specializes in health treatments, with spa hotels including the **Löwe and Bär**, **t** +43 (0)5476 6058, *www.loewebaer.com*, **Wellnesshotel Cervosa**, **t** +43 (0)5476 62110, *www.cervosa.com*, and **Wellnesshotel Schalber**, **t** +43 (0)5476 6770, *www.schalber.at*. **Gourmet-Hotel Maximilian**, **t** +43 (0)5476 6520, *www.maximilian.at*, is, as its name suggests, renowned for its food. Four-stars at Fiss include **Hotel Bergblick**, **t** +43 (0)5476 6364, *www.bergblick.com*, **Verwöhnhotel Chesa-Monte**, **t** +43 (0)5476 6406, *www.chesa-monte.at*, and **Hotel Gebhard**, **t** +43 (0)5476 6617, *www.hotel-gebhard.at*. In Ladis **Hotel Goies**, **t** +43 (0)5472 6133, *www.hotel-goies.at*, houses the **Vitality Schlössl spa**.

Serrada-Folgaria, Italy

t +39 0464 720 538, *www.folgariaski.com*
Altitude 1169m (3,835ft)–2060m (6,758ft)
Lifts 42
Tour operators Equity/Rocket Ski, Sloping Off

Good-value, mainly beginner and easy intermediate ski area in the Dolomites that is popular with school groups. Folgaria (not to be confused with Folgarida, linked to Madonna di Campiglio) is made up of seven hamlets, of which Serrada has the low-cost accommodation. **Golf Hotel**, **t** +39 0464 723114, *www.golfhotelfolgaria.it*, in the Costa area, has a choice of hotels or apartments. The resort also has over 20 three-star hotels and *rèsidences*.

Serre Chevalier, France

Page 229
Tour operators Alpine Elements, Club Med, Crystal, Equity/Rocket Ski, Erna Low, First Choice, French Freedom, Hannibals, Inghams, Lagrange, Momentum, Neilson, Peak Retreats, Ski Activity, Ski Arrangements, Ski

Expectations, Ski France, Ski Miquel, Skitopia, Sloping Off, Thomson, Tops

Sestriere, Italy

Page 303
Tour operators Alpine Answers Select, Crystal, Equity/Rocket Ski, First Choice, Inghams, Interhome, Momentum, Mountain Leap, Neilson, Ski Arrangements, Thomson

Shiga Kogen, Japan

t +44 (0)20 7734 6870, *www.snowjapan.co.uk*
Altitude 1228m (4,028ft)–2305m (7,562ft)
Lifts 71

Nagano's largest ski area, and venue for the majority of ski events at the 1998 Winter Olympics. It is a mixture of 21 different ski bases, served by 71 lifts, dotted over six interlinked mountains. None of the sectors is big or particularly difficult; in alpine terms, the whole area would make up just three or four linked resorts of reasonable size. A competent skier could cover all the terrain in a couple of days. Accommodation includes **Villa Alpen**, **t** +81 (0)269 34 2731, which has its own ski school and equipment rental shop in the Sun Valley resort, and **Hotel La Neige Higashikan**, **t** +81 (0)261 72 7111, at Shiga Kogen.

Sierra-at-Tahoe, California, USA

t +1 530 659 7453, *www.sierrattahoe.com*
Altitude 2024m (6,640ft)–2698m (8,852ft)
Lifts 9
Tour operator Ski Dream

Lake Tahoe resort set in 2,000 acres with plenty of sunny intermediate skiing and no less than six terrain parks with two half-pipes for skiers and riders. 'One decent mountain restaurant with stunning views, and lots of tree-lined runs, so good in poor weather,' said a reporter.

Sierra Nevada, Spain

t +34 958 24 91 00, *www.sierranevadaski.com*
Altitude 2100m (6,888ft)–3470m (11,385ft)
Lifts 19
Tour operator Thomson

An Andalucian resort 32km from Granada, offering mainland Europe's most southerly skiing. The presence of a ski resort here seems at complete odds with the nearby resorts of Marbella and Malaga, under two hours away. The purpose-built and somewhat charmless village of Pradollano is where most skiers stay. 'The resort has been built up the side of the mountain so it is best to stay at the bottom around the square, otherwise it's a long walk home uphill with your skis,' warned a reader. The ski area is vulnerable to bad weather, the mountain range is often exposed to high winds, and skiing is as likely to be interrupted by too much snow as too little. But when conditions are good, the skiing can be excellent and is best suited to beginners and intermediates. On a clear day you can see from the top across to North Africa. During fiesta time the resort can be crowded due to its proximity to Granada and the Costa del Sol. Accommodation includes **Hotel Sol Melia Sol y Nieve**, **t** +34 958 48 03 00, and the four-star **Sol Melia Sierra Nevada**, **t** +34 958 24 91 11 (both *www.solmelia.com*), which are convenient and pleasant. Four-star **Hotel Maribel**, **t** +34 958 24 91 11, is highly rated.

Silver Star, BC, Canada

Page 129
Tour operators Alpine Answers Select, American Ski Classics, AWWT, Frontier Ski, Ski Activity, Ski All America, Ski Dream, Ski Independence, Ski Safari

Sinaia, Romania

t +40 (0)1 614 5160 or **t** +44 (0)20 7224 3692, *www.romaniantourism.com*
Altitude 855m (2,805ft)–2219m (7,280ft)
Lifts 10

Spa town where the Romanian royal family used to spend their summers after King Karol I built beautiful Peles Castle in the 1870s. Its once-smart hotels and casinos have an air of faded grandeur. The skiing is basic, but the setting is delightful. The long and easy runs down the front of the mountain are poorly marked and therefore challenging in uncertain visibility. The main area is on exposed slopes behind the mountain. Four-star hotels include **New Montana**, **t** +40 (0)244 312 751, *www.newmontana.ro*, **Hotel Anda**, **t** +40 (0)244 306 020, *www.hotel.anda.tourneo.ro*, and the recently renovated **Palace Hotel**, **t** +40 (0)244 312 051, *www.sinaia.biz*. Three-star **Hotel Sinaia**, **t** +40 (0)244 311 551, *www.sinaia.hotel.tourneo.ro*, is rated.

Siviez, Switzerland

t +41 (0)27 289 5589, *www.nendaz.ch*
Altitude 1730m (5,676ft)–3330m (10,925ft)
Lifts 89 in Four Valleys
Tour operator Interhome

Budget option for those wanting to ski the Four Valleys. A high-speed chair links to the Gentianes-Mont-Fort cable cars of Verbier. Accommodation is in one hotel, a soulless apartment block and a youth hostel.

Sixt-Fer-à-Cheval, France

t +33 (0)4 50 34 49 36, *www.sixtferacheval.com*
Altitude 1600m (5,248ft)–2480m (8,134ft)
Lifts 73 in Grand Massif
Tour operators Lagrange, Peak Retreats

Small 9th-century village in the Grand Massif ski area linked via the Piste des Cascades, a 14km blue trail, with Flaine.

SkiWelt, Austria

See Söll and the SkiWelt, page 94

Smiggins, Australia

See Perisher-Blue, page 491

Smugglers' Notch, Vermont, USA

t +1 800 169 8219, *www.smuggs.com*
Altitude 314m (1,030ft)–1109m (3,640ft)
Lifts 8

Resort that has carved a niche for itself in the family market, but you would not choose to come here if you did not have small children. The key is convenience, with the lifts and accommodation within a 1,000ft radius, and apartments designed with families in mind. Smuggs is a small, unadorned village consisting mainly of condos, with a swimming-pool and several restaurants.

Morse is the beginners' mountain, conveniently situated in the village centre. Another novice area, Morse Highlands, is set halfway up the mountain. More adept skiers move on from Morse to the other two mountains, which are reached by bus or on skis. Madonna Mountain offers some pleasant trails, and Sterling has long intermediate runs. **Snow Sport University**, t +1 802 644 1293, is the ski and snowboard school. Kids are cared for at **Treasures Child Care Center**, t +1 800 451 8752, which features giant fishtanks and a magic carpet lift for skiers from two and a half years.

Snowbird and Alta, Utah, USA

Page 429
Tour operators Alpine Answers Select, American Ski Classics, AWWT, Momentum, Ski All America, Ski Dream, Ski Independence, Ski Safari, United Vacations

Snow King, Wyoming, USA

t +1 307 733 5200, *www.snowking.com*
Altitude 1901m (6,237ft)–2380m (7,808ft)
Lifts 4

Small, quiet ski area in Jackson town but quite separate from Jackson Hole resort. There is ample scope here for a day's (or night's) skiing. The closest accommodation is the **Snow King Resort Hotel and Condominiums**, **t** +1 307 733 5200, at the base.

Snowmass, USA

See Aspen and Snowmass, page 384

Solda, Italy

t +39 0473 737 060, *www.sulden.com*
Altitude 1905m (6,185ft)–2625m (8,612ft)
Lifts 11 in Solda, 74 in area
Tour operator Pyrenean Mountain Tours

South Tyrol village with 40km of piste offering extensive skiing. The resort is home to the magnificent four-star **Hotel Post**, **t** +39 0473 613 024, *www.hotelpost.it*, with an indoor pool and spa. Solda is part of the Ortler Skiarena, with 13 separate resorts sharing one lift pass. A total 260km of piste is served by eight cableways and 66 chairs and draglifts.

Sölden, Austria

Page 93
Tour operators Momentum, Neilson

Soldeu, Andorra

Page 41
Tour operators Crystal, Directski, Elegant Resorts, First Choice, Inghams, J2Ski, Lagrange, Neilson, Thomson, Ski Wild

Solitude Mountain Resort, Utah, USA

t +1 801 534 1400, *www.skisolitude.com*
Altitude 2435m (7,988ft)–3059m (10,035ft)
Lifts 8
Tour operators Ski Dream, Ski Independence, Ski Safari

Underrated ski in, ski out village 45 minutes' drive from Salt Lake City in the heart of Big Cottonwood Canyon in Utah's Wasatch National Forest. The resort is family-owned and full of charm, with 50 per cent of the trails rated as intermediate.

All accommodation, **t** +1 801 536 5707 for reservations, is of a good standard, with comfortable ski in, ski out apartments in **Creekside Lodge** and **Powderhorn Lodge**, as well as at the four-star **Inn at Solitude**, which houses the St Bernard's restaurant and a spa. **The Crossings** town houses are well equipped. **Silver Fork Lodge**, **t** +1 801 533 9977, in the Wasatch National Forest, overlooks Solitude.

Söll, Austria

See Söll and the SkiWelt, page 94
Tour operators Crystal, Directski, First Choice, Inghams, Neilson, Ski Activity, Ski Hillwood, Ski Wild, Thomson

Squaw Valley, California, USA

Page 432
Tour operators American Ski Classics, AWWT, Crystal, Ski All America, Ski Dream, Ski Expectations, Ski Independence, Ski Safari, United Vacations

Staffa, Italy

See Macugnaga, page 482

Steamboat, Colorado, USA

Page 434
Tour operators American Ski Classics, Crystal, Lotus Supertravel, Ski Activity, Ski All America, Ski Dream, Ski Independence, Ski Safari, Skiworld, Thomson, United Vacations, Virgin Snow

Stoneham, Québec, Canada

t +1 418 848 2415, *www.ski-stoneham.com*
Altitude 420m (695ft)–632m (2,075ft)
Lifts 8
Tour operators Frontier Ski, Ski All America, Ski Dream, SkiBound, Ski Safari, Tops

Resort with the most extensive night-skiing in Canada. Its 17 illuminated trails are open daily from 3pm to 10pm, making it popular with local skiers from Québec City – only a 20-minute drive away – on weekday evenings. With 32 trails spread over four mountains, Stoneham is one of the three largest ski areas in the province. It boasts three terrain parks, including a super-pipe with 17ft walls, and a 1km-long boardercross course. It is covered by the Carte Blanche lift pass which includes Mont-Ste-Anne and Le Massif. **Stoneham Hotel**, **t** +1 418 848 2411, is the only lodging.

Stowe, Vermont, USA

Page 437
Tour operators American Ski Classics, Crystal, Ski All America, Ski Dream, Ski Arrangements, Ski Independence, Ski Safari, Tops, Virgin Snow

Stubaital, Austria

See Neustift and the Stubaital, page 68

Stuben, Austria

t +43 (0)5582 399, *www.stuben.com*
Altitude 1407m (4,616ft)–2811m (9,222ft)
Lifts 86 on Arlberg Ski Pass

The village is called after the warm parlour – or *Stube* – of a solitary house on the Arlberg Pass where pilgrims used to shelter in the 18th century. Only 32 houses have been added since. Four-star **Hotel Post**, **t** +43 (0)5582 7616, *www.hotelpost.com*, was where mail-coach drivers changed horses for the steep journey up the pass. With its small collection of five hotels and restaurants, Stuben makes a pleasant base for exploring St Anton and the Arlberg.

Sun Peaks, BC, Canada

Page 132
Tour operators Alpine Answers Select, American Ski Classics, AWWT, Frontier Ski, Ski Activity, Ski All America, Ski Dream, Ski Independence, Ski Safari

Sun Valley, Idaho

Page 440
Tour operators AWWT, Ski Activity, Ski All America, Ski Dream, Ski Independence, Ski Safari

Sundance, Utah, USA

t +1 801 225 4107, *www.sundanceresort.com*
Altitude 6,100ft (1,859m)–8,250ft (2,515m)
Lifts 4
Tour operators Ski All America, Ski Dream, Ski Independence, Ski Safari

Traditional little Utah resort, created by film star Robert Redford, with old boardwalks and the atmosphere of a bygone era. It is a 55-minute drive from Salt Lake City and lift queues are rare. Sundance offers a variety of terrain ranging from wide, open trails to bowl skiing, and is recommended for families. Accommodation is in the elegant-rustic **Sundance Cottages**, **t** +1 801 225 4107.

Sunday River, Maine, USA

t +1 207 824 3000, *www.sundayriver.com*
Altitude 244m (800ft)–957m (3,140ft)
Lifts 18
Tour operators American Ski Classics, Ski Dream, Ski Independence, Ski Safari, Virgin Snow

One of the largest East Coast resorts, based six miles north of Bethel in Maine. The state suffers at times from sparse natural snow, but given low temperatures this is of little consequence thanks to the snow-cannon that can cover up to 92 per cent of the total terrain. 'A good selection of runs,' said a reporter; 'the resort offers blacks and double-blacks with steep inclines.' The quality of the skiing compares well with that of a medium-sized Alpine resort. Fortunately, Sunday River is far enough from New York not to suffer from the overcrowding of other Vermont resorts.

Sunday River is flanked at one end by the **Grand Summit Hotel**, **t** +1 207 824 3500, and at the other by the **Jordan Grand Resort**, **t** +1 207 824 5000. In between lies the base area beneath a ridge of eight peaks offering a variety of terrain. 'Après-ski is non-existent, with the village of Bethel a ghost town at night with the exception of a few poky bars,' complained a reporter.

Superdévoluy, France

t +33 (0)4 92 58 91 91, *www.superdevoluy.com*
Altitude 1500m (4,921ft)–2500m (8,202ft)
Lifts 25
Tour operators Crystal, Erna Low, Snow-Line, Thomson

Southern Alps resort to the south of Gap and Grenoble, featuring 100km of mainly intermediate piste. The resort attracts skiers and snowboarders, as well as families on a budget.

Les Sybelles, France

See Le Corbier, page 467; St-Jean d'Arves, page 467; St-Sorlin d'Arves, page 497 and La Toussuire, page 507

La Tania, France

Page 233
Tour operators Alpine Action, Alpine Answers Select, Crystal, Directski, Erna Low, Family Friendly Ski, First Choice, French Freedom, Lagrange, Le Ski, Momentum, Neilson, Silver Ski, Ski Activity, Ski Amis, Ski Arrangements, Ski Beat, Ski-Dazzle, Ski Deep, Ski France, Ski Independence, Ski Power, Ski Solutions, Skiweekends, Snowline, Thomson

Taos, New Mexico, USA

Page 442
Tour operators AWWT, Ski Activity, Ski Dream, Ski Independence, Ski Safari

El Tarter, Andorra

See Soldeu-El Tarter, page 41
Tour operators Directski, First Choice, Neilson

Telfes, Austria

See Neustift and the Stubaital, page 68

Telluride, Colorado, USA

Page 445
Tour operators American Ski Classics, AWWT, Ski All America, Ski Dream, Ski Independence, Ski Safari, United Vacations

Termas de Chillán, Chile

t +562 233 1313, *www.andesweb.com*
Altitude 1800m (5,900ft)–2500m (8,200ft)
Lifts 9
Tour operators Andes, Momentum, Scott Dunn Latin America, Ski Dream, Ski Safari

South America's most exotic resort, set against a backdrop of smoking volcanoes and bubbling sulphur springs 480km south of Santiago and 80km east of Chillán. The resort boasts some of the country's longest runs, with some 28 groomed trails spread across varied terrain. The excellent off-piste includes the 14km Shangri-La run, and Pirigallo – one of the resort's most celebrated itineraries, which comes complete with fumaroles belching sulphur fumes. 'Lifts are dated when compared with US and European resorts, but scenery to die for,' commented a reporter. The **Gran Hotel**, **t** +562 233 1313, has expensive ski in, ski out accommodation and a steaming indoor/outdoor pool fed by pipes from the volcano. Reporters recommend renting a cabin in the village, which is cheaper than any of the hotels. 'Restaurants excellent albeit some queues on weekends, but otherwise food is cheap but good – try the outside BBQ,' said a reader.

Termignon, France

t +33 (0)4 79 20 51 67, *www.termignon-la-vanoise.com*
Altitude 1300m (4,265ft)–2500m (8,202ft)
Lifts 5
Tour operator Lagrange, Peak Retreats

Traditional village in the upper Maurienne Valley with a 35km ski area that has only been in existence since 1985. The simple accommodation includes a two-star hotel and a *gîte d'étape*. Future plans include a lift link to nearby Val Cenis.

Thierbach, Austria

See Niederau, page 70

Thredbo, Australia

t +61 (0)2 6459 4100, *www.thredbo.com.au*
Altitude 1365m (4,478ft)–2037m (6,683ft)
Lifts 12

Australia's leading resort, set in the Kosciuszko National Park of New South Wales. It was founded in the early 1950s by Austrian and Czech immigrants who helped build the Snowy Mountain hydroelectric scheme. Aussies make either a six-hour drive from Sydney or the 2½hr journey by road from Canberra, but you can also fly to Cooma, 80km away. The lifts serve some of the best intermediate terrain in the country and this is therefore Australia's nearest equivalent to a European ski resort – with the addition of gum trees. Four quads among the dozen lifts whisk skiers and boarders above the tree-line. From here you progress to the summit on T-bars, which are better suited to the altitude's windier conditions. Because the snow record is unpredictable, the resort has invested heavily in snowmaking, and boasts the largest system in the southern hemisphere.

Hotels include the **Alpenhorn**, **t** +61 (0)2 6457 6223, *www.alphorn.com.au*, **Black Bear Inn**, **t** +61 (0)2 6457 6216, *www.blackbearinn.com.au*, **Candlelight Lodge**, **t** +61 (0)2 6457 6049, *www.candlelightlodge.com.au*, **High Country Mountain Resort**, **t** +61 (0)2 6456 2511, and **Thredbo Alpine Hotel**, **t** +61 (0)2 6459 4100, which has a new-look pub called **The Pub**. Nearby **Crackenback Farm**, **t** +61 (0)2 6456 2198, *www.crackenback.com.au*, is a four-star country guesthouse. **Eagle's Nest**, at the top of the Kosciuszko Express, is the highest mountain restaurant in Australia and sometimes opens for sunset dinners. Reporters rated the resort 'astonishingly expensive for what it offers'.

La Thuile, Italy

Page 306
Tour operators Alpine Answers Select, Crystal, Inghams, Interski, Momentum, Neilson, Ski Arrangements, Thomson

Thyon-Les Collons, Switzerland

t +41 (0)27 281 27 27, *www.thyon-region.ch*
Altitude 1500m (4,920ft)–3330m (10,925ft)
Lifts 89 in Four Valleys
Tour operator Alpine Tours

Unexpected piste-side community situated at the top of the Mayen-de-L'Ours gondola. It is little more than a collection of apartment blocks and a hotel linked into the Four Valley's ski area, of which Verbier is the major resort.

Tignes, France

Page 235
Tour operators Alpine Answers Select, Alpine Elements, Club Med, Crystal/Crystal Finest, Directski, Erna Low, Esprit, First Choice, Inghams, Interhome, J2Ski, Lagrange, Made to Measure, Mark Warner, Momentum, Mountain Leap, Mountain Sun, Mountain Tracks, Neilson, On the Piste, Peak Retreats, Ski Activity, Ski Amis, Ski Arrangements, Ski Collection, Ski Expectations, Ski France, Ski Freshtracks, Ski in Luxury, Ski Olympic, Ski Solutions, Ski Supreme, Skitopia, Skiworld, Snowstar, Thomson, Total Ski, Wasteland, White Roc

Torgon, Switzerland

t +41 (0)24 481 3131, *www.torgon.ch*

Altitude 1100m (3,608ft)–2350m (7,708ft)
Lifts 207 in Portes du Soleil

One of the least visited resorts of the Portes du Soleil, a small purpose-built Swiss outpost of 1960s A-frame buildings on a balcony above the Rhône and close to Lac Lèman. It is reached on skis either from Châtel or from La Chapelle d'Abondance. Accommodation is in modest apartments. The resort is best suited to families looking for a quiet holiday spot with no distractions apart from skiing.

La Toussuire, France

t +33 (0)4 79 83 06 06, *www.la-toussuire.com* or *www.sybelles.com*
Altitude 1800m (5,905ft)–2620m (8,596ft)
Lifts 75
Tour operators Erna Low, Lagrange, Ski Collection, Ski Independence

Village in the 310km Les Sybelles ski area in the Maurienne Valley, linked to St-Jean, Le Corbier and St-Sorlin. It is a compact resort with shops, ski school, ice rink and an outdoor pool within easy walking distance. Accommodation is in ugly apartment blocks, but there are one or two prettier hotels and chalets. The two three-star hotels are **Les Airelles, t** +33 (0)4 79 56 75 88, *www.hotel-les-airelles.com*, and **Les Soldanelles, t** +33 (0)4 79 56 75 29, *www.hotelsoldanelles.com*.

Trafoi, Italy

t +39 0473 613015, *www.inmontagna.net/trafoi.htm*
Altitude 1570m (5,151ft)–2550m (8,366ft)
Lifts 74 in area

Small resort in the South Tirol with four lifts and 15km of piste, but plenty of other skiing within a short drive of the village. The resort is part of the Ortler Skiarena – 13 unconnected resorts covered by one lift pass. There is a total 260km of piste in the area. Three-star **Hotel Madatsch, t** +39 0473 611 767, at Trafoi, is a comfortable spot.

Treble Cone, New Zealand

See Wanaka (Cardona and Treble Cone), page 513

Tremblant, Québec, Canada

Page 133

Tour operators American Ski Classics, Crystal, Elegant Resorts, Erna Low, Frontier Ski, Inghams, Neilson, Ski All America, Ski Dream, Ski Independence, Ski Safari, Ski Solutions, Ski Wild, Thomson, Tops, Trailfinders, United Vacations, Virgin Snow

Trois Vallées, France

See Brides-les-Bains, page 462; Courchevel, page 173; Les Menuires, page 196; Méribel, page 199; St-Martin-de-Belleville, page 225; La Tania, page 233; Val Thorens and the Belleville Valley, page 248

Trysil, Norway

t +47 624 51000, *www.trysil.com*
Altitude 600m (1,969ft)–1132m (3,714ft)
Lifts 31
Tour operator Alpine Tracks

Norway's largest ski area, ideal for families. 'An awesome resort,' said reporters. Trysil is a 2½hr drive from Oslo and has some of the most reliable snow-cover in Norway. The village is not pretty compared to Alpine resorts and does not offer much après ski. Its pistes spread across the wooded slopes of Trysilfjellet, and run 75 is rated for adventurous skiers and boarders. Instruction is highly rated and teachers speak good English. The recently added six-person chairlift has heated seats. The excellent accommodation is in hotels, apartments, and the many new *hyttes* (cabins). **Trysilfjell Aparthotel, t** +47 624 52350, is on the slopes. **Norlandia Trysil Hotel, t** +47 624 50833, *www.norlandia.no/trysil*, and **Trysil-Knut, t** +47 624 48000, are based in the old village of Trysil, 2km away from the slopes. Avoid staying in the Fageråsen area as the slopes are quite flat.

Tschagguns, Austria

t +43 (0)5556 721660, *www.schruns-tschagguns.at*
Altitude 1430m (4,692ft)–2300m (7,546ft)
Lifts 62 in area

Part of the vast Montafon region with its 11 villages and a total 222km of piste and 62 lifts, as well as extensive ski-touring on the Sillvretta glaciers and 100km of cross-country trails. Four-star **Alpenhotel Bitschnau, t** +43 (0)5556 75700, *www.alpenhotel-bitschnau.at*, is a traditional hotel with a an excellent modern spa.

Turoa, New Zealand

See Whakapapa and Turoa, page 513

Tux im Zillertal, Austria

t +43 (0)5287 8506, *www.tux.at*
Altitude 1500m (4,920ft)–3250m (10,663ft)
Lifts 59 in Ski & Glacier World 3000
Tour operator Redpoint Holidays

'The best skiing ever – I have been there in summer and also in winter. You can ski for a week and every day would be different, with lots of slopes and great connecting lifts. The food here is also fantastic,' said a reporter. Tux im Zillertal is made up of five villages in the Tuxer valley – Hintertux is the main one. It boasts the steepest glacier skiing in Austria and is usually open all year (20km of the piste is open all summer). It also offers the most advanced skiing and snowboarding on the otherwise low-altitude Zillertal Superskipass.

The glacier is prone to overcrowding when conditions are poor elsewhere, but hotel guests have priority in the lift queue. The skiing isn't terribly challenging, with most runs groomed and free of bumps. However, the pistes are thought to be the best all-year downhill training ground in Europe, and national teams spend much of the summer here. The 2008–9 season sees the opening of the new Gletscherbus cable car.

'The B&Bs are charming and friendly. Not too many huge hotels, which only adds on the picturesque atmosphere,' said a reader. The handful of four-stars include **Hotel Bergfried**, **t** +43 (0)5287 87239, *www.bergfried.at*, which has a pool surrounded by rock walls.

Vail, Colorado, USA

Page 449
Tour operators American Ski Classics, Alpine Answers Select, Alpine Tracks, AWWT, Carrier, Crystal/Crystal Finest, Elegant Resorts, Erna Low, Inghams, Lotus Supertravel, Momentum, Ski Activity, Ski All America, Ski Dream, Ski Expectations, Ski Freshtracks, Ski Independence, Ski-Line, Ski Safari, Ski Solutions, Ski Wild, Skiworld, Thomson, Trailfinders, United Vacations, Virgin Snow

Val Cenis, France

t +33 (0)4 79 05 23 66, *www.valcenis.com*
Altitude 1400m (4,593ft)–2800m (9,186ft)
Lifts 22
Tour operators AWWT, Crystal, Erna Low, Lagrange, MGS Ski, Peak Retreats, Ski Collection, Snowcoach

The old unspoilt villages of Lanslebourg and Lanslevillard in the Haute Maurienne join together to form the resort of Val Cenis. The villages have a traditional community ambience. 'A good value family holiday,' commented one reporter. The skiing is for all standards, particularly beginners to intermediates ('though limited in comparison with the bigger resorts, some nice cruising red runs on which to improve style and a few tricky blacks'). The village crèche takes babies from three months. The eight two-star hotels include **La Vieille Poste**, **t** +33 (0)4 79 05 93 47, *www.lavieilleposte.com*, ('too much good food') and **Le Val Cenis**, **t** +33 (0)4 79 05 80 31. **CIS Centre International de Sejour**, **t** +33 (0)4 79 05 92 30, is warmly recommended.

Val Fiscalina, Italy

See Alta Pusteria, page 456

Val di Fassa, Italy

See Canazei and the Val di Fassa, page 260
Tour operators Crystal, Exodus, Thomson

Val di Fiemme, Italy

See Cavalese, page 464
Tour operator Ramblers

Val Fiscalina, Italy

See Alta Pusteria, page 456

Val d'Isère, France

Page 240
Tour operators Alpine Answers Select, Alpine Elements, Alpine Weekends, Altitude Holidays, Club Med, Corporate Ski Company, Crystal/Crystal Finest, Descent International, Directski, Elegant Resorts, Erna Low, Esprit, Flexiski, Finlay's, First Choice, Indigo Lodges, Inghams, J2Ski, Lagrange, Le Ski, Lotus Supertravel, Made to Measure, Mark Warner, Momentum, Mountain Leap, Mountain Rooms & Chalets, Mountain Tracks, Neilson, On the

Piste, Oxford Ski Company, Powder White, Scott Dunn Ski, Seasons in Style, Silver Ski, Ski Activity, Ski Amis, Ski Arrangements, Ski Beat, Ski Collection, Ski Expectations, Ski France, Ski Freshtracks, Ski-Line, Ski in Luxury, Ski Olympic, Ski Solutions, Ski Supreme, Ski Val, Ski Weekend, Skiworld, Snowline, Thomson, Total Ski, Val d'Isère à la Carte, VIP, White Roc, YSE

Val d'Ultimo, Italy

See Monte San Vigilio, page 485

Valfréjus, France

t +33 (0)4 79 05 33 83, *www.valfrejus.com*
Altitude 1550m (5,085ft)–2737m (8,980ft)
Lifts 12
Tour operators Erna Low, Lagrange, Peak Retreats

Modern resort built around the old wood-and-stone hamlet of Charmaix above the town of Modane ('prices are pretty cheap'). The skiing is mainly above the treeline on steep and sometimes mogulled slopes. Ski tuition here is highly rated: 'Use Ecole de Ski Internationale for lessons – good English spoken and a good ski school.' **Hotel Club MMV Le Valfréjus**, **t** +33 (0)4 92 12 62 12, is a Savoyard-style three-star in the centre of the village, while **Le Grand Vallon**, **t** +33 (0)4 79 05 08 07, is a two-star with good views.

Valle Nevado, Chile

t +56 2 206 0027, *www.vallenevado.com*
Altitude 3200m (7,972ft)–3670m (12,040ft)
Lifts 11
Tour operators Andes, Crystal Finest, Momentum, Scott Dunn Latin America, Ski Dream, Ski Safari

Situated just 64km from Santiago, making it the closest resort to a capital city. The resort is linked by lift to the resorts of La Parva and El Colorado to create a small version of an alpine ski circuit. A variety of slopes offer mainly intermediate skiing, and experienced skiers and riders can take advantage of some of the world's best-value heli-skiing, which goes up to a breathtaking 5000m. Pistes are 'pretty well maintained', according to reporters. The most comfortable accommodation is in **Hotel Valle Nevado**. The slightly cheaper options are **La Puerta del Sol** and **Tres Puntas** (bookings advisable through tour operators). **La Parva** is an enclave of smart holiday homes for wealthy city dwellers, while **El Colorado** is a purpose-built base for the adjoining old village of Farellones. Owing to the extremely high altitude, visitors arriving from sea level may feel some discomfort for the first few days and are advised to drink plenty of water and refrain from drinking alcohol.

Vallnord, Andorra

See Pal-Arinsal, page 34

Valloire, France

t +33 (0)4 79 59 03 96, *www.valloire.net*
Altitude 1430m (4,690ft)–2600m (8,528ft)
Lifts 33
Tour operators Crystal, Erna Low, Ski France, Lagrange, Peak Retreats, Thomson

Large, attractive village set in an isolated bowl above the Maurienne Valley ('a lovely atmosphere and wonderful scenery'). It is still very much a traditional French farming community, without a lot of nightlife. The skiing, linked to Valmeinier, is divided between three areas on adjacent mountains accessed by two gondolas a few minutes' walk from the village centre. The ski area is mainly intermediate with some long runs ('surprisingly quiet, even over half term'). Accommodation includes three-stars **Les Oursons**, **t** +33 (0)4 79 59 01 37, *www.hotel-les-oursons.com*, with a pool, **Grand Hôtel de Valloire et du Galibier**, **t** +33 (0)4 79 59 00 95, *www.grand-hotel-valloire.com*, opposite the lifts, **Hôtel Rapin**, **t** +33 (0)4 79 59 06 02, *www.hotel-rapin.com*, which has a gastronomic restaurant **Le Matafan**, and a wide range of chalets and apartments. 'Very quiet in the evenings but some reasonable restaurants,' said a reporter.

Valmeinier, France

t +33 (0)4 79 59 53 69, *www.valmeinier.com*
Altitude 1430m (4,690ft)–2600m (8,528ft)
Lifts 33
Tour operators Crystal, Erna Low, French Freedom, Frontier Ski, Lagrange, On the Piste, Peak Retreats, Snowcoach, Thomson, Wasteland

'Not the place to come if you choose France for its food, but you can get standard Savoyard fare and pizzas for about half the price of the Trois Vallées or Espace Killy,' said a reporter.

'A wonderful resort – small but perfectly performed. Great for beginners and intermediate skiers,' added another. The skiing is linked to that of Valloire in the Maurienne Valley (*see* above). Accommodation choices include **Auberge Le Grand Fourchon**, **t** +33 (0)4 79 59 21 01, *www.fourchon.com*, **Hôtel L'Aigle**, **t** +33 (0)4 79 59 24 31, with an outdoor hot tub, and **Hôtel Club Les Carrettes**, **t** +33 (0)4 79 59 25 45, which provides full-board, a mini-club, and evening entertainment. 'Few Brits, but everyone very friendly,' said one reader.

Valmorel, France

t +33 (0)4 79 09 85 55, *www.valmorel.com*
Altitude 1400m (4,592ft)–2550m (8,364ft)
Lifts 49 in Grand Domaine
Tour operators Crystal, Erna Low, Lagrange, Neilson, Ski Amis, Ski Supreme, Thomson

Attractive ski resort, constructed in 1976 in a style sympathetic to its mountain setting. Over the years it has matured into a family-friendly resort. The large ski area extends into the Maurienne Valley and to the resort of St-François-Longchamp. It is also connected to the beginner resort of Doucy Combelouvière. The skiing stretches in one direction to the 1981m Col du Gollet and to the other across a gorge to mainly intermediate terrain. The nursery slopes are exceptional, and the area offers some excellent off-piste. **ESF**, **t** +33 (0)4 79 09 81 86, is the main ski school, and **Les Piou-Piou** is their children's club. At lunchtime, **L'Altipiano**, **t** +33 (0)4 79 09 86 31, and **Le Prariond**, **t** +33 (0)4 79 09 87 17, have *à la carte* specialities, **Banquise 2000**, **t** +33 (0)4 79 59 10 60, is rustic, **Les Mazots**, **t** +33 (0)4 79 59 10 01, has Savoyard dishes, and **L'Alpage**, **t** +33 (0)4 79 09 83 81, is a recommended self-service.

In the evening, **La Marmite** has a cosy atmosphere. **L'Aigle Blanc**, in the forest outside the village, has local dishes. **Le Jimbo Lolo** is 'a nice Mexican restaurant with good food and atmosphere', **Café Alpin**, **t** +33 (0)4 79 06 90 22, offers wood-fired pizzas, and **Le Ski Roc**, **t** +33 (0)4 79 09 83 17, has more sophisticated fare. **La Cordée** has music and **Les Nuits Blanches** complex contains two discos. For accommodation, two-star **Hôtel du Bourg**, **t** +33 (0)4 79 09 86 66, *www.hoteldubourg.com*, is said to be welcoming. **Les Marmottons**, **t** +33 (0)4 79 09 86 66, *www.hotel-les-marmottons.com*, is a hotel in La Charmette village.

Val Senales (Schnalstal), Italy

t +39 0473 662 171, *www.schnalstal.com*
Altitude 2005m (6,578ft)–3250m (10,663ft)
Lifts 12
Tour operator Mountain Tracks

Principal destination in the Ortler Skiarena, with 13 unconnected resorts all covered by one lift pass. A total 260km of prepared piste is served by eight cableways and 66 chair and draglifts. This is the main village of the scenic Vinschgau and base for one of Europe's largest year-round ski areas, with guaranteed snow, six lifts in summer at the top of the Ghiacciai cable car and another five in winter. **Berghotel Grawand**, **t** +39 0473 662 118, *www.grawand.com*, located at 3212m on the glacier, is a two-star hotel that houses the only on-mountain eatery and a small museum dedicated to Ötzi, the Neolithic man found preserved in the ice above the ski area in 1991. Other hotels include three-star **Hotel Schwarzer Adler**, **t** +39 0473 669 652, which has been in the same family for four generations.

Val Thorens, France

See Val Thorens and the Belleville Valley, page 248
Tour operators Alpine Elements, Crystal, Directski, Erna Low, First Choice, French Freedom, Inghams, Interhome, Lagrange, Made to Measure, Momentum, Neilson, On the Piste, Ski Activity, Ski Amis, Ski Arrangements, Ski Collection, Ski Expectations, Ski France, Ski Freshtracks, Ski-Line, Ski Solutions, Ski Supreme, Skiworld, Solo's, Thomson, Total Ski, Wasteland

Valtournenche, Italy

t +39 0166 92055, *www.cervinia.it*
Altitude 1524m (5,000ft)–3883m (12,740ft)
Lifts 59 with Zermatt
Tour operator J2Ski

Old village 9km by road from Cervinia, but linked into the same ski area. There is good-value accommodation in a genuine, unspoilt village ambience. **Albergo Grandes Murailles**, **t** +39 0166 932 956, *www.hotelgmurailles.com*, is a small hotel with lots of atmosphere.

Vars 1850, France

t +33 (0)4 92 46 51 31, *www.vars-ski.com*
Altitude 1850m (6,068ft)–2750m (9,020ft)
Lifts 57 with Risoul
Tour operators Crystal, Erna Low, Equity/Rocket Ski, Lagrange, Thomson, Tops

Larger, less attractive neighbour of Risoul 1850 ('locals very friendly and welcoming, some good places to eat out, and not many Brits'). The resort is linked by draglift to the modern station, but you have to walk across town to reach the Vars gondola and chair to Risoul 1850. Vars-Ste-Marie is more picturesque than the larger main centre of Vars-Les Claux, but without much nightlife. Beginners can learn in the village, where there are two drags and some gentle green runs. Intermediates have a choice of runs above and below the tree-line, and some wide-open bowl skiing. Accommodation is in apartments – **Résidence l'Albane** and **l'Ecrin des Neiges** – and in two-star **Hôtel Vallon, t** +33 (0)4 92 46 54 72, *www.hotelvallon.com*, which has friendly staff (though small rooms) and is close to the main ski lift in Vars-Ste-Marie.

Vaujany, France

Page 252
Tour operators Erna Low, J2Ski, Kick Ski, Peak Retreats, Ski Independence, Ski Peak

Venosc, France

t +33 (0)4 76 80 06 82, *www.venosc.com*
Altitude 1650m (5,412ft)–3600m (11,808ft)
Lifts 51
Tour operator Peak Retreats

Attractive hamlet with cobblestone streets set below Les Deux Alpes, with which it shares a ski area. **Hôtel Les Amis de la Montagne, t** +33 (0)4 76 11 76 11 10, *www.hotel-venosc-deux-alpes.com*, has 29 rooms, and a restaurant serving grills and fondue.

Vent, Austria

t +43 (0)57200 261, *www.vent.at*
Altitude 1900m (6,234ft)–2680m (8,793ft)
Lifts 4
Tour operator Pyrenean Mountain Tours

Small village offering 15km of piste and some good off-piste skiing. The seven hotels include **Familyhotel Vent, t** +43 (0)5254 8102, which houses a kindergarten. A free ski-bus links with Sölden and Obergurgl.

Verbier, Switzerland

Page 365
Tour operators Alpine Answers Select, Alpine Weekends, Altitude Inspires, Belvedere Chalets, Bramble Ski, CK Verbier, Crystal, Crystal Finest, Descent International, Elegant Resorts, Erna Low, First Choice, Flexiski, Indigo Lodges, Inghams, Interhome, Kaluma, Lotus Supertravel, Made to Measure, Momentum, Mountain Leap, Oxford Ski Company, Peak Ski, Powder Byrne, The Powder Company, Powder White, Ski Activity, Ski Armadillo, Ski Expectations, Ski Freshtracks, Ski Independence, Ski-Line, Ski Solutions, Ski Verbier, Ski Weekend, Ski with Julia, Skiworld, Total Ski, Swiss Travel Service, Thomson, White Roc

Veysonnaz, Switzerland

t +41 (0)27 207 1053, *www.veysonnaz.ch*
Altitude 1400m (4,593ft)–3330m (10,925ft)
Lifts 89 in Four Valleys

Used as a training base by the Swiss national ski team and reached by a 13km mountain road from Sion. It is part of the 412km Four Valleys circuit and is a useful backdoor into Mont Fort. An eight-person gondola brings you up to the mid-station, and Veysonnaz' own considerable ski area can be accessed from a second base area 3km away at Mayen-de-L'Ours. A bus connects the two. **Hotel Magrappé, t** +41 (0)27 207 1817, is comfortable and friendly.

La Villa, Italy

See San Cassiano, page 293
Tour operators J2Ski, Powder Byrne

Villach, Austria

t +43 (0)4242 57047, *www.verditz.at*
Altitude 600m (1,968ft)–1900m (6,234ft)
Lifts 5 (3 chairs, 2 drags)
Tour operator BoardnLodge

Carinthia's most attractive provincial town, with medieval and renaissance buildings. **Blue Mountain Hotel, t** +43 (0)4247 2084, *www.bluemountainhotel.at*, is Australian-run and has a mix of bedrooms and multi-share loft rooms. Nightlife here is better than in the larger local town of Klagenfurt.

Villard-de-Lans, France

t +33 (0)4 76 95 10 38, *www.ot-villard-de-lans.fr*
Altitude 1160m (3,806ft)–2170m (7,119ft)
Lifts 29
Tour operators AWWT, J2Ski, Lagrange

Rural French community attracting weekend skiers from nearby Grenoble rather than an international clientèle. The pistes, best suited to beginners and low intermediates, are at Côte 2000 – a rather unappealing *station de ski* situated a 2km bus ride from the resort. Together with the resort of Corrençon, Villard-de-Lans is also a popular venue for cross-country skiing. Recommended hotels include three-star **Le Christiania, t** +33 (0)4 76 95 12 51, **Le Dauphin**, **t** +33 (0)4 76 95 95 25, and two-star **Les Bruyères, t** +33 (0)4 76 95 11 83.

Villard-Reculas, France

t +33 (0)4 76 80 45 69, *www.villard-reculas.com*
Altitude 1500m (4,921ft)–3330m (10,922ft)
Lifts 84 in area
Tour operator La Source

One of those hidden jewels in the Alps, but only a chairlift away from the vast ski runs of Alpe d'Huez. The large farming village is perched on the mountain below Alpe d'Huez and above the valley town of Bourg d'Oisans. A quad-chair links it to the top of Signal and the rest of the large Alpe d'Huez circuit, which includes Vaujany, Auris, and Oz-en-Oisans. **Bonsoir Clara, t** +33 (0)4 76 80 37 20, is warmly recommended for dinner. Accommodation is at **Hôtel Beaux Monts, t** +33 (0)4 76 80 43 14, and in good *gîtes* and independent chalets. The website, *www.villard-reculas.com*, has lists of self-catering apartments and chalets.

Villaroger, France

See Les Arcs, page 159
Tour operator Optimum Ski

Villars, Switzerland

Page 371
Tour operators Altitude Inspires, Club Med, Crystal, Inghams, Interhome, Kuoni, Lagrange, Made to Measure, Momentum, Ski Independence, Ski Solutions, Ski Weekend, Swiss Travel Service, Switzerland Travel Centre, Thomson

Vorderlansersbach, Austria

Small village up the valley from Mayrhofen.

Voss, Norway

t +47 565 20800, *www.visitvoss.no*
Altitude 91m (300ft)–945m (3,100ft)
Lifts 9
Tour operators Alpine Tours, Alpine Tracks, Crystal, Inghams

Reasonable ski area for beginners and lower intermediates, but it can become busy at weekends. 'Extremely quiet slopes and very well groomed,' enthused a reporter, and, 'The mountain is deserted during the week,' said another. But 'On the minus side, very poor mountain restaurants – cheeseburgers pall a little after six days and there is no beer on the mountain.' For more experienced skiers and boaders, the resort has three black runs and some off-piste. Cross-country skiers will not be disappointed with 60km of prepared *loipe* close to the centre, with more on offer in the valleys around the area. **Hotel Fleischer, t** +47 565 20500, *www.fleischers.no*, is traditional.

Wagrain, Austria

Page 98
Tour operator Ski Astons, Sloping Off

Waidring, Austria

t +43 (0)5353 5242, *www.tiscover.com/waidring*
Altitude 780m (2,558ft)–1860m (6,102ft)
Lifts 8
Tour operators Thomson, Tyrolean Adventures

Unspoilt village under 20km away from St Johann in Tirol and in the same snowpocket as Fieberbrunn. The peaceful resort is known for its family skiing, with convenient nursery slopes in the village centre. The main skiing is at Steinplatte, 4km from the village and ideal for beginners and intermediates ('the slopes can be challenging, there is only one black run but some of the red runs can be just as difficult'). The ski school was said to be friendly and very helpful, with English-speaking instructors. **Hotel Waidringerhof, t** +43 (0)5353 5228, *www.waidringerhof.at*, has a pool, and the central **Hotel Tiroler Adler, t** +43 (0)5353 5311, *www.tiroler-adler.at*, is also rated.

Wanaka (Cardrona and Treble Cone), New Zealand

Cardrona, **t** +64 (0)3 443 8651 / **Treble Cone**, **t** +64 (0)3 443 7443, *www.cardrona.com* or *www.lakewanaka.co.nz* or *www.treblecone.co.nz*
Altitude Cardrona 1670m (5,479ft)–2060m (6,759ft), Treble Cone 1200m (3,936ft)–1860m (6,102ft)
Lifts 9 in Cardona and Treble Cone
Tour operators Original Travel, Scott Dunn Asia Pacific

Alternative bed base to Queenstown from which to explore the main South Island skiing. From here, the ski areas of Cardrona and Treble Cone, as well as the Waiorau Nordic Ski Area and the Wanaka Snow Park (New Zealand's first whole-mountain terrain park) are all within a 30-minute drive. The road between Queenstown and Wanaka is sealed, but reporters warn it is 'a test of nerves'. making the other Southern Lakelands resorts of Coronet Peak and The Remarkables even more accessible.Cardrona's ski field is suited to beginners and intermediates, with several wide, gentle slopes. It is known for its dry snow and reliable season, which runs from late June until early October. The area has the country's largest terrain park and four half-pipes.

Wanaka is also the gateway to Treble Cone, with 'scenery that has to be seen to be believed'. One of the country's top resorts, it boasts New Zealand's first six-seater chair. Advanced skiers – and snowboarders in particular – are well catered for, but the area is quite limited for beginners. One reporter recommended Cardrona as a great place for families – 'the mountain is set up for kids'. The area's best off-piste is found by hiking 20 minutes to the summit. There is good heli-skiing nearby in the Harris Mountains.

Wengen, Switzerland

Page 374
Tour operators Club Med, Crystal, Inghams, Kuoni, Made to Measure, Momentum, Ski Expectations, Ski Freshtracks, Ski Solutions, Swiss Travel Service, Switzerland Travel Centre, Thomson

Westendorf, Austria

Page 100
Tour operators Inghams, Ski Astons, Thomson

Whakapapa and Turoa, New Zealand

See Mount Ruapehu, page 487

Whistler, BC, Canada

Page 137
Tour operators Alpine Answers Select, American Ski Classics, AWWT, Carrier, Cold Comforts, Crystal/Crystal Finest, Directski, Elegant Resorts, Erna Low, First Choice, Frontier Ski, Inghams, Kaluma, Lotus Supertravel, Mark Warner, Momentum, Neilson, Non Stop Ski, Original Travel, Ski Activity, Ski Arrangements, SkiBound, Ski Dream, Ski Expectations, Ski Freshtracks, Ski Independence, Ski-Line, Ski Miquel, Ski Safari, Ski Solutions, Ski Wild, Skiworld, Thomson, Trailfinders, United Vacations, Virgin Snow

Whitewater, BC, Canada

t +1 250 354 4944, *www.skiwhitewater.com* or *www.nelsonbc.ca*
Altitude 1646m (5,400ft)–2042m (6,700ft)
Lifts 3

Pleasant small ski area close to the atmospheric Victorian town of Nelson. Its two lifts give direct access to challenging trails through the trees as well as some great – but avalanche-prone – off-piste. Some 20 per cent of the terrain is made up of easy runs, while the remainder is divided equally between intermediate and advanced skiing. But the real attraction is Nelson. The lakeside town, close to the Montana border, was the point of arrival in Canada for hundreds of hippies fleeing the draft during the Vietnam War. Some of them travelled no further. **Inn the Garden**, **t** +1 250 352 3226, is recommended.

Wildschönau, Austria

See Niederau, page 70

Winter Park, Colorado, USA

Page 453
Tour operators American Ski Classics, AWWT, Crystal, Erna Low, Lotus Supertravel, Ski Activity, Ski All America, SkiBound, Ski Dream,

Ski Independence, Skiworld, Thomson, United Vacations, Virgin Snow

Wirl, Austria

See Galtür, page 471

Xiling Snow Mountain, China

www.china.org.cn or *www.chengdu.cn*

Resort that opened in 2004 and claims to be the leading resort in China, with the potential to grow into a major international resort. It has a gondola, double- and quad-chairs serving 10 trails for all standards. Xiling Snow Mountain extends to over 5300m, giving one of the world's biggest lift-served verticals.

Xiling aims to attract international tourists who have so far avoided China owing to its reputation for having limited facilities and often basic standards. Xiling is a 90-minute drive by modern road from the regional capital, Chengdu. The resort has invested in high quality skis and bought over 30 snowmobiles, as well as setting up a tubing park.

China's tourism industry is reported to have grown by 15 per cent last year and the country is now the world's fourth largest destination for inbound tourism and has the largest domestic tourism market. Chengdu's growth has outstripped even this rapid rise.

Yabuli, China

t +86 (0)451 345 5088, *www.yabuliski resort.com*
Altitude 1374m (4,508ft)–1944m (6,378ft)
Lifts 9

This vies with Xiling for the position of China's most important resort. It was initially developed at a cost of $210m, and was the venue for the 1996 Asian Winter Games. Situated 194km northwest of the city of Harbin, the resort is open 120 days a year and is attempting to double its present ski terrain. However, development is being held back by an apparent lack of agreement between the government and the 10 Chinese investors. The longest run is 5km and there is a vertical drop of 600m. Yabuli is also the location for a separate, private ski area used until now for competitions and by army skiers. There is a plan to link the two areas to create China's most extensive ski area. The hotel of choice is four-star **Windmill Villa**, **t** +86 451 345 5168, close to the slopes.

Yellowstone Club, Montana, USA

t +1 406 995 4900, *www.theyellowstone club.com*
Altitude 2182m (7,160ft)–3005m (9,860ft)
Lifts 13

The world's only private ski resort covers an area of 6,000 acres of perfectly manicured piste – that's an area bigger than Breckenridge – but you'll never see more than 30 people on the slopes on a busy day. Of the total 12 lifts, 11 are high-speed covered chairs; the pistes are so smooth that you never see a mogul. The ski area is supplemented by neighbouring Big Sky, with its 11 lifts and 150 runs that can be skied by YC members but not vice versa.

To join you have to be proposed by another member. Then you have to buy property here, with prices starting at $795,000. Three lodges house restaurants, bars, and a ski shop. Some 20 lovely little log cabins are available to members' friends and to prospective buyers.

Zakopane, Poland

t +48 18 2020400, *www.zakopane.pl*
Altitude 838m (2,749ft)–2301m (7,549ft)
Lifts 16
Tour operators Pyrenean Mountain Tours

Skiing has been popular in Zakopane for over a hundred years. The earliest international ski competition took place here in 1910. The resort offers plenty of scope, from beginner to more difficult. The best skiing can usually be found in the Kasprowy Wierch area. However, 'There was no great evidence of people looking up the slope before launching themselves,' warned a reporter. Eating out is quite cheap and varied. 'You can get a good three course meal for less than £15 with drinks extra,' said a reader.

Zao, Japan

Zao Onsen Eko, **t** +23 694 9533 or **t** +44 (0)20 7734 6870, *www.zao-spa.or.jp* or *www.snow japan.com*
Altitude 780m (2,599ft)–1736m (5,696ft)
Lifts 42

Spa town in the Yamagata Prefecture that is one of the biggest resorts in Japan. It is located 2½hrs from Tokyo by bullet train, and its slopes are reached by ancient cable car. They are famous throughout the country because of a huge forest of 'snow-ghosts' – fir trees that become encrusted with hoar frost to form a vast collection of monster shapes. Some 90 per cent of this large ski area is suited to beginners and intermediates – the resort has little to entice advanced skiers. Accommodation is mainly in *ryokan* inns, which include the recommended **Zao Onsen Eko**, **t** +23 694 9533.

Zauchensee, Austria

See Wagrain and the Salzburger Sportwelt, page 98
Tour operators Made to Measure, Ski Hillwood

Zell am See, Austria

See Zell am See and Kaprun, page 102
Tour operators Club Europe, Crystal, Directski, Erna Low, First Choice, Inghams, Interhome, Neilson, Ski Activity, Ski Astons, Ski Wild, Snowscape, Thomson

Zell am Ziller, Austria

t +43 (0)5282 22810, *www.zell.at*
Altitude 1250m (4,101ft)–2505m (8,219ft)
Lifts 55 in area
Tour operators Interhome, Redpoint

Second most substantial valley resort in the Zillertal area after Mayrhofen. The two areas, Kreuzjoch and Gerlosstein, are set away from the town. Kreuzjoch is reached by swift eight-person gondola, and Gerlosstein has twin cable cars. There is an influx of visitors from Germany each weekend. Four-star **Sport und Wellnesshotel Theresa**, **t** +43 (0)5282 22860, *www.theresa.at*, and three-star **Hotel Englhof**, **t** +43 (0)5282 3134, are rated.

Zermatt, Switzerland

Page 378
Tour operators Alpine Answers Select, Alpine Weekends, Altitude Inspires, Carrier, Corporate Ski Company, Crystal/Crystal Finest, Descent International, Elegant Resorts, Erna Low, Indigo Lodges, Inghams, J2Ski, Kuoni, Lagrange, Lotus Supertravel, Momentum, Oak Hall, Powder Byrne, Scott Dunn Ski, Seasons in Style, Ski Dream, Ski Expectations, Ski Freshtracks, Ski Independence, Ski-Line, Ski Solutions, Swiss Travel Service, Switzerland Travel Centre, Thomson, Total Ski, VIP, White Roc, Zermatt Holidays

Zillertal 3000, Austria

See Mayrhofen, page 64
Tour operator Oak Hall

Zug, Austria

See Lech and Zürs, page 59

Zürs, Austria

See Lech and Zürs, page 59
Tour operators Alpine Answers Select, Altitude Inspires, Corporate Ski Company, Crystal, Elegant Resorts, Inghams, Kaluma, Made to Measure, Momentum, Powder Byrne, Ski Independence

Directory

Tour Operators

Over 200 ski and board operators listed below offer inclusive ski and board holiday packages, but you should be aware that not all of them are fully bonded. Before parting with any money, it makes sense to discover what would happen in the event of a company going bust before you travel or while you are abroad. One extra safeguard which may entitle you to a refund in such an event is to pay by credit card direct to the company rather than to a travel agent.

Albus Travel: Hill Farm Barn, Angel Hill, Earl Stonham, Stowmarket IP14 5DP
t +44 (0)1449 711 952,
www.albustravel.com
Winter ski holidays with flights from Gatwick and Manchester to four catered chalets and an apartment in St Anton. *See* page 83

Alp Leisure: La Nouvaz, 73120 Courchevel, France
t +33 (0)4 79 00 59 42,
www.alpleisure.com
Tailor-made luxury holidays to privately owned luxury chalets in Méribel and Courchevel 1850. Selected chalets available all year round.

Alpine Action: Marine Suite, The Old Town Hall, Southwick BN42 4AX
t +44 (0)1273 597 940,
www.alpineaction.co.uk
Small family-run operator with chalets in Méribel and La Tania.

Alpine Answers: Office 204, 250 York Road, London SW11 3SJ
t +44 (0)20 7801 1080,
www.alpineanswers.co.uk
Well-established tailor-made arm of specialist ski travel agency, with holidays in Andorra, Austria, Canada, France, Italy, Switzerland and the USA.

The Alpine Club: 24 Argos Lofts, Robert Street, Brighton BN1 4AY
t + 44 (0)630 226 215,
www.thealpineclub.co.uk
Two bespoke chalets in St-Martin-de-Belleville.

Alpine Elements: 3 Wigton Place, London SE11 4AN
t +44 (0)844 815 3530,
www.alpineelements.co.uk
Luxury chalets and value ski holidays in the French Alps

Alpine Tours: The Ardmore Group, Hall Place, Berkshire College, Burchetts Green SL6 6QR
t +44 (0)1628 826 699,
www.theardmoregroup.com
Long-established schools and groups operator to Austria, Canada, Italy, Norway, Spain and Switzerland.

Alpine Tracks: 40 High Street, Menai Bridge, Anglesey LL59 5EF
t +44 (0)800 0282 546,
www.alpine-tracks.co.uk
Chalet and hotel holidays to resorts in France, Switzerland and Norway. Also short breaks, off-piste courses, mountain awareness and ski-touring. *See* page 6

Alpine Weekends: 95 Dora Road, London SW19 7JT
t +44 (0)20 8944 9762,
www.alpineweekends.com
Bespoke breaks in France, Italy and Switzerland, with off-piste, heli-skiing and ski-touring.

Alps Accommodation:
t +33 (0)4 50 90 83 55,
www.alpsaccommodation.com
Premier chalets and apartments in Samoëns. Catered and self-catered holidays for individuals, families and groups.

Altitude Holidays: Suite 787, 2 Old Brompton Road, London SW7 3DQ
t +44 (0)870 870 7669,
www.altitudeholidays.com
Chalets and apartments, catered and self-catered in France. Also Argentina and Chile. Accommodation-finding agency across the Alps.

Altitude Inspires: 7 Albert Court, Prince Consort Road, London SW7 2BJ

t +44 (0)20 7591 4970, *www.altitudeinspires.com*
Specializes in bespoke corporate ski programmes and events throughout. Europe.

American Ski Classics: PO Box 250,Twickenham TW1 2XX
t +44 (0)870 242 0623, *www.americanskiclassics.com*
Hotels and condos in 27 resorts in North America.

Andes: 37A St Andrews Street, Castle Douglas DG7 1EN
t +44 (0)1556 503 929, *www.andes.org.uk*
South American skiing and climbing specialist, with holidays and ski tours to Chile and Patagonia.

AWWT: 1 Lonsdale Gardens, Tunbridge Wells TN1 1NU
t +44 (0)1892 511 894, *www.awwt.co.uk*
Tailor-made holidays to North America

Balkan Holidays: Sofia House, 19 Conduit Street, London W1S 2BH
t +44 (0)845 130 1114, *www.balkanholidays.co.uk*
Mass-market operator to Bulgaria, Romania, Slovenia and Serbia.

Balkan Tours: 61 Ann Street, Belfast BT1 4EE
t +44 (0)845 1301114, *www.balkan.co.uk*
Long-established holiday specialist to Bulgaria and Romania, with direct flights from Belfast and Dublin.

Barrelli Ski: 19 Sefton Park Road, St Andrews, Bristol BS7 9AN
t +44 (0)117 940 1500, *www.barrelliski.co.uk*
Self-catered and catered chalet holidays in 12 properties in Les Houches, Chamonix and Champagny-en-Vanoise.

Belvedere Chalets:Peach House, Gangbridge Lane, St Mary Bourne SP11 6EW
t +44 (0)1264 738 257, *www.belvedereproperties.net*
Small specialist operator with six superb catered chalets in Méribel and Verbier.

Bigfoot Travel: 5b Résidence le Mummery, 27 ave du Savoy, Chamonix, France 74400
t +44 (0)870 300 5874, *www.bigfoot-travel.co.uk*
Hotels, chalets and apartments in the Chamonix Valley.

BoardnLodge.com: 18 Belsize Grove, London NW3 4UN
t +44 (0)20 3239 8181, *www.boardnlodge.com*
Snowboarding holidays in Austria, France, Bulgaria, Slovakia, Slovenia and Chile.

Borderline: Borderline Holidays, 16 Place St Clement, 65120 Luz St Sauveur, France
t +33 (0)562 92 68 95, *www.borderlinehols.com*
Well-established operator with own hotel and self-catering properties in Barèges.

Bramble Ski: Cariocca Business Park, 2 Sawley Road, Manchester M40 8BB
t +33 (0)871 218 0988, *www.brambleski.com*
New luxury operator with six catered chalets and in-house instruction in Verbier. Also apartments and three chalets in Kicking Horse.

Canterbury Travel: 42 High Street, Northwood HA6 1BL
t +44 (0)1923 457 017, *www.laplandmagic.com*
Lapland specialist with holidays to Luosto in Finland.

Carrier: 1 Lakeside, Cheadle SK8 3GW
t +44 (0)161 491 7600, *www.carrier.co.uk*
Luxury tailor-made holidays to Austria, France, Italy, Switzerland and North America.

The Chalet Company: 262 Res Sabaudia, Les Bois Venants, 74110 Morzine, France
t +44 (0)871 717 4208 (UK) or t +33 (0)450 79 68 40 (France),

www.thechaletco.com
Accommodation-only holidays in eight luxury catered chalets in Morzine and Ardent in the Portes du Soleil.

Chalet Snowboard: Dell House, Bodham NR25 6NG
t +44 (0)20 8133 4180, *www.chaletsnowboard.co.uk*
Specialist snowboard holidays and freestyle camps based in the company's own chalets in Morzine and Avoriaz.

Challenge Activ: Chalet Flori, L'Ele, Montriond 74110, France
t +44 (0)871 717 4113, *www.challenge-activ.com*
Activity holiday specialist with catered chalet in Morzine.

Chamonix Locations: Les Chalets de Philippe, 700 route du Chapeau, Le Lavancher, 74400 Chamonix, France
t +33 (0)33 607 23 17 26, *www.chamonixlocations.com*
Luxury catered chalets and restored *mazots* in Chamonix. Transport can be arranged.

CK Verbier: Chalet Kernow, 49 Chemin des Vernes, 1936 Verbier, Switzerland
t +41 794280172, *www.ckverbier.com*
Small company with two luxury catered chalets in Verbier with gourmet cuisine.

Classic Ski: Ober Road, Brockenhurst SO42 7ST
t +44 (0)1590 623 400, *www.classicski.co.uk*
Established operator with holidays in the French Alps, including tuition for singles and couples over 50yrs, weekday flights and flexible-length stays.

Club Europe: Fairway House, 53 Dartmouth Road, London SE23 3HN
t +44 (0)800 496 4996, *www.club-europe.co.uk*
Schools operator with all-inclusive ski programmes in Austria, France and Italy.

Club Med: 1st Floor, Gemini House, 10–18 Putney Hill, London SW15 6AA
t +44 (0)871 424 4044, *www.clubmed.co.uk*
Club villages in France, Italy, Japan and Switzerland. Flights, transfers, full-board accommodation, ski pass, tuition, après ski entertainment and insurance all included in the price, as well as childcare in many resorts.

Cold Comforts: 22 Chilbolton Avenue, Winchester SO22 5HD
t +44 (0)800 881 8429 or **t** (0)20 7993 8544, *www.cold-comforts.com*
Tailor-made holidays to Whistler, with ski guiding, flexible-length holidays and Vancouver add-ons. *See* page 142

Collineige: The Galloway Barn, Units 1 & 2 Home Farm, Loseley Park, Guildford GU3 1HS
t +44 (0)1276 24262, *www.collineige.com*
Large portfolio of catered and uncatered chalets in Chamonix and Argentière. Guiding/instruction and childcare available on request. Chalets available year-round.

Concept One: 3 Cholswell Court, Shippon, Abingdon OX13 6HX
t +44 (0)1865 390 807, *www.conceptchalets.com*
Luxury gourmet chalet with spa in Chamonix.

Contiki: Wells House, 15 Elmfield Road, Bromley BR1 1LS
t +44 (0)20 8290 6422, *www.contiki.com*
Holidays for 18–35s in Hopfgarten, Austria by coach or air.

Cooltip Mountain Holidays: Suffield, St Judes Road, Sulby, Isle of Man IM7 2ES
t +44 (0)1964 563 563, *www.cooltip.com*
Small operator with two catered chalet-apartments in Méribel.

The Corporate Ski Company: Olympic House, 196 The Broadway, London SW19 1RY
t +44 (0)20 8542 8555, *www.thecorporateskicompany.co.uk*
Bespoke ski trips to 30 resorts in the Alps. Incentive travel, conferences and special events. *See* page 29

Crystal Finest: King's Place, 12–42 Wood Street, Kingston-upon-Thames KT1 1JY
t +44 (0)871 971 0364, *www.crystalfinest.co.uk*
Stylish hotels and ski chalets in premier resorts in Europe, North America, Chile and Japan.

Crystal Ski/Crystal Family Ski: King's Place, 12–42 Wood Street, Kingston-upon-Thames KT1 1JY
t +44 (0)871 231 2256 / **t** +44 (0)871 230 8146, *www.crystalski.co.uk / www.crystalfamilies.co.uk*
Ski specialist with UK's largest choice of resorts and properties throughout Europe, North and South America, Japan.

Descent International: Riverbank House, Putney Bridge Approach, London SW6 3JD
t +44 (0)20 7384 3854, *www.descent.co.uk*
Luxury operator positioned at the extreme upper end of the chalet market, with properties in Courchevel, Davos, Les Gets, Klosters, Méribel, Sainte Foy, Val d'Isère, Verbier and Zermatt. *See* page 351

Directski.com: Block 10–4, Blanchardstown Corporate Park, Dublin 15, Ireland
t +44 (0)800 358 0448, *www.directski.com*
Major Dublin-based online operator with holidays to Andorra, Austria, Bulgaria, Canada, France, Italy, Norway, Slovenia, Switzerland and USA. *See* pages 45, 155

Discover The World: Arctic House, 8 Bolters Lane, Banstead SM7 2AR
t + 44 (0)1737 218 800, *www.discover-the-world.co.uk*
Off-piste and heli-skiing in Bjorkliden in northern Sweden, combined with the Swedish Ice Hotel.

Elegant Resorts: The Old Palace, Chester CH1 1RB
t +44 (0)1244 897 333, *www.elegantresorts.co.uk*
Effortlessly stylish ski holidays at exclusive hotels, resorts and chalets throughout Europe and North America. The company is now owned by Thomas Cook.

Elemental Adventure: 3rd Floor, Bedford Chambers, The Piazza, Covent Garden, London WC2E 8HA
t +44 (0)20 7836 3547, *www.eaheliskiing.com*
Heli-skiing in Alaska, Canada, Greenland, Himalayas, India, Italy, Russia, Sweden, Switzerland and Turkey.

Elevation Holidays: **t** +44 (0)845 644 3578, or **t** +43 (0)6584 23407, *www.elevationholidays.com*
Haus Salzburg, Hinterthal 48, A-5761 Maria Alm, Austria
Austrian specialist with holidays to Hintermoos and Hinterthal in the Hochkönig area.

Equity Ski: One Jubilee Street, Brighton BN1 1GE
t +44 (0)1273 622 111, *www.equityski.co.uk*
All-inclusive ski holidays to 23 resorts in Austria, France and Italy.

Erna Low: 9 Reece Mews, London SW7 3HE
t +44 (0)870 750 6820 or **t** +44 (0)20 7584 7820 (brochure line), *www.ernalow.co.uk*
The oldest independent ski tour operator, with a wide selection of apartments in Austria, France, Italy and Switzerland, as well as hotels. Also offers ski programme to selected resorts in North America, spa holidays, and ski properties for sale. *See* page 21

Esprit Ski: 185 Fleet Road, Fleet GU51 3BL
t +44 (0)1252 618 300, *www.esprit-holidays.co.uk*
Family specialist to 18 resorts in Austria, France, Italy and Switzerland, with dedicated nurseries, ski classes and activity clubs. *See* page 23

Exodus: Grange Mills, Weir Road, London SW12 0NE
t +44 (0)845 863 9600, *www.exodus.co.uk*

Long-established cross-country ski operator with flexible-length holidays to hotels in Andorra, Italy, Switzerland, Norway, Finland, Slovakia and Slovenia. Also snowshoeing, multi-activity, and hut-to-hut tours.

Exsus Travel: 23 Heddon Street, London W1B 4BQ
t +44 (0)20 7292 5060,
www.exsus.com
Luxury tailor-made holidays to Baqueira-Beret in Spain, and Argentina.

Family Friendly Skiing: 419 Manchester Road, Bury BL9 9RY
t +44 + (0)161 764 4520,
www.familyfriendlyskiing.com
Catered chalets in Courchevel and La Tania with in-house nannies.

Family Ski Company: Bank Chambers, Walwyn Road, Colwall, Malvern WR13 6QG
t +44 (0)1684 540 333,
www.familyski.co.uk
Family ski specialist with dedicated child facilities. Catered chalets in Portes du Soleil, Paradiski and the Trois Vallées. Provides helpers at the ski schools' *jardins de neige* working with Family Ski Company. *See* page 25

Finlays: 2 Abbotsford Court Business Centre, Kelso TD5 7BQ
t +44 (0)1573 226 611,
www.finlayski.com
Long-established small Scottish chalet company with a dedicated following in Courchevel, La Plagne, Les Coches and Val d'Isère. *See* page 155

First Choice Ski: King's Place, 12–42 Wood street, Kingston upon Thames KT1 1JY
t +44 (0)871 200 7799,
www.firstchoice.co.uk/ski
Mainstream winter sports operator with a collection of chalets, hotels and apartments across Europe and North America.

Flexiski: Olivier House, 18 Marine Parade, Brighton BN2 1TL
t +44 (0)1273 244 668,
www.flexiski.com
Specializes in tailor-made ski holidays and weekend breaks for individuals and groups to luxury catered chalets and hotels in 13 European resorts.

Four Winds Meriski: Carpenters Buildings, Carpenters Lane, Cirencester GL7 1EE
t +44 (0)1285 648 510, *www.meriski.co.uk*
Luxury family operator in Méribel with 10 chalets and a dedicated crèche.
See page 201

French Freedom Holidays: 44 Newdown Road, Southpark, Scunthorpe DN17 2TX
t +44 (0)1724 290 660,
www.skifrance4less.co.uk
Self-drive and fly-drive holidays to the French Alps.

Frontier Ski: 6 Sydenham Avenue, London SE26 6UH
t +44 (0)20 8776 8709,
www.frontier-ski.co.uk
Canadian specialist with tailor-made holidays to 17 resorts. Also heli-skiing, dog-sledding, cat-skiing, and holidays to Alaska. *See* page 142

Hannibals: Farriers, Little Olantigh Road, Wye, Ashford TN25 5DQ
t +44 (0)1233 813 105,
www.hannibals.co.uk
Established specialist operator with family-run hotels, chalets and self-catering apartments in Serre Chevalier.

Headwater: The Old School House, Chester Road, Northwich CW8 1LE
t +44 (0)1606 720 033,
www.headwater.com
Cross-country ski programme in Austria, the French Jura, Italy, Lapland, Norway, Switzerland and USA.

HF Holidays: Catalyst House, 720 Centennial Court, Centennial Park, Elstree, Herts WD6 3SY
t +44 (0)20 8732 1220,
www.hfholidays.co.uk
Group holidays with instruction in skiing, cross-country skiing and snowshoeing in Austria, France, Italy and Switzerland.

High Mountain Holidays: 39 Bartholomew Close, Ducklington OX29 7UJ
t +44 (0)1993 775 540, *www.highmountain.co.uk*
Chamonix specialist with apartments, hotels and eight chalets. Weekends and short stays, off-piste courses.

Hucksters Lodge: Colliford Lake Park, Bodmin Moor, Cornwall, PL14 6PZ
t +44 (0)1208 821 100, *www.huckstersIodge.com*
Small, independent tour operator offering value-for-money holidays in Tignes, Les Arcs and La Tania.

Huski Chalet Holidays: 14 Warren Road, Nork, Banstead SM7 1LA
t +44 (0)8000 971 760, *www.huski.com*
Long-established Chamonix chalet operator, with six chalets. Also offers hotels and weekend skiing.

Independent Luxury Travel: 350 Route la Mernaz, Morzine 74410, France
t +44 (0)845 474 2417 or
t +33 (0)4 50 796 569, *www.independent-luxury.co.uk*
Ultra-luxury, flexible chalet holidays in St-Jean d'Aulps in the Portes du Soleil. Also holidays to other resorts in Austria, France and Switzerland.

Indigo Lodges: 28 Quai de Seujet, CP 580, 1211 Geneva 12, Switzerland
t +44 (0)79 7950 6913, *www.indigolodges.co.uk*
Luxury chalets in over a dozen resorts in Austria, France, Italy and Switzerland, with or without catering.

Inghams: 10–18 Putney Hill, London SW15 6AX
t +44 (0)20 8780 4433, *www.inghams.co.uk*
Major tour operator with chalet and hotel holidays in 95 resorts in 14 countries. Top end of the mass market but also has separate luxury programme. *See* inside front cover

Inntravel: Nr Castle Howard, York YO60 7JU
t +44 (0)1653 617 920, *www.inntravel.co.uk*
Cross-country, snowshoeing and Alpine skiing in Austria, Italy, Finland, France, Italy, Norway, Switzerland and Scandinavia.

Interhome: 383 Richmond Road, Twickenham TW1 2EF
t +44 (0)20 8891 1294, *www.interhome.co.uk*
Impressive selection of privately owned chalets and apartments for rent throughout the Alps. Flexible durations and short breaks.

In Resort Services: Suite 787, 2 Old Brompton Road, London, SW7 3DQ
t +44 (0) 870 870 7669, *www.inresortservices.com*
Chalets and apartments in Flaine and the other resorts of Le Grand Massif.

Interski: Acorn Park, Commercial Gate, Mansfield NG18 1EX
t +44 (0)1623 456 333, *www.interski.co.uk*
Long-established schools operator to Courmayeur and the Aosta Valley. Also has own BASI ski school, gap year programme, and equipment rental.

J2Ski: *www.j2ski.com*
Web-based operator with apartment and chalet holidays throughout the Alps.

James Orr Heliski: 12 Rose & Crown Walk, Saffron Walden CB10 1JH
t +44 (0)1799 516 964, *www.heliski.co.uk*
Established agent for heli-skiing holidays in Canada.

Jeffersons Private Jet Holidays: Mill House, Millers Way W6 7NH
t +44 (0)20 8746 2496, *www.jeffersons.com*
Short breaks by private jet/helicopter to selected resorts with nearby airfield. Limousine transfers and luxury accommodation

Just Slovenia: The Barns, Woodlands End, Mells, Frome BA11 3QD

t +44 (0)1373 814 230,
www.justslovenia.co.uk
Specialist tour operator offering tailor-made holidays to Kranjska Gora.

Kaluma Travel: 263 Putney Bridge Road SW15 2PU
t +44 (0)870 442 8044,
www.kalumatravel.co.uk
Luxury ski holiday specialist to eight resorts in France, Austria, Switzerland and Canada. Tailor-made flexible-length trips and weekend breaks available. Also incentive travel and special events.

Kick Ski: 13 Acacia Avenue, Brant Road, Lincoln LN5 9BX
t +44 (0)845 625 6025
www.kickski.co.uk
Apartment holidays in Vaujany, France.

Kuoni Travel: Kuoni House, Deepdene Avenue, Dorking RH5 4AZ
t +44 (0)1306 747 002,
www.kuoni.co.uk
Long-established mainstream operator with 16 resorts in Austria, Canada, France, Italy, Japan, Switzerland and USA.

Lagrange: 168 Shepherds Bush Road, London W6 7PB
t +44 (0)20 7371 6111,
www.lagrange-holidays.co.uk
British branch of giant French operator with a wide range of self-catering accommodation in 110 resorts in the French Alps, Jura and Pyrenees.
See page 213

La Source: 14 The Grove, Brookmans Park, Hatfield AL9 7RN
t +44 (0)1707 655988,
www.lasource.org.uk
Self-catering chalets, *gîtes*, and a hotel in the small resort of Villard Reculas in the Alpe d'Huez ski area.

Le Ski: Stirling House,139 Netheroyd Hill Road, Huddersfield HD2 2LX
t +44 (0)1484 548996,
www.leski.com
Family-run chalet company with a long-established pedigree to 29 chalets in Courchevel 1650, Val d'Isère and La Tania. Offers crèches in La Tania, own ski school in Courchevel, free ski guiding, pre-season ski clinics. *See* pages 175, 237

Lotus Supertravel: Sandpiper House, 39 Queen Elizabeth Street, London SE1 2BT
t +44 (0)20 7295 1650,
www.supertravel.co.uk
High-quality chalets and tailor-made holidays to Austria, Canada, France, Switzerland and USA

Made to Measure: 1 South Street, Chichester PO19 1EH
t +44 (0)1243 533 333,
www.mtmhols.co.uk
Long-established operator specializing in tailor-made and flexible holidays to a wide range of resorts in Austria, France, Italy and Switzerland.

Mark Warner: 10 Old Court Place, London W8 4PL
t +44 (0)871 703 3888,
www.markwarner.co.uk
With over 33 years' experience, Mark Warner Holidays are experts in ski holidays for families, singles, couples and groups. Chalet-hotel holidays in 10 major resorts in France, Italy, Austria and Canada. Also heli-skiing in Revelstoke.
See inside back cover

McNab Mountain Sports: Harbour House, Crinen, Lochgilphead PA31 8SW
t +44 (0)141 416 3828,
www.mcnabsnowboarding.com
Off-piste, freeride and freestyle specialists based at catered chalet in Argentière. Also freeriding in the Caucus Mountains, snowboard camps and heli-skiing.

MGS Ski Ltd: 109 Castle Street, Saffron Walden CB10 1BQ
t +44 (0)1799 525 984,
www.mgsski.com
Small, well-established family operator offering apartments and hotels in Val Cenis, France.

Momentum Ski: 162 Munster Road, London SW6 6AT
t +44 (0)20 7371 9111,

www.momentumski.com
Tailor-made operator specializing in weeks and weekends to the Alps and North America for individuals, families and groups, together with alpine corporate event programmes. Italy and Switzerland are a particular strength. *See* page 29

Moswin's Germany: The Birds Building, Fleckney Road, Kibworth LE8 0HJ
t +44 (0)844 4488 999, *www.moswin.com*
Holidays in Garmisch-Partenkirchen in Germany and cross-country skiing in Berchtesgarten.

Mountain Heaven: 1 Cholmondeley Road, West Kirby, Wirral CH48 7HB
t +44 (0)151 625 1921, *www.mountainheaven.co.uk*
Comfortable chalet-style apartments in La Plagne, Plagne-Montalbert, La Rosière and Les Sept Laux in France, Grimentz in Switzerland.

Mountain Highs: Chalet Marcassin, Le Clos de Reneve, Seytroux 74430, France
t +33 (0)4 50 79 29 54 or
t +33 (0)6 24 79 07 09, *www.mountainhighs.co.uk*
Catered and self-catered chalets in Morzine, with optional transfers and childcare.

Mountain Leap Events: 25 Eccleston Square, London SW1V 1NS
t +44 (0)20 7931 0621, *www.mountainleap.com*
Ski weekends and corporate events in Austria, France, Italy, Sweden and Switzerland. Also conferences and private parties.

Mountain Paradise: 3 Regent Court, Altrincham WA14 1PQ
t +44 (0)845 602 5874, *www.mountainparadise.co.uk*
Leading ski, snowboard and cross-country specialists to the Tatra mountains of Slovakia.

Mountain Retreats: Guilton Ash, Tile Barn, Woolton Hill, Newbury RG20 9UX
t +44 (0)1635 253 946 or
t +33 (0)686 54 72 40, *www.mountainretreats.co.uk*
Small company offering luxury catered and self-catered ski in, ski out accommodation in Chamonix valley.

Mountain Rooms & Chalets: Pulse House, 1a Lonsdale Square, London N1 1EN
t +44 (0)700 2000 456, *www.mountainrooms.com*
Flexible 'scatered' holidays, which are cross between fully catered and self catered board with three evening meals instead of six.
Create your own holiday with add-ons like meals and cleaning.

Mountain Sun: Fillis Cottage, The Street, Kingston, Lewes BN7 3NT
t +44 (0)7941 196 517, *www.mountainsunltd.com*
Catered and self-catered chalets in La Plagne, Les Coches, Tignes and San Cassiano.

Mountain Tracks: 250 York Road, London SW11 3SJ
t +44 (0)20 8123 2978, *www.mountaintracks.co.uk*
Off-piste performance, weekends, heli-skiing and avalanche awareness, alpine skills for teens, ice-climbing, ski-touring in Southern Turkey and Morocco, off-piste in Sainte-Foy, Japan and Kashmir.

Neilson Ski & Snowboard: Locksview, Brighton Marina, Brighton BN2 5HA
t +44 (0)870 333 3356, *www.neilson.co.uk*
Major tour operator with hotels, chalets and apartments in Andorra, Austria, Bulgaria, Canada, Finland, France, Italy, Norway, Romania, Sweden and Switzerland The company now incorporates Airtours and Panorama Holidays. *See* page 139

Nonstopski: 3b The Plough Brewery, 516 Wandsworth Road, London SW8 3JX
t +44 (0)845 365 1525, *www.nonstopski.com* and *www.nonstopsnowboard.com*
Learn-to-be-a-ski-instructor courses in

Banff, Fernie, Red Mountain and Whistler in Canada. Also has its own hotel in Fernie

Oak Hall Skiing and Snowboarding: Oak Hall, Otford TN15 6XF
t +44 (0)1732 763 131,
www.oakhall.co.uk
Christian holidays for 20s and 30s to Austria and Switzerland. Also off-piste and personal performance courses.

On the Piste: 28 Great King Street, Macclesfield SK11 6PL
t +44 (0)1625 503 111,
www.onthepiste.com
Leading student and schools specialist to French Alps. Also music and snowsports festivals .

Optimum Ski: Chalet Tarentaise, Le Pré, 73640 Villaroger, France
t +44 (0)131 208 1154,
www.optimumski.com
BASI trainer-run ski courses in large chalet in Villaroger, Les Arcs with superb cuisine, sauna and in-house massage.

Original Travel Company: Crombie Mews, 11a Abercrombie Street, London SW11 2JB
t +44 (0)20 7978 7333,
www.originaltravel.co.uk
Upmarket short-break specialist offering heli-skiing, ski-touring, ski safaris, and off-piste in Austria, Canada, France, Italy, Norway, Switzerland and Sweden.

The Oxford Ski Company: Magdalen Centre, Robert Robinson Avenue, Oxford OX4 4GA
t +44 (0)870 787 1785,
www.oxfordski.com
Tailor-made luxury holidays to Switzerland, France, Austria and North America.

Outgoing Ski: The Stables, Wilmslow Road, Manchester M20 5PG
t +44 (0)845 331 3040,
www.outgoing.co.uk
All-inclusive holidays for students and groups to Austria and France.

Peak Leisure: The Old Post Office, Steventon, Basingstoke, RG25 3BA
t +44 (0)870 760 5610,
www.peak-leisure.co.uk
Independent catered chalet in Ste-Foy, flexible-length stays, multi-resort skiing.

Peak Retreats: 2.4 Central Point, Kirpal Road, Portsmouth PO3 6FH
t +44 (0)844 576 0123,
www.peakretreats.co.uk
French Alps specialist for self-catering chalets, apartments and family-run hotels in 25 offbeat and backdoor resorts. *See* page 209, 228

Peak Ski: White Lilacs House, Water Lane, Bovingdon HP3 0NA
t +44 (0)1442 832 629, *www.peakski.co.uk*
Small independent operator offering seven catered chalets in Verbier. Ski courses arranged with Warren Smith Ski Academy.

PGL Ski: Alton Court, Penyard Lane, Ross-on-Wye HR9 5GL
t +44 (0)8700 507 507,
www.pgl.co.uk
Major schools operator with all-inclusive holidays to Kitzsteinhorn glacier.

Pollen-Brooks Leisure: St Anthony, Portnall Drive, Wentworth GU25 4NN
t +44 (0)1344 849 135,
www.pollenbrooks.com
Hotels, apartments and six luxury catered chalets in the Chamonix Valley, as well as heli-skiing and corporate events. Also offers life coaching on skis.

Powder Byrne: 250 Upper Richmond Road, London SW15 6TG
t +44 (0)20 8246 5300,
www.powderbyrne.com
Luxury family ski holidays to 12 resorts in Austria, Italy, France and Switzerland, with ski instruction, children's clubs and crèches.

The Powder Company: CP 1454, Verbier 1936, Switzerland
t +44 (0)7788 136 622,
www.thepowderco.com
Luxury fully-staffed chalet in Verbier.

Powder White: 11b Osiers Road, London SW18 1NR
t +44 (0)20 8877 8888, *www.powderwhite.com*
Luxury chalets in Courchevel, Méribel, St Anton, Val d'Isère, Verbier and Whistler, with flexible catering.

Première Neige: 19 East London Street, Edinburgh EH7 4ZD
t +44 (0)870 383 1000
www.premiere-neige.com
Apartments and 10 luxury catered chalets in Ste-Foy. Private crèche, concierge service and ski safaris to other resorts in the region.

Purple Ski: 4 Cruxwell Street, Bromyard HR7 4EB
t +44 (0)1885 488799, *www.purpleski.com*
Small luxury chalet operator in Méribel.

Pyrenean Mountain Tours: 2 Rectory Cottages, Wolverton, Tadley RG26 5RS
t +44 (0)1635 297 209, *www.pyrenees.co.uk*
Small operator with comprehensive ski-touring, snowshoeing and telemark holidays, as well as children's programmes. Hotels and self-catering apartments in Austria, France, Italy, Poland, Spain and Switzerland.

Ramblers Holidays: Lemsford Mill, Lemsford, Welwyn Garden City AL8 6PQ
t +44 (0)1707 331 133, *www.ramblersholidays.co.uk*
Walking holidays specialist with ski holidays in Courchevel and Val Thorens, and cross-country programme to Achenkirch in Austria, Dobbiaco in Italy, and the Engadine in Switzerland.

Reach4theAlps: Chalet Sol Re, Essert La Pierre, 74430 St-Jean d'Aulps, France
t +44 (0)845 680 1947, *www.reach4theAlps.com*
Independent chalet company offering a high standard of catered accommodation with chalets in Morzine, Les Gets and Montriond.

Redpoint Holidays: BCM BOX 1785, London, WC1N
t +33 (0)845 6801214, *www.redpoint.co.uk*
Solo ski, snowboard and activity holidays based in the Ziller Valley in Austria. Also weekends, ski courses, adaptive programme and summer skiing.

Rocket Ski: Dukes Lane House, 47 Middle Street, Brighton BN1 1AL
t +44 (0)1273 810 777, *www.rocketski.com*
Online booking service for components of holidays to Austria, France and Italy.

Rudechalets: Salix Farm, Great Sampford, Saffron Walden, CB10 2QE
t +(0)870 068 7030, *www.rudechalets.com*
Catered ski and snowboard holidays in chalets and apartments in Avoriaz/Morzine and Chamonix.

Scott Dunn: Fovant Mews, 12 Noyna Road, London SW17 7PH
t +44 (0)20 8682 5050, *www.scottdunn.com*
Luxury operator with a portfolio of luxury catered chalets with experienced chefs, hosts and childcare in Courchevel 1850, Méribel, St Anton, Val d'Isère, and Zermatt. Handpicked hotels in leading resorts across the Alps. Also tailor-made holidays to Argentina, Chile and New Zealand. *See* page 3

Seasons in Style: Lakeside, St David's Park, Chester CH5 3YE
t +44 (0)1244 202 000, *www.seasonsinstyle.co.uk*
Five-star worldwide hotel operator with a ski programme to Austria, France, Italy, Switzerland and USA. Also three luxury catered chalets in France.

Silver Ski: Conifers House, Grove Green Lane, Maidstone ME14 5JW
t +44 (0)1622 735 544, *www.silverski.co.uk*
No-nonsense catered chalets in La Plagne, Courchevel, Méribel, Réberty-Les Menuires, La Tania Val d'Isère.

Simon Butler Skiing: Portsmouth Road, Ripley GU23 6EY
t +44 (0)1483 212726, *www.simonbutlerskiing.co.uk*
Holidays to chalet-hotels in Megève, including instruction.

Ski 2: The Old Forge, High Street, Twyford SO21 1RF
t +44 (0)1962 713 330, *www.ski-2.com*
Champoluc and San Cassiano specialist, offering total flexibility of travel dates and length of stay, with its own crèche. Also corporate groups and own ski/snowboard school.
See pages, 269, 295

Ski4you: Spring Mill, Earby, Barnoldswick BB94 0AA
t +44 (0)870 197 6692, *www.french-life-ski-resorts.co.uk*
Budget ski holidays for the independent traveller, mainly focused on self-drive to France and Switzerland. Also short breaks.

Ski Activity: Lawmuir House, Methven PH1 3SZ
t +44 (0)1738 840 888, *www.skiactivity.com*
Chalets, hotels and apartments in Andorra, Austria, Canada, France, Italy, Switzerland and USA.

Ski Addiction: The Cottage, Fontridge Lane, Etchingham TN19 7DD
t +44 (0)1580 819 354 or
t +33 (0)4 50 73 39 83, *www.skiaddiction.co.uk*
Holidays in Châtel and La Chapelle d'Abondance in the Portes du Soleil and Ischgl in Austria. Short breaks, catered chalet and hotels, instruction and guiding.

Ski Adventures: 10 Graham Road, Malvern WR14 2HN
t +33 (0)479 07 97 15, *www.skiadventures.co.uk*
Small operator with three chalets in Les Arcs 1600. In-house childcare, ski guiding, and transfers can be arranged.

Ski All America: 117 St Margarets Road, Twickenham TW1 2LH
t +44 (0)8701 676 676, *www.skiallamerica.com*
Chalets, hotels and apartments in a large portfolio of resorts in North and South America.

Skialot: Chalet Chataigne, 438 Route du Boude, 74390 Châtel, France
t + 44 (0)845 004 3622, *www.skialot.com*
Catered chalet in Châtel, with draught beer on tap from chalet's own micro-brewery

Ski Amis: 122–126 High Road, London NW6 4HY
t +44 (0)20 7692 0850, *www.skiamis.com*
Well-established tour operator offering catered and self-catered apartments and chalets in the French Alps.

Ski Armadillo: Rocquaine House, Route du Coudre, St Peter's, Guernsey GY7 9HX
t +44 (0)1799 586 652, *www.skiarmadillo.com*
Independent operator with 12 catered chalets in Verbier.

Ski Arrangements: The Reading Rooms, Sandy Lane, Crich, Matlock DE4 5DE
t +44 (0)8700 110 565, *www.skiarrangements.com*
Weekends and flexible-length holidays to France, Italy and North America, staying in apartments, chalets and hotels.

Ski Astons: Clerkenleap, Broomhall, Worcester WR5 3HR
t +44 (0)1905 829 200, *www.skiastons.co.uk*
Schools specialist with all-inclusive holidays to resorts in Austria and Switzerland.

Ski Barrett-Boyce: 3 Mayfields, Brighton Road KT20 6QZ
t +44 (0)1737 831 184, *www.skibb.com*
Family-run company offering catered

chalet holidays in Megève, with instruction and childcare.

Ski Basics: 95 West Avenue, Oldfield Park, Bath BA2 3QB
t +44 (0)1225 444 143, *www.skibasics.co.uk*
Méribel specialist with 12 good-value catered chalets, offering ski courses.

Ski Beat: Metro House, Northgate, Chichester PO19 1BE
t +44 (0)1243 780 405, *www.skibeat.co.uk*
Long-established operator with chalets in La Plagne, Les Arcs, Méribel, Paradiski, La Tania, La Rosière and Val d'Isère. Crèches in four resorts, and some childfree chalets.

Ski Blanc: 89 Palmerston Road, Buckhurst Hill IG9 5NH
t +44 (0)20 8502 9082, *www.skiblanc.co.uk*
Small operator with six catered chalets in Méribel-les-Allues.

SkiBound: Olivier House, 18 Marine Parade, Brighton BN2 1TL
t +44 (0)1273 244 500, *www.skibound.co.uk*
Market leader for school trips to Austria, Bulgaria, Canada, France, Italy, Switzerland and USA. Part of the First Choice group .

Ski Chamois: 18 Lawn Road, Doncaster DN1 2JF
t +44 (0)1302 369 006, *www.skichamois.co.uk*
Small chalet-hotel operator in Morzine, with crèche. Sleeper coach from Dover and Manchester.

Ski Collection: 2.4 Central Point, Kirpal Road, Portsmouth PO3 6FH
t +44 (0)844 576 0175, *www.skicollection.com*
Ski-in ski-out four-star self-catering specialist to 31 French resorts. Accommodation-only or packaged with a ferry or Eurotunnel crossing.
See pages 8

Ski Cuisine: 49 Burges Road, Southend-on-Sea SS1 3AX
t +44 (0)1702 589 543, *www.skicuisine.co.uk*
Small company with six gourmet-catered chalets in Méribel.

Ski-Dazzle: 16 Birchwood, Thorpe St Andrew, Norwich NR7 0RL
t +33 (0)479 00 17 25, *www.ski-dazzle.com*
Independent family-run company with three catered chalets in La Tania.

Ski Dream: Welby House, 96 Wilton Road, London SW1V 1DW
t +44 (0)845 277 3333, *www.skidream.com*
The UK's original independent ski holiday specialist operator to North America, now part of Western and Oriental.

Ski Equipe: Victoria House, 19/21 Ack Lane East, Bramhall SK7 2PR
t +44 (0)1625 599 988, *www.ski-equipe.co.uk*
Small operator with chalets and hotels in Beaver Creek, Cortina d'Ampezzo and St Anton.

Ski Etoile: 94 Hopkins Heath, Shawbirch TF1 0LZ
t +44 (0)1952 253 252, *www.skietoile.co.uk*
Flexible holidays to Montgenèvre with hotels, chalets and apartments.

Ski Expectations: Jasmine Cottage, Manor Lane, Great Chesterford CB10 1PJ
t +44 (0)1799 531 888, *www.skiexpectations.com*
Small tailor-made hotel and catered chalet operator to major resorts in Austria, Canada, Italy, Switzerland and USA.

Ski Famille: Suite 3e Westmead House, Westmead, Farnborough GU14 7LP
t +44 (0)845 644 3764, *www.skifamille.co.uk*
Specialist family-run chalet operator in Les Gets, with free childcare programme.
See page 25

Ski France: Linkline House
65 Church Road, Hove BN3 2BP
t +44 (0)870 251 0005,
www.skifrance.co.uk
Travel by rail, air or self-drive to France, with chalets, hotels and apartments in 27 resorts.

Ski Freshtracks: The White House, 57–63 Church Road, Wimbledon, London SW19 5SB
t +44 (0)20 8410 2022,
www.skifreshtracks.co.uk
The Ski Club of Great Britain's own ski programme to resorts in Andorra, Austria, Canada, France, Italy, Switzerland and USA. with off-piste holidays, family weeks, instructional courses, and weekend breaks with leaders, instructors and guides.

Ski High Days: Fireclay House, Netham Road, Bristol BS5 9PJ
t +44 (0)117 955 1814,
www.skihighdays.com
Group ski and snowboard specialist, including schools, with holidays in eight resorts in France, Italy and Switzerland.

Ski Hillwood: Lavender Lodge, Dunny Lane, Chipperfield WD4 9DD
t +44 (0)1923 290 700,
www.hillwood-holidays.co.uk
Long-established specialist family operator with childcare programme to Söll and Zauchensee in Austria, Les Gets in France.

Ski Hiver: 29 Place House, Close, Fareham PO15 5BH
t +44 (0)1329 847 788,
www.skihiver.co.uk
Luxury apartments and three catered chalets with childcare in Peisey-Nancroix, Paradiski.

Ski Independence: 5 Thistle Street, Edinburgh EH2 1DF
t +44 (0)845 310 3030, *www.ski-i.com*
Largest independent operator to the USA and Canada, with hotels, chalets and apartments in 40 North American resorts. Also an extensive programme to 44 French, 8 Swiss and 5 Austrian resorts, with option to fly or drive for week or weekend stays.
See page 141

Ski in Luxury: Bristol and West House, Post Office Road, Bournemouth BH1 1BL
t +44 (0)1202 313 693,
www.skiinluxury.com
Luxury chalets and hotels in Austria, France and Switzerland.

Ski-Line: 29 London Road, Bromley BR1 1DG
t +33 (0)20 8313 3999, *www.skiline.co.uk*
Independent ski chalet specialist to a wide choice of resorts in Austria, also hotels and self-catering. *See* page 209

Ski-Link: 5 Hopfield Avenue, West Byfleet KT14 7PE
t +44 (0)871 218 0175, *www.ski-link.co.uk*
Independent chalet operator in Courchevel as well as a comprehensive airport transfers service throughout the French Alps.

Ski La Côte: 33 Dale Road, Welton, Brough HU15 1PE
t +44 (0)1482 668 357,
www.ski-la-cote.karoo.net
Catered chalet in La Chapelle d'Abondance, with airport transfers and instruction, but not flights.

Ski Miquel: 73 High Street, Uppermill, Oldham OL3 6AP
t +44 (0)1457 821 200,
www.miquelhols.co.uk
Long-established since 1981, chalet, chalet-hotel, hotel and apartment operator to Alpe d'Huez, Bad Gastein, Baqueira, Lauterbrunnen, Saalbach and Serre Chevalier. Uses own properties and provides ski guiding. *See* page 142

Ski Morgins: The Barn House, 1 Bury Court Barns, Wigmore HR6 9US
t +44 (0)1568 770 681,
www.skimorgins.com
Small specialist operator with catered chalets in Morgins, Switzerland. Also

choral workshops, snowshoeing and property sales.

Ski Norwest: 8 Foxholes Cottages, Foxholes Road, Horwich, Bolton BL6 6AL
t +44 (0)1204 668 468, *www.skinorwest.com*
Weekend and midweek ski and snowboarding breaks to Aviemore.

Ski Olympic: PO Box 396, Doncaster DN5 7YS
t +44 (0)1302 328 820, *www.skiolympic.com*
Chalets and chalet-hotels in eight French resorts, with in-house equipment hire.

Ski Peak: Barts End, Crossways Road, Grayshott GU26 6HD
t +44 (0)1428 608 070, *www.skipeak.com*
Small, dedicated operator with its own chalets, apartments and hotel in Vaujany in the Alpe d'Huez ski area. Provides a British nanny for the resort crèche. Chalets available all year round. *See* page 253

Ski Power: 6 Fitzroy Place, Blackborough Road, Reigate RH2 7AD
t +44 (0)1737 306 029, *www.skipower.co.uk*
Catered chalets in La Tania and Courchevel 1550.

Ski Rosie: L'Alpage 8B, route du Petit Châtel, 74390 Châtel, France
t +33 (0)4 50 81 31 00, *www.skirosie.com*
Long-established operator with one catered chalet in Morgins; apartments in Châtel.

Ski Safari: 1 Amber House, St Johns Road, Hove BN3 2EZ
t +44 (0)1273 224 060, *www.skisafari.com*
North America expert with high-quality hotels and apartments. Self-drive adventures a speciality. Also flexible-length holidays in Austria, Switzerland, Chile and Japan. *See* page 143

Skisafe Travel: Strandarrif Farm, Greenock Road, Inchinnan, Renfrewshire PA4 9LB
t +44 (0)141 812 0925, *www.osatravel.co.uk*
Family-run operation with weekends in Aviemore, Nevis Range and Glenshee.

Ski Solutions à la Carte: 84 Pembroke Road, London W8 6NX
t +44 (0)20 7471 7777, *www.skisolutions.com*
Tailor-made arm of specialist ski travel agency, with hotels and apartments in all major resorts in Austria, France, Switzerland and North America. Staff have intimate knowledge of the resorts and properties.
See page 61

Ski Supreme 24 Howard Court, Neraton Estate, East Kilbride G74 4QZ
t +44 (0)845 194 7541, *www.skisupreme.co.uk*
Self-drive and accommodation-only holidays in France, schools skiing in Italy.

Skitopia: 40 Lemon Street, Truro TR1 2NS
t +44 (0)844 412 9919, *www.skitopia.com*
Catered chalets and club-hotels to the Trois Vallées, Montgenèvre and Serre Chevalier.

Ski Val: The Ski Barn, Middlemoor, Tavistock PL19 9DY
t +44 (0)1822 611 200, *www.skival.co.uk*
Catered chalets and chalet-hotels in Courchevel, Val d'Isère and St Anton.

Ski Verbier: Skyline House, 200 Union Street, London SE1 0LX
t: +44 (0)20 7401 1101, *www.skiverbier.com*
Established upmarket operator in Verbier, with 20 catered chalets offering gourmet cuisine, and its own four-star boutique hotel. Suitable for families and corporate groups. *See* page 367

Ski Weekend: Darts Farm Village, Topsham, Exeter EX3 0QH
t +44 (0)139 287 8350, *www.skiweekend.com*
Weekends and short breaks combined with high-mountain guiding and specialist courses, to Chamonix Valley and other destinations in Switzerland

and Italy. Corporate programme also available.

Skiweekends and Skiweeks: 4 Post Office Walk, Fore Street, Hertford SG14 1DL
t +44 (0)870 442 3400, *www.skiweekends.com* or *www.skiweeks.co.uk*
Budget weekends and flexible breaks. Coach and air packages to Brides-les-Bains, La Châble, Chamonix, Courmayeur, Les Houches, La Tania and Täsch.

Ski Wild: 26 Prey Heath Close, Woking, Surrey GU22 0SP
t +44 (0)870 746 9668, *www.skiwild.co.uk*
Tailor-made holidays in Andorra, Austria, France, Italy and North America.

Ski with Julia: East Lodge Farm, Stanton, Broadway WR12 7NH
t +44 (0)1386 584 478, *www.skijulia.co.uk*
Three chalets and two hotels in Verbier.

Skiworld: Skiworld House, 3 Vencourt Place, London W6 9NU
t +44 (0)870 241 6723 (Europe) or t +44 (0)870 787 9720 (North America), *www.skiworld.ltd.uk*
Large independent ski tour operator, with major chalet, self-catering and hotel programme in the Alps and North America.

Sloping Off: 1 Jubilee Street, Brighton BN1 1GE
t +44 (0)1273 648 200, *www.sloping-off.co.uk*
Schools and groups operator to resorts in Andorra, Austria, France, Italy, Spain and Switzerland.

Snowbizz Vacances: 69 High Street, Maxey PE6 9EE
t +44 (0)1778 341 455, *www.snowbizz.co.uk*
Small, long-established operator to Puy-St-Vincent in France, with extensive childcare and own ski-school programme with race-training for children 10–16yrs.

Snowcoach: 146–148 London Road, St Albans AL1 1PQ
t +44 (0)1727 866 177, *www.snowcoach.co.uk*
Specialist ski and snowboard operator offering good-value holidays to France and Austria.

Snowfocus: Chalet La Sonnaille, 74390 Châtel, France
t +44 (0)1392 479 555, *www.snowfocus.com*
Catered chalet in Châtel for weeks and weekend breaks, with in-house ski school and nannies.

Snowlife: Chanson de la Mer, rue de la Falaise, Trinity, Jersey JE3 5BD
t +44 (0)1534 863 630, *www.snowlife.co.uk*
Catered chalet with childcare in La Clusaz.

Snowline: Collingbourne House, 140–142 Wandsworth High Street, London SW18 4JJ
t +44 (0)870 112 3118, *www.snowline.co.uk*
Well-established operator with a wide range of smart catered ski chalets in Val d'Isère, Méribel, La Tania and Morzine, La Plagne. Piste-side locations, ski hosting, excellent childcare.
See page 209

Snow Safari: Chalet Savoy, 1351 route des Chavants, 74310 Les Houches, France
t +33 (0)4 50 54 56 63, *www.chaletsavoy.com*
Small chalet specialist to Chamonix Valley with mountain guiding, safaris, snowshoeing and instruction.

Snowscape: Restdale House, 32–33 Foregate Street, Worcester WR1 1EE
t +44 (0)845 370 8570, *www.snowscape.co.uk*
Weekends and flexible holidays to Austria for groups and individuals, and heli-skiing in Canada.

Snowstar: 38 Nicola Close, South Croydon CR2 6NB
t +44 (0)870 068 6611,

www.snowstarholidays.com
Catered chalet holidays in Tignes.

Snowy Pockets: Chalet Runca, Wetterweide, 7050 Arosa, Switzerland
t +44 (0)798 333 608, *www.snowypockets.com*
Arosa specialist with catered chalet and apartments.

Solo's Holidays: 30 City Road, London EC1Y 2AB
t +44 (0)844 815 0005, *www.solosholidays.co.uk*
Holidays for singles in 14 resorts in Andorra, France, Italy, Switzerland, Romania, Slovenia, North America.

Stanford Skiing: 479 Unthank Road, Norwich NR4 7QN
t +44 (0)1603 477 471, *www.stanfordskiing.co.uk*
Megève specialist and long-established family-run operator with chalets, apartments and hotels. Also weekends and short breaks. *See* page 193

Swiss Travel Service/Cresta Holidays: Holiday House, Sandbrook Park, Sandbrook Way, Rochdale OL11 1SA
t +44 (0)871 664 7963, *www.crestaholidays.co.uk*
Holidays to hotels in Switzerland. Travel by scheduled flight, with rail transfers or by rail or car from the UK.

Switzerland Travel Centre: 30 Bedford Street, London WC2E 9ED
t +44 (0)20 7420 4900,*www.stc.co.uk*
Switzerland specialist offering holidays in 13 resorts, plus igloo accommodation in Engelberg, Gstaad and Zermatt.

Ted Bentley Chalet Holidays: Winthill House, Winthill, Banwell BS29 6NN
t +44 (0)1934 820 854, *www.tedbentley.co.uk*
Luxury operator with three chalets in Haute Nendaz, Switzerland, with gourmet cuisine.

TG Ski: The Glebe, Sandhurst Lane, Sandhurst, GL2 9NP
t +44 (0)1452 731 000, *www.tgski.co.uk*
Four catered chalets in Morzine with chauffeur service, and a professional photographer to record the holiday.

Thomson Ski: King's Place, 12–42 Wood Street, Kingston-upon-Thames KT1 1JY
t +44 (0)871 971 0578, *www.thomson-ski.co.uk*
Major ski tour operator offering hotels, chalets and apartments throughout Europe and North America.

Total Ski: 185 Fleet Road, Fleet GU51 3BL
t +44 (0)870 163 3633, *www.skitotal.com*
Large portfolio of quality catered chalets in premier resorts of Austria, France, Switzerland and Italy.

Trail Alpine: Cordelia House, James Park, Dyserth, Rhyl LL18 6AG
t +44 (0)870 750 6560, *www.trailalpine.co.uk*
Small personal chalet operator in Morzine-Avoriaz. High level of service and comfort.

Trailfinders: 194 Kensington High Street, London W8 7RG
t +44 (0)845 050 5900, *www.trailfinders.com*
Largest independent travel company in UK, with tailor-made holidays to USA and Canada.

Tyrolean Adventures: 33 Ingra Walk, Roborough, Plymouth PL6 7DF
t +44 (0)7779 764 858, *www.tyroleanadventures.com*
Small operator offering holidays to the Tyrol by coach, inclusive of ski pass and ski hire.

United Vacations: PO Box 377, Bromley BR1 1LY
t +44 (0)844 499 0033, *www.unitedvacations.co.uk*
Tour operator arm of United Airlines, offering tailor-made service to 18 resorts across the USA and Canada.

Val d'Isère à la Carte: La Hure, rue de la Motte, St Martins, Guernsey GY4 6ER
t +44 (0)1481 236 800,

www.skivaldisere.co.uk
Tailor-made holidays and booking service for all components of holidays to Val d'Isère, but not flights. *See* page 247

Vanilla Ski: Avoca Cottage, Woodside Road, Chiddingfold GU8 4RJ
t +44 (0)1932 860 696,
www.vanillaski.com
Catered chalet near Bourg-St-Maurice, with day trips organized to nearby resorts.

VIP: Collingbourne House, 140–142 Wandsworth High Street, London SW18 4JJ
t +44 (0)870 1123 119,
www.vip-chalets.com
Well-established luxury chalet operator with stylish catered chalets in Val d'Isère, Méribel, and Zermatt. Ski hosting and exemplary VIP service. Childcare and nannies also available.
See page 247

Virgin Snow: The Galleria, Station Road, Crawley RH10 1WW
t +44 (0)871 222 5825,
www.virginholidays.co.uk
The tour-operator arm of Virgin Atlantic with hotel and fly-drive holidays to resorts across Canada and USA.

Warren Smith Ski Academy: Merlewood, Kenyon Lane, Dinckley BB6 8AN
t +44 (0)7775 500 599,
www.warrensmith-skiacademy.com
Specialist ski clinics including freeride, personal performance, powder skiing, heli-skiing and summer skiing in Saas-Fee, Verbier, New Zealand and Japan.
See page 7

Wasteland: 9 Disraeli Road, London SW15 2DR
t +44 (0)20 8246 6677,
www.wastelandski.com
Cross-country ski operator Waymark Holidays is now part of Exodus, with flexible-length holidays to hotels in Austria, Finland, France, Italy, Norway, Slovenia and the Urals. Also snowshoeing, dog-sledding, reindeer safaris, ice-fishing and hut-to-hut tours.

White Roc Weekends: 69 Westbourne Grove, London W2 4UJ
t +44 (0)20 7792 1188,
www.whiteroc.co.uk
Weekend and longer tailor-made holidays for individual and corporate clients to Austria, France, Italy, Spain and Switzerland, with a choice of 26 resorts and good-quality hotels.

YSE: Church House, Abbey Close, Sherborne DT9 3LQ
t +44 (0)845 122 1414,
www.yseski.co.uk
Large Val d'Isère specialist with a wide range of chalets, from comfortable to luxurious, with travel by charter flights.

Ski Property

Alpine Homes International
t +41 (0)27 323 7777,
www.alpinehomesintl.com
Austria, France, Switzerland

Alpine Property Investments
t +44 (0)1722 743 662,
www.alpinepropertyinvestments.co.uk
Colorado, Switzerland

Chesterton
t +44 (0)20 7201 2070,
www.chesterton.co.uk
Valais area of Switzerland

Descent International
t +33 (0)6 26 29 29 03,
www.descent.co.uk
Alpine properties

Erna Low Property
t +44 (0)20 7590 1624,
www.ernalowproperty.co.uk
Properties in 30 Alpine locations, including Intrawest properties in Canada and France

4 Property
t +33 (0)4 79 40 18 48,
www.4propertysales.co.uk

Properties in Val d'Isère, Ste-Foy and Lake Tahoe

Hartmann Singleton
t +44 (0)1845 597 795,
www.hartmansingleton.com
Switzerland

Homes in Bulgaria
t +44 (0)870 777 3370,
www.homesinbulgaria.co.uk
Bulgaria

Investors in Property
t +44 (0)20 8905 5511,
www.investorsinproperty.com
Austrian, French and Swiss property

Pure
t +44 (0)20 7331 4500,
www.pureintl.com
Austria, Canada and France

Savills International
t +44 (0)20 7016 3740,
www.savills.co.uk/abroad
Austria, Bulgaria, Canada, France, Switzerland

UK Overseas
t + 44 (0)8701 149 807,
www.ukoverseas.com
Austria and France

Undiscovered Properties
t +44 (0)870 734 7968,
www.undiscoveredproperties.com
BC and Québec in Canada

Ski Travel Agents

Alpine Answers
t +44 (0)20 7801 1080,
www.alpineanswers.co.uk
Also a tour operator

Chalet World (London)
t +44 (0)20 3080 0202,
www.chaletworld.co.uk
Agency for tour operator chalets

Chalet World Ski
t +44 (0)1743 231 199,
www.chaletworldski.co.uk
Chalet agents to major alpine resorts

Erna Low
t +44 (0)845 863 0525,
www.ernalow.co.uk
Agent for Serre Chevalier, Intrawest Europe and MGM apartments. Also a tour operator and ski property specialist.

The First Resort
t +44 (0)800 027 3882,
www.thefirstresort.com
Online holiday booking, cheap flights and information for snow users

Ifyouski
www.ifyouski.com
Online agency

Iglu
t +44 (0)20 8542 6658, *www.iglu.com*
Online travel and accommodation

Independent Ski Links
t +44 (0)1964 533 905, *www.ski-links.com*
Agency offering holidays to the Alps and North America

Momentum Ski
t +44 (0)20 7371 9111,
www.momentumski.com
Tailor-made holidays to Austria, Chile, France, Italy, Switzerland and North America. Short break, corporate travel and special events specialist.

Mountain Beds
t +44 (0)20 7924 2650,
www.mountainbeds.co.uk
Apartment bookings for Verbier

Packyourskis
t +44 (0)800 652 8552,
www.packyourskis.com
Online agents for ski destinations and flights

Satellite Travel
t +44 (0)8643 3666,
www.satellitetravel.co.uk
Low cost ski flights to Chambéry from Gatwick, Stansted, Manchester and Bristol. One of the leading providers of flight seats to the UK ski industry.

Ski Deals
t +44 (0)800 027 3158, *www.skideals.com*
Online holiday agency

Ski McNeill
t +44 (0)870 600 1359, *www.skimcneill.com*
Independent ski travel agency

Ski Solutions
t +44 (0)20 7471 7700, *www.skisolutions.com*
The original independent ski travel agency, also a tour operator

Ski Travel Centre
t +44 (0)1416 499 696, *www.skitravelcentre.co.uk*
Scotland's biggest ski travel agency

Snow Finders
t +44 (0)1858 466 888, *www.snowfinders.com*
Independent ski and board travel agency

Snowhounds
t +44 (0)1243 788 487, *www.snowhounds.co.uk*
Ski specialist agency arm of Ski Beat

Snow-Line
t +44 (0)871 222 6000, *www.snow-line.co.uk*
Large and long-established ski travel agency

World Ski & Travel
t +44 (0)870 428 8706, *www.worldski.co.uk*
Specialist ski travel agency

Travelling by Air

Airlines

Air Canada
t +44 (0)871 700 1777, *www.aircanada.ca*

Air France
t +44 (0)870 142 4343, *www.airfrance.co.uk*

Air 2000 /First Choice
t +44 (0)871 200 7799, *www.firstchoice.co.uk*

Alitalia
t +44 (0)844 493 1234, *www.alitalia.co.uk*

American Airlines
t +44 (0)20 7365 0777, *www.aa.com*

Austrian Airlines
t +44 (0)20 7766 0300, *www.aua.com*

bmibaby
t +44 (0)871 224 0224, *www.bmibaby.com*

British Airways
t +44 (0)844 493 0787, *www.ba.com*

Continental Airlines
www.continental.com

Darwin Airline
t +41 800 177 177, *www.darwinairline.com*

Delta Airlines
t +44 (0)845 600 0950, *www.delta.com*

easyJet
t +44 (0)905 821 0905, *www.easyjet.com*

Excel Airways
t +44 (0)871 911 4220, *www.xl.com*

Flybe
t +44 (0)871 700 0535, *www.flybe.com*

Jet 2
t +44 (0)871 386 0000, *www.jet2.com*

JMC /Thomas Cook
t +44 (0)870 750 5711, *www.thomascook.com*

Lufthansa
t +44 (0)871 945 9747, *www.lufthansa.com*

Monarch Airlines
t +44 (0)870 040 5040, *www.flymonarch.com*

Northwest Airlines
www.nwa.com

Mytravel /Airtours
www.mytravel.com

Ryanair
www.ryanair.com

SnowJet
t +44 (0)20 8652 1222,
www.snowjet.co.uk
See page 9

Swiss International Airlines
t +44 (0)845 601 0956,
www.swiss.com

Thomsonfly
t +44 (0)871 231 4691,
www.thomsonfly.com

United Airlines
www.unitedairlines.co.uk

Virgin Atlantic Airways
t +44 (0)8710 380 2007,
www.virgin-atlantic.com

Zoom
t +44 (0)870 240 0055,
www.flyzoom.com

Airport Extras

Airport Parking Shop
www.airport-parking-shop.co.uk
Online comparison of car parks and meet-and-greet prices at UK airports.

First Luggage
t +44 (0)800 083 5503,
www.firstluggage.com
Skis and suitcases collected from your home and delivered to any European resort.

Holiday Extras
www.holidayextras.co.uk
Hotels, car parks and lounges at UK airports, chauffeur transfers, car hire, foreign exchange and travel insurance.

Ski Hoppa
t +44 (0)871 855 0350,
www.skihoppa.com
Airport shuttle bus and heli-transfers in Andorra, Austria, Bulgaria, France, Italy, Norway and Switzerland.

Ski Taxis
t +44 (0)870 443 4192,
www.skitaxis.com
Transfers from 18 airports in Austria, Bulgaria, France, Italy, Switzerland and USA.

Travel Supermarket
www.travelsupermarket.com
Price comparisons for flights and car hire.

Travelling by Car

Breakdown Insurance

AA European Breakdown Cover
t +44 (0)800 085 7253 ,
www.theaa.com
10 per cent online discount

Autohome
t +44 (0)800 371 280,
www.autohome.co.uk

Britannia Rescue
t +44 (0)800 591 563,
www.britanniarescue.com

Direct Line European Breakdown Cover
t +44 (0)845 246 0940,
www.directline.com

Europ Assistance
t +44 (0)870 737 5720,
www.europ-assistance.co.uk

Green Flag National Breakdown
t +44 (0)845 246 1557,
www.greenflag.com

Mondial Assistance
www.mondial-assistance.co.uk

RAC Travel Services
t +44 (0)8705 722 722,
www.rac.co.uk

Channel Crossings

Brittany Ferries
www.brittanyferries.com

Eurotunnel
t +44 (0)8705 35 35 35,
www.eurotunnel.com

Norfolkline
t +44 (0)870 870 1020,
www.norfolkline-ferries.co.uk
See page 5

P&O Ferries
t +44 (0)8716 645 645,
www.poferries.com

Seafrance
t +44 (0)871 633 2557,
www.seafranceski.com
Stena Line
t +44 (0)870 570 7070,
www.stenaline.com

Ski Roof-boxes

Karrite
t +44 (0)1275 340 404,
www.karrite.co.uk
The Roof Box Company
t +44 (0)1539 621 884,
www.roofbox.co.uk
Thule
t +44 (0)1275 340 404,
www.thule.co.uk

Snow Chains

AA
www.theaa.com
Brindley Chains
www.brindley-chains.co.uk
Polar Automotive
www.snowchains.com
RAC
www.rac.co.uk
Rud
www.rud.co.uk
Snowchains
www.snowchains.co.uk

Travelling by Rail

Eurostar
t +44 (0)870 518 6186,
www.eurostar.com
A daytime and overnight ski-train service leaves St Pancras International, London, arriving in the Tarentaise Valley on either Fridays or Saturdays. Return trains depart either Saturday mornings or evenings.
French Rail SNCF (including the TGV)
www.sncf.com
Rail Europe
t +44 (0)0844 8484 071 (for travel on French Motorail and SnowTrain).
www.raileurope.co.uk
Rail Europe are operators of the Snow Train, which carries skiers overnight to the French Alps. Travelling from London, with a change of platforms in Gare du Nord in Paris, the Snow Train offers *couchette* accommodation and a bar-disco carriage. Trains depart London on Friday evening, arriving in the Alps on Saturday morning, and from the Alps on Saturday evening, arriving in London on Sunday morning.
Switzerland Travel Centre
t + 44 (0)0800 100 20030,
www.myswitzerland.com/rail
Discount rail cards bought in advance. Also bookings and (compulsory) seat reservations on Swiss Railways and the Glacier Express.

National Tourist Offices

Andorran Delegation
www.andorra.ad
Argentinian Embassy
t +44 (0)20 7318 1300,
www.argentina-embass-uk.org
Australia
www.australia.com
Austria
t +44 (0)845 101 1818,
www.austria.info
Bulgaria
www.bulgariaski.com
Canada
www.travelcanada.ca
Chile
www.visitchile.org
Czech Republic
www.visitczechia.cz
France
t (09068) 244 123 (brochure line)
www.franceguide.com or
www.skifrance.fr

Finland
t +44 (0)20 7365 2512,
www.visitfinland.com

Italy
t +44 (0)20 7408 1254,
www.enit.it

Japan
t +44 (0)20 7734 9638,
www.seejapan.co.uk

New Zealand
t +44 (0)9050 606 060,
www.newzealand.com

Norway
t +44 (0)9063 022 003 (brochure line),
www.visitnorway.com

Poland
t +44 (0)8700 675 010 (brochure line),
www.poland.dial.pipex.com

Romania
t +44 (0)20 7224 3692,
www.romaniatourism.com

Scotland
t +44 (0)1313 322 433,
www.visitscotland.com

Slovenia
t +44 (0)870 225 5305,
www.slovenia.info

Spain
t +44 (0)20 7486 8077,
www.tourspain.co.uk / www.spain.info

Sweden
t +44 (0)800 3080 3080
(international freephone),
www.visit-sweden.com

Switzerland
t +44 (0)20 7420 4900,
www.myswitzerland.com

United States
Switchboard t +44 (0)20 7499 9000
Visa Information t +44 (0)9068 200 290 (24hr)
www.unitedstatesvisas.gov

California
www.visitcalifornia.com

Colorado
www.visitcolorado.com

Maine
www.visitmaine.com

Nevada
t +44 (0)87 0523 8832 (brochure line),
www.visitnevada.com

New Hampshire
www.visitnh.gov

Rocky Mountain International
t +44 (0)9063 640 655,
www.rmi-realamerica.com

Official Organizations

Association of British Tour Operators to France (ABTOF)
t +44 (0)1989 769 140, *www.abtof.org.uk*

Association of British Travel Agents (ABTA)
www.abta.com

Association of Independent Tour Operators (AITO)
t +44 (0)20 8744 9280, *www.aito.co.uk*

The Back Up Trust
t +44 (0)20 8875 1805,
www.backuptrust.org.uk
Charity for disabled skiers.

British Association of Ski Patrollers
t +44 (0)1855 811443,
www.basp.org.uk
Safety officers at Scottish resorts and UK artificial slopes.Also runs first aid courses

British Association of Snowsport Instructors (BASI)
t +44 (0)1479 861 717,
www.basi.org.uk

British Bobskeleton Association
t +44 (0)1225 323 696,
www.bobskeleton.org.uk

British Mountain Guides
www.bmg.org.uk

British Ski Academy
t +44 (0)20 8399 1181,
www.britskiacad.org.uk
Race training with academic study for 8–16yrs at residential centre in Les Houches, also summer courses on glaciers.

British Ski Club for the Disabled
t +44 (0)1747 828 515,
www.bscd.org.uk
British Universities Snowsports Council
www.buscevents.co.uk
DHO Ski Club
www.downhillonly.com
Wengen-based junior race training, and organizers of British Schoolboys Races.
Disability Snowsport
t +44 (0)1479 861 272,
www.disabilitysnowsport.org.uk
Freestyle Snowsports
www.freestylesnowsports.co.uk
International School of Mountaineering
t +44 (0)1766 890 441,
www.alpin-ism.com
Lectures and courses.
Kandahar Ski Club
t +44 (0)20 8762 0705,
www.kandahar.org.uk
Junior race training, and organizers of the British Schoolgirls Races in Flaine.
Ski 2 Freedom Foundation
t +44 (0)1460 76212,
www.ski2freedom.com
Information for disabled skiers.
Ski Club of Great Britain
t +44 (0)845 458 0780,
www.skiclub.co.uk
Snowsport Industries of Great Britain
www.snowlife.org.uk
Snowsport England
t +44 (0)121 501 2314,
www.snowsportengland.co.uk
The governing body for Engish snowsports.
Snowsport GB
t +44 (0)131 445 7676,
www.snowsportgb.com
Snowsport Wales
t +44 (0)29 2056 1904
www.snowsportwales.net
Snowsport Scotland
t +44 (0)131 445 4151,
www.snowsportscotland.org

UK Ski Slopes

Artificial Slopes

A full list of all 70 slopes is available from the Ski Club of Great Britain
Bearsden Ski Club, Glasgow
t +44 (0)141 943 1500,
www.skibearsden.co.uk
Gloucester Ski and Snowboard Centre
t +44 (0)870 240 0375,
www.gloucesterski.co.uk
Hemel Ski Centre, Hemel Hempstead
t +44 (0)1442 241 321,
www.hemel-ski.co.uk
Llandudno Ski and Snowboard Centre
t +44 (0)1492 874 707,
www.llandudnoskislope.co.uk
Midlothian Ski Centre, Edinburgh
t +44 (0)131 445 4433,
www.midlothian.gov.uk
Rossendale Ski Centre, Lancashire
t +44 (0)1706 226 457,
www.ski-rossendale.co.uk
Sheffield Ski Village
t +44 (0)114 276 9459,
www.sheffieldskivillage.co.uk
Wycombe Summit, High Wycombe
t +44 (0)1494 474 711,
www.wycombesummit.com
Realli-ski, Canterbury, Kent and Watford, Herts **t** +44 (0)845 83 82 81 1,
www.realli-ski.co.uk

Real Snow Slopes

Opening times are dependent on snow conditions
Allenheads, Northumberland
t +44 (0)1670 715 719,
www.ski-allenheads.co.uk
Carlisle Ski Club, Alston, Cumbria
t +44 (0)1228 561 634,
www.thepriceofcheese.com
Chill Factore, nr Manchester
t +44 (0)161 749 2222,
www.chillfactore.com

Tamworth SnowDome, Staffordshire
t +44 (0)870 500 0011,
www.snowdome.co.uk
Xscape Snozone
Castleford, West Yorkshire
t +44 (0)871 222 5671
Milton Keynes
t +44 (0)871 222 5670,
Braehead-Glasgow
t +44 (0)871 222 5672
www.xscape.co.uk
Weardale Ski Club, Shield, Northumberland
t +44 (0)191 534 6251,
www.skiweardale.co.uk

Ski Recruitment Agencies

Free Radicals
www.freeradicals.co.uk
Jobs in the Alps
www.jobs-in-the-alps.com
Natives
t +44 (0)870 046 3377, *www.natives.co.uk*
Ski Connection
www.skiconnection.co.uk
Voovs.com
t +44 (0)1707 396 511,
www.voovs.com

Gap Year Skiing

Base Camp Group
t +44 (0)20 7243 6222,
www.basecampgroup.com
Ski and snowboard instructor courses in Europe and North America. Also seasonal jobs, powder and freestyle camps.
Bunac/Gap Canada
t +44 (0)20 7251 3472,
www.bunac.org
Student work opportunities in Australia, New Zealand and North America.
Interski
t +44 (0)1623 456 333, *www.interski.co.uk*
BASI gap year programme in Italy.
Mind The Gap Year
t +44 (0)1428 664 265,
www.mindthegapyear.co.uk
Gap year travel insurance .
Nonstop Ski
t +44 (0)870 241 8070,
www.nonstopski.com
Intensive instruction in Fernie, Red Mountain and Banff, with the aim of qualifying as a Level 1 Canadian ski or board instructor.
Peak Leaders
t +44 (0)1337 860 079,
www.peakleaders.co.uk
Gap-year instructor courses in in Whistler,Verbier, Zermatt, Bariloche and Queenstown.
Ski Le Gap
t +44 (0)800 328 0345,
www.skilegap.com
Ski and snowboard instructor courses in Tremblant, Quebec.
Warren Smith Ski Academy
t +44 (0)7775 500 599,
www.warrensmith-skiacademy.com
Gap year BASI courses in Verbier.

Clothing and Equipment Retailers

For a full list see *www.snowlife.org.uk*
47 Degrees
t +44 (0)20 7731 5415 (Fulham) or
t +44 (0)20 7730 8447 (Chelsea),
www.47degrees.com
Anatom Innovative Products
t +44 (0)800 032 3505,
www.anatom.co.uk
Anything Technical
t +44 (0)1539 734 701, *www.skiequipmentuk.co.uk*
Blacks
t +44 (0)800 665 410,
www.blacks.co.uk
Boardwise
t +44 (0)8707 504 421,
www.boardwise.com

Cotswold Outdoor
t +44 (0)870 442 7755, *www.cotswoldoutdoor.com*

Ellis Brigham
t +44 (0)161 833 0746, *www.ellis-brigham.com*

Lockwoods
t +44 (0)1926 339 388, *www.lockwoods.com*

Sheactive
t +44 (0)870 766 3227, *www.sheactive.co.uk*

Snow + Rock
t +44 (0)845 100 1000, *www.snowandrock.com*

Ski Clothing Rental

Captain's Cabin
t +44 (0)1732 464 463, *www.theski-shop.co.uk*
Clothing and equipment hire.

edge2edge
t +44 (0)1293 649 300, *www.edge2edge.co.uk*
Clothing, equipment, roof box and snowchain hire.

Ski Togs Hire
t +44 (0)20 8993 9883, *www.skitogshire.co.uk*
Clothing and après ski boots.

Ski West
t +44 (0)1453 819 247, *www.ski-west.co.uk*
Clothing and accessories.

Weather and Snow

www.lawine.at
Avalanche warnings for Austria.

www.meteo.fr
French weather forecasts.

www.skiclub.co.uk
Snow reports and six-day weather forecasts on 250 resorts across Europe and North America.

www.slf.ch
Avalanche warnings for Switzerland.

www.snow-forecast.com
Worldwide snow data.

www.welove2ski.com
Snow reports and weather maps and forecasts updated daily.

Ski Travel Insurance

American Express
t +44 (0)800 028 7573, *www.americanexpress.co.uk*

BIBA
t +44 (0) 0901 814 0015, *www.biba.org.uk*

Columbus Direct
t +44 (0)870 033 9988, *www.columbusdirect.com*

Direct Travel Insurance
t +44 (0)845 605 2700, *www.direct-travel.co.uk*

Endsleigh Insurance Services
t +44 (0)800 028 3571, *www.endsleigh.co.uk*

Europ Assistance
t +44 (0)870 737 5720, *www.europ-assistance.co.uk*

Fogg Travel Insurance
t +44 (0)1623 631 331, *www.fogginsure.co.uk*

Insure & Go
t +44 (0)870 901 3674, *www.insureandgo.com*

Liverpool Victoria
t +44 (0)800 373 905, *www.liverpool-victoria.co.uk*

Medicover
t +44 (0)870 735 3600, *www.medi-cover.co.uk*

Mondial Assistance
t +44 (0)20 8681 2525, *www.mondial-assistance.co.uk*

MPI
t +44 (0)1428 664 265, *www.mpibrokers.com*

MRL Insurance Direct
t +44 (0)845 676 0689, *www.mrlinsurance.co.uk*

Options Travel Insurance
t +44 (0)870 876 7878,
www.optionsinsurance.co.uk

Primary Insurance
t +44 (0)870 220 0634,
www.primaryinsurance.co.uk

Ski Club of Great Britain
t +44 (0)845 601 9422, *www.skiclub.co.uk*

Snowcard Insurance Services
t +44 (0)1327 262 805,
www.snowcard.co.uk

Sportscover Direct
t +44 (0)845 120 6400,
www.sportscover.co.uk

Travel & General Group
t +44 (0)845 345 3456,
www.tgic-online.com

WorldSki
t +44 (0)870 428 8706,
www.worldski.co.uk

Worldwide Insure
t +44 (0)870 112 8100,
www.worldwideinsure.com

Miscellaneous

O'Neill TV
www.oneilleurope.com/tv
Digital TV platform with free action sports footage.

www.pistehors.com
The latest news on ski resorts.

www.snoweye.com
Links to webcams in all major resorts in Europe, North and South America, Japan, New Zealand and Australia.

www.snowzone.tv
Showcasing the best resorts and ski destinations worldwide, also film trailers produced by industry leaders.

www.welove2ski.com
All you need to know about skiing and snowboarding.

ski atlas of the world

THE COMPLETE REFERENCE TO THE BEST RESORTS

CONTRIBUTING EDITOR **Arnie Wilson**

ISBN 978 1 84537 467 9 £35.00

NEW HOLLAND PUBLISHERS (UK) LTD
GARFIELD HOUSE
86–88 EDGWARE ROAD
LONDON W2 2EA
TELEPHONE: 020 7724 7773

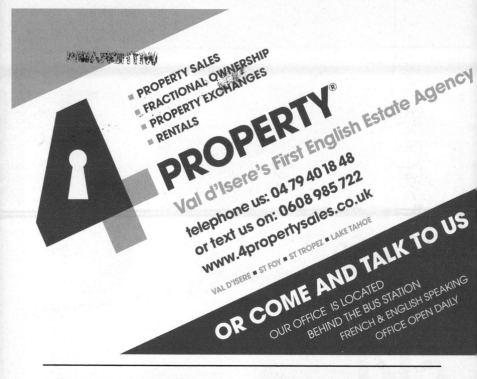

■ PROPERTY SALES
■ FRACTIONAL OWNERSHIP
■ PROPERTY EXCHANGES
■ RENTALS

4 PROPERTY®

Val d'Isere's First English Estate Agency

telephone us: 04 79 40 18 48
or text us on: 0608 985 722
www.4propertysales.co.uk

VAL D'ISERE ■ ST FOY ■ ST TROPEZ ■ LAKE TAHOE

OR COME AND TALK TO US
OUR OFFICE IS LOCATED
BEHIND THE BUS STATION
FRENCH & ENGLISH SPEAKING
OFFICE OPEN DAILY

New 'Scatered' service now available
OUR CROSS BETWEEN CATERED & SELF CATERED BOARD

CALL US NOW
In the UK: 0700 2000 456
Abroad: +44 20 7607 9936
E: sales@mrooms.co.uk
www.mountainrooms.com
ENGLISH AND FRENCH SPEAKING. RESORT OFFICE IS LOCATED BEHIND THE BUS STATION IN 4 PROPERTY OFFICE - OPEN DAILY

MANAGEMENT SOLUTIONS FOR PRIVATE OWNERS AND OPERATORS
Three-tier Property Management contracts
Renovation of your new or existing property
Linen rental of quality bed linen, bath towels, bath robes & bath mats. Private laundry service

FOR A BROCHURE OR FURTHER ENQUIRIES, REFER TO OUR WEBSITE OR CALL OR EMAIL US ON
Tel: 04 79 06 29 79 contact@valservice.com
www.valservice.com
ENGLISH & FRENCH SPEAKING
RESORT OFFICE IS LOCATED BEHIND THE BUS STATION IN 4 PROPERTY OFFICE - OPEN DAILY